EXPERT ADVISOR

dBASE III PLUS™

EXPERT ADVISOR

dBASE III PLUS™

Tom Rettig
Debby Moody

Addison-Wesley Publishing Company, Inc.
Reading, Massachusetts Menlo Park, California New York
Don Mills, Ontario Wokingham, England Amsterdam Bonn
Sydney Singapore Tokyo Madrid San Juan

Library of Congress Cataloging-in-Publication Data
Rettig, Tom.
Expert advisor: dBASE III PLUS / Tom Rettig and Debby Moody.
p. cm.
Includes index.
ISBN 0-201-17197-X (pbk.)
1. Data base management. 2. dBASE III PLUS (Computer program)
I. Moody, Debby. II. Title.
QA76.9.D3R478 1988
005.75'65—dc19 87-28800CIP

Technical Reviewer: Laurie Miller
Series Editor: Barbara Graves
Cover Design by Corey & Company: Designers
Text Design by Joyce Weston
Set in 10.5-point Palatino by Publication Services Inc.

ISBN 0-201-17197-X
ABCDEFGHIJ - HA - 898
First printing, August, 1988

For my father, Frank Moody, who always allowed me to be myself and make my own decisions. I miss you.
Debby

For my first grandchild who, at the time of this writing, is still in development.
Tom

Contents

Acknowledgments

We, the authors, would like to acknowledge several people for their contributions to this book. Laurie Miller's work as technical editor of this book was invaluable. Leonard Zerman contributed an assembly language program that captures printed output (including @...SAY commands) to a text file; thanks to Leonard for providing dBASE users with a much requested feature. Finally, we would like to thank Carole Alden, Barbara Graves, and Alexandra McDowell for their patience and personal attention every step of the way.

Introduction

This book is a complete reference to dBASE III PLUS, including the network commands and functions. The alphabetical arrangement of the commands, functions, and general topics provides every level of user with easy access to the dBASE language. Each topic is described with practical programming examples and cross-references to related topics.

Each topic is organized using the following headings:

Syntax

The syntax is described at the beginning of each command or function to show you what options are available and how to form the command or function correctly. The syntax representations use the special symbols listed below. Don't use any of these symbols in the actual command or function. They only represent the syntax. For example, you would never put angle brackets around a file name in the formation of a command; instead, you would substitute the actual file name for the < filename > symbol in the syntax representation. For a quick reference, Appendix D provides a complete list of the syntax of each command and function.

SYMBOL	MEANING
< >	Angle brackets indicate that the item they enclose in the syntax is to be provided by the user. For example, < filename > means that you are supposed to supply a file name, such as Mail, as part of the command or function syntax.
[ ]	Square brackets indicate that the part of the syntax they surround is optional. For example, `[FOR <condition>]` means that you can use a FOR keyword followed by a logical condition as part of the command. Only the portions of the command or function that are not enclosed in square brackets are required.

SYMBOL	MEANING
¦	A vertical bar separates two or more items in the syntax that are mutually exclusive (i.e., only one item can be used. For example, SET BELL ON ¦ OFF means that you must use either the word ON or the word OFF in the SET BELL syntax. The use of the vertical bar instead of the slash (/) is a deviation from the usual dBASE syntax representation; however, its use eliminates a conflict when the slash symbol must be used, literally, as part of a command. (See SORT for an example.)
...	Ellipses indicate that you can repeat a particular part of the syntax as many times as you want. For example, `REPLACE <fieldname> WITH <exp> [, <fieldname> WITH <exp>...]` means that you can specify as many field names with expression clauses as you want by separating them with commas.

The following items are also commonly used in the syntax representations and each has a special meaning:

<filename>	A <filename> is the name of a disk file that may include a drive letter, path name, and extension. The default file name extension depends on the command or function. File names can be up to eight characters in length. The first character must be a letter, and the remaining seven can be any combination of letters, numbers, and underscores as can the extension.
<fieldname>	A <fieldname> is the name of a field in a database file that may include an alias name followed by the arrow symbol (– >) as a prefix. Field names can be up to ten characters in length. The first character must be a letter, and the remaining nine can be any combination of letters, numbers, and underscores.
<memory variable>	A <memory variable> is the name of a memory variable that can be prefixed by the memory variable arrow symbol (M– >) to distinguish it from a field with the same name. Memory variable names can be up to ten characters in length. The first character must be a letter, and the remaining nine can be any combination of letters, numbers, and underscores.
<expression> *or* <exp>	An <expression> is any type of expression. It may also be represented as <exp>. (See Expression.)
<expC>	An <expC> is a character type expression.
<expD>	An <expD> is a date type expression.
<expN>	An <expN> is a numeric type expression.
<condition>	A <condition> is a logical expression. It may also be represented as <expL>.

<list> — You will not see <list> alone in a command or function syntax; instead you will see <filename list>, <field list>, or <expression list>. A <list> is a list of a specific type of item separated by commas if there is more than one item in the list.

Overview

This section describes each dBASE feature in general terms. It also describes the effect of using the various optional parameters for commands and functions.

Procedure

This section describes how to use a particular feature in an application. It lists the rules for using the optional parameters for commands and functions. It also outlines any prerequisites to using a feature, such as opening files, and lists related commands and functions. Read this section if you want to know how and where to use a feature.

Examples

This section provides programming and interactive examples for each feature. The purpose of the example and its outcome are described. The programs are practical and make liberal use of comments so that the programs are easy to understand.

Some of the examples in this book use database files to illustrate how a particular command or function affects the data. Each example assumes that the file has its original contents and structure, although some examples may change the file.

All database files used in this book are listed in Appendix E. The listing for each file includes its file structure and contents. If you want to execute the examples, you can create these files and add the data. (See CREATE, APPEND.)

Warnings

This section describes common errors in using a particular feature and how to correct them. There is no complete list of error messages in this book; instead, the Warnings section explains error messages and pitfalls associated with each feature.

Tips

This section provides tips to help you use each feature more efficiently.

EXPERT ADVISOR

dBASE III PLUS™

Alphabetical Entries

! (Exclamation Point)

Syntax `!|RUN <command> |<program>|<batch file>`

Overview

The ! command, pronounced "bang", executes DOS commands and other external programs, including batch files, from within dBASE III PLUS. It does not close any files and does not affect existing memory variables.

If you do not explicitly specify a file extension when you execute a program, the ! command first looks for a file with a .COM extension, then for one with a .EXE extension, and finally for a .BAT extension.

RUN is an alternative syntax for the ! command.

Procedure

Use the ! command to execute a DOS command or to use another program without leaving dBASE III PLUS. When the command or program that you execute is finished, control is returned to dBASE III PLUS with all open files and memory variables intact.

You may want to use the ! command from the dot prompt to access some of the DOS commands that are more powerful than their dBASE counterparts. For example, because ERASE in dBASE III PLUS does not allow wildcard characters, you might want to use the DOS ERASE command.

In an applications program, you can allow a user to gain access to a favorite word processor or spreadsheet program by using the ! command in a menu program.

Examples

The following example illustrates how to use the ! command from the dot prompt. It allows you to create and use a new directory without ever leaving dBASE III PLUS:

```
. ! md \dbase\programs  && Creates a DOS directory
. SET PATH TO \dbase\programs  && Puts new directory in path
```

Warnings

You must have sufficient memory in your computer to use the ! command successfully. Attempting to use ! without sufficient memory results in the error message *Insufficient memory*. You need enough additional memory (above the 256K used by dBASE III PLUS) to load a copy of the DOS command interpreter, Command.COM, and to load the program that you want to execute.

When you issue the ! command, dBASE III PLUS must load another copy of Command.COM into memory before it can execute the named command or program. dBASE III PLUS uses a DOS environmental variable, COMSPEC, to find this file. The error message *Unable to load COMMAND-.COM* means that the command interpreter is not where COMSPEC thinks it is. Usually, you will not get this error because the command interpreter is kept in the root directory of your hard disk, and the default setting for COMSPEC is correct; however, you may encounter this error if you have a two-floppy disk system.

You can make the dBASE III PLUS System Disk #1 bootable using the DOS program Sys.COM. This is not much help, however, since System Disk #2 must remain in Drive A, and there is not enough room on this disk for a copy of the Command.COM. If you do not use the help system, you can erase the file called Help.DBS from System Disk #2 to make enough room for Command.COM; otherwise, you will have to put a copy of Command.COM on the disk in Drive B and use the DOS command SET COMSPEC=B:\Command.COM in the Autoexec.BAT file on the disk that you use to boot your computer.

Don't use the ! command to execute programs that are designed to remain resident in memory after their execution (e.g., Mode and Assign); instead, execute them before entering dBASE III PLUS.

Tips

To leave dBASE III PLUS and access the DOS command interpreter, issue `! Command.COM` from within dBASE III PLUS. You will be presented with the DOS prompt and can execute any command that you want. When you want to return to dBASE III PLUS, type `EXIT` at the DOS prompt.

To execute binary programs from within dBASE III PLUS, use the LOAD and CALL commands. (See LOAD, CALL.)

& (Ampersand). *See* Macro Substitution

&& (Double Ampersand)

Syntax `<command> && <text>`

Overview

The && (double ampersand) symbol places a comment on the same line as a command in a program file, format file, or procedure. This symbol is not a command, but an optional keyword for any dBASE III PLUS command. Using && is often referred to as "in-line commenting" because the comment occurs in the same line as the command.

As soon as && is encountered in a command, the remainder of the command line is ignored by the interpreter.

Procedure

The && symbol is most commonly used in program files and procedures to document the individual commands in the code. Include the symbol at the end of the command line. Any text can follow.

Examples

The following example illustrates how to use the && to comment commands in a program:

```
* Two examples of in-line commenting follow.
USE Mail   && Open the mailing list database file
LIST       && List its contents
```

Warnings

Although the text following && in a command line is not executed by the command interpreter, using a semicolon at the end of an in-line comment indicates that the comment continues on the next line. Do not use a semicolon as the last character of a comment; if you do, the next line of the program will not be executed. For example, the following sequence

```
USE Mail  && Open database file ;
SET INDEX TO Zip
```

is equivalent to

```
USE Mail && Open database file SET INDEX TO Zip
```

Neither one opens the Zip index file. The correct command sequence is:

```
USE Mail  && Open database file
SET INDEX TO Zip
```

You can use this feature for making lengthy in-line comments, though these types of comments are usually better stated using *.

Tips

See * (asterisk) for more information on commenting your programs.

* (Asterisk)

Syntax `*|NOTE <text>`

Overview

The * (asterisk), or NOTE, command comments program files, format files, and procedures in dBASE III PLUS. The command indicates that what follows is a comment to be ignored by the command interpreter.

Procedure

The * command is most commonly used to document the code in program files. You can include as many comments in a program as you want to make it more understandable. The comments will help if you need to make changes to the program at a later date.

You may use a single * to comment a single line in a program, but commenting large blocks of code, such as a DO WHILE or DO CASE construct, may take more than one comment line.

As a general rule, you will not see NOTE used very often for commenting, because it is easier to read the comment if you use * instead.

Examples

The following example illustrates a program that makes liberal use of comments using *. NOTE can be substituted for *, if you prefer.

```
* Letter.PRG

*****************************************************************
*                                                               *
* This program uses the LOCATE and CONTINUE commands to print   *
* delinquent payment notices for customers who are late in      *
* making payment.                                               *
*                                                               *
*****************************************************************
```

```
SET TALK OFF
SET DEVICE TO PRINTER
USE Customer

* LOCATE is used to find the first delinquent customer.
LOCATE FOR Deadline < DATE()

* This DO WHILE loop prints a letter for each record meeting
* the LOCATE condition.
DO WHILE FOUND()
   @  6, 0      SAY TRIM(First_Name) + " " + Last_Name
   @  7, 0      SAY TRIM(Address1)
   @  8, 0      SAY TRIM(City) + ", " + State + "  " + Zip
   @  9,70      SAY DATE()
   @ 10, 0      SAY "Dear " + TRIM(First_Name) + " "
   @ 10, PCOL() SAY TRIM(Last_Name) + ":"
   @ 12, 0      SAY "Our records show that your account is "
   @ 12, PCOL() SAY "overdue.  "
   @ 12, PCOL() SAY "Your balance is $"
   @ 12, PCOL() SAY LTRIM(STR(Amt_Owed, 10, 2)) + "."
   @ 13, 0      SAY "This amount was due and payable on "
   @ 13, PCOL() SAY Deadline
   @ 13, PCOL() SAY ".  Please send payment immediately."
   @ 14, 0      SAY "If you have already submitted your payment,"
   @ 14, PCOL() SAY " disregard this notice."

   * CONTINUE finds the rest of the records.
   CONTINUE

ENDDO
USE
EJECT
SET DEVICE TO SCREEN
SET TALK ON
```

Warnings

The * command can be continued on the next line by using a semicolon followed by a carriage return. For this reason, you cannot use a semicolon as the last character on a comment command line; if you do so, the next command line will be considered a part of the comment. For example, the following sequence

```
* The next command opens the database file;
USE Mail
```

is equivalent to

```
* The next command opens the database file USE Mail
```

Neither one opens the Mail database file. The correct way to do this is

```
* The next command opens the database file.
USE Mail
```

Tips

The * command is one way of commenting programs. You can also comment programs with the && symbol, which allows you to perform in-line commenting. See && (Double Ampersand) for more information.

Remember that the most valuable comments describe *why* you did something a certain way in the code. The literal meaning of the code is apparent to anyone who understands the language.

; (Semicolon)

Overview

The ; (semicolon) has a special meaning in dBASE III PLUS command, procedure, and format files as the command line continuation character. It is used as the last character on a command line in order to continue the command on the next line.

If you use the built-in text editor (see MODIFY COMMAND) to create your files, the lines automatically wrap around to the next line when you are typing. In that case, you do not really need to use the semicolon for continuation; however, you may not agree with a particular line break. To make long command lines more readable, use the semicolon followed by a hard carriage return (i.e., press Enter) to break the line at a logical place. A hard carriage return is indicated by the < symbol on the right side of the screen, but a soft carriage return is not indicated.

The semicolon has another special meaning to the REPORT FORM command. If a semicolon is encountered in the contents of a column, it is not displayed; instead, a carriage return is used in its place. (See CREATE REPORT for an example.)

In function key settings, the semicolon is also interpreted as a carriage return. If you include a semicolon, the command that you store in the function key is executed automatically when you press the key. You can also store several commands to be executed consecutively in a single function key by placing a semicolon after each one. (See SET FUNCTION.)

Warnings You cannot use the semicolon to continue commands entered at the dot prompt. The command line in the interactive mode automatically scrolls to accommodate the longest possible command (254 characters).

Tips The semicolon can be used to continue a comment line, thus eliminating the need for a leading asterisk on continued lines; however, this use of the semicolon makes the program difficult to read and is not recommended.

? (Question Mark)

Syntax
```
? [<expression list>]
?? [<expression list>]
```

Overview The ? (question mark) command and its secondary form, ?? (double question mark), display the value of one or more expressions. The expressions are supplied to the command in the form of a list separated by commas, and can evaluate to any data type. The values are displayed on the screen and, if SET PRINTER is ON, they are also printed.

The only difference between the two forms of this command is that the single question mark issues a carriage return/linefeed pair before displaying the expression values, while ?? does the display at the current cursor location or print position.

The ? command with no parameters displays a blank line; the ?? command with no parameters has no effect.

Procedure Use the ? command to display the contents of one or more expressions when you do not want the information displayed at specific coordinates.

Use the ?? command to display the contents of one or more expressions on the current line. This form of the command does not generate a carriage return/linefeed pair before displaying the information.

SET PRINTER ON before issuing either form of this command if you want to print its results.

Examples The ? command can be used at the dot prompt to turn dBASE III PLUS into a calculator. The following example shows you how to do mathematical calculations at the dot prompt:

```
. ? 5.97 * 257
 1534.29
. ? 1534.29/3
  511.43
. ? SQRT(511.43)
 22.61
. ? 22.61 ^ 2
  511.21
```

The following routine uses the ? command to print the name and birthday of everyone in your mailing list. The First_Name and Last_Name are formatted with an initial capital letter followed by lowercase letters.

```
USE Mail
SET TALK OFF
* Console turned off so printed output is not seen on screen.
SET CONSOLE OFF
SET PRINTER ON
DO WHILE .NOT. EOF()
   ? UPPER(LEFT(First_Name, 1)) + LOWER(SUBSTR(First_Name, 2))
   * Last_Name is printed on the same line as First_Name using ??
   ?? SPACE(1) + UPPER(LEFT(Last_Name, 1)) +;
                 LOWER(SUBSTR(Last_Name, 2))
   ? Birthday
   * Two blank lines are printed between each record.
   ?
   ?
   SKIP
ENDDO
SET PRINTER OFF
SET CONSOLE ON
SET TALK ON
CLOSE DATABASES
```

Warnings

Since the ? command deals with expressions, many error messages are possible. The most common expression evaluation errors are *Data type mismatch* and *Variable not found*.

One cause of *Data type mismatch* might be that you have attempted to add a number and a character string. Users of dBASE III PLUS must be very careful when forming expressions; subtracting a number from a date is one of only a few operations permitted between differing data types. With

?, however, this error should not occur often because there is no need to use such complex expressions. Remember that this command allows a list of expressions separated by commas. Instead of having one long complicated expression that uses many conversion functions in order to add simple expressions together, you can just list the simple expressions and eliminate the conversion functions altogether.

Variable not found indicates that you used a variable name before initializing the variable. This error will be displayed if you misspell a field or variable name, use a field name when its database file is not in use, or use a memory variable name that you have neglected to initialize.

Tips

The most common method for sending control characters to the printer is the ?? command with SET PRINTER ON. Use ?? instead of ? to avoid an unwanted linefeed on your printed output. (*See* CHR( ) for an example of sending control characters to your printer.)

Remember that the screen output is not suppressed if you SET PRINTER ON to print the result of this command. Use SET CONSOLE OFF if you want to suppress the screen output when you are printing with the ? or ?? commands.

Because there are no formatting options with this output command as there are with the @...SAY command, it is considered an "unformatted output" command. Formatting the output of ? can be achieved using the TRANSFORM( ) function. (See TRANSFORM( ) for an example that is easily adaptable for use with this command.)

If you use ?? at the dot prompt, the result of the command will overwrite the command itself. If this is not desired, use ? for interactive use at the dot prompt.

?? (Double Question Mark) *See* ? (Question Mark)

@...CLEAR

Syntax `@ <coordinates> CLEAR [TO <coordinates>]`

Overview The @...CLEAR command erases a rectangular portion of the screen defined by coordinates that you supply as command line parameters. The coordinates are a pair of numeric expressions separated by a comma.

The first set of coordinates specifies the top-left corner of the rectangle to be erased. If the TO option is used, its coordinates specify the bottom-right corner of the rectangle; otherwise, the bottom-right corner is assumed to be the extreme lower-right position of the screen (e.g., 24, 79 on a 25-by-80 screen).

The CLEAR command is designed to clear the entire screen, and is equivalent to @ 0, 0 CLEAR.

Procedure Use @...CLEAR to erase a rectangular portion of the screen. This command is not affected by SET DEVICE TO PRINTER.

Examples The @...TO command is used to draw boxes on the screen. You can use @...CLEAR to clear the interior portion of a box without erasing the box itself. For example, the following routine draws a box on the screen, displays a message on the screen, and clears the message from the box:

```
* Box.PRG
*
SET TALK OFF
m_continue = SPACE(1)
@  8,15 TO 18,45 DOUBLE
@ 10,18 SAY "This message will be"
@ 12,18 SAY "erased as soon as you"
@ 14,18 SAY "press any key, but the"
@ 16,18 SAY "box border will remain."
@ 17,28 GET m_continue
READ
@  9,16 CLEAR TO 17,44 && Erase what is inside the box
SET TALK ON
```

Warnings The @...CLEAR command does not check the SET STATUS flag. If SET STATUS is ON, it is possible to erase part or all of the status bar with this

command. Be sure that you limit the TO coordinates to row 21 if SET STATUS is ON.

The error message *Position is off the screen* is displayed if any coordinate does not match an addressable screen position. Screen positions are addressed beginning with zero, not one. For example, if your screen is 25 rows by 80 columns, the addressable screen positions are rows zero through 24 and columns zero through 79. @ 0, 0 CLEAR TO 24,80 causes this error message because the eightieth column is addressed as 79.

Tips

In the above example, @...CLEAR was used to clear the interior portion of a box drawn with @...TO. It can also be used to erase the entire box (including interior) by making the coordinates of @...CLEAR exactly the same as those used to draw the box with @...TO.

@...GET

Syntax

```
@ <coordinates> GET <variable>
[PICTURE <template>] [RANGE [<exp>], [<exp>]]
```

Overview

The @...GET command displays for editing the contents of a variable (i.e., a field or a memory variable) on the screen. When this command is executed, the variable is shown with the enhanced display. (See SET COLOR.) You must use READ or a format file (see SET FORMAT) in conjunction with one of the full-screen editing commands to actually edit the variable.

The <coordinates> are screen coordinates represented by a pair of numeric expressions separated by a comma. The first expression represents the row, or line, and the second one represents the column. These coordinates specify where the @...GET variable is displayed on the screen. Row and column numbering begin with zero, not one.

Data validation and display criteria can be imposed on the variable using the PICTURE and RANGE keywords. (See PICTURE and RANGE for more information on these keywords.) A FUNCTION option similar to PICTURE is also available. (See PICTURE for information on using FUNCTION.)

Procedure

Use @...GET along with READ or in a format file with APPEND or EDIT to edit fields or memory variables.

Examples

The following example shows how to display several fields and memory variables on the screen and edit them. If you want to edit the record of a particular name in your mailing list, you can use the following routine:

```
* MailEdit.PRG
*
SET TALK OFF
USE Mail INDEX Last

* Set up the screen so that the user can enter a last name.
* The labels for the other fields are displayed here because
* they are the same for each record and need only be shown once.

CLEAR
@ 3, 5 SAY "Last Name"
@ 4, 5 SAY "First Name"
@ 5, 5 SAY "Street"
@ 6, 5 SAY "Apartment"
@ 7, 5 SAY "City"
@ 8, 5 SAY "State"
@ 9, 5 SAY "Zip Code"

m_error = .F.  && Initialize error flag

DO WHILE .T.

   * A different prompt is displayed depending on the error flag.
   IF m_error
      @ 1,5 SAY "The name you entered was not found.  Try again."
      m_error = .F.  && Reset error flag
   ELSE
      @ 1,5 SAY "Enter the last name of the person to find.      "
   ENDIF

   m_last = SPACE(20)    && Make m_last blank
   @ 3,17 GET m_last     && Enter a name into a memory variable
   @ 4,17 CLEAR TO 9,79  && Clear previous record from screen
   READ

   IF "" = TRIM(m_last)
      EXIT   && Exit from the loop if no name is entered
   ENDIF

   SEEK m_last  && Locate the last name entered
```

```
    IF .NOT. FOUND()   && Test to make sure that name is on file

       * If the name is not found, set the error flag to true
       * and start the loop over.
       m_error = .T.
       LOOP

    ELSE  && Display contents of record on screen for editing

       @ 1, 5  && Erase prompt
       @ 3,17 GET Last_Name
       @ 4,17 GET First_Name
       @ 5,17 GET Address1
       @ 6,17 GET Address2
       @ 7,17 GET City
       @ 8,17 GET State
       @ 9,17 GET Zip

       READ  && Allow user to edit the fields
    ENDIF
ENDDO
CLEAR
CLOSE DATABASES
SET TALK ON
```

If you execute this program, your screen should look like the one in Figure 1. Entering a name that is not in the database file results in a different prompt. When a name is found, the prompt is erased and you can edit the contents of that person's record.

Warnings The @...GET command is ignored when SET DEVICE TO PRINTER is in effect.

You can use @...GET to edit the contents of a memo field only if you do so using a format file. (See SET FORMAT.) Otherwise, the memo icon is displayed, but you cannot access the contents of the field.

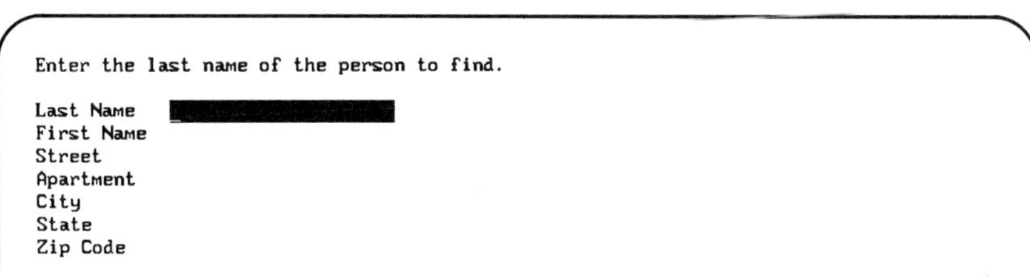

Figure 1

If you receive the error message *Variable not found* with @...GET, you probably neglected to initialize a memory variable that you want to edit. Remember that @...GET is not capable of creating a memory variable; it can only edit an existing one. Initialize the variable using either STORE or the assignment statement <memory variable> = <expression> before doing @...GET. This error message also occurs if you neglect to open the appropriate database file before doing an @...GET with a field name, or if you misspell a field name.

If you are using dBASE III PLUS in a network environment, you must obtain a manual file or record lock (See FLOCK( ), RLOCK( )), or open the database file for exclusive use (See SET EXCLUSIVE, USE) before using @...GET on a field followed by a READ. The error message *Record is not locked* is displayed if you attempt to READ an @...GET under these circumstances.

Remember when using this command that row and column numbering start at zero, and this means that the first line on your screen is row zero.

If you want to use row zero effectively, you must either SET STATUS ON or SET SCOREBOARD OFF. This is necessary because when SET STATUS is OFF, dBASE III PLUS reserves line zero for displaying certain messages to you (i.e., the status of Caps Lock, Num Lock, and Ins keys, as well as data entry errors). SET SCOREBOARD OFF suppresses the display of these messages, allowing you to use line zero. SET STATUS ON causes this information to be displayed on the status bar or the message line, also allowing you to use line zero.

Tips

The @...SAY and @...GET commands can be combined into a single command that is referred to as @...SAY...GET. To use this command, omit the @ <coordinates> portion of @...GET and concatenate the remainder with any @...SAY command. The GET variable is automatically placed one space to the right of the SAY expression. For example,

```
yourname = SPACE(30)
CLEAR
@ 10, 0 SAY "Enter your name:" GET yourname
READ
```

The complete syntax for using @...SAY and @...GET together is

```
@ <coordinates> SAY <expression> [PICTURE <template>]
                GET <variable> [PICTURE <template>]
                [RANGE [<exp>], [<exp>]]
```

@...SAY

Syntax

```
@ <coordinates> [SAY <expression>
[PICTURE <template>]]
```

Overview

The @...SAY command displays the result of any expression (except a memo field) on the screen or printer; SET DEVICE determines where the output goes. When @...SAY is executed with SET DEVICE TO SCREEN in effect, the expression is evaluated and its result is displayed on the screen using the standard display. (See SET COLOR.) SET DEVICE TO PRINTER causes the @...SAY result to be printed. (See SET DEVICE for more information.)

The <coordinates> are represented by a pair of numeric expressions separated by a comma. The first expression represents the row, or line, and the second one represents the column. These coordinates specify where the @...SAY expression result is displayed on the screen or printer. Row and column numbering begin with zero, not one.

Data display criteria can be imposed on the expression result using the PICTURE keyword. (See PICTURE for more information on this keyword.) A FUNCTION option similar to PICTURE is also available. (See PICTURE for information on using FUNCTION.)

As the syntax of the command indicates, you can use @ <coordinates> without the SAY keyword. This form of the command erases the screen beginning at the point specified by the coordinates and continuing to the end of the line. For example, @ 3, 0 erases line 3 completely, and @ 3,39 erases only the right half of line 3.

Procedure

The @...SAY command can be used to display the contents of a field or a memory variable on the screen or printer. It can also be used to display the result of a more complicated expression or to output a literal character string.

Examples

The following example shows you how to use @...SAY to display simple as well as more complicated expressions. In the following routine, invoices are printed using the Customer, Orders, and Inventry files. The invoices are assumed to be pre-printed forms, which makes using @...SAY an appropriate choice.

```
* Invoice.PRG
*
SET TALK OFF
SET DEVICE TO PRINTER  && Send @...SAY result to printer

* Establish environment for printing invoices.
SELECT 3
USE Inventry INDEX Part_No
SELECT 2
USE Customer INDEX Cust_No
SELECT 1
USE Orders INDEX O_CustNo
SET RELATION TO Part_No INTO Inventry

* The memory variable, previous, is used to determine if the
* current customer number is the same as the record before in
* the Orders file.  This way, Orders for the same customer go
* on a single invoice.
previous = SPACE(4)

DO WHILE .NOT. EOF()

   * Since there may be more than one order for a particular
   * customer number, this IF...ENDIF block prints the customer
   * number, name, and address only once per invoice.
   IF Cust_No <> previous

      * Find the Customer record for this order.
      SELECT Customer
      SEEK Orders->Cust_No
      SELECT Orders

      * The @...SAY command is used to print a single character
      * field from the Orders file and to print fields from the
      * Customer file that are concatenated with other fields
      * and character string contents.  Functions are also
      * applied to some fields, demonstrating the ability of
      * the @...SAY command to work with complicated character
      * expressions.

      @ 2,50  SAY Cust_No
      @ 3, 5  SAY TRIM(Customer->First_Name) + " " + ;
                  Customer->Last_Name
      @ 4, 5  SAY Customer->Address1
      @ 5, 5  SAY Customer->Address2
```

```
      @ 6, 5  SAY TRIM(Customer->City) + ", " + ;
                  Customer->State + "  " + Customer->Zip
   ENDIF

   * This next DO WHILE loop prints the line items on the
   * invoice.  A line counter, next_line, and total price
   * accumulator are initialized.
   next_line = 10
   tot_price = 0

   * The previous customer number becomes the current customer
   * number before the line items are printed.
   previous = Cust_No

   * The printing of line items continues until the customer
   * number changes.
   DO WHILE Cust_No = previous

      * The @...SAY command is used with a variable row number
      * to print fields from Orders and Inventry.

      @ next_line, 0 SAY Part_No
      @ next_line, 8 SAY SUBSTR(Inventry->Descrip, 1, 45)
      @ next_line,54 SAY Quantity

      * The @...SAY command is used to calculate a numeric
      * expression and print its result.
      @ next_line,57 SAY Quantity * Inventry->Price

      * The total price accumulator for this customer is updated.
      tot_price = tot_price + Quantity * Inventry->Price

     * Time to print the next line item of the invoice.
      SKIP
      next_line = next_line + 1

   ENDDO

   * The @...SAY command is used to print the total price
   * which is stored in the memory variable, tot_price.
   @ next_line,65 SAY tot_price

ENDDO
EJECT
CLOSE DATABASES
SET DEVICE TO SCREEN
SET TALK ON
```

Warnings

When using a series of @...SAY commands with SET DEVICE TO PRINTER, remember to always put the commands in order of increasing row numbers. If the row number of an @...SAY command is less than the row number of the previous one, a page eject occurs. The example above shows the correct way to order a series of @...SAY commands for printing.

You cannot display the contents of a memo field using @...SAY. If you attempt to do so, the error message *Operation with a Memo field invalid* is displayed.

Since the @...SAY command evaluates an expression, several error messages are possible. The two most common are *Variable not found* and *Data type mismatch*.

If *Variable not found* occurs, you probably neglected either to initialize a memory variable that you want to display or to enclose a literal character string in delimiters. This message also occurs if you neglect to open the appropriate database file before doing an @...SAY with a field name, or if you misspell a field name.

Data type mismatch occurs when you attempt to form an expression by doing operations between differing data types. Check the expression and, if necessary, use data type conversion functions to correct the problem.

Remember when using this command that row and column numbering start at zero. This means that the first line on your screen is row zero.

To use row zero effectively, you must either SET STATUS ON or SET SCOREBOARD OFF. This is necessary because when SET STATUS is OFF, dBASE III PLUS reserves line zero for displaying certain messages to you (i.e., the status of Caps Lock, Num Lock, and Ins keys, as well as data entry errors). SET SCOREBOARD OFF suppresses the display of these messages, thereby allowing you to use line zero. SET STATUS ON causes this information to be displayed on the status bar or the message line, also allowing you to use line zero.

Tips

The @...SAY and @...GET commands can be combined into the single command @...SAY...GET. To use this command, omit the @ <coordinates> portion of the @...GET command and concatenate the remainder with any @...SAY command. The GET variable is automatically placed one space to the right of the SAY expression. For example,

```
yourname = SPACE(30)
CLEAR
```

```
@ 10, 0 SAY "Enter your name:" GET yourname
READ
```

The complete syntax for using @...SAY and @...GET together is

```
@ <coordinates> SAY <expression> [PICTURE <template>]
                GET <variable> [PICTURE <template>]
                [RANGE [<exp>], [<exp>]]
```

@...TO

Syntax `@ <coordinates> TO <coordinates> [DOUBLE]`

Overview The @...TO command draws a rectangular box on the screen. The dimensions of the rectangle and the border character are defined by command line parameters.

Both sets of coordinates are given as a pair of numeric expressions separated by a comma. The first set of coordinates specify the top-left corner, and the TO coordinates specify the bottom-right corner of the box to be drawn. A single-line is used as the box border unless the DOUBLE keyword is used, in which case a double-line border is used.

Procedure Use @...TO command to draw single- and double-line boxes on the screen. When you use this command, boxes can be drawn on the screen, but not on the printer (i.e., @...TO is not affected by the SET DEVICE TO PRINTER).

Examples The @...TO command can be used in a format file to draw attention to certain areas of the screen, such as important messages or instructions, or simply to make your data entry screen more attractive. The following example of a format file borders the entire data entry screen with a double-line bordered box, and displays a message on the screen in a single-line bordered box.

```
* Emp_Add.FMT
*
* Screen is enclosed in a double line bordered box.
@  0, 0  TO 20,79 DOUBLE
@  2, 7  SAY "Employee Number"
@  2,24  GET  Emp_Code PICTURE "@! A999"
```

```
@  2,42  SAY "Hire Date"
@  2,59  GET  Hire_Date
@  3,42  SAY "Social Security"
@  3,59  GET  Ssn PICTURE "999-99-9999"
@  4,42  SAY "Starting Salary"
@  4,59  GET  Salary
@  6, 4  SAY "Name"
@  6,13  GET  Last_Name PICTURE "AAAAAAAAAAAAAAAAAAAAA"
@  6,35  GET  First_Name PICTURE "AAAAAAAAAAAA"
@  7,16  SAY "(last)                  (first)"
@  9, 4  SAY "Address"
@  9,13  GET  Address1
@ 10,16  SAY "(street)"
@ 11,13  GET  Address2
@ 12,16  SAY "(apartment #)"
@ 13,13  GET  City
@ 13,46  GET  State PICTURE "@! AA"
@ 13,55  GET  Zip PICTURE "99999"
@ 14,16  SAY "(city)                        (state)    (zip)"
@ 16, 4  SAY "Phone"
@ 16,13  GET  Phone PICTURE "(999)999-9999"
@ 18, 4  SAY "Comments"
@ 18,13  GET  Comment PICTURE "@S64"
* Draw a single line bordered box and display a message.
@  7,47  TO 12,75
@  8,51  SAY "Make sure all fields"
@  9,51  SAY "are filled in before"
@ 10,51  SAY "going on to the next"
@ 11,51  SAY "record."
```

If you issue the following commands, your screen should look like the one in Figure 2.

```
USE Employee
SET FORMAT TO Emp_Add
SET STATUS ON
APPEND
```

Warnings

The @...TO command does not check the SET STATUS flag. If SET STATUS is ON, it is possible to draw a box that overwrites all or part of the status bar with this command. Be sure that you limit the TO coordinates to row 21 if SET STATUS is ON.

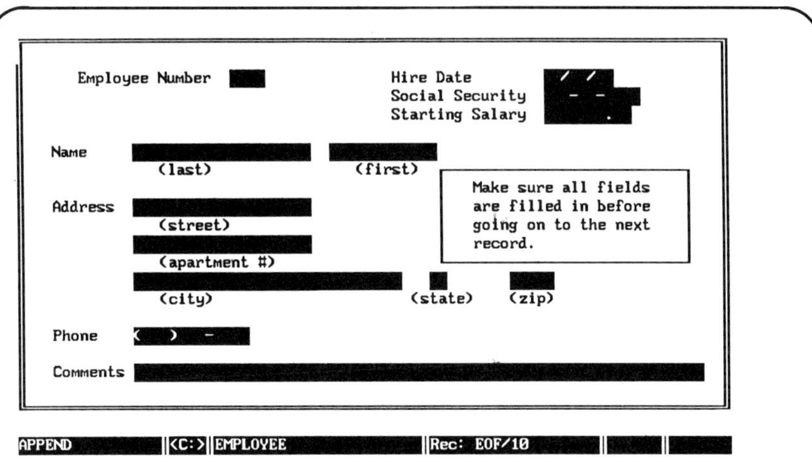

Figure 2

The error message *Position is off the screen* is displayed if any coordinate does not match an addressable screen position. Screen positions are addressed beginning with zero, not one. For example, if your screen is 25 rows by 80 columns, the addressable screen positions are rows zero through 24 and columns zero through 79. @ 0, 0 TO 24,80 causes this error message because the eightieth column should be addressed as 79.

Tips

Using the same row number in both sets of coordinates with @...TO results in a horizontal line; using the same column number results in a vertical line.

Use @...CLEAR to erase boxes drawn with @...TO. The command can be used to erase either the entire box or just its interior. (See @...CLEAR for an example.)

ABS( )

Syntax `ABS(<expN>)`

Overview

The ABS( ) function, short for absolute value, accepts a numeric expression as its argument. The function evaluates the expression and returns the absolute value of the resulting number.

If the number is negative, the function is computed by multiplying the number by −1, which results in a positive number; if the number is greater than or equal to zero, the absolute value is the number itself.

Procedure

ABS( ) returns a number and can be used anywhere in the language where a numeric expression is appropriate.

Examples

ABS( ) can be used when you want to show a negative number as positive. The following routine uses the Customer file and prints a letter for each customer who has a credit in the Amt_Owed field. ABS( ) is used to show the negative Amt_Owed as a positive number.

```
* Promo.PRG
*
SET TALK OFF
SET DEVICE TO PRINTER
USE Customer
DO WHILE .NOT. EOF()

   * Print a promotional letter of each person with a credit.
   IF Amt_Owed < 0

      * ABS(Amt_Owed) is passed as a parameter to Credit.PRG so
      * the number will print on the letter as a positive number.
      DO Credit WITH ABS(Amt_Owed)

   ENDIF
   SKIP
ENDDO
EJECT
CLOSE DATABASES
SET TALK ON
SET DEVICE TO SCREEN
```

The Credit.PRG program prints a letter informing the customer of the credit amount and invites the customer to come into the store.

```
* Credit.PRG - Prints a letter using the ABS(Amt_Owed) as
*              a parameter called amount.
*

PARAMETERS amount
```

```
@  7, 8 SAY DATE()

@  9, 8 SAY TRIM(First_Name) + " " + TRIM(Last_Name)
@ 10, 8 SAY Address1
@ 11, 8 SAY TRIM(City) + ", " + State + "  " + Zip

@ 13, 8 SAY "Dear " + TRIM(First_Name) + ":"

@ 15, 8 SAY "Our records show that you have a credit in the " + ;
             "amount of " + LTRIM(STR(amount, 10, 2)) + "."
@ 16, 8 SAY "You can claim this amount as a cash refund or " + ;
             "use it as credit"
@ 17, 8 SAY "against your next purchase.  Come into the " + ;
            "store and shop around."

@ 20, 8 SAY "Sincerely,"
@ 25, 8 SAY "Debby Moody"
@ 26, 8 SAY "Proprietor"

RETURN
```

Warnings If the function argument evaluates to a data type other than numeric, the error message *Invalid function argument* is displayed.

ACCEPT

Syntax `ACCEPT [<prompt>] TO <memory variable>`

Overview The ACCEPT command waits for the user to enter data and creates a character memory variable which stores this data. Data entry is terminated by pressing the Enter key.

If used, the <prompt> is supplied in the form of a character expression. The expression is evaluated and the resulting character string is displayed on the screen to prompt the user for specific input.

Procedure Use ACCEPT to prompt a user for character input and to save that input in a memory variable for later use.

Examples

The following example uses ACCEPT to prompt for the user's name and uses the name for the SET MESSAGE value:

```
* Name.PRG
*
SET TALK OFF
ACCEPT "Enter your first name: " TO m_first
SET STATUS ON
SET MESSAGE TO "This copy of dBASE III PLUS belongs to " +;
               m_first + "."
```

Warnings

If used, the <prompt> must be a character expression. If the error message *Variable not found* occurs, you probably used a literal character string as the prompt and did not enclose the string in single quotes, double quotes, or square brackets. If the expression used for the prompt evaluates to a data type other than character, the error message *Not a Character expression* is displayed.

Tips

Note that ACCEPT creates the named memory variable so that it does not have to be initialized before the command is executed; in fact, if the memory variable does exist, it is overwritten without any warning.

INPUT is very similar to ACCEPT, but it allows you to create any type of memory variable, depending on what you enter in response to it. (See INPUT for more details.)

WAIT is also similar to ACCEPT, but it allows only a single character to be entered. (See WAIT for more details.)

Pressing Enter (and typing nothing else) in response to ACCEPT creates a memory variable containing a null string. If you want to force the user to enter something, put ACCEPT in a DO WHILE loop that tests for the null value. For example,

```
* The memory variable, value, is initialized to a null string
* so that the DO WHILE condition is true until the user enters
* something.
value = ""
DO WHILE "" = value
   ACCEPT "Enter a value " TO value
ENDDO
```

ACCESS( )

Syntax ACCESS()

Overview If using dBASE III PLUS in a network environment, you have the option of installing a security utility. (See Protect.) The Protect facility assigns an access level number between 1 and 8 to each user and corresponding access level numbers to files and fields. ACCESS( ) returns a value between 1 and 8, inclusive signifying the access level number of the current user. This function is effective only if you are using dBASE III PLUS in a network environment and have installed Protect; ACCESS( ) returns a value of zero if these conditions are not met.

Procedure The function is usually used in a menu program to determine which options are available to what access levels, but it cannot override the access level file and field privilege settings assigned by Protect. When using ACCESS( ) remember that users with lower access level numbers are more privileged than those with higher level numbers. A user with an ACCESS( ) value of 1 usually has full access to all field and file privileges, whereas a user with an ACCESS( ) of 8 is highly restricted.

ACCESS( ) returns a numeric value and can be used anywhere in the language where a numeric expression is appropriate.

Examples The following example is a main menu program that allows a user access to particular menu options based on the ACCESS( ) level of the user:

```
* AccsMenu.PRG
*
SET TALK OFF
CLEAR

DO WHILE .T.

   * Menu is displayed.
   @ 4, 10 SAY "0 - Exit"
   @ 5, 10 SAY "1 - Add Records"
   @ 6, 10 SAY "2 - Edit Records"
   @ 7, 10 SAY "3 - Print Reports"

   choice = 0
```

```
* The user is prompted for a value between zero and three.
@ 11, 0 SAY "Enter your selection";
      GET choice PICTURE "9" RANGE 0, 3
READ
@  9, 0   && Clear error message, if any

* The user's response is evaluated in order to determine
* what to do next.
DO CASE

   * All users can exit the menu, no access check necessary.
   CASE choice = 0
      SET TALK ON
      RETURN

   CASE choice = 1
      * Only users with access level of 4 or less
      * can add records.
      IF ACCESS( ) <= 4
         DO Add_Recs
      ELSE
         @ 9, 0 SAY "Unauthorized access level.  Try again."
         LOOP
      ENDIF

   CASE choice = 2
      * Only users with access level of 2 or less
      * can change records.
      IF ACCESS( ) <= 2
         DO EditRecs
      ELSE
         @ 9, 0 SAY "Unauthorized access level.  Try again."
         LOOP
      ENDIF

   * All users can print reports, no access check necessary.
   CASE choice = 3
      DO PrtRprts

  ENDCASE
ENDDO
```

Warnings

Some access level checking is done automatically using the access levels numbers that were assigned using Protect. (See Protect for more

information.) Hence, a user with an access level number of 5 cannot open a database file with a read access level of 3. For example,

```
IF ACCESS() <= 5
   USE Mail   && Assume mail has read access level of 3
ENDIF
```

results in the error message *Unauthorized access level* when USE is executed because the access level of the user is 5, which is greater than the file read access level of 3. The access levels assigned in Protect always take precedence, and the user access level must be less than or equal to the file access level in order to perform the file operation (i.e., Read, Update, Extend, or Delete).

Certain fields may be inaccessible even if the user has an access level that allows any operation on a particular database file. For example, assume that the current user has an access level of 2 and that the mailing list database file has an access level of 3 for all file operations. Although it seems that this user should be able to perform any operation at all on the mailing list file, individual field access levels must be considered. Using Protect, all fields in a database file can be assigned different privileges (i.e., FULL, NONE, or R/O) for each access level. Assuming that for access level 2 the Phone field had been assigned a privilege of NONE, the user would not be able to access the Phone number of an individual, much less change its value. For example,

```
IF ACCESS() <= 2
   USE Mail
   EDIT FIELDS Last_Name, Phone
ENDIF
```

results in the error message *Unauthorized access level* when the EDIT command is executed because a user with access level 2 has no access to the Phone field.

Tips

Note that ACCESS( ), if used correctly, is designed so that a program using it will operate in a single-user environment or in a network environment on which Protect has not been installed. (ACCESS( ) is always zero in these cases.) The function value should never be compared for equality to a particular value; it should be compared to see if it is at least as large as a particular value (i.e., ACCESS( ) < = <value>). For example, the program that is listed under Examples above works under any environment. Since ACCESS( ) is zero, any user satisfies both IF conditions and can add and edit records.

ALIAS

Overview

dBASE III PLUS provides the capability of assigning an alias name to a database file when you open the file. (See USE.) The naming convention used for alias names is identical to that of fields and memory variables. An alias name

- can be anywhere from one to ten characters in length,
- must begin with a letter, and
- can contain only letters, numbers, and underscores.

Procedure

You may use the ALIAS keyword of USE (see USE) to specify an alias name for a database file when you open the file; otherwise, dBASE III PLUS assigns a default alias name to the file using the root portion of the database file name (i.e., the eight-letter file name without the drive letter, path name, or file extension).

In addition to the database alias name that is assigned either by you or by the system, the work area in which the database file is opened also has an alias name that relates to its work area number. The work areas are numbered from 1 to 10 and assigned the alias names of A through J, respectively.

Once the database file is opened, either the database alias name or the work area alias name can be used in place of the file name to refer to the database. The alias name is generally used to SELECT the work area (see SELECT) containing the database file when you are working with more than one file (see SET RELATION) and to identify fields in a file that is not active (i.e., it is in USE in an unselected work area). To identify a field using the alias name of a database file, use the alias name followed by the arrow symbol (– >) as a prefix to the field name (e.g., Mail – >Last_Name).

The JOIN, UPDATE, and SET RELATION commands also allow an alias name as part of their syntax. Any command that allows a fields list (see FIELDS) as part of its syntax can use the alias name to refer to a field in an unselected database file using the <alias name> – > <field name> form.

Examples The following example illustrates the use of alias names with several commands:

```
* Clients.PRG
*

* For the Orders file, no alias name is specified.  Instead, the
* file name is used as the alias.
USE Orders

* Customers is assigned an alias name of Clients.
SELECT 2
USE Customer INDEX Cust_No ALIAS Clients

* Activate the Orders file using its alias name.
SELECT Orders

* Relate Orders file to Customer file using the alias Clients.
SET RELATION TO Cust_No INTO Clients

* List fields from both files.  Fields from the unselected file,
* Customer, are referred to by using the alias Clients.
LIST Part_No, Cust_No, Clients->Last_Name, Clients->Phone

CLOSE DATABASES  && Close both files
```

To execute this program and see its results,

```
. DO Clients
Record#  Part_No Cust_No Clients->Last_Name   Clients->Phone
      1  R-123   A254    SMITH                (803)255-1635
      2  B-254   F126    Moore                (803)235-3205
      3  G-165   A452    Schaefer             (213)465-5723
      4  R-123   A452    Schaefer             (213)465-5723
```

Warnings

You cannot open a database file with a name that is the same as one of the default work area alias names (i.e., the letters A through J) because these names are reserved by dBASE III PLUS. Similarly, you cannot explicitly specify a database alias name using any of these reserved names unless it happens to correspond to the current work area. The error message *ALIAS name already in use* is displayed after the USE command if you attempt to do either of these things. For example, if you have a file named A.DBF:

```
. USE A                  && A is a reserved alias name
ALIAS name already in use.
      ?
USE A
. USE Mail ALIAS B       && B is reserved for another work area
ALIAS name already in use.
                 ?
USE Mail ALIAS B
. USE Mail ALIAS A       && A is okay as ALIAS only in work area 1
```

Although it will not produce an error message, using the letter M for a database file or alias name should be avoided. This letter is reserved to distinguish a memory variable from a field name when a conflict exists. (See Memory Variables for more information.)

Tips

The maximum allowable length of a single command line in dBASE III PLUS is 254 characters, including blank spaces. Often with commands such as JOIN and UPDATE, the command line can get quite long. You can shorten the length of a command line that uses the alias name by using the default work area alias name instead of the database alias name or by assigning a shorter alias name to the file when you open it. For example, assuming that the Orders and Inventry files are set up for a JOIN (see JOIN), the command

```
JOIN WITH B FOR Part_No = B->Part_No FIELDS Part_No, Cust_No,;
     Quantity, B->Descrip, B->Price TO NewFile
```

is much shorter, albeit less readable, than

```
JOIN WITH Inventry FOR Part_No = Inventry->Part_No FIELDS;
     Part_No, Cust_No, Quantity, Inventry->Descrip,;
     Inventry->Price TO NewFile
```

Although the alias name is only required to access fields in unselected files, it is occasionally used to specify the selected file in order to enhance the readability of complex expressions.

ALL. *See* Scope

APPEND

Syntax `APPEND[BLANK]`

Overview The APPEND command adds new records interactively to an existing database file. It is one of the full-screen editing commands and, as such, is able to make use of the full-screen cursor movement and editing keys. These keys are listed in a table in Appendix A.

APPEND BLANK is a special form of this command which adds a blank record to the file without entering the interactive append mode.

The append mode can be exited in one of three ways by pressing

- Enter on the first character of a new record. The current, blank record is not saved.
- Ctrl-End at any time. The current record is saved.
- Esc at any time. The current record is not saved.

Procedure Use APPEND to add records to an existing database file and input data interactively. Use APPEND BLANK to add a single blank record.

Examples The following example shows how using APPEND with and without a format file affects screen appearance. If you enter the following commands to enter APPEND without a format file, the screen should look like the one in Figure 3 (assuming SET MENUS OFF and SET STATUS OFF).

```
. USE Mail
. APPEND
```

Figure 3

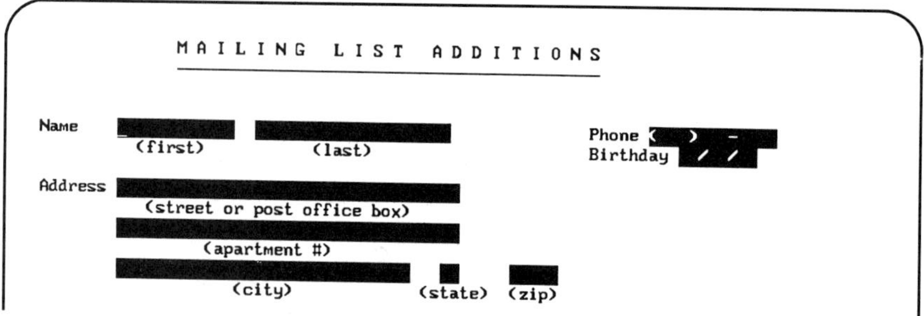

Figure 4

Activating a format file can make the screen more attractive, like the one in Figure 4. The following commands open a format file for use with APPEND:

```
. SET FORMAT TO Mail_Add
. APPEND
```

Warnings

If SET CARRY is ON, pressing PgDn on the first character of a new record adds the new record instead of exiting the append mode. This is inconsistent with the way PgDn works when SET CARRY is OFF.

Pressing Ctrl-End on a new, blank record saves the blank record to the database file. To avoid saving a blank record to your file, either press Esc or press Enter on the first character of the blank record.

If you are using dBASE III PLUS in a network environment, APPEND attempts an automatic file lock unless the database file is already locked (see FLOCK( )) or is opened for exclusive use (see SET EXCLUSIVE, USE). If the command cannot lock the database file for any reason, the error message *File is in use by another* is displayed.

Tips

APPEND BLANK is most frequently used in applications where the level of data validation sophistication must exceed what is provided by @...GET. Data validation is achieved by initializing a set of memory variables that match in length and type the fields in the database file. A format file is employed that contains a series of @...GET commands for these memory variables, and the READ command is used to activate the format file. The user inputs data into the memory variables, and a data validation routine is then invoked which may require the user to make some corrections. For example, the validation routine might do a SEEK on a key field to ensure it doesn't already exist in the database file, or test to see if a particular value is a member of a list of valid values. When all of the data is valid, an APPEND BLANK is issued followed by one or more REPLACE commands to put the memory variable values into the blank fields. (See SEEK for a good example of this.)

Use a format file if the default screen provided for the APPEND command does not appeal to you. You can use CREATE SCREEN to design format files using a screen painter approach, or you can simply enter the appropriate @ commands in a text file with an .FMT extension using MODIFY COMMAND. SET FORMAT TO activates a format file for use with the active database file.

APPEND FROM can be used to add records from another file.

APPEND FROM

Syntax

```
APPEND FROM <filename>¦? [FOR <condition>] [[TYPE]
WKS¦SYLK¦DIF¦SDF¦DELIMITED [WITH <delimiter>¦BLANK]]
```

Overview

The APPEND FROM command adds records from an existing file to the active database file. The type of file to be appended from is specified by a command line argument.

A FOR clause can be specified to limit the records that are processed. (See FOR.) Unless a FOR clause is specified, all records in the FROM file are appended.

If no TYPE is specified, the FROM file is assumed to be another database (.DBF) file. All records in the FROM file are added to the active file by field name; field names in the FROM file not found in the active file are ignored. The fields do not have to match in data type or length since APPEND FROM attempts to convert and truncate fields when necessary. Date, numeric, and logical to character conversions are always successful. Character to date, numeric, and logical conversions are successful provided that the data in the field is correct.

The ?, or catalog query clause, can be used if there is an open catalog (see SET CATALOG) to activate a menu of cataloged database files. You can select the FROM file using this menu.

The other types of files are described in turn. In appending from any of the following file types, memo fields are ignored and dates are assumed to be eight-digit numbers of the form CCYYMMDD (where CC is the century, YY is the year, MM is the month, and DD is the day).

TYPE WKS is a Lotus 1-2-3 worksheet, and the file is assumed to have a WKS extension; TYPE SYLK is a Microsoft Multiplan file, assumed to have no extension; TYPE DIF is a VisiCalc file, assumed to have a .DIF extension. All spreadsheet files are assumed to be in row major order with no leading blank columns. Any titles in the first few rows are appended into the database file. Be sure to delete title rows from the spreadsheet before doing APPEND FROM if you want only the data in your database file.

SDF, short for system data format, is an ASCII text file with fixed length fields and records. The file is assumed to have a .TXT extension. Each field is its full potential length with no delimiting or termination characters. Each record is terminated by a carriage return/linefeed pair. If appending data from an SDF file, be sure that the field lengths in your database file structure exactly match those in the SDF file ; otherwise, the data will not be appended properly. An example of an SDF file follows:

```
John        Doe        19640305      234.87
Janie       Jones      19570201       12.42
Mike        McCollough 19490505     1263.00
Susan       Simons     19591220     3562.11
Alexander   Adams      19630425        0.00
```

A DELIMITED file is also an ASCII text file, but the fields and records can be of varying lengths. As with SDF files, a .TXT extension is assumed and each record is terminated by a carriage return/linefeed pair. The fields in each record are separated by commas, and the character fields are enclosed between delimiters that you can specify using the WITH option. Double quotes are assumed if you do not specify a delimiter. An example of a file that is DELIMITED WITH ' (single quote mark) follows:

```
'John','Doe',19640305,234.87
'Janie','Jones',19570201,12.42
'Mike','McCollough',19490505,1263.00
'Susan','Simons',19591220,3562.11
'Alexander','Adams',19630425,0.00
```

In a delimited file, logical values are represented by a single character (i.e., T, F, N, or Y) that may be uppercase or lowercase. Logical and date values may be delimited like character values.

DELIMITED WITH BLANK is a special text file in which each field is separated from the next by a blank space with no other delimiters.

Procedure

Use APPEND FROM to add the records from another file to the active database file. The command has various forms designed to add records from several different types of file. These are listed below:

- APPEND FROM < filename > adds records from another dBASE III PLUS database (.DBF) file.

- APPEND FROM <filename> DIF adds records from a VisiCalc (.DIF) file.
- APPEND FROM <filename> SYLK adds records from a Microsoft Multiplan file.
- APPEND FROM <filename> WKS adds records from a Lotus 1-2-3 work sheet (.WKS) file.
- APPEND FROM <filename> SDF adds records from an ASCII text (.TXT) file in system data format.
- APPEND FROM <filename> DELIMITED adds records from an ASCII text (.TXT) file that is delimited.

Examples

The following example appends an ASCII text file with several record types, each of which is identified by a character in the first position of each record. The text file is delimited with double quote marks; an uppercase letter in the first position indicates a newly hired individual. The example can be used to update the Employee file by adding the new hires from this text file.

```
* New_Hire.PRG
*
SET TALK OFF
USE Employee
* Save last record number before adding new hires.
GO BOTTOM
last = RECNO()
* Add records from the DELIMITED file.
APPEND FROM Master FOR ISUPPER(Emp_Code) DELIMITED
* Go to the last record before new hires were added.
GO last + 1
* List the rest of the records to see newly added records.
LIST REST Emp_Code, Last_Name, Salary
CLOSE DATABASES
SET TALK ON
```

In order to demonstrate the result of this program on the Employee database file, the file Master.TXT is listed before the program is executed:

```
. USE Employee
. TYPE Master.TXT
"A033","David","Gurly",45000.00
"b123","Perry","Lester"
"9870","Doug","Smith"
"@143","Wade","Adams"
"F375","Lawrence","Arthur",37389.00
"A333","Jeff","Potter",47823.98
"0178","Jerry","Samuels"
"9999","Chris","Whiteside"

. DO New_Hire
Record#  Emp_Code Last_Name           Salary
     11  A033     Gurly               45000.00
     12  F375     Arthur              37389.00
     13  A333     Potter              47823.98
```

Warnings If the named file cannot be found, the error message *File does not exist* is displayed. Be sure that you have specified the correct file name extension if it differs from the default for the type of file that you APPEND FROM.

If you attempt to APPEND FROM a database file that is open in another work area, the error message *File is already open* is displayed. Do a DISPLAY STATUS to find out which work area contains the FROM file, SELECT that work area, and issue a USE command with no parameters to close the file. Then, SELECT the original work area and issue APPEND FROM again.

If you are using dBASE III PLUS in a network environment, APPEND FROM attempts an automatic file lock unless the database file is already locked (see FLOCK( )) or is opened for exclusive use (see SET EXCLUSIVE, USE). If the command cannot lock the database file for any reason, the error message *File is in use by another* is displayed.

Tips dBASE III PLUS also has the capability of reading PFS:File files using IMPORT. In addition to appending the records from the file, this command creates the appropriate database file structure for you. (See IMPORT for more information.)

ASC( )

Syntax `ASC(<expC>)`

Overview The ASC( ) function, short for ASCII, accepts a character expression as its argument. The function evaluates the expression to obtain the resulting character string and then returns the numeric ASCII code for the first character in that string. The code that is returned is a decimal number between zero and 255, inclusive. (See the table in Appendix C for a list of the ASCII codes.)

Procedure ASC( ) returns a number, and can be used anywhere in the language where a numeric expression is appropriate.

Examples ASC( ) can be used whenever you want the ASCII code for a single character. The following example program generates a portion of the table in Appendix C, beginning with a character that is entered from the console:

```
* Ascii.PRG
*
SET TALK OFF
CLEAR
WAIT "Enter any character:" TO symbol
decimal = ASC(symbol)
* ASC() determines the decimal ASCII code for the character.
? "        ASCII CODE TABLE"
? "     Decimal        Symbol"
DO WHILE decimal < 255
   symbol = CHR(decimal)
   ? decimal, SPACE(10), symbol
   decimal = decimal + 1
ENDDO
SET TALK ON
```

Warnings If the function argument evaluates to a data type other than character, the error message *Invalid function argument* is displayed.

If the function results in the error message *Variable not found*, you probably used a literal character string as the function argument, and it is being interpreted as a variable name. The character string, in this case, must be enclosed in single quotes, double quotes, or square brackets.

ASSIST

Syntax `ASSIST`

Overview The ASSIST command invokes the Assistant, the menu-driven system that allows you to use a series of menu selections to construct and execute many of the dBASE III PLUS commands.

Procedure Use ASSIST if you are unfamiliar with the dBASE III PLUS commands and their syntax. When using ASSIST, you construct and execute commands by making a series of menu selections. Navigation instructions are always shown just below the status bar; below these instructions is a message explaining the current menu selection. Just above the status bar is the Command line on which the Assistant displays the command that you are constructing. The menu navigation and selection keys are detailed in Appendix B.

The Set Up menu allows you to open various types of files and to quit out of dBASE III PLUS. As with all other menu options in the Assistant, each option in this menu corresponds to a single command. (For more information on a particular command, see the entry for that command.) The Set Up menu and its corresponding commands are shown in Figure 5.

The Create menu allows you to create files. This menu and its corresponding commands are shown in Figure 6.

The Update menu allows you to make changes to the active database file. Some of the changes you can make include adding new records,

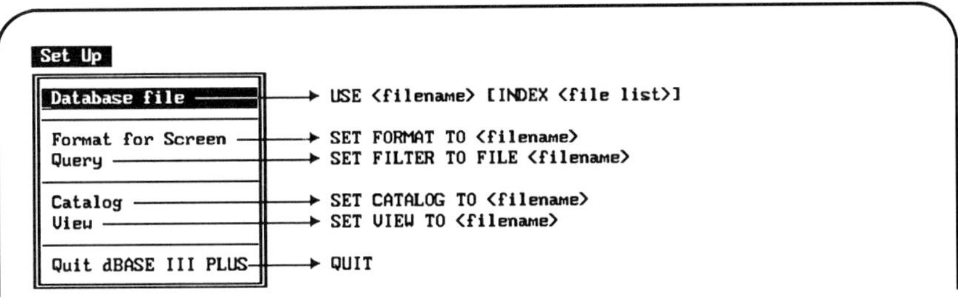

Figure 5

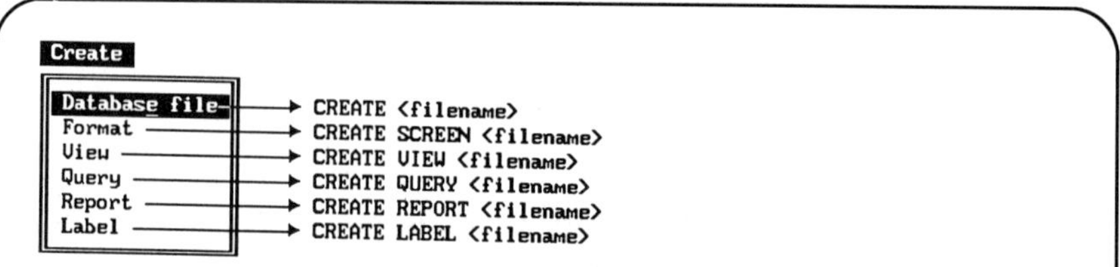

Figure 6

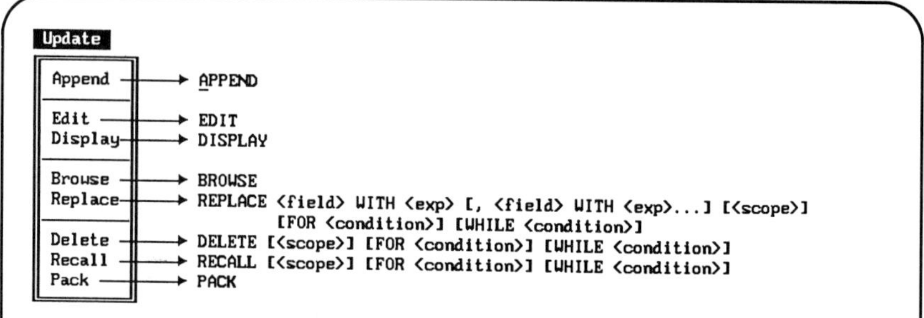

Figure 7

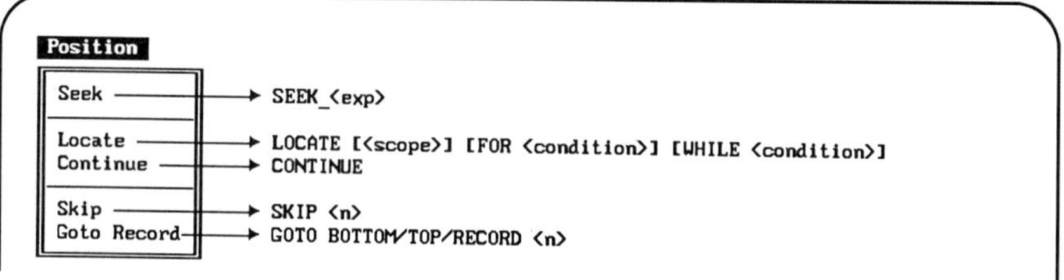

Figure 8

editing individual records with EDIT and BROWSE, and making mass updates with REPLACE. The Update menu and its corresponding commands are shown in Figure 7.

The Position menu allows you to move the record pointer in the active database file. You can LOCATE records based on conditions, SEEK records based on an index key value, or position the record pointer to a specific record number. This menu and its corresponding commands are shown in Figure 8.

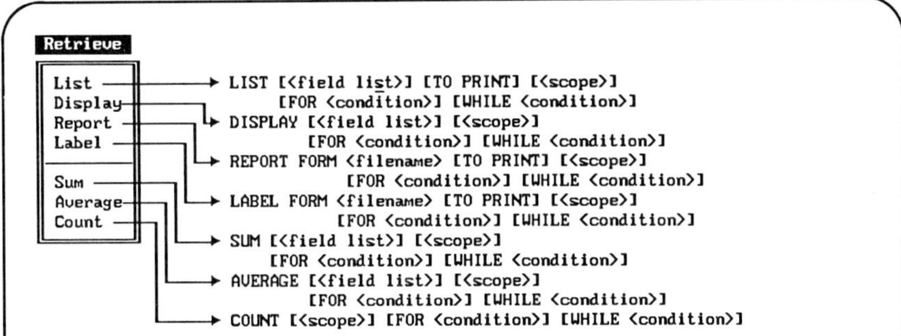

Figure 9

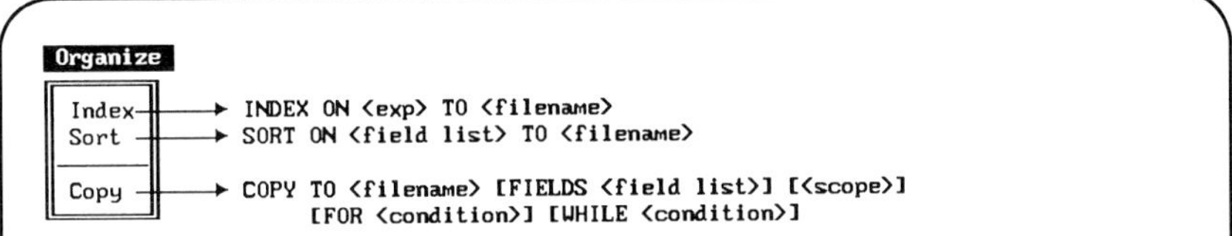

Figure 10

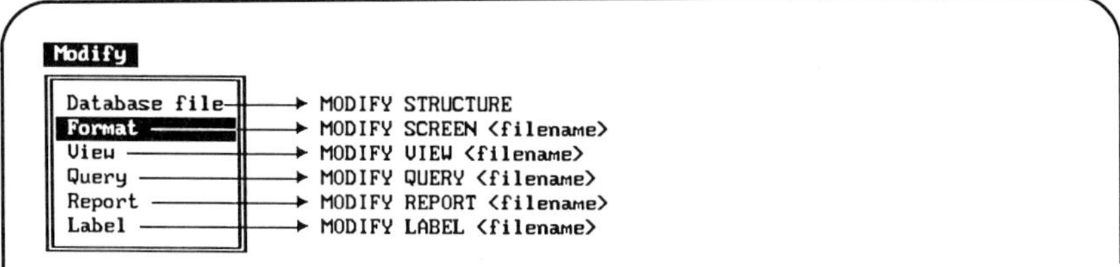

Figure 11

The Retrieve menu retrieves and displays data from the active database file. This menu and its corresponding commands are shown in Figure 9.

The Organize menu allows you to SORT and INDEX your database file so that the records are organized in a particular order. It also allows you to make a copy of the active database file. The Organize menu and its corresponding commands are shown in Figure 10.

The Modify menu allows you make changes to your files. This menu and its corresponding commands are shown in Figure 11.

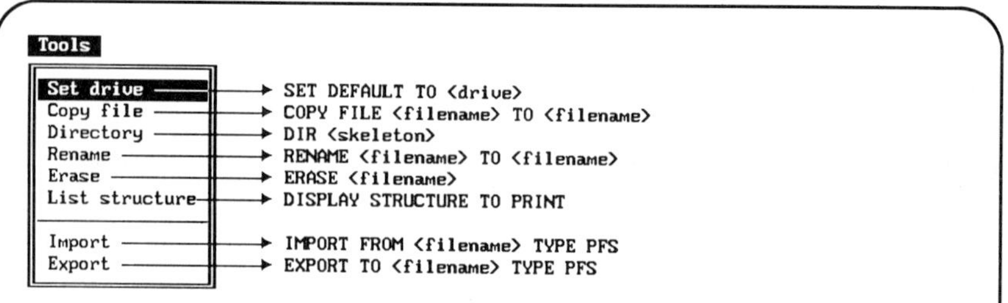

Figure 12

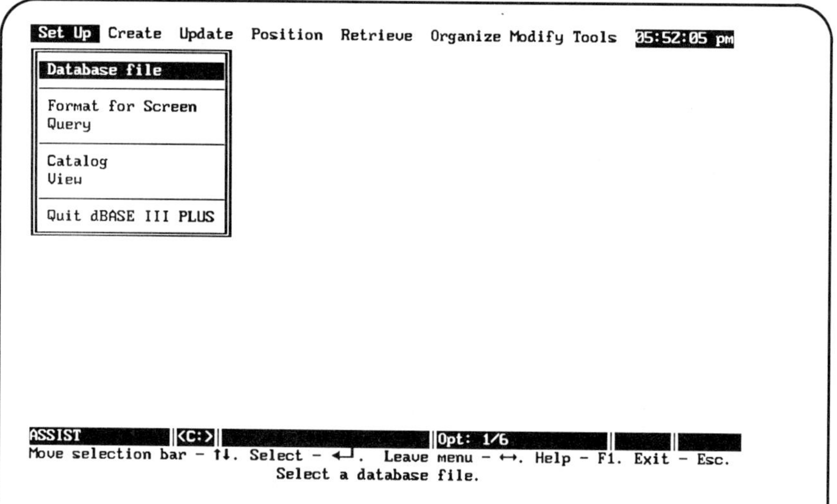

Figure 13

The Tools menu gives you access to the disk utilities that are available in the dBASE III PLUS command language. These include setting the default drive, getting a disk directory, and COPY, RENAME, and ERASE commands. Import/Export capabilities are also in this menu. This menu and its corresponding commands are shown in Figure 12.

Examples

The following example steps you through the execution of a LIST command with a FIELDS list and a FOR condition. This illustration shows many of the submenus that occur in ASSIST. At the dot prompt, enter ASSIST to invoke the Assistant. The menu bar of the Assistant is shown in Figure 13.

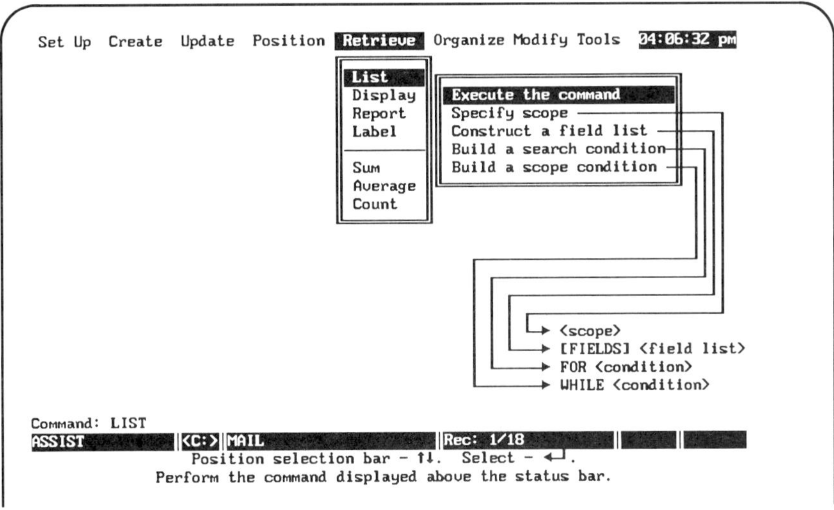

Figure 14

To open a database file, press Enter to select the highlighted Database file option. Select the drive letter that contains your database file, and select MAIL.DBF from the list of database files. Type N at the index prompt. You are now ready to use the Assistant menus to construct and execute the following LIST command.

```
LIST First_Name, Last_Name, Birthday FOR Phone = "(213)"
```

Navigate to the Retrieve menu by typing an R. (Any item on the menu bar can be selected quickly by using the first letter of its name.) Select List, the first item in the menu, by pressing Enter. The screen should look something like the one in Figure 14. You will often see this submenu when you use the Assistant. The submenu is annotated to show the command line parameter that results with each menu option.

You need a FIELDS list and a FOR condition for the LIST command that you want to build. Use the Down Arrow key to highlight the *Construct a field list* option and press Enter. A list of the available fields in the mailing list will be displayed as in Figure 15.

Select FIRST_NAME, LAST_NAME, and BIRTHDAY from the list by highlighting each one and pressing Enter. After selecting the three fields,

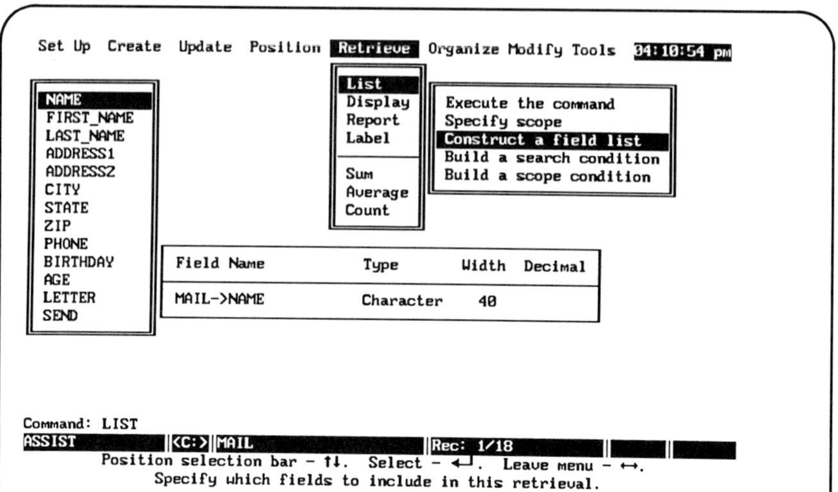

Figure 15

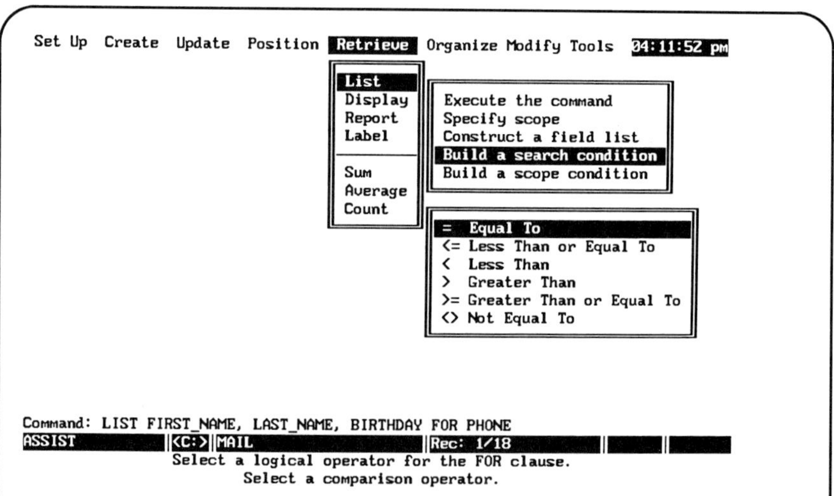

Figure 16

press the Right Arrow to close the fields list. Next, select *Build a search condition* from the submenu, then select the Phone field from the available fields list. Your screen should look like the one in Figure 16.

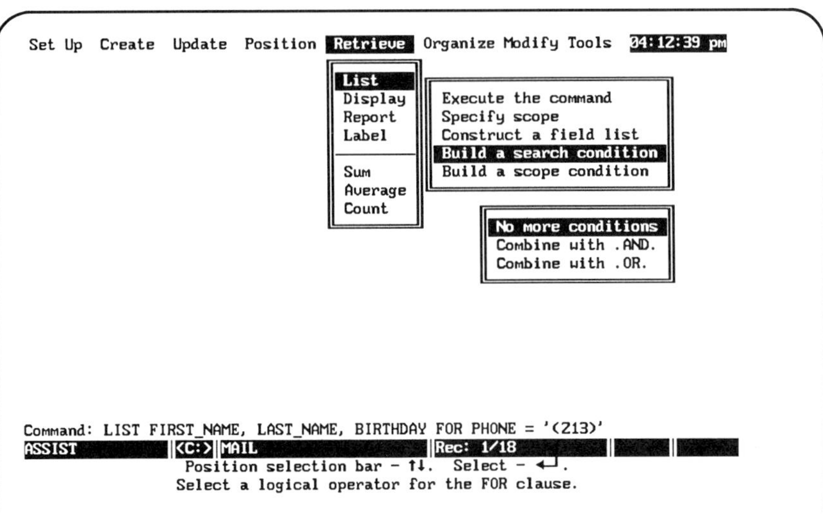

Figure 17

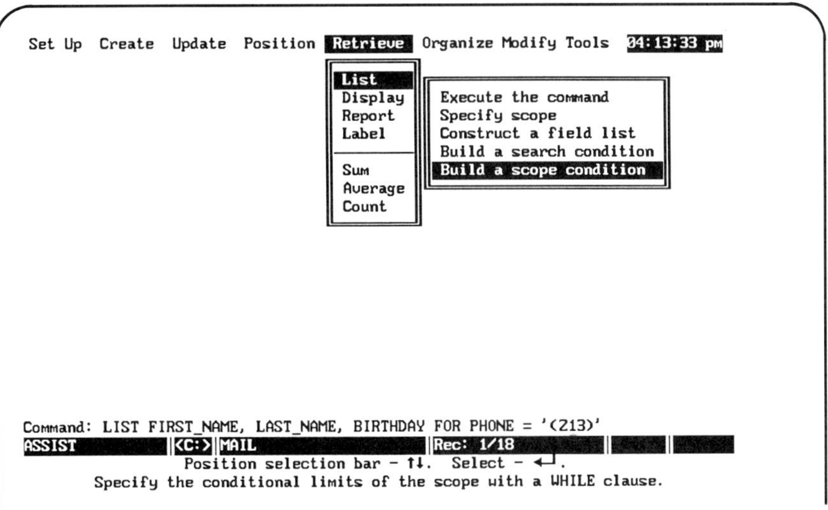

Figure 18

Select the *Equal to* option. At the prompt, enter a character string without quotes. Type (213) and press Enter, and you are presented with the submenu that you see in Figure 17.

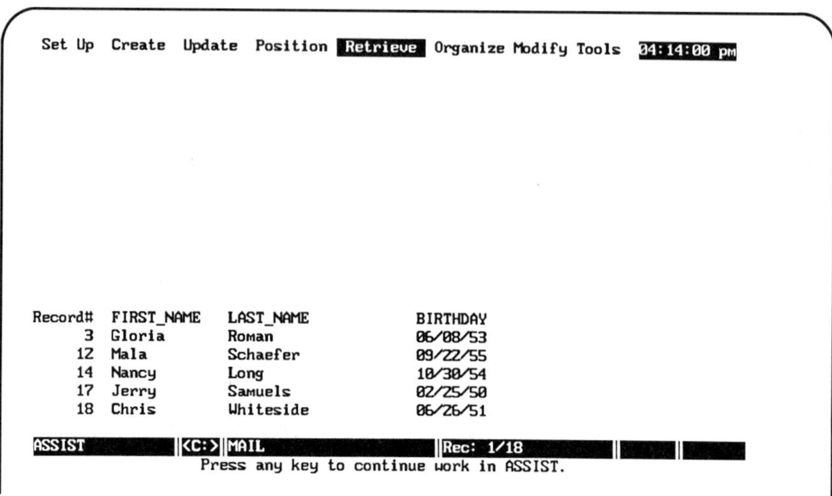

Figure 19

At this point, you can continue to construct a more complicated FOR condition by selecting either of the logical connectors (.AND. or .OR.) from the submenu. You will then be led through the series of menus where you select a field, select an operator, and enter a value. For this example, you don't want any additional conditions, so select *No more conditions*. You will be back in the original submenu, with your completed command displayed on the Command line as you see in Figure 18.

Select *Execute the command*, and you will get a chance to print the LIST command result. Since you don't want to print it, press Enter, and LIST is executed. The result is displayed in Figure 19.

The message line will prompt you to press any key to return to the Assistant.

Tips

The commands executed from ASSIST are recorded in the history buffer if SET HISTORY is ON. This is a helpful feature if you use the Assistant to execute the same procedure repeatedly, as you can easily put the series of commands into a program file.

Before going into the Assistant, be sure that the history buffer is set to a large enough value to hold all of the commands. The following command file increases the buffer size to 100, invokes ASSIST, and saves the resulting output to a command file:

```
* Make_Prg.PRG
*
SET DOHISTORY OFF
SET HISTORY ON      && Just to make sure
SET TALK OFF
SET HISTORY TO 0    && Clear history buffer
SET HISTORY TO 100  && Change number if 100 lines is not enough
ASSIST
prg_name = SPACE(8)
@ 10, 0 SAY "Enter a name for this program file " GET prg_name
READ
* Use SET ALTERNATE and LIST HISTORY to create a .PRG file.
prg_name = TRIM(prg_name) + ".PRG"
SET ALTERNATE TO &prg_name
SET ALTERNATE ON
LIST HISTORY
CLOSE ALTERNATE
SET HISTORY TO 20    && Reset history buffer
SET TALK ON
```

Instead of typing ASSIST at the dot prompt, type `DO Make_Prg`. The program then sets up the history buffer and invokes the Assistant. As you make menu selections in ASSIST, the corresponding commands are recorded in the history buffer. When you exit the Assistant by pressing Esc, the program asks you to enter the name of a program file and then writes the contents of the history buffer to that file. Now, instead of repeating this series of commands using ASSIST, simply DO <filename>, where <filename> is the name that you entered.

AT()

Syntax `AT(<expC1>, <expC2>)`

Overview The AT() function asks, "What is the starting position of one character string within another?". It requires two character expressions for its arguments. The function evaluates the expressions to obtain the resulting character strings and then returns the starting position of the first string within the second.

Since the length of character strings in dBASE III PLUS is limited to 254 characters (including spaces), the result of AT( ) is a number between zero and 254, inclusive. A result of zero indicates that the first string was not found anywhere within the second string.

Procedure

AT( ) returns a number and can be used anywhere in the language where a numeric expression is appropriate.

Examples

AT( ) is useful in extracting phrases from a long character field where the phrases are separated by a designated character such as a comma. An example is a medical application in which the symptoms of a patient's illness are kept in a single field. Assuming that each symptom in the field is separated from the next symptom by a comma, the following program extracts each symptom from the field and displays the symptoms on the screen:

```
* NextWord.PRG
*
SET TALK OFF
USE Medical
rest_word = Symptoms
last_word = .F.
DO WHILE .NOT. last_word .AND. LEN(TRIM(rest_word)) > 0
   word_end = AT(",", rest_word) - 1
   * AT() is used to determine the position of the separator,
   * which determines where one word ends and the next begins.
   next_word = word_end + 2
   IF word_end < 0
      last_word = .T.
      ? TRIM(LTRIM(rest_word))
   ELSE
      ? SUBSTR(rest_word, 1, word_end)
      rest_word = LTRIM(SUBSTR(rest_word, next_word))
   ENDIF
ENDDO
CLOSE DATABASES
SET TALK ON
```

To execute this program and see the results,

```
. DO NextWord
Sniffles
headache
scratchy throat
aching muscles
```

Warnings If either function argument evaluates to a data type other than character, the error message *Invalid function argument* is displayed.

If the function results in the error message *Variable not found*, you probably used a literal character string as one or both of the function arguments and the string is being interpreted as a variable name. The character string, in this case, must be enclosed in single quotes, double quotes, or square brackets.

Tips In dBASE III PLUS, all character string comparisons are case-sensitive (e.g., a lowercase "a" is not equal to an uppercase "A"). Use UPPER() if you want to ignore the distinction between lowercase and uppercase when using AT( ). UPPER( ) converts a character string to all uppercase letters. For example,

```
. USE Medical
. ? AT("SNIFFLES", Symptoms)
         0
```

The result in this case is zero because the symptom was entered as "Sniffles". You could use

```
. ? AT("SNIFFLES", UPPER(Symptoms))
         1
```

to determine more accurately if a patient has the sniffles.

Similarly, LOWER( ), which converts a character string to all lowercase letters, can be used. For example,

```
. ? AT("sniffles", LOWER(Symptoms))
        1
```

would also accurately determine if a patient has the sniffles.

AVERAGE

Syntax `AVERAGE [<scope>] [WHILE <condition>] [FOR <condition>] [<expN list>] [TO <memory variable list>]`

Overview The AVERAGE command computes the arithmetic mean, or average, of one or more numbers by processing a specified set of records in the active database file. If this command is issued when there is no file in use in the current work area, you are prompted to enter the name of a database file. The average is computed by taking a running sum of each numeric field and dividing it by the total number of records processed.

The result of the command is displayed on the screen with headings if both SET HEADING and SET TALK are ON. SET HEADING OFF suppresses the field name headings, and SET TALK OFF completely suppresses the screen output of AVERAGE.

In its simplest form (i.e., no command line arguments are specified), AVERAGE calculates the arithmetic mean of all numeric fields for each record in the active database file.

A scope, a FOR clause, and a WHILE clause can be specified to limit the records which are processed. Each of these command line options is discussed separately. (See Scope, FOR, and WHILE.) The default scope of AVERAGE is all records.

The expression list is used to limit the fields and to specify more complicated numbers to be averaged. If used, the list must consist of one or more numeric expressions separated by commas.

The result of AVERAGE can be saved in one or more memory variables using the TO clause. Items in the memory variable list are separated by commas.

Procedure

Use AVERAGE to compute the arithmetic mean of one or more fields in the active database file. The result is displayed if SET TALK is ON and can be saved in one or more memory variables for later use.

Examples

The following example uses a database file of the scores of students who have taken one of three tests. The average score is computed for all students, and then an average for each test is computed.

```
. USE Tests
. AVERAGE Score
      6 records averaged
Score
   87
. AVERAGE Score FOR Test_Num = 1
      2 records averaged
Score
   85
. AVERAGE Score FOR Test_Num = 2
      2 records averaged
Score
   80
. AVERAGE Score FOR Test_Num = 3
      2 records averaged
Score
   95
. CLOSE DATABASES
```

Warnings

If the number of memory variables listed in the TO clause does not match the number of numbers to be averaged (i.e., the number of expressions in the list or the number of numeric fields in the database file), the error message *Syntax error* is displayed.

If an expression in the expression list evaluates to a data type other than numeric, the error message *Not a numeric expression* is displayed.

If you misspell a field name or include a memory variable that has not been initialized in the expression list, the error message *Variable not found* is displayed.

If you are using dBASE III PLUS in a network environment, AVERAGE attempts an automatic file lock unless the database file is already locked (see FLOCK( )) or is opened for exclusive use (see SET EXCLUSIVE, USE). If for any reason the command cannot lock the database file, the error message *File is in use by another* is displayed.

Tips

dBASE III PLUS also has a SUM command to compute the sum of one or more numbers. AVERAGE and SUM are the only statistical functions available in the command language at this time. (See SET PROCEDURE for an example that calculates a few other statistical values.)

BOF( )

Syntax `BOF()`

Overview

The BOF( ) function, short for beginning of file, has no argument. The function returns a logical True (.T.) if the active database file is positioned at the beginning of the file; otherwise, it returns a logical False (.F.).

Procedure

In order to use BOF( ) effectively, a database file must be in use in the current work area. (See USE.) BOF( ) returns a logical false (.F.) if there is no open database file.

BOF( ) returns a logical value, and can be used anywhere in the language where a logical expression (i.e., condition) is appropriate.

Examples

BOF( ) is useful when you process a database file starting with the last record. To do this, you must skip backward through the file, then test for the beginning of the file to stop the process. This procedure is illustrated in the following routine which lists customer names in descending order according to the amount that each one owes. The example assumes that you already have an index on the Amt_Owed field called Amount.

```
* Backward.PRG
*
SET TALK OFF
USE Customer INDEX Amount
GO BOTTOM
DO WHILE .NOT. BOF()
   ? Last_Name, Amt_Owed
   SKIP -1
ENDDO
CLOSE DATABASES
SET TALK ON
```

To execute the program and see its results,

```
. DO BackWard
Moore              1500.43
King               1500.00
SMITH              1000.00
Schaefer            193.79
Long                 75.98
Roman                30.00
Richardson           27.50
Roberts               0.00
MOODY               -10.00
Corbbit             -25.00
```

Warnings

Unlike the EOF( ) function, the RECNO( ) function cannot be used to detect the BOF( ) condition. When EOF( ) is true, RECNO( ) is always equal to one plus the total number of records in the file. This is the only time RECNO( ) takes on this value. When BOF( ) is true, RECNO( ) is always equal to one; however, this condition is also true when the record pointer is positioned on the first record.

If BOF( ) is true and an attempt is made to SKIP using a negative number (e.g., SKIP-1) the error message *Beginning of file encountered* is displayed.

Tips

Unless you force it to process a database file in reverse order with a routine like the one above, dBASE III PLUS always processes all database files from top to bottom. Therefore, the only way to make BOF( ) true is to issue a SKIP -x command when the active database file is positioned at a record whose record number is less than or equal to x. (This is considerably different from EOF( ) which can be made true with many commands.)

BROWSE

Syntax

```
BROWSE [FIELDS <field list>] [LOCK <expN>]
[FREEZE <fieldname>] [WIDTH <expN>] [NOAPPEND]
[NOFOLLOW] [NOMENU]
```

Overview

The BROWSE command provides a tabular view of the records in your database file and allows you to edit existing data and to add new records. As one of the full-screen editing commands, it is able to make use of the full-screen cursor movement and editing keys. These keys are listed in a table in Appendix A.

When used in its simplest form with no command line options, BROWSE presents you with a table of records beginning with the current record in the active database file. The first field in the file is the first column in the table, the second field is the second column, and so on. Each field uses a width equal to its length in the database file structure, and all records are accessible using the proper cursor navigation keys.

The fields included in the table can be limited using the FIELDS list. The FIELDS list is discussed separately under its own heading.

Usually, all fields in the BROWSE table can move in and out of view when you pan the screen left and right. The LOCK option allows you to specify one or more fields on the left side of the screen that won't move (i.e., you LOCK them into place) when you pan the screen. The number of fields is specified with a numeric expression.

By default, you can edit all fields that you see in the BROWSE table. The FREEZE option limits your ability to edit to a single field that you specify by name.

The WIDTH option uses a numeric expression to specify the maximum display width for character fields in the BROWSE table. Fields that exceed the specified WIDTH are horizontally scrolled. Character fields that are shorter in width and other field types are unaffected by the WIDTH option.

The NOAPPEND option disables your ability to add records in BROWSE. If you don't use this option and you attempt to navigate past the last record in the database file, you are prompted as to whether or not you want to add new records. If you type Y, you enter the append mode of BROWSE and can add as many records as you want.

The NOFOLLOW option is effective only if an index file is in use with the active database file. When an index file is in use and you update a key field in BROWSE, the record is repositioned according to its new index key. If NOFOLLOW is specified, the record pointer is moved to the next record before the index file is updated (i.e., the record pointer does not follow the index file). Without NOFOLLOW, the record pointer is moved to the next record after the index file is updated.

BROWSE has a menu bar that is accessed by pressing F10. The menu bar allows you to navigate quickly through the database file and to specify LOCK and FREEZE options. The NOMENU option disables the user's ability to access the menu bar in BROWSE.

Procedure

Use BROWSE to view more than one record at a time when editing records in your database file. Once the BROWSE table is displayed on the screen, you can navigate through your database file and make any necessary changes. Editing and navigation are straightforward using the standard keys. If your file has more fields than can fit on a single screen, you can pan the other fields into view. Ctrl-Right Arrow pans the entire screen to the left to bring new fields into view on the right side of the screen; Ctrl-Left Arrow pans the entire screen to the right to bring new fields into view on the left side of the screen.

You can access a menu bar (see Figure 20) that gives you several navigation shortcuts and allows you to FREEZE and LOCK by pressing F10. For this reason, the BROWSE table always has a status bar and a message, regardless of SET STATUS and SET MESSAGE. Once the menu bar is displayed, you navigate it using the Left Arrow and Right Arrow keys, and select an option by pressing Enter when it is highlighted. The menu bar options are discussed in the list below:

- The *Bottom* option moves the record pointer to the last record in the table.
- The *Top* option moves the record pointer to the first record in the table.

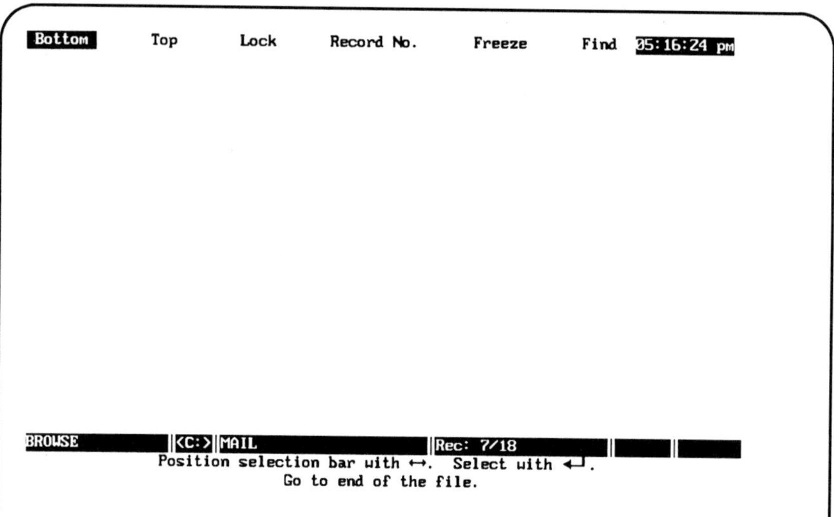

Figure 20

- The *Lock* option prompts you with *Change number of columns to lock to* and expects you to enter a number. It is equivalent to the LOCK command line option.
- The *Record No.* option prompts you with *Enter new record number* and expects you to enter a number. The record pointer is moved to the record number that you enter.
- The *Freeze* option prompts you with *Enter field name to freeze* and expects you to enter a field name. It is equivalent to the FREEZE command line option.
- The *Find* option appears on the menu bar only if there is an index file in use. It prompts you with *Enter search string* and expects you to enter a literal value (i.e., a value that is not enclosed by delimiters). The record pointer is positioned to the first record in the database file with an index key that matches the value that you enter. You are reprompted if the key value is not found.

You can press the Escape key to remove the menu bar.

Examples

The following example illustrates how to use BROWSE with several of its options. In the example, a FIELDS list is defined to limit the fields that are in the table, the first field which happens to be the index key field is locked

into place for reference, the WIDTH option is used so that long fields display in thirty columns or less, and the NOAPPEND option is specified to prevent the addition of more records in this particular BROWSE session.

```
. USE Employee INDEX Emp_Code
. BROWSE FIELDS Emp_Code, Last_Name, Hire_Date, Comment, Salary
LOCK 1 WIDTH 30 NOAPPEND
```

Because of the command line options, the BROWSE command on the previous screen wraps around. If you enter this command at the dot prompt, do not press the Enter key until after you type the entire command. Your screen should look like the one in Figure 21.

Notice how the Comment field is shortened to thirty characters. If you pan the screen to the left using Ctrl-Right Arrow, you notice that the Emp_Code field remains stationary and the Salary field comes into view. Your screen should look like the one in Figure 22.

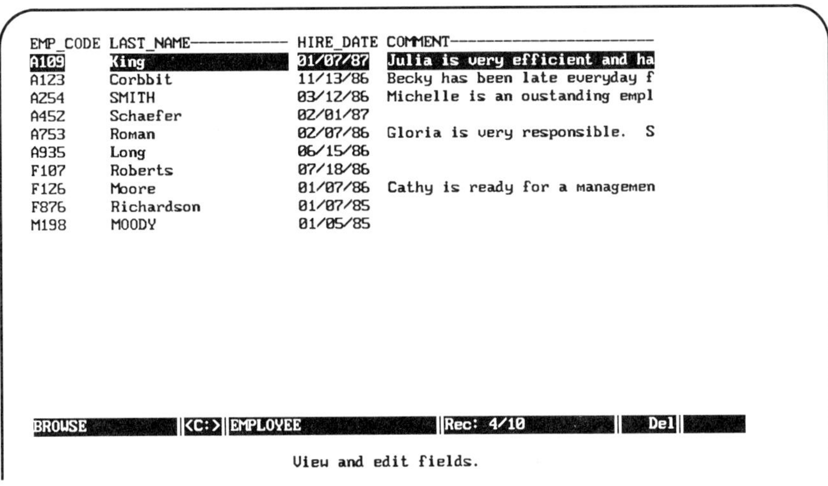

EMP_CODE LAST_NAME HIRE_DATE COMMENT
A109 King 01/07/87 Julia is very efficient and ha
A123 Corbbit 11/13/86 Becky has been late everyday f
A254 SMITH 03/12/86 Michelle is an oustanding empl
A452 Schaefer 02/01/87
A753 Roman 02/07/86 Gloria is very responsible. S
A935 Long 06/15/86
F107 Roberts 07/18/86
F126 Moore 01/07/86 Cathy is ready for a managemen
F876 Richardson 01/07/85
M198 MOODY 01/05/85
BROWSE <C:> EMPLOYEE Rec: 4/10 Del
View and edit fields.

Figure 21

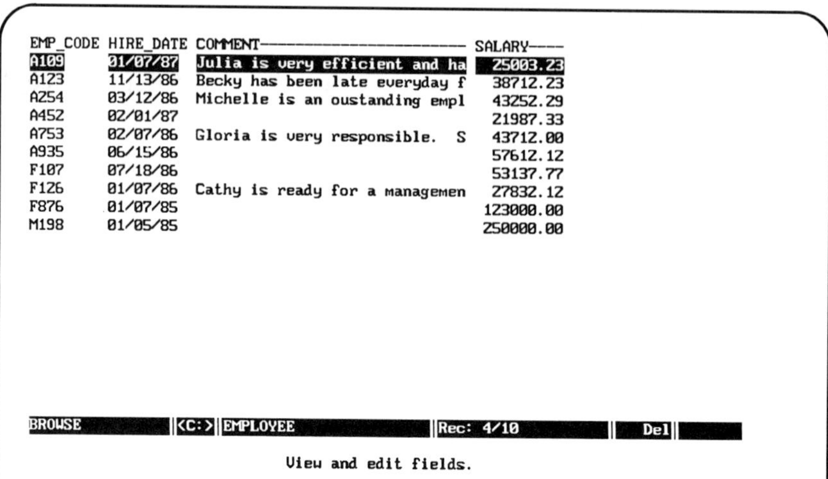

EMP_CODE HIRE_DATE COMMENT---------------------- SALARY----
A109 01/07/87 Julia is very efficient and ha 25003.23
A123 11/13/86 Becky has been late everyday f 38712.23
A254 03/12/86 Michelle is an oustanding empl 43252.29
A452 02/01/87 21987.33
A753 02/07/86 Gloria is very responsible. S 43712.00
A935 06/15/86 57612.12
F107 07/18/86 53137.77
F126 01/07/86 Cathy is ready for a managemen 27832.12
F876 01/07/85 123000.00
M198 01/05/85 250000.00
BROWSE
<C:>
EMPLOYEE
Rec: 4/10
Del
View and edit fields.

Figure 22

Warnings You cannot edit memo fields in BROWSE.

If you have a SET RELATION TO in effect for the active database file with a SET FIELDS list with fields from both files, BROWSE allows you to edit fields from both files but does not allow you to add records, regardless of whether you use the NOAPPEND option.

The BROWSE table does not automatically pan when entering data. To edit fields that are not on the screen, you must pan left or right using the Ctrl-Right Arrow and Ctrl-Left Arrow keys, until the field that you are looking for comes into view.

If you have a character field that is wider than the remaining number of columns on the screen, you may have to pan the screen several times before you are able to see that field.

Both the LOCK and WIDTH options can cause the error message *Not a numeric expression* if the corresponding expression evaluates to a data type other than numeric. Each can also cause the error message *Variable not found* if the expression cannot be evaluated.

If the value of the LOCK expression is greater than the number of fields in the table, the error message *Illegal value* is displayed.

The value of the WIDTH expression must be between four and ninety-nine, inclusive; otherwise, a *Syntax error* is displayed.

If either the FREEZE field name or any of the fields in the FIELDS list cannot be found, the error message *Variable not found* is displayed.

If you are using dBASE III PLUS in a network environment, BROWSE attempts an automatic file lock unless the database file is already locked (see FLOCK( )) or is opened for exclusive use (see SET EXCLUSIVE, USE). If for any reason the command cannot lock the database file, the error message *File is in use by another* is displayed.

CALL

Syntax

```
CALL <binary module name>
[WITH <memory variable>¦<expC>]
```

Overview

The CALL command executes a binary program. The CS (code segment) register points to the beginning address of the module when it is executed with CALL.

The WITH option is used to pass a single parameter to the binary program. This parameter can be passed as a memory variable of any type or as a character expression. The DS:BX registers contain the address of the first byte of the WITH parameter when the module is called.

Procedure

In order to CALL a module, you must first use LOAD to place the binary file in memory. Then, use CALL followed by the root portion of the binary file name (i.e., the name of the file with no extension or path name) to execute the program.

Use the WITH option to pass a parameter to the binary program. A memory variable name used as the parameter can be of any data type; the binary program can change its value but not its length. If the binary program expects a character string as the parameter and does not change its value, you can pass it as a character expression.

In order to LOAD and CALL programs from within dBASE III PLUS, you must have additional memory above the 256K required memory.

Examples See LOAD for a complete example of loading a binary file into memory and executing it using CALL.

Warnings If you attempt to CALL a module without first using LOAD to load it from disk file to memory, the error message *File was not LOADed* is displayed.

Tips Modules are put into memory using LOAD and released using RELEASE MODULE.

CANCEL

Syntax `CANCEL`

Overview The CANCEL command terminates a program and returns control to the dot prompt. When the command is executed, the warning message *Do cancelled* is displayed.

Procedure Occasionally, an anticipated error condition prevents recovery and normal program execution. In this situation, use CANCEL to indicate an abnormal ending to a program. Never use CANCEL as the normal ending of a command file; use RETURN instead.

Examples The following program segment uses CANCEL to stop an application if there is an error in attempting to open the Employee database file (e.g., the file cannot be found or the file header is corrupted). ON ERROR is used to trap and detect an error. This program is assumed to be a subroutine of a main menu program, or else RETURN could have been used instead of CANCEL. Since the application cannot continue without this database file, it is acceptable to stop the application at a level other than the main program.

```
* GetFile.PRG
*
    .
    .
    .
ON ERROR CANCEL  && Enable error branch
```

```
USE Employee
ON ERROR          && Disable error branch
    .
    .
    .
```

Warnings Allowing only one entry and one exit point from any application is a good programming practice. (An application is one or more programs that work together to accomplish a task.) Usually, there is a main program that presents the user with a list of choices, one of which is to exit the program; however, instead of using CANCEL, it is more appropriate to use RETURN to return control to the dot prompt. At the level of the main program, the two commands are equivalent except that CANCEL displays a warning message and RETURN does not.

The other choices in the list cause the execution of other programs that perform specific tasks. Each of these other programs is called a subroutine and, in keeping with the one entry/one exit rule, should RETURN to the main program when its task is complete rather than CANCEL the entire application.

Tips Like RETURN, CANCEL closes program files, but not the procedure file. Use CLOSE PROCEDURE to close an open procedure file.

The message that is displayed when CANCEL is executed can be suppressed only by using SET CONSOLE OFF. SET TALK OFF has no effect on this message.

CASE. *See* DO CASE

Catalogs

Overview

dBASE III PLUS has a built-in cataloging system that you can use to keep track of what files belong to which database files. (See File Types.) This feature can be useful for organizing the many report form, label form, index, query, screen, and format files on your disk. Unless you keep a record or use a file-naming convention, you have no way of knowing to which database file each item belongs.

Create your catalog, then open it whenever you want to use it. (See SET CATALOG for information on creating and opening catalog files.) A master catalog named Catalog.CAT is automatically created and maintained by the system to keep track of all other catalogs.

Each time you create a new file or use an existing file, the file name is added to the catalog along with other information that allows the cataloging system to connect the file with a particular database file. The following commands add files to the catalog:

COMMAND	FILES ADDED TO CATALOG
COPY STRUCTURE	Database
COPY STRUCTURE EXTENDED	Database
COPY TO	Database
CREATE	Database
CREATE FROM	Database
CREATE LABEL	Label
CREATE QUERY	Query
CREATE REPORT	Report
CREATE SCREEN	Format, Screen
CREATE VIEW	View
IMPORT	Database, Format, View
INDEX	Index
SET FORMAT	Format
SET INDEX	Index
SET VIEW	View
SORT	Database
TOTAL	Database
USE	Database, Index

DELETE FILE and ERASE remove files from the catalog; RENAME changes the file name in the catalog.

All catalogs are database files with a .CAT extension, and all have the same structure as listed in Table 1.

TABLE 1

Data Catalog File Structure

FIELD	FIELD NAME	TYPE	WIDTH	DEC
1	PATH	Character	70	
2	FILE_NAME	Character	12	
3	ALIAS	Character	8	
4	TYPE	Character	3	
5	TITLE	Character	80	
6	CODE	Numeric	3	0
7	TAG	Character	4	

The Path field is used to store the path name of the file. File_Name stores the eight-letter file name plus the dot and the extension. Alias is used to store the eight-letter root portion of each file name without the extension; this field has nothing to do with the ALIAS keyword. (See USE.) The Alias field is not used further in the cataloging system. The Type field stores the file type so that the catalog can accommodate files with non-standard extensions; the Type field is used along with the Code field to determine which file names are listed in the menu when ?, the catalog query clause, is used to open a file. The Title field is used to store the title that is entered when the file is first added to the catalog. (See SET TITLE.) For index files, this field stores the index key expression. (See INDEX.) The Code field is used to determine what ancillary files belong to which database files. The Tag field is extra and is not used.

Each time a database file is added to the catalog, the next highest code number is stored in the Code field. In other words, the first database file added to the catalog has a Code of 1, the next one has a Code of 2, and so on. All other ancillary files that are added when that database file is active are assigned the same Code as the database file. The exception to this is view files, which are always given a Code of zero. Thus, all files with the same Code as a particular database file can be associated with that file.

Warnings Avoid using SET VIEW to open your files if you are using a catalog. (See SET VIEW for more information.)

RENAME presents a peculiarity if used with a catalog. This command is supposed to work in conjunction with the catalog to change file names in the catalog as they are changed on the disk; however, RENAME requires that you explicitly specify a file name extension, and the catalog does not seem to understand this fact. A similar peculiarity exists with the ERASE and DELETE FILE commands. If you use RENAME, ERASE, or DELETE FILE with a file that does not have an extension, the catalog assumes that you are referring to a .DBF file and acts accordingly. For example, if there happens to be a database file in the catalog with the same root file name as the one you RENAME, that file gets renamed in the catalog by mistake. Be sure that you SET CATALOG OFF in this event to prevent the active catalog from becoming confused.

CDOW( )

Syntax `CDOW(<expD>)`

Overview The CDOW( ) function, short for character day of week, accepts any date expression as its argument. The function evaluates the expression and returns the day of the week corresponding to the date. The result of this function is the unabbreviated name of the day, with the first letter capitalized.

Procedure CDOW( ) returns a character string and can be used anywhere in the language where a character expression is appropriate.

Examples CDOW( ) can be used to improve the appearance of date output, or to obtain the day of the week for a particular date. In the example below, a date of birth is entered, and the day of the week is displayed:

```
* Birthday.PRG
*
SET TALK OFF
```

```
SET BELL OFF
birthday = CTOD("  /  /  ")
CLEAR
@ 10,20 SAY "Enter your date of birth: " GET birthday
READ
@ 12,20 SAY "You were born on a " + CDOW(birthday) + "."
SET BELL ON
SET TALK ON
```

Warnings If the function argument evaluates to a data type other than date, the error message *Invalid function argument* is displayed.

Tips CDOW( ) returns the full name of the day. Use the LEFT( ) function to extract the standard three-letter abbreviation for the day of the week with the formula (LEFT(CDOW(<expD>), 3).

CHANGE

Syntax

```
CHANGE [<scope>] [FIELDS <field list>]
[WHILE <condition>] [FOR <condition>]
```

Overview The CHANGE command is functionally identical to the EDIT command. (See EDIT.)

CHR( )

Syntax

```
CHR(<expN>)
```

Overview The CHR( ) function accepts a numeric expression as its argument. The function evaluates the expression to obtain the resulting decimal number and then returns the ASCII symbol for that number. See the table in Appendix C for a list of the ASCII codes.

Procedure CHR( ) returns a character string and can be used anywhere in the language where a character expression is appropriate.

Examples

CHR( ) is commonly used to send control characters to the printer. The following example is for the Epson FX-80 printer:

```
* Condense.PRG
* This program selects condensed print mode, displays some
* sample output, and restores the printer to the normal mode.
SET PRINTER ON
?? CHR(15)
? "This sentence is in condensed print."
?? CHR(18)
EJECT
SET PRINTER OFF
```

Warnings

If the function argument evaluates to a data type other than character, the error message *Invalid function argument* is displayed.

The CHR( ) function argument must evaluate to a number between zero and 255, inclusive; otherwise, the error message ****Execution error on CHR( ): Out of range* is displayed.

Tips

You can use either @...SAY with SET DEVICE TO PRINTER, or ?? with SET PRINTER ON to send control codes to your printer with the CHR( ) function. The ?? command is used to prevent the carriage-return/linefeed pair associated with the single question mark. (See ? (Question Mark).)

Since CHR( ) returns a character value, it can be concatenated with other character strings. This feature allows you to print a line of output with several different print styles using a single command line. For example,

```
SET DEVICE TO PRINTER
@ 5,10 SAY "Normal, " + CHR(15) + "condensed, " + CHR(18) + ;
           "normal again."
EJECT
SET DEVICE TO SCREEN
```

Use ? CHR(7) to ring the bell in programs to alert the user when an input error has been made.

Note that for n equal to the values 7, 10, and 13, the ? CHR(n) command does not produce the same result as @...SAY CHR(n) because each of these ASCII codes performs a special function: CHR(7) rings the bell, CHR(10) performs a line feed, and CHR(13) performs a form feed. In addition to their special functions, these ASCII codes have associated graphics symbols. In dBASE III PLUS, the ? command performs the function, and @...SAY displays the graphics symbol.

CLEAR

Syntax `CLEAR`

Overview The CLEAR command erases the entire screen.

Procedure Use CLEAR interactively whenever the screen is cluttered and you want a fresh, blank display. Also, use CLEAR at the beginning of any program that uses the screen for display and editing of data. (See @...SAY and @...GET.) This ensures starting with a blank screen.

Examples In the following example, CLEAR erases the screen before a series of @...SAY...GET commands:

```
* Clr_Scrn.PRG
*
USE Mail

CLEAR  && Erase the screen before displaying the record

@ 3, 5 SAY "Last Name " GET Last_Name
@ 4, 5 SAY "First Name" GET First_Name
@ 5, 5 SAY "Street    " GET Address1
@ 6, 5 SAY "Apartment " GET Address2
@ 7, 5 SAY "City      " GET City
@ 8, 5 SAY "State     " GET State
@ 9, 5 SAY "Zip Code  " GET Zip

READ

CLEAR  && Erase the screen before exiting the program
CLOSE DATABASES
```

Tips To erase a single line, use @ <coordinates> with no other keywords or parameters. (See @...SAY for details.) To erase a rectangular portion of the screen, use @...CLEAR.

CLEAR ALL

Syntax `CLEAR ALL`

Overview

The CLEAR ALL command closes all open database files including all catalog, format, and index files, releases all memory variables (both PUBLIC and PRIVATE), and selects work area one. (See SELECT.)

Procedure

Use CLEAR ALL at the end of a program that uses PUBLIC memory variables and one or more database files and/or a data catalog. (See SET CATALOG.) You can then release the variables from memory and close the database files and the catalog with a single command. It is a good programming practice to reset the dBASE III PLUS environment to its default state before exiting a program.

Examples

In the following example, an existing data catalog is used and the user selects a cataloged database file with which to work. Since both a database file and a catalog are used in this example, CLEAR ALL is used at the end of the program to close them both.

```
* Main.PRG
*
SET TALK OFF
SET CATALOG TO Business
USE ?
DO WHILE .T.
   * Allow user to enter commands to execute.
   ACCEPT "Enter a dBASE III PLUS command:" TO m_command
   * If no command is entered, exit the loop.
   IF "" = TRIM(m_command)
      EXIT
   * Otherwise, execute the command using macro substitution.
   ELSE
      &m_command
   ENDIF
ENDDO
* Close database file and catalog.
CLEAR ALL
SET TALK ON
```

Tips If your program uses only PRIVATE variables and does not use a data catalog, use CLOSE DATABASES to close all the database files and to select work area one. The advantage of this command over CLEAR ALL is that it makes the program code easier to understand. If you use a data catalog, however, CLOSE DATABASES does not close the catalog. You must use either CLEAR ALL, CLOSE ALL, or SET CATALOG TO to close the active data catalog.

CLEAR FIELDS

Syntax `CLEAR FIELDS`

Overview The CLEAR FIELDS command releases all fields from all database files from the SET FIELDS TO field list and does a SET FIELDS OFF. (See SET FIELDS.) In effect, this command completely disables the SET FIELDS TO field list and returns dBASE III PLUS to its original state of working with all fields in the active database file.

Procedure Use CLEAR FIELDS if there is a SET FIELDS TO field list in effect and you want to return to working with only the fields in the active database file.

Examples In the following example, a fields list is defined for the mailing list using SET FIELDS TO. The information in these fields is listed to the printer. CLEAR FIELDS is then used to disable the fields list so that you can print a report that uses other fields in the database file.

```
USE Mail
SET FIELDS TO Last_Name, First_Name, Phone
LIST OFF TO PRINTER
CLEAR FIELDS
REPORT FORM Mailing TO PRINTER
```

Tips Using CLEAR FIELDS is a permanent way of disabling the SET FIELDS TO field list. If you want to be able to resume working with the SET FIELDS TO field list at any time, use SET FIELDS OFF instead. This command only disables the field list temporarily, and you can reinstate it whenever you want by using SET FIELDS ON.

CLEAR GETS

Syntax `CLEAR GETS`

Overview The CLEAR GETS command frees all previously issued @...GET commands from the access of the READ command.

Procedure CLEAR GETS is not often used in dBASE III PLUS because, unlike in dBASE II, READ automatically does a CLEAR GETS. In dBASE III PLUS, the @...GETs are not saved unless you use READ SAVE . (See READ.) You can issue only up to 128 @...GETs in dBASE III PLUS, before you must do a CLEAR GETS (either directly, using this command, or by doing a CLEAR or a READ).

Examples The following example shows how to use CLEAR GETS so that READ has access only to a portion of the @...GET variables issued. The routine lets you edit a single record in the Inventry database file based on a part number that you enter. If the record is found in the database file, it is displayed on the screen for editing. Note that the key field, Part_No, is displayed to look like the other fields, but cannot be edited.

```
* NoEdit.PRG
*
SET TALK OFF
USE Inventry INDEX Part_No
m_part_no = SPACE(5)

CLEAR
@  2, 5 SAY "Enter the part number to find." GET m_part_no
READ

SEEK m_part_no

IF FOUND()    && Only edit record if key is found
   @  2, 0  && Erase the prompt from line 2

   * Display key field on screen and release it from READ access.
   @  3, 5 SAY "Part Number       " GET Part_No
   CLEAR GETS
   * PICTURE "@S40" limits the display width to 40 characters.
```

```
    @  4, 5 SAY "Description      " GET Descrip PICTURE "@S40"
    @  5, 5 SAY "Quantity on Hand " GET Quantity
    @  6, 5 SAY "Reorder Point    " GET Reorder
    @  7, 5 SAY "Price per Unit   " GET Price
    READ  && Only accesses GETs after the CLEAR GETS command
ENDIF

CLOSE DATABASES
```

Warnings If you issue more than 128 @...GETs without executing a CLEAR, CLEAR GETS, or READ command to release those GET variables from subsequent READ accesses, the error message *Insufficient memory* is displayed.

Tips You can use @...GET to display data on the screen using the enhanced display (see SET COLOR) without allowing the data to be edited. To do this, issue the @...GET commands without doing a READ. If you issue more than 128 @...GET commands without doing a READ, remember to do a CLEAR GETS.

CLEAR MEMORY

Syntax `CLEAR MEMORY`

Overview The CLEAR MEMORY command releases all memory variables, both PUBLIC and PRIVATE, from memory.

Procedure Use CLEAR MEMORY at the end of an application that uses PUBLIC memory variables but no database files. It is a good programming practice to release memory variables at the end of a program so that their existence in one program does not interfere with another program that might use a memory variable with the same name.

Warnings CLEAR MEMORY should be used sparingly; in fact, if you never use PUBLIC memory variables, there is no reason to use CLEAR MEMORY at all.

If, however, you use PUBLIC memory variables in your programs, CLEAR MEMORY is the only way (other than CLEAR ALL) to release them in the program. At the dot prompt, RELEASE ALL also releases PUBLIC memory variables. In a program, RELEASE ALL releases only PRIVATE memory variables that would be released anyway at the end of the program.

Tips

If your program uses only PRIVATE memory variables, CLEAR MEMORY is not necessary since these variables are automatically released from memory when the program is finished executing.

If the program also uses database files, use CLEAR ALL instead of CLEAR MEMORY to release the PUBLIC memory variables and to close the database files with a single command.

CLEAR TYPEAHEAD

Syntax `CLEAR TYPEAHEAD`

Overview

The CLEAR TYPEAHEAD command empties the typeahead buffer. (See SET TYPEAHEAD.)

Procedure

In a program, you may want to display a message on the screen and have the user press a key to acknowledge the message. After you display the message, CLEAR TYPEAHEAD before prompting the user. Without this command, the message may be unnoticed because the prompt will be answered by the next keystroke in the typeahead buffer. CLEAR TYPEAHEAD discards all of the keystrokes in the buffer and ensures that the user will acknowledge the message.

Examples

The following is an example of a main menu program. In order to make the user notice the menu with each selection, the typeahead buffer is emptied using CLEAR TYPEAHEAD before the user is prompted to make a menu selection.

```
* Menu.PRG
*
SET TALK OFF
SET STATUS ON
SET MESSAGE TO "Enter a menu choice."
```

```
CLEAR
DO WHILE .T.  && Display the menu until the user selects Exit.
   choice = 0

   * Display menu and prompt for user's choice.
   @  6,29 SAY "0 - Exit"
   @  8,29 SAY "1 - Add Records"
   @ 10,29 SAY "2 - Edit Records"
   @ 12,29 SAY "3 - Print Reports"
   @  4,20 TO 14, 54 DOUBLE

   * Empty the typeahead buffer so that user is forced to look
   * at the menu before making a selection.
   CLEAR TYPEAHEAD
   @ 14,37 GET choice PICTURE "9" RANGE 0, 3
   READ

   * Use DO CASE to execute a different program for each choice.
   DO CASE

      * If the user chooses 0, QUIT dBASE III PLUS.
      CASE choice = 0
         QUIT

      * If the user chooses 1, do program to add records.
      CASE choice = 1
         DO Add_Recs

      * If the user chooses 2, do program to edit records.
      CASE choice = 2
         DO EditRecs

      * If the user chooses 3, do program to print reports.
      CASE choice = 3
         DO Reports

   ENDCASE  && End the DO CASE control structure
ENDDO
```

Tips

Use CLEAR TYPEAHEAD when you want the user to look at the screen before giving a response. You may want to use this feature for ensuring that the user reads instructions, messages, or prompts.

CLOSE

Syntax `CLOSE ALL¦ALTERNATE¦DATABASES¦ FORMAT¦INDEXES¦PROCEDURE`

Overview The CLOSE command closes a particular type of file that you name with one of the many command line parameters.

CLOSE ALL	Closes all open database files, including the catalog, all format files, all index files, the alternate file, and the procedure file
CLOSE ALTERNATE	Closes the alternate file
CLOSE DATABASES	Closes all open database files except the catalog. (All format and index files are also closed)
CLOSE FORMAT	Closes the format file in the active work area only
CLOSE INDEXES	Closes all index files in the active work area only
CLOSE PROCEDURE	Closes the procedure file

Procedure In a program that uses an alternate file (see SET ALTERNATE), you must close the alternate file when you are finished writing to it. Use CLOSE ALTERNATE to close the file. CLOSE ALTERNATE is equivalent (and preferable since it is more readable) to SET ALTERNATE TO with no parameters.

At the end of a program that uses one or more database files, issue CLOSE DATABASES to close all of these files. Use CLOSE ALL if a catalog file is being used, since CLOSE DATABASES does not affect the catalog.

CLOSE FORMAT is equivalent (and preferable since it is more readable) to SET FORMAT TO with no parameters. Use this command if you want to close the format file in the active work area and continue working with the database file.

CLOSE INDEXES is equivalent (and preferable since it is more readable) to SET INDEX TO with no parameters. Use this command if you want to close the index files in the active work area and continue working with the database file in its natural, record number order.

At the end of an application that uses a procedure file (see SET PROCEDURE), always do a CLOSE PROCEDURE to close the file so that it does not interfere with the execution of other program files that may have the same name as procedures in the file. CLOSE PROCEDURE is equivalent

(and preferable since it is more readable) to SET PROCEDURE TO with no parameters.

Examples

The following routine opens a procedure file to execute several of its procedures. The routine also opens a database file to work with. At the end of the program, CLOSE PROCEDURE and CLOSE DATABASES close the procedure file and the database file that are opened by the program:

```
* Compute.PRG
*
SET TALK OFF
SET PROCEDURE TO Stats  && Open the procedure file
USE Mail
* The field name on which you want to gather statistics
* must be passed as a character string.
field_name = "Age"
* The variables used in the procedure are initialized.
STORE 0 TO mean, sum_total, variance, std_dev
* Statistics are computed.
DO Sum_Total WITH field_name
DO Mean WITH field_name
DO Variance WITH field_name, mean
DO Std_Dev WITH variance
* Statistics are displayed.
? "Sum: " + LTRIM(STR(sum_total, 10, 2))
? "Mean: " + LTRIM(STR(mean, 10, 2))
? "Variance: " + LTRIM(STR(variance, 10, 2))
? "Standard deviation: " + LTRIM(STR(std_dev, 10, 2))
CLOSE DATABASES
CLOSE PROCEDURE
SET TALK ON
```

Tips

You can make the program code easier to read by using CLOSE <file type> instead of SET <file type> TO with no parameters.

CMONTH( )

Syntax `CMONTH(<expD>)`

Overview

The CMONTH( ) function, short for character month, accepts any date expression as its argument. The function evaluates the expression and returns the name of the month corresponding to the date. The result of this function is the unabbreviated name of the month, with only the first letter capitalized.

Procedure

CMONTH( ) returns a character string and can be used anywhere in the language where a character expression is appropriate.

Examples

dBASE III PLUS usually displays dates in a standard format that depends on SET DATE. SET CENTURY can also be used to control whether or not the century is displayed as part of the year. Even with this control, the format of the date display is still not very interesting. Use CMONTH( ) in combination with some of the other date manipulation functions to get a wide variety of date displays. The following routine displays the current date in several different formats:

```
* Dates.PRG
*
SET TALK OFF
today = DATE()
? today
? LEFT(CMONTH(today), 3) + " " + LTRIM(STR(DAY(today))) + ", " +;
  LTRIM(STR(YEAR(today)))
? CMONTH(today) + " " + LTRIM(STR(DAY(today))) + ", " +;
  LTRIM(STR(YEAR(today)))
? CDOW(today) + ", " + LTRIM(STR(DAY(today))) + " " +;
  CMONTH(today)
? LTRIM(STR(DAY(today))) + " " + LEFT(CMONTH(today), 3) + " " +;
  LTRIM(STR(YEAR(today)))
SET TALK ON
```

Assuming that today's date is June 19, 1987, executing this routine results in the following output:

```
. DO Dates
06/19/87
Jun 19, 1987
June 19, 1987
Friday, 19 June
19 Jun 1987
```

Warnings If the function argument evaluates to a data type other than date, the error message *Invalid function argument* is displayed.

Tips CMONTH( ) returns the full name of the month. Use the LEFT( ) function (as in the above example) to extract the standard three-letter abbreviation for the month.

COL( )

Syntax `COL()`

Overview The COL( ) function, short for column, has no arguments. This function determines and returns the column number of the current screen position.

Procedure COL( ) returns a number and can be used anywhere in the language where a numeric expression is appropriate.

Examples COL( ) is used most frequently when it is necessary to use relative screen addressing (i.e., displaying data at screen coordinates relative to where the last screen output ended). Since the maximum command line length in dBASE III PLUS is 254 characters (including blank spaces), it is not always possible to accomplish what you want with a single command. This is especially true of @...SAY which can become very long with all of its parameters.

To avoid @...SAY commands that are too long, use COL( ) to make one @...SAY command pick up where the previous one left off. Use of this function is illustrated in the following routine which allows you to page through all of the customers in the Customer database file who have an outstanding balance that exceeds $1000.00. The first and last names are displayed on line 10, and the amount owed is shown on the same line, one column to the right of where the name ends.

```
* Amt_Owed.PRG
*
SET TALK OFF
USE Customer
LOCATE FOR Amt_Owed >= 1000.00
DO WHILE FOUND()
    CLEAR
    @ 10,5 SAY TRIM(First_Name) + " " + TRIM(Last_Name) + ": "
    @ 10,COL() SAY "$" + LTRIM(STR(Amt_Owed, 10, 2)) + "."
    WAIT
    CONTINUE
ENDDO
CLOSE DATABASES
SET TALK ON
```

Warnings CLEAR resets the value of the COL( ) function to zero.

COL( ) works only when addressing the screen. When directing output to the printer with SET DEVICE TO PRINTER, use PCOL( ).

Tips The $ symbol can be used in place of COL( ) only when used in conjunction with @...SAY...GET. This carryover from dBASE II maintains consistency with that language.

Condition. *See* Expression

Config.DB

Overview dBASE III PLUS provides users the option to create a configuration file that can change the default values of certain SET commands and specify other configuration elements not available in the dBASE language. When you enter dBASE III PLUS, a Config.DB file is searched for in the current directory. If the file is not found, the DOS path setting is searched for a file with that name. If the file is found, its contents are read and put into effect.

Procedure

To use the configuration file, create a text file called Config.DB in the same directory as Dbase.EXE or in your DOS path setting. Using Table 2, type on a separate line each entry that you want to include in the file. (An entry consists of one of the words from the Keyword column, an equals sign (=), and a value as specified in the Value column.)

TABLE 2

Config.DB Entries

KEYWORD	VALUE	COMMAND OR DESCRIPTION
ALTERNATE	<filename>	SET ALTERNATE TO <filename>
BELL	ON ¦ OFF	SET BELL ON ¦ OFF
BUCKET	1 to 31	The amount of memory available for storing PICTURE and RANGE values for @...GET commands. The number that you specify is in kilobytes, and the default is 2. Specifying more than 2K requires memory beyond the minimum requirement for dBASE III PLUS. For 256K machines, you should use BUCKET = 1 for maximum efficiency.
CARRY	ON ¦ OFF	SET CARRY ON ¦ OFF
CATALOG	<filename>	SET CATALOG TO <filename>
COLOR	<color specs>	SET COLOR TO <color specs>
COMMAND	<command>	The named <command> is executed automatically when you enter dBASE III PLUS. It can be any valid command with any command line options that you want to use.
CONFIRM	ON ¦ OFF	SET CONFIRM ON ¦ OFF
CONSOLE	ON ¦ OFF	SET CONSOLE ON ¦ OFF
DEBUG	ON ¦ OFF	SET DEBUG ON ¦ OFF
DECIMALS	0 to 15	SET DECIMALS TO <number>
DEFAULT	<drive>	SET DEFAULT TO <drive>
DELETED	ON ¦ OFF	SET DELETED ON ¦ OFF
DELIMITERS	<characters>	SET DELIMITERS TO "<characters>"
DELIMITERS	ON ¦ OFF	SET DELIMITERS ON ¦ OFF
DEVICE	SCREEN ¦ PRINTER	SET DEVICE TO SCREEN ¦ PRINTER

Table 2 continues

KEYWORD	VALUE	COMMAND OR DESCRIPTION
ECHO	ON ¦ OFF	SET ECHO ON ¦ OFF
ENCRYPTION	ON ¦ OFF	SET ENCRYPTION ON ¦ OFF
ESCAPE	ON ¦ OFF	SET ESCAPE ON ¦ OFF
EXACT	ON ¦ OFF	SET EXACT ON ¦ OFF
EXCLUSIVE	ON ¦ OFF	SET EXCLUSIVE ON ¦ OFF
F2	<expC>	SET FUNCTION 2 TO <expC>
F3	<expC>	SET FUNCTION 3 TO <expC>
F4	<expC>	SET FUNCTION4 TO <expC>
F5	<expC>	SET FUNCTION 5 TO <expC>
F6	<expC>	SET FUNCTION 6 TO <expC>
F7	<expC>	SET FUNCTION 7 TO <expC>
F8	<expC>	SET FUNCTION 8 TO <expC>
F9	<expC>	SET FUNCTION 9 TO <expC>
F10	<expC>	SET FUNCTION 10 TO <expC>
GETS	35 to 1023	The number of @...GETs that you can issue before doing a READ or CLEAR GETS. The default number is 128. For 256K machines, you should use GETS = 35 for maximum efficiency. Larger numbers require more memory.
HEADING	ON ¦ OFF	SET HEADING ON ¦ OFF
HELP	ON ¦ OFF	SET HELP ON ¦ OFF
HISTORY	0 to 16000	SET HISTORY TO <number>
INTENSITY	ON ¦ OFF	SET INTENSITY ON ¦ OFF
MARGIN	0 to 254	SET MARGIN TO <number>
MEMOWIDTH	5 to 254	SET MEMOWIDTH TO <number>
MENUS	ON ¦ OFF	SET MENUS ON ¦ OFF
MVARSIZ	1 to 31	The maximum amount of memory, in kilobytes, allocated for memory variable storage. The default is 6000 bytes, but on a 256K machine you should set MVARSIZ = 3 for maximum efficiency.
PATH	<path list>	SET PATH TO <path list>

Table 2 continues

KEYWORD	VALUE	COMMAND OR DESCRIPTION
PRINT	ON ¦ OFF	SET PRINTER ON ¦ OFF
PROMPT	<string>	The <string> that you specify replaces the dot (.) as the interactive prompt.
SAFETY	ON ¦ OFF	SET SAFETY ON ¦ OFF
SCOREBOARD	ON ¦ OFF	SET SCOREBOARD ON ¦ OFF
STATUS	ON ¦ OFF	SET STATUS ON ¦ OFF
STEP	ON ¦ OFF	SET STEP ON ¦ OFF
TALK	ON ¦ OFF	SET TALK ON ¦ OFF
TEDIT	<program>	Each time you use MODIFY COMMAND, the named <program> is invoked as your editor.
TYPEAHEAD	0 to 32000	SET TYPEAHEAD TO <number>
UNIQUE	ON ¦ OFF	SET UNIQUE ON ¦ OFF
VIEW	<filename>	SET VIEW TO <filename>
WP	<program>	Each time you edit a memo field, the named <program> is invoked as your word processor.

For more information on the effect of using a particular entry, see the SET command that corresponds to the keyword in the table. Putting an entry of <keyword> = <value> in Config.DB is equivalent to executing the command SET <keyword> with <value> as its command line parameter. For example, BELL = ON is the same as SET BELL ON, and DECIMALS = 5 is the same as SET DECIMALS TO 5.

For information on setting the function keys, see SET FUNCTION. Instead of using F<n> = <expC>, you can use the alternative syntax, FUNCTION = <n>, <expC>, to specify function keys in Config.DB. For example, F3 = "LIST HISTORY;" is the same as FUNCTION = 3, "LIST HISTORY;". The function key entries in Config.DB are the only ones that require you to quote the value that you use.

The keywords BUCKET, COMMAND, GETS, MVARSIZ, PROMPT, TEDIT, and WP are special configuration items and do not correspond to any dBASE III PLUS command. BUCKET, GETS, and MVARSIZ allow you to customize dBASE within the limits of available memory. TEDIT and WP let you use your favorite word processor for MODIFY COMMAND and memo field editing instead of the more rudimentary editor built into dBASE III PLUS. These entries require sufficient memory to load both dBASE and the other program at the same time. PROMPT lets you change the dot prompt to something else. COMMAND lets you specify a command that you want to execute automatically when you execute dBASE.

Examples

The following is a listing of a configuration file that turns off the safety and other help features:

```
* Config.DB
*
HELP = OFF
SAFETY = OFF
MENUS = OFF
```

Note that you can include comments in the Config.DB by using an asterisk (*) at the beginning of a line.

Warnings

If you put an invalid entry in the configuration file, the error message ^---*Keyword not found* is displayed below each bad entry and only the valid entries are put into effect.

If you use a value with an entry that does not fall in the allowable range, the error message ^---*Out of range* is displayed. See Table 2 for the valid ranges.

If you use a keyword in a configuration file that expects a value of ON or OFF with some other value, the error message ^---*Expected ON or OFF* is displayed.

The COMMAND entry in Config.DB is overridden if you specify a program name when you enter dBASE. To do this, execute dBASE by typing dBASE < program name > at the DOS prompt.

If you specify more than one entry with the same keyword, each one sets the parameter so that only the last one in the file is effective. The exception is DELIMITERS which allows two entries.

If you specify a CATALOG or VIEW that does not exist, no error message is displayed.

Tips

Although the configuration file has a special name and syntax so that dBASE III PLUS can find and understand it, the file is simply an ASCII text file; therefore, you can change it with MODIFY COMMAND while using dBASE III PLUS. However, if you make changes, be aware that they will not become effective until the next time you execute dBASE. It is only when you first enter dBASE that the configuration file is read and its contents put into effect.

Note that although the valid range of values for the MEMOWIDTH setting is from 5 to 254, SET MEMOWIDTH TO does not allow a setting less than 8. (See SET, the full-screen set command, for information on this peculiarity.)

CONTINUE

Syntax `CONTINUE`

Overview The CONTINUE command is used after LOCATE has been executed to find the next record in the active database file that meets the locate condition. This command continues the search initiated by the LOCATE command.

Procedure Use CONTINUE in a DO WHILE...ENDDO loop to find all of the subsequent records that meet the LOCATE condition.

Examples The following program uses the LOCATE and CONTINUE commands to print delinquent payment notices for customers who are late in making payment:

```
* Letter.PRG
*
SET TALK OFF
SET DEVICE TO PRINTER
USE Customer

* LOCATE is used to find the first delinquent customer.
LOCATE FOR Deadline < DATE()

* DO WHILE FOUND() processes records meeting the LOCATE condition.
DO WHILE FOUND()
```

```
    @  6, 0       SAY TRIM(First_Name) + " " + Last_Name
    @  7, 0       SAY TRIM(Address1)
    @  8, 0       SAY TRIM(City) + ", " + State + "  " + Zip
    @  9,70       SAY DATE()
    @ 10, 0       SAY "Dear " + TRIM(First_Name) + " "
    @ 10, PCOL() SAY TRIM(Last_Name) + ":"
    @ 12, 0       SAY "Our records show that your account is "
    @ 12, PCOL() SAY "overdue.  "
    @ 12, PCOL() SAY "Your balance is $"
    @ 12, PCOL() SAY LTRIM(STR(Amt_Owed, 10, 2)) + "."
    @ 13, 0       SAY "This amount was due and payable on "
    @ 13, PCOL() SAY Deadline
    @ 13, PCOL() SAY ".  Please send payment immediately."
    @ 14, 0       SAY "If you have already submitted your payment,"
    @ 14, PCOL() SAY " disregard this notice."

    * CONTINUE finds the rest of the records.
    CONTINUE

ENDDO
USE
EJECT
SET DEVICE TO SCREEN
SET TALK ON
```

Warnings

If you issue a CONTINUE command without having previously issued a LOCATE command in the current work area the error message *CONTINUE without LOCATE* is displayed.

Tips

Remember that there is a separate LOCATE condition for each work area. The CONTINUE command applies to the last LOCATE command issued in the current work area.

Copy. *See* COPY TO

COPY FILE

Syntax `COPY FILE <filename> TO <new filename>`

Overview The COPY FILE command makes a duplicate copy of any file. The file name extension must be specified for both files.

Procedure Use COPY FILE whenever you want to copy a file, whether it is a program file, a report form file, or a database file. The command provides a convenient way of making a backup copy of a file to another disk and of creating new reports, labels, and programs that are similar to existing ones. Use COPY FILE to make a copy of the similar file and to modify the new file instead of starting from scratch.

Examples The following routine makes a backup copy of the Employee database file to Drive A:

```
. COPY FILE Employee.DBF TO A:Emp_Back.DBF
   4608 bytes copied
```

The next example shows you how to make a copy of a report form file. Since the file structures for the Employee and Customer database files are very much alike, the Emp_Name report that is designed for use with the Employee file can be modified easily to work with the Customer file.

```
COPY FILE Emp_Name.FRM TO CustName.FRM
USE Customer
MODIFY REPORT CustName
```

Warnings If you use COPY FILE to copy a file that is open, the error message *File is already open* is displayed. Close the file using one of the forms of the CLOSE command and try COPY FILE again.

COPY FILE cannot be interrupted by pressing Esc, regardless of the status of SET ESCAPE.

Tips Use COPY FILE rather than COPY TO to make a faster duplicate copy of a database file. If there are any memo fields in the file, make sure that you also copy the .DBT file.

COPY FILE is very similar to the DOS Copy command; however, unlike the DOS Copy command, it cannot be used to copy more than one file at a time using a file skeleton with wildcard characters. dBASE III PLUS has no command for copying multiple files. If you have enough memory, you can ! Copy <parameters> to execute the DOS Copy command from within dBASE III PLUS.

COPY STRUCTURE

Syntax `COPY STRUCTURE [FIELDS <field list>] TO <filename>`

Overview The COPY STRUCTURE command copies the database file structure of the active database file to a new database file. The new file is assumed to have a .DBF extension.

The fields in the structure that are copied can be limited using the FIELDS list. (See FIELDS for a separate discussion.) By default, all fields are copied.

Note that unlike COPY TO which copies the entire database file (i.e., the structure and the data records), COPY STRUCTURE copies only the file structure and not the data.

Procedure To create a new database file that is similar (or identical) in structure to an existing one, use COPY STRUCTURE. USE the new file and then MODIFY STRUCTURE, if necessary, to make the changes.

Examples The following example copies the structure of the mailing list file to a new file, Supplier. Then, the new file is opened and MODIFY STRUCTURE removes unwanted fields and inserts additional fields.

```
. USE Mail
. COPY STRUCTURE TO Supplier
. USE Supplier
. MODIFY STRUCTURE
```

Warnings If it already exists, the file that you COPY STRUCTURE TO is overwritten without warning unless SET SAFETY is ON.

If you are using dBASE III PLUS in a network environment, COPY STRUCTURE attempts an automatic file lock unless the database file is already locked (see FLOCK( )) or is opened for exclusive use (see SET EXCLUSIVE, USE). If for any reason the command cannot lock the database file, the error message *File is in use by another* is displayed.

Tips

Using COPY STRUCTURE is one way to ensure that an application starts each time with an empty file structure. Suppose, for example, that every day you record new orders and that you want to keep the orders for each day in a separate file to be appended to the main Orders database file at the end of the day. You also like to save orders for a week. The following routine uses COPY STRUCTURE to accomplish this:

```
* Daily.PRG
*
SET SAFETY OFF
* Number of day of the week is converted to a character string.
weekday = STR(DOW(DATE()), 1)
* Main Orders file is used to create structure of daily orders
* file if it has not already been created today.
USE Orders&weekday
IF LUPDATE() <> DATE()
   USE Orders

   * Daily orders file is called Orders1, Orders2, etc...
   * depending on the day of the week.  Macro substitution of
   * the day of week as part of the file name is used to do
   * this. By naming the daily orders file after the day of the
   * week, you can keep the daily orders for up to a week.  For
   * example, the orders for last Tuesday are always in
   * Orders3.DBF.

   COPY STRUCTURE TO Orders&weekday
ENDIF

* Daily orders file is opened and records are added using a
* format file.
USE Orders&weekday
SET FORMAT TO AddOrder
APPEND
SET SAFETY ON
CLOSE DATABASES
```

The program is designed to run any number of times during a day. Sometime at the end of the day, you might want to run a program that adds the daily orders to the main Orders database file. It should contain the following commands:

```
* Number of day of the week is converted to a character string.
weekday = STR(DOW(DATE()), 1)

* Daily orders are added to the main Orders file.
USE Orders
APPEND FROM Orders&weekday
```

If you are using dBASE III PLUS in a network environment and the database file whose structure you want to copy is encrypted (see Protect), the new file that you create with COPY STRUCTURE is also encrypted unless you SET ENCRYPTION OFF (see SET ENCRYPTION).

COPY STRUCTURE EXTENDED

Syntax `COPY STRUCTURE EXTENDED TO <filename>`

Overview

The COPY STRUCTURE EXTENDED command creates a database file of which records are the field attributes (i.e., field name, field type, field length, and number of decimals) of the active database file. This file is called an extended file, and its file structure is fixed as shown in Table 3.

TABLE 3

Extended File Structure

FIELD	FIELD NAME	TYPE	WIDTH	DEC
1	FIELD_NAME	Character	10	
2	FIELD_TYPE	Character	1	
3	FIELD_LEN	Numeric	3	
4	FIELD_DEC	Numeric	3	
** Total **			18	

The number of records in the extended file is equal to the number of fields in the active database file (i.e., one record for each field). The extended file is assigned a .DBF extension unless you supply another extension as part of the file name.

Procedure The sole use of COPY STRUCTURE EXTENDED is to work in conjunction with CREATE FROM to program a database file creation routine.

Examples The following program creates a database file from information entered into an extended file. COPY STRUCTURE EXTENDED creates the extended file, a record for each field is added to the file using a series of @...GET and READ commands, and some data validation is performed. When a blank field name is entered, CREATE FROM creates a new database file from the information entered.

```
* MyCreate.PRG
*
SET TALK OFF
SET SAFETY OFF

* Open any existing database file in order to create the
* extended file.
USE Mail
COPY STRUCTURE EXTENDED TO ExteFile

* Open the extended file, and delete all of its records.
* This application must begin with a blank file.
USE ExteFile
ZAP

* Set up the screen for data entry.
CLEAR
@  5, 0  SAY "Field Name"
@  6, 0  SAY "Field Type"
@  7, 0  SAY "Field Length"
@  8, 0  SAY "Number of Decimals"

DO WHILE RECCOUNT() < 128

   * Add a new, blank record to the extended file
   APPEND BLANK

   * Clear previous field from screen and read field name.
   * Field name is capitalized and begins with a letter.
   * The remaining character can be letters and numbers -
```

```
* this application does not allow underscores.
@  5,20 GET Field_Name PICTURE "@! ANNNNNNNNN"
@  6,20
@  7,20
@  8,20

READ

* Exit loop when user does not enter a field name.
IF "" = TRIM(Field_Name)
   * Delete the last blank record from the file.
   DELETE
   PACK
   * If there are any records, CREATE a database file.
   IF RECCOUNT() > 0

      * A database file called YourFile is created
      * using the information entered into the
      * extended file.
      CREATE YourFile FROM ExteFile

   ENDIF
   EXIT
ENDIF

* Read the field type.  It must be C, D, L, M or N.
DO WHILE .NOT. Field_Type $ "CDLMN"
   REPLACE Field_Type WITH "C"
   @  6,20  GET Field_Type PICTURE "@A!"
   READ
ENDDO

* The CASE structure either assigns a field length or allows
* the user to enter one, depending on the field type.  For
* numeric fields, the number of decimals is also defined in
* this CASE structure.

DO CASE

   CASE Field_Type = "M"
      REPLACE Field_Len WITH 10  && Memos are 10 in length

   CASE Field_Type = "L"
      REPLACE Field_Len WITH 1   && Logicals are 1 in length
```

```
      CASE Field_Type = "D"
         REPLACE Field_Len WITH 8   && Dates are 8 in length

      * Numeric fields have a user-defined length that must be
      * between one and 19.
      CASE Field_Type = "N"
         @  7,20 GET Field_Len RANGE 1, 19
         READ

         * The upper limit on the number of decimal places
         * is determined by the field length.
         IF Field_Len < 3
            limit = 0
         ELSE
            limit = Field_Len - 2
         ENDIF

         @  8,20 GET Field_Dec RANGE 0, limit
         READ

      * Character fields have a user-defined length that must
      * be between one and 254.
      CASE Field_Type = "C"
         @  7,20 GET Field_Len RANGE 1, 19
         READ
   ENDCASE
ENDDO
CLOSE DATABASES
SET TALK ON
SET SAFETY ON
```

After running this program and entering the information for one or more fields, USE YourFile and see that its structure matches what you entered.

Note that this program is incomplete because it does not check for duplicate field names and does not allow the underscore character in field names. Also, this create routine does not allow you to edit field information after you have entered it. It does, however, demonstrate the use of COPY STRUCTURE EXTENDED and CREATE FROM and can be modified to be more complete.

Warnings

If it already exists, the file that you COPY STRUCTURE EXTENDED TO is overwritten without warning unless SET SAFETY is ON.

If you are using dBASE III PLUS in a network environment and the active database file is encrypted (see Protect), you cannot use COPY STRUCTURE EXTENDED unless SET ENCRYPTION is OFF. If you neglect this, the error message *Database is encrypted* is displayed. (See SET ENCRYPTION.)

Tips

Be sure to follow the proper field-naming conventions when adding records to a database file that you have created using COPY STRUCTURE EXTENDED. Also, be sure that the data type is valid and that the length of the field (and the number of decimal places for numerics) is correct for its type; otherwise, you will encounter errors when you use CREATE FROM to create a new database file.

COPY TO

Syntax

```
COPY TO <filename> [FIELDS <field list>] [<scope>]
[WHILE <condition>] [FOR <condition>] [[TYPE]
WKS¦SYLK¦DIF¦SDF¦DELIMITED [WITH <delimiter>¦BLANK]]
```

Overview

The COPY TO command copies records from the active database file to a new file. The type of file to be copied to is specified by a command line argument.

A scope, a FOR clause, and a WHILE clause can be specified to limit the records that are processed. Each of these command line options is discussed separately. (See Scope, FOR, and WHILE). Unless one of these clauses is specified, all records in the active database file are copied.

The fields that are copied can be limited using the FIELDS list. (See FIELDS for a separate discussion.) By default, all fields are copied.

If no TYPE is specified, the TO file is another database (.DBF) file.

The other types of files are described in turn. In copying to any of the following file types, memo fields are ignored and dates are copied as eight-digit numbers of the form CCYYMMDD, where CC is the century, YY is the year, MM is the month and DD is the day.

TYPE WKS is a Lotus 1-2-3 worksheet, and the file is given a WKS extension. TYPE SYLK is a Microsoft Multiplan file, and the file is given no extension. TYPE DIF is a VisiCalc file and is given a .DIF extension. All

spreadsheet files are copied in row major order with no leading blank columns. The field names are copied to the first row of the spreadsheet as headings.

SDF stands for system data format, and the file is given a .TXT extension. An SDF type file is an ASCII text file with fixed length fields and records. Each record is terminated by a carriage return/linefeed pair. An example of an SDF file follows:

```
John        Doe        19640305      234.87
Janie       Jones      19570201       12.42
Mike        McCollough 19490505     1263.00
Susan       Simons     19591220     3562.11
Alexander   Adams      19630425        0.00
```

A DELIMITED file is also an ASCII text file, but the fields and records can be of varying lengths. As with SDF files, a .TXT extension is assigned and each record is terminated by a carriage return/linefeed pair. The fields in each record are separated by commas, and the character fields are enclosed between delimiters that you can specify using the WITH option. If you do not specify a delimiter, double quotes are assumed. An example of a file that is DELIMITED WITH ' (single quote mark) follows:

```
'John','Doe',19640305,234.87
'Janie','Jones',19570201,12.42
'Mike','McCollough',19490505,1263.00
'Susan','Simons',19591220,3562.11
'Alexander','Adams',19630425,0.00
```

DELIMITED WITH BLANK is a special text file in which each field is separated from the next by a blank space with no other delimiters.

Procedure

Use COPY TO when you want to copy records from the active database file to another file. The command has various forms designed to copy to several different types of file. These are listed below:

- COPY TO <filename> copies records to another dBASE III PLUS database (.DBF) file.
- COPY TO <filename> DIF copies records to a VisiCalc (.DIF) file.
- COPY TO <filename> SYLK copies records to a Microsoft Multiplan file.
- COPY TO <filename> WKS copies records to a Lotus 1-2-3 work sheet (.WKS) file.
- COPY TO <filename> SDF copies records to an ASCII text (.TXT) file in system data format.

- COPY TO <filename> DELIMITED copies records to an ASCII text (.TXT) file that is delimited.

Examples

The following example copies a portion of the Inventory file to an ASCII text file. Only parts of the file that need to be reordered are copied. This is accomplished by using a FOR clause.

```
. USE Inventry
. COPY TO Reorder FOR Quantity < Reorder SDF
     2 records copied
```

Next, a subset of the fields in the Employee file are copied to a Lotus 1-2-3 spreadsheet.

```
. USE Employee
. COPY TO Emp FIELDS Emp_Code, Salary, Hire_Date TYPE WKS
    10 records copied
. CLOSE DATABASES
```

Warnings

If it already exists, the file that you COPY TO is overwritten without warning unless SET SAFETY is ON.

If you are using dBASE III PLUS in a network environment, COPY attempts an automatic file lock unless the database file is already locked (see FLOCK( )) or is opened for exclusive use (see SET EXCLUSIVE, USE). If for any reason the command cannot lock the database file, the error message *File is in use by another* is displayed.

In the network version, you must SET ENCRYPTION OFF before specifying a file TYPE to create a non-database file with COPY; otherwise, the error message *Database is encrypted* is displayed.

Tips

dBASE III PLUS also has the capability of creating PFS:File files using EXPORT. This command, in addition to copying the records from the file, uses an open format file to determine the screen design on the new file. (See EXPORT.)

If you are using dBASE III PLUS in a network environment and the database file that you COPY is encrypted (see Protect), the new file is also encrypted unless you SET ENCRYPTION OFF (see SET ENCRYPTION).

COUNT

Syntax `COUNT [<scope>] [WHILE <condition>] [FOR <condition>] [TO <memory variable>]`

Overview

The COUNT command counts a specified set of records in the active database file. If this command is issued when there is no file in use in the current work area, you are prompted to enter the name of a database file.

The result of the command is displayed on the screen if SET TALK is ON. SET TALK OFF completely suppresses the screen output of the COUNT command.

In its simplest form (i.e., no command line arguments are specified), COUNT counts all the records in the active database file.

A scope, a FOR clause, and a WHILE clause can be specified to limit the records which are processed. Each of these command line options is discussed separately. (See Scope, FOR, and WHILE.)

The result of COUNT can be saved in a memory variable using the TO clause.

Procedure

Use COUNT to count records that meet a particular condition in the active database file. The result is displayed if SET TALK is ON and can be saved in a memory variable for later use.

Examples

The following example calculates the number of parts that need to be reordered using the Inventry file:

```
. Use Inventry
. COUNT FOR Quantity < Reorder
      2 records
```

The next example counts the number of people in the mailing list who have a birthday this month. To do this, an index file is opened with the database file. The index key is MONTH(Birthday), so that SEEK MONTH (DATE( )) locates the first person in the mailing list whose birthday is this month. COUNT is then used with a WHILE clause, which is much faster than counting the entire file with a FOR clause.

```
. USE Mail INDEX BrthMnth
. SEEK MONTH(DATE())
. COUNT WHILE MONTH(Birthday) = MONTH(DATE())
     4 records
. CLOSE DATABASES
```

Warnings

If you are using dBASE III PLUS in a network environment, COUNT attempts an automatic file lock unless the database file is already locked (see FLOCK( )) or is opened for exclusive use (see SET EXCLUSIVE, USE). If for any reason the command cannot lock the database file, the error message *File is in use by another* is displayed.

Tips

It is inefficient to use COUNT to count all of the records in a database file. Instead, use RECCOUNT ( ), which returns the total number of records in the active database file. RECCOUNT( ) is much faster than COUNT especially on a database file with many records. Save COUNT for those times when you need to know how many records meet a particular condition.

CREATE

Syntax `CREATE <filename>`

Overview

The CREATE command designs a new database (.DBF) file structure which can contain a maximum of 128 fields or 4000 bytes (whichever occurs first). When designing a database file structure, you must provide the following information for each field:

FIELD ATTRIBUTE	EXPLANATION
Name	The field name can be up to ten characters long. It must begin with a letter; the remaining characters can be any combination of letters, numbers, and underscores.
Type	The available field types are Character, Date, Logical, Memo, and Numeric.

Width	The width depends on the field type. Date, Logical, and Memo fields are automatically assigned a field width. Character fields can be from 1 to 254 characters in length. Numeric fields can be between 1 and 19, including the decimal point and sign, if any.
Decimals	Decimals are only available for Numeric fields. The number of decimal places must be at least two less than the field width to allow for the decimal point plus the initial zero dBASE III PLUS displays on values between zero and 1. Negative numbers between −1 and zero require the number of decimal places to be three less than the field width to accommodate the sign.

Procedure

Issuing CREATE <filename> invokes a full-screen database file structure design mode. Any database file that is open in the current work area is automatically closed.

The cursor appears in the first column, labeled Field Name. A field name can be up to ten characters in length. The first character in the field name must be a letter of the alphabet; the remaining characters can be any combination of letters, numbers, and underscores. To enter a field name, simply type it in; CREATE will not let you enter an incorrect field name. If you use all ten characters of the field name, the cursor automatically moves to the next column; otherwise, you must press Enter to move the cursor to the Type column.

You must specify a field type for each field. The available types are as follows:

FIELD TYPE	USAGE
Character	For storing text, such as names and addresses, and for storing numbers that are never used in mathematical calculations, such as zip codes, phone numbers, and social security numbers.
Numeric	For storing numbers that are used in mathematical calculations, such as salaries, prices, and quantities.
Date	For storing dates, such as birthdays and shipping dates.
Logical	For storing yes/no values (e.g., a field called Paid that tells you whether or not a customer has paid his bill).
Memo	For storing large amounts of text, such as a letter.

You can select a field type by entering the first letter of the type that you want. For example, you would type `N` for a Numeric field. If you use this method for selecting the field type, the cursor automatically moves to the next column; another method for selecting a field type is to use the space bar to scroll through the available data types. When the data type you want to use appears in the Type column, press Enter to select it and advance the cursor.

Depending on the field type that you choose, the cursor moves to a different column. For Date, Logical, and Memo fields, CREATE automatically assigns the field width, and the cursor moves down one line, back to the Field Name column. Date fields are eight characters, Logical fields are one, and Memo fields use ten positions in the file structure. With Memo fields, the actual data that you enter into the field is stored in a separate file that is automatically created and given the same name as the database file, but with a .DBT extension. This is called the memo file. The ten characters in the file structure are used internally by dBASE III PLUS to keep track of the information in that file.

For Character and Numeric fields, the cursor moves to the Width column where you enter a number. For Character fields, the range is between 1 and 254; for Numerics, the range is 1 to 19. The width of a Numeric field must be large enough for the decimal point and sign, if any. If you use three digits in the field width, the cursor automatically moves to the next column; otherwise, you must press Enter to advance the cursor. CREATE will not let you enter an incorrect field width. If you do, you are prompted with an error message reminding you of the legal range of values, and you must then press any key to reenter the field width.

For Character fields, the cursor advances to the Field Name column on the next line after you enter the field width.

For Numeric fields, the cursor moves to the column labeled Dec, short for decimal places. If the field is to have digits to the right of the decimal place, you must enter that number here. The number of decimal places can be any number between 0 and 15, as long as the number of decimal places is at least two less than the field width. CREATE will not let you enter a number that is outside of the allowable range. If you do, you are prompted with an error message reminding you of the legal range of values, and you must then press any key to reenter the decimal places. After you enter the number of decimals required, press Enter to advance the cursor to the Field Name column on the next line.

You can enter up to 128 fields in this way, as long as the sum of all of the field widths does not exceed 4000 characters.

Once all of the attributes for a single field are defined, you can go back and make changes to them as you would with MODIFY STRUCTURE. All of the full-screen editing and cursor control keys listed in Appendix A are available in CREATE. Ctrl-N is used to insert a new field before the current field, and Ctrl-U deletes the current field.

Ctrl-End saves the database file structure when you are finished with the design. Before the file structure is saved, you are prompted to *Press ENTER to confirm. Any other key to resume.* If you press any key other than Enter, the CREATE session is resumed. Pressing Enter saves the file structure as database file with the name that you entered on the CREATE command line. By default, the file is given a .DBF extension. If there are any Memo fields, a memo file with the same name as the database file and a .DBT extension is also created. You are prompted with *Input data records now? (Y/N).* If you respond by typing `Y`, you enter the append mode. (See APPENDEND.) A response of `N` ends the full-screen CREATE mode.

If you decide that you do not want to save the database file structure, press Esc to abandon the CREATE session without saving the file; you will be prompted to confirm your decision. If you respond by typing `N`, the CREATE session is resumed. A response of `Y` ends the full-screen CREATE mode without saving the file.

Examples

The following example guides you through the design of a database file designed to help you keep track of the people who owe you money. The structure of the file that you will create is listed in Table 4.

TABLE 4

Collect.DBF Database File Structure

FIELD NAME	TYPE	LENGTH	DECIMALS
Name	Character	30	
Amt_Owed	Numeric	10	2
Due_Date	Date	8	
Paid	Logical	1	
Notes	Memo	10	

Enter the following command to begin designing the database file:

```
. CREATE Collect
```

To begin designing the database file, enter the first field name in the column labeled Field Name by typing NAME. Press Enter to indicate that you are finished entering the field name; the cursor moves to the column labeled Type. Since this field is a Character field, press Enter to accept the default; the cursor moves to the Width column. Type 30 for the field width and press Enter; the cursor moves to the next line of the Field Name column. You have defined the first field. Your screen should look like the one in Figure 23.

For the second field name, type Amt_Owed and press Enter. Type N to select the Numeric field type. For the field width, type 10 and press Enter. Finally, type 2 for the decimal places and press Enter to go on to the next field definition.

For the final three fields, you need only enter the field name and type. The width is automatically assigned for Date, Memo, and Logical fields. Use the following steps to complete the database file design:

1. Type Due_Date and press Enter.
2. Type D to select the Date field type.

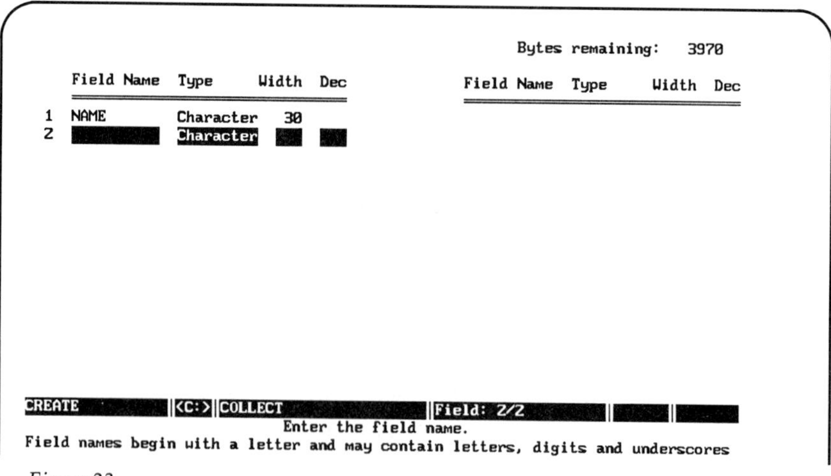

Figure 23

3. Type Paid and press Enter.
4. Type L to select the Logical field type.
5. Type Notes and press Enter.
6. Type M to select the Memo field type.

The database file design is complete. Your screen should look like the one in Figure 24.

Press Ctrl-End to save the database file structure. You are prompted with *Press ENTER to confirm. Any other key to resume.* Press Enter to indicate that you want to save the database file structure. When you are prompted with *Input data records now? (Y/N)* type Y. Your screen should look like the one in Figure 25.

You can add records to the new file if you want to. (See APPEND.) Press Esc or Ctrl-End when you are finished.

Warnings Since the letters A through J are reserved as default alias names for the ten work areas (see SELECT), you cannot create database files with these names. If you use CREATE with one of these reserved alias names, the error message *ALIAS name already in use* is displayed.

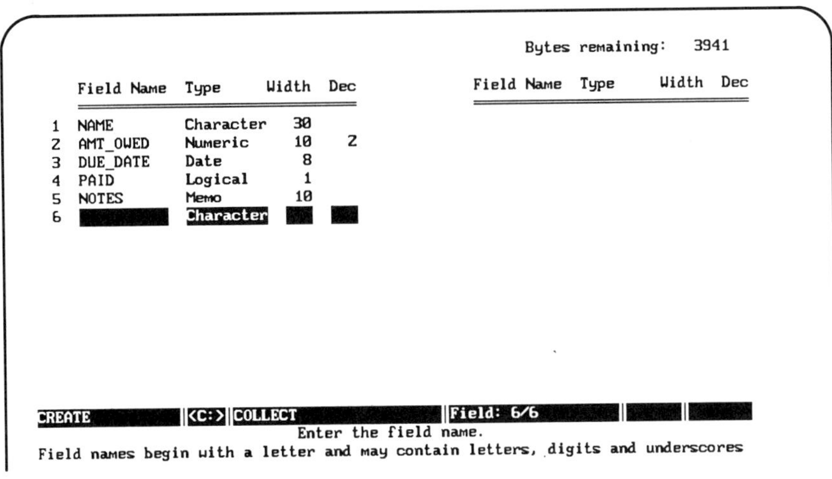

Figure 24

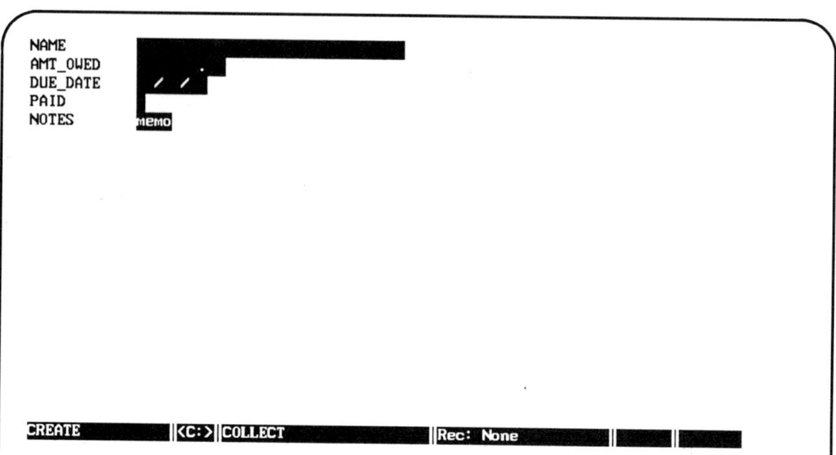

Figure 25

If you attempt during the CREATE session to enter another field when there are already 128 fields in the file structure, the error message *Maximum number of fields already reached* is displayed.

If you attempt to enter a new field whose width would cause the total record length to exceed the 4000-byte maximum, the error message *Maximum record length exceeded* is displayed.

If you attempt to enter a field name for the second time, the message *Field name already in use* is displayed.

If you enter a width for a Character field that is not between 1 and 254, the error message *Illegal data length* is displayed.

For Numeric fields, the field width must be in the range of 1 to 19. If you enter a number outside of that range, the error message *Illegal Numeric data length* is displayed. Because dBASE III PLUS must have a place to display at least one number before the decimal, the number of decimal places must be at least two less than the field width; fifteen is the maximum number of decimal places that is allowed. If you enter an incorrect number of decimal places, the error message *Illegal Decimal length* is displayed.

Tips

Once you have designed a database file and defined its structure by using CREATE, you can change it later without losing any data. (See MODIFY STRUCTURE.)

CREATE FROM

Syntax `CREATE <filename> FROM <extended filename>`

Overview

The CREATE FROM command creates a database file from an extended file. (See COPY STRUCTURE EXTENDED.) The structure of the database file is contained in the records of the extended file. The number of fields in the new database file is equal to the number of records in the extended file.

The first file name in the command syntax is the name of the new database file that you want to create and the second file is the name of an extended file. Both files are assumed to have a .DBF extension. The extended file may be open in the active work area when CREATE FROM is executed, but it does not have to be. After the command is executed, the new database file is automatically put into use in the active work area.

Procedure

CREATE FROM is only used in conjunction with COPY STRUCTURE EXTENDED to program your own database file creation routine, if you don't like the CREATE command provided by dBASE III PLUS.

Examples

Assuming that you have previously created an extended file with COPY STRUCTURE EXTENDED, use CREATE FROM to turn the extended file back into a database file.

```
. CREATE NewFile FROM ExteFile
```

Warnings

The extended file may be open in the current work area when CREATE FROM is executed; however, if it is open in any other work area, the error message *File is already open* is displayed.

The new database file is overwritten without warning unless SET SAFETY is ON.

When you are adding records to a database file that you have created using COPY STRUCTURE EXTENDED, be sure that you follow the proper field-naming conventions. Also, be sure that the data type is valid and that the length of the field (and the number of decimal places for numerics) is correct for its type. Otherwise, you will encounter errors when you use CREATE FROM to create a new database file.

The possible error messages are listed below. They are self-explanatory, and any one of them prevents the new database file from being created:

Illegal field name-- detected on field <*n*>
Illegal field type-- detected on field <*n*>
Illegal Decimal length-- detected on field <*n*>
Field name is already in use.-- detected on field <*n*>

<*n*> is the record number in the extended file for which the error was detected.

Tips

See COPY STRUCTURE EXTENDED for a programming example that uses CREATE FROM to create a database file.

CREATE LABEL

Syntax `CREATE¦MODIFY LABEL <filename>¦?`

Overview

The CREATE LABEL command designs mailing labels for the active database file. When designing labels, you specify the label dimensions and contents using a menu-driven system. Labels can contain up to sixteen lines of information; one to five labels can be displayed across the page.

The label design is saved in a label (.LBL) file so that you can display the labels whenever you want without having to redesign them.

Procedure

In order to design labels for a database file, the file must be open in the current work area. (See USE.) You then issue CREATE LABEL to invoke the menu-driven label design mode. The file name that you specify is assumed to have a .LBL extension. If the file already exists, the existing label file is brought up for you to edit; otherwise, a new label file is created, and you must design the labels from scratch.

If you are using a catalog (see SET CATALOG), you can use the catalog query clause, ?, instead of specifying a label file name. This presents you with a menu of the label files in the catalog that are associated with the active database file. Select from this menu the label file that you want to modify by highlighting its file name and pressing Enter.

After you issue CREATE LABEL, you see the screen pictured in Figure 26 in the Examples section below. The menu navigation and selection keys are detailed in Appendix B.

Options The first menu that you see is called Options. This menu specifies the dimensions of the labels and how they are to be displayed.

The first option is *Predefined size* with which you can choose from five standard label sizes that are listed in order of their appearance in the menu in Table 5. The Enter key selects the next predefined label size in the list. Changing this menu option also changes the menu options below it to correspond to the new label size.

TABLE 5 **Predefined Label Sizes**

WIDTH	HEIGHT	NUMBER ACROSS
3 1/2″	15/16″	1
3 1/2″	15/16″	2
3 1/2″	15/16″	3
4″	1 7/16″	1
3 2/10″	11/12″	3

If you want to specify label dimensions that do not correspond to any of the predefined sizes, use the other selections in the Options menu. Each of the remaining options requires that you enter a number. To change the value, highlight the option and press Enter. Type in the number that you want, and press Enter to indicate that you are finished. The range of allowable values for each menu option is listed in Table 6. If you enter an incorrect value for any of these menu options, you are prompted with an error message and must press the space bar before you can continue.

TABLE 6

Ranges for Options Menu Selections

MENU OPTION	RANGE
Label width	1–120
Label height	1–16
Left margin	0–120
Lines between labels	0–16
Spaces between labels	0–120
Labels across page	1–5

The *Label width* option is the maximum number of characters that can appear on any label line. *Label height* is the number of lines to use for each label. *Left margin* is the number of blank spaces to leave on the left of the page when the labels are printed; this value is added to the SET MARGIN value. (See SET MARGIN.) *Lines between labels* is the number of blank lines between the labels going down the page. *Spaces between labels* is the number of blank spaces between the labels going across the page. (This option is pertinent only if there is more than one label across the page.) *Labels across page* is the number of labels going across the page.

Contents The next menu is Contents. This menu allows you to specify the fields that have contents you want to display on the labels. The number of items in this menu is equal to the value of the *Label height* in the Options menu.

To define the contents of a label line, highlight its line number and press Enter. Then, type in the names of the fields that you want to display on that line, or press F10 and select them from a menu of available fields. To select a field from this menu, highlight it and press Enter. The field name appears in the menu just as if you had typed it. In either case, separate the field names with a comma if you use more than one field on a line . When the label is printed, the blank spaces are automatically trimmed (see TRIM( )) from the end of each field and a single blank space is placed between the fields. You can enter any expression list as the label line contents, not just a field list; however, you cannot use Memo and Logical fields for the label contents. You can use a memory variable as part of the label contents; keep in mind, however, that if you do this, the variable must exist (see STORE) when you create the label file, any time you modify it, and when you display the labels. Press Enter when you are finished defining the label line. If you make a mistake in entering the contents, you are prompted with an error message, and must press the space bar to correct the mistake.

Exit The Exit menu is used to leave the label design mode. The available options are *Save* and *Abandon*.

If you select *Abandon*, you are indicating that you do not want to save the changes made during this session of CREATE LABEL. Selecting *Abandon* is equivalent to pressing Esc, and you will be prompted to confirm your decision. If you respond by typing `N`, the CREATE LABEL session is resumed. A response of `Y` ends the full-screen CREATE LABEL mode without saving the changes that you have made to the file.

If you select *Save*, the label file you designed is saved to disk. The file name is the name that you used as the CREATE LABEL command line option. By default, the file is given a .LBL extension.

See LABEL FORM for information on displaying labels once you have designed them.

Examples

The following example guides you through designing a set of labels for the people in the mailing list. A program example is then given that prints party invitations and mailing labels for selected individuals. Before CREATE LABEL is issued, the database file must be in use.

```
. USE Mail
. CREATE LABEL Party
```

When you first issue the CREATE LABEL command, the *Predefined Size* option is highlighted. Your screen should look like the one in Figure 26.

To begin the label design, specify the label dimensions if they differ from the default values. In this example, you will use the default label size. Type `C` to go directly to the label Contents menu. (Typing the first letter of a menu name is a shortcut for selecting any menu in dBASE III PLUS.)

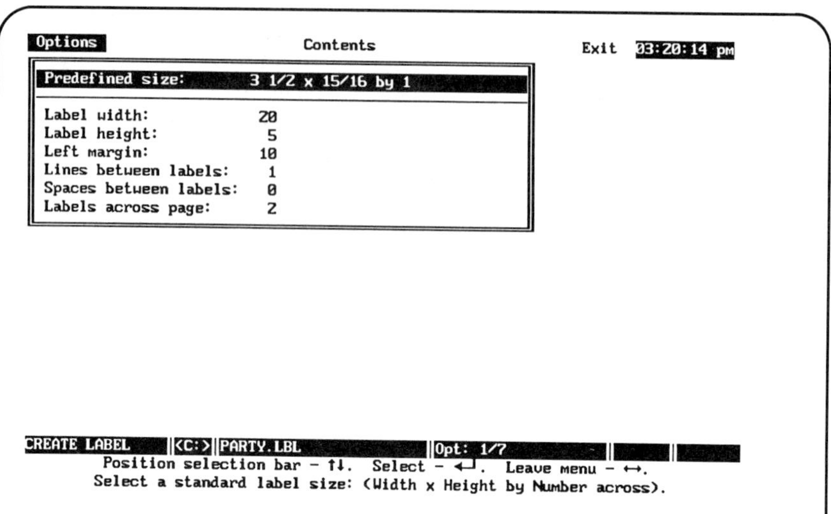

Figure 26

The label that you will design is fairly standard and includes the first and last name on line 1, the street address on line 2, the apartment number on line 3, and the city, state, and zip code on line 4. To begin, press Enter to select the line 1 option from the contents menu.

Since the first line is used for First_Name and Last_Name, press F10 to obtain the fields list menu, then highlight the First_Name field and press Enter. When the field name appears in the menu, type a comma (,) to separate it from the next field name. Press F10 again and select the Last_Name field. You are finished with line 1; press Enter.

The comma between the First_Name and Last_Name fields causes the fields to be displayed as you would expect on the label. First_Name is trimmed of trailing spaces (see TRIM( )), and a single space is placed between it and Last_Name.

Press the Down Arrow key to highlight line 2, and press Enter. At this point, you can either type the field name, `Address1`, or select it from the fields menu as you did with the First_Name and Last_Name fields. In either case, press Enter when you are finished.

In the same manner as you entered Address1 on line 2, enter Address2 on line 3. Many of the people in the mailing list do not have a second address line, but when the labels are printed, they will not have a blank third line. The command that displays the labels is designed to adjust spacing in the label lines.

Mailing labels usually have the city and state separated by a comma, and the state and zip code separated by two spaces. For this reason, the final line of the label is slightly more complicated than the other lines because it requires that you enter an expression. Highlight line 4, press Enter, and type `City + ", " + State + "  " + Zip`. Notice the label line definition scrolls horizontally to accommodate the length of this line's contents. Press Enter when you are finished.

When you are finished defining the label, your screen should look like the one in Figure 27.

To save the label design, type `E` to access the Exit menu then press Enter to select the *Save* option. The label file is saved to disk. If you display a single label on the screen, you will see the following screen:

```
. LABEL FORM Party NEXT 1

         MICHELLE SMITH
         510 Mabel Street
         Columbia
```

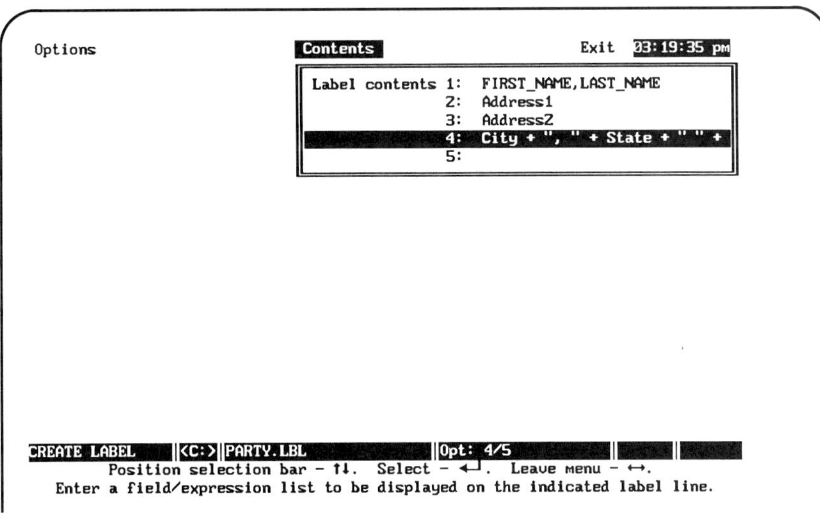

Figure 27

However, this is not exactly what you want; the last line does not properly display the State and Zip fields because the City field is too long. You can rectify this problem by removing the trailing blank spaces from City. Type `MODIFY LABEL Party` to correct the problem.

Access line 4 of the Contents menu by typing `C` and pressing the Down Arrow key until the line is highlighted. You are going to use TRIM( ) with the City field to remove the trailing spaces. Press Enter to change the expression, and press the Ins key to go from overwrite mode into insert mode (look at the status bar for the *Ins* indicator to make sure that you are in insert mode). Using the Left Arrow, highlight the beginning of the City field and type `TRIM(`. Press the Right Arrow key four times to get to the space following the City field name. Your screen should look like the one in Figure 28. Type `)`, and press Enter to indicate that you are finished making changes.

Save the label design using the Exit menu.

You are ready to print the party invitations and mailing labels. For this particular party, you are going to invite only those people over twenty-five who live in the 213 area code. The following routine assumes that you have two printers attached to your computer which allows the program to

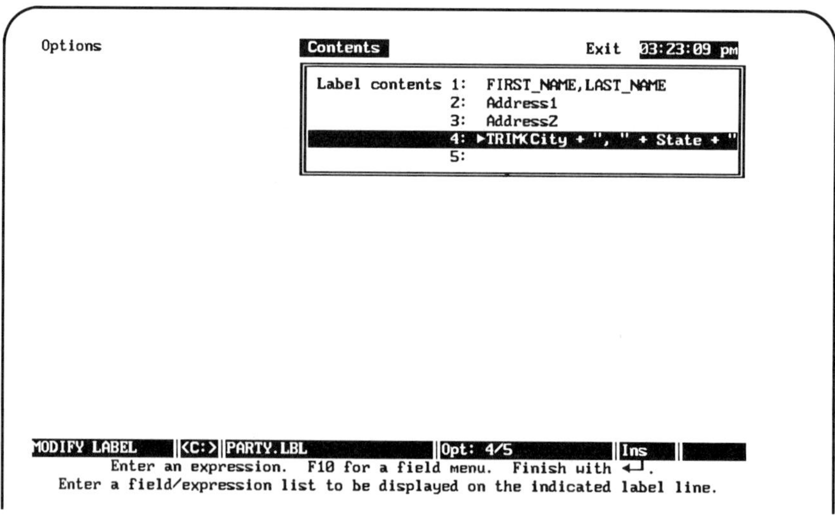

Figure 28

switch back and forth between the two printers. (See SET PRINTER TO.) One printer is set up with regular paper for printing the invitations, and the other is set up for printing mailing labels.

```
* Party.PRG
*
USE Mail
DO WHILE .NOT. EOF()
   * Only invite people over 25 years of age who live nearby
   IF Age > 25 .AND. Phone = "(213)"

      * Switch to second printer and print a single label.
      SET PRINTER TO LPT2
      LABEL FORM Party NEXT 1 TO PRINTER

      * Switch to first printer and print an invitation.
      SET PRINTER TO LPT1
      DO Invite && Invite.PRG is the invitation print program

   ENDIF

   SKIP
ENDDO

CLOSE DATABASES
```

Warnings Several self-explanatory error messages are possible when you are designing labels. For example, if you make an error in entering one of the Label widths, the error message *RANGE is 1 to 120 (press SPACE)* is displayed. There is a similar message for each of the label dimension options, but the range values differ.

The only other error that you can make is in entering the label Contents. If you enter the name of a Memo or Logical field, the error message *Memo and Logical fields are not allowed here. Press any key to continue.* is displayed. You must press any key and erase the field name. If you enter an expression that cannot be evaluated, the error message *This must be a valid dBASE expression. Press any key to continue.* is displayed. This same error message is displayed regardless of the mistake which could be a data type mismatch or an unknown field or variable name. Examine the expression to determine the mistake, and press any key to correct it.

Tips

The LABEL FORM command is equipped with some features that make designing labels much easier.

- The contents of each label line are truncated to the label width that you specify, rather than being wrapped around. This feature prevents the labels from becoming misaligned when label lines are very long.
- A field or expression list separated by commas and used as the contents of a label line in the design gets special treatment when the labels are displayed. Each expression in the list is trimmed of trailing spaces (see TRIM( )), and a single space is displayed between each field or expression. This feature avoids the necessity of having to form a more complicated expression in the label design to accomplish the same task. For example, when you design the label using CREATE LABEL, you can use `First_Name, Last_Name` rather than `TRIM(First_Name) + "" + Last_Name.`
- Blank label lines are not shown in the label. All blank lines are moved to the top of the label which causes the non-blank lines to appear consecutively on the label.

CREATE LABEL is functionally identical to MODIFY LABEL; however, the CREATE form of the command is generally used to design a new label form, while the MODIFY form is used to edit an existing label form.

It is possible to design labels that use fields from more than one file. The database files you want to use must be open (see USE) when you use CREATE LABEL to create or modify the label file. If SET FIELDS is ON when you use F10 to access the optional fields list menu from the Contents menu, all of the available fields from all of the files appear in the menu; however, if SET FIELDS is OFF, only the fields from the active database file appear in the menu. In the latter case, you must type the <alias name> -> <field name> form of the field name that you want to include from an unselected file . When you display the labels using LABEL FORM, all database files that are used in the label design must be open, and the relationships between those files must be established. (See SET RELATION.)

CREATE QUERY

Syntax `CREATE¦MODIFY QUERY <filename>¦?`

Overview The CREATE QUERY command constructs a logical condition, or query, to filter the active database file. (See SET FILTER). When constructing a query, you specify up to seven individual conditions and combine them into a single condition using logical operators through a menu-driven system.

The query is saved in a query (.QRY) file so that you can use it whenever you want without having to reconstruct it. Each time you activate the query file with SET FILTER TO FILE, only the records in the database file that meet the query condition (i.e., it evaluates to a logical .T.) are accessible.

Procedure When designing a query for a database file, be sure that the file is open in the current work area. (See USE.) Then, issue CREATE QUERY to invoke the menu-driven query design mode. The file name that you specify is assumed to have a .QRY extension. If the file already exists, the existing query file is brought up for you to edit; otherwise, a new file is created, and you must design the query from scratch.

You can use the catalog query clause, ?, instead of specifying a query file name if you are using a catalog. (See SET CATALOG.) This presents you with a menu of all of the query files in the catalog that are associated with the active database file. From this menu, select the query that you want to modify by highlighting its file name and pressing Enter.

The menu navigation and selection keys for CREATE QUERY and all other menu-driven commands are detailed in Appendix B.

Set Filter The first menu is Set Filter. You use this menu to specify a single logical condition in order to filter the database file. (See SET FILTER.) The condition that you define can consist of up to seven individual conditions connected by logical operators. Each of the individual conditions is limited to comparing the value of a field to an expression. (See Expression for more information on the subject of logical conditions and how they are formed.)

As you define conditions using the Set Filter menu, they appear in the box below the menu.

The *Field Name* option selects the field that you want to use in the condition. To use this menu option, highlight it and press Enter. A menu of available fields appears to the right of the Set Filter menu (memo fields are not allowed as part of a condition). Highlight the name of the field that you want and select it by pressing Enter.

The *Operator* option lets you select the comparison operator that you want to use in the condition. When you select this menu option by pressing Enter, a menu of comparison operators appears to the right of the Set Filter menu. The contents of this menu depends on the type of the field that you chose for the *Field Name*. For Date and Numeric fields, the menu contains all available operators for that data type. (See Expression.) For Character fields, the menu contains all of the available operators, plus some additional ones. For Logical fields, the menu contains only two options, *Is True* and *Is False*. In all cases, the operators in the menu are represented by the symbolic operator (e.g., >, =, etc..) and an explanation. To select an operator, highlight it and press Enter.

The *Constant/Expression* menu option enables you to define to what the field name is to be compared. This option is not available for Logical fields since it is not necessary to convert them to a logical expression. To use this option, press Enter and type in an expression that matches the data type of the *Field Name*.

The expression that you enter can be as simple or as complicated as you want it to be. For example, you can enter a constant value (for a Character field, this would be a quoted character string; for a Numeric field, it would be a number). A constant date value is usually represented using CTOD( ), since there is no direct representation for dates in dBASE III PLUS. (For example, the date of January 22, 1984 would be CTOD("01/22/84")); however, CREATE QUERY is forgiving when it comes to dates. You can enter dates in the form of MM/DD/YY, (where MM is the month, DD is the day, and YY is the year), and CREATE QUERY will understand what you mean. If the date format has been changed to something other than American (see SET DATE), you must be sure to format the date correctly; although CREATE QUERY lets you specify the dates in this simplified form, it does not verify that the elements of the date are in order or that you have used the correct date delimiter.

The expression may be another field that you want to compare to the field name. For example, you might want to compare the Quantity of an order to establish that it is less than or equal to the Quantity in stock. An optional field list menu is available to you by pressing F10. To select a field from this menu, highlight its field name and press Enter. The fields list menu disappears and the field name appears in the menu just as if you had typed it.

Any expression you choose must match the data type of the *Field name*. If it does not, an error message is displayed below the status bar when you press Enter to indicate that you are finished with the *Constant/Expression*. CREATE QUERY forces you to correct the error.

The *Connect* option allows you to define a condition that is more complicated than a simple condition which only compares one value to another. Complex conditions are created by stringing together two or more simple conditions using logical operators. (See Expression.) If you want to define a complex condition, select this menu option by pressing Enter for a menu containing these operators. When the menu of operators appears on your screen, highlight the one you want to use and press Enter.

When you are defining conditions to create a new query, the Set Filter menu automatically goes to a new *Line Number* when you select an operator using the *Connect* option. If you want to change any of the options for a particular condition, locate its number in the box below the menu, highlight the *Line Number* option in the menu, press Enter, and type in the number of the condition line that you want to change.

You can delete a condition line using Ctrl-U when the line appears in the Set Filter menu. You can also insert a condition line between two existing lines. To do this, use the *Line Number* menu option to locate the condition line before which you want to insert the new condition and press Ctrl-N.

Nest If you have a very complicated Set Filter condition, you may want to use parentheses to nest the individual lines of the condition to alter the order of precedence. (See Expression.) Use the Nest menu to add parentheses to the condition. The options in this menu are designed to allow you to add and remove parentheses at the beginning and end of a line number that you specify.

To add a set of parentheses, select the *Start* option under the word *Add* by highlighting it and pressing Enter. Then, type in the line number where you want to place the left parenthesis. To determine the line number, look at the filter box in the middle of the screen. Press Enter after you type in the line number, and the left parenthesis appears in the filter box. Now, select the *End* option under *Add*. Enter the line number after which you want to place the right parenthesis, and it appears in the filter box. The lines in the condition box starting with the *Start* number and ending with the *End* number are now grouped together.

If you add a set of parentheses that you do not want, use the *Start* and *End* options under the word *Remove*. These options are used like the *Add* options to take parentheses out of the condition.

Display After the condition is defined and nested properly, you can use the *Display* menu bar option to display the records that meet the condition. This menu bar option is unusual because it does not have a menu. You select it just like any other menu, but to make it work you must press Enter when it is highlighted.

Selecting *Display* shows you, one at a time, the records that meet the filter condition. The records are displayed using a screen format that looks like the default edit screen. (See EDIT.) You cannot, however, edit records from within CREATE QUERY. Use PgDn and PgUp to page through the records and use F1 to turn off the filter box so that you can use that part of the screen for the record display.

You can use this menu bar option to view the records that meet the query condition. If you have made a mistake in the logic when defining the condition, you may be able to detect that error and correct it. For example, if you are inexperienced in forming complicated logical expressions, you may not know how to express the condition "all records of people who live in Los Angeles who are at least twenty-five years old or who will turn twenty-five this year, 1987." You might try the following condition:

```
City = "Los Angeles" .AND. Age >= 25 .OR. YEAR(Birthday) = 1962
```

If you use this as your Set Filter condition, *Display* shows all people who are having their twenty-fifth birthday in 1987 even if they do not live in Los Angeles because the .AND. is evaluated before the .OR. which gives the .AND. precedence over the .OR.. (See Expression for a discussion of the order of precedence.) In this case the correct condition must use parentheses to change the order in which the components of the condition are evaluated:

```
City = "Los Angeles" .AND. (Age >= 25 .OR. YEAR(Birthday) = 1962)
```

Grouping the .OR. condition forces it to be evaluated before the .AND. condition, which gives the .OR. precedence over the .AND.

Exit The Exit menu is used to leave the query design mode. The available options are *Save* and *Abandon*.

If you select *Abandon*, you are indicating that you do not want to save the changes that you have made during this session of CREATE QUERY. It is equivalent to pressing Esc, and you are prompted to confirm your decision. If you respond by typing `N`, the CREATE QUERY session is resumed. A response of `Y` ends the full-screen CREATE QUERY mode without saving the changes that you made to the file.

If you select *Save*, the query condition that you have defined is saved to disk as a query file. The file name is the name that you used as the CREATE QUERY command line option. By default, the file is given a .QRY extension. A SET FILTER TO FILE is automatically executed to put the query condition into effect.

See SET FILTER for information on how to disable a query condition once you have designed it, and how to enable it again when you want to use it.

Examples

The following example guides you through designing a query condition for the mailing list. The query that you will design includes all of the people who live in either the 213 or the 818 area code and who were at least twenty-five years of age on July 1, 1987. Before CREATE QUERY is issued, the database file must be in use.

```
. USE Mail
. CREATE QUERY Local
```

When you first issue CREATE QUERY, you see the Set Filter menu, and the *Field Name* option is highlighted like the screen in Figure 29.

To begin the query design, specify each of the individual conditions that go together to make the entire query condition. The query condition is all of the people who live in either the 213 or the 818 area code and who were at least twenty-five years of age by July 1, 1987. In the mailing list database file, the area code is part of the Phone field. Select the *Field Name* option by pressing Enter. A fields list menu opens up to the right of the Set Filter menu. Select the Phone field from this menu by highlighting it and pressing Enter.

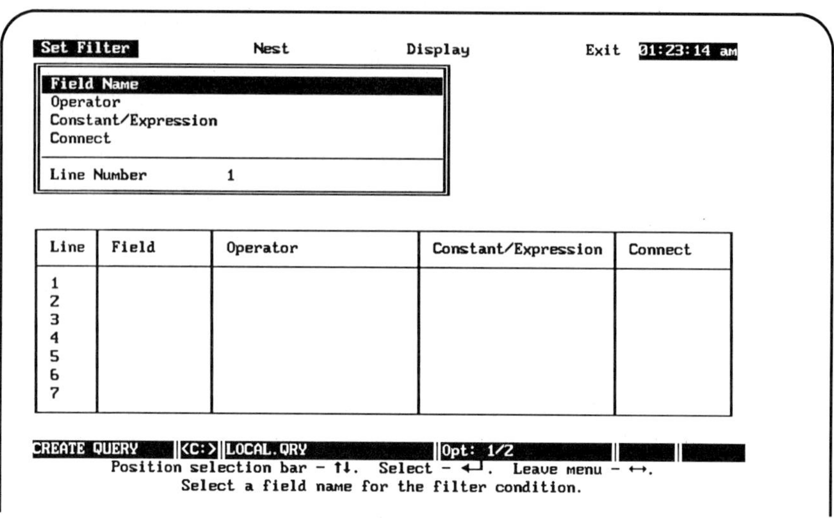

Figure 29

The Phone field name appears in the filter box in the middle of the screen, and the menu highlight automatically moves to the *Operator* option. Select this option by pressing Enter, and you are presented with a submenu of operators. Your screen should look like the one in Figure 30. In this case, you are interested in all of the phone numbers that begin with area code 213 or 818. Highlight the *Begins with* options and press Enter.

The operator that you selected appears in the filter box, and the menu highlight automatically moves to the *Constant/Expression* option. Press Enter, and type "(213)". (You must type the quotation marks in order to form a valid character expression.) Press Enter to indicate that you are finished entering the expression.

The value that you entered appears in the filter box, and the menu highlight automatically moves to the *Connect* option. Select this menu option by pressing Enter, and you are presented with a submenu of logical connectors. Since you are interested in phone numbers that begin with the area code 213 or 818, select the option labeled *Combine with .OR.*

The connector appears in the filter box, and the menu moves on for you to enter line 2 of the condition. Use the following list to define line 2 in the same way as you defined line 1:

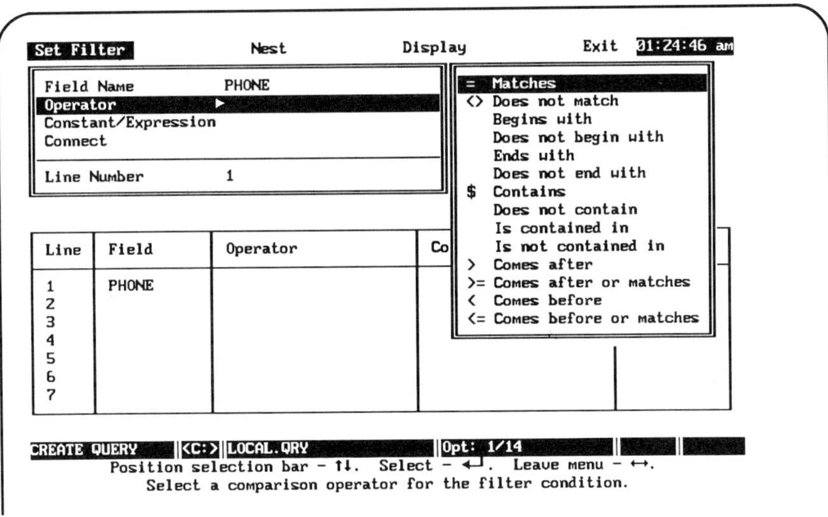

Figure 30

1. Press Enter and select the Phone field from the submenu.
2. Press Enter and select *Begins with* from the submenu.
3. Press Enter and type "(818)".
4. Press Enter to indicate that you are through.

After you define line 2, the *Connect* option will be highlighted, and your screen will look like the one in Figure 31.

Select the *Connect* option, and this time select *Combine with .AND.* from the submenu. Remembering the statement of the query in words will help you to decide which connector to use. The original statement called for "people who live in either the 213 or the 818 area code, and who were at least twenty-five years of age on July 1, 1987."

Define the last line of the query condition so that you will see only records of people who were twenty-five years old by July 1, 1987. The definition of this condition is not as straightforward as the other two conditions but it is not too difficult when you analyze it. There is a field in the mailing list called Birthday that contains the birth date of the individual. In order to be twenty-five by 07/01/87, one must have been born on or before 07/01/62; therefore, the condition is that the Birthday field be less than or equal to 07/01/62.

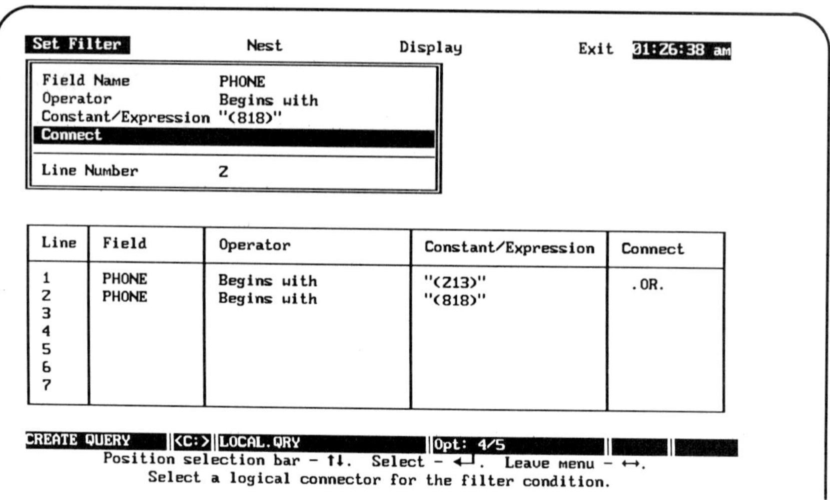

Figure 31

Select the Birthday field for the *Field Name* option, then select the option labeled < = *Less than or equal* for the *Operator*. For the *Constant/Expression* option, type 07/01/62. Use the following list if you cannot remember how to proceed:

1. Press Enter and select the Birthday field from the submenu.
2. Press Enter and select < = *Less than or equal* from the submenu.
3. Press Enter and type 07/01/62.
4. Press Enter to indicate that you are through.

You are positioned on the *Connect* option and your screen should look like the one in Figure 32.

At this point, you are almost through with defining the query condition, but the rules of logic creep in to spoil it for you. Because of the order in which logical conditions are evaluated, the condition that you have defined does not mean what you think.

The logical connectors, or operators, have a precedence associated with them, in much the same way as mathematical operators do. (See Expression). In this example, .AND. takes precedence over .OR., which means that the two conditions that are connected with .AND. are evaluated together

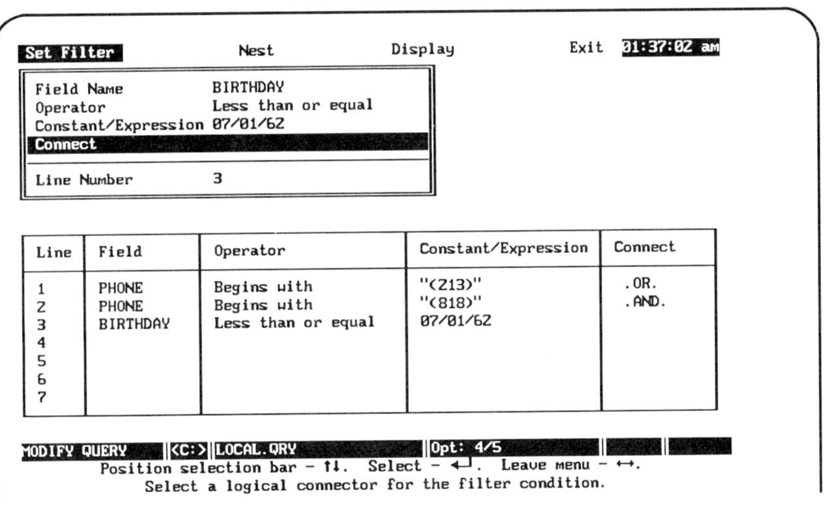

Figure 32

as a single condition. Hence, the Birthday condition is only considered in conjunction with the Phone condition to which it is connected (i.e., Phone = "(818)"). The entire query condition will be true for anybody who lives in the 213 area code, regardless of their date of birth.

You can change the order in which the conditions are evaluated by grouping them with parentheses using the Nest menu to group the conditions that you want evaluated together. In this example, you must first determine if the person lives in either of the designated area codes. Only after that is established do you want to determine whether or not they are old enough to be included. You accomplish this by grouping the first two lines of the conditions together.

Type N to get to the Nest menu, and select the *Start* option under the menu heading *Add.* Type 1 to indicate that you want to place the left parenthesis before line 1 of the condition. Press Enter, and press Down Arrow to highlight the *End* option. To place the ending, or right, parenthesis after line 2 of the condition, press Enter, type 2, and press Enter again to indicate that you are finished. Your screen should look like the one in Figure 33. (See Expression for more information on precedence and operators.)

To save the query condition to a file, type E to access the Exit menu, and press Enter to select the *Save* option. The query file is saved to disk and put

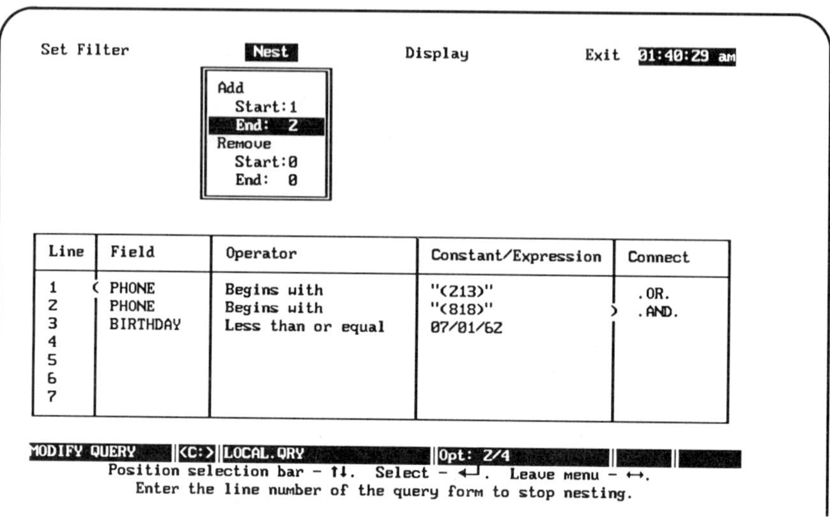

Figure 33

into effect. The following LIST command shows the effect of the query condition on the database file:

```
. LIST First_Name, Phone, Birthday
Record#  First_Name  Phone          Birthday
      3  Gloria      (213)485-5955  06/08/53
     12  Mala        (213)465-5723  09/22/55
     14  Nancy       (213)444-7732  10/30/54
     17  Jerry       (213)635-1235  02/25/50
     18  Chris       (213)622-5597  06/26/51
```

You can disable the query condition and view the entire database file with SET FILTER TO. SET FILTER TO FILE Local puts the query condition back into effect.

Warnings

It is difficult to make a mistake when using CREATE QUERY because almost everything is selected from a submenu rather than entered.

An exception to this rule in the Set Filter menu is the *Constant/Expression* option for which you must enter an expression. If you make an error such as neglecting to enclose a character string constant in quotation marks or attempting to add two data elements of differing data types, the error message *This field must contain a valid dBASE expression. Press any key to continue.* is displayed. The specific error might be caused by neglecting to quote a character string, using a field name that does not exist, using a memory variable that you have not initialized (see STORE), or using mixed data types in the same expression.

The *Line Number* option in this menu displays the error message *RANGE is 1 to 7 (press SPACE)* if you enter a line number that is outside of the allowable range. All of the Nest menu options cause this same error message if you enter an incorrect line number.

Additionally, the Nest options can cause some other error messages if you do not balance the parentheses (for example, you might add a left parenthesis without adding the corresponding right parenthesis). If you make an error of this nature and attempt to save the query condition, the error message *Cannot save an invalid filter. Press any key to continue.* is displayed. A similar error message comes from attempting to *Display* such a query condition. Look at the filter box in the middle of the screen and *Add* or *Remove* parentheses as necessary to correct this problem.

This same error message occurs if you have a logical connector at the end of the last line in the query condition. This can occur, for example, if you delete the last line of a condition using Ctrl-U, which leaves the previous line with its connector. To remove the connector, locate the last line of the condition in the Set Filter menu using the *Line Number* option, select the *Connect* option, and select *No combination* from the submenu.

Unlike most other full-screen commands, CREATE QUERY does not have a cursor navigation menu. F1 has no effect unless you are using the Display menu. For this menu, it toggles the Filter Box on and off the screen.

Tips

CREATE QUERY is functionally identical to MODIFY QUERY; however, the CREATE form of the command is normally used to create a new query file, while the MODIFY form is used to edit an existing query file.

Formulating very complicated query conditions may be difficult if you do not understand logical expressions thoroughly. Although CREATE QUERY is supposed to make this task easier, you still need to understand logical operators and expressions. (See Expression for more information.)

There are certain conditions that you cannot define using CREATE QUERY because of the simplicity of the form of condition that it allows. In its full form, a simple condition is any expression compared to another expression of the same type, and complex conditions are formed by connecting simple conditions using logical operators. CREATE QUERY only allows you to compare a field to an expression so that, for example, it is not possible to form a query condition that involves comparing a particular substring (see SUBSTR( )) of a Character field to a string.

You can always use SET FILTER TO <condition> to form a more complicated query condition, but you will not be able to save it to a query file; instead, you can save SET FILTER TO as a program file (see MODIFY COMMAND) once you have formulated the condition. This allows you to use the filter condition repeatedly by executing the program. (See DO.)

If you use a memory variable as part of the CREATE QUERY condition, the variable must exist (see STORE) when you create the query condition, each time you modify it, and when you use it.

CREATE REPORT

Syntax `CREATE¦MODIFY REPORT <filename>¦?`

Overview

The CREATE REPORT command designs columnar report forms for the active database file. When designing reports, you specify the title, dimensions, and contents of the report using a menu-driven system.

Reports can contain up to twenty-four columns, each of which can be used to display a single field or a more complicated expression (e.g., a calculation involving two or more fields). Columns that are used to display numeric values can be totalled automatically with up to two levels of subtotals that you must define.

The report design is saved in a report form (.FRM) file so that you can print the report whenever you want without having to redesign it.

Procedure

In order to design a columnar report form for a database file, the file must be open in the current work area. (See USE.) (You can also define a report

form for more than one database file as illustrated later in this section under Examples.) You then issue CREATE REPORT to invoke the menu-driven report form design mode. The file name that you specify is assumed to have a .FRM extension. If the file already exists, the existing report form is brought up for you to edit; otherwise, a new report form is created, and you must design the report from scratch.

If you are using a catalog (see SET CATALOG), you can use the catalog query clause, ?, instead of specifying a report form name. This presents you with a menu of all of the report forms in the catalog that are associated with the active database file. From this menu, select the report form that you want to modify by highlighting its file name and pressing Enter.

After issuing CREATE REPORT, you see the screen pictured in Figure 34. The menu navigation and selection keys are detailed in Appendix B.

You will probably notice the cursor navigation menu that appears on the screen. CREATE REPORT displays this regardless of the status of SET MENUS. When the Columns menu is open, the cursor navigation menu is replaced by the *Report Format* box. You can switch back and forth at any time between the two by pressing F1.

Options The first menu is Options. This menu specifies the page title and dimensions of the report, as well as other options that affect how the report is to be displayed.

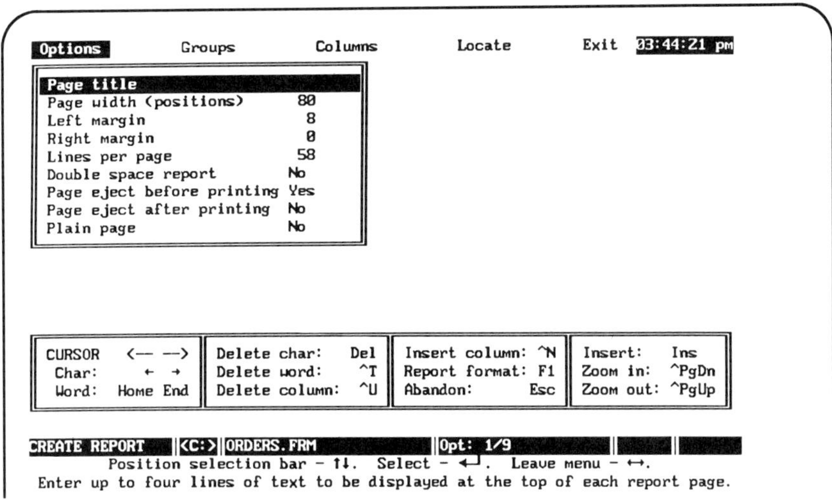

Figure 34

The first option is *Page title.* To enter a page title, press Enter when this option is highlighted and a data entry box opens up to the right of the Options menu. You can enter up to four lines of text in this box. Although the data entry box is not very wide, each line in it is horizontally scrolled when the cursor reaches the edge of the box. Each line can contain up to sixty characters. In the page title data entry box, type in the text that you want to appear at the top of each new page of the report. All of the full-screen editing and cursor navigation keys listed in Appendix A can be used when you are entering the page title. Ctrl-End closes the data entry box when you are finished.

The next four options in the menu specify the report dimensions. To change one of the report dimension options, highlight it and press Enter. You can then type in the new value and press Enter to indicate that you are finished. The range of allowable values for each of these options is listed in Table 7. If you enter an incorrect value for any of these menu options, you are prompted with an error message and must press the space bar before you can continue.

TABLE 7

Ranges for Report Dimensions

MENU OPTION	RANGE	DEFAULT
Page width (positions)	1–500	80
Left margin	0–499	8
Right margin	0–499	0
Lines per page	1–500	58

The default values for these menu options are designed for standard 8½-by-11 inch paper.

The *Page width* is the maximum number of characters that can appear on a single line of the report.

Left margin is the number of blank spaces you want to leave on the left of the page when the report is printed; this value is added to the SET MARGIN value. (See SET MARGIN for more information.) The value that you specify for *Left margin* must be at least one less than the *Page width.*

Right margin is supposed to specify the number of blank spaces to leave on the right side of the page, but it does not. You can define report

Columns that move into the right margin without getting any error messages. The actual right margin is defined by the report columns that you define, the left margin and the page width. You can ignore the *Right margin* menu option without losing any functionality in your report.

The *Lines per page* option allows you to specify the number of lines that you want to print on each page of the report. This number does not include the lines that are used for the Page title, the standard report headings (date and page number), and the additional HEADING that you can specify when you print the report. This is the reason that the default value for this menu option is 58, even though there are sixty-six lines available on standard 8½-by-11 inch paper.

The final four options in the Options menu are Yes/No toggles. Change any of these options by highlighting it and pressing Enter. If its value is *Yes*, it will change to *No*, and vice versa.

Double space report determines whether the report is single- or double-spaced. By default, all reports are single-spaced, but if you change this menu option to *Yes*, the report will be double-spaced.

Page eject before printing determines whether or not there is an initial page eject before the report is printed. By default, all reports begin with a page eject. If you change this menu option to *No*, the report will begin printing at the current print location, which is useful if you want to print several short reports on the same page. This menu option is overridden if you print the report using the NOEJECT option. (See REPORT FORM.)

Page eject after printing determines whether or not there is a page eject after the report is printed. By default, the printer position remains wherever the report happens to finish, which is useful if you want to print several short reports on the same page; however, if you prefer to have an automatic page eject at the end of a report, change this menu option to *Yes*.

Plain page determines whether or not the date and page number are printed at the top of each page of the report just before the page title, and whether or not the page title appears on all pages. By default, a page number and the current date are displayed on the first two lines of each report page, and the page title is printed at the top of each page. To display the page title only on the first page and to suppress the other headings (as well as the HEADING that you can specify when you display the report), change *Plain page* to *Yes*. This menu option is overridden if you display the report using the PLAIN option. (See REPORT FORM.)

Groups The next menu on the menu bar is Groups. This menu specifies how the detail lines of the report are to be grouped together.

Detail lines in a report are grouped together according to an expression that you specify with the *Group on expression* menu option. This expression is usually the name of a single field, and the database file for which the report is being designed is assumed to be ordered by that field. (See INDEX, SORT.)

To enter the field name (or expression), press Enter when this menu option is highlighted and type in the name of the field. If you want, select the field from a field list menu by pressing F10. Highlight the field that you want to use and press Enter. The field name appears in the menu just as if you had typed it. Press Enter to indicate that you are finished.

When the report is displayed, each line with the same value for the group field (or expression) is displayed together as a group. Each group is preceded by the value of its group field. When the value of the group field changes, subtotals are displayed for all report Columns that are totalled, and the next group of report lines begins.

You can specify a heading to appear before each group of report lines using the *Group heading* menu option. To enter a group heading, highlight this menu option and press Enter. Type in the text that you want to use, and press Enter when you are finished. The text will appear at the beginning of each group just before the group field value.

The *Summary report only* option is a Yes/No toggle that lets you specify whether or not the report detail lines are displayed. By default, the detail lines are displayed along with subtotal and total lines. You can suppress the detail lines and display only the subtotal and total lines of the report by changing the value of this menu option to *Yes*. To change the *Summary report only* option, highlight it and press Enter. This menu option is overridden if you display the report using the SUMMARY option.

Once you have defined a *Group on expression*, the *Page eject after group* option becomes available. This is a Yes/No toggle that you can change by highlighting it and pressing Enter. By default, the value of this menu option is *No* and the report groups are not separated by a page eject. If you change it to *Yes*, each group of report lines begins on a new page.

The last two options in the Groups menu are *Sub-group on expression* and *Sub-group heading*. These options become available only after you have defined a *Group on expression*, and they are specified just like *Group on expression* and *Group heading*. A sub-group is treated as a group within the main group.

If you want to have a sub-group in your report, the database file should be ordered using the sub-group field for the secondary sort or index key. In other words, if the database file is ordered using an index file, the INDEX ON key expression should be the group expression concatenated with the sub-group key expression (e.g., INDEX ON <group expression> + <sub-group expression> TO <filename>). This ensures that all of the records with the same group and sub-group values are in consecutive order and will be displayed on the report in that order.

Columns The next menu is Columns. With this menu, you define the report one column at a time. The column number that you are defining appears at the bottom of the screen on the status bar. You can use the PgDn and PgUp keys to move from one column to another. As you add new columns and make changes to existing ones, the columns are reflected in the *Report Format* box that appears in the middle of the screen.

This box gives you an example of what your report will look like when you display it by showing the column heading and width, as well as the type of data that appears in the column. It also indicates the left- and right-margin settings. The following list explains the symbols that are used in the *Report Format* box:

SYMBOL	EXPLANATION
X	Contents is character data type
9	Contents is numeric data type, and not totalled
#	Contents is numeric data type, and totalled
mm/dd/yy	Contents is date data type
.L.	Contents is logical data type
M	Contents is a memo field
<	Indicates a position in the right margin
>	Indicates a position in the left margin
?	Indicates that something in the column is undefined

You can switch back and forth between the *Report Format* box and the cursor navigation menu by pressing F1.

The first option in the Columns menu is called *Contents*, which is where you type in the field name or expression that has a value you want to appear in the current report column. To enter the column contents, highlight the *Contents* option, press Enter, and type in the field or expression that you want to use. Instead of typing in a field name, you can select from a menu of available fields by pressing F10. When the menu of fields appears, highlight the one you want, press Enter, and the field name appears in the menu just as if you had typed it. Press Enter when you are finished entering the column contents.

If you make a mistake in entering the contents, CREATE REPORT forces you to correct it before allowing you to continue. If you use an expression for the column contents, remember that if you want to use a memory variable it must exist (see STORE) when you create the report form, any time you modify it, and when you display the report.

For each column, you can have up to four lines of text as a column *Heading*. Defining a column heading is identical to defining the *Page title* in the Options menu. Highlight the option, and press Enter to open a data entry box into which you enter the column heading. Ctrl-End indicates that you are finished with the heading.

CREATE REPORT automatically assigns a width for the column based on the expression and heading that you enter. You can change the column width by highlighting the *Width* option, pressing Enter, and entering a new number. If the column contents are wider when the report is displayed, it is wrapped around using the width that you specify.

The *Decimal Places* and *Total this column* options are available for numeric columns.

The number of decimal places defaults to a value based on the expression that you enter for *Contents*. You can change it by highlighting the *Decimal places* option, pressing Enter, typing a number, and pressing Enter again when you are finished. When the report is displayed, the value that is printed in the column is rounded to this number of decimal places.

The *Total this column* option is a Yes/No toggle that you can change by pressing Enter. Its default value is *Yes* for all numeric columns, which means that a total for the column will be displayed at the end of the report. Additionally, if you have defined any Groups, the column will be subtotalled. Changing this option to *No* prevents the column from being totalled.

Locate After you use the Columns menu to define the columns of a report form, you may decide to change one or more of them. To change a column definition, simply locate the column in the Columns menu and

edit the options that you want. You can even insert and delete columns using the Ctrl-N and Ctrl-U keys, respectively.

You could use the PgUp and PgDn keys with the Columns menu to locate the column that you are interested in, but using the Locate menu allows you to access the column you want more quickly – especially if you have many columns.

The Locate menu has as its menu options the expressions you entered for each report column that you have defined. They are in order by column number. To quickly bring a column up for editing, highlight the expression that defines the column contents and press Enter. The Columns menu opens up immediately, showing the column that you selected.

Exit The Exit menu is used to leave the report form design mode. The available options are *Save* and *Abandon*.

If you select *Abandon*, you are indicating that you do not want to save the changes that you have made during this session of CREATE REPORT. It is equivalent to pressing Esc, and you are prompted to confirm your decision. If you respond by typing `N`, the CREATE REPORT session is resumed. A response of `Y` ends the full-screen CREATE REPORT mode without saving the changes that you have made to the file.

If you select *Save*, the report form file that you have designed is saved to disk. The file name is the name that you used as the CREATE REPORT command line option. By default, the file is given a .FRM extension.

See REPORT FORM for information on how to display the report once you have designed it.

Examples The following example guides you through the design of a report form that uses fields from the Orders and the Inventry files. Before CREATE REPORT is issued, the database file environment must first be established.

```
. SELECT 2
. USE Inventry INDEX Part_No
. SET FIELDS TO ALL  && Select all fields from Inventry file
. SELECT 1
. USE Orders
. SET FIELDS TO ALL  && Select all fields from Orders file
. SET RELATION TO Part_No INTO Inventry  && Link files on Part_No
. CREATE REPORT Orders
```

Note that SET FIELDS TO ALL is issued for each database file. As a result you will be presented with all fields from both files if you want to select fields from the fields menu when you are designing the report . If SET FIELDS is OFF, only the fields from the active database file appear in the fields menu. (See SET FIELDS.)

To begin designing the report, give the report a page title. When you first enter the report form design mode, this option is already highlighted. Press Enter, type `Monthly Orders` into the box, and press Ctrl-End to indicate that you are finished entering the report page title.

Since this report is being designed to print on standard 8½-by-11 inch paper, you need not change the Options concerning the report dimensions; however, the page eject options for the report will be changed to do a page eject after the report has printed, rather than before. Use the Down Arrow key to highlight *Page eject before printing,* and change its value to *No* by pressing Enter. Press Down Arrow once more to change the *Page eject after printing* option to *Yes* in the same way. Your screen should look like the one in Figure 35.

The Groups menu will not be used yet. Later in this example, you will modify this report and define grouping criteria for it.

Open the Columns menu by typing `C`. (You can access a particular menu in all dBASE III PLUS menus simply by typing the first letter of its name on the menu bar.)

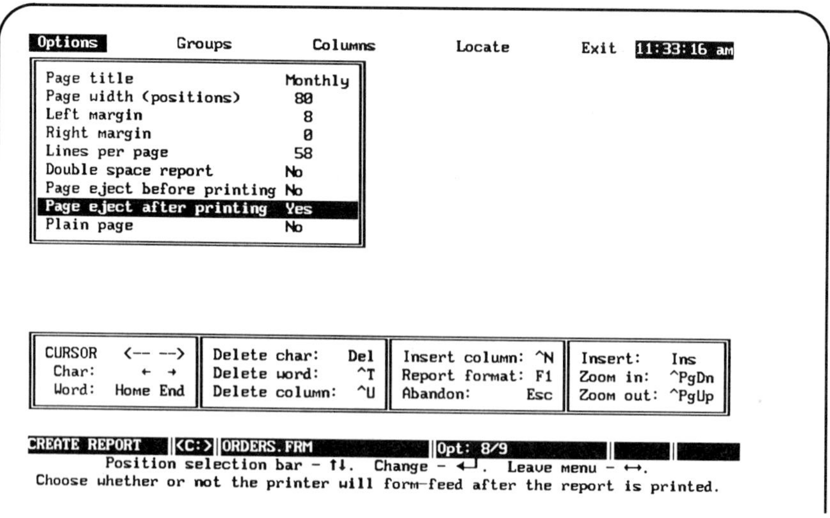

Figure 35

The first column in the report will be the Part_No field from the Orders database file. Press Enter when the *Contents* option is highlighted, and press F10 to open the fields list menu. This menu contains all fields in the SET FIELDS TO list which, in this case, is all fields from both the Orders and the Inventry files. Select the second field in the list, Orders – > Part_No, by pressing the Down Arrow to highlight it and pressing Enter. The field name appears in the Columns menu, just as if you had typed it. The alias name is automatically attached to the field name to avoid ambiguity when there is more than one data file open or if memory variables have the same names as fields. Press Enter to indicate that you are finished with the *Contents*, and press the Down Arrow key to highlight the *Heading* option.

Press Enter to specify a column heading. A data entry box similar to the one used for the *Page title* is displayed for you to type in a column heading. Type `Part`, press Enter to go to the second line of the box, and type `Number`. Press Ctrl-End. Your screen should look like the one in Figure 36. For this column, take the default for the column *Width* option, and press PgDn to define the next column.

In the same manner as you entered the Part Number column, use Table 8 to enter the next four report columns. Take the default Width for all of these columns and, for the three Numeric fields, change *Total this column* to *No* by highlighting the option and pressing Enter.

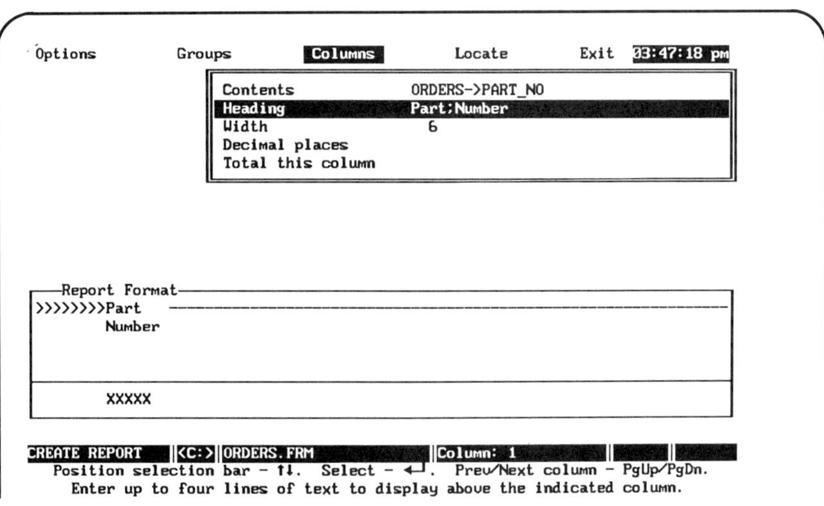

Figure 36

TABLE 8

Report Column Definitions

CONTENTS	HEADING
Inventry – > Descrip	Product Description
Orders – > Quantity	Quantity Ordered
Inventry – > Quantity	Quantity On Hand
Inventry – > Price	Price Per Unit

The final report column is the total price for each order, which involves using a calculation, but the *Report Format* box indicates that there is no room on the report to add another column (see Figure 37).

You can decrease the width of one of the other columns to make enough room to add the final report column. The best choice is the Inventry – > Descrip column since it is the widest. In order to change this

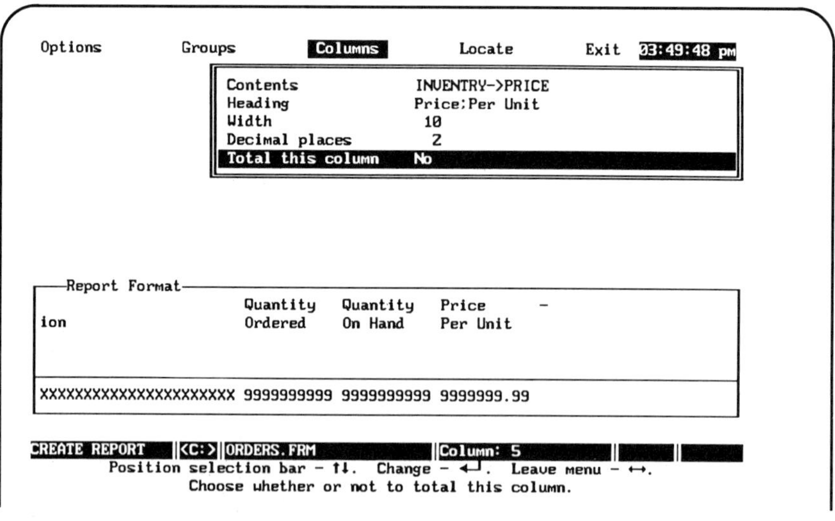

Figure 37

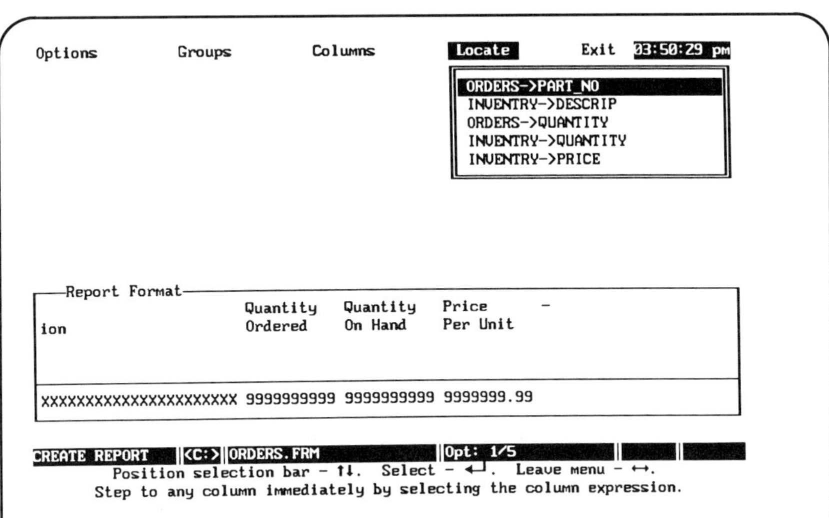

Figure 38

column, first locate it in the Columns menu. Press the Right Arrow key to access the Locate menu, and you will see all of the columns that you have defined so far. Your screen should look like the one in Figure 38.

Since the description column is the second one in the report, it is the second item in the menu. Highlight it by pressing the Down Arrow key, and press Enter to select it. As soon as you do, the Columns menu reappears showing the Inventry – > Descrip column, and you can make any changes to the column that you want.

You need about ten spaces to add the final column. Highlight the *Width* option, press Enter, change it from 30 to `20`, and press Enter. The entire contents of the Descrip field will appear when you display the report, but it will be wrapped around using only twenty columns.

You are now ready to add the final column. Press PgDn until the Columns menu is empty, and define the Contents of the last column using the following steps:

1. Press Enter
2. Type `Orders->Quantity * Inventry->Price`
3. Press Enter

Enter the column heading using the word `Total` on the first line and the word `Price` on the second line, just as you did for the other columns. Press Ctrl-End to indicate that you are finished. You want a total for this column, so do nothing to the Total option.

To save the report design, type `E` to access the Exit menu, then press Enter to select the *Save* option. The report form file is saved to disk. To print it, enter the following command:

```
. REPORT FORM Orders TO PRINTER
```

The printout should look like the one in Figure 39.

You can easily group the report lines with the same part number together by creating an index file (see INDEX) for the Orders file and modifying the report design. (Note that Orders.DBF is still in use.)

```
. INDEX ON Part_No TO O_PartNo
  100% indexed              4 Records indexed
. MODIFY REPORT Orders
```

Access the Groups menu by typing `G`. For the *Group on expression,* use the Orders– >Part_No field, which is the same as the index key field. Press Enter, and type `Orders->Part_No`, followed by Enter. Highlight *Group heading,* press Enter, and type `Part Number`, followed by Enter.

Save the modified report design using the *Save* option in the Exit menu, and print the report again.

```
. REPORT FORM Orders TO PRINTER
```

Notice how the part numbers are divided into groups on the printout in Figure 40.

```
Page No.     1
07/27/87
                                        Monthly Orders

Part   Product                          Quantity  Quantity     Price      Total
Number Description                       Ordered   On Hand  Per Unit      Price


R-123  Red high top tennis                     1         2     23.95      23.95
       shoe.
B-254  Blue leather pump.                      2         5     65.99     131.98
G-165  Green leather slip                      2         7     23.98      47.96
       on.
R-123  Red high top tennis                     1         2     23.95      23.95
       shoe.
*** Total ***
                                                                         227.84
```

Figure 39

```
Page No.     1
07/27/87
                                        Monthly Orders

Part   Product                          Quantity  Quantity     Price      Total
Number Description                       Ordered   On Hand  Per Unit      Price


** Part Number B-254
 B-254  Blue leather pump.                     2         5     65.99     131.98
** Subtotal **
                                                                         131.98

** Part Number G-165
 G-165  Green leather slip                     2         7     23.98      47.96
        on.
** Subtotal **
                                                                          47.96

** Part Number R-123
 R-123  Red high top tennis                    1         2     23.95      23.95
        shoe.
 R-123  Red high top tennis                    1         2     23.95      23.95
        shoe.
** Subtotal **
                                                                          47.90
*** Total ***
                                                                         227.84
```

Figure 40

Warnings You cannot use memory variables in the report *Page title* or in any of the headings, such as group, sub-group, and column that you specify using CREATE REPORT. If you attempt to do this using macro substitution, the macro won't be expanded when the report is displayed using the REPORT FORM command; instead, the ampersand and the memory variable are displayed.

You can, however, use a memory variable anywhere in the report form that calls for an expression. Just make sure that the variable is initialized (see STORE) at the time that you create the report form and when you display the report.

There are a number of errors that you might make when designing a report form, but CREATE REPORT attempts to catch these errors as they occur. If you make an error such as entering a numeric value that is out of range or an invalid expression, an appropriate error message is displayed below the status bar. You must then press a key and correct the error before you are allowed to continue. If, somehow, CREATE REPORT does not detect a particular error in the report design, REPORT FORM will detect it when you display the report. If REPORT FORM gives you an error message, use CREATE REPORT to correct the error and try REPORT FORM again.

Tips

When you are defining a report column, including a semicolon as part of the contents expression will cause a carriage return to occur on the report when it is displayed (the semicolon will not be displayed). You can use this feature to your advantage in designing report forms that do not conform to the strict columnar format towards which CREATE REPORT is geared. You can cause fields on the report to be displayed, one on top of the other rather than side by side. For example, the following rather complicated expression, if entered as a report column contents, will display the First_Name and Last_Name field on top of the street Address, similar to a mailing label:

```
TRIM(First_Name) + " " + Last_Name + ";" + Address1
```

If you have a report that is designed to display information from two or more related database files, it may be cumbersome to establish the environment each time you want to display the report. You can establish the environment once, save it in a view file (see CREATE VIEW or CREATE VIEW FROM ENVIRONMENT) with the same name as the report form file, and use SET VIEW TO <filename> to reestablish the environment before you issue REPORT FORM <filename>.

CREATE REPORT is functionally identical to MODIFY REPORT; the CREATE form of the command is normally used to design a new report form, while the MODIFY form is used to edit an existing report form.

CREATE SCREEN

Syntax CREATE¦MODIFY SCREEN <filename>¦?

Overview

The primary use of the CREATE SCREEN command is to design format files using a full-screen approach rather than entering the individual @ commands (see @...GET, @...SAY, and @...TO) with a text editor (see MODIFY COMMAND). CREATE SCREEN can also be used to design a new database file structure and to modify the structure of an existing file. Note, however, that these aspects of CREATE SCREEN are less straightforward and not as easy to use as the commands of which the main intent is to create and modify database file structures. (See CREATE, MODIFY STRUCTURE).

Use CREATE SCREEN to design format files that take advantage of every available feature of the @ commands. With CREATE SCREEN, you can place fields at any location on the screen and choose whether the field should be displayed or edited; specify any PICTURE or FUNCTION template (see PICTURE) that you want to use; display text, boxes, and lines at various locations on the screen, and design multi-page format files with up to thirty-two pages. Using the menus and the blackboard allows you to place and move objects on the screen without needing to know the corresponding @ commands that will ultimately be generated by CREATE SCREEN when you save your work.

To accomplish the generation of the format file that you design, CREATE SCREEN uses a special file called a screen file. The file name is specified on the command line and is assigned a default extension of .SCR. When you are using CREATE SCREEN, it is the file that you are working with, and only when you exit the command and save the changes is the format file generated. The format file has the same name as the .SCR file but with a .FMT extension.

Procedure

To design a format file, you must first establish the database file environment. You can do this before you enter CREATE SCREEN (see SELECT, USE), or you can use the Set Up menu after you enter CREATE SCREEN. Both methods are equally effective; however, if you are designing a format file that involves more than one database file, you should establish the environment (including relating the files and establishing the fields list) before entering CREATE SCREEN. (See SET RELATION, SET FIELDS.) Doing all of this work before entering CREATE SCREEN allows you to deal with all of the files as a single entity rather than using the menu to switch back and forth between the individual database files. It does not matter which method you use if you are designing a format file for a single database file.

When you enter CREATE SCREEN, the file name that you specify is assumed to have a .SCR extension. A file with the same name and a .FMT extension is generated when you exit the command by saving the changes. If the file already exists, the existing screen file is brought up for you to edit; otherwise, a new screen file is created, and you must design it from scratch.

If you are using a catalog (see SET CATALOG), you can use the catalog query clause, ?, instead of specifying a screen file name. This presents you with a menu of all of the screens in the catalog that are associated with the active database file. Select from this menu the screen file that you want to modify by highlighting its file name and pressing Enter.

After entering CREATE SCREEN, you see the screen pictured in Figure 41. The menu navigation and selection keys are detailed in Appendix B.

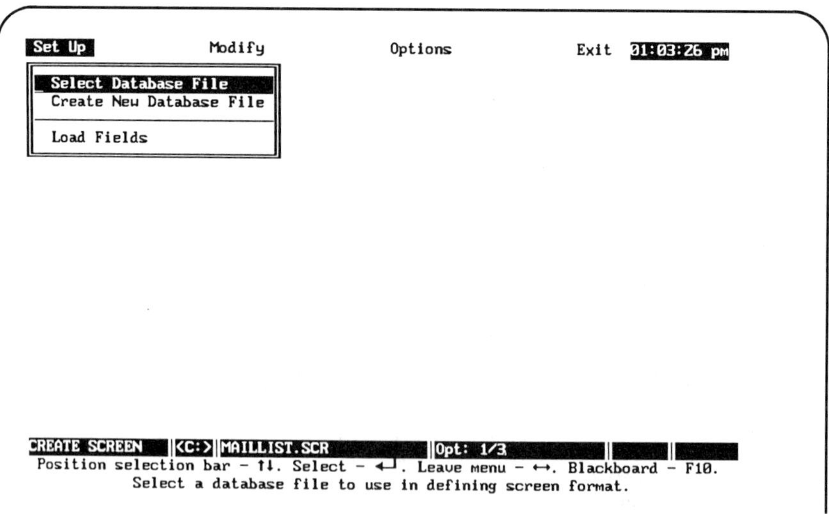

Figure 41

Set Up To use the Set Up menu to add files to the database file environment, choose the *Select Database File* menu option. Selecting this option presents you with a submenu of available database files. The options in this submenu are all of the .DBF files in the current directory, or in the catalog if you are using one. (See SET CATALOG.)

Unlike other menu-driven commands, CREATE SCREEN does not indicate which database files are already open. This is because *Select Database File* serves two purposes: it opens the database file (see USE) or selects it to be the active database file (see SELECT), depending on whether or not the file you select is already open. Since you cannot use this menu option to close an already open database file, open files are not indicated in the submenu. Select a database file with which to work by highlighting it and pressing Enter.

If you are working with more than one database file and no relationship has been established between the files (see SET RELATION) prior to entering CREATE SCREEN, you will have to use the *Select Database File* menu option each time you want to access fields from a different file. You should never have to use this menu option, however, if you have fully established the database file environment prior to entering CREATE SCREEN.

The next option in the Set Up menu is labeled *Create New Database File.* This option is used to indicate that you want to create a database file as you design the format file. Creating a database file using CREATE SCREEN is sloppy and difficult, and should be avoided under any circumstance. (See CREATE for how to create a database file.) After the file structure has been designed, use CREATE SCREEN to design a format file for it.

Once you have opened the database file(s) that you want to use, you are ready to begin the format file design. To do this, you must understand the blackboard, which is a unique feature of CREATE SCREEN. The easiest way to begin is to pick the fields that you want to include from the Set Up menu.

If you highlight and select the *Load Fields* menu option, a submenu of fields opens up to the right of the Set Up menu. This submenu shows all available fields (i.e., all fields in the active database file, or all fields in the SET FIELDS list if SET FIELDS is ON prior to entering CREATE SCREEN). From this submenu, highlight and select all of the fields that you want to include as part of the format file. When you are done, press F10 to access the blackboard. You will see all of the fields you selected on an otherwise blank screen.

The Blackboard The blackboard shows what your screen is going to look like when you use the generated format file. The fields are highlighted on the screen with symbols that indicate their data types. The following symbols are used:

SYMBOL	FIELD TYPE
X	Character
99/99/99	Date
L	Logical
MEMO	Memo
9	Numeric

You can move the fields on the screen to wherever you want them, lengthen or shorten their display width, remove fields that you no longer want to use, give the fields new titles, and type additional text on the screen—all without accessing the menu bar.

Once you have the fields loaded onto the blackboard, designing the format file is a matter of moving items around until you are satisfied with the way the screen looks. All of the full-screen cursor navigation and editing keys (see Appendix A) are available when the blackboard is activated.

To move a field to a new location on the screen, move the cursor to the beginning of the field and press Enter. Then, move the cursor to the desired location. There is no visual indication of moving the field until you press Enter again to drop the field at its new location. The labels that appear next to the field on the screen are not linked to the field; they are only text that happens to appear next to the field. Thus, you leave the field label behind when you move a field. There is no corresponding method for moving text around on the screen. To give a field a new label, you must type the label on the blackboard screen wherever you want it to appear and delete the old label.

You can type text other than field labels on the blackboard screen. For example, you may want to include a screen title and some instructions and notes to the user. As with field labels, type whatever you want, wherever you want it to appear on the screen. Again, the keys that are available for text editing on the blackboard are detailed in Appendix A.

To change the display width of a field, move the cursor to the beginning of the field. When the cursor is positioned on a field on the blackboard, the

Ins and Del keys take on a special function. Pressing Ins inserts a character into the display width; pressing Del deletes a character from the display width. This is a shortcut to using the Modify menu, described later on, in order to define a PICTURE for the field.

To remove a field that you put on the screen and no longer want, delete the line on which it appears using Ctrl-Y, or move the cursor to the field and press Ctrl-U to remove only the field and not the rest of the line. Depending on the database file environment, using Ctrl-U may prompt you to also delete the field from the file structure. Respond with N unless this is what you really want. A positive response will alter your database file structure and may lose data.

Once you are satisfied with the way the screen looks, you can add finishing touches to it using the line and box drawing capabilities available in the CREATE SCREEN Options menu. If you don't want any lines or boxes on your screen, move on to the Modify section. To activate the menu bar again, press F10, and the Modify menu appears. Press the Right Arrow to open the Options menu.

Options The Options menu is primarily used to draw lines and boxes on the blackboard; however, it has another option, *Generate text file image*. Selecting this menu option causes the generation of an additional file when you exit CREATE SCREEN and save the changes. The file will have the same name as the screen and format files, but with a .TXT extension. Our experience is that the format file provides sufficient documentation and that the text file image is superfluous. Select this option by pressing Enter; after you exit CREATE SCREEN, type the text file. (See TYPE.) You can then decide if the text file is useful.

To draw a box or line on your screen, select *Single bar* or *Double bar* from the menu. These menu options determine the character that is used to draw the box or line. (See @...TO.) The blackboard is automatically activated as soon as you select the option.

To draw, move the cursor to the location where you want to begin (i.e., the upper-left corner of the box) and press Enter. Make sure that you do not move the cursor to a line that already has text and/or fields on it since the box border will overwrite them. To draw a line instead of a box, move the cursor to the right on the same line where you began to draw and press Enter. To draw a box, locate the position of its lower-right corner with the cursor and press Enter. The box or line is drawn on the screen with either a single- or double-bar, depending on your menu selection.

Use F10 to access the Options menu to draw as many boxes and lines as you want. Once a line or box is on the blackboard, you can change its size and move the entire box to a new location on the screen. To change the size of a box on the blackboard, position the cursor on the side or corner that you want to move. If you position the cursor on a corner, you can move both sides of the box that it connects; if you position the cursor on a box side, you can move only that side. When the cursor is positioned, press Enter. Use the arrow keys to move the box side in whatever direction you want. When you are finished, press Enter.

To remove a box or line from the screen, move the cursor to any point on its border and press Ctrl-U.

Modify When you are satisfied with the way the screen looks, use the Modify menu to define data entry and display criteria for the fields on the screen. To use the Modify menu, move the cursor to the field on the blackboard with which you want to work and press F10 to activate the menu bar. This menu looks complicated at first, but there are only four options you should ever need to use.

The first menu option that you will use is *Action,* which lets you change a field on the screen to display only. This feature is useful if you are designing a screen that is going to be used to edit existing records when there are fields that you do not want the user to be able to change. For example, you may not want to give the user the capability of changing the hire date in an employee database file, but you would want to display the field on the screen for their information. By default, when you put a field on the blackboard it has an *Action* value of *Edit/GET* which means that you can change the value in that field when you use the format file. If you want to change the field that you see in the Modify menu to display only, press Enter when the *Action* option is highlighted. This changes the *Action* value to *Display/SAY.* Essentially, *Action* is a toggle. If you change your mind about a particular field, you can press Enter when its value is *Display/ SAY* to change it back to *Edit/GET.*

The other menu options that you will commonly use are located at the bottom of the Modify menu below the line. The first two options are *Picture Function* and *Picture Template.* When you select either of these options, you must type in the PICTURE function or template that you want to use for the current field. A help box appears on the screen to remind you of the template and function characters that you can use, but you need to know something about the correct formation of picture functions and templates to use this. (See PICTURE for more information.)

Basically, the *Picture Function* lets you specify a code letter that applies to the contents of the entire field, and *Picture Template* lets you specify several code letters that provide a character-for-character mask for the field. You can specify both a picture function and a picture template. Do not use quotation marks when you type the function and template code letter(s). Press Enter when you are finished.

The *Range* option is simpler than the picture options. It can be used only with Numeric and Date fields, and only if the *Action* for the field is *Edit/GET*. When you select *Range* from the menu, you are prompted in a submenu to enter a *Lower limit* and an *Upper limit* for the current field. You need only select each option, enter a value and press Enter when you are done.

After you have used the Modify menu to designate all of the necessary data entry and display criteria for the current field, press F10 to go back to the blackboard, move the cursor to the next field you want to use, and press F10 to use the Modify menu for the new field.

The remaining options in the menu, *Content*, *Type*, *Width*, and *Decimal*, show the characteristics of the current field on the blackboard. If used, they will change the structure of your database file. These options should be avoided because changing them might result in lost data. (See Warnings section below.) See MODIFY STRUCTURE for a command that is more reliable if you want to make changes to your file structure.

Exit The Exit menu is used to leave the screen design mode. The available options are *Save* and *Abandon*.

If you select *Abandon*, you are indicating that you do not want to save the changes that you have made during this session of CREATE SCREEN. It is equivalent to pressing Esc, and you are prompted to confirm your decision. If you respond by typing `N`, the CREATE SCREEN session is resumed. A response of `Y` ends the full-screen CREATE SCREEN mode without saving the changes that you have made to the screen file and without generating the new format file.

If you select *Save*, the new screen file is saved to disk and the corresponding format file is generated and saved to disk. If during the CREATE SCREEN session you selected the *Generate text file image* option of the

Options menu, a text file is also generated and saved to disk. All file names have the name that you used as the CREATE SCREEN command line option but with different extensions. By default, the screen file is given a .SCR extension. The corresponding format and text files are assigned .FMT and .TXT extensions, respectively.

The format file is automatically opened when you exit CREATE SCREEN and save the changes. Any database files that you opened using the Set Up menu are left open. (See CLOSE for information on how to close the files that CREATE SCREEN leaves in use; and see SET FORMAT for information on how to use the format file that you have designed.)

Examples

In the following example, you are going to use CREATE SCREEN to design a screen that will be used to add records to the mailing list. When you are done, the screen will look like the one in Figure 42. Before you enter the CREATE SCREEN design mode, establish the database file environment with the following commands:

```
. USE Mail
. CREATE SCREEN MailList
```

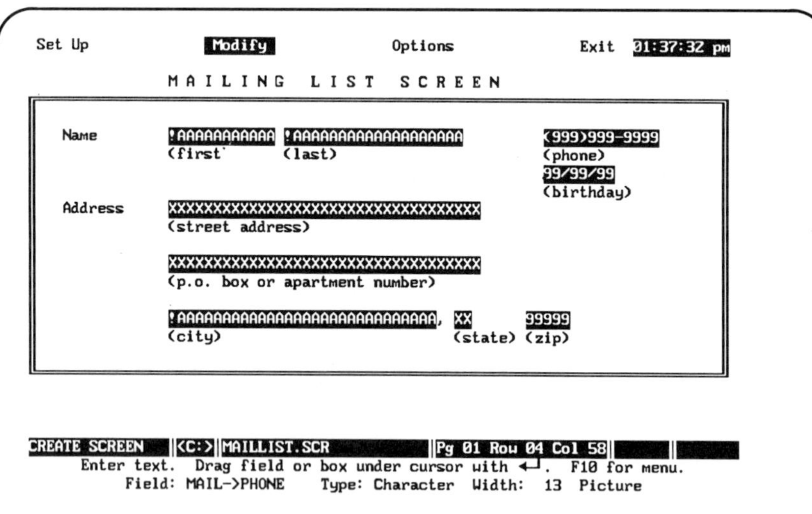

Figure 42

To begin designing the screen, select several fields to load onto the blackboard. Highlight the *Load Fields* option and press Enter, and a fields list submenu opens to the right to the Set Up menu. Select all of the fields between and including FIRST_NAME and BIRTHDAY by highlighting each field name and pressing Enter. After you select the fields, your screen should look like the one in Figure 43.

Press F10 to activate the blackboard and you will see that the selected fields are there, as in Figure 44. The fields are highlighted on the blackboard with the field names to the left as labels.

You can now move the fields around on the blackboard. First, press Ctrl-N four times to move the fields down a little on the screen. Ctrl-N inserts a blank line at the current cursor location.

Next, move the Last_Name field up beside the First_Name by moving the cursor to the first position of the Last_Name field and pressing Enter. Then, move the cursor one position to the right of the First_Name field and press Enter again to drop off the Last_Name. Similarly, move the Phone field approximately eight positions to the right of Last_Name.

Now, press Home to move the cursor to the beginning of the line that now contains the First_Name, Last_Name, and Phone fields. Type the word Name over the label that is already there (it reads FIRST_NAME), and

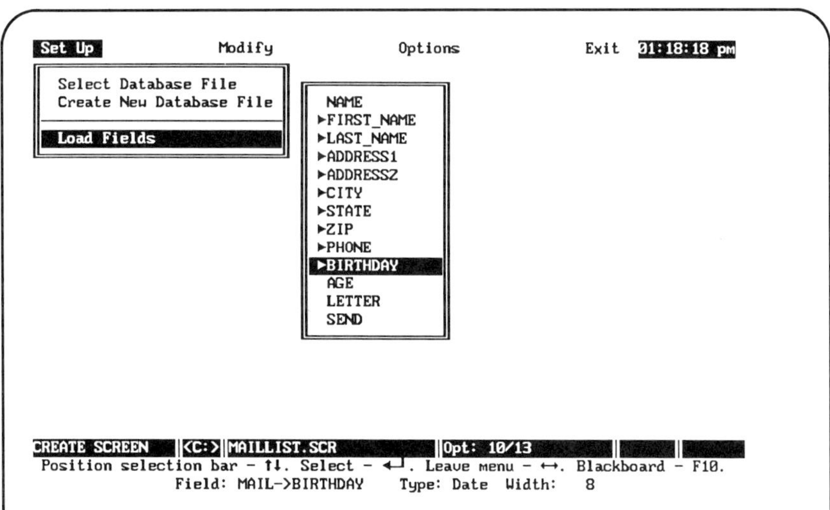

Figure 43

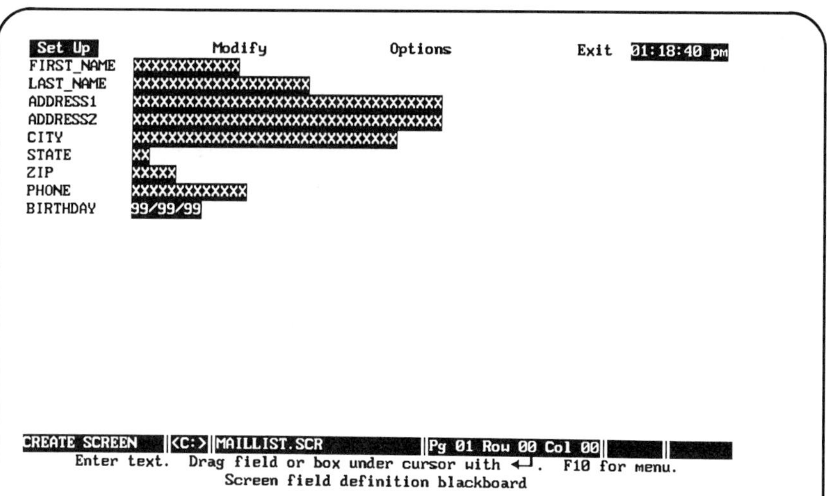

Figure 44

press the space bar several times to erase the remaining portion of the old label. Move the cursor once again to the beginning of this line and press the Ins key to go from overwrite to insert mode. Check the status bar if you are not sure what mode you are currently using. The word *Ins* appears there when you are in insert mode, and the Ins key acts as a toggle between the two modes. When you know you are in insert mode, press the space bar four times to move the entire line over four spaces to the right.

Move the cursor to the beginning of the next line and erase the LAST_NAME label by pressing Ctrl-T. Then, type `(first)`, `(last)`, and `(phone)` underneath their corresponding fields so that your screen looks like the one in Figure 45.

Move the cursor to the beginning of the line containing the Address1 field and press Ctrl-N two times to insert two blank lines. Next, move the Birthday field two lines below the Phone field, directly underneath the word (phone) on the screen. Just as you did with the Phone and Last_Name fields, move the cursor to the Birthday field, press Enter, move the cursor below the (phone) label, and press Enter to drop off the field at the new screen location. After moving the field, type `(birthday)` underneath it as in Figure 46.

Use Ctrl-T to delete the remaining field labels for Address1, Address2, City, State, and Zip fields and the old labels for Phone and Birthday. Ctrl-T

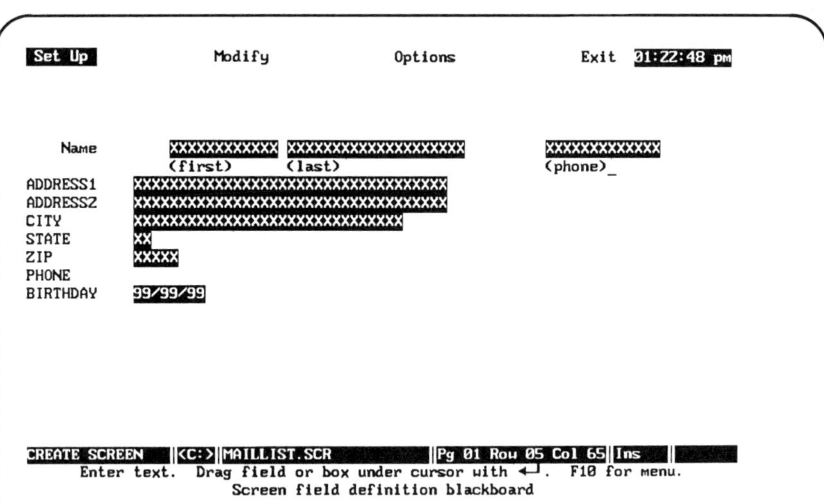

Figure 45

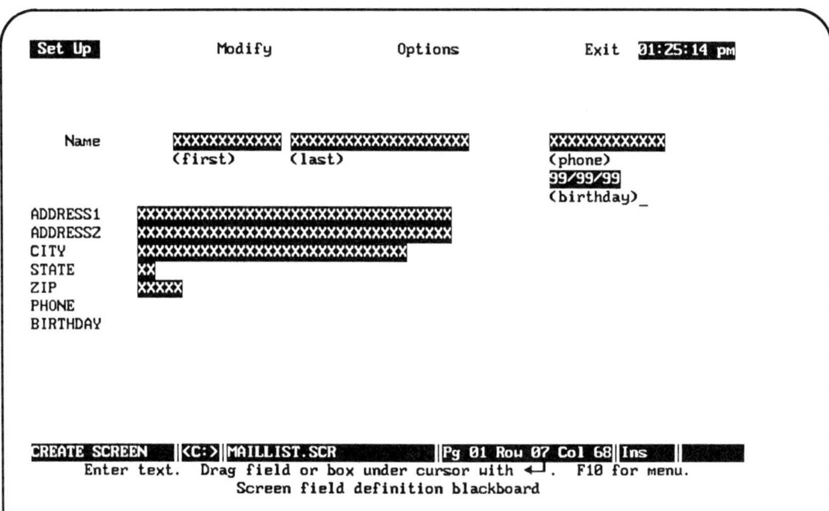

Figure 46

deletes starting at the current cursor location to the end of the word. For example, to delete the word ADDRESS1, move the cursor to the A and press Ctrl-T.

When the labels are gone, use Ctrl-N to insert two blank lines between the Address1, Address2, and City fields. Using the space bar while in insert mode, move these three fields over so that they each line up with the First_Name field.

Move the cursor to the beginning of the line containing the Address1 field, toggle to overwrite mode using the Ins key, and type the word `Address` so that it lines up with the word Name several lines above.

Move the State and Zip fields up to the line with City just as you did with the Birthday field earlier. Leave a few spaces between the fields so that there will be enough room for the new labels to go underneath them.

Finally, type in the remaining field labels underneath the fields as you see in Figure 47.

You are now ready to put a box around the screen. Press F10 to activate the menu bar, and press Right Arrow to open the Options menu. Select *Double bar* from the menu by highlighting it and pressing Enter, and the blackboard is automatically activated for you to draw the box. Using the Arrow keys, move the cursor to the first column of the line that is two lines above the First_Name field and press Enter. To complete the box, move

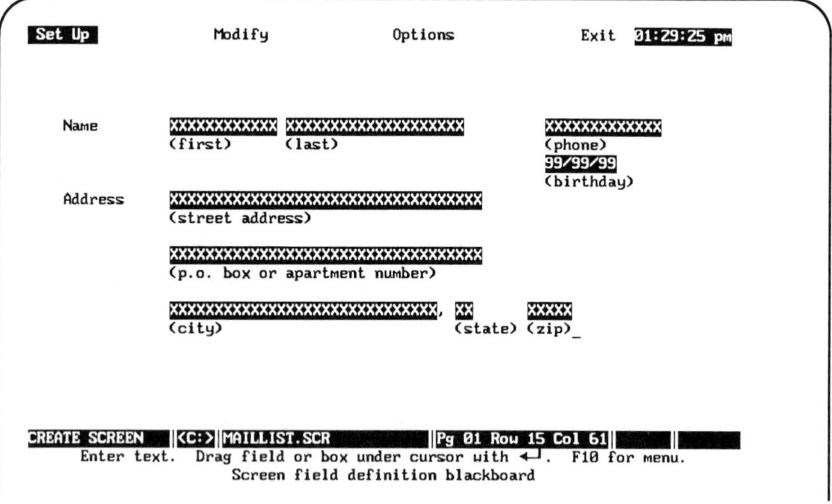

Figure 47

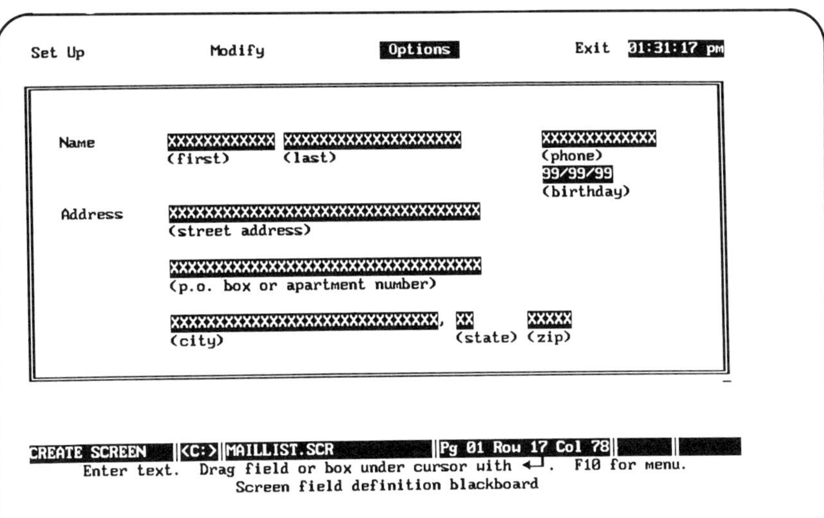

Figure 48

the cursor so that it is a couple of lines below the Zip field and a few spaces to the right of the Phone field and press Enter. The box appears on the screen as you see in Figure 48.

Move the cursor to the line just above the top of the box, and type

```
M A I L I N G   L I S T   S C R E E N
```

so that the title appears centered. You are now done with the drawing part of the screen design. The next step is to specify data entry criteria for some of the fields using the Modify menu.

For the First_Name, Last_Name, and City fields, you will use a picture template to capitalize the first letter and to make sure that the user can only enter letters into the fields. To begin, move the cursor to the First_Name field and press F10. Your screen should look like the one in Figure 49 where you see the First_Name field and its characteristics in the Modify menu.

Select *Picture Template* from the menu and type

```
!AAAAAAAAAAA
```

followed by Enter. The ! symbol capitalizes the first character, and the A symbols restrict data entry to letters. Press F10 to return to the blackboard and move the cursor to the Last_Name field. Press F10, and for this *Picture Template* type

```
!AAAAAAAAAAAAAAAAAAA
```

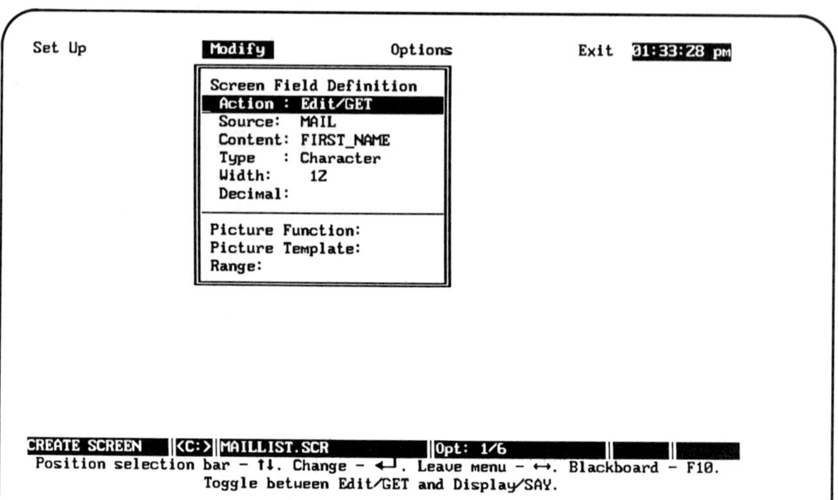

Figure 49

followed by Enter. Press F10 to return to the blackboard, and do the same for City using

!AAAAAAAAAAAAAAAAAAAAAAAAAAAAA

for its *Picture Template*. In each case, the picture template must be as long as the field itself. The template symbols appear in each of the field highlights as you see in Figure 50.

For the State field, capitalize the entire field and make sure that only letters are entered. On the blackboard, move the cursor to the State field and press F10. Select *Picture Function* from the menu, type !A, and press Enter. The !A symbol entered as a picture function applies the uppercase and alphabetic symbols to the entire field. Press F10 to return to the blackboard.

Only numbers can be entered in the Zip field. Similar to the way you entered the *Picture Template* for the First_Name field, type 99999 for the Zip field.

Finally, format the Phone field so that the area code is enclosed in parentheses and the parts of the number are separated by a dash. Again, be sure that only numbers are entered. Type a *Picture Template* of (999)999-9999 for this field. Activate the blackboard, and your screen should look like the one in Figure 42 at the beginning of the example.

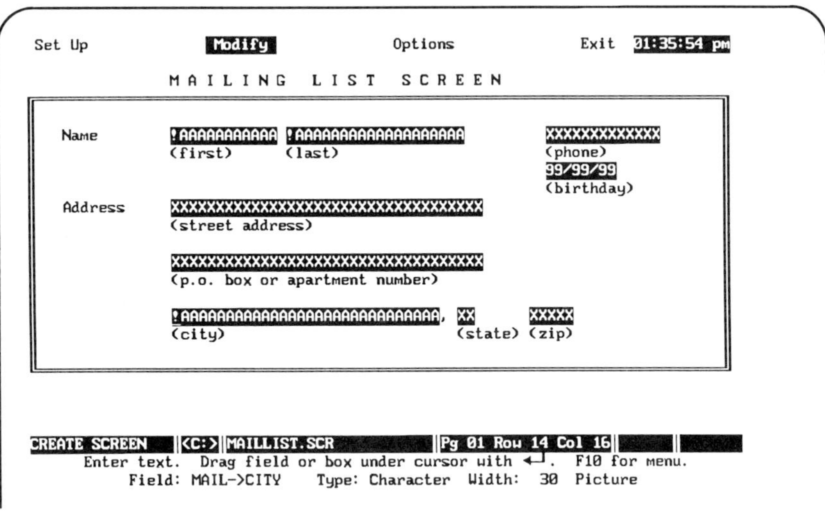

Figure 50

To save the screen design, activate the menu bar and type E to access the Exit menu, then press Enter to select the *Save* option. The screen file is saved to disk and the corresponding format file is generated, saved to disk, and put into use with the database file in the active work area. To see the format file in action, type

```
. EDIT
```

Your screen should look like the one in Figure 51.

Warnings

The screen file is only understood by CREATE SCREEN and cannot be modified or used by any other command in dBASE III PLUS.

If you elect to use the CREATE SCREEN Modify menu and the Ctrl-U feature on the blackboard to make changes to your database file structure, you may find some of your data missing when you return to the dot prompt. Most changes that you make to the file structure using the Modify menu are kept in memory and not saved to disk until you elect to save the screen design; however, adding a new field commits all structure modifications that you have made up to that point; deleting a field from the file

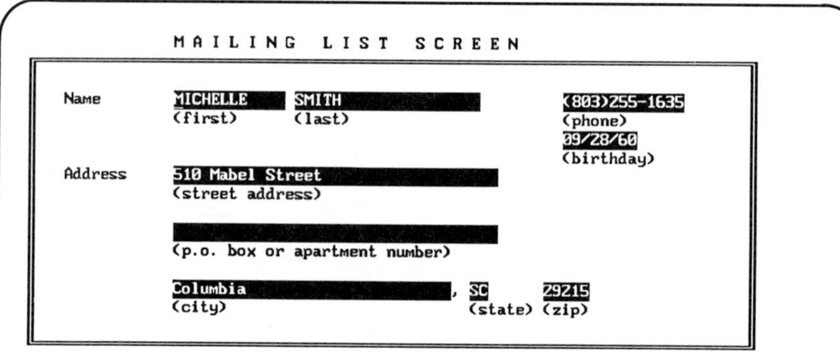

Figure 51

structure with Ctrl-U commits all previous structure changes. CREATE SCREEN attempts to save your data by making a backup of the database file (see MODIFY STRUCTURE) before saving the new structure; however, since the command may save more than one new structure, the final backup file may not be of the original database file. To avoid this kind of problem, refrain from using CREATE SCREEN to make database file structure changes (even if you can figure out how).

Tips Although CREATE SCREEN is functionally identical to MODIFY SCREEN, the CREATE form of the command is normally used to design a new screen format, while the MODIFY form is used to edit an existing screen format.

CREATE VIEW

Syntax `CREATE¦MODIFY VIEW <filename>¦?`

Overview A view in dBASE III PLUS is defined by certain components that combine to establish the current environment. Those components are the open database and index files (see USE and SET INDEX), the work areas containing (see SELECT) and the relationships between those files (see SET RELATION), the fields that are accessible in those files (see SET FIELDS), and the format file and filter (see SET FORMAT and SET FILTER) associated with the active database file.

In its simplest form, a view is a single database file, including all of its fields and records, with no ancillary files. At its most complicated, a view is several indexed database files that are related to one another, with only selected records and fields included; the fields, when presented for full-screen editing, are always shown in a particular format. There are, of course, many views in between these two extremes, but almost all of the components are optional when you are designing a view using CREATE VIEW. In effect, a view can be as simple or as complicated as you want it to be.

The CREATE VIEW command uses a menu-driven system to design a view. The view design is saved in a view (.VUE) file so that you can establish the environment that is stored in the file whenever you want without having to redesign it.

Procedure

It is not necessary to have any files open in order to design a view. Simply issue the CREATE VIEW command to invoke the menu-driven view design mode. The file name that you specify is assumed to have a .VUE extension.

If the file already exists, the existing view file is brought up for you to edit. The view is put into effect as the current environment; any other files in use are closed.

If the view file does not exist, a new view is created using the current environment. (See CREATE VIEW FROM ENVIRONMENT.) This view is then brought up for you to edit. If there are no open files in the current environment, you must design the view from scratch.

You can use the catalog query clause, ?, instead of specifying a view file name if you are using a catalog. (See SET CATALOG.) The catalog query clause, ?, presents you with a menu of all of the view files in the catalog. From this menu, you select the view that you want to modify by highlighting its file name and pressing Enter.

The menu navigation and selection keys for CREATE VIEW and all other menu-driven commands are detailed in Appendix B.

Set Up The first menu is Set Up. Use this menu to select the database and index files that you want to include in the view. (See USE.)

The options in this menu are all of the .DBF files in the current directory, or in the catalog if you are using one. (See SET CATALOG.) To open one of these database files, highlight it and press Enter. The open database files are indicated by a triangle to the left of the file name. You can close an open database file by highlighting it and pressing Enter.

When you open a database file, a menu of index files opens up to the right of the database file menu. Like the database file menu, the contents of this menu depends on whether or not you are using a catalog. If you are, all of the index files that belong to the database file that you selected are displayed; otherwise, all index files in the current directory are included in the menu. You can select up to seven index files for use with the database file by highlighting each file name and pressing Enter.

The open index files are indicated by a triangle to the left of the file name but, unlike database files, you cannot close a single index file. This is because the controlling index (see SET INDEX and SET ORDER) is the first index file that you select from this menu. Thus, if you were allowed to close individual files, you could close the controlling index file, and then CREATE VIEW would need a way to decide on a new one. Instead of allowing you to close individual index files, a way to close all of the index files is provided.

If you make an error in selecting index files, you can start over by pressing the Esc key. Unfortunately, this key also closes the index file menu and leaves the associated database file open; therefore, you have to close the database file by pressing Enter, and open it again with the same key. The index file list reappears and you can start over.

Relate Once you have opened all of the database and index files that you want to include in the view, you establish the relationships between the files using the Relate menu. To establish a relation between two files, you must identify the files and define the relationship between them. In dBASE III PLUS, there are two methods to relate files: by record number or by index key. (See SET RELATION for details on both of these methods.)

In CREATE VIEW, if you want to relate two files by record number, the file that you relate to (the second file) cannot be indexed. If you want to relate two files by the index key, the second file must be indexed; the relation is based on the index key expression for the controlling index file.

To use the Relate menu to establish a relationship between two files, select the first file from the menu by highlighting its file name and pressing Enter. This action causes a submenu containing the remaining, eligible database files to open up to the right of the main menu. The database files that appear in this submenu depend on the *Relation chain* that is displayed just above the status bar. If no relation chain has been established, all files in the main menu, except for the file that you have selected, are included in the submenu. If there is a relation chain, both the files that are not already a part of the chain as well as those that appear in the chain to the right of the selected file appear in the submenu.

From this submenu, select the file into which you want to relate the first file by highlighting its name and pressing Enter.

When you select the second file name, a triangle appears to the right of the file name, and you are expected to enter the expression that defines the relationship between the two files.

If the second file is indexed, its controlling index expression is shown on the bottom line of the screen, and you are expected to enter a field name or expression from the first file that corresponds to that index key expression. It is a good idea when you design your database files to give the same field name to a data element every time you use it (e.g., Part Number is always called Part_No in every file where it is used). If you follow this practice, the field name or expression that you enter will be identical to the index key expression that you see on the last line of the screen; otherwise, you have to remember that you used one name for the relating field in the first file and another name in the second file.

If the second file is not indexed, the message at the bottom of the screen indicates that the files will be related by record number. You can enter RECNO( ) or any other numeric expression.

In either case, you must type in the name of the field (or expression) that you want to use to define the relationship between the files. Instead of typing a particular field name, you can select it from a menu by pressing F10. When the fields list menu appears, highlight the field name that you want to use and press Enter. The field name appears in the menu just as if you had typed it. When you are finished with the relation expression, press Enter. The expression that you enter must be valid and it must be of the correct data type (i.e., Numeric if relating by record number, or the same type as the controlling index key expression if relating by index key).

Unlike most submenus in dBASE III PLUS, this one does not close automatically after you have entered the relation expression – you must close it using the Left Arrow or the Right Arrow. You can then relate more files using this same procedure. In general, when you are designing a view, the next file that you select from the main Relate menu is the one that you last selected in the submenu (i.e., the last file name in the *Relation chain* that appears just above the status bar). This procedure establishes a relation chain between all of the files in the view.

When you have successfully established the relationship between two files, their file names appear on the line labeled *Relation chain* just above the status bar. This line gives you a superficial glance at how the files in the view are connected. When you save the view, the first file in this list will be the active database file.

Once you have established a relation chain involving two or more database files, you can modify the relationships between the files. To change the file to which another file is related, select the first file from the main-Relate menu and then select a different file from the submenu. All files that come after the second file in the relation chain will be dropped from the relation chain, and you will have to redefine all of the other relationships. To change the relation expression between two files, select the first file from the main menu and the other file from the submenu and enter the new expression. No files will be dropped from the relation chain.

Set Fields After you have defined the relationships between the database files in the view, you can specify the fields that you want to include from each database file. (See SET FIELDS.) As in the Relate menu, the options in the Set Fields menu consist of the database file names that are indicated in the Set Up menu.

To select fields from a particular file, highlight the file name and press Enter. A submenu containing all of the fields in that file appears to the left of the main menu. Fields that are already selected are indicated by a triangle to the left of the field name. To select a field that is not already selected, highlight it, press Enter, and the select marker appears beside the field name. To unselect a field that is already marked on the left by a triangle, highlight and press Enter. The triangle disappears, and the field is no longer included. When you are finished with the fields submenu for a particular database file, all of the fields that you want to use from that file should be marked on the left; those that you do not want to use should not be marked. Press the Left Arrow or Right Arrow key to close the menu.

Repeat this process for each database file in the Set Fields menu.

Options Once you have defined the files, relationships, and fields that you want to include in the view, the only other components that are

left to define are the format file and the filter condition. These components are defined using the Options menu.

The first menu option is labeled *Filter*, and it specifies a condition that is used to filter (see SET FILTER) the records in the active database file (i.e., the first file displayed in the Relation chain above the status bar). To specify a filter condition, highlight this menu option, press Enter, and type in any valid logical condition. The filter condition usually involves at least one field from the active database file. If you press F10, you are presented with a list of all fields from this file. To select a field, highlight it and press Enter. The field name appears in the menu, just as if you had typed it. When you are finished entering the filter condition, press Enter.

The final component of the view is the format file which you specify using the *Format* menu option. To select a format file to use as part of the view, highlight this menu and press Enter. You are presented with a submenu of all of the available format files. To select a file, highlight its name and press Enter. The format file submenu closes automatically.

If you are modifying an existing view and you want to change the format file that you have selected, simply select the *Format* option and pick a new file when the submenu appears. The new file takes over as the format file for the view. To remove the format file all together, press the Esc key when the submenu appears.

If you are designing a view for the first time, it is unlikely that you have already designed a format file for the view. Since this menu option allows you to select an existing format file, you may want to ignore it when you are designing a new view. After the view is designed and saved to disk, you can use CREATE SCREEN or MODIFY COMMAND to create a format file for the view. You can then use MODIFY VIEW to add the format file to the view design.

Exit The Exit menu is used to leave the view design mode. The available options are *Save* and *Abandon*.

If you select *Abandon*, you are indicating that you do not want to save the changes that you have made during this session of CREATE VIEW. It is equivalent to pressing Esc, and you are prompted to confirm your decision. If you respond by typing `N`, the CREATE VIEW session is resumed. A response of `Y` ends the full-screen CREATE VIEW mode without saving the changes that you have made to the file. If you were modifying an existing view, that view remains in effect as your current environment after the CREATE VIEW session is over.

If you select *Save*, the view that you have defined is saved to disk as a view file. The file name is the name that you used as the CREATE VIEW command line option. By default, the file is given a .VUE extension. A SET VIEW TO is automatically executed to put the new view into effect.

See CLOSE for information on how to disable a view once it is established, and see SET VIEW for information on how to establish a view that is stored in a view file when you want to use it again.

Examples

The following example guides you through the design of a view that links the Orders, Inventry, and Supplier files. The Orders file contains information about orders that customers have placed and includes the customer number (Cust_No), the part number (Part_No) ordered, and the amount (Quantity) ordered. Inventry contains the inventory information on each product that your company carries, including part number (Part_No), quantity on hand (Quantity), the reorder point (Reorder), and the price per unit (Price); there is one record in this file for each part number. The Supplier file contains information about the companies who supply products to your company when your inventory is low. This information includes supplier number (Supplier) and the part number (Part_No) of the product they supply. There may be more than one record per supplier since a supplier is likely to supply more than one product.

You want this view to create a list of the part numbers ordered, the quantity ordered, the price per unit, and the supplier number (if the quantity on hand minus the quantity ordered is less than or equal to the reorder point). The Orders file is connected to the Inventry file on Part_No, and the Inventry file is connected to Supplier on Part_No.

To begin designing this view, be sure that there are no files in use. Enter the following commands:

```
. CLOSE DATABASES
. CREATE VIEW Orders
```

The first menu that you see differs depending on the database files that you have saved on your disk, but your screen should look something like the one in Figure 52. The file names are not in any logical order, so it may not be easy to locate a particular one if you have many files. For this example, you want to use Orders, Inventry, and Supplier.

Highlight the Orders file, and press Enter to select it. A triangle appears to the left of the file name indicating that it is selected, and a submenu of index files appears to the right of the Set Up menu. You do not want to use any index files for the Orders file, so press Left Arrow to close the submenu.

Highlight the Inventry file, and press Enter to select it. This time, you want an index file so that you can relate this file with Orders using the Part_No field. The name of the index file that uses Part_No as its key is Part_No. Highlight this index file and press Enter. You do not want to open any more index files, so press Left Arrow to close the submenu.

Open Supplier with S_Part as its index file in the same way you opened Inventry with its index, Part_No.

You are now ready to relate the files. Press R to open the Relate menu. The database files that you see are the same ones that you selected using

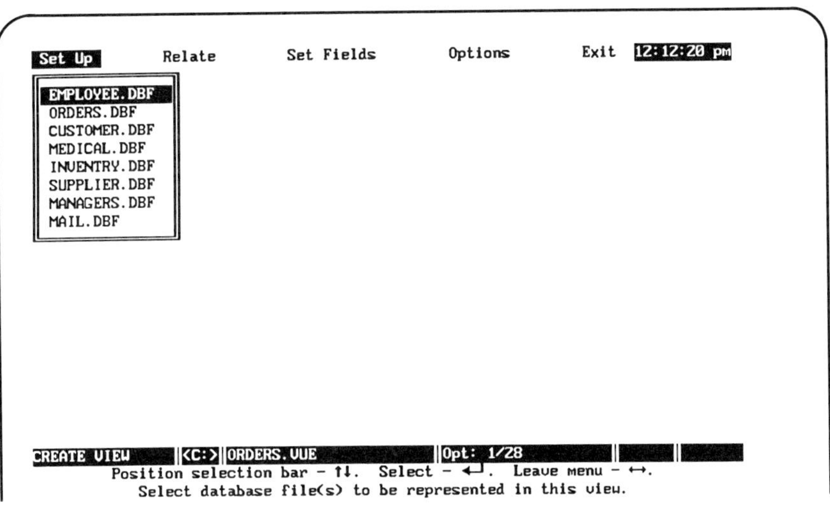

Figure 52

the Set Up menu, and they are in the order that you selected them. Your screen should look like the one in Figure 53.

Select the first file in the list, Orders, by pressing Enter. A submenu containing Inventry and Supplier opens up to the right of the main menu. Since you want to relate Orders to Inventry on the Part_No field, select Inventry from the submenu by pressing Enter, and type `Part_No`, followed by Enter. The submenu does not close automatically like most others that you encounter in dBASE III PLUS, so you must close it manually by pressing Left Arrow. Your screen should look like the one in Figure 54. Notice that just above the status bar, the *Relation chain* indicates that you have successfully established a link between Orders and Inventry.

To finish the relation chain, you want to link Inventry to Supplier based on Part_No. Select Inventry from the Relate menu, and select Supplier from its submenu. Type `Part_No` as the field that you want to use to relate the two files, and press Enter to indicate that you are finished. Press Left Arrow to close the menu. The line just above the status bar should read *Relation chain: ORDERS.DBF - >INVENTRY.DBF - >SUPPLIER.DBF,* indicating that you have successfully linked all three files.

To indicate the fields that you want to include in the view, press the Right Arrow to open the Set Fields menu. You want the part number,

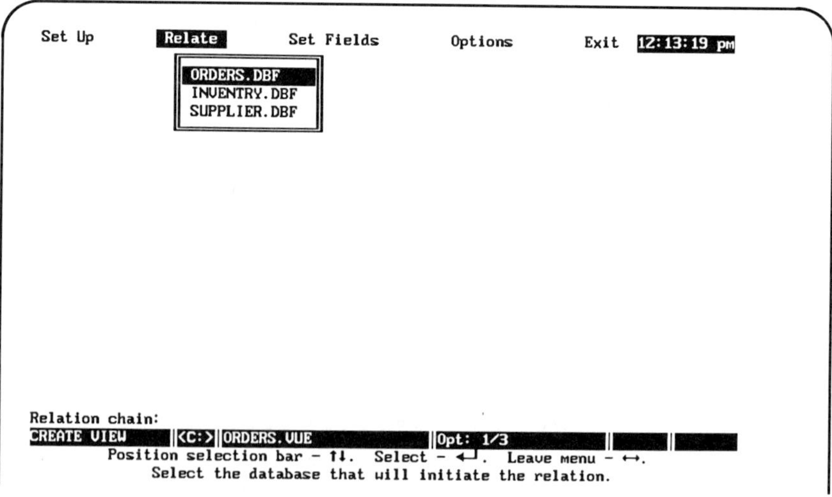

Figure 53

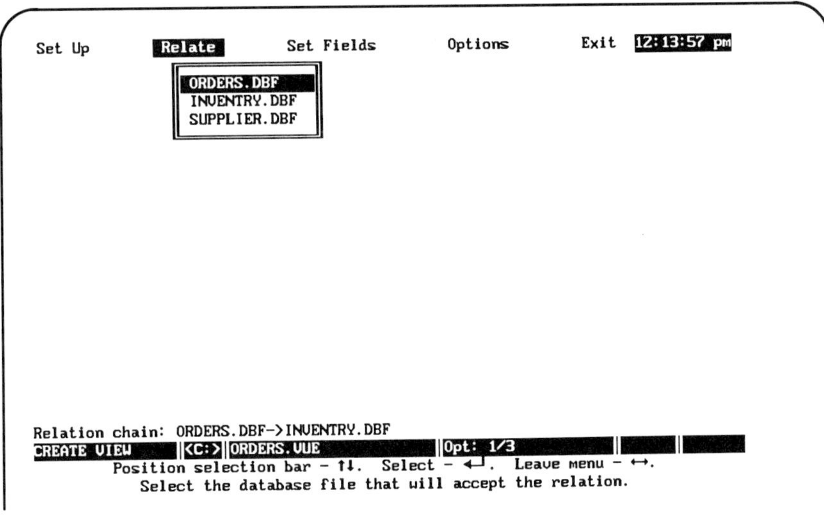

Figure 54

quantity ordered, price per unit, and supplier number fields. The first two fields come from the Orders file, the third from Inventry, and the last one from Supplier.

The Orders database file is the first in the menu. Select it by pressing Enter, and a submenu of all its fields appears to the left of the main menu. Each field in the submenu is marked on the left with a triangle, like in Figure 55, indicating that all of the fields are to be included. Because you are creating a new view, the assumption is that you want to use all fields from all files. You must unselect the fields that you do not want to include, rather than selecting the fields that you want.

Unselect the Cust_No field by pressing Enter when the field name is highlighted. Since this is the only field from Orders that you do not want to include, press the Left Arrow to close the fields submenu.

From the main Set Fields menu, press the Down Arrow to highlight the Inventry file name, and press Enter to open a submenu of its fields. Again, all fields in the submenu are marked. Unselect all fields in this menu except Price by highlighting each field name and pressing Enter. Close the file using the Left Arrow when you are finished.

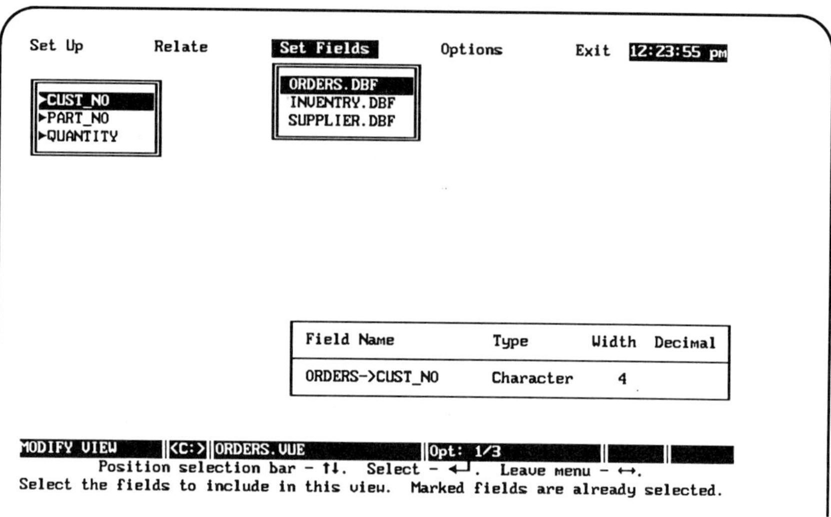

Figure 55

For the Suppliers file, unselect all fields except Supplier in the same manner as you did with the Inventry file. Close the submenu with Left Arrow, and open the Options (type O) menu to define a filter.

The first option in this menu is *Filter*. For this view, you only want to see those orders that cause the inventory quantity to reach or go below the reorder point. Select the *Filter* option by pressing Enter, and type the following condition:

```
Inventry->Quantity - Orders->Quantity <= Inventry->Reorder
```

This condition takes the quantity on hand and subtracts the quantity ordered because after the order is filled the quantity on hand will have to be reduced by the amount ordered to obtain a new value for the quantity on hand. The part must be reordered if this new amount is less than or equal to the reorder point value.

Press Enter when you are finished. Your screen should look like the one in Figure 56.

To save the view design, type E to access the Exit menu and press Enter to select the *Save* option. The view file is saved to disk, and the view is put into effect as the new environment. Enter the following command to see the result of this view:

```
. LIST
Record#  PART_NO   QUANTITY       PRICE SUPPLIER
      1  R-123            1       23.95 A198
      2  B-254            2       65.99 A951
      3  G-165            2       23.98 S861
      4  R-123            1       23.95 A198
```

Warnings

When you are selecting files from the Set Up menu, the error message *Too many files are open* indicates that you have selected more files than the maximum allowed. The maximum is fifteen open files at one time, but you will not be able to open that many unless your Config.SYS file has the entry FILES = 20.

When you are selecting index files for a database file in the Set Up menu, the error message *Index does not match database* indicates that the file you selected belongs to a database file other than the one that you have selected. If you select the maximum of seven index files for one database file, the index file submenu closes automatically and no message is displayed.

In the Relate menu, if you select the database file that is last in the relation chain, the error message *No file available to form this relation* is

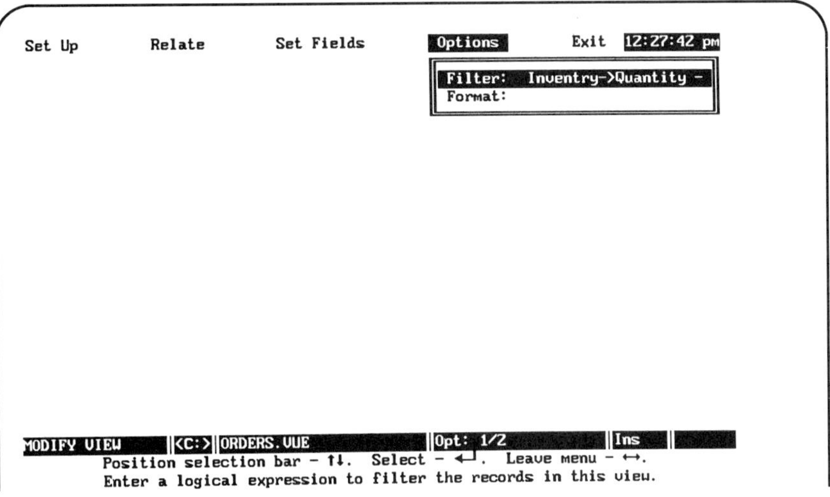

Figure 56

displayed if all files in the menu are already a part of the relation chain. This prevents you from forming a cyclic relation like A→B→A.

In the Options menu, you must enter an expression if you use the *Filter* option. If you make a mistake in entering the filter expression, a number of error messages are possible. The most common are *Variable not found* and *Data type mismatch.*

Variable not found indicates that you have entered a field or memory variable name that is not recognized in the *Filter* expression. A memory variable used as part of the filter condition must exist (see STORE) prior to creating the view. To use a field name from a file other than the first file in the relation chain, you must specify the alias name as part of the field name (e.g., <alias name> – > <field name>).

Data type mismatch means that you have attempted to form a *Filter* expression using two different data types. Part_No = 1254 causes this message because Part_No is a Character field and 1254 is a Numeric constant. The correct expression would be Part_No = "1254".

Unlike most other full-screen commands, CREATE VIEW does not have a cursor navigation menu. F1 has no effect when you are using this command.

Tips

CREATE VIEW is functionally identical to MODIFY VIEW; the CREATE form of the command is normally used to create a new view, while the MODIFY form is used to edit an existing view.

When you modify an existing view, the current environment is lost because the view is put into effect (see SET VIEW) for you to make changes, and the current environment is not saved. The view remains in effect even if you choose to abandon the MODIFY VIEW session without making any changes .

If you are interested in returning to your original environment after a MODIFY VIEW session, use CREATE VIEW FROM ENVIRONMENT to save the current environment to a view file. Then, after you are finished with the MODIFY VIEW session, use SET VIEW TO to reestablish the original view. For example,

```
CREATE VIEW Original FROM ENVIRONMENT
MODIFY VIEW Old_View
SET VIEW TO Original
```

When you are creating a new view with CREATE VIEW, any current environment is saved automatically to a view that is brought up for modification. If you create a new view in this way, the view file will save all open format files and filter conditions, not just those in the current work area. If you want to ignore the current environment and start a new view from scratch, use CLOSE DATABASES to start with a clean slate.

A view can be established using the commands referenced above without using CREATE VIEW; however, it can be cumbersome to issue all of the necessary commands if you use a particular view often. An alternative is to use CREATE VIEW FROM ENVIRONMENT to save an established view to a file. (See CREATE VIEW FROM ENVIRONMENT for more information.)

CREATE VIEW FROM ENVIRONMENT

Syntax `CREATE VIEW <filename> FROM ENVIRONMENT`

Overview

The CREATE VIEW FROM ENVIRONMENT command lets you save the current database file environment to a view file without going through the full-screen view design process. (See CREATE VIEW.) When you issue this command, the following information is recorded in the view file:

- The current work area number
- All open database files and their work area numbers
- The open index files for each database file and their order
- All open format files
- The filter condition for each work area
- The SET FIELDS list, if SET FIELDS is ON
- The relationships between files that have a SET RELATION in effect

Procedure

To save a view to a file with CREATE VIEW FROM ENVIRONMENT, you must first issue all of the commands necessary to set up the view.

SELECT and USE are used to open database and index files in different work areas. SET FORMAT activates a format file in the current work area, SET FILTER establishes a filter condition for the active database file, SET

RELATION defines the relationships between the open database files, and SET FIELDS indicates which fields you want to use. (See the entries for these commands for more information on their usage.)

Once the database environment is established, enter CREATE VIEW FROM ENVIRONMENT. The view file is created with the default extension of .VUE. Use SET VIEW to activate the view that is saved in the file any time you want to use this environment.

Examples The following commands illustrate how to establish a view using several dBASE III PLUS commands and how to save that view to a file:

```
. USE Orders
. SET FIELDS TO Part_No, Quantity
. SELECT 2
. USE Inventry INDEX Part_No
. SET FIELDS TO Price
. SELECT Orders
. SET RELATION TO Part_No INTO Inventry
. CREATE VIEW OrdList FROM ENVIRONMENT
```

Once the view is saved to a file, you can close all files in the current environment and recall the view from the file:

```
. CLOSE DATABASES  && Closes all files in the current environment
. SET VIEW TO OrdList  && Reestablished environment in view file
. LIST  && Shows view result
Record#  PART_NO   QUANTITY      PRICE
      1  R-123            1      23.95
      2  B-254            2      65.99
      3  G-165            2      23.98
      4  R-123            1      23.95
```

Tips If you use CREATE VIEW FROM ENVIRONMENT, the view that you create includes all open format files and filter conditions, not just those in the current work area.

CTOD( )

Syntax `CTOD(<expC>)`

Overview The CTOD( ) function, short for character-to-date, accepts any character expression as its argument. The function evaluates the expression and converts the resulting character string to a date.

The character expression is of the form "MM/DD/[CC]YY", where M, D, C, and Y are numbers that represent the month, day, century, and year, respectively. The year can be two or four digits in length; use two digits for the current century and four to specify another century. The (/) used for the separating character can be replaced by any other character, but the separator in the resulting date is changed to conform to the SET DATE setting. (See SET DATE.)

Procedure CTOD( ) returns a date and can be used anywhere in the language where a date expression is appropriate.

Examples Since there is no direct representation for dates in dBASE III PLUS, CTOD( ) is essential in creating date memory variables. The following example shows how to initialize a blank date memory variable. Notice that although the "-" character is used as the date separator when the date variable is created, dBASE III PLUS changes it to the "/" character.

```
. date = CTOD("  -  -  ")
  /  /
. ? date
  /  /
. ? TYPE("date")
D
```

Warnings If the function argument evaluates to a data type other than character, the error message *Invalid function argument* is displayed.

Tips Note that the form in which dates are input and returned is controlled by SET DATE. The explanation here assumes SET DATE AMERICAN, which is the default for the U.S. version of dBASE III PLUS. If you change the date format with the SET DATE command, the order of the month, day, and year in the character string must be supplied in the correct format. (For example, SET DATE ANSI requires that you use CTOD(" <YY/MM/DD> ").)

Data Type. *See* Expression

DATE( )

Syntax `DATE()`

Overview The DATE( ) function has no arguments. The function returns the system date.

Procedure DATE( ) returns a date and can be used anywhere in the language where a date expression is appropriate.

Examples DATE( ) can be used whenever you want the current date. For example, the following routine prompts you for your birthday and, using the current date along with some simple date arithmetic, calculates your age in days:

```
* How_Old.PRG
*
SET TALK OFF
SET BELL OFF
birthday = CTOD("  /  /  ")
CLEAR
@ 10,20 SAY "Enter your date of birth: " GET birthday
READ
days = DATE() - birthday
years = INT(days / 365)
@ 12,15 SAY "You are " + LTRIM(STR(days)) + " days old, "
@ 12,COL() SAY "which is about " + LTRIM(STR(years)) + " years."
SET BELL ON
SET TALK ON
```

Warnings There are no error messages associated with the DATE( ) function because of its simple syntax.

Tips See TIME( ) for a function that returns the system time.

DAY( )

Syntax `DAY(<expD>)`

Overview The DAY( ) function accepts any date expression as its argument. The function evaluates the expression and returns the day portion as a number.

Procedure DAY( ) returns a number and can be used anywhere in the language where a numeric expression is appropriate.

Examples Using DAY( ) in combination with some of the other date manipulation functions makes possible a wide variety of date displays. The following routine displays the current date in several different formats:

```
* Dates.PRG
*
SET TALK OFF
today = DATE()
? today
? LEFT(CMONTH(today), 3) + " " + LTRIM(STR(DAY(today))) + ", " +;
  LTRIM(STR(YEAR(today)))
? CMONTH(today) + " " + LTRIM(STR(DAY(today))) + ", " +;
  LTRIM(STR(YEAR(today)))
? CDOW(today) + ", " + LTRIM(STR(DAY(today))) + " " +;
  CMONTH(today)
? LTRIM(STR(DAY(today))) + " " + LEFT(CMONTH(today), 3) + " " +;
  LTRIM(STR(YEAR(today)))
SET TALK ON
```

If today's date is June 19, 1987, executing this routine results in the following output:

```
. DO Dates
06/19/87
Jun 19, 1987
June 19, 1987
Friday, 19 June
19 Jun 1987
```

Warnings If the function argument evaluates to a data type other than date, the error message *Invalid function argument* is displayed.

DBF( )

Syntax `DBF()`

Overview The DBF( ) function asks, "What is the name of the active database file?" This function returns the name of the active database file, including the drive letter, the path name, and the extension.

Procedure In order to use DBF( ) effectively, there must be a database file in use in the current work area. (See USE.) Otherwise, the function automatically returns a null string.

DBF( ) returns a character string and can be used anywhere in the language where a character expression is appropriate.

Examples DBF( ) can be used to determine whether or not there is a database file in USE in the current work area. In applications that may use many database files, it is often faster to open all of the files in different work areas and SELECT between the files than to use the same work area for all files. The following routine starts in work area 1 and checks to see if there is an open database file. If so, the routine selects the next work area and tests again. As soon as an available work area is found, a database file whose name is passed to the routine is opened. If no available work area is found, an error message is displayed.

```
* Open.PRG
*
PARAMETERS database
opened = .F.
n = "1"
DO WHILE VAL(n) <= 10 .AND. .NOT. opened
   SELECT &n
   IF "" = DBF()
      USE &database
      opened = .T.
   ELSE
      n = n + 1
      n = LTRIM(STR(VAL(n) + 1))
   ENDIF
ENDDO
IF .NOT. opened
   ? CHR(7) + "There are no available work areas."
   ?
   WAIT
ENDIF
RETURN
```

Assuming that this routine is called Open.PRG, and that you want to open the Customer database file in the next available work area, you would issue the following command either from the dot prompt or from within another program:

```
DO Open WITH "Customer"
```

Use DISPLAY STATUS to see in which work area Customer was opened.

Warnings

Because of its simple syntax, there are no error messages associated with DBF( ).

Tips

In order to determine if a particular database file is in USE in the active work area, you must be aware that this function returns the entire file name which includes the drive letter, the path name, and the extension. Furthermore, the file name is returned using a combination of uppercase and lowercase letters; the actual combination depends on how the file name was entered with USE and whether or not a SET PATH TO is in effect.

Apply UPPER( ) to DBF( ), and then compare the result to a character string that is in uppercase letters. For example,

```
. USE Customer
. ? DBF() = "C:CUSTOMER.DBF"
.F.
. ? UPPER(DBF()) = "C:CUSTOMER.DBF"
.T.
```

DELETE

Syntax `DELETE [<scope>] [WHILE <condition>] [FOR <condition>]`

Overview

The DELETE command is used to mark records in the active database file for deletion. If used with no parameters, it marks only the current record for deletion; however, a scope, a FOR clause, and a WHILE clause can be used to mark records within a specific range that meet certain conditions. Each of these command line options is discussed separately. (See Scope, FOR, and WHILE.)

A record marked for deletion is indicated by an asterisk when the record is displayed using LIST or DISPLAY. In full-screen editing, the word *Del* on the scoreboard or the status bar indicates that a record is marked for deletion. The Ctrl-U key is used in full-screen editing as a toggle to mark records for deletion and reinstate them.

Procedure

Use DELETE when you have records in your database file that you no longer need. If you have only a few records that have nothing in common, position the record pointer to each record using GOTO, LOCATE, or some other command, and enter DELETE with no parameters. Use DELETE with a FOR or WHILE clause to mark a group of records that meet a particular condition.

Suppose you want to discontinue the Black patent leather shoe due to lack of sales. The following commands DELETE this record from the Inventry file and permanently remove it using PACK:

```
. USE Inventry INDEX Part_No
. SEEK "BL861"  && The shoe has BL861 as the part number
. DISPLAY Part_No, Descrip
Record#  Part_No Descrip
      5  BL861   Black high heel patent leather pump.

. DELETE
      1 record deleted
. DISPLAY Part_No, Descrip  && Note the asterisk in the display
Record#  Part_No Descrip
      5 *BL861   Black high heel patent leather pump.

. PACK
      5 records copied
Rebuilding index - C:Part_No.ndx
  100% indexed           5 Records indexed
. CLOSE DATABASES
```

Warnings PACK permanently removes records marked for deletion from the active database file. Before you PACK the database file, you can reinstate records marked for deletion using RECALL; however, the deleted records cannot be recovered once you have PACKed a database file.

If you are using dBASE III PLUS in a network environment, DELETE, if used with a scope, FOR, or WHILE clause, attempts an automatic file lock unless the database file is already locked (see FLOCK( )) or is opened for exclusive use (see SET EXCLUSIVE, USE). If for any reason the command cannot lock the database file, the error message *File is in use by another* is displayed. DELETE with no scope, FOR, or WHILE clause attempts a record lock instead. (See RLOCK( ).) The error message *Record is in use by another* is displayed.

Tips In dBASE III PLUS, records marked for deletion are processed by other commands just like any other record. In order to make a particular command ignore deleted records, use the clause FOR .NOT. DELETED( ) as part of the command syntax. To make all commands ignore deleted records, SET DELETED ON or SET FILTER TO .NOT. DELETED( ).

DELETE FILE

Syntax `DELETE FILE <filename>¦?`

Overview The DELETE FILE command is functionally identical to the ERASE command. (See ERASE for more information regarding the use of this command.)

DELETED( )

Syntax `DELETED()`

Overview The DELETED( ) function has no arguments. The function tests the current record in the active database file and returns a logical True (.T.) if the record is marked for deletion; otherwise, it returns a logical False (.F.).

Procedure In order to use DELETED( ) effectively, a database file must be in use in the current work area. (See USE.) If there is no open database file, the function automatically returns a logical false (.F.).

DELETED( ) returns a logical value and can be used anywhere in the language where a logical expression (i.e., condition) is appropriate.

Examples DELETED( ) can be used when you want to process only the records marked for deletion in a database file. For example, to close the account of a particular customer, you might mark his record for deletion in the Customer database file. The following routine prints a report showing each closed account before permanently removing those customers from the database file. This report can be sent to an agency specializing in delinquent accounts.

```
Mala Schaefer
1822 Hollywood Blvd.

Los Angeles, CA  90038

Outstanding Balance: 193.79
```

Figure 57

```
* Collect.PRG
*
SET TALK OFF
SET DEVICE TO PRINTER
USE Customer
DO WHILE .NOT. EOF()
   IF DELETED() .AND. Amt_Owed > 0.00
      @ 4, 0 SAY TRIM(First_Name) + " " + Last_Name
      @ 5, 0 SAY Address1
      @ 6, 0 SAY Address2
      @ 7, 0 SAY TRIM(City) + ", " + TRIM(State) + "  " + Zip
      @ 9, 0 SAY "Outstanding Balance: " + ;
                 LTRIM(STR(Amt_Owed, 10, 2))
   ENDIF
   SKIP
ENDDO
EJECT
PACK   && Remove deleted records permanently
CLOSE DATABASES
SET DEVICE TO SCREEN
SET TALK ON
```

To execute this program, type `DO Collect`. A sample of the printed output is shown in Figure 57.

Warnings Because of its simple syntax, there are no error messages associated with the DELETED( ) function.

Tips SET DELETED ON eliminates the need for testing each record with the DELETED( ) function. SET DELETED is normally OFF which means that dBASE III PLUS acknowledges records that are marked for deletion and processes them like any other record.

DIR

Syntax `DIR [[ON] <drive>] [[LIKE] <skeleton>]`

Overview The DIR command, short for DIRECTORY, lists the file names on a particular drive or directory. Used with no parameters, DIR displays the database files (i.e., all files with a .DBF extension) on the current drive and directory. In addition to the database file names, the number of records, date of last update, and file size are displayed.

The ON <drive> option causes DIR to look on a drive other than the default.

The LIKE <skeleton>, or more simply, <skeleton>, option causes DIR to list only the file names that match a particular pattern. (See Skeleton for information.)

If there are more files in the directory listing than fit on a single screen, you are prompted to *Press any key to continue* after each full screen is displayed.

Procedure The dBASE III PLUS DIR command is very similar to the DOS Dir command. Use DIR to get a directory listing without leaving dBASE III PLUS if you are not sure what files are on your disk or if you forget the name of a particular file that you want to work with.

Examples The following examples show you how to use DIR with various skeletons:

```
. DIR  && Shows the .DBF files only
Database Files     # Records    Last Update     Size
EMPLOYEE.DBF              13    05/14/87        6144
CUSTOMER.DBF              10    05/05/87        2136
MEDICAL.DBF                1    03/02/87         643
INVENTRY.DBF               6    06/03/87        1934
MAIL.DBF                  18    05/26/87        4608
ORDERS.DBF                 4    05/14/87         250
NUMBERS.DBF               25    05/04/87         341
ANSWERS.DBF                3    05/08/87        1787
REORDER.DBF                2    05/29/87         774
EXTEFILE.DBF               7    06/01/87         288
```

continued

```
  18905 bytes in    10 files.
1839104 bytes remaining on drive.

. DIR *.FMT  && Shows all of the format files
CUST_ADD.FMT        MAILEDIT.FMT        EMP_ADD.FMT        INVOICES.FMT
MAIL_ADD.FMT

   5030 bytes in     5 files.
1839104 bytes remaining on drive.

. DIR ON A:  && Shows all .DBF files on the A drive
Database Files    # Records    Last Update    Size

None

  37888 bytes remaining on drive.

. DIR LIKE C:\*.*  && Shows all files in the root directory
COMMAND.COM         CONFIG.SYS          AUTOEXEC.BAT

  23693 bytes in     3 files.
1839104 bytes remaining on drive.
```

Tips DISPLAY FILES is functionally identical to DIR except for one important difference: DISPLAY FILES has a TO PRINTER option to print the directory listing. DIR does not have such an option, but if you SET PRINTER ON before issuing the DIR command, its result is printed.

DISKSPACE( )

Syntax `DISKSPACE()`

Overview The DISKSPACE( ) function does not have any arguments. The function returns the amount of disk space available (in bytes) on the default drive.

Procedure DISKSPACE( ) returns a number and can be used anywhere in the language where a numeric expression is appropriate.

Examples

DISKSPACE( ) is useful when you want to avoid getting a disk full error in a program. Before writing to a disk drive, approximate the amount of space needed to do the write, and compare that value to the DISKSPACE( ) result. The following example is a routine that copies the Customer database file from a hard disk to a text file on a floppy disk. It checks the amount of space available on the floppy and compares that to the amount of space needed to copy the file. The program warns the user if there is insufficient space on the floppy disk.

```
* Backup.PRG
*
SET TALK OFF
USE Customer
size = RECCOUNT() * RECSIZE()
SET DEFAULT TO A
available = DISKSPACE()
SET DEFAULT TO C
IF available < size
   ?? CHR(7)
   ? "There is not enough room on the floppy disk to copy the"
   ? "Customer file."
   WAIT
ELSE
   COPY TO A:Customer SDF
ENDIF
CLOSE DATABASES
SET TALK ON
```

The example uses RECCOUNT( ) and RECSIZE( ) to calculate the size of the resulting text file. These functions return the number of records and the record size for the active database file. Multiplying these numbers together gives an approximation of the amount of disk space used by the data. The SDF option of COPY copies the data from the Customer database file to a text file.

Warnings

Because of its simple syntax, there are no error messages associated with DISKSPACE( ).

Tips

To check the amount of available space on a drive other than the current default drive, change the default drive using SET DEFAULT TO. Because dBASE III PLUS keeps track of the default drive internally, the default drive may be different from the operating system default drive.

DISPLAY

Syntax

```
DISPLAY [[FIELDS] <expression list>] [<scope>]
[WHILE <condition>] [FOR <condition>]
[OFF] [TO PRINTER]
```

Overview

The DISPLAY command is used to display database information on the screen or printer. Used without parameters, DISPLAY displays all of the fields in the current record of the active database file with a record number and headings (if SET HEADING is ON). Memo fields are represented by an icon.

A scope, a FOR clause, and a WHILE clause can be used to display records within a specific range that meet certain conditions. Each of these command line options is discussed separately. (See Scope, FOR, and WHILE.) If there is more information than can fit on a single screen, you are prompted to *Press any key to continue* after each full screen.

An expression list can specify which fields are shown and which other expression results (e.g., calculations involving fields, memory variables) are displayed. Because it is a list of expressions, not just fields, the expression list may be preceded by the FIELDS keyword. Memo field contents are displayed if you specify them in the expression list by name.

The OFF keyword suppresses the display of the record number. TO PRINTER causes the display to be printed.

Procedure

Use DISPLAY to view the fields in your database file. Use the expression list for including calculations involving the fields and to display Memo fields.

Examples

The following example uses DISPLAY to show both the part numbers that must be reordered as well as the amounts that must be reordered to restore the quantity on hand to the reorder point:

```
. USE Inventry
. DISPLAY Part_No, Reorder - Quantity FOR Quantity - Reorder < 0
Record#  Part_No  Reorder - Quantity
      1  R-123                     3
      4  B-735                     5
. CLOSE DATABASES
```

Warnings If you have fields with the same name as other DISPLAY keywords (e.g., HISTORY, MEMORY, STATUS), you won't be able to display them without using the FIELDS keyword. For example, a field named Status cannot be shown using the command, DISPLAY Status, because this is another dBASE III PLUS command; however, you can DISPLAY FIELDS Status. Refrain from naming fields with dBASE III PLUS keywords, and you will avoid such conflicts.

Tips The TO PRINTER option prints the display, but the display remains on the screen. In order to suppress the screen output, SET CONSOLE OFF before doing a DISPLAY TO PRINTER. SET CONSOLE ON again after the command is executed.

DISPLAY is very similar to LIST except that the default scope for LIST is ALL records; another difference is that LIST is not interrupted with the *Press any key to continue* message.

DISPLAY FILES

Syntax

```
DISPLAY FILES [[ON] <drive>] [[LIKE] <skeleton>]
[TO PRINTER]
```

Overview Except for the TO PRINTER option, DISPLAY FILES is functionally identical to DIR. (See DIR for more information regarding the use of this command.)

Tips Use DISPLAY FILES or DIR for viewing the directory on the screen and LIST FILES TO PRINTER for printing it. If you DISPLAY FILES TO PRINTER, the *Press any key to continue* message is printed also.

DISPLAY HISTORY

Syntax `DISPLAY HISTORY [LAST <expN>] [TO PRINTER]`

Overview

The DISPLAY HISTORY command is functionally identical to LIST HISTORY, except that it prompts you to *Press any key to continue* if there is more information than will fit on a single screen. (See LIST HISTORY for more information regarding the use of this command.)

Tips

Use DISPLAY HISTORY for viewing the commands in the history buffer on the screen and LIST HISTORY TO PRINTER for printing them. If you DISPLAY HISTORY TO PRINTER, the *Press any key to continue* message is printed also.

DISPLAY MEMORY

Syntax `DISPLAY MEMORY [TO PRINTER]`

Overview

The DISPLAY MEMORY command is functionally identical to LIST MEMORY, except that it prompts you to *Press any key to continue* if there is more information than will fit on a single screen. (See LIST MEMORY for more information regarding the use of this command.)

Tips

Use DISPLAY MEMORY for viewing the memory variable contents on the screen and LIST MEMORY TO PRINTER for printing this information. If you DISPLAY MEMORY TO PRINTER, the *Press any key to continue* message is printed also.

DISPLAY STATUS

Syntax `DISPLAY STATUS [TO PRINTER]`

Overview The DISPLAY STATUS command is functionally identical to LIST STATUS, except that it prompts you to *Press any key to continue* if there is more information than will fit on a single screen. (See LIST STATUS for more information regarding the use of this command.)

Tips Use DISPLAY STATUS for viewing the status information on the screen and LIST STATUS TO PRINTER for printing it. If you DISPLAY STATUS TO PRINTER, the *Press any key to continue* message is printed also.

DISPLAY STRUCTURE

Syntax `DISPLAY STRUCTURE [TO PRINTER]`

Overview The DISPLAY STRUCTURE command is functionally identical to LIST STRUCTURE, except that it prompts you to *Press any key to continue* if there is more information than will fit on a single screen. (See LIST STRUCTURE for more information regarding the use of this command.)

Tips Use DISPLAY STRUCTURE for viewing the database file structure on the screen and LIST STRUCTURE TO PRINTER for printing it. If you DISPLAY STRUCTURE TO PRINTER, the *Press any key to continue* message is printed also.

DISPLAY USERS

Syntax `DISPLAY USERS [TO PRINTER]`

Overview

The DISPLAY USERS command is functionally identical to LIST USERS, except that it prompts you to *Press any key to continue* if there is more information than will fit on a single screen. (See LIST USERS for more information regarding the use of this command.)

Tips

Use DISPLAY USERS for viewing the user names on the screen and LIST USERS TO PRINTER for printing it. If you DISPLAY USERS TO PRINTER, the *Press any key to continue* message is printed also.

DISPLAY USERS has no effect in a single-user environment.

DO

Syntax

```
DO <command filename>¦<procedure name>
[WITH <parameter list>]
```

Overview

The DO command executes a dBASE III PLUS command file or procedure.

A command file is an ASCII text file containing dBASE III PLUS commands. It is assumed to have a .PRG extension.

A procedure is like a command file in that it is a group of dBASE III PLUS commands that performs a specific task; it differs from a command file, however, because it is a part of another file called a procedure file. A procedure file is an ASCII text file that is assumed to have a .PRG extension. The file can contain up to thirty-two procedures, each of which begins with the command PROCEDURE <procedure name>. Once a procedure file is open with SET PROCEDURE TO <filename>, any procedure in the file can be executed by issuing DO <procedure name>.

Parameters can be passed to the command file or procedure using the WITH clause, provided there is a corresponding PARAMETERS statement in the command file or procedure. The PARAMETERS statement must be the first statement in the command file and the first statement following the PROCEDURE command in a procedure. The number of parameters in the WITH list and the PARAMETERS list must be the same. (See PARAMETERS for more information on passing parameters back and forth between programs.)

Command and procedure files can be created using MODIFY COMMAND or any other word processor capable of generating an ASCII text file. The dBASE III PLUS commands are typed into the file in the order in which you want them to be performed. The programming constructs (see DO CASE, DO WHILE, and IF) can be used to alter the order of execution.

Procedure

If you have a task more complicated than a single command that you perform frequently, store the commands in a dBASE III PLUS command file or procedure. Then, instead of entering the sequence of commands to perform the task again and again, simply DO the command file or procedure in which the commands are stored.

You may also have tasks that require decisions to be made and a different set of commands to be performed based on those decisions. For these tasks, it is necessary to write a program using the dBASE III PLUS programming constructs DO WHILE, DO CASE, and IF. These constructs allow you to test conditions and perform a different set of commands for different conditions.

Use the WITH option to pass one or more parameters to a program that expects them (i.e., a program that has a PARAMETERS command as its first statement).

You can nest programs by using DO inside another program. There is, however, a limit to the number of files that can be open at one time which, in turn, limits the nesting of command files in this manner. Note that DO <command file> opens a file, but DO <procedure> does not.

Examples

Many of the examples for the other entries in this book are programs that are executed using DO. The following example illustrates the execution of several procedures that use a parameter list:

```
* Compute.PRG - This is a command file that opens a procedure
*               file and executes several of the procedures in
*               it.
*
SET TALK OFF
SET PROCEDURE TO Stats  && Open the procedure file
```

```
USE Mail

* The field name on which you want to gather statistics
* must be passed as a character string.
field_name = "Age"

* The variables used in the procedure are initialized.
STORE 0 TO mean, sum_total, variance, std_dev

* Statistics are computed by executing the procedures stored in
* the Stats.PRG procedure file.
DO Sum_Total WITH field_name
DO Mean WITH field_name
DO Variance WITH field_name, mean
DO Std_Dev WITH variance

* Statistics are displayed.
? "Sum: " + LTRIM(STR(sum_total, 10, 2))
? "Mean: " + LTRIM(STR(mean, 10, 2))
? "Variance: " + LTRIM(STR(variance, 10, 2))
? "Standard deviation: " + LTRIM(STR(std_dev, 10, 2))
CLOSE DATABASES
CLOSE PROCEDURE
SET TALK ON
```

The Stats procedure file is listed below:

```
* Stats.PRG is a procedure file that computes statistical
* values based on a field name that is passed to the individual
* procedures.

PROCEDURE Sum_Total
* This procedure computes the sum of the numbers stored in the
* field name that is passed as a parameter, field_name.
PARAMETERS field_name
SUM &field_name TO sum_total
RETURN

PROCEDURE Mean
* This procedure computes the mean of the numbers stored in the
* field name that is passed as a parameter, field_name.
PARAMETERS field_name
AVERAGE &field_name TO mean
RETURN

PROCEDURE Variance
* This procedure computes the variance of the numbers stored in
```

```
* the field name that is passed as a parameter, field_name.
PARAMETERS field_name, mean
square_sum = 0
GO TOP
DO WHILE .NOT. EOF()
   square_sum = &field_name ^ 2 + square_sum
   SKIP
ENDDO
variance = square_sum / RECCOUNT() - mean ^ 2
RETURN

PROCEDURE Std_Dev
* This procedure computes the standard deviation of the numbers
* stored in the field name passed as a parameter, field_name.
PARAMETERS variance
std_dev = SQRT(variance)
RETURN
```

If you execute the program, you will get the following statistics based on the age of the people in the mailing list:

```
. DO Compute
Sum: 583.00
Mean: 32.39
Variance: 40.68
Standard deviation: 6.38
```

Warnings

When you execute a program with DO, the commands that are listed in the command file or procedure are executed. If there is an error in a command, the error message appears on your screen, and you are given the opportunity to *Cancel, Ignore, or Suspend? (C, I, or S).* If you choose to Suspend, be sure that you enter `RESUME` to continue with the program execution; using DO results in a *File is already open* message. Enter `CANCEL` if you want to close the program file (`CLOSE PROCEDURE` for a procedure file) to modify it. (See MODIFY COMMAND.)

Tips

When a procedure file is open, procedure names take precedence over command file names; therefore, DO executes the procedure if a procedure in the file has the same name as a command file. Remember this when naming your procedures, and you will avoid conflicts.

(See SET PROCEDURE for information on procedures or procedure files.)

DO CASE

Syntax

```
DO CASE
   CASE <condition 1>
      <commands>
  [CASE <condition 2>
      <commands>
   .
   .
   .
   CASE <condition n>
      <commands>]
  [OTHERWISE
      <commands>]
ENDCASE
```

Overview The DO CASE command indicates the beginning of a DO CASE...ENDCASE control structure in dBASE III PLUS. This control structure is designed to evaluate several conditions, only one of which is expected to be true. A different set of commands is executed depending on which of the conditions is true.

The CASE and OTHERWISE statements are part of the DO CASE...ENDCASE program control structure; as such, they must be nested properly between DO CASE and ENDCASE. Each CASE statement inside of the control structure specifies a condition and is followed by a set of other commands that are executed if the condition is true. The OTHERWISE statement is used to specify a path to take if none of the CASE conditions is true.

When DO CASE is encountered, dBASE III PLUS scans for a CASE statement. The associated condition is evaluated as soon as it is encountered.

If the condition is true, the commands following the CASE statement are executed until the next CASE, OTHERWISE, or ENDCASE statement is encountered. Program control is then transferred to the command immediately following the ENDCASE.

If the condition is false, dBASE III PLUS scans for the next CASE statement in the DO CASE...ENDCASE structure, and the above process is repeated until there are no more CASE statements in the control structure.

If all of the CASE conditions evaluate to false, and there is an OTHERWISE statement in the control structure, the commands following it are executed until the ENDCASE is encountered. Program control is then transferred to the command immediately following the ENDCASE.

Procedure

Use a DO CASE...ENDCASE control structure when you want to perform a different operation for each of a set of mutually exclusive conditions (i.e., only one of the conditions is true at any given point in time).

The statements that go together to make up the control structure must be arranged correctly in order for it to work properly. Begin with the DO CASE command. The first CASE statement is on the next line. Following this statement are the commands to be executed if the associated condition is true. After all of these commands comes the next CASE statement (if any), followed by its associated commands. After all CASE statements are complete, include an OTHERWISE statement if you want to specify a group of commands to be executed in the event that none of the CASE conditions is true. Finally, you must mark the end of the control structure with an ENDCASE statement.

You can nest other control structures (i.e., DO CASE, DO WHILE, and IF) inside of a DO CASE...ENDCASE structure.

All of the control structures are designed for use in programs (e.g., a command file or a procedure) and cannot be used at the dot prompt.

Examples

The following example is a menu program that uses a DO CASE...ENDCASE control structure to determine what choice the user made and to execute the appropriate commands based on that choice:

```
* Menu.PRG
*
SET TALK OFF
SET STATUS ON
SET MESSAGE TO "Enter a menu choice."
CLEAR
DO WHILE .T.  && Display the menu until the user selects Exit
   choice = 0

   * Display menu and prompt for user's choice.
   @  6,29 SAY "0 - Exit"
   @  8,29 SAY "1 - Add Records"
   @ 10,29 SAY "2 - Edit Records"
   @ 12,29 SAY "3 - Print Reports"
   @  4,20 TO 14, 54 DOUBLE
   CLEAR TYPEAHEAD
```

```
@ 14,37 GET choice PICTURE "9" RANGE 0, 3
READ

* Use DO CASE to execute a different program for each choice.
DO CASE

   * If the user chooses 0, QUIT dBASE III PLUS.
   CASE choice = 0
      QUIT

   * If the user chooses 1, do program to add records.
   CASE choice = 1
      DO Add_Recs

   * If the user chooses 2, do program to edit records.
   CASE choice = 2
      DO EditRecs

   * If the user chooses 3, do program to print reports.
   CASE choice = 3
      DO Rpt_Menu

ENDCASE  && End the DO CASE control structure
ENDDO
```

Warnings

If any of the CASE conditions evaluates to other than a logical expression, the error message *Not a Logical expression* is displayed.

If you attempt a DO CASE at the dot prompt, the error message *Valid only in programs* is displayed.

CASE statements encountered after an OTHERWISE statement in a DO CASE...ENDCASE control structure are always ignored because of the order in which the statements are executed. Commands encountered between the DO CASE command and the first CASE statement are also ignored for the same reason. These are logic errors that do not produce error messages.

Neglecting to mark the end of a DO CASE...ENDCASE control structure with an ENDCASE statement does not cause an error message. Instead, all of the commands following the last CASE or OTHERWISE command are executed as part of the control structure because dBASE III PLUS continues to execute commands until it finds the ENDCASE. For this reason and the reasons stated above, be sure to construct this control structure properly.

Tips

The DO CASE...ENDCASE program control structure is an expanded version of the IF...ENDIF control structure. In fact, any DO CASE...ENDCASE control structure can be written as a set of nested IF...ENDIF structures. IF...ENDIF only handles one condition. If the condition is true, one set of commands is executed; otherwise, you can optionally specify a second set of commands to be executed using the ELSE statement.

There are many decisions of this more simple nature to be made in programs. Use IF...ENDIF instead of DO CASE...ENDCASE in these cases because it is faster and more straightforward. Reserve using the DO CASE...ENDCASE for times when you want to choose one of two or more possible conditions.

Using indentation with the DO CASE...ENDCASE structure (as with other control structures) makes it easier to identify and read in your program. Using indentation also allows you to see quickly that you have properly closed the structure.

DO WHILE

Syntax

```
DO WHILE <condition>
    <commands>
    [LOOP]
    [EXIT]
ENDDO
```

Overview

The DO WHILE command indicates the beginning of a DO WHILE...ENDDO control structure in dBASE III PLUS. This control structure is designed to execute a group of dBASE III PLUS commands as long as the specified DO WHILE condition is true.

The LOOP and EXIT statements are optional parts of the DO WHILE...ENDDO control structure and, as such, must be nested properly between a DO WHILE and an ENDDO command. The LOOP command transfers control to the DO WHILE statement, and the EXIT command transfers control to the command immediately following the ENDDO statement.

When a DO WHILE command is encountered, dBASE III PLUS evaluates the condition. If it evaluates to true, all of the commands following the DO WHILE command are executed until the next ENDDO statement is encountered. When ENDDO is encountered, control is transferred back to the DO WHILE command, and the process is continued. If the DO WHILE condition is false, control is transferred to the command immediately following the next ENDDO command.

Procedure

Use a DO WHILE...ENDDO control structure (also called a "DO WHILE loop") to continue performing a group of dBASE III PLUS commands until a particular condition changes from true to false.

In order for a DO WHILE loop to work correctly, either the DO WHILE condition must change to false somewhere within the loop, or the EXIT command must be used; otherwise, the result is a loop which executes forever.

The EXIT statement, if used, is generally part of an IF...ENDIF structure. This is also true of the LOOP statement. Use the EXIT statement to get out of an otherwise infinite loop (e.g., DO WHILE .T.). Use the LOOP statement to force the DO WHILE loop to start over.

You can nest other control structures (i.e., DO CASE, DO WHILE, and IF) inside of a DO WHILE...ENDDO structure.

All of the control structures are designed for use in programs (e.g., a command file or a procedure) and cannot be used at the dot prompt.

Examples

Probably the most common use of the DO WHILE loop is to process sequentially the records in a database file. The following routine uses a DO WHILE loop to perform a series of commands for each record in a database file. This program is designed to fill the orders in the Orders file. When an order is filled, the quantity in the Inventry file must be updated and a shipping label printed for the customer.

```
* OrderFil.PRG
*
SET TALK OFF
SELECT 3
USE Customer INDEX Cust_No
SELECT 2
USE Inventry INDEX Part_No
SELECT 1
```

```
USE Orders

DO WHILE .NOT. EOF()  && Process all records in the Orders file

   * Find the part number in the inventory file and decrease
   * the quantity by the number ordered.
   SELECT Inventry
   SEEK Orders->Part_No
   IF FOUND()
      REPLACE Quantity WITH Quantity - Orders->Quantity
   ENDIF

   * Find Customer for this order and print a single shipping
   * Label.  The LABEL FORM Shipping.LBL is already designed
   * for this.
   SELECT Customer
   SEEK Orders->Cust_No
   IF FOUND()
      LABEL FORM Shipping NEXT 1 TO PRINTER
   ENDIF

   * Go back to the Orders file to process the next order.
   SELECT Orders
   SKIP

ENDDO  && Close the DO WHILE loop
CLOSE DATABASES
SET TALK ON
```

The next example shows how to use the EXIT statement from within a DO WHILE loop when you want to test for the exit condition somewhere in the middle of the loop rather than at the beginning. This example also uses the LOOP statement to start the loop over if an incorrect name is entered.

```
* MailEdit.PRG
*
SET TALK OFF
USE Mail INDEX Last

* Set up the screen so that the user can enter a last name.
* The labels for the other fields are displayed here because
* they are the same for each record and need only be shown once.

CLEAR
```

```
@ 3, 5 SAY "Last Name"
@ 4, 5 SAY "First Name"
@ 5, 5 SAY "Street"
@ 6, 5 SAY "Apartment"
@ 7, 5 SAY "City"
@ 8, 5 SAY "State"
@ 9, 5 SAY "Zip Code"

m_error = .F.  && Initialize error flag for a record not found

DO WHILE .T.

   * A different prompt is displayed depending on the error flag.
   * If the error flag is true, that means that the name entered
   * could not be found.
   IF m_error
      @ 1,5 SAY "The name you entered was not found.  Try again."
      m_error = .F.  && Reset error flag
   ELSE
      @ 1,5 SAY "Enter the last name of the person to find.      "
   ENDIF

   m_last = SPACE(20)    && Make m_last blank
   @ 3,17 GET m_last     && Enter a name into a memory variable
   @ 4,17 CLEAR TO 9,79  && Clear previous record from screen
   READ

   * The loop is exited if the user does not enter a name.
   IF "" = TRIM(m_last)
      EXIT   && Exit from the loop if no name is entered
   ENDIF

   SEEK m_last  && Locate the last name entered
   IF .NOT. FOUND()   && Test to make sure that name is on file

      * If the name is not found, set the error flag to true
      * and start the loop over.
      m_error = .T.
      LOOP

   ELSE  && Display contents of record on screen for editing

      @ 1, 5  && Erase prompt
      @ 3,17 GET Last_Name
      @ 4,17 GET First_Name
```

```
      @ 5,17 GET Address1
      @ 6,17 GET Address2
      @ 7,17 GET City
      @ 8,17 GET State
      @ 9,17 GET Zip

      READ  && Allow user to edit the fields
   ENDIF
ENDDO
CLEAR
CLOSE DATABASES
SET TALK ON
```

Warnings

The use of macro substitution in the DO WHILE condition is limited because of the way in which the condition is interpreted. In order to increase the execution time of DO WHILE loops, dBASE III PLUS only interprets the expression the first time through the loop (i.e., the macro substitution only occurs once). The interpreted form is kept in memory and used for subsequent passes through the loop. Consequently, it is not possible to have a DO WHILE expression that changes, though the condition or evaluation of the expression may change. For example, you might try this sequence to display non-blank fields in a database file that are similarly named:

```
    .
    .
    .
number = "1"
DO WHILE "" <> TRIM(Symptom&number)
   ? Symptom&number
   number = LTRIM(STR(VAL(number) + 1, 2))
ENDDO
    .
    .
    .
```

What happens with this loop, as with all others, is that the DO WHILE expression is interpreted only the first time through. When this occurs, the expression looks like " " < > TRIM(Symptom1), and the condition represented by that expression is evaluated each time through the loop. Although it may seem that the condition should change each time through the loop because the variable changes, this is not the case. In order to make the loop work correctly, you could use the following commands:

```
    .
    .
    .
number = "1"
DO WHILE .T.
   IF "" <> TRIM(Symptom&number)
      ? Symptom&number
   ELSE
      EXIT
   ENDIF
   number = LTRIM(STR(VAL(number) + 1, 2))
ENDDO
    .
    .
    .
```

The only way to use macro substitution effectively as part of the DO WHILE condition is if the variable being substituted does not change in value. This may seem unimportant, but it allows you to do something like this:

```
    .
    .
    .
ACCEPT "Enter a condition"  TO condition
IF TYPE(condition) = "L"
   DO WHILE &condition
      .
      .
      .
   ENDDO
ELSE
   ? condition + " is not a logical expression."
ENDIF
    .
    .
    .
```

If the DO WHILE condition evaluates to anything other than a logical expression, the error message *Not a Logical expression* is displayed.

If you attempt a DO WHILE at the dot prompt, the error message *Valid only in programs* is displayed.

EXIT and LOOP statements encountered outside of a DO WHILE loop do not produce error messages; instead, each of these commands behaves like a RETURN.

Neglecting to mark the end of a DO WHILE loop with an ENDDO statement does not cause an error message; instead, all of the commands following the DO WHILE command are executed as part of the loop; the loop never starts over because no ENDDO is ever encountered. For this reason and the one stated above, use indentation to make sure that you properly construct each DO WHILE loop.

Tips

Using indentation with the DO WHILE...ENDDO structure (as with other control structures) makes it easier to identify and read in your program. Using indentation also allows you to see quickly that you have properly closed the structure.

DOW( )

Syntax `DOW(<expD>)`

Overview

The DOW( ) function, short for day of week, accepts any date expression as its argument. The function evaluates the expression and returns the number that corresponds to the day of week. The days are numbered from 1 to 7, beginning with Sunday.

Procedure

DOW( ) returns a number and can be used anywhere in the language where a numeric expression is appropriate.

Examples

DOW( ) can be used as the index into a pseudo-array involving the days of the week. For example, the following routine sets up a counter memory variable for each day of the week and counts how many of the people in your mailing list were born on each day. To accomplish this, DOW( ) is used along with macro substitution to determine which of the counter memory variables to increment.

```
* Array.PRG
*
SET TALK OFF
USE Mail
* Pseudo array of days of the week is initialized.
STORE 0 TO day1, day2, day3, day4, day5, day6, day7
```

```
DO WHILE .NOT. EOF()
   * The day of birth is converted to a character string so
   * that it can be used in macro substitution.
   num = STR(DOW(Birthday), 1)
   * The variable num is now a number between 1 and 7 that is
   * stored as a character string.  day&num will result in one
   * of the elements of the pseudo array.
   day&num = day&num + 1
   SKIP
ENDDO
* Now the pseudo array is displayed.
CLEAR
num = "1"
* The days memory variable is a list of all the days of the
* week. It is used below for displaying the name of the day.
days = "Sunday   Monday   Tuesday  Wednesday";
     + "Thursday Friday   Saturday "
start = 1
DO WHILE VAL(num) <= 7
   @ VAL(num), 0 SAY STR(day&num, 1) + " born on ";
                  + SUBSTR(days, start, 9)
   num = STR(VAL(num) + 1, 1)
   start = start + 9
ENDDO
CLOSE DATABASES
SET TALK ON
```

To execute this program, you type `DO Array` and see the following:

```
2 born on Sunday
2 born on Monday
2 born on Tuesday
3 born on Wednesday
4 born on Thursday
1 born on Friday
4 born on Saturday
```

Warnings If the function argument evaluates to a data type other than date, the error message *Invalid function argument* is displayed.

DTOC( )

Syntax `DTOC(<expD>)`

Overview The DTOC( ) function, short for date-to-character, accepts a date expression as its argument. The function evaluates the expression and then returns the date as a character string. The format of the resulting character string depends on the SET DATE and SET CENTURY settings. By default, the result of the DTOC( ) function is of the form "MM/DD/YY."

Procedure DTOC( ) returns a character string and can be used anywhere in the language where a character expression is appropriate.

Examples DTOC( ) converts dates to character strings and is useful when you want to display a date next to a character string. The following routine displays all of the Customers with a payment deadline that falls on or before the current date:

```
* Past_Due.PRG
*
SET TALK OFF
USE Customer
CLEAR
s_row = 1
DO WHILE .NOT. EOF()
   IF Deadline <= DATE()
      @ s_row, 1 SAY TRIM(Last_Name) + " " + DTOC(Deadline)
      s_row = s_row + 1
   ENDIF
   SKIP
ENDDO
CLOSE DATABASES
SET TALK ON
```

Warnings If the function argument evaluates to a data type other than date, the error message *Invalid function argument* is displayed.

Tips dBASE III PLUS stores dates as numbers so that dates can be compared chronologically and certain arithmetic operations can be performed with

them. The date 02/01/85 comes before 01/01/86 in a chronological sense, but if these two dates are converted to character strings using CTOD( ), the string "02/01/85" comes after "01/01/86". To avoid this problem, do not use CTOD( ) if you are concatenating a date with a character string in order to create an INDEX. Instead, use the following more complicated expression.

```
STR(YEAR(<expD>), 2) + STR(MONTH(<expD>), 2) +;
STR(DAY(<expD>), 2)
```

This expression results in a character string with the year at the beginning, and the string "850201" before "860101".

EDIT

Syntax

```
EDIT [FIELDS <field list>] [<scope>]
[WHILE <condition>] [FOR <condition>]
```

Overview

The EDIT command allows you to make changes interactively to existing records in a database file. As one of the full-screen editing commands, it is able to make use of the full-screen cursor movement and editing keys listed in Appendix A.

If EDIT is used with no parameters and without an open format file, all of the fields in the current record of the active database file are presented on the screen for editing. A FIELDS list can be specified to limit the fields that you see on the screen and to change the order in which they appear, but the placement of the fields is in a standard format. If a format file is open in the current work area (see SET FORMAT), it determines which fields are presented and the placement of the fields on the screen.

A scope, a FOR clause, and a WHILE clause can be used to limit the records which can be changed. Each of these command line options is discussed separately. (See Scope, FOR, and WHILE.) The default scope for EDIT is ALL records.

When EDIT is executed, dBASE III PLUS enters the interactive edit mode, which remains in effect until you choose to leave it. You can exit from the edit mode in one of three ways:

- Press PgDn on the last record in the scope of the EDIT command. The changes to the current record are saved.
- Press Ctrl-End at any time. The changes to the current record are saved.
- Press Esc at any time. The changes to the current record are not saved.

Procedure

Use EDIT to make changes to the records in a database file.

Examples

The following examples show the difference in screen appearance using EDIT with and without a format file:

```
. USE Mail
. EDIT
```

Without a format file, the screen looks like the one in Figure 58 (assuming that SET MENUS OFF and SET STATUS OFF).

Using the following commands to activate a format file can make the screen more appealing, like in Figure 59.

```
. SET FORMAT TO MailEdit
. EDIT
```

Figure 58

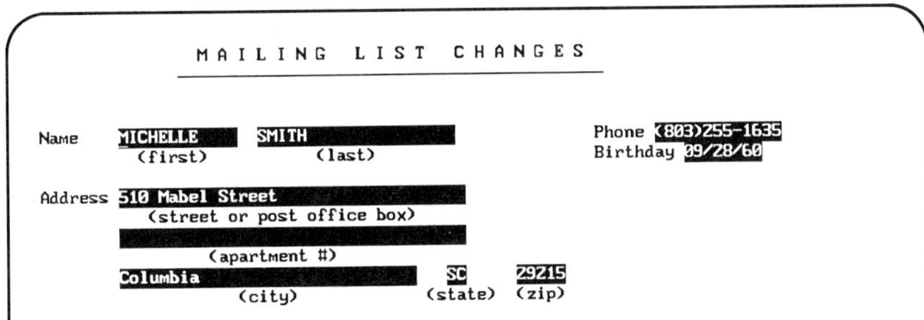
MAILING LIST CHANGES

Name MICHELLE SMITH
(first) (last)

Phone (803)255-1635
Birthday 09/28/60

Address 510 Mabel Street
(street or post office box)

(apartment #)
Columbia SC 29215
(city) (state) (zip)

Figure 59

Warnings Even with a format file, the EDIT command does not allow very precise data validation and, therefore, may not be sufficient in applications programming. All changes may not be written to the disk until you close the database file. (See CLOSE.)

Tips When using dBASE III PLUS in a network environment, use Ctrl-O to lock and unlock records interactively while in EDIT. You must obtain a record lock in order to change a record in EDIT unless the database file was opened for exclusive use (see SET EXCLUSIVE, USE), or the file or record was locked before entering EDIT (see FLOCK( ), RLOCK( )).

If a view that involves fields from two or more database files is in effect, EDIT can be used to make changes to several database files simultaneously.

Use a format file if the default screen provided for EDIT does not appeal to you. You can use CREATE SCREEN to design format files using a screen painter approach, or you can simply enter the appropriate @ commands in a text file with an .FMT extension using MODIFY COMMAND. SET FORMAT activates a format file for use with the active database file.

BROWSE is another way to make changes to your database file interactively. This command presents you with a tabular view of the records in your file, while EDIT presents you with a form view.

CHANGE is functionally identical to EDIT.

EJECT

Syntax `EJECT`

Overview

The EJECT command sends a form feed (i.e., CHR(12)) to the printer, which causes a page eject to occur. This command works regardless of the status of SET PRINTER or SET DEVICE. After an EJECT, PROW( ) and PCOL( ) are reset to zero.

Procedure

Use EJECT to start printing on a new sheet of paper or to eject the last printed page.

Examples

The following routine prints the names, addresses, and phone numbers from your mailing list using the ? command with SET PRINTER ON. In order to print each name on a new page, the EJECT command is issued after each record is printed.

```
SET TALK OFF
SET PRINTER ON
USE Mail
DO WHILE .NOT. EOF()
   ? TRIM(First_Name) + " " + Last_Name
   ? Address1
   ? Address2
   ? TRIM(City) + ", " + State + "  " + Zip
   SKIP
   EJECT
ENDDO
CLOSE DATABASES
SET PRINTER OFF
SET TALK ON
```

Warnings

Before using EJECT or any other printing command, be sure that your printer is properly connected to your computer, and that it is turned on and is on-line. dBASE III PLUS tries to be forgiving about printing errors, either by providing an error message or by simply not printing; there are some printing errors, however, that can cause a program to hang. If this happens to you, check the printer to make sure that it is turned on and is on-line before making the decision to reboot your machine, and possibly losing some of your data. Sometimes turning on the printer and/or bringing it on-line will make dBASE III PLUS operational again.

Closing (see CLOSE) and reopening your files between data entry and printing will prevent data loss, even if you reboot your computer.

Tips

If @...SAY is used with SET DEVICE TO PRINTER, a form feed is automatically sent to the printer, provided the row coordinate is less than the current printer row. The following example is like the one above, except that it uses @...SAY instead of the ? command to display the data. For this reason, EJECT is necessary only after the last record is printed.

```
SET TALK OFF
SET DEVICE TO PRINTER
USE Mail
DO WHILE .NOT. EOF()

   * Each record is automatically printed on a new page using
   * the @...SAY command.
   @ 0,25 SAY Phone
   @ 1, 5 SAY TRIM(First_Name) + " " + Last_Name
   @ 2, 5 SAY Address1
   @ 3, 5 SAY Address2
   @ 4, 5 SAY TRIM(City) + ", " + State + "  " + Zip

   SKIP
ENDDO

EJECT  && To eject the page with the last record in the file

CLOSE DATABASES
SET DEVICE TO SCREEN
SET TALK ON
```

ELSE. *See* IF

ENDCASE. *See* DO CASE

ENDDO. *See* DO WHILE

ENDIF. *See* IF

ENDTEXT. *See* TEXT

EOF( )

Syntax `EOF()`

Overview The EOF( ) function, short for end of file, does not have any arguments. The function returns a logical True (.T.) if the active database file is positioned at the end of file; otherwise, it returns a logical False (.F.).

Procedure In order to use EOF( ) effectively, a database file must be in use in the current work area. (See USE.) EOF( ) returns a logical false (.F.) if there is no open database file.

EOF( ) returns a logical value and can be used anywhere in the language where a logical expression (i.e., condition) is appropriate.

Examples EOF( ) is used to process a database sequentially, record by record. There are many dBASE III PLUS commands that process an entire database file sequentially, but often you will want more control than any single command can give you. The following example updates the area code for a particular range of zip codes and displays each record that is changed:

```
* New_Zip1.PRG
*
SET TALK OFF
```

```
USE Customer
DO WHILE .NOT. EOF()
   IF "90029" <= Zip .AND. Zip <= "90037"
      REPLACE Phone WITH STUFF(Phone, 2, 3, "818")
      ? Last_Name, Zip, Phone
   ENDIF
   SKIP
ENDDO
CLOSE DATABASES
SET TALK ON
```

To execute this program and see its results,

```
. DO New_Zip1
Roman                  90029 (818)485-5955
```

You could accomplish the same thing with the following, much shorter routine, but it would take about twice as long because both REPLACE and LIST process the entire database file, while the previous routine processes the file only once:

```
* New_Zip2.PRG
*
SET TALK OFF
SET HEADING OFF
USE Customer
REPLACE Phone WITH STUFF(Phone, 2, 3, "818");
   FOR "90029" <= Zip .AND. Zip <= "90037"
LIST OFF Last_Name, Zip, Phone;
   FOR "90029" <= Zip .AND. Zip <= "90037"
CLOSE DATABASES
SET HEADING ON
SET TALK ON
```

To execute this program and see its results,

```
. DO New_Zip2
Roman                  90029 (818)485-5955
```

Warnings If EOF( ) is true and an attempt is made to SKIP, the error message *End of file encountered* is displayed.

Tips EOF( ) can be used to test the success or failure of a FIND or SEEK operation. If either of these commands results in a no-find situation, EOF( ) is set to True. This is not always true of the LOCATE/CONTINUE command pair because you can specify a scope that does not encompass the entire file. With all of these commands, it is better to use FOUND( ) to test the success or failure of the search command. FOUND( ) is designed to work with all of these commands and with SET RELATION TO. It also makes the code more readable and consistent.

ERASE

Syntax `ERASE <filename>¦?`

Overview The ERASE command is used to delete a single file from a disk; you must specify an extension as part of the file name. If the file is located on a drive or directory other than the default, you must also specify these as part of the file name.

The ?, or catalog query clause, can be used instead of a file name if there is an open catalog. (See SET CATALOG.) This activates a menu of all cataloged files from which you select the one you want to delete. The file is deleted from the catalog and from the disk.

Procedure Use ERASE to delete files that you no longer need and you will recover the disk space used by those files.

Examples The following routine uses the mailing list to put the local (i.e., 213 and 818 area codes) names and addresses in another file. It is assumed that the other file (Local.DBF) already contains other records that you want to keep, which means that you cannot simply COPY the records from one file

to the other. Instead, the program makes use of a temporary file to accomplish the task and deletes the file at the end.

```
* Local.PRG
*
SET TALK OFF
USE Mail

* Local records are put in a temporary file.
COPY TO TempMail FOR Phone = "(213)" .OR. Phone = "(818)"

* Records in the temporary file are added to Local file.
USE Local
APPEND FROM TempMail

* Temporary file is deleted.  Note the .DBF file extension
* must be specified as part of the file name.
ERASE TempMail.DBF

CLOSE DATABASES
SET TALK ON
```

Now if you USE Local, you will see all of the records from Mail that contained either area code (213) or (818) in the phone field.

Warnings

The message *File does not exist* is displayed if the file name that you are trying to ERASE cannot be found. This is a warning message rather than an error, and the message is suppressed using SET TALK OFF. Be sure to specify the correct drive, directory, and extension as part of the file name.

In dBASE III PLUS, you cannot delete a file that is open. If you attempt to do this, the error message *Cannot erase a file which is open* is displayed. Use the appropriate CLOSE command to close the file, and try ERASE again.

Tips

ERASE is designed to delete a single file at a time. It does not accept a file skeleton that enables you to delete several files using a wildcard symbol, but if you have enough memory, you can execute the DOS Erase command with RUN Erase <skeleton> to delete multiple files with a single command.

DELETE FILE is functionally identical to ERASE.

ERROR( )

Syntax `ERROR()`

Overview The ERROR( ) function has no arguments. The function returns the error number of the last error encountered by dBASE III PLUS. The error messages and their corresponding numbers are listed in the dBASE III PLUS documentation.

Procedure In order for ERROR( ) to work effectively, you must use it in conjunction with ON ERROR; otherwise, the function automatically returns a value of zero.

ERROR( ) returns a number and can be used anywhere in the language where a numeric expression is appropriate.

Examples ERROR( ) can be used when you want to trap particular errors and handle them programmatically. The following error routine traps the *Record is not in index* error, which has an ERROR( ) number of 20. The routine reindexes the active database file and returns to the calling program to RETRY the command that caused the error.

```
* Err_Trap.PRG
*
IF ERROR() = 20
   REINDEX
   RETRY
ENDIF
RETURN
```

To enable this routine so that it is invoked whenever an error is encountered, issue the following command either from a program or from the dot prompt:

```
ON ERROR DO Err_Trap
```

To clear the error procedure when you no longer need it, issue `ON ERROR` with no parameters.

Warnings Because of its simple syntax, there are no error messages associated with ERROR( ).

Tips If you clear the ON ERROR procedure as soon as it is no longer needed, it will not be triggered by an unrelated error.

EXIT. *See* DO WHILE

EXP( )

Syntax EXP(<expN>)

Overview The EXP( ) function, short for exponential, accepts any valid numeric expression as its argument. The function evaluates the expression and returns e raised to that power. Approximately equal to 2.71828183, e is the base for the natural logarithm.

Procedure EXP( ) returns a number and can be used anywhere in the language where a numeric expression is appropriate.

Examples EXP( ) is often used in statistical analysis; calculating the Poisson, the chi-square, and the normal distributions are several of its uses. The following routine displays a portion of the exponential table found in many mathematics textbooks:

```
* ExpTable.PRG
*
SET TALK OFF
SET DECIMALS TO 5
x = 1.00
CLEAR
? "         +----------+----------+-------------+"
? "         ¦    x     ¦ EXP(x)   ¦   EXP(-x)   ¦"
? "         +----------+----------+-------------+"
DO WHILE x <= 2
   ? x, EXP(x), EXP(-x)
   x = x + .05
ENDDO
SET DECIMALS TO 2
SET TALK ON
```

If you execute this program by typing `DO ExpTable`, you will see the following table:

```
+----------+----------+-------------+
|    x     |  EXP(x)  |   EXP(-x)   |
+----------+----------+-------------+
   1.00      2.71828       0.36788
   1.05      2.85765       0.34994
   1.10      3.00417       0.33287
   1.15      3.15819       0.31664
   1.20      3.32012       0.30119
   1.25      3.49034       0.28650
   1.30      3.66930       0.27253
   1.35      3.85743       0.25924
   1.40      4.05520       0.24660
   1.45      4.26311       0.23457
   1.50      4.48169       0.22313
   1.55      4.71147       0.21225
   1.60      4.95303       0.20190
   1.65      5.20698       0.19205
   1.70      5.47395       0.18268
   1.75      5.75460       0.17377
   1.80      6.04965       0.16530
   1.85      6.35982       0.15724
   1.90      6.68589       0.14957
   1.95      7.02869       0.14227
   2.00      7.38906       0.13534
```

Warnings If the function argument evaluates to a data type other than numeric, the the error message *Invalid function argument* is displayed.

Tips EXP( ) is the inverse of LOG( ) (i.e., EXP(LOG(x)) = x for every value of x).

EXPORT

Syntax

```
EXPORT TO <filename> [TYPE] PFS [FIELDS <field list>]
[<scope>] [WHILE <condition>] [FOR <condition>]
```

Overview

The EXPORT command is very similar to COPY TO. It copies records from the active database file to a new file using the format of PFS:File. By default, the new file has no file extension.

A scope, a FOR clause, and a WHILE clause can be specified to limit the records which are processed. Each of these command line options is discussed separately. (See Scope, FOR, and WHILE.) Unless one of these clauses is specified, all records in the active database file are copied.

If no format file is open in the current work area, the fields that are copied can be limited using the FIELDS list. (See FIELDS for a separate discussion.) By default, all fields except Memo fields are copied.

If a format file is in use when EXPORT is executed, the format file is used to determine which fields are copied and how the screen will appear when the new file is used in PFS:File. The essential difference between EXPORT and COPY TO is that EXPORT includes a screen format and COPY TO does not.

Procedure

Use EXPORT to copy records from the active database file to a file in the format of PFS:File.

Examples

The following example copies the entire Customer file to a PFS:File type file. When you use this file in PFS:File, the screen design will be the same as the default screen used by dBASE III PLUS because no format file is open.

```
. USE Customer
. EXPORT TO Cust TYPE PFS
     10 records copied
```

Next, a subset of the mailing list is copied to a PFS:File type file with a format file in use. Because the MailEdit format file is in use at the time the mailing list file is exported, the screen design that you see when you use this file in PFS:File is determined by the format file.

```
. USE Mail
. SET FORMAT TO MailEdit
. EXPORT TO Mail_It FOR ZIP = "900" PFS
      6 records copied
```

Warnings

If it already exists, the file that you EXPORT TO is overwritten without warning unless SET SAFETY is ON.

If you are using dBASE III PLUS in a network environment and the database file that you want to EXPORT is encrypted (see Protect), you must SET ENCRYPTION OFF (see SET ENCRYPTION) before issuing the EXPORT command. If you attempt to EXPORT an encrypted database, the error message *Database is encrypted* is displayed.

Tips

Use COPY TO to create file types other than PFS:File.

Expression

Overview

The term "expression" occurs very often in discussions of the dBASE language. The following representations of the term are frequently seen in the command and function syntax:

REPRESENTATION	MEANING
<condition> or <expL>	Condition, or Logical expression
<expC>	Character expression
<expD>	Date expression
<expN>	Numeric expression
<exp>	Expression of no specific type
<expression>	Expression of no specific type
<expression list>	List of expressions separated by commas

In simple terms, an expression is any value that takes on one of the four data types: character, date, logical, or numeric. In order to understand what an expression is, you must first understand how data types are assigned to the basic expression elements, which are fields, constants, memory variables, and functions.

You assign the data type of a field when you first design its database file structure. (See CREATE.) (You can specify memo fields as part of the file structure, but memo is not a true data type and is not included in this discussion.) (See memo fields.) The field is an example of the most simple expression in the dBASE language.

Another example of a simple expression is a constant. The data type of a constant value is determined by how it is represented. Although there is no constant representation for the Date data type, the rules for representing the other data types as constant values are listed below:

DATA TYPE	RULES FOR CONSTANT REPRESENTATION
Character	Any string of characters enclosed in single quotes, double quotes, or square brackets. "Debby Moody", '12345 #A$B (testing)', and [This is a character constant.] are all examples of character constants.
Numeric	Any string of digits with no intervening spaces. A leading sign and imbedded decimal point are optional. For example, 729, −345.634, and +0.875 are all numeric constants. No embedded commas or currency symbols are allowed in the number representation.
Logical	The letter T, F, Y, or N enclosed between two periods. For example, .T. represents a logical True and .n. a logical False. The letter may be uppercase or lowercase.

The third basic expression is the memory variable. (See Memory Variable.) You assign both a value and that value's data type to a memory variable when you create it. The commands that create memory variables and the data types of the memory variables that they create are listed below:

COMMAND	DATA TYPE OF MEMORY VARIABLE
ACCEPT	Character
AVERAGE	Numeric
COUNT	Numeric
INPUT	Same as expression the user enters in response
PARAMETERS	Same as corresponding WITH variable (see DO)
PUBLIC	Logical
STORE	Determined by expression type used (see STORE)
SUM	Numeric
WAIT	Character

The fourth basic expression is the function. The data type of the function is determined by the value that it returns. For example, LOG( ) returns a number; therefore, its data type is numeric. Note that all functions except IIF( ) return a single data type. The data type of the IIF( ) return value depends on the function arguments. (See IIF( ).)

You can form more complicated expressions by using the appropriate operators to string expressions together. The data type of an expression is ultimately determined by either the data type of the individual elements that go together to make it up or by the type of operator used to combine the elements. In general, you cannot perform an operation between two expressions with differing data types. The exception to this rule is described below under date and numeric operators.

Character operators Character operators connect two character expressions to form a more complicated character expression. You can then combine more complicated expressions to achieve higher levels of expression complexity.

OPERATOR	OPERATION
+	Concatenates the results of two character expressions.
−	Concatenates the results of two character expressions and moves the trailing blank spaces of the first string to the end of the resulting string.

Date operators Date operators are used to perform a special kind of mathematical operation using one date expression and one numeric expression to form a more complicated date expression.

OPERATOR	OPERATION
+	Addition
−	Subtraction

In each case, the numeric expression represents the number of days that is added to or subtracted from the date to arrive at a new date. The date expression must come first when using the subtraction operator.

Numeric operators Numeric operators are used to perform a mathematical operation using one or two numeric expressions to form a more complicated numeric expression.

OPERATOR	OPERATION
+	Addition and unary positive sign
−	Subtraction and unary negative sign
*	Multiplication
/	Division
**	Exponentiation
^	Exponentiation

The plus and minus signs can be used as signs that precede a single numeric expression. When used this way, they are called unary operators because they operate on a single number. A mathematical operator that operates on two numbers is called a binary operator. The subtraction operator can be used to subtract two date expressions and arrive at a number that represents the number of days between the two dates; this is considered a numeric expression.

Relational operators Relational operators are used to compare two expressions of the same data type to form a logical expression, or condition.

OPERATOR	OPERATION
>	Greater than
<	Less than
=	Equal
> =	Greater than or equal
< =	Less than or equal
< >	Not equal
#	Not equal
$	Substring

All of the relational operators except $ can compare character, date, and numeric expressions; $ can be used only with character expressions to determine if one string is contained in another.

Logical operators Logical operators are used to perform a logical operation using one or two logical expressions to form a more complicated condition.

OPERATOR	OPERATION
.NOT.	Changes a logical True to False and vice versa.
.AND.	Performs a logical AND between two values. If both are True, the result is True; otherwise, the result is False.
.OR.	Performs a logical OR between two values. If both are False, the result is False; otherwise, the result is True.

.AND. and .OR. are binary operators, and .NOT. is a unary operator. (In other words, .AND. and .OR. combine two expressions, and .NOT. operates on a single expression.)

The operators in each group have an order of precedence that is used when the expression is evaluated. This order of precedence guarantees that the method used to evaluate expressions is always the same.

The operators in character and date expressions are evaluated in order from left to right. Neither operator has precedence over the other.

The operators in a numeric expression are evaluated in the following order:

1. Unary signs
2. Exponentiation
3. Division and multiplication
4. Addition and subtraction

For each step, all occurrences of the named operator are evaluated in order from left to right before moving on to the next step.

For a condition, or logical expression, all relational operators must be evaluated first to determine their logical value. The logical operators are then evaluated in the following order:

1. .NOT.
2. .AND.
3. .OR.

For each step, all occurrences of the named operator are evaluated in order from left to right before moving on to the next step.

For any expression, you can override the order of evaluation by including parentheses around the parts of the expression that you want to be evaluated first.

Procedure

The dBASE language uses expressions more often than any other single element. For example, several commands have FOR and WHILE clauses as part of their syntax, both of which require that you specify a condition (i.e., logical expression). All functions require expressions as their arguments, and most commands require that you specify values in the form of an expression.

Whenever the language syntax calls for a particular expression type, you must be able to express correctly the value that you want to use, whether it is a constant, a field name, a memory variable, a function, or some valid combination of these elements that go together to form a more complex expression.

Examples

The following examples use the ? command to show how various expressions are formed and evaluated. The first set of commands listed on page 221 opens the mailing list file and establishes several memory variables using constant expressions of varying data types.

```
. USE Mail
. string1 = 'string one is a character memory variable'
string one is a character memory variable
. string2 = [so is string two]
so is string two
. number1 = 120
120
. number2 = -2
-2
. number3 = 1.5
1.5
. date = DATE()
08/26/87
. truth = .t.
.T.
. DISPLAY MEMORY
STRING1      pub   C  "string one is a character memory
                      variable"
STRING2      pub   C  "so is string two"
NUMBER1      pub   N          120  (        120.00000000)
NUMBER2      pub   N           -2  (         -2.00000000)
NUMBER3      pub   N          1.5  (          1.50000000)
DATE         pub   D  08/26/87
TRUTH        pub   L  .T.
    7 variables defined,       99 bytes used
  249 variables available,   5901 bytes available
```

The next set of commands demonstrates character expressions:

```
. ? string1 + string2
string one is a character memory variableso is string two
. ? string1 + " and " + string2
string one is a character memory variable and so is string two
. ? First_Name
MICHELLE
. ? First_Name + Last_Name
MICHELLE     SMITH
. ? First_Name - Last_Name
MICHELLESMITH
. ? TRIM(First_Name) + " " + Last_Name - string1
MICHELLE SMITHstring one is a character memory variable
```

The next set of commands demonstrates numeric expressions:

```
. ? (date - Birthday)/365
        26.93
. ? number1 * number2
                -240
. ? number1 * -number2
                 240
. ? -number1 * number2 / number3
                    160.00
. ? -number1 * number2 / number3 + 5
                     165.00
. ? -number1 * number2 / (number3 + 5)
                     36.92
. ? SQRT(number1) ** 5 / Age
   6067.08
. ? SQRT(number1) ** (5 / Age)
                                  1.58
```

The last set of commands demonstrates logical expressions:

```
. ? Age < 30
.T.
. ? Last_Name = "SMITH"
.T.
. ? First_Name = "Cathy"
.F.
. ? Last_Name = "SMITH" .OR. First_Name = "Cathy"
.T.
. ? Last_Name = "SMITH" .AND. First_Name = "Cathy"
.F.
. ? Last_Name = "SMITH" .AND. .NOT. First_Name = "Cathy"
.T.
. ? City = "Glendale" .OR. CITY = "Los Angeles" .OR. Zip = "29"
.T.
. ? EOF()
.F.
. ? EOF() .OR. RECNO() = 1
.T.
. CLOSE DATABASES
```

Warnings

The error message *Data type mismatch* indicates that you have used a valid operator to combine expressions of differing data types in an attempted new expression, (e.g., Name < = Number, or Name + Number).

The error message *Invalid operator* indicates that you have used an operator that cannot be used with the expression type that you have specified (e.g., Date / Number).

The error message *Variable not found* indicates that some basic element in the expression cannot be identified. Although dBASE III PLUS assumes that it is the name of a memory variable that you have not defined, this may not be the case. It may also mean that you are using a field name in the expression when its database file is either not open or is in use in an unselected work area, or that you misspelled a field or variable name. In a character expression, this error message may mean that you forgot to put quotes around a constant value.

The error messages *Not a character expression, Not a Logical expression*, and *Not a numeric expression* indicate that the command did not expect the type of expression you used.

Tips

You can include parentheses in any expression, even though you may not want to change the order of precedence used to evaluate the expression. Parentheses often make an expression more readable, especially when the expression has complicated conditions. For example, the following condition could be used with a FOR clause to LIST all customers who are due to pay their bill and have not, and those who are due to pay today:

```
Due_Date > DATE() .AND. .NOT. Paid .OR. Due_Date = DATE()
```

Since .AND. takes precedence over .OR., you do not need parentheses for this condition; however, parentheses make it easier to understand which conditions belong together.

```
(Due_Date > DATE() .AND. .NOT. Paid) .OR. Due_Date = DATE()
```

dBASE III PLUS does not provide the logical operator to do an "exclusive or" between two logical expressions, but you can create one using a combination of the operators that are provided. An exclusive or operation is True if exactly one of the logical expressions is True. Assuming that A and B represent the two expressions, use the following condition to get an exclusive or:

```
(A .AND. .NOT. B) .OR. (B .AND. .NOT. A)
```

FIELD( )

Syntax `FIELD(<expN>)`

Overview

The FIELD( ) function accepts any numeric expression as its argument. The function evaluates the expression and then returns the name of the field corresponding to that number in the active database file structure. The field name is returned in all uppercase letters.

Procedure

To use FIELD( ) effectively, there must be an open database file in the current work area. (See USE.) The function automatically returns a null string if there is no open database file.

FIELD( ) returns a character string and can be used anywhere in the language where a character expression is appropriate.

Examples

FIELD( ) can be used whenever you want to manipulate for display purposes the names of the fields in a database file. The following routine lists the field names in the Employee database file. The field names are formatted with an initial capital letter with the rest of the letters in lowercase.

```
* Fld_List.PRG
*
SET TALK OFF
USE Employee
x = 1
? "This is a list of the fields in the Employee database file:"
DO WHILE "" <> FIELD(x)
   ? LEFT(FIELD(x), 1) + LOWER(SUBSTR(FIELD(x), 2))
   x = x + 1
ENDDO
CLOSE DATABASES
SET TALK ON
```

To execute this program and see its results:

```
This is a list of the fields in the Employee database file:
Emp_code
First_name
Last_name
Salary
Address1
Address2
City
State
Zip
Phone
Hire_date
Ssn
Comment
```

Warnings

If the function argument evaluates to a data type other than numeric, the error message *Invalid function argument* is displayed.

Tips

FIELD( ) returns a null string if there is no corresponding field in the active database file structure.

FIELDS

Syntax `FIELDS <field list>`

Overview

The FIELDS phrase limits or expands the fields used by a particular command. The FIELDS keyword is followed by a list of field names separated by commas.

Commands that allow a FIELDS phrase as an optional part of their syntax operate on a default set of fields unless the FIELDS phrase is specified.

The default set of fields depends on the status of the SET FIELDS command. If it is OFF, the default field list is all of the fields in the active database file.

If SET FIELDS is ON, the default field list is defined by one or more SET FIELDS TO commands. Each SET FIELDS TO <field list> command adds the fields in the list to the existing fields list. The default fields list is all of the fields in this fields list that come from the active database and any of its related files.

Procedure

Use a FIELDS phrase with any command that allows it in order to limit or expand the fields which the command normally includes.

Examples

The following example uses a FIELDS phrase with LIST to include fields from the active database file and a related file. The Orders and Inventry file are related using SET RELATION TO.

```
. SELECT 2
. USE Inventry INDEX Part_No
. SELECT 1
. USE Orders
. SET RELATION TO Part_No INTO Inventry
. LIST FIELDS Part_No, Quantity, Inventry->Price
Record#  Part_No   Quantity Inventry->Price
      1  R-123            1           23.95
      2  B-254            2           65.99
      3  G-165            2           23.98
      4  R-123            1           23.95

. CLOSE DATABASES
```

Warnings

If you include a field name in the FIELDS list that is not recognized, the error message *Variable not found* is displayed. Remember that to gain access to a field in an unselected database file, you may have to specify the alias name of the file as part of the field name (e.g., <alias name> – > <field name>). Also, if SET FIELDS is ON, you can access only field names that are part of the SET FIELDS TO field list.

Tips

See SET FIELDS for more information on changing the default field list.

File Types

Overview

You will encounter various types of files in the dBASE command language. Some files are used to store your data, while others are used to manipulate data stored elsewhere. Many commands require that you specify file names as part of the syntax to indicate a new file that you want to create or an existing file that you want to use.

Wherever the syntax of a command or function calls for a < filename >, it is referring to one of the file types listed in Table 9.

TABLE 9

dBASE III PLUS File Types

DEFAULT EXTENSION	FILE TYPE	DESCRIPTION
BIN	Binary	A binary file is an executable program in binary form that can be loaded into memory (see LOAD) and executed (see CALL).
CAT	Catalog	A catalog file is a special form of database file that keeps track of which ancillary files (e.g., format, report form) belong to what database files. (See Catalogs, SET CATALOG.)
DBF	Database	A database file stores your data so that you can manipulate it in any way that you want. (See CREATE, JOIN, TOTAL, USE.)
FMT	Format	A format file is a special program file that contains only @ commands (see @...CLEAR, @...GET, @...SAY, and @...TO) and comments (see *). It is used with the full-screen editing commands (see APPEND, EDIT, INSERT, and READ) to determine what data is used and how the data is displayed on the screen. You can create a format file using MODIFY COMMAND if you explicitly provide the .FMT extension as part of the file name. (See CREATE SCREEN and SET FORMAT for more information on creating and using format files.)

Table 9 continues

DEFAULT EXTENSION	FILE TYPE	DESCRIPTION
FRM	Report form	A report form file stores report definitions that you design. (See CREATE REPORT.) The report is displayed with the REPORT FORM command.
LBL	Label form	A label form file stores label definitions that you design. (See CREATE LABEL.) The labels are displayed with the LABEL FORM command.
MEM	Memory variable	A memory variable file saves existing memory variables for later use. (See SAVE, RESTORE.)
NDX	Index	An index file allows you to view your database file in a particular order without having to sort the file physically. It is also used to locate records quickly in the database file based on the index key value. (See INDEX for information on creating index files; see USE, SEEK, SET INDEX, and SET ORDER for information on how to use them.)
PRG	Program and procedure	A program file stores a group of dBASE commands to do a task that you want to perform repeatedly. A procedure file is a special form of program file that stores up to thirty-two command groups that are individually identifiable. You can use MODIFY COMMAND or any other word processor to create program and procedure files. (See DO, PROCEDURE, and SET PROCEDURE for more information on the use of program and procedure files.)
QRY	Query	A query file stores a logical condition that you specify. (See CREATE QUERY.) Use SET FILTER TO FILE to activate the logical condition as a filter to your database file. (See SET FILTER.)
SCR	Screen	Screen files are used by CREATE SCREEN to generate format files. You use a screen file each time you activate CREATE SCREEN to design a new format file or to make changes to an existing one.

Table 9 continues

DEFAULT EXTENSION	FILE TYPE	DESCRIPTION
TXT	Text	A text file is any file that stores ASCII text. In dBASE III PLUS, you create a text file anytime you use the TO FILE option of a command. (See LABEL FORM, REPORT FORM.) SET ALTERNATE also creates a text file, as does CREATE SCREEN if you select the *Generate text file image* menu option. You can view the contents of a text file using TYPE and change its contents with MODIFY COMMAND as long as you explicitly specify the .TXT extension as part of the file name.
VUE	View	A view file stores a view that you design. (See CREATE VIEW.) Activating the view file with the SET VIEW command opens all of the files in the view.

Specify the name of the file that you want to use as a command line parameter. If the command is designed to create a new file (e.g., CREATE, CREATE QUERY, MODIFY COMMAND), you must know the rules for assigning a file name. A file name can be up to eight characters in length. The first character must be a letter; the remaining seven can be any combination of letters, numbers, and underscores. In almost every case (see COPY FILE, RENAME, and TYPE for exceptions), a default file name extension (see Table 9) is assigned to the file that you create unless you explicitly specify a different extension as part of the file name. It is a good idea to use the default extension; otherwise, you must remember the file extension whenever you want to use the file you have created. You can include a drive letter and/or path name before the file name if you want to locate it on a drive or directory other than the default. (See SET DEFAULT.)

If the command is designed to use an existing file (e.g., LABEL FORM, MODIFY REPORT), you must specify the file name that you assigned when you originally created the file. If you assigned a file name extension

of your own, you must specify it each time you use the file. If the file is on a drive other than the default (see SET DEFAULT) or in a directory other than the current one that is not in the path setting (see SET PATH), you must include the drive letter and/or path name before the file name.

There are three other file types listed in Table 10 that exist in dBASE III PLUS, but a user cannot control them. These files are created and used automatically.

TABLE 10

Other File Types

DEFAULT EXTENSION	FILE TYPE	DESCRIPTION
BAK	Backup	Backup database files are automatically created by CREATE SCREEN and MODIFY STRUCTURE if you save the changes. For your protection, MODIFY COMMAND creates a backup of the program (or other) file if you save the changes. If you decide after saving a file that you prefer the old version, you can recover the original file from the backup file. (See MODIFY STRUCTURE for an example.)
DBT	Memo file	A memo file is automatically created when you design a database file to include one or more memo fields. (See CREATE, MODIFY STRUCTURE.) This file is opened each time you USE the database file.
TBK	Backup memo file	In addition to making a backup database file, MODIFY STRUCTURE and CREATE SCREEN also create a backup memo file if you save changes made to a database file structure. (See MODIFY STRUCTURE for information on recovering a database file from a backup.)

FILE( )

Syntax `FILE(<expC>)`

Overview The FILE( ) function accepts any character expression as its argument. The function evaluates the expression and then tries to find a file with a name that matches the resulting character string. First, the current drive and directory are searched, then the path list specified by SET PATH TO is searched. If the file is found, the function returns a logical True (.T.); otherwise, it returns a logical False (.F.).

Procedure FILE( ) returns a logical value and can be used anywhere in the language where a logical expression (i.e., condition) is appropriate.

Examples FILE( ) is used to test for the existence of a file in order to prevent a program from resulting in an error condition. This can also be done using ERROR( ) in conjunction with ON ERROR, but using FILE( ) is more straightforward and less cumbersome. The use of this function is illustrated in the following routine which prompts the user for a database file name and tests for its existence before issuing the USE command:

```
* FileTest.PRG
*
SET TALK OFF
ACCEPT "Enter the name of your database file:" TO dbf_file
IF FILE(dbf_file + ".DBF")
   USE &dbf_file
ELSE
   ? "There is no database file called " + dbf_file
ENDIF
SET TALK ON
```

Warnings If the function argument evaluates to a data type other than character, the error message *Invalid function argument* is displayed.

If the function results in the error message *Variable not found*, you probably used a literal character string as the function argument and it is being interpreted as a variable name. The character string, in this case, must be enclosed in single quotes, double quotes, or square brackets.

Tips

FILE( ) is not case-sensitive to its argument, and has the same result whether or not the drive letter and path are specified for files in the current directory. This means that the file name can be entered any way you like, as long as the file extension is specified.

To test for the existence of a file in a directory other than the default, either put that directory in the path list with SET PATH TO or specify the path name as part of the file name.

To test for the existence of a file on a drive other than the default, either make that drive the default with SET DEFAULT TO or specify the drive letter as part of the file name.

SET SAFETY ON will prevent existing files from being overwritten without warning, but this command does not work with SET ALTERNATE TO. Use FILE( ) in order to warn a user when an alternate file is about to be overwritten.

FIND

Syntax `FIND <string>`

Overview

The FIND command locates the first record with a particular index key value in the active database file. The key value is specified as an unquoted string.

If the key value is a character string with leading blanks, you must put the FIND string in quotes and include the correct number of blanks at the beginning. Using quotes with other types of strings is optional.

Procedure

Use FIND with an indexed database file to locate a record with a particular key value in the controlling index file. (See SET INDEX or SET ORDER.) FIND can only be used if the index key is a character or a numeric data type. If your index key is a date, you must use SEEK instead.

Usually, you want to use FIND with a character memory variable, but the command expects an unquoted character string rather than a character expression as its parameter. Consequently, you must use macro substitution (see Macro substitution) to use FIND with a character type memory variable. Using SEEK with no macro is a preferable and faster alternative.

After FIND is issued, FOUND( ) can be used to determine whether or not the record was located. A WHILE clause can be used with any command to process all occurrences of the same key.

Examples

To illustrate the correct use of FIND, some examples follow that use various index files and methods for using the command:

```
. USE Inventry INDEX Part_No
. FIND b-254  && No find because "b" must be capitalized
No find.
. FIND B-254  && Correct the problem, and record is found
. DISPLAY Part_No
Record#  Part_No
      2  B-254
. key = "G-165"  && Use a memory variable for the key
G-165
. FIND key   && No find because FIND can't work with expressions
No find.
. FIND &key  && Using macro substitution corrects the problem
. DISPLAY Part_No
Record#  Part_No
      6  G-165

. key = "BL"  && You don't have to use the entire key value
BL
. FIND &key
. DISPLAY Part_No WHILE Part_No = key  && Show all BL records
Record#  Part_No
      5  BL861
      3  BL890
```

Next, an index that has a more complicated key is used. STR( ) is used to convert the Price field to a character string to be indexed with the part number. This example illustrates how to use FIND when the key field is likely to have leading blank spaces:

```
. INDEX ON STR(Price, 10, 2) + Part_No TO Prices
  100% indexed           6 Records indexed
. FIND 23.95  && STR() puts leading spaces in the key
No find.
. key = STR(23.95, 10, 2)  && Try using a memory variable
     23.95
. FIND &key  && No find because & strips leading blanks
No find.
. FIND "&key" && Quoting string forces FIND to use the blanks.
. DISPLAY Price, Part_No
Record#       Price Part_No
      1       23.95 R-123
```

In the above examples, macro substitution is used with FIND to illustrate how to use the command, but in each case, using SEEK is faster and requires fewer keystrokes. Macro substitution should be avoided whenever possible. (See SEEK for a programming example.)

Warnings

If you use FIND with a database file that does not have an open index file, the error message *Database is not indexed* is displayed.

The warning message *No find* is displayed if FIND is unsuccessful. You can suppress this message with SET TALK OFF.

Tips

SEEK was an improvement in the original version of dBASE III. FIND was left in the product only to maintain compatibility with dBASE II. FIND has almost no advantages over SEEK, and you will find that in almost all cases SEEK is much easier to use and more straightforward than FIND—especially in programs where the key value is stored in a memory variable. Another advantage of SEEK is that it uses an expression as its command line argument. As a result, you can avoid macro substitution in the command, and the command executes faster. For these reasons, it is probably a good idea to use SEEK instead of FIND. (You might want to use FIND, however, if you are working at the dot prompt and the key is not in a memory variable because you won't have to type the quotes.)

If you use FIND and know that the key value you are looking for has leading blanks (e.g., the index key expression uses STR( )), you must include the blanks. To do this, enclose the key value in quotes, even if you are using macro substitution. Since this method for using FIND with a memory variable is cumbersome, you would probably use SEEK with a memory variable instead. For example,

```
USE Mail INDEX Ages   && Ages is indexed on STR(Age, 3, 0)
age_var = STR(31, 3, 0)
FIND "&age_var" is equivalent to

USE Mail INDEX Ages   && Ages is indexed on STR(Age, 3, 0)
SEEK STR(31, 3, 0)
```

If there are multiple occurrences of the same key in your database file, FIND can only locate the first one. In order to process all occurrences of a particular key, use a DO WHILE loop with the SKIP command. For example,

```
FIND &key
DO WHILE key = KeyField
   <commands>
   SKIP
ENDDO
```

You can also use a WHILE clause with any command that allows it to process all of the keys. For example,

```
FIND &key
LIST WHILE key = KeyField
```

FKLABEL( )

Syntax `FKLABEL(<expN>)`

Overview

The FKLABEL( ) function, short for function key label, accepts any numeric expression as its argument. The function evaluates the expression and returns the name of the function key that corresponds to that number. Only the names of programmable function keys are returned by this function.

Procedure

FKLABEL( ) returns a character string and can be used anywhere in the language where a character expression is appropriate.

Examples FKLABEL( ) can be used with FKMAX( ) to program the function keys without knowing their names. This is useful when you want an application to be generic rather than machine specific, because not all machines address the function keys in the same way. The following routine prompts the user in order to program all the available function keys, and will work on any machine capable of running dBASE III PLUS. Each command is terminated with a semicolon (;) to simulate a carriage return. (See SET FUNCTION.):

```
* FKeys.PRG
*
SET TALK OFF
num_key = 1
DO WHILE num_key <= FKMAX()
   ACCEPT "Enter the command to perform when ";
          + FKLABEL(num_key) + " is pressed: " TO command
   SET FUNCTION FKLABEL(num_key) TO command + ";"
   num_key = num_key + 1
ENDDO
SET TALK ON
```

Warnings If the function argument evaluates to a data type other than numeric, the error message *Invalid function argument* is displayed.

Tips You can use the following routine to set all of the programmable function keys to null strings. This step can prevent unwanted results from an accidental keypress (e.g., user presses F2 during an EDIT and the word "assist" is entered into the database file record).

```
* Null_Key.PRG
*
SET TALK OFF
num_key = 1
null = ""
DO WHILE num_key <= FKMAX()
   SET FUNCTION FKLABEL(num_key) TO null
   num_key = num_key + 1
ENDDO
SET TALK ON
```

FKMAX( )

Syntax `FKMAX()`

Overview The FKMAX( ) function has no arguments. It returns the number of programmable function keys that are available.

Procedure The FKMAX( ) function returns a number and can be used anywhere in the language where a numeric expression is appropriate.

Examples FKMAX( ) can be used in conjunction with FKLABEL( ) to program the function keys without knowing how many are available on a particular machine. This is useful when you want an application to be generic rather than machine specific because not all machines have the same number of function keys.

The following routine prompts the user in order to program all the available function keys, and will work on any machine capable of running dBASE III PLUS:

```
* FKeys.PRG
*
SET TALK OFF
num_key = 1
DO WHILE num_key <= FKMAX()
   ACCEPT "Enter the command to perform when ";
          + FKLABEL(num_key) + " is pressed: " TO command
   SET FUNCTION FKLABEL(num_key) TO command + ";"
   num_key = num_key + 1
ENDDO
SET TALK ON
```

Warnings Because of its simple syntax, there are no error messages associated with FKMAX( ).

Tips The first function key is not programmable because it is reserved by dBASE III PLUS for help; therefore, if there are ten function keys on your keyboard, FKMAX( ) returns a value of 9.

FLOCK( )

Syntax `FLOCK()`

Overview The FLOCK( ) function, short for file lock, does not have any arguments. It can be used effectively only if you are using dBASE III PLUS in a network environment.

The function attempts to lock the database file in the current work area, all files to which it is related (see SET RELATION), and any index files that are open with these database files. If no other user on the network has a file or record lock (see RLOCK( )) on any of these files and, if no other user has exclusive use of any of the files (see SET EXCLUSIVE, USE), all necessary files are locked and the function returns a logical True (.T.). A separate file lock can be obtained for each work area that has an open file.

If any of the files cannot be locked, the function returns a logical False (.F.) and none of the files are locked.

Procedure FLOCK( ) is used in network programming to prevent a user from making mass changes to a database while others may also be changing data in the same file. Use file locking only if the file was opened with shared access (i.e., SET EXCLUSIVE was OFF when the file was opened and USE was issued without the EXCLUSIVE keyword). FLOCK( ) is unnecessary if you have exclusive use of the file, since no other user can open it (much less make changes to it).

One use of FLOCK( ) is to EDIT a block of records in a database file that meets a specific condition. If you do not lock the file before issuing the command, another user may change a record so that it no longer meets a specified condition. Once a file is locked, other users on the network can still open the file, but cannot make any changes. Locking the file ensures that the records you originally intended to EDIT are actually the records that you get.

To use FLOCK( ) in a program, you must first open all of the database and index files that you want to lock and establish the relationships between them. (See SELECT, SET RELATION, USE.) Next, you use FLOCK( ) in a DO WHILE loop that has a time-out capability. After the DO WHILE loop, check again to make sure that the loop did not time-out. If you obtain the file lock before running out of time, perform the commands that you want (e.g., EDIT FOR Last_Name = "Smith") and unlock the files. (See CLOSE, UNLOCK.) If you run out of time without obtaining the file lock, display an error message for the user.

Examples

The following example illustrates the correct use of FLOCK( ). The file is locked before issuing REPLACE to do a global update on the Salary in the Employee file.

```
* Raise.PRG
*
SET TALK OFF
SET EXCLUSIVE OFF  && Want shared access to files

err_flag = .F.

ON ERROR DO ErrTrap  && Trap any file open errors

* If someone else has exclusive use of this file, the ErrTrap
* program is executed.
USE Employee
ON ERROR  && disable error trap

* Exit program if file cannot be opened.
IF err_flag
   RETURN
ENDIF

time_out = 0

* Try to lock the file 100 times.
DO WHILE .NOT. FLOCK() .AND. time_out < 100
   time_out = time_out + 1  && Increment time_out variable
ENDDO

* If time_out equals 100, it means that the DO WHILE loop
* timed out without obtaining a file lock.  ErrTrap
* will handle this error also.
IF time_out = 100  && File lock was not successful
  DO ErrTrap
  RETURN  && Exit program if file could not be locked
ELSE  && Otherwise, the file lock was successful
  REPLACE ALL Salary WITH Salary * 1.1
ENDIF
```

```
UNLOCK  && Unlock file so that others can make changes
LIST Last_Name, Salary  && See result of REPLACE

CLOSE DATABASES
SET TALK ON
SET EXCLUSIVE ON  && Return exclusive flag to default
```

The ErrTrap program is listed below:

```
* ErrTrap.PRG
*

* This is the error trap routine for the program Raise.PRG.
* Only two errors are possible.  Either the database file
* Employee.DBF could not be opened because another user had
* exclusive use, or the FLOCK() routine timed out.

IF ERROR() = 108  && File is in use by another
  ? "Another user has exclusive use of the Employee file."
ELSE
  ? "File lock could not be obtained in 100 tries."
ENDIF
WAIT

err_flag = .T.

CLOSE DATABASES
SET TALK ON
SET EXCLUSIVE ON  && Return exclusive flag to its default value
RETURN
```

To execute this program and see its results if the file lock was successful:

```
. DO Raise
Record#  Last_Name             Salary
      1  SMITH               47577.52
      2  Corbbit             42583.45
      3  Roman               48083.20
      4  King                27503.55
      5  Moore               30615.33
      6  Richardson         135300.00
      7  MOODY              275000.00
      8  Schaefer            24186.06
      9  Long                63373.33
     10  Roberts             58451.55
```

Warnings

FLOCK( ) does not produce an error message if the file lock is unsuccessful because this is not considered an error. The function tells you with its return value whether or not it succeeded; you can continue to try the file lock until it succeeds.

Always allow for a time-out when using FLOCK( ); otherwise, your program will get stuck in an infinite loop if another user forgets to release a lock or close an exclusively used database file.

Note that certain commands in dBASE III PLUS (see BROWSE and UPDATE, for example) automatically attempt a file lock unless there is already one in place or the file(s) involved are being used exclusively. This may lead you to believe that FLOCK( ) is unnecessary, but this is not the case. FLOCK( ) allows you to control how an unsuccessful file lock is handled, whereas automatic file locking simply results in the error message *File is in use by another* if it is unsuccessful.

Unlike most other commands that operate on the entire database file, LABEL FORM does not attempt an automatic file lock before executing. (The reason for this is unclear since REPORT FORM does, in fact, attempt the automatic file lock). If you do not obtain a file lock manually using FLOCK( ) before running a LABEL FORM, the LABEL FORM will be interrupted if another user has a record lock.

Tips

FLOCK( ) always returns a logical True (.T.) if used with the single-user version of dBASE III PLUS. As a result, programs written for the network version can be used by the single-user version without producing an error.

Certain operations in dBASE III PLUS (see INSERT, MODIFY STRUCTURE, PACK, REINDEX, and ZAP) require that the database file be used exclusively. (See SET EXCLUSIVE, USE.) In these cases, using FLOCK( ) to lock the file is insufficient.

See RLOCK( ) for information on locking a single record at a time. FLOCK( ) and RLOCK( ) are unique among the dBASE III PLUS functions because they not only return a value but also perform an operation.

A user-controlled time-out provides a more flexible interface. If a file is locked, display a message stating that the program is waiting for a locked file and that the user can press a key to stop waiting. Then, enter a loop that tests for INKEY( ) while trying to lock the file rather than counting to a fixed number. (See INKEY( ) for more information.)

FOR

Syntax `FOR <condition>`

Overview

When you use a FOR clause as part of a command, you specify a logical condition that is evaluated for each record that the command processes. If the condition evaluates to true (.T.), the record is processed by the command; if it evaluates to false (.F.), the command ignores the record.

Procedure

Many dBASE III PLUS commands allow a FOR clause as part of their syntax. The command processes the records in the active database file unconditionally unless you use a FOR clause to impose a condition that each record must meet to be processed by the command.

Examples

The following example uses the LIST command with a FOR clause to list all people in the local Los Angeles zip code area with June birthdays:

```
. USE Mail
. LIST Last_Name FOR Zip = "900" .AND. CMONTH(Birthday) = "June"
Record#  Last_Name
      3  Roman
     18  Whiteside
```

The next example shows all of the people with a 213 or an 818 area code:

```
. LIST Last_Name FOR Phone = "(213)" .OR. Phone = "(818)"
Record#  Last_Name
      3  Roman
      6  Lester
     12  Schaefer
     14  Long
     17  Samuels
     18  Whiteside

. CLOSE DATABASES
```

Warnings The error message *Not a Logical expression* is displayed if the FOR condition evaluates to a data type other than logical.

Tips With database files containing many records, using a WHILE clause with an index file is faster than using a FOR clause. (See WHILE for more information on its use alone and with FOR.)

FOUND( )

Syntax `FOUND()`

Overview The FOUND( ) function has no arguments. The function determines whether or not the previously issued search command was successful. The search commands are LOCATE, CONTINUE, FIND, and SEEK. If the command was successful, the function returns a logical True (.T.); otherwise, it returns logical False (.F.).

Procedure To use FOUND( ) effectively, there must be an open database file in the current work area. (See USE.) Issue a search command to locate a particular record, then use FOUND( ) to test whether or not the command was successful. You can use the following program code skeleton with the LOCATE command to process all records meeting a condition:

```
USE <filename>
LOCATE FOR <condition>
DO WHILE FOUND()
   <commands>
   CONTINUE
ENDDO
```

FOUND( ) returns a logical value and can be used anywhere in the language where a logical expression (i.e., condition) is appropriate.

Examples FOUND( ) is used in conjunction with one of the search commands to determine its success or failure in accessing a particular record in the active database file. The following routine uses the LOCATE/CONTINUE command pair to find and examine all records in the Customer file with an outstanding balance in excess of $1000.00:

```
* Amt_Owed.PRG
*
SET TALK OFF
SET HEADING OFF
USE Customer
LOCATE FOR Amt_Owed > 1000
DO WHILE FOUND()
   DISPLAY OFF Last_Name, Amt_Owed
   CONTINUE
ENDDO
CLOSE DATABASES
SET HEADING ON
SET TALK ON
```

To execute this program and see its results,

```
. DO Amt_Owed
King                 1500.00

Moore                1500.43
```

Warnings Because of its simple syntax, there are no error messages associated with FOUND( ).

Tips FOUND( ) is evaluated separately for each of the ten available work areas. Within a work area, issuing a database command other than one of the search commands resets the value of FOUND( ) to False. Using SELECT to use a different work area, however, does not affect FOUND( ) for the current work area. FOUND( ) is designed this way to enable you to keep track of what is happening in more than one work area.

GETENV( )

Syntax `GETENV(<expC>)`

Overview The GETENV( ) function, short for get environment, accepts a character expression for its argument. This expression should evaluate to a character string that corresponds to a DOS environmental variable name such as "path" or "comspec". The function returns either the setting of the operating system environmental variable specified or a null string if there is no such environmental variable.

Procedure

GETENV( ) returns a character string and can be used anywhere in the language where a character expression is appropriate.

Examples

Use GETENV( ) whenever you want to access a DOS setting. For example, you may get the error message *Unable to load COMMAND.COM* when you attempt to RUN an external program from within dBASE III PLUS. (See !.) This message occurs because the DOS environmental variable "COMSPEC" is set to a directory, but the command interpreter, COMMAND.COM, is not located there. Use GETENV( ) as follows to determine where dBASE III PLUS is looking for the command interpreter:

```
. ? GETENV("Comspec")
C:\COMMAND.COM
```

Warnings

If the function results in the error message *Variable not found*, you probably used a literal character string as the function argument and it is being interpreted as a variable name. The character string, in this case, must be enclosed in single quotes, double quotes, or square brackets.

Tips

Although you can use GETENV( ) to examine the DOS path setting, dBASE III PLUS has its own path setting and does not use the DOS path. You can use the following commands to make the dBASE III PLUS path setting the same as the DOS path setting:

```
path = GETENV("path")
SET PATH TO &path
```

GETENV("COMSPEC") is the same as GETENV("comspec") because GETENV( ) is not case-sensitive.

GO

Syntax `GO¦GOTO [RECORD] <expN>`
`GO¦GOTO BOTTOM¦TOP`

Overview The GO, or GOTO, command moves the record pointer in the active database file to the specified record number. If the first form of the command, GO RECORD <expN>, is used, you specify the record number using a numeric expression. If the second form is used, you specify TOP or BOTTOM to move the record pointer to the first or last record in the file, respectively. If there is an index file engaged, this refers to the first and last records in the controlling index.

Procedure Use GO to gain access to a specific record in the active database file.

Examples The following routine is a record-editing routine that allows the user to navigate to the previous record, the next record, the first record, the last record, or a specified record number. GO is used to accomplish the latter three.

```
* MailEdit.PRG
*
SET TALK OFF
USE Mail

* Clear the screen and display the prompts for the edit screen
* only once.
CLEAR
@  2,19 SAY "M A I L I N G   L I S T   C H A N G E S"
@  6, 3 SAY "Name"
@  6,59 SAY "Phone"
@  7,13 SAY "(first)          (last)"
@  7,58 SAY "Birthday"
@  9, 3 SAY "Address"
@ 10,14 SAY "(street or post office box)"
@ 12,20 SAY "(apartment #)"
@ 14,23 SAY "(city)              (state)  (zip)"
@  3,17 TO  3,59

* Editing is done in an infinite loop.  The only way to get out
* is to select the Quit option when the menu is displayed.
DO WHILE .T.
```

```
@  6,11 GET First_Name
@  6,25 GET Last_Name
@  6,65 GET Phone PICTURE "(999)999-9999"
@  7,68 GET Birthday
@  9,11 GET Address1
@ 11,11 GET Address2
@ 13,11 GET City
@ 13,44 GET State PICTURE "!!"
@ 13,51 GET Zip PICTURE "99999"
@ 22, 0
@ 24, 0
READ

* After each record, initialize first menu prompt to one and
* execute the WhatNext menu program.
choice = "one"
DO WhatNext

DO CASE

   * Choice one is the Next record, so do a SKIP.
   CASE choice = "one"
      SKIP
      IF EOF()
         GO BOTTOM
      ENDIF

   * Choice two is the Previous record, so do a SKIP -1.
   CASE choice = "two"
      SKIP -1
      IF BOF()
         GO TOP
      ENDIF

   * Choice three is the Top record, so do a GO TOP.
   CASE choice = "three"
      GO TOP

   * Choice four is the Bottom record, so do a GO BOTTOM.
   CASE choice = "four"
      GO BOTTOM

   * Choice five is Record #, so the user is prompted for
   * a record number.
   CASE choice = "five"

      recnbr = 1
      @ 24, 0 SAY "Enter the record number that you want:";
              GET recnbr RANGE 1, RECCOUNT()
      READ
```

```
            * GO to the specified record number.
            GO RECORD recnbr

         * Choice six is to Quit dBASE III PLUS.
         CASE choice = "six"
            QUIT
      ENDCASE
   ENDDO
```

The WhatNext menu program is also listed below:

```
* WhatNext.PRG
*

* Initialize prompts for the menu.
prompt1 = " Next "
prompt2 = " Previous "
prompt3 = " Top "
prompt4 = " Bottom "
prompt5 = " Record # "
prompt6 = " Quit "

* Display menu in its initial state with instruction message.
@ 22, 0 GET prompt1
@ 22, 7 SAY prompt2
@ 22,18 SAY prompt3
@ 22,24 SAY prompt4
@ 22,33 SAY prompt5
@ 22,44 SAY prompt6
@ 24, 0 SAY "Use arrow keys to navigate and Enter to select."
DO WHILE .T.
   key = 0

   * Continuously poll keyboard for next key press.
   DO WHILE key = 0
      key = INKEY()
   ENDDO

   DO CASE

      * If the current menu choice is prompt1 and the Right
      * Arrow is pressed, or if the current menu choice is
      * prompt3 and the Left Arrow is pressed, prompt2 becomes
      * the current choice.
      CASE (choice = "one" .AND. key = 4) .OR.;
           (choice = "three" .AND. key = 19)
         @ 22, 0 SAY prompt1
         @ 22, 7 GET prompt2
```

```
   @ 22,18 SAY prompt3
   choice = "two"

* If the current menu choice is prompt2 and the Right
* Arrow is pressed, or if the current menu choice is
* prompt4 and the Left Arrow is pressed, prompt3 becomes
* the current choice.
CASE (choice = "two" .AND. key = 4) .OR.;
     (choice = "four" .AND. key = 19)
   @ 22, 7 SAY prompt2
   @ 22,18 GET prompt3
   @ 22,24 SAY prompt4
   choice = "three"

* If the current menu choice is prompt3 and the Right
* Arrow is pressed, or if the current menu choice is
* prompt5 and the Left Arrow is pressed, prompt4 becomes
* the current choice.
CASE (choice = "three" .AND. key = 4) .OR.;
     (choice = "five" .AND. key = 19)
   @ 22,18 SAY prompt3
   @ 22,24 GET prompt4
   @ 22,33 SAY prompt5
   choice = "four"

* If the current menu choice is prompt4 and the Right
* Arrow is pressed, or if the current menu choice is
* prompt6 and the Left Arrow is pressed, prompt5 becomes
* the current choice.
CASE (choice = "four" .AND. key = 4) .OR.;
     (choice = "six" .AND. kcy = 19)
   @ 22,24 SAY prompt4
   @ 22,33 GET prompt5
   @ 22,44 SAY prompt6
   choice = "five"

* If the current menu choice is prompt5 and the Right
* Arrow is pressed, or if the current menu choice is
* prompt1 and the Left Arrow is pressed, prompt6 becomes
* the current choice.
CASE (choice = "five" .AND. key = 4) .OR.;
     (choice = "one" .AND. key = 19)
   @ 22, 0 SAY prompt1
   @ 22,33 SAY prompt5
   @ 22,44 GET prompt6
   choice = "six"
```

```
     * If the current menu choice is prompt6 and the Right
     * Arrow is pressed, or if the current menu choice is
     * prompt2 and the Left Arrow is pressed, prompt1 becomes
     * the current choice.
     CASE (choice = "six" .AND. key = 4) .OR.;
          (choice = "two" .AND. key = 19)
        @ 22, 0 GET prompt1
        @ 22, 7 SAY prompt2
        @ 22,44 SAY prompt6
        choice = "one"

     * As soon as the user selects a menu choice using the
     * Enter key, exit the loop.
     CASE key = 13
        EXIT

  ENDCASE
ENDDO

* Since no READ is done for any of the @...GET commands, must
* do a CLEAR GETS.  GETs were used, in this case, only to change
* the display color and not to do data entry.
CLEAR GETS
RETURN
```

Warnings

The error message *Record is out of range* is displayed if the record number that you specify is either negative or larger than the actual number of records in the database file.

The error message *Record is not in index* is displayed if you attempt to GO to a record number that is not in the controlling index file. If you get this message, it probably means that records have been added to the database file without the knowledge of the index file. REINDEX and try again.

Tips

As a shortcut, you can simply use the record number instead of GO followed by the record number, but this shortcut works only if the record number is a literal number and not another numeric expression. This shortcut is useful when working interactively, but makes programs difficult to understand and should be avoided.

It is often necessary to do a GO TOP after using SET FILTER. (See SET FILTER for more information.)

GOTO. *See* GO

HELP

Syntax `HELP [<screen name>]`

Overview The HELP command is used to access the dBASE III PLUS help system, which is a series of named screens. When you are using HELP, the screen name is always located in the upper-right corner of the screen. If you know its name, any screen can be accessed directly by using the HELP <screen name>.

There is a screen for each dBASE III PLUS command and function that shows the complete syntax of the command or function, along with a brief explanation. Each of these screens can be reached using the name of the command or function. Enter `HELP <command name>` or `HELP <function name>` to get help on a particular command or function.

In addition to these screens, other screens describe dBASE III PLUS elements, such as expressions and operators. These screens are directly accessible and are listed in Table 11.

TABLE 11 **HELP Screen Names**

HELP SCREEN NAME	SCREEN DESCRIPTION
MAIN MENU	The main menu screen
STARTING	Getting started—Page 1
USING HELP	Page 2
HELP KEYS	Page 3
SYNTAX	Page 4
WHAT IS A ...	WHAT IS A ...? menu screen
COMMAND	Describes a command
EXPRESSION	Describes expressions—Page 1
EXP2	Page 2
CONDITION	Page 3

Table 11 continues

HELP SCREEN NAME	SCREEN DESCRIPTION
FIELD LIST	Describes a field list
FILES	Describes various file types
KEY FIELD	Describes a key field
MEMORY VARIABLE	Describes a memory variable
OPERATOR	OPERATOR menu screen
MATHEMATICAL OP	Describes the mathematical operators
RELATIONAL OP	Describes the relational operators
LOGICAL OP	Describes the logical operators
STRING OP	Describes the string operators
RECORD	Describes a record
SCOPE	Describes a scope
SKELETON	Describes a skeleton
HOW DO I ...	HOW DO I ...? menu screen
SAVING	Describes how to save a database file
CREATING	Creating a database file menu screen
NARRATIVE	Description of creating – Page 1
TYPES	Page 2
DEFINING	Page 3
CREATE EXAMPLE	Page 4
DATABASE NAME	Database file naming conventions
FIELD NAME	Field naming conventions
FIELD TYPE	Describes various field types
FIELD SIZE	Describes field width and decimal places
USING A DATABASE	Using a database menu screen
EDITING	Menu to editing commands
EXTRACTING	Menu to commands that extract data
INDEX/SORT	Menu to INDEX and SORT commands
LOCATING	Menu to commands used to locate records
RECORD COPY	Menu to copying commands

Table 11 continues

HELP SCREEN NAME	SCREEN DESCRIPTION
RECORD DELETE	Menu to deletion commands
COMMANDS/FUNCTIONS	Menu to all commands and functions
STARTER	Menu to starter commands
ADVANCED	Menu to advanced commands
DISPLAY CMDS	Menu to DISPLAY commands
LIST CMDS	Menu to LIST commands
MODIFY CMDS	Menu to CREATE ¦ MODIFY commands
FUNCTIONS	Menu to functions
DATABASE FUNC	Database functions – Page 1
DATABASE FUNC 2	Page 2
DATE FUNCTIONS	Date functions
ENVIRONMENT FUNC	Environment functions – Page 1
ENV FUNC 2	Page 2
ENV FUNC 3	Page 3
NUMERIC FUNCTIONS	Numeric functions – Page 1
NUM FUNC 2	Page 2
NUM FUNC 3	Page 3
STRING FUNCTIONS	String functions – Page 1
STR FUNC 2	Page 2
STR FUNC 3	Page 3
SET TO	Menu to SET...TO commands
SET ON/OFF	SET...ON ¦ OFF commands – Page 1
SET ON/OFF 2	Page 2
SET ON/OFF 3	Page 3
SET ON/OFF 4	Page 4

If you need help, simply access the appropriate screen. For example, if you want help on dBASE III PLUS field-naming conventions, enter HELP FIELD NAME.

Due to the lack of extra space on System Disk #2, there is not a separate HELP screen for each SET ON ¦ OFF command; instead, there is a series of four screens that briefly describe these commands in alphabetical order. For example, entering HELP SET BELL presents you with the SET ON/OFF screen, and entering HELP SET UNIQUE gives you the SET ON/OFF 4 screen. The same is true for the functions.

All help screens are available using HELP with no parameter. This calls up the main menu of the help system from which you make selections. The F1 function key is permanently set to "HELP;"; therefore, pressing this key is equivalent to entering HELP with no parameter.

Examples To get help with the syntax and use of the TOTAL command,

```
. HELP TOTAL
```

Your screen should look like the one in Figure 60.

Warnings If HELP does not recognize the screen name that you use as its command line parameter, no error message is displayed; instead, the main menu screen is displayed.

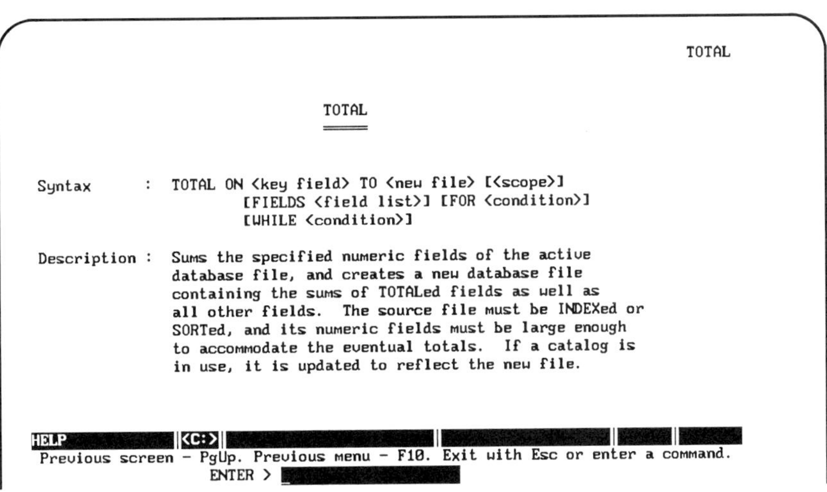

```
                                                              TOTAL

                                  TOTAL

Syntax      :  TOTAL ON <key field> TO <new file> [<scope>]
                       [FIELDS <field list>] [FOR <condition>]
                       [WHILE <condition>]

Description :  Sums the specified numeric fields of the active
               database file, and creates a new database file
               containing the sums of TOTALed fields as well as
               all other fields.  The source file must be INDEXed or
               SORTed, and its numeric fields must be large enough
               to accommodate the eventual totals.  If a catalog is
               in use, it is updated to reflect the new file.

HELP            <C:>
 Previous screen - PgUp. Previous menu - F10. Exit with Esc or enter a command.
                    ENTER >
```

Figure 60

If the help file, Help.DBS, is not on your disk, the error message *Help text not found* is displayed. This file is located on your original System Disk #2. If you want to use the help facility, you should copy it onto the same disk and directory as your other dBASE III PLUS system files.

Tips

If SET HELP is ON and you make an error in entering a command, you are prompted with *Do you want some help?* If you answer yes, you are presented with the same help screen as if you had entered HELP followed by the erroneous command. SET HELP OFF suppresses this prompt.

History Buffer

Overview

When you enter commands interactively at the dot prompt, the commands that you type are automatically recorded in the history buffer. By default, the last twenty commands that you have typed are saved in the buffer, but you can adjust this number to suit your needs. (See SET HISTORY.)

As you enter commands, they are saved in the buffer in LIFO (last in, first out) order. When the buffer is full, the oldest commands are pushed out of the buffer to make room for the new ones.

The history buffer saves time when you are working in the interactive mode. For example, if you enter a command that returns an error message, you would not want to retype the entire command just to correct two transposed letters. The history buffer allows you to correct your error rather than retyping the command.

Procedure

To retrieve any command that you have entered from the history buffer, press Up Arrow key until the command appears beside the dot prompt. The commands are displayed in LIFO (last in, first out) order. When the command that you want appears, you can use the full-screen editing keys (see Appendix A) to edit it just as you would edit a field or variable value. You do not have to edit the command unless you need to correct something. In other words, you can use the history buffer to reexecute the same command (or group of commands) a number of times.

A command from the history buffer is displayed as if you had typed it. Press Enter to execute it, and add it to the history buffer as the last command entered. After the command you enter is executed, you are returned to the dot prompt.

If you access the history buffer by accident and do not want to execute any previously entered command, press Ctrl-Y to erase the current line, or press Down Arrow until you get to a blank line.

See SET HISTORY for information on how to control which commands are recorded in the history buffer and which are not. See LIST HISTORY for information on how to view the contents of the history buffer.

Tips

Commands that you construct and execute from the Assistant (see ASSIST) are recorded in the history buffer just as if you had typed them at the dot prompt. (See SET DOHISTORY for information on how to record commands executed from a program or a procedure in the history buffer.)

IF

Syntax

```
IF <condition>
   <commands>
[ELSE
   <commands>]
ENDIF
```

Overview

The IF command indicates the beginning of an IF...ENDIF control structure in dBASE III PLUS. This control structure is designed to execute one of two sets of commands. The choice is based on the evaluation of a single condition that is part of the IF command.

The first set of commands is executed if the specified condition is true. These commands immediately follow the IF command in the control structure and continue until either the ELSE or the ENDIF statement is encountered.

The second set of commands to be executed if the condition is false is optional. If included, these commands must follow the first set of commands and must be preceded by an ELSE statement.

Procedure

Use an IF...ENDIF control structure to evaluate a condition and perform one set of commands if it is true and, optionally, another if it is false.

The statements that go together to make up the control structure must be arranged correctly in order for it to work properly. Begin with the IF command. On the following lines, continue with commands that are to be executed if the specified condition is true. After these commands, you may put an ELSE statement followed by the commands that you want to execute if the condition is false. Finally, mark the end of the control structure with an ENDIF statement.

You can nest other control structures (i.e., DO CASE, DO WHILE, and IF) inside of an IF...ENDIF structure.

All of the control structures are designed for use in programs (e.g., a command file or a procedure) and cannot be used at the dot prompt.

Examples

The following example illustrates the use of an IF...ENDIF structure with and without an ELSE statement. The routine allows you to edit records in the Customer database file based on the index key field, Cust_No. The IF...ENDIF control structure tests whether or not you enter a value. If you do not, the DO WHILE loop is terminated. Next, another IF...ENDIF tests whether or not the value you enter is in the file.

```
* Edit Cust.PRG
SET TALK OFF
USE Customer INDEX Cust_No
DO WHILE .T.  && Exit condition for this loop is below

   m_cust = SPACE(4)
   @ 10, 0 SAY "Customer number" GET m_cust PICTURE "@! A999"
   READ

   * If you do not enter a customer number, terminate the loop.
   IF "" = TRIM(m_cust)
      EXIT
   ENDIF  && Mark the end of the IF structure

   SEEK m_cust

   * After the SEEK, FOUND() function is either True or False.
   * If the customer number is FOUND(), EDIT the record and
   * CLEAR the screen.
```

```
      IF FOUND()
         EDIT NEXT 1
         CLEAR

      * If the customer number is not FOUND(), display a message.
      ELSE
         @ 12, 0 SAY "Record not found.  Please, try again."

      ENDIF  && Mark the end of the IF structure

   ENDDO
   CLOSE DATABASES
   SET TALK ON
```

Warnings

If the IF condition evaluates to other than a logical expression, the error message *Not a Logical expression* is displayed.

If you attempt an IF command at the dot prompt, the error message *Valid only in programs* is displayed.

If more than one ELSE statement is encountered in an IF...ENDIF control structure, all commands between the superfluous ELSE and the ENDIF are ignored because of the way in which the statements are executed. This is a logic error that does not cause an error message.

Neglecting to mark the end of a IF...ENDIF control structure with an ENDIF statement does not cause an error message; instead, all of the commands following the IF command are executed as part of the control structure because dBASE III PLUS continues to execute commands until it finds the ENDIF. For this reason and the one stated above, be sure that you construct this control structure properly.

Tips

The DO CASE...ENDCASE program control structure is an expanded version of the IF...ENDIF control structure. Use the DO CASE...ENDCASE structure when you want to choose from several possible conditions.

Using indentation with the IF...ENDIF structure (as with other control structures) makes it easier to identify in your program and allows you to see quickly that you have properly closed the structure.

IIF( )

Syntax `IIF(<condition>, <expl>, <exp2>)`

Overview

The IIF( ) function, short for immediate if, requires three arguments:

- A condition that is evaluated to determine what value the function returns.
- An expression that is evaluated and its value returned if the condition evaluates to True. This expression can be character, date, logical, or numeric.
- A second expression that is evaluated and its value returned if the condition evaluates to False. This expression must have the same data type as the first expression.

IIF( ) evaluates the condition and returns the value of the first expression if the condition is True; otherwise, the value of the second expression is returned.

Procedure

The data type of the result of IIF( ) is the same as the data type of its second and third arguments, which must be the same. It can be used anywhere in the language where the data type it returns is appropriate.

Examples

IIF( ) can be used to format logical values. For example, the following routine prints a reorder status report using the Inventry database file. The Quantity and Reorder fields represent the quantity on hand and the reorder point for a particular part. These amounts are compared using IIF( ) to determine if the part needs to be reordered. If the part needs to be reordered (i.e., Quantity is less than or equal to Reorder), "Yes" is printed in the Reorder column of the report; otherwise, "No" is printed.

```
* Reorder.PRG
*
SET TALK OFF
SET PRINTER ON
USE Inventry
? "          Reorder Status Report"
? "Part  Reorder?  Quantity   Reorder Point"
? "----- --------  ---------- ------------- "
DO WHILE .NOT. EOF()
```

```
   ?  Part_No, IIF(Quantity <= Reorder, "Yes", "No ")
   ?? Quantity, Reorder
   SKIP
ENDDO
EJECT
CLOSE DATABASES
SET PRINTER OFF
SET TALK ON
```

The resulting report is shown in Figure 61.

```
        Reorder Status Report
Part  Reorder?  Quantity   Reorder Point
----- --------  ---------- -------------
R-123 Yes          2           5
B-254 No           5           4
BL890 Yes         10          10
B-735 Yes         15          20
BL861 Yes          3           3
G-165 No           7           6
```

Figure 61

Warnings

If any of the function arguments evaluates to a data type other than what is expected, the error message *Invalid function argument* is displayed.

If you attempt to use this function with memo fields, the error message *Operation with Memo field invalid* is displayed.

Tips

Whenever possible, use IIF( ) to replace IF...ELSE...ENDIF constructs in your programs. The function will execute faster, making your programs more efficient. Also, use IIF( ) where the IF...ENDIF structure cannot be used, such as in report and label forms.

IMPORT

Syntax `IMPORT FROM <filename> [TYPE] PFS`

Overview

The IMPORT command is used to create a database file from a PFS:File type file. In addition to the database file, this command also creates a format file and a view file. All files that it creates have the same name as the PFS:File

file name, with appropriate extensions (i.e., .DBF, .FMT, and .VUE, respectively). The PFS:File file is assumed to have no extension.

The database file that is created has fields with names that are assigned automatically by the command. The first field is called Field01, the second is Field02, and so on. The format file that is created contains the field names you assigned in PFS:File, so that when you open the view file (i.e., the database file with the format file), your screen looks just as it did in PFS:File if you EDIT or APPEND records.

Procedure

Use IMPORT when you want to use an existing PFS:File type file to create a dBASE III PLUS database file. The command creates a database file, a format file, and a view file, and opens these files for your use.

To open the files at a later time, SET VIEW TO <filename>, where the file name is the same as the original PFS:File file.

Once the files are open, use APPEND to add new records, EDIT to change existing records, or use any other dBASE III PLUS command.

Examples

The following example imports a PFS:File file into dBASE III PLUS. DIR is then executed to show you the files that IMPORT created.

```
. IMPORT FROM Names TYPE PFS
     18 records added
. DIR Names.*  && Show all files created by IMPORT command
NAMES               NAMES.FMT           NAMES.DBF           NAMES.VUE

  35877 bytes in     4 files.
1564672 bytes remaining on drive.

. CLOSE DATABASES   && Closes the database and format files
. SET VIEW TO Names  && Opens the database and format files again
```

Warnings

If the named file cannot be found, the error message *File does not exist* is displayed. Note that IMPORT assumes that the file name does not have an extension. If it has an extension, you must specify it as part of the file name.

Tips

dBASE III PLUS also has the capability of reading other file types using APPEND FROM.

INDEX

Syntax `INDEX ON <key expression> TO <filename> [UNIQUE]`

Overview

The INDEX command creates an index (.NDX) file for the active database file. An index file is used to make the database file appear to be in a particular order. That order is determined by a key expression that you specify as a command line argument.

If the UNIQUE option is used, only the first record in the database file with a particular key value is indexed. In other words, once a key value is encountered, subsequent records with the same key value are ignored by INDEX. Without the UNIQUE option, all records are included in the index file.

INDEX leaves the newly created index file open with the database file in the current work area.

Procedure

Use INDEX to create a new index file for the active database file.

The key expression may be a single field name or any expression that involves at least one field. To make an index key that includes several fields of differing data types, use the appropriate conversion functions (see CTOD( ), DTOC( ), STR( ), and VAL( )) to construct the key expression (e.g., INDEX ON Last_Name + STR(Salary, 10, 2) creates an index key using a character and a numeric field). The key expression cannot involve memo or logical fields, and the resulting key must be the same size for every record in the file.

Do not use a key expression that may result in a key value that is not the same length for each record in the file (e.g., where TRIM(Last_Name) is five characters long for one record and ten for another). Ignoring this warning does not result in an error message, but the resulting index file will not behave as you expect.

Once the index file is created, you can open it (see SET INDEX and USE) along with up to six other index files with the database file. When index files are open with a database file, each one is automatically updated if you make changes to the database file. The database file is processed in order according to the controlling index. (See SET INDEX and SET ORDER.) If you use its key value, a record can be quickly located. (See SEEK and FIND.)

INDEX is needed only to create new index files. Once an index file is created, it can be kept up-to-date as long as you remember to engage it when making changes and additions to the database file. If you neglect to do this and an index file becomes inconsistent with the database file, use REINDEX to rebuild the index file.

Examples

The following examples show the effect of various index key expressions on the mailing list:

```
SET TALK OFF
USE Mail
INDEX ON Last_Name + First_Name TO Names
LIST Last_Name  && Lists in alphabetical order by Last_Name
INDEX ON Age TO Ages
LIST Age, Last_Name  && Lists in order according to Age
INDEX ON STR(Age, 2) + Last_Name TO Age_Name
LIST Age, Last_Name  && Lists in order by Age then by Last_Name
CLOSE DATABASES
SET TALK ON
```

Warnings

The INDEX ON key expression should not contain any memory variables, but no error message is displayed if it does. Instead, if you use a memory variable and it does not exist the next time you use the index file, the error message *Variable not found* is displayed for such operations as CHANGE, EDIT, and REPLACE.

If you are using dBASE III PLUS in a network environment, INDEX attempts an automatic file lock unless the database file is already locked (see FLOCK( )) or is opened for exclusive use (see SET EXCLUSIVE, USE). If the command cannot lock the database file for any reason, the error message *File is in use by another* is displayed.

If you use STR( ) as part of the INDEX ON key expression, be sure to include the length parameter. No error message is displayed if you omit this argument, but you will not be able to locate records using FIND or SEEK.

Do not use a key expression whose value may be of a different length for any two records (e.g., avoid STR( ) and SUBSTR( ) with a variable length argument, and never use TRIM( )). Although this does not cause an error message, you should avoid using variable length index keys.

The length of the index key expression cannot exceed 220 characters, and the length of the resulting key cannot exceed 100 characters. The error messages *Index expression is too big (220 char maximum)* and *Index too big (100 char maximum)* are displayed if these conditions occur.

When you INDEX on a character field and a date field together, you must convert one to the other to make up the index expression. Usually, the date is converted to a character string using CTOD( ). At first glance, this conversion may seem correct, but it does not work correctly. (See CTOD( ) for an explanation of this problem, as well as a good solution.)

Since SET DATE ANSI converts a date into a format suitable for ordering when concatenated with character strings, a natural use for this command might seem to be indexing dates with character fields. This will work correctly; however, if you choose this method, SET DATE ANSI must be in effect not only when the index file is created, but also whenever the index file is updated. Therefore, when you add records, the date will have to be entered as ANSI, which may not seem natural to a user. It is better to use the method described under the entry for DTOC( ) since this method works for all dates, regardless of the status of SET DATE.

Tips

INDEX opens the newly created index file in the current work area. Any other index files are closed by this command. If you want the new index and the other index files open, be sure that you issue SET INDEX TO after you create a new index file.

INDEX does not have an option to create an index file that is in descending order, but you can accomplish a descending order index if the key expression is numeric. Simply precede the expression by a minus sign when you create the index file. The following example creates an index file that is in descending age order:

```
USE Mail
INDEX ON -Age TO Age_Desc
```

If you INDEX ON one or more character fields, and the data in these fields is a combination of upper and lowercase letters, the order of the records in the resulting index may not be what you expect. Remember that INDEX uses ASCII order (see Appendix C), which means that all uppercase letters come before lowercase letters; thus,the name "SMITH" would come before "adams." If you want INDEX to ignore this distinction between capital and lowercase letters, apply either LOWER( ) or UPPER( ) to the key expression. (For example, instead of INDEX ON Last_Name + First_Name, use INDEX ON UPPER(Last_Name + First_Name).) Remember to use the same expression when you SEEK index key values.

INKEY( )

Syntax `INKEY()`

Overview

The INKEY( ) function has no arguments. The function returns a decimal number representing the ASCII code equivalent of the first keystroke that is stored in the typeahead buffer. Querying INKEY( ) removes the first keystroke from the typeahead buffer. If there are no keystrokes remaining in the typeahead buffer, the function returns a value of zero. The following table shows the INKEY( ) value for the non-printable keys:

KEY	INKEY()	KEY	INKEY()	KEY	INKEY()
Home	1	Enter	13	F1	28
END	6	Esc	27	F2	−1
⇧	5	Ins	22	F3	−2
⇩	24	Del	7	F4	−3
⇦	19	Ctrl ⇨	2	F5	−4
⇨	4	Ctrl ⇦	26	F6	−5
PgUp	18	Ctrl END	23	F7	−6
PgDn	3	Ctrl Home	29	F8	−7
Backspace	127	Ctrl PgUp	30	F9	−8
Tab	9	Ctrl PgDn	31	F10	−9
Backtab	15				

Procedure

INKEY( ) returns a number and can be used anywhere in the language where a numeric expression is appropriate.

Examples

dBASE III PLUS maintains a typeahead buffer that holds a certain number of keystrokes specified by SET TYPEAHEAD TO. This allows you to continue typing while another command is executing. INKEY( ) allows you to detect and utilize the keystrokes that are stored in this buffer.

A common use for this function is in designing menu systems that use the non-printable keys for navigation and selection. In general, the menu is displayed on the screen with adequate instructions for the user; the program is then put into an infinite loop which continuously queries INKEY( ) to determine the user's choice. For example, the following routine displays a menu bar on the first line of the screen and allows the user to navigate using the Left and Right Arrow keys as well as Home and End. Selections are made with the Enter key.

```
* Menu.PRG
*
SET TALK OFF
SET SCOREBOARD OFF

prompt1 = "Add"
prompt2 = "Edit"
prompt3 = "Quit"

DO WHILE .T.  && Display menu continuously
   CLEAR
   * The menu display always starts on prompt one.  GET is used
   * to enhance the display of the current prompt.
   current = 'one'
   @  0, 0 GET prompt1
   @  0,10 SAY prompt2
   @  0,20 SAY prompt3
   @ 21, 0 SAY "Use arrow keys to navigate and Enter to select."

   * Infinite loop that constantly updates the menu display as
   * the user navigates until a selection is made.
   DO WHILE .T.

      key = 0
      * Waits for a key to be pressed using INKEY() function.
      DO WHILE key = 0
         key = INKEY()
      ENDDO

      DO CASE
      * If prompt1 is highlighted and the Right Arrow is
      * pressed, or if prompt1 is highlighted and the Left Arrow
      * is pressed, highlight prompt2.
      CASE (current = 'one' .AND. key = 4) .OR.;
           (current = 'three' .AND. key = 19)
         @ 0, 0 SAY prompt1
         @ 0,10 GET prompt2
         @ 0,20 SAY prompt3
         current = 'two'
```

```
            * If prompt2 is highlighted and the Right Arrow is
            * pressed, or if prompt1 is highlighted and the Left Arrow
            * is pressed, or if the End key is pressed, highlight
            * prompt3.
            CASE (current = 'two' .AND. key = 4) .OR.;
                 (current = 'one' .AND. key = 19) .OR.;
                 (key = 6)
               @ 0, 0 SAY prompt1
               @ 0,10 SAY prompt2
               @ 0,20 GET prompt3
               current = 'three'

            * If prompt3 is highlighted and the Right Arrow is pressed
            * or if prompt2 is highlighted and the Left Arrow is
            * pressed, or if Home is pressed, highlight prompt1.
            CASE (current = 'three' .AND. key = 4) .OR.;
                 (current = 'two' .AND. key = 19) .OR.;
                 (key = 1)
               @ 0, 0 GET prompt1
               @ 0,10 SAY prompt2
               @ 0,20 SAY prompt3
               current = 'one'

            * If Enter is pressed...
            CASE key = 13

               * ...this nested DO CASE performs menu selection.
               DO CASE
               * If menu prompt one was selected, DO Add_Recs.
               CASE current = 'one'
                  DO Add_Recs
                  EXIT  && Exit to outermost loop to begin menu

               * If menu prompt two was selected, DO Edit_Recs.
               CASE current = 'two'
                  DO Edit_Recs
                  EXIT  && Exit to outermost loop to begin menu

               * If prompt three was selected, QUIT dBASE III PLUS.
               CASE current = 'three'
                  QUIT
               ENDCASE
            ENDCASE
         ENDDO  && End menu navigation loop
      ENDDO  && End menu display loop
      SET TALK ON
      SET SCOREBOARD ON
```

Warnings SET ESCAPE must be OFF to trap the Esc key with INKEY( ).

Tips Certain commands in dBASE III PLUS are designed to use the typeahead buffer themselves, and INKEY( ) is superseded by them. These commands are referred to as the full-screen commands and include APPEND, EDIT, and READ. READKEY( ) works with these commands to detect what keystroke was used to exit the full-screen mode.

INPUT

Syntax `INPUT [<prompt>] TO <memory variable>`

Overview The INPUT command waits for the user to enter an expression and creates a memory variable that stores the value of the expression. This is the only dBASE III PLUS command that allows you to enter expressions of any data type. Data entry is terminated by pressing the Enter key.

The type of memory variable created depends on what the user enters. For example, if the user enters the name of another memory variable or a field, the INPUT memory variable will be the same type as the memory variable or field; if the user enters a number, the memory variable will be numeric, and if the user enters a quoted character string, the memory variable will be character.

If used, the <prompt> is supplied in the form of a character expression. The expression is evaluated and the resulting character string is displayed on the screen in order to prompt the user for specific input.

Procedure Although INPUT is very flexible and can create memory variables of all types, it is most commonly used to prompt a user for numeric input and to save that input in a memory variable for later use. Use TYPE( ) to determine the data type of the expression entered.

Examples The following example uses INPUT after a menu is displayed on the screen in order to prompt the user for a selection:

```
* Inp_Menu.PRG
*
SET TALK OFF
CLEAR
```

```
DO WHILE .T.

* Menu is displayed using TEXT...ENDTEXT construct.
TEXT

          0 - Exit
          1 - Add Records
          2 - Edit Records
          3 - Print Reports

ENDTEXT

* choice memory variable is initialized to -1 so that it will
* pass the first time through the loop.
choice = -1

* The user is prompted until a value between zero and three
* is entered.  The cursor is positioned to line 10 before the
* INPUT command to make sure that the INPUT prompt is always
* displayed on line 11.
DO WHILE choice < 0 .OR. choice > 3
   @ 10, 0 SAY ""
   INPUT "Enter your selection " TO choice

   * If the user enters something other than a number, change
   * the variable back to a number, -1, and the loop will
   * execute once again.
   IF TYPE("choice") <> "N"
      choice = -1
   ENDIF
ENDDO

* The users response is evaluated in order to determine what to
* do next.
DO CASE
   CASE choice = 0
      SET TALK ON
      RETURN
   CASE choice = 1
      DO Add_Recs
   CASE choice = 2
      DO EditRecs
   CASE choice = 3
      DO PrtRprts
ENDCASE

ENDDO
```

INPUT introduces two difficulties into this program: it cannot force the user to enter a number (much less, an integer), and it is not capable of doing any range checking on the value entered. As a result, special tests for these situations had to be included in the program. The @...GET command offers greater control than INPUT and is the preferred method of input in most programs. In the above example, the innermost DO WHILE loop can be replaced by the following two commands:

```
@ 11, 0 SAY "Enter your selection";
        GET choice PICTURE "9" RANGE 0, 3
READ
```

Warnings

If used, the <prompt> must be a character expression. If you get the error message *Variable not found*, you probably used a literal character string as the prompt and did not enclose the string in single quotes, double quotes or square brackets. If the expression used for the prompt evaluates to a data type other than character, the error message *Not a Character expression* is displayed.

If you press Enter in response to the INPUT command without typing anything else, the command continues to prompt you until you enter a valid expression.

If you enter an invalid expression in response to the INPUT command, a variety of error messages are possible, the most common of which is *Variable not found*. If you get this error message, you probably entered an unquoted character string in response to the INPUT prompt, similar to the way you would with ACCEPT; however, since INPUT expects your response to be an expression, an unquoted character string is interpreted as a variable. If you want to enter a character string in response to the INPUT command, you must enclose the string between delimiters.

Tips

Since INPUT creates the named memory variable, you do not have to initialize it before the command is executed. In fact, if it does exist, the INPUT memory variable is overwritten without any warning.

Since INPUT has no real positioning capability, the prompt and input area occur on the screen at the current cursor location. However, you can use @...SAY to display a null value on the line before where you want the INPUT prompt to be displayed, and use SPACE( ) as part of the INPUT prompt to position it vertically. For example, if you want the prompt to appear on line 11 beginning in column 25, use the following sequence:

```
@ 10, 0 SAY ""
INPUT SPACE(24) + "Input a value" TO value
```

ACCEPT is very similar to INPUT, but only allows you to create a character type memory variable. (See ACCEPT for more details.)

INSERT

Syntax `INSERT [BEFORE] [BLANK]`

Overview The INSERT command allows you to insert a single record into the active database file. As one of the full-screen editing commands, it is able to make use of the full-screen cursor movement and editing keys listed in Appendix A. The record is inserted after the current record unless the BEFORE option is used.

The BLANK option inserts a blank record in the file without entering the interactive mode. If the BLANK option is not specified, INSERT enters the interactive insert mode which allows you to insert a single record interactively.

If the active database file is indexed, or if you INSERT a record after the last one in the file, INSERT is identical to APPEND and allows you to add multiple records to the end of the active database file.

The insert mode can be exited in one of three ways by pressing:

- Enter on the first character of the record. The record is not saved.
- Ctrl-End at any time. The record is saved.
- Esc at any time. The record is not saved.

Procedure Use INSERT when you want to keep the records in a database file in a particular physical order. Instead of using APPEND to add records to the end of the file, locate the record (e.g., use LOCATE or GOTO) before or after which you want the new record to appear. Then, use INSERT BEFORE or INSERT, depending on which command form is appropriate for your application. Do not use this command when you are also using index files.

If you are using dBASE III PLUS in a network environment, exclusive use (see SET EXCLUSIVE, USE) of the active database file is required to do an INSERT.

INSERT is seldom used because it is cumbersome to keep a database file in order using this method. One particular problem is the difficulty in determining where a record should go in the file. In general, it is much easier to have an index file that keeps your file in order and APPEND records to the end of the file; however, if your application calls for it, INSERT can be used to keep your database file in order.

If there is a format file open in the current work area, INSERT uses it as the APPEND and EDIT commands do.

Examples

The following example shows the difference in screen appearance using the INSERT command with and without a format file:

```
. USE Mail
. SET STATUS ON
. INSERT
```

Without a format file, the screen should look like the one in Figure 62.

Using the following commands to activate a format file can make the screen more attractive, like in Figure 63.

```
. SET FORMAT TO Mail_Add
. INSERT
```

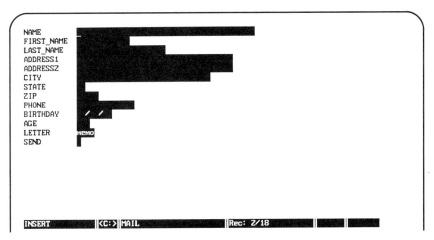

Figure 62

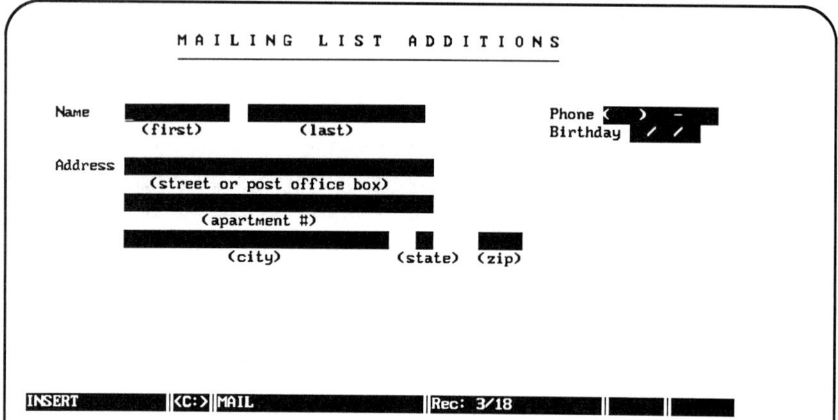

Figure 63

Warnings

If there are one or more index files in use with the active database file, INSERT is identical to APPEND in that you cannot insert records into an indexed database file but can add them to the end of the file.

The message *Record is not inserted* is displayed if you press a key that exits the insert mode without saving the new record (e.g., Esc or Enter on the first character of the first field). This is a warning message rather than an error. SET TALK OFF suppresses this message.

The interactive INSERT command carries the data from the previous record if SET CARRY is ON. In this case, pressing PgDn on the first character of a new record adds the new record instead of exiting the insert mode without saving the record. This is inconsistent with the way PgDn works when SET CARRY is OFF.

Pressing Ctrl-End while in the insert mode saves the blank record to the database file. To avoid saving a blank record to your file, either press Esc or press Enter on the first character of the blank record.

If you use INSERT in the network version of dBASE III PLUS, exclusive use of the active database file is required, and the error message *Exclusive open of file is required* is displayed if you attempt to INSERT a record into a database file that was opened for shared use. Either SET EXCLUSIVE ON and reopen the file, or reopen the file with USE <filename> EXCLUSIVE, and issue INSERT again.

Tips

Use a format file if the default screen provided for INSERT does not appeal to you. You can use CREATE SCREEN to design format files using a screen painter approach, or you can simply enter the appropriate @ commands in a text file with an .FMT extension using MODIFY COMMAND. SET FORMAT activates a format file for use with the active database file.

Instead of using INSERT to ensure a particular physical order in your database file, you can SORT the file to a new file, ERASE the original file and RENAME the new file to the original file name. For example,

```
USE YourFile
SORT ON KeyField TO NewFile
CLOSE DATABASES
ERASE YourFile.DBF
RENAME NewFile.DBF TO YourFile.DBF
```

INT( )

Syntax `INT(<expN>)`

Overview

The INT( ) function, short for integer, accepts a numeric expression as its argument. The function evaluates the expression and returns the integer portion of the resulting number.

Procedure

INT( ) returns a number and can be used anywhere in the language where a numeric expression is appropriate.

Examples

INT( ) can be used when you want only the integer portion of a number. The floor function, which returns the largest integer less than or equal to its argument, is not a part of the dBASE III PLUS language; however, it can be computed using INT( ):

```
* Floor.PRG
*
SET TALK OFF
INPUT "Enter any number: " TO number
IF number >= 0 .OR. INT(number) = number
   floor = INT(number)
ELSE
   floor = INT(number) - 1
```

```
ENDIF
? "FLOOR(", number, ") = " + LTRIM(STR(floor))
SET TALK ON
```

Warnings If the function argument evaluates to a data type other than numeric, the error message *Invalid function argument* is displayed.

Tips INT( ) returns the integer portion of a number by truncating all numbers to the right of the decimal place. Use ROUND( ) with zero decimal places to get the rounded integer. For example,

```
. ? INT(2.6)
  2
. ? ROUND(2.6, 0)
  3.0
```

ISALPHA( )

Syntax `ISALPHA(<expC>)`

Overview The ISALPHA( ) function requires a character expression for its argument. The function evaluates the expression to obtain the resulting character string and then returns a logical True (.T.) if that string begins with an alpha character (i.e., any letter of the alphabet, either lowercase or uppercase).

If the string begins with a number or some symbol other than a letter, ISALPHA( ) returns a logical False (.F.).

Procedure ISALPHA( ) returns a logical value and can be used anywhere in the language where a logical expression (i.e., condition) is appropriate.

Examples ISALPHA( ) is useful in data validation when the first character in a field or variable must be a letter. For example, the following routine uses ACCEPT, which, unlike @...GET, does not have its own data validation capabilities. The routine tests the input to make sure that it begins with a letter and continues to prompt until the input meets this condition:

```
* Code.PRG
*
ACCEPT "Enter the code: " TO code
* Continue prompting for the code until it is entered correctly.
DO WHILE .NOT. ISALPHA(code)
   ? "The code must begin with a letter.  Please, reenter."
   ACCEPT "Enter the code: " TO code
ENDDO
```

Warnings If the function argument evaluates to a data type other than character, the error message *Invalid function argument* is displayed.

ISCOLOR( )

Syntax `ISCOLOR()`

Overview The ISCOLOR( ) function has no arguments. The function returns a logical True (.T.) if the primary display is attached to a color graphics board; otherwise, it returns a logical False (.F.).

Procedure ISCOLOR( ) returns a logical value and can be used anywhere in the language where a logical expression (i.e., condition) is appropriate.

Examples ISCOLOR( ) is used to make programs that use SET COLOR TO compatible with both color and monochrome screen systems. This is useful if you want to make your application generic because you are not sure of what kind of system it will be used on. For example, the following routine sets up the color for a dBASE III PLUS session based on whether the program is running in color or monochrome mode:

```
* ColorSet.PRG
*
SET TALK OFF
IF ISCOLOR()
   standard = "R"
   enhanced = "GR+/B"
ELSE
   standard = ""
```

```
   enhanced = "U"
ENDIF
SET COLOR TO &standard, &enhanced
SET TALK ON
```

For a color system, this routine sets the standard display to red on black, and the enhanced display to yellow on blue. For a monochrome system, it leaves the standard display unchanged and makes the enhanced display underlined. Notice the use of memory variables to store the color values and the use of macro substitution with SET COLOR TO. (See Macro Substitution.)

Warnings Occasionally, a system has a monochrome monitor attached to a color graphics board. In this case, ISCOLOR( ) returns a .T., but you may be experimenting with SET COLOR thinking that you are dealing with a monochrome system.

Be aware that certain color settings can cause the standard display to disappear and cause the dBASE III PLUS system to appear locked when it is not. Even though you are unable to see what you are typing, enter SET COLOR TO with no further parameters to return the color settings to their default values.

ISLOWER( )

Syntax `ISLOWER(<expC>)`

Overview The ISLOWER( ) function asks, "Is the first character of this string a lowercase letter?" It requires a character expression for its argument. The function evaluates the expression to obtain the resulting character string and then returns a logical True (.T.) if that string begins with a lowercase letter.

If the string begins with an uppercase letter, a number, or any symbol other than a letter, ISLOWER( ) returns a logical False (.F.).

Procedure ISLOWER( ) returns a logical value and can be used anywhere in the language where a logical expression (i.e., condition) is appropriate.

Examples ISLOWER( ) is useful in data validation when the first character in a field or variable must be a lowercase letter. Although @...GET has a PICTURE function and template symbol to force letters to uppercase, there is no corresponding capability for lowercase letters. The following routine forces the input to lowercase if the first character is not a lowercase letter:

```
* Code.PRG
*
code = SPACE(4)
@ 10, 0 SAY "Enter the code: " GET code PICTURE "A999"
READ
IF .NOT. ISLOWER(code)
   code = LOWER(code)
ENDIF
```

Warnings If the function argument evaluates to a data type other than character, the error message *Invalid function argument* is displayed.

ISUPPER( )

Syntax `ISUPPER(<expC>)`

Overview The ISUPPER( ) function asks, "Is the first character of this string an uppercase letter?" It requires a character expression for its argument. The function evaluates the expression to obtain the resulting character string and then returns a logical True (.T.) if that string begins with an uppercase letter.

If the string begins with a lowercase letter, a number, or any symbol other than a letter, ISUPPER( ) returns a logical False (.F.).

Procedure ISUPPER( ) returns a logical value and can be used anywhere in the language where a logical expression (i.e., condition) is appropriate.

Examples ISUPPER( ) is useful in data validation when the first character in a field or variable must be an uppercase letter. Suppose that there is an ASCII text file with several record types, each of which is identified by a character in the first position of each record. If an uppercase letter in the first position indicates a newly hired individual, the following routine could be used to update the Employee file by adding the new hires from this text file:

```
* NewHires.PRG
*
SET TALK OFF
USE Employee
GO BOTTOM
last = RECNO()
APPEND FROM Master FOR ISUPPER(Emp_Code) SDF
GO last + 1
LIST REST Emp_Code, Last_Name, Salary
CLOSE DATABASES
SET TALK ON
```

To demonstrate the result of this program on the Employee database file, the file Master.TXT is listed before the program is executed.

```
. TYPE Master.TXT
A033David       Gurly                    45000.00
b123Perry       Lester
9870Doug        Smith
@143Wade        Adams
F375Lawrence    Arthur                   37389.00
A333Jeff        Potter                   47823.98
0178Jerry       Samuels
9999Chris       Whiteside

. DO NewHires
Record#  Emp_Code Last_Name                Salary
     11  A033     Gurly                  45000.00
     12  F375     Arthur                 37389.00
     13  A333     Potter                 47823.98
```

Warnings

If the function argument evaluates to a data type other than character, the error message *Invalid function argument* is displayed.

JOIN

Syntax
```
JOIN WITH <alias> TO <filename>
FOR <condition> [FIELDS <field list>]
```

Overview

The JOIN command merges two open database files together into a new database file.

When the command is executed, each record in the active database file is processed until the end of file is encountered. For each record processed, the FOR condition is evaluated for every record in the WITH database file. If the condition is true (.T.), a new record is added to the end of the TO database file. This implies that if there are ten records in one file and one hundred in the other, the resulting file can potentially have one thousand (i.e., 10 * 100) records.This command can be time-consuming with large database files.

If no FIELDS phrase is specified, the resulting file contains the union of the fields from both files (i.e., all fields minus duplicates) excluding all memo fields. If there is a duplicate field, it is taken from the active database file. Specifying a FIELDS list limits the fields that are included in the resulting file, but you cannot use memo fields in this list. (See FIELDS list for more information.)

Procedure

In order to JOIN two database files, you must first open both files in separate work areas. Use the SELECT and USE commands to accomplish this.

Then, issue a JOIN WITH the alias name of the unselected database file. The alias name is the name of the file, unless you specify another one using the ALIAS keyword with the USE command.

Next, specify a FOR condition. This condition usually compares a field in one file to a field in the other file for equality, but the condition can be any valid logical expression. Remember that you must use the <alias name> – > <field name> form if you want to use a field in the unselected database file as part of the FOR condition.

Finally, specify the name of the resulting file using a TO <filename> clause. You may also indicate which fields to include in the resulting file with a FIELDS list.

Once JOIN has executed, the two original files remain in use. To view the contents of the new database file, USE the file, and CLOSE DATABASES to close all of the files when you are done.

Examples

In the following example, JOIN is used to build a database file for all employees who make more money than their managers:

```
* More.PRG
* Creates a file of all employees who make more money
* than their manager.

SET TALK OFF

* Set up environment for using the JOIN command.
SELECT 2
USE Managers
SELECT 1
USE Employee

* The JOIN command uses a FOR condition to test if the employee
* works for a particular manager (Emp_Code = Managers->Mg_Code),
* and then if the employee's Salary is greater than that of the
* manager.  If both conditions are true, a record is written to
* the new file, More.DBF.
JOIN WITH Managers FOR Emp_Code = Managers->Mg_Code .AND.;
          Salary > Managers->Salary;
          FIELDS Emp_Code, Salary, Managers->Last_Name TO More

* New file is opened and listed, and all files are closed.
USE More
LIST
CLOSE DATABASES
```

If you execute the preceding program, you will find that four employees have a higher salary than their manager:

```
. DO More
Record#  EMP_CODE      SALARY LAST_NAME
      1  A254        43252.29 Simpkins
      2  A753        43712.00 Simpkins
      3  F876       123000.00 Johansen
      4  A935        57612.12 Simpkins
```

Warnings

Because of both the preliminary set up required in order to JOIN two files and the complicated syntax, several errors are possible.

If you neglect to open the file that you want to JOIN WITH in another work area, the error message *ALIAS not found* is displayed.

Unlike most other commands that allow a FOR condition as an optional part of their syntax, JOIN requires it. If you do not specify a FOR clause, the result is a *Syntax error*. This same error message occurs if you omit the TO <filename> clause.

If you use a memo field in the FIELDS list, the error message *Operation with Memo field invalid* is displayed.

If a variable name that you use as part of the FIELDS list or FOR condition is not recognized the error message *Variable not found* is displayed. Be sure to specify the alias name as part of the field name if you are using a field name from the unselected database file.

You may find that your application calls for a JOIN of a particular database file with itself, but dBASE III PLUS does not allow this. If you attempt such a JOIN, the error message *Cannot JOIN a file with itself* is displayed. To accomplish the JOIN of a file with itself, COPY the file to a temporary file, and JOIN the original file with the temporary one.

If you are using dBASE III PLUS in a network environment, JOIN attempts an automatic file lock unless the database file is already locked (see FLOCK( )) or is opened for exclusive use (see SET EXCLUSIVE, USE). If for any reason the command cannot lock the database file, the error message *File is in use by another* is displayed.

Also in the network version, you cannot JOIN an encrypted file WITH an unencrypted file. (*See* Protect.) If you attempt to do this the error message *Database is encrypted* is displayed.

Tips

The JOIN command does not require that you use any index files. In fact, having an INDEX file engaged slows down the execution of the command.

If the JOIN condition compares a field in the active database file to a field in the WITH file to see if they are equal, and if you do not want the result saved in a database file, you may find it more convenient to obtain the join using SET RELATION. SET RELATION requires an index file to be open but, other than this exception, is no more complicated to set up than the JOIN command, and is much faster. There is, however, a hitch to using SET

RELATION to obtain a join—the unselected database file must have unique index keys. (See SET RELATION for more information.)

If you are using dBASE III PLUS in a network environment and the database files involved in the JOIN are encrypted (see Protect), the new file is also encrypted unless you SET ENCRYPTION OFF (see SET ENCRYPTION).

LABEL FORM

Syntax

```
LABEL FORM <filename>¦? [SAMPLE] [<scope>]
[WHILE <condition>] [FOR <condition>] [TO PRINTER]
[TO FILE <filename>]
```

Overview

The LABEL FORM command is used to display the labels defined in a label file on the screen or the printer. Label files are created and changed using the CREATE LABEL command (see CREATE LABEL) and are assumed to have a .LBL extension.

The ?, or catalog query clause, can be used instead of a file name if there is an active catalog. (See SET CATALOG.) This activates a menu of all cataloged label files that belong to the active database file and allows you to select the label design that you want to use.

A scope, a FOR clause, and a WHILE clause can be used to display records that meet certain conditions within a specific range. Each of these command line options is discussed separately. (See Scope, FOR, and WHILE.) The default scope for LABEL FORM is ALL records in the active database file.

The TO PRINTER option prints the labels on the printer. The labels are displayed on the screen if the option is not specified. The labels can be directed to a text (.TXT) file using the TO FILE option.

The SAMPLE option is used to print sample labels. This option is normally used with TO PRINTER to ensure that the labels are properly lined up in the printer. A sample label is displayed using a series of X's to show you what the actual labels will look like. After each row of labels is displayed, you are prompted with *Do you want more samples*? If you want more samples, type Y. Otherwise, type N and the real labels are displayed.

Procedure

Use LABEL FORM to print labels that you have already defined using CREATE LABEL. The database file (or files) for which the labels were designed must be open. (See USE.) Before you issue LABEL FORM, any memory variables that are used in the label design must be initialized. (See STORE.)

Examples

In the following example, mailing labels are printed for all of the people in the mailing list who live nearby:

```
* Party.PRG
*
USE Mail
LABEL FORM Party TO PRINTER FOR Phone = "(213)" .OR.;
                                Phone = "(818)"
CLOSE DATABASES
```

Warnings

If the label file cannot be found, the error message *File does not exist* is displayed.

If you are using dBASE III PLUS in a network environment, be aware that, unlike most other commands that operate on the entire database file, LABEL FORM does not attempt an automatic file lock before executing. The reason for this is unclear, since REPORT FORM attempts the lock. If you do not obtain a file lock manually using FLOCK( ) before running a LABEL FORM, the labels will be interrupted if another user has a record lock. The label display will simply end and return you to the dot prompt without an error message as soon as it encounters a locked record.

Tips

If you issue LABEL FORM...TO PRINTER and the printer is not turned on- or off-line, one of two things may happen.

If the prompt *Printer not ready. Retry? (Y/N)* is displayed, you should correct the problem and then type `Y`. If you get this prompt and type `N`, the labels go to the screen.

Instead of this prompt, however, there may be a long pause with no warning message; the labels then go to the screen. If you turn the printer on before the screen display begins, the labels will print.

LABEL FORM is equipped with some features that make designing labels (see CREATE LABEL) much easier.

- The contents of each label line is truncated to the label width that you specify, rather than being wrapped around, preventing the labels from becoming misaligned for label lines that are too long.
- A field or expression list separated by commas, used as the contents of a label line in the design, gets special treatment when the labels are displayed—each expression in the list is trimmed of trailing spaces (see TRIM( )), and a single space is displayed between each field or expression. This feature prevents you from having to form a more complicated expression in the label design to accomplish the same task. For example, when you design the label using CREATE LABEL, instead of using TRIM(First_Name) + " " + Last_Name, you can accomplish the same thing using First_Name, Last_Name.
- Label lines that are blank are not shown as a blank line in the middle of the label. All blank lines are moved to the top of the label causing the non-blank lines to appear consecutively on the label.

LEFT( )

Syntax `LEFT(<expC>, <expN>)`

Overview

The LEFT( ) function, short for left substring, requires two arguments:

- A character expression representing the original string from which substring is to be extracted
- A numeric expression representing the number of characters to be extracted from the original string

After evaluating the expressions, the function returns the substring of the original string starting in the first position and extending right the specified number of characters.

Procedure

LEFT( ) returns a character string and can be used anywhere in the language where a character expression is appropriate.

Examples LEFT( ) is just a special case of SUBSTR( ) to be used when the desired substring is known to start in the first position of the string. Suppose, for example, that you want to display only the first twenty characters of a very long character field. The following two commands produce identical results:

```
? SUBSTR(Long_Field, 1, 20)
? LEFT(Long_Field, 20)
```

Warnings If the function argument evaluates to a data type other than character, the error message *Invalid function argument* is displayed.

If the numeric expression evaluates to a number other than an integer, the numbers after the decimal place are truncated before LEFT( ) is executed (e.g., 2.9 becomes 2, not 3).

LEN( )

Syntax `LEN(<expC>)`

Overview The LEN( ) function accepts a character expression as its argument. The function evaluates the expression to obtain the resulting character string and then returns the length of that string.

Since the length of character strings in dBASE III PLUS is limited to 254 characters, the result of LEN( ) is a number between zero and 254, inclusive. A result of zero indicates that character string is a null string.

Procedure LEN( ) returns a number and can be used anywhere in the language where a numeric expression is appropriate.

Examples LEN( ) is commonly used with TRIM( ) to determine if a character string is blank. The relationship between these functions is that the TRIM( ) of a blank string is always a null string, and the LEN( ) of a null string is always zero. The following example lists the contents of a mailing list database. Since the second address field is not always used, it is only displayed if it is not blank.

```
* MailList.PRG
*
SET TALK OFF
USE Mail
DO WHILE .NOT. EOF()
   ? TRIM(First_Name), TRIM(Last_Name)
   ? TRIM(Address1)
   * Address2 is displayed only if it is not blank.
   IF LEN(TRIM(Address2)) > 0
      ? TRIM(Address2)
   ENDIF
   ? TRIM(City), State, Zip
   ?
   ?
   SKIP
ENDDO
CLOSE DATABASES
SET TALK ON
```

Warnings If the function argument evaluates to a data type other than character, the error message *Invalid function argument* is displayed.

Tips To determine the length of a field, use LEN(TRIM(< field name >)). If you do not use TRIM( ), the result of LEN( ) will be the length of the field as defined in the file structure, rather than the length of the actual field contents.

LIST

Syntax

```
LIST [[FIELDS] <expression list>] [<scope>]
[WHILE <condition>] [FOR <condition>]
[OFF] [TO PRINTER]
```

Overview The LIST command displays the information in a database file on the screen or printer. Used with no parameters, LIST displays all of the fields for each record in the active database file with record numbers and headings (if SET HEADING is ON). Memo field contents are not displayed; instead, the word Memo is displayed.

A scope, a FOR clause, and a WHILE clause can be used to display records within a specific range that meet certain conditions. Each of these command line options is discussed separately. (See Scope, FOR, and WHILE.)

An expression list can be specified to explicitly state which fields are to be shown and to include other expression results (e.g., calculations involving fields, or memory variables) in the display. The expression list may be preceded by the FIELDS keyword, but this is not necessary since this is a list of expressions, not just fields. The only way to get LIST to show memo field contents is to include an expression list containing the memo field names.

The OFF keyword suppresses the display of the record number. TO PRINTER causes the display to be printed.

Procedure

Use LIST to view the fields in your database file. Use the expression list for including calculations involving the fields. Press Ctrl-S to pause and resume the listing.

Examples

The following example uses LIST to show both the part numbers that need to be reordered along with the amounts that must be reordered to restore the quantity on hand to the reorder point. The record numbers are suppressed using the OFF option.

```
. USE Inventry
. LIST OFF Part_No, Reorder - Quantity FOR Quantity - Reorder < 0
 Part_No  Reorder - Quantity
 R-123                    3
 B-735                    5

. CLOSE DATABASES
```

Warnings

If you have fields with the same name as other LIST keywords (e.g., HISTORY, MEMORY, STATUS), you won't be able to display them without using the FIELDS keyword. For example, a field named Status cannot be shown using the command, LIST Status, because this is another dBASE III PLUS command; however, you can LIST FIELDS Status. Refrain from naming fields with dBASE III PLUS keywords, and you will avoid such conflicts.

The contents of Memo fields are not displayed unless you explicitly specify the field names in the expression list as part of the command.

Tips

The TO PRINTER option prints the display, but it is still shown on the screen. SET CONSOLE OFF before doing a LIST TO PRINTER in order to suppress the screen output, and SET CONSOLE ON again after the command is executed.

LIST is very similar to DISPLAY except that the default scope for LIST is ALL records; another difference is that LIST is not interrupted with the *Press any key to continue* message.

LIST FILES

Syntax

```
LIST FILES [[ON] <drive>] [[LIKE] <skeleton>]
[TO PRINTER]
```

Overview Except for the TO PRINTER option and the fact that its directory listing does not pause, the LIST FILES command is functionally identical to the DIR command. (See DIR for more information regarding the use of this command.)

Tips Use DISPLAY FILES or DIR for viewing the directory on the screen and LIST FILES TO PRINTER for printing it. If you DISPLAY FILES TO PRINTER, the *Press any key to continue* message is also printed.

LIST HISTORY

Syntax

```
LIST HISTORY [LAST <expN>] [TO PRINTER]
```

Overview The LIST HISTORY command shows you the commands that are stored in the history buffer. The TO PRINTER option allows you to print the history buffer, and the LAST < expN > lets you specify how many commands you want to see.

Procedure Use LIST HISTORY along with SET DOHISTORY ON when debugging a newly written command file. If something goes wrong when the program is executing, you can either SUSPEND or CANCEL the program and use LIST HISTORY to determine what commands have been executed and in what order.

Use LIST HISTORY at the dot prompt to see what commands have been entered and to locate the position of a particular command in the history buffer.

Press Ctrl-S to pause the listing, and press it again to resume.

Examples

In following example, the LIST HISTORY command is issued at the dot prompt to show what commands have been executed so far:

```
. LIST HISTORY
USE Mail
LIST STRUCTURE
LIST STATUS
name = "Debby"
age = 27
birthday = CTOD("12/20/59")
female = .T.
LIST MEMORY
LIST HISTORY
```

Warnings

Unless you SET DOHISTORY ON, only commands that are issued at the dot prompt and from ASSIST are recorded in the history buffer. Remember this if you want to use LIST HISTORY for debugging a program.

By default, the maximum number of commands saved in the history buffer is twenty. You can change this using the SET HISTORY TO command.

Tips

LIST HISTORY and DISPLAY HISTORY are very similar commands. Use DISPLAY HISTORY for viewing the commands in the history buffer on the screen and LIST HISTORY TO PRINTER for printing them. If you DISPLAY HISTORY TO PRINTER, the *Press any key to continue* message is also printed.

Use SET CONSOLE OFF before LIST HISTORY TO PRINTER to suppress the screen output while printing. SET CONSOLE ON after the command has executed.

See ASSIST for an example on how to create a dBASE III PLUS command file using LIST HISTORY with SET ALTERNATE. (See History Buffer.)

LIST MEMORY

Syntax `LIST MEMORY [TO PRINTER]`

Overview The LIST MEMORY command is used to view the contents of the current memory variables. The result can be printed using the TO PRINTER option.

Procedure Use LIST MEMORY whenever you want to view the contents of your memory variables or when you want to find out how much space is available for new variables.

This feature is useful in debugging a newly written program to determine if the memory variables have the values that you expect at any given point. If the program is interrupted with SUSPEND, you can LIST MEMORY at the dot prompt, or you can imbed the command in your program at strategic points when you want to check on memory contents.

Press Ctrl-S to pause the listing, and press it again to resume.

Examples In the following example, LIST MEMORY is issued at the dot prompt after initializing several memory variables. Notice the number of bytes used by the memory variables that have been initialized. In dBASE III PLUS, numeric and date variables always use nine bytes, logical variables use two, and character variables use two more than their length. A default

```
. name = "Debby"
Debby
. age = 27
27
. birthday = CTOD("12/20/59")
12/20/59
. female = .T.
.T.
. LIST MEMORY
NAME        pub   C  "Debby"
AGE         pub   N          27  (         27.00000000)
BIRTHDAY    pub   D  12/20/59
FEMALE      pub   L  .T.
    4 variables defined,       27 bytes used
  252 variables available,   5973 bytes available
```

maximum of 6000 bytes is available for memory variables (see Config.DB for information on increasing this maximum); a maximum of 256 variables can be in existence at one time.

Tips LIST MEMORY and DISPLAY MEMORY are very similar commands. Use DISPLAY MEMORY for viewing the memory variable contents on the screen and LIST MEMORY TO PRINTER for printing this information. If you DISPLAY MEMORY TO PRINTER, the *Press any key to continue* message is also printed.

Use SET CONSOLE OFF before LIST MEMORY TO PRINTER if you want to suppress the screen output while printing. SET CONSOLE ON after the command has executed.

See STORE for information on how to create memory variables; see CLEAR MEMORY and RELEASE for information on how to get rid of memory variables that you no longer need.

LIST STATUS

Syntax `LIST STATUS [TO PRINTER]`

Overview The LIST STATUS command is used to view the status of the SET parameters and to see what files are open in which work areas. Any binary modules that you have loaded in memory (see LOAD) are also shown in the status display. If you are using dBASE III PLUS in a network environment, LIST STATUS also shows file and record locks. (See FLOCK( ), RLOCK( ).) The result can be printed using the TO PRINTER option.

Procedure Use LIST STATUS whenever you want to view the status of the SET parameters including the function key settings, the margin setting, any open alternate and procedure file, and the SET ON | OFF parameters. This command also shows what database files, index files, and format files are open in each work area, which is the controlling index, what the relationships between the files are, and which is the current work area.

Press Ctrl-S to pause the listing, and press it again to resume.

Examples

In the following example, LIST STATUS is used at the dot prompt to see what files are open and the status of the SET parameters:

```
. LIST STATUS

Currently Selected Database:
Select area:  1, Database in Use: C:Mail.dbf   Alias: MAIL
           Memo file:   C:Mail.dbt

File search path:
Default disk drive: C:
Print destination:  PRN:
Margin =     0
Current work area =    1

ALTERNATE  - ON    DELETED    - OFF  FIXED      - OFF  SAFETY     - OFF
BELL       - OFF   DELIMITERS - OFF  HEADING    - ON   SCOREBOARD - ON
CARRY      - OFF   DEVICE     - SCRN HELP       - OFF  STATUS     - OFF
CATALOG    - OFF   DOHISTORY  - OFF  HISTORY    - ON   STEP       - OFF
CENTURY    - OFF   ECHO       - OFF  INTENSITY  - ON   TALK       - ON
CONFIRM    - OFF   ESCAPE     - ON   MENU       - OFF  TITLE      - ON
CONSOLE    - ON    EXACT      - OFF  PRINT      - OFF  UNIQUE     - OFF
DEBUG      - OFF   FIELDS     - OFF

Programmable function keys:
F2  - assist;
F3  - list;
F4  - dir;
F5  - display structure;
F6  - display status;
F7  - display memory;
F8  - display;
F9  - append;
F10 - edit;
```

LIST STATUS and DISPLAY STATUS are very similar commands. Use DISPLAY STATUS for viewing the status information on the screen and LIST STATUS TO PRINTER for printing it. If you DISPLAY STATUS TO PRINTER, the *Press any key to continue* message is also printed.

Use SET CONSOLE OFF before LIST STATUS TO PRINTER if you want to suppress the screen output while printing. SET CONSOLE ON after the command has executed.

If you use SET VIEW to establish a view and you are unsure what files are involved and what their relationships are, use LIST STATUS after SET VIEW to find out.

LIST STRUCTURE

Syntax `LIST STRUCTURE [TO PRINTER]`

Overview

The LIST STRUCTURE command shows the structure (field numbers, names, types, lengths, and number of decimal places) of the active database file. The structure can be printed using the TO PRINTER option.

Procedure

LIST STRUCTURE is normally used at the dot prompt to see what fields are available in the active database file. This is useful if you forget a field name or its spelling.

Press Ctrl-S to pause the listing, and press it again to resume.

You can use LIST STRUCTURE TO PRINTER to get a printout of a database file structure for documentation purposes and use while programming.

Examples

In the example on page 296, an attempt is made to LIST the names and addresses in the mailing list but the result is an error message. LIST STRUCTURE is used to check the field names and the mistake is corrected.

```
. USE Mail
. LIST Last_Name, Address

Variable not found.
                                ?
LIST Last_Name, Address
. LIST STRUCTURE  && To find the correct spelling of address
Structure for database: C:Mail.dbf
Number of data records:       18
Date of last update   : 06/10/87
Field  Field Name  Type       Width    Dec
    1  NAME        Character     40
    2  FIRST_NAME  Character     12
    3  LAST_NAME   Character     20
    4  ADDRESS1    Character     35
    5  ADDRESS2    Character     35
    6  CITY        Character     30
    7  STATE       Character      2
    8  ZIP         Character      5
    9  PHONE       Character     13
   10  BIRTHDAY    Date           8
   11  AGE         Numeric        3
   12  LETTER      Memo          10
   13  SEND        Logical        1
** Total **                     215

. LIST Last_Name, Address1  && Correct spelling of address field
Record#  Last_Name            Address1
      1  SMITH                510 Mabel Street
      2  Corbbit              22 Winner Circle
      3  Roman                1922 Kant Street
      4  Gurly                P.O. Box 3640
      5  King                 447 Spring Road
      6  Lester               38 Merrily Circle
      7  Moore                88 Chris Street
      8  Smith                7902 Queen Road
      9  Adams                343 Sarah Drive
     10  Richardson           51 Constance Road
     11  MOODY                23 Clemson Drive
     12  Schaefer             1822 Hollywood Blvd.
     13  Arthur               703 Main Street
     14  Long                 242 Beach Road
     15  Potter               858 Laughing Lane
     16  Roberts              138 Briarpatch Road
     17  Samuels              4184 Maryland Road
     18  Whiteside            1432 Gentleman Avenue
```

Warnings

If SET FIELDS is ON, the fields in the active database file that are included in the fields list are indicated by a > symbol. Fields that are not marked are not accessible unless you SET FIELDS OFF or include them in the fields list with additional SET FIELDS TO commands. So, although you can see all of the field names in the structure listing, you may not be able to use all of them. If you attempt to access a field that is not in the SET FIELDS list, *Variable not found* or a similar error message is displayed.

Tips

LIST STRUCTURE and DISPLAY STRUCTURE are very similar commands. Use DISPLAY STRUCTURE for viewing the database file structure on the screen and LIST STRUCTURE TO PRINTER for printing it. If you DISPLAY STRUCTURE TO PRINTER, the Press any key to continue message is also printed.

Use SET CONSOLE OFF before LIST STRUCTURE TO PRINTER if you want to suppress the screen output while printing. SET CONSOLE ON after the command has executed.

LIST USERS

Syntax `LIST USERS [TO PRINTER]`

Overview

The LIST USERS command is available only if you are using dBASE III PLUS in a network environment. This command shows the computer (or user) names of all workstations on the network that are using dBASE III PLUS and indicates which user is at the current workstation.

The TO PRINTER option can be used to send the result of the command to the printer.

Procedure

LIST USERS is most often used interactively at the dot prompt to guarantee that all users are out of dBASE III PLUS (see LOGOUT, QUIT) before performing a crucial task, such as a daily backup. When the command is issued, all users who are still in dBASE III PLUS are listed, and the name of the user who issued the command is marked on the left by the > symbol.

Examples The following example illustrates the LIST USERS command:

```
. LIST USERS
  Computer name
  -------------
 >DEBBY
  TOM
  LEONARD
  CHRIS
  MARK
```

This listing tells you that there are five users on your network who are currently using dBASE III PLUS. The name of the user who issued this command is DEBBY. If the command had been issued from Tom's workstation, the result would have been

```
. LIST USERS
  Computer name
  -------------
  DEBBY
 >TOM
  LEONARD
  CHRIS
  MARK
```

Warnings Always use LIST USERS to ensure that no one is using dBASE III PLUS before uninstalling the dBASE ADMINISTRATOR. Continue issuing LIST USERS until you are the only user, then QUIT and do the necessary task.

Like all other commands that are intended for use in a network environment, LIST USERS is ignored if you are using dBASE III PLUS in a single-user environment.

Tips LIST USERS and DISPLAY USERS are very similar commands. Use DISPLAY USERS for viewing the user names on the screen and LIST USERS TO PRINTER for printing it. If you DISPLAY USERS TO PRINTER, the *Press any key to continue* message is also printed.

Use SET CONSOLE OFF before LIST USERS TO PRINTER if you want to suppress the screen output while printing; use SET CONSOLE ON after the command has executed.

LOAD

Syntax `LOAD <binary module filename>`

Overview

The LOAD command loads a binary (.BIN) file into memory and assigns a module name to it. The module name is the root portion of the file name (i.e., the eight letter file name without the extension or directory) that you LOAD; this is the name you use when you CALL the module.

Provided that you have enough available memory, you can LOAD up to sixteen different binary modules, and each can be a maximum of 32,000 bytes. dBASE III PLUS uses the size of the binary file to determine how much memory to allocate for it; therefore, the binary program must not allocate or use more memory than its actual size.

Procedure

To LOAD a binary program file and later execute it with CALL, you must first design and write the program. When designing your program, be sure that it conforms to the following rules:

- The program must ORG the first executable instruction at an offset of zero.
- If the program is to be called with a memory variable parameter (see CALL...WITH), it must not change the length of the memory variable. The DS (data segment) and BX registers contain the address of the first byte of the WITH parameter.
- It must restore the CS (code segment) and SS (stack segment) registers before returning to dBASE III PLUS.
- When the program returns control to dBASE III PLUS, it must use a far return rather than an exit call. Programs that use an exit call can be executed from dBASE III PLUS using RUN, but not with LOAD and CALL.

Once the program is loaded into memory, it is executed using CALL. RELEASE MODULE removes the module from memory when you are finished using it.

Examples

The following assembly language program, Redirect.ASM, redirects all printer output to a text file. It works with SET PRINTER and SET DEVICE. Using this program, you can send the result of the @...SAY command to a file:

```
;  Redirect.asm
;
;  by Leonard Zerman
;
;  Placed in the public domain by Tom Rettig Associates, 1987.
;----------------------------------------------------------------
;
;  Syntax: CALL REDIRECT WITH <Filespec> ¦ ""
;
;  Notes: This is a .BIN file to be LOADed into dBASE III PLUS.
;         It redirects all printer output to a specified disk
;         file.  This includes all @...SAYs, ? commands, and
;         anything else that would normally go to the printer.
;
;         If the specified file exists, it will be overwritten
;         without warning; otherwise, it will simply be created.
;
;         If an error occurs writing the file, an asterisk will
;         replace the first character in the file name as an
;         error message.
;
;         If a null character ("") is specified in place of a
;         file name, any previous redirection is cancelled.
;
;         Example of use:
;
;            * Open a file to receive redirected output.
;            memvar = "Filename.txt"
;            CALL REDIRECT WITH memvar
;            IF memvar = "*ilename.txt"
;               ? "Error: Redirected file could not be opened."
;               RETURN
;            ENDIF
;
```

```
;           * Formatted output.
;           SET DEVICE TO PRINTER
;           <@...SAY commands redirected from printer to file>
;           SET DEVICE TO SCREEN
;
;           * Unformatted output.
;           SET PRINTER ON
;           <? and TEXT commands redirected from printer to file>
;           SET PRINTER OFF
;
;           * Close redirected file.
;           CALL REDIRECT WITH ""
;           IF memvar = "*ilename.txt"
;              ? "Error: Redirected file could not be closed."
;              RETURN
;           ENDIF
;
;----------------------------------------------------------------

;----------- assign names to constants -------------------------
stdprn          equ     04h     ; printer's file handle
dos_int         equ     21h     ; dos interrupt number
file_create     equ     3Ch     ; create file function
file_close      equ     3Eh     ; close file function
file_attrib     equ     00h     ; normal (read/write) mode
file_write      equ     40h     ; file write function
dup_handle      equ     45h     ; get dupe file handle function
force_dup       equ     46h     ; force dupe handle function
toggle_switch   equ     0FFh    ; toggles is_file_open on/off

;----------- code area -----------------------------------------
prog        segment
            assume  cs:prog, ds:prog  ; data/code share segment

redirect        proc    far           ; force a far return

                jmp     start         ; jump over data storage

; Reserve data storage in code segment.
old_handle      dw      ?       ; storage for old prn handle
new_handle      dw      ?       ; storage for new file handle
is_file_open    db      0       ; is file redirected flag
parm_ptr        dw      ?       ; offset from ds points to parm
eof             db      0Dh,0Ah,1Ah ; cr, lf, and eof bytes
```

```
start:          push    ds          ; save the registers that
                push    dx          ; will be used
                push    cx
                push    bx
                push    ax

                mov     cs:parm_ptr,bx       ; save parm pointer
chk_file_open:  mov     al,cs:is_file_open   ; check to see if we
                or      al,al                ; are now redirected
                jnz     file_is_open         ; if now redirected

open_file:      mov     dx,cs:parm_ptr    ; point to file name
                mov     ah,file_create    ; file create function
                mov     cx,file_attrib    ; read/write mode
                int     dos_int           ; create the file
                jc      error             ; error opening file

                mov     cs:new_handle,ax ; save the file handle
                or      cs:is_file_open,toggle_switch
                                          ; toggle we are active

redir_out:      mov     ah,dup_handle     ; get dupe file handle
                mov     bx,stdprn         ; of the stdprn handle
                int     dos_int
                jc      error
                mov     cs:old_handle,ax ; dupe handle in ax
                mov     ah,force_dup      ; swap handles
                mov     bx,cs:new_handle ; swap file with prn
                mov     cx,stdprn         ; to redirect file
                int     dos_int
                jc      error
                jmp     exit

file_is_open:
swap_back:      push    ds                    ; write cr,lf,eof bytes
                mov     ah,file_write
                mov     bx,cs:new_handle
                mov     cx,3
                mov     dx,cs
                mov     ds,dx
                mov     dx,offset cs:eof
                int     dos_int
                pop     ds
                jc      error
```

```
                mov     ah,force_dup       ; force dupe back to prn
                mov     bx,cs:old_handle   ; swap handles back
                mov     cx,stdprn
                int     dos_int
                jc      error

close_file:     mov     ah,file_close      ; close the old_handle
                mov     bx,cs:old_handle
                int     dos_int
                jc      error

                mov     ah,file_close      ; close the disk file
                mov     bx,cs:new_handle
                int     dos_int
                jc      error

                mov     bx,cs:parm_ptr     ; ds:bx points to filename
                cmp     byte ptr [bx],0    ; if null passed, close
                jnz     open_file          ; or else open new file
                mov     cs:is_file_open,0  ; reset redirected flag
                jmp     exit

error:          mov     bx,cs:parm_ptr     ; put * in filename
                mov     byte ptr [bx],'*'  ;   if any error

exit:           pop     ax                 ; restore all registers
                pop     bx
                pop     cx
                pop     dx
                pop     ds
                ret                        ; far return is forced

redirect        endp                       ; end procedure

prog            ends                       ; end code segment
                end                        ; end file
;----------- eof redirect --------------------------------------
```

To LOAD this assembly language program into dBASE III PLUS, it must be assembled, linked, and turned into a binary file. The following commands are issued from DOS to create a binary file:

```
C> MASM Redirect;
C> LINK Redirect;
C> EXE2BIN Redirect
```

The following example illustrates how to use this binary file in dBASE III PLUS:

```
* AtToFile.PRG
* This program uses the assembly language program, Redirect, to
* send the result of @...SAY commands to a file when SET DEVICE
* TO PRINTER is in effect.

SET TALK OFF
LOAD Redirect  && Loads binary program, Redirect.BIN, into memory

* Execute binary program with the file name, Atsay.TXT, as a
* parameter.
filename = "Atsay.TXT"
CALL Redirect WITH filename

* Error check to make sure that the binary program was able to
* successfully open the file.
IF filename = "*ilename.txt"
   ? "Error: Redirected file could not be opened."
   RELEASE MODULE Redirect  && Release binary file from memory
   RETURN
ENDIF

* Formatted output is now sent to the file Atsay.TXT instead of
* to the printer.
SET DEVICE TO PRINTER
@ 10, 0 SAY "This is an example"
@ 12, 5 SAY "just to show how the binary program"
@ 15, 2 SAY "Redirect.BIN works"
SET DEVICE TO SCREEN

* Close the file so that printed output is no longer redirected
* to a file by calling the binary file with a null parameter.
CALL Redirect WITH ""

* Error check to make sure that the binary program was able to
* successfully close the file.
IF filename = "*ilename.txt"
```

```
   ? "Error: Redirected file could not be closed."
   RELEASE MODULE Redirect  && Release binary file from memory
   RETURN
ENDIF

RELEASE MODULE Redirect  && Release binary file from memory
TYPE Atsay.TXT  && Show the resulting text file contents
SET TALK ON
```

If you execute this program, you get the following result:

```
. DO AtToFile

This is an example

     just to show how the binary program

  Redirect.BIN works
```

Warnings

If you do not specify another extension as part of the file name, LOAD assumes that the binary file has a .BIN extension. Because of the way the command assigns the module name, you can see that if you LOAD a binary file with the same name as one that you have previously loaded (but with a different extension) the second one will have the same module name as the first. In fact, the second module takes the place of the first module in memory. There is no warning.

LOAD does not check the integrity of the binary file before loading it into memory. You must be sure that the program functions properly before using LOAD and CALL to execute it from within dBASE III PLUS.

Tips

The DOS operating system comes equipped with a linker and an executable-to-binary file conversion program. If you also have access to a macro assembler, you can use these tools in order to create a .BIN file from an assembly language (8086/8088) program, using the following as a guideline:

```
MASM <assembly program filename>;
LINK <object filename>;
EXE2BIN <executable filename>
```

The MASM program assembles the program and creates an object (.OBJ) file. LINK creates an executable (.EXE) file from the object file. EXE2BIN converts the executable file to a binary (.BIN) file.

See your DOS manual or other documentation for more information on using these utility programs.

LOCATE

Syntax `LOCATE [<scope>] [WHILE <condition>] [FOR <condition>]`

Overview

The LOCATE command finds the first record in the active database file that meets a condition that you specify (usually in the form of a FOR clause). A scope and a WHILE clause can also be specified to limit the records that are searched. Each of these command line options is discussed separately. (See Scope, FOR, and WHILE.)

If you study the syntax carefully, you will notice that LOCATE can be used without parameters, but this form of the command is almost never used since it only positions the record pointer to the beginning of the database file.

The WHILE option is seldom used because doing a LOCATE WHILE assumes that the current record meets the search criteria. Use IF...ENDIF or DO WHILE...ENDDO if you want to know if the current record meets a particular condition.

Procedure

LOCATE is most commonly used with a FOR condition to find the first record in the active database file that meets the specified search condition. This form of LOCATE works faster if used with an unindexed database file.

After LOCATE, use FOUND( ) to find out whether or not the search was successful. Use CONTINUE to find subsequent records that meet the LOCATE condition.

If you want to process all records in the file that meet the condition, use the following program skeleton:

```
LOCATE FOR <condition>
DO WHILE FOUND()
   <commands>
   CONTINUE
ENDDO
```

Examples

In the following example, LOCATE is used in a program that sends party invitations to all of the people in the local area codes who are between the ages of twenty five and thirty. An invitation and a mailing label are printed for each of these individuals. Since these must be printed on separate forms, SET PRINTER TO is used to switch back and forth between two printers; the first is loaded with mailing label forms and the other with regular paper.

```
* Party.PRG
*
SET TALK OFF
USE Mail

* The LOCATE condition finds the first record that meets all of
* the party criteria.  Local people are in the 213 or 818 area
* code.  The $ is the substring operator.
LOCATE FOR LEFT(Phone,5)$ "(213) (818)" .AND. Age >= 25 .AND. Age <= 30

* A successful LOCATE or CONTINUE sets the FOUND() function to
* .T.  An unsuccessful search sets the function to .F. and drops
* out of the loop.
DO WHILE FOUND()

   * Printer 1 is set up for mailing labels.
   SET PRINTER TO LPT1
   LABEL FORM Party NEXT 1 TO PRINTER

   * Printer 2 is set up for invitations.
   SET PRINTER TO LPT2
   DO Invite WITH First_Name  && Invite.PRG prints invitations

   CONTINUE  && Next record
ENDDO
CLOSE DATABASES
SET TALK ON
```

Warnings

The message *End of LOCATE scope* is displayed after an unsuccessful LOCATE or CONTINUE. This is a warning message rather than an error and is suppressed with SET TALK OFF.

Tips

A separate LOCATE condition can be maintained for each of the ten available work areas. Because of this feature, you can LOCATE a record in a work area based on one condition, and LOCATE a record in another work area based on an entirely different condition. Then, depending on which work area is selected at the time you issue a CONTINUE, the correct condition is reevaluated to find the next record. Similarly, FOUND( ) reports the result of the previously issued LOCATE or CONTINUE in each separate work area.

Use LOCATE when the search criteria is more complicated than comparing a single field to a particular value; otherwise, it is more efficient to use an index file with FIND or SEEK. For example, if you want to find the people in your mailing list who live either in Los Angeles or in Glendale and who are between the ages of twenty-five and thirty, you might use this command sequence:

```
SET TALK OFF
USE Mail
LOCATE FOR TRIM(City) $ "Los Angeles Glendale" .AND.;
           Age >= 25 .AND. Age <=30
DO WHILE FOUND()
   DISPLAY First_Name, Phone
   CONTINUE
ENDDO
CLOSE DATABASES
SET TALK ON
```

On the other hand, if you are interested only in those people who live in the city of Los Angeles, you could use the following command sequence:

```
SET TALK OFF
USE Mail INDEX Cities  && Cities is indexed on the City field
SEEK "Los Angeles"
DO WHILE City = "Los Angeles"
   DISPLAY First_Name, Phone
   SKIP
ENDDO
CLOSE DATABASES
SET TALK ON
```

If you must use LOCATE, remember that the command operates more quickly on an unindexed database file.

LOCK( ). *See* RLOCK( )

LOG( )

Syntax `LOG(<expN>)`

Overview The LOG( ) function accepts any numeric expression as its argument. The function evaluates the expression and returns the natural logarithm of the resulting number.

Procedure LOG( ) returns a number and can be used anywhere in the language where a numeric expression is appropriate.

Examples LOG( ) is often used in statistical analysis such as calculating the Poisson, the chi-square, and the normal distributions. The following routine displays a portion of the natural logarithm table that is found in many mathematics textbooks:

```
* LogTable.PRG
*
SET TALK OFF
SET DECIMALS TO 4
x = 0.1
? "     +-----------+--------------+"
? "     |     x     |    LOG(x)    |"
? "     +-----------+--------------+"
DO WHILE x <= 2
   ? x, LOG(x)
   x = x + .1
ENDDO
SET DECIMALS TO 2
SET TALK ON
```

If you execute this program by typing `DO LogTable`, you will see the following table:

```
+-----------+--------------+
¦     x     ¦    LOG(x)    ¦
+-----------+--------------+
     0.1         -2.3026
     0.2         -1.6094
     0.3         -1.2040
     0.4         -0.9163
     0.5         -0.6931
     0.6         -0.5108
     0.7         -0.3567
     0.8         -0.2231
     0.9         -0.1054
     1.0          0.0000
     1.1          0.0953
     1.2          0.1823
     1.3          0.2624
     1.4          0.3365
     1.5          0.4055
     1.6          0.4700
     1.7          0.5306
     1.8          0.5878
     1.9          0.6419
     2.0          0.6931
```

Warnings

If the function argument evaluates to a data type other than numeric, the error message *Invalid function argument* is displayed.

If the function argument evaluates to a number that is less than or equal to zero, the error message ****Execution error on LOG( ) : Zero or negative* is displayed.

Tips

dBASE III PLUS does not have a base 10 logarithm function, but the formula LOG(x) / LOG(10) gives the base 10 logarithm of any positive number, x, based on the natural logarithm function.

LOGOUT

Syntax `LOGOUT`

Overview

If you are using dBASE III PLUS in a network environment, you have the option of installing a security utility called Protect. (See Protect.) When a user accesses dBASE III PLUS with PROTECT installed, a log-in screen is presented, and the user must enter a group name, user name, and password.

LOGOUT is used to log the current user out of dBASE III PLUS (see QUIT) and to set up the screen for a new user to log in. Functionally, LOGOUT is almost the equivalent of QUIT because it closes all files (see CLOSE) and releases all objects from memory (see RELEASE, RELEASE MODULE); however, LOGOUT has the added capability of reexecuting dBASE III PLUS so that a log-in screen is presented after quitting.

LOGOUT is functional only if you are using dBASE III PLUS in a network environment and have installed Protect.

Procedure

In general, LOGOUT has very limited utility because it saves the user only one step. In most cases, you could just as easily use QUIT to exit to the operating system prompt, thereby giving other users the freedom to execute whatever program or command is desired. Using LOGOUT is superior to QUIT if the users on the network are using only dBASE III PLUS. If this is the case, use LOGOUT because it quits to the dBASE III PLUS log-in screen instead of to the operating system prompt and saves the next user the trouble of having to execute dBASE.

Examples

The following example shows how to use LOGOUT instead of QUIT to force the current workstation to go to the dBASE III PLUS log-in screen when the user selects the Exit menu option. The example assumes that Protect has already been installed.

```
* MainMenu.PRG
*
SET TALK OFF
CLEAR

DO WHILE .T.
```

```
      * Menu is displayed.
      @ 4, 10 SAY "0 - Exit"
      @ 5, 10 SAY "1 - Add Records"
      @ 6, 10 SAY "2 - Edit Records"
      @ 7, 10 SAY "3 - Print Reports"

      choice = 0

      * The user is prompted for a value between zero and three.
      @ 11, 0 SAY "Enter your selection";
              GET choice PICTURE "9" RANGE 0, 3
      READ
      @  9, 0   && Clear error message, if any

      * The users response is evaluated in order to determine
      * what to do next.
      DO CASE

         * All users can exit the menu, no access check necessary.
         CASE choice = 0
            LOGOUT  && exits to log-in screen, not operating system

         CASE choice = 1
            * Only users with access level of 4 or less
            * can add records.
            IF ACCESS() <= 4
               DO Add_Recs
            ELSE
               @ 9, 0 SAY "Unauthorized access level.  Try again."
               LOOP
            ENDIF

         CASE choice = 2
            * Only users with access level of 2 or less
            * can change records.
            IF ACCESS() <= 2
               DO EditRecs
            ELSE
               @ 12, 0 SAY "Unauthorized access level.  Try again."
               LOOP
            ENDIF

         * All users can print reports, no access check necessary.
         CASE choice = 3
            DO PrtRprts

      ENDCASE
   ENDDO
```

Warnings LOGOUT is ignored completely if you are using dBASE III PLUS in a single-user environment. Using it in a network environment without having installed Protect, it is equivalent to cancelling the program. (See CANCEL.) Thus, using the LOGOUT command instead of QUIT in a program makes the program incompatible with the single user version of dBASE III PLUS, as well as with other network versions that do not use the Protect facility.

Tips If you use Dba #DF = <drive>: <program name> to execute a program automatically when you enter dBASE III PLUS, LOGOUT does not cause the same program to be executed for the next user. If you want the workstation to always execute a program when any user enters dBASE III PLUS, use the COMMAND = DO <program name> in the Config.DB file (see Config.DB) for that workstation instead of putting the program name on the command line that you use to execute Dba.

LOOP. *See* DO WHILE

LOWER( )

Syntax `LOWER(<expC>)`

Overview The LOWER( ) function accepts a character expression as its argument. The function evaluates the expression to obtain the resulting character string and then returns that character string in all lowercase letters.

Procedure LOWER( ) returns a character string and can be used anywhere in the language where a character expression is appropriate.

Examples In dBASE III PLUS, all character string comparisons are case-sensitive. The ASCII chart in Appendix C shows the numerical values used for each character when comparisons are made. These values make a lowercase "a" greater in value than an uppercase "A". As a result, you may be unable to query the database based on character data unless you know exactly how that data is entered into a database file. For example, if you are trying to find all of the people with a Last_Name of Smith in your mailing list, you might issue the following commands:

```
. USE Mail
. LIST First_Name, Last_Name FOR Last_Name = "Smith"
```

These commands would exclude all records for which the Last_Name field was SMITH, for example, since "SMITH" is not equal to "Smith".

Issuing the same query using LOWER( ) converts the Last_Name field to all lowercase letters so that the comparison can be done. For example,

```
. LIST First_Name, Last_Name FOR LOWER(Last_Name) = "smith"
```

Warnings If the function argument evaluates to a data type other than character, the error message *Invalid function argument* is displayed.

LTRIM( )

Syntax `LTRIM(<expC>)`

Overview The LTRIM( ) function, short for left trim, accepts a character expression as its argument. The function evaluates the expression to obtain the resulting character string and then returns that character string without any leading blank spaces.

Procedure LTRIM( ) returns a character string and can be used anywhere in the language where a character expression is appropriate.

Examples LTRIM( ) can be used to remove the leading blanks that are inevitable when numbers are converted to character strings with STR( ).

In dBASE III PLUS, numeric output is always right justified. In order to left justify a set of numbers, use LTRIM( ) and STR( ) together. The following routine shows how the format of numeric output can be changed using the LTRIM( ) function:

```
* Justify.PRG
*
SET HEADING OFF
USE Customer
LIST OFF NEXT 5 STR(Amt_Owed, 10, 2)
GO TOP
LIST OFF NEXT 5 LTRIM(STR(Amt_Owed, 10, 2))
CLOSE DATABASES
SET HEADING ON
```

To execute this program and see its results,

```
. DO Justify
    1000.00
     -25.00
      30.00
    1500.00
    1500.43

 1000.00
 -25.00
 30.00
 1500.00
 1500.43
```

Warnings If the function argument evaluates to a data type other than character, the error message *Invalid function argument* is displayed.

Tips LTRIM( ) can be applied to RTRIM( ) to trim all leading and trailing blank spaces from a character string.

LUPDATE( )

Syntax `LUPDATE()`

Overview

The LUPDATE( ) function, short for last update, has no arguments. The function returns the date on which the active database file was last updated. This function is possible because the system DATE( ) is written to the header record of a database file whenever a change is made to that file. The header record is the record that dBASE III PLUS uses to keep track of the database file structure.

If it is used with no open database file, LUPDATE( ) returns a blank date (i.e., CTOD(" / / ").

Procedure

In order to use LUPDATE( ) effectively, you must have a database file in use in the current work area. (See USE.) Otherwise, the function automatically returns a blank date (i.e., CTOD(" / / ")).

LUPDATE( ) returns a date value and can be used anywhere in the language where a date expression is appropriate.

Examples

LUPDATE( ) can be used to determine if changes have been made to a particular database file today. For example, suppose that you add new customers to the Customer database file once a day. You can use the following routine to ensure that the batch of new customers is added to the file only once:

```
* Add_Test.PRG
*
SET TALK OFF
USE Customer
IF LUPDATE() < DATE()
   DO Cust_Add
ELSE
   ? CHR(7) + "The Customer file has already been updated "
   ?? "today."
ENDIF
CLOSE DATABASES
SET TALK ON
```

Warnings Because of its simple syntax, there are no error messages associated with LUPDATE( ).

Tips For LUPDATE( ) to work correctly, you must either have a built-in system clock or set the date and time whenever you boot your computer; otherwise, the date that gets posted to the database file header may be incorrect. (This is also true for the DATE( ) and TIME( ) functions.)

Macro Substitution

Syntax `&<character memory variable>[.<literal string>]`

Overview The macro substitution symbol, &, is a part of the dBASE language that is neither a command nor a function. It is most accurately described as a unary operator (see Expression) that can only be used with a character memory variable.

When & is followed immediately by the name of a character memory variable (i.e., no spaces between the ampersand and the variable name) the contents of the memory variable are literally substituted in place of the & and variable name.

Procedure You can use & anywhere in the dBASE language to substitute a literal value (i.e., an unquoted string of characters) that is stored in a memory variable. For example, FIND accepts a literal, unquoted string as its command line argument. This means that you cannot use a memory variable with FIND unless you use it with & so that the contents of the memory variable are substituted.

Commands and functions generally do not use literal values as their arguments. Instead, you are required to specify values as expressions. Some exceptions to this are file, field, and memory variable names, and the commands, functions, and reserved keywords themselves.

If you want to specify a file name as part of a command and it is stored in a memory variable, use & before the memory variable name in the command wherever the file name is supposed to be. (For example, USE &file_name.)

Use the optional period to concatenate the memory variable contents with a literal character string. This tells the macro where the variable name ends and where the string begins.

Examples A common use of macro substitution is in the implementation and use of pseudo-arrays. (See DOW( ) and VAL( ) for examples showing the use of a one-dimensional and a two-dimensional pseudo-array using macro substitution to give like names to a group of memory variables.)

Warnings You cannot use & symbol with anything other than a character memory variable. For example, if it is used with a character field, *Syntax error* is displayed.

Macro substitution is a slow process and makes programs difficult to understand; it is best avoided whenever possible.

Tips See GETENV( ), ISCOLOR( ), and TYPE( ) for other examples that use macro substitution.

MAX( )

Syntax `MAX(<expN1>, <expN2>)`

Overview The MAX( ) function requires two arguments, both of which must be numeric expressions. The function evaluates both expressions, compares the results, and returns the larger of the two values.

Procedure MAX( ) returns a number and can be used anywhere in the language where a numeric expression is appropriate.

Examples MAX( ) is used to select the larger of two values. For example, you could calculate a bonus based on the salary of an employee that would not be less than a stated minimum with the following commands:

```
. USE Employee
. LIST Emp_Code, MAX(500, Salary * .02)
 Emp_Code MAX(500, Salary * .02)
 A254                   865.0458
 A123                   774.2446
 A753                   874.2400
 A109                   500.0646
 F126                   556.6424
 F876                  2460.0000
 M198                  5000.0000
 A452                   500.0000
 A935                  1152.2424
 F107                  1062.7554

. CLOSE DATABASES
```

In this example, an employee gets the minimum bonus amount of $500.00 if two percent of the employee's salary is less than $500.00.

Warnings If either function argument evaluates to a data type other than numeric, the error message *Invalid function argument* is displayed.

Tips MAX( ) cannot be used with dates or character strings, but you can get the equivalent by using IIF( ). For example, the function

```
IIF(<exp1> > <exp2>, <exp1>, <exp2>)
```

is equivalent to MAX( ) and can be used with either numbers, dates, or character strings.

Memo Fields

Overview Memo fields hold text that exceeds the 254 character limit of character fields. However, the use of memo fields is very limited in dBASE III PLUS. Memo is not a data type (see Expression), which means that there is no such thing as a memo expression. Therefore, wherever an expression is called for, memo fields are automatically excluded from the command or function. The exceptions to this rule are ?, ??, DISPLAY, and LIST, all of which allow memo fields in a list with other expressions.

The only other place in the language where you can use memo fields is when a field name or field list is required; even this rule has exceptions. For example, COPY excludes the use of memo fields when creating non-dBASE files; memo fields cannot be used as the key fields in SORT, TOTAL, or UPDATE; you cannot edit memo fields in BROWSE, and you cannot display the contents of a memo field with @...SAY. The @...GET command can only be used to edit a memo field if it is used in a format file. (See SET FORMAT.)

Also, memo fields cannot be compared relationally (see Expression) to other memo fields, their values cannot be replaced programmatically, and there is no function in dBASE III PLUS that can manipulate a memo field.

In spite of its limitations, memo fields have several important uses. The following is a complete list of what you can do with memo fields:

1. Enter and edit data with APPEND, EDIT or INSERT
2. Edit the data with READ if you use a format file (see SET FORMAT)
3. View data with ?, ??, DISPLAY, LIST, and REPORT FORM
4. COPY and APPEND FROM other database files
5. Change display width with SET MEMOWIDTH

Memo fields are stored in a separate .DBT file that is automatically linked to the .DBF database file. Regardless of the length of its contents, each memo field occupies only ten bytes in the database file.

Warnings If you try to use a memo field name when you are not supposed to the error message *Operation with Memo field invalid* is displayed.

Tips Because of the limitations of memo fields, you may prefer to use a long character field (the maximum length is 254 characters).

Memory Variables

Overview You can create and use memory variables in dBASE III PLUS to store temporary values that you do not want to store in a database file. You can then use the memory variable names anywhere in the language where an expression (see Expression) can be used.

The following commands are the only ones capable of creating memory variables:

- ACCEPT
- AVERAGE
- COUNT
- INPUT
- PARAMETERS
- PUBLIC
- STORE
- SUM
- WAIT

When using any of these commands, the memory variable name can be up to ten characters in length. The first character must be a letter; the remaining nine can be any combination of letters, numbers, and underscores.

There can be a maximum of 256 memory variables in memory at one time, as long as the amount of space used by all of them does not exceed 6,000 bytes. (See Config.DB for information on how to increase the MVARSIZ.) Character variables use their length plus two extra bytes; numeric and date variables each use nine bytes, and Logical variables use two bytes.

The @...GET command followed by READ is the only way to edit the contents of an existing memory variable.

Tips

If you have a field with the same name as a memory variable, the field name takes precedence over the memory variable. As a result, any reference to that name as part of a command or function assumes that you are talking about the field, rather than the memory variable. To override this precedence, use the prefix M – > before the name to indicate that you are referring to the memory variable even if there happens to be a database file with M as its alias name. (See Alias.) For example, if you have a field and a memory variable called Last_Name, you might use these commands:

```
? Last_Name     && Displays the field
? M->last_name && Displays the memory variable
```

See PRIVATE and PUBLIC for information on different kinds of memory variables.

MESSAGE( )

Syntax `MESSAGE()`

Overview

The MESSAGE( ) function has no arguments. The function returns as a character string the error message text of the last error encountered by dBASE III PLUS. The error messages and numbers are listed in the dBASE III PLUS documentation.

Procedure

In order to use MESSAGE( ) effectively, you must use it with ON ERROR; otherwise, the function automatically returns a null string.

MESSAGE( ) returns a character string and can be used anywhere in the language where a character expression is appropriate.

Examples

MESSAGE( ) can be used to display a particular error message while handling the error programmatically. The following is a modification of the error routine shown for ERROR( ) that displays the error message along with other text before it reindexes the active database file:

```
* Err_Trap.PRG
*
IF ERROR() = 20
   ? MESSAGE()
   ? "Please, wait while the database file is reindexed"
   REINDEX
   RETRY
ENDIF
RETURN
```

To enable this routine so that it is invoked whenever an error is encountered, issue the following command either from a program or from the dot prompt:

```
ON ERROR DO Err_Trap
```

To clear the error procedure when you no longer need it, issue `ON ERROR` with no parameters.

Warnings

Because of its simple syntax there are no error messages associated with MESSAGE( ).

Tips As soon as it is no longer useful, clear the ON ERROR procedure so that it will not be triggered by an unrelated error.

MIN( )

Syntax `MIN(<expN1>, <expN2>)`

Overview The MIN( ) function requires two arguments, both of which must be numeric expressions. The function evaluates both expressions, compares the results, and returns the smaller of the two values.

Procedure MIN( ) returns a number and can be used anywhere in the language where a numeric expression is appropriate.

Examples MIN( ) is used to select the smaller of two values. For example, if you want to give each employee a ten percent raise but you do not want any individual raise to exceed $3000.00, the following commands update the Salary field appropriately:

```
. USE Employee
. REPLACE ALL Salary WITH MIN(Salary + 3000, Salary * 1.1)
    10 records replaced
. CLOSE DATABASES
```

In this example, the employee gets only a $3000.00 raise if ten percent of the employee's salary is more than $3000.00.

Warnings If either function argument evaluates to a data type other than numeric, the error message *Invalid function argument* is displayed.

Tips MIN( ) cannot be used with dates or character strings, but you can get the equivalent by using IIF( ). For example, the function

```
IIF(<expl> < <exp2>, <expl>, <exp2>)
```

is equivalent to MIN( ) and can be used with either numbers, dates, or character strings.

MOD( )

Syntax `MOD(<expN1>, <expN2>)`

Overview The MOD( ) function, short for modulus, accepts two numeric expressions as its arguments. The function evaluates the expressions, divides the first number by the second, and returns the remainder of the division.

Procedure MOD( ) returns a number and can be used anywhere in the language where a numeric expression is appropriate.

Examples MOD( ) is useful for converting one set of units to another. For example, the following example converts inches to feet and inches:

```
* Inches.PRG
*
SET TALK OFF
INPUT "Enter the number of inches to convert: " TO total
feet = INT(total / 12)
inches = MOD(total, 12)
? Total, "inches equals", feet, "feet and", inches, "inches."
SET TALK ON
```

MOD( ) is also very useful in limiting numbers. A common problem arises when using a variable line number in printing with @...SAY. First, a page heading is printed and after each line is printed the line number is incremented. The following example uses a routine similar to the one used in LOG( ) to limit the line number variable so that it does not exceed the page length. The logarithm table is printed out up to LOG(10).

```
* Limit.PRG
*
SET TALK OFF
SET DECIMALS TO 4
SET DEVICE TO PRINTER
x = 0.1
line = 0
DO WHILE x <= 10
   * When line gets back to zero, it is time to start new page.
```

```
    IF line = 0
       @ 1, 9 SAY "+-----------+--------------+"
       @ 2, 9 SAY "¦     x     ¦    LOG(x)    ¦"
       @ 3, 9 SAY "+-----------+--------------+"
       line = 4
    ENDIF
    @ line, 5 SAY x
    @ line, PCOL() SAY LOG(x)
    x = x + .1
    * The MOD() function limits line, so that it does
    * not exceed 64 lines per page.
    line = MOD(line + 1, 64)
ENDDO
EJECT
SET DEVICE TO SCREEN
SET DECIMALS TO 2
SET TALK ON
```

If you execute this program, you will get a printed logarithm table with about sixty entries per page and a new heading on each page.

Warnings If either function argument evaluates to a data type other than numeric, the error message *Invalid function argument* is displayed.

Tips The formula for computing MOD( ) involves dividing the first argument by the second. Because division by zero is undefined, however, MOD( ) is defined separately if the second argument evaluates to zero. (MOD(x,0) = x for every value of x.)

MODIFY COMMAND

Syntax `MODIFY COMMAND <filename>`

Overview MODIFY COMMAND invokes the dBASE III PLUS text editor. The file name that you specify is assumed to be a program file with a .PRG extension, but you can specify another extension if you want to edit a different kind of text file.

If the file does not already exist, a new file is created; if it does exist, the file contents are brought up for you to edit.

Procedure

MODIFY COMMAND is generally used to create program and format files and to make changes to these files, but you can use it to create and edit any text file.

To create a new program file, enter MODIFY COMMAND with a new file name. The editor is invoked, and you are presented with a blank screen for entering text. Each line of text that you enter should be a valid dBASE III PLUS command. The line will automatically wrap around to the next line after you type sixty-six characters.

If you have a long command line that you want to wrap at a particular location, type a semicolon at the place where you want to break up the command, then press Enter to continue with the rest of the command on the next line. The semicolon is the command line continuation character (see ;), and signals the dBASE III PLUS interpreter to look on the next line for the rest of the command.

When you force a line to wrap in this manner, a < symbol appears at the right of the screen. In the MODIFY COMMAND editor, this symbol indicates a hard carriage return represented by the ASCII character CHR(13). This symbol does not appear on lines that automatically wrap around; such lines are terminated with a CHR(141).

After typing in an entire command, press Enter to get to the next line and enter the next command. Use the full-screen cursor navigation and editing keys listed in Appendix A whenever you want to go back to change a line you have already typed.

When you finish entering commands, press Ctrl-End to save the file. If you decide that you do not want to save the new file, press Esc instead of Ctrl-End. You will be asked to verify your decision.

If you want to create a text file that is not a program file (such as a format file), use the correct file name extension with the file name when you enter MODIFY COMMAND. For a format file, enter only @ commands (see @...CLEAR, @...GET, @...SAY, and @...TO) and comments. (See *.)

To modify an existing file, use MODIFY COMMAND with the name of the file that you want to edit. The editor is invoked, and the file contents appear on the screen. You can use the full-screen cursor navigation and editing keys listed in Appendix A to make the changes that you want. Ctrl-End then saves the file with all of the changes that you make. If you decide that you have made changes that you do not want to save, press Esc to abandon MODIFY COMMAND. You will be asked to verify your decision.

There are several control key commands unique to MODIFY COMMAND which appear in the cursor control menu. (See SET MENUS.) They are listed below:

KEY	OPERATION
^KB	Reformat
^KF	Find
^KL	Refind
^KR	Read text file
^KW	Write text file

^KB reformats the current line. This command ensures that lines with inserted text will wrap around correctly. Position the cursor anywhere on the line and press ^KR to reformat.

^KF is used to find the first occurrence of a character string in the file. When you press ^KF, the *Find?* prompt appears at the top of the screen. Type in the string that you want to locate; the string is taken literally and, therefore, should not be quoted. The Find command is case-sensitive, so you must type the string exactly as it appears in the file. This is another reason to use strict case conventions for commands, keywords, memory variables, fields, and file names in your programs. Press Enter after you type the string, and MODIFY COMMAND locates it for you by repositioning the cursor. If the string is not found, you are warned and must press the space bar to continue. ^KF begins its search for the specified string starting at the current cursor position and continuing to the end of the file, but does not wrap around to the top of the file.

^KL finds subsequent occurrences of the Find string. After finding the first occurrence with ^KF, press ^KL as many times as you want to find the rest. Like ^KF, ^KL only searches to the end of the file. If the string is not found again, you are warned and must press the space bar to continue.

^KR is used to read the contents of a text file into the file that you are editing. To use this feature, position the cursor to the beginning of the line before which you want the read file contents to be inserted. Then press ^KR, and the *Enter file name* prompt appears. Type in the name of the file that you want to read (including the extension if it is other than .TXT), and press Enter when you are finished. The entire contents of the named file is read into your file following the current position of the cursor.

^KW is used to write the contents of the file that you are editing to another text file. When you press ^KW, the *Enter file name* prompt appears. Type in the name of the file that you want to write, including the extension if it is other than .TXT, and press Enter. Regardless of the cursor position, the entire file contents are written to the new file.

After creating or modifying a program file with MODIFY COMMAND, you can execute the program (see DO) to make sure that the new program works. See SET FORMAT for information on how to use a format file.

See TYPE for information on listing the text file. You must specify the file name extension when you TYPE it.

Warnings

If you get the error message *File is currently open* when you enter MODIFY COMMAND, it means that the file you are attempting to edit is open and must be closed before you can edit it. If this error message occurs when you are attempting to edit a program file, you are probably in suspend mode (See SUSPEND), and should enter CANCEL at the dot prompt to close all program files. When the error occurs with a format file, use CLOSE FORMAT. Use CLOSE PROCEDURE to close a procedure file.

The dBASE III PLUS text editor cannot handle files larger than 5000 bytes. An attempt to edit a larger file results in the warning message *File too large, some data may be lost.* Data will indeed be lost if you make changes to a file and save the file after seeing this message. If you see this message, abandon MODIFY COMMAND using the Esc key to guarantee that you do not lose any part of your file.

Inserting characters into a large file is very slow. For all but the quickest changes to small files, using a more fully-featured editor will save you time and frustration (See Config.DB.)

Tips

When you use MODIFY COMMAND to edit an existing text file, a backup of that file is created before you are allowed to make any changes. The backup file is given the same name as the file that you are editing, but with a .BAK extension. If you make some changes to a program file that you do not want to keep, you can recover the previous version of the file with the following commands:

```
COPY FILE <filename>.BAK TO <filename>.PRG
```

If you have sufficient memory in your computer, you can use your own word processor instead of the built-in text editor of dBASE III PLUS. Use the entry TEDIT = <program name> in the Config.DB file to define the program that you want to use whenever you enter MODIFY COMMAND, and use WP = <program name> to specify the program that you want to use for editing memo fields. (See Config.DB for more information.)

Unless you specify your own memo field word processor in Config.DB, the MODIFY COMMAND editor is used when you edit the contents of a memo field.

MODIFY FILE

Syntax `MODIFY FILE <filename>`

Overview MODIFY FILE is identical to MODIFY COMMAND, except that the file name is assumed to have no extension. (See MODIFY COMMAND for information on this command.)

MODIFY LABEL. *See* CREATE LABEL

MODIFY QUERY. *See* CREATE QUERY

MODIFY REPORT. *See* CREATE REPORT

MODIFY SCREEN. *See* CREATE SCREEN

MODIFY STRUCTURE

Syntax `MODIFY STRUCTURE`

Overview

The MODIFY STRUCTURE command is very similar to CREATE, except that it edits an existing database file structure rather than creating a new one.

Before allowing you to make any changes, MODIFY STRUCTURE makes a backup of the database file and the memo file (if there is one) to ensure that you do not lose any data. The backup files are given the same name as the database file, but with a .BAK extension for the database file and a .TBK extension for the memo file.

Procedure

To use MODIFY STRUCTURE, the database file of which you want to change the structure must be open in the current work area. (See USE.) If you are using dBASE III PLUS in a network environment, exclusive use (See SET EXCLUSIVE, USE) of the active database file is required. Once the database file is open, enter MODIFY STRUCTURE.

Except for the fact that you cannot use it to create a new database file, MODIFY STRUCTURE is identical to CREATE. (See CREATE for information on using MODIFY STRUCTURE.)

In addition to the features discussed under CREATE, a menu bar is available to locate more quickly a particular field. Pressing Ctrl-Home activates the menu shown in Figure 64. If you do not want to make a selection from the menu, press Esc to deactivate it.

As with all other menu bars in dBASE III PLUS, use the Left Arrow and Right Arrow keys to highlight the option that you want and press Enter to select the option. *Bottom* moves the cursor to the last field name in the file structure, and *Top* moves it to the first field. The *Field #* prompts you to enter the number of the field that you want to locate, and the cursor moves to the field number that you type. The other menu options, *Save* and *Abandon,* are equivalent to pressing Ctrl-End and Esc, respectively.

Pressing Esc at any time during the MODIFY STRUCTURE indicates that you want to abandon the changes you have made to the database file structure. Before allowing you to do this, MODIFY STRUCTURE prompts for verification. A positive response to this prompt leaves the file structure

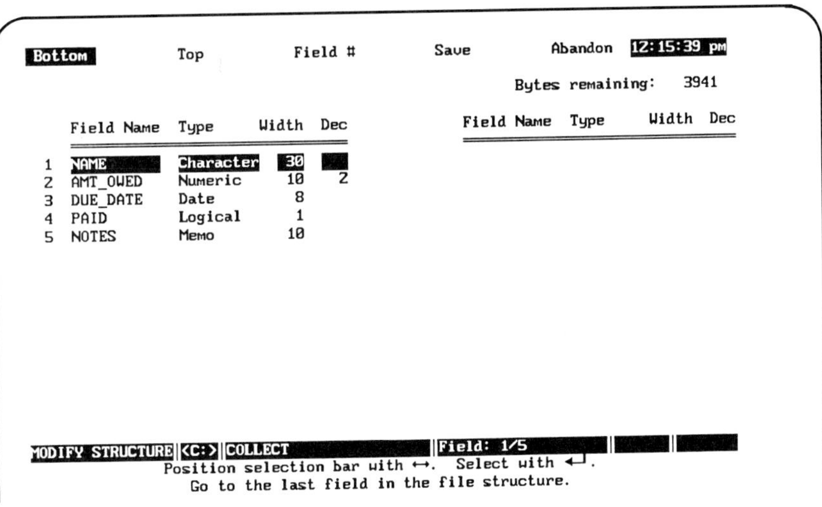

Figure 64

as it was when you entered MODIFY STRUCTURE, and a negative response resumes the MODIFY STRUCTURE session.

Ctrl-End indicates that you are finished making changes and that you want to save the changes made to the database file structure. Depending on the kinds of changes that you made to the structure, one of two things can happen.

The prompt *Should data be COPIED from backup for all fields? (Y/N)* is displayed if you made changes to field names only. Typing `Y`, indicates that you want to retain all of the data in your original database file; typing `N` indicates that you do not want to retain the data from those fields whose name you have changed.

If you change the data type of any existing field, add or insert fields, delete fields, or change the length of any field, you are not given a choice about how the data is retrieved from the backup; the data from the original file is retained only for those fields where names have not been changed.

In any case, you are prompted to *Press ENTER to confirm. Any other key to resume.* If you are satisfied that you want to save the new database file structure in light of any data loss that you have been warned about, press Enter. Otherwise, press any other key to resume the MODIFY STRUCTURE session, and press Esc to abandon the changes.

After you save the MODIFY STRUCTURE changes, the data is appended from the backup file, and the database file is left open in the current work area. Any index files that may have been open when you entered MODIFY STRUCTURE are closed because of the possibility of their invalidation. If you change any of the attributes of a field used as part of an index key, the index file can no longer be used and must be recreated. (See INDEX.)

If you know that the changes made to the fields do not involve index key expressions, use SET INDEX TO to reopen all of the index files and continue to work with the database file.

Examples

The Collect database file that was designed in a previous example (see CREATE) has a single Name field. In this example, the structure of this file is modified to replace Name with First_Name and Last_Name. In order to prevent data loss, the new fields are added and these changes are saved before Name is deleted. Enter the following commands, and your screen should look like the one in Figure 65.

```
. USE Collect
. MODIFY STRUCTURE
```

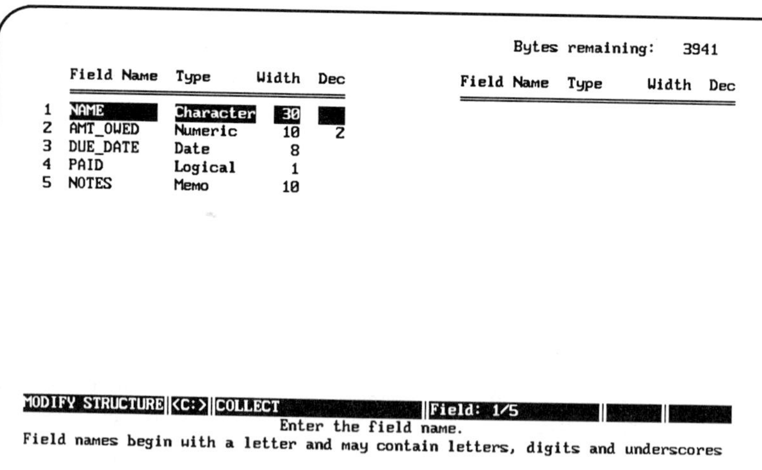

Figure 65

To insert the First_Name field before the Name field, press Ctrl-N. A blank line appears, and all of the existing fields are moved down. Type `First_Name`, press Enter to accept the Character data type, and type 30 for the field width. When you are finished entering the field width, press Enter.

To insert the Last_Name field before the Name field, press Ctrl-N. A blank line appears, and all of the existing fields are moved down. Type `Last_Name`, and press Enter when you are finished. Press Enter to accept the Character data type, and type 30 for the field width. When you are finished entering the field width, press Enter. Your screen should look like the one in Figure 66.

Save the file structure by pressing Ctrl-End, and press Enter to confirm that you want to save the changes. Use the following commands to split the Name field into First_Name and Last_Name, assuming that there is a space between the first and last names in the Name field. Note that this is a simple example and does not take into consideration any titles, initials, or middle names.

```
. REPLACE ALL First_Name WITH SUBSTR(Name, 1, AT(" ", Name))
. REPLACE ALL Last_Name WITH SUBSTR(Name, AT(" ", Name) + 1)
```

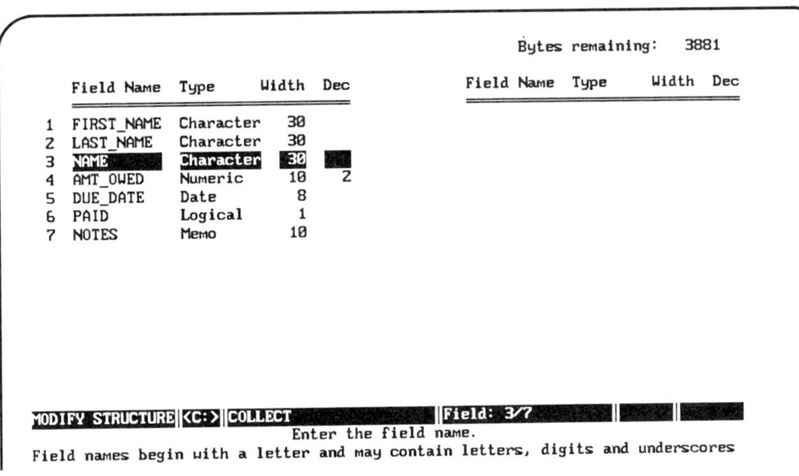

Figure 66

Now, you are ready to remove the Name field that you no longer need. Enter

```
. MODIFY STRUCTURE
```

Press Ctrl-Home, select the Field # option by typing F, and type 3 followed by Enter to locate the Name field. Press Ctrl-U when Name is highlighted to delete the field from the file structure, and save the file with Ctrl-End. Press Enter to confirm the save.

Warnings

You can avoid data loss when using MODIFY STRUCTURE by following one simple rule: Make field name changes in a separate session—never in the same session as you make any other changes.

You can change field names in one session of MODIFY STRUCTURE and retain all of the data, if you wish, in the original file. Then, in a second MODIFY STRUCTURE session, you can add fields, insert fields, delete fields, and change field types and lengths.

If you use MODIFY STRUCTURE in the network version of dBASE III PLUS, exclusive use of the active database file is required and the error message *Exclusive open of file is required* is displayed if you attempt to modify the structure of a database file that was opened for shared use. Either SET EXCLUSIVE ON and reopen file, or reopen the file with USE <filename> EXCLUSIVE and issue the MODIFY STRUCTURE command again.

Tips

If you find immediately after saving changes made during a MODIFY STRUCTURE session that some of the data in your file is missing, you can recover the data from the backup file. Substitute the name of your file, and use the following commands to copy the backup files to the originals:

```
CLOSE DATABASES
COPY FILE <filename>.BAK TO <filename>.DBF
COPY FILE <filename>.TBK TO <filename>.DBT
```

Use the second COPY FILE command only if you have one or more memo fields in the original file.

As an added safeguard, you may want to make an additional backup of the database file on another disk before attempting to recover the data.

MODIFY VIEW. *See* CREATE VIEW

MONTH( )

Syntax `MONTH(<expD>)`

Overview The MONTH( ) function accepts any date expression as its argument. The function evaluates the expression and returns the month portion as a number.

Procedure The MONTH( ) function returns a number and can be used anywhere in the language where a numeric expression is appropriate.

Examples In the following example, MONTH( ) is used to update the ages of the people in your mailing list. The age of an individual is usually computed by subtracting the year of birth from the current year, but you must subtract one from the current year for birthdays that have not yet occurred this year:

```
* Age.PRG
*
SET TALK OFF
USE Mail
DO WHILE .NOT. EOF()
   IF MONTH(DATE()) >= MONTH(Birthday) .AND.;
      DAY(DATE()) >= DAY(Birthday)
      REPLACE Age WITH YEAR(DATE()) - YEAR(Birthday)
   ELSE
      REPLACE Age WITH YEAR(DATE()) - YEAR(Birthday) - 1
   ENDIF
   SKIP
ENDDO
CLOSE DATABASES
SET TALK ON
```

Warnings If the function argument evaluates to a data type other than date, the error message *Invalid function argument* is displayed.

NDX( )

Syntax `NDX(<expN>)`

Overview

The NDX( ) function accepts a numeric expression as its argument. The function evaluates the expression and returns the name of the index file in that position in the index order for the active database file. The index order is determined by the position of the file names in the index file list when the files are opened using either USE...INDEX <index file list> or SET INDEX TO <index file list>.

The numeric expression must evaluate to a number between 1 and 7, inclusive. If the number is in this range and there is no index in the specified position, NDX( ) returns a null string.

Procedure

To use NDX( ) effectively, a database file must be in use in the current work area (see USE); otherwise, the function automatically returns a null string.

NDX( ) returns a character string and can be used anywhere in the language where a character expression is appropriate.

Examples

NDX( ) can be used to select a particular file for the controlling index when you are unsure of the index order. For example, to determine the index order position of the Names index file, you could use the following routine:

```
* Order.PRG
*
DO WHILE "" < NDX(control)
   IF UPPER(NDX(control)) = "C:NAMES.NDX"
      EXIT
   ELSE
      control = control + 1
   ENDIF
ENDDO
RETURN
```

Assuming there is a database file in use in the current work area with an index file called Names, you could make Names the controlling index by issuing the following commands in a program or from the dot prompt:

```
control = 1
DO Order
SET ORDER TO control
```

Warnings If the function argument evaluates to a data type other than numeric, the error message *Invalid function argument* is displayed.

If the function argument evaluates to a number that is greater than 7 or less than 1, the error message ****Execution error on NDX( ) : Invalid index number* is displayed.

Tips Note that NDX( ) returns the entire file name which includes the drive letter, the path name, and the extension. Furthermore, the file name is returned using a combination of uppercase and lowercase letters; the actual combination depends on how the file name was entered when the file was opened and whether or not a SET PATH TO is in effect. As in the above example, apply UPPER( ) to NDX( ) and then compare the result to a character string that is in all uppercase letters.

NEXT. *See* Scope

NOTE. *See* * (asterisk)

ON ERROR

Syntax `ON ERROR [<command>]`

Overview

The ON ERROR command prevents dBASE III PLUS from interrupting with messages when errors are encountered. Usually, ON ERROR is used in programs to trap potential errors that can result from certain commands, but it can be used at the dot prompt also.

After ON ERROR < command > is executed, a message does not display when an error is encountered; instead, dBASE III PLUS executes the command that you specify as the ON ERROR command line argument. The rerouting of error control continues until you discontinue the error trap by issuing ON ERROR with no argument.

Procedure

Although it can be used at the dot prompt, ON ERROR is almost always used in a program. It can be used as a sort of global error trap, but is normally used to trap a specific subset of potential errors.

In order to use ON ERROR to trap errors, you must first decide what errors you want to trap and how they should be remedied. To make this decision, you must first determine which commands in your program are likely to produce errors that can be corrected programmatically. For example, suppose you have a program that opens a database file. If you are not sure what directory the file is in and cannot depend on the path setting (see SET PATH) to be accurate, you may want to trap any potential errors resulting from the USE command that opens the database file.

Deciding how to correct the error is up to you. To recover from an error almost always requires more than a single command, which means that you must design and write a program to handle error recovery. In situations such as the above example of the database file, you may want to allow the user to change the path setting or, more simply, to enter the directory where the file is stored.

In designing an error recovery program, use ERROR( ) or MESSAGE( ) if you need to know exactly what error has occurred. (See ERROR( ) and MESSAGE( ).) If you are interested in several specific errors, use a DO CASE construct (see DO CASE), and check the error number (see ERROR( )) in each CASE statement to make a decision based on the particular error.

These steps will allow you to have a single error recovery program that handles all of the potential errors in an application. You can reexecute the erroneous command in your recovery program after you have corrected the error. (See RETRY.)

Once you have isolated the commands that you want to monitor for potential errors and have written your error recovery program, place the ON ERROR DO <recovery program name> command, before each command or group of commands that you want to monitor. After the command or group of commands, place an ON ERROR command with no parameter to disable the error trap. The result is that you isolate and trap only those commands that have the potential for errors, and you allow your error recovery program to decide exactly what error it must deal with.

Examples

The following example traps illustrates ON ERROR. The first listing below, Open.PRG, is a partial program that is called from a main menu.

```
* Open.PRG
*
   .
   .
   .

* The recovery program for database and index open errors is
* called Recover.PRG.  The ON ERROR trap is activated to execute
* this recovery program in case the USE...INDEX command results
* in an error.

ON ERROR DO Recover
USE Inventry INDEX Part_No
ON ERROR  && Disable error trap

   .
   .
   .
```

The next listing is of the error recovery program, Recover.PRG. This program tests for certain known errors that are likely to occur as the result of the USE...INDEX command that is isolated in the Open.PRG program. Depending on the error, a different recovery path is taken.

```
* Recover.PRG
*
* This is a recovery program for trapping potential database
* and index file opening errors.
```

```
DO CASE

   * ALIAS name already in use, or File is already open.
   CASE ERROR() = 24 .OR. ERROR() = 3

      * Both of these errors can be corrected by closing
      * all database files and reexecuting the USE...INDEX.
      CLOSE DATABASES
      RETRY

   * File does not exist.
   CASE ERROR() = 1

      * If the file does not exist, it is assumed that
      * the path is not set to the directory where the file
      * is stored.  This gives the user the opportunity to
      * enter the correct directory name.
      setpath = SPACE(40)
      CLEAR
      @ 10, 0 SAY "Either the Inventory file or its index"
      @ 11, 0 SAY "file cannot be found.  Enter the name"
      @ 12, 0 SAY "of the directory where the file is stored."
      @ 14, 0 GET setpath
      READ
      SET PATH TO &setpath
      RETRY

   * Index file does not match database.
   CASE ERROR() = 19

      * The index must be recreated from scratch to recover
      * from this error.  RETRY is used to reopen the database
      * and the newly created index file just to make sure that
      * the complete index file is written to disk.
      INDEX ON Part_No TO Part_No
      RETRY

   * Not a dBASE database file.
   CASE ERROR() = 15

      * This is a serious error that requires restoring the
      * database file from a backup.
      go_ahead = SPACE(1)
      CLEAR
      @ 10, 0 SAY "The Inventory file is corrupted."
      @ 11, 0 SAY "Insert the backup diskette in drive A."
```

```
    @ 12, 0 SAY "Press any key to restore from backup." ;
            GET go_ahead
    READ
    COPY FILE A:Inventry.DBF TO Inventry.DBF
    USE Inventry

    * The index is recreated from scratch just in case it
    * is also corrupted.
    INDEX ON Part_No TO Part_No
    RETRY

  OTHERWISE

    * This takes care of any unexpected error.
    CLEAR
    @ 10, 0 SAY "Unanticipated error encountered."
    @ 11, 0 SAY "No recovery available."

    * All files are closed.
    CLOSE DATABASES

    * The ON ERROR trap is disabled here since there will
    * not be a return to the calling program.
    ON ERROR

    * The application cannot continue due to an
    * unrecoverable error.
    RETURN TO MASTER

ENDCASE
```

Warnings In dBASE III PLUS, only error messages with corresponding ERROR( ) numbers can be trapped with ON ERROR. Errors without ERROR( ) numbers fall into one of four categories:

1. Errors that occur in one of the full-screen commands, such as *Invalid date* in APPEND or EDIT, or *Cannot save an invalid filter* in CREATE QUERY.
2. Errors that occur when dBASE III PLUS relinquishes control to the operating system. This includes all file I/O errors and most printing errors (e.g., *Printer not ready. Retry? (Y/N)*).
3. Errors that are considered "internal" errors to dBASE III PLUS. The error messages are usually prefaced by the word internal (e.g., *Internal error: EVAL work area overflow*).

4. Errors that are unique to a particular command. Because of the architecture of dBASE III PLUS, an error message cannot be trapped if it is isolated as part of a command rather than shared in a pool of common error messages. An example of this is the message *Syntax error in field expression* when you run a REPORT FORM, or *Illegal field name* when you use CREATE FROM.

The dBASE III PLUS documentation lists all error messages with ERROR( ) numbers in a separate section at the end of the main reference section. The message listing is comprehensive, and the ERROR( ) numbers reflect exactly which errors can be trapped and which cannot.

The validity of the command used as the ON ERROR command line option is not checked when ON ERROR is executed. Instead, the command is interpreted when an error triggers ON ERROR.

Tips

Remember to disable the error trap when it is no longer needed; otherwise, you will end up trapping errors that you do not want, and the recovery that you have designated may not be appropriate.

You can disable all error trapping with ON ERROR * which tells dBASE III PLUS to do nothing. This is confusing when working interactively, but can be useful in large applications because known errors are bypassed until they are fixed.

ON ERROR SUSPEND can save time and keystrokes during debugging.

ON ESCAPE

Syntax `ON ESCAPE [<command>]`

Overview

ON ESCAPE controls what action is taken when a user presses the Esc key during the execution of certain dBASE III PLUS commands. It affects all commands except the full-screen commands (e.g., APPEND, MODIFY STRUCTURE, CREATE REPORT). In programs, ON ESCAPE is used to change the function of the Esc key, which is generally used to suspend program execution. (See SET ESCAPE.) ON ESCAPE can also be used at the dot prompt.

After ON ESCAPE <command> is executed, dBASE III PLUS executes the command that you specify as the ON ESCAPE command line argument rather than displaying the *** *INTERRUPTED* *** message when a command is interrupted by pressing the Esc key. The redefinition of the Esc key continues until you restore the key to its original function by issuing ON ESCAPE with no arguments.The keypress is discarded and not saved in the typeahead buffer.

Procedure

Although it can be used at the dot prompt, ON ESCAPE is almost always used in a program. To use ON ESCAPE effectively, SET ESCAPE must be ON. You then must decide under what circumstances you want the Esc key redefined and how you want it redefined.

Deciding when you want Esc redefined depends on your application, but it is generally used to allow interruption of a command or group of commands without interfering with the rest of the application. Ordinarily, pressing Esc during the program execution interrupts not only the command that is currently executing, but the entire application. There may be occasions, however, when you want to stop only the executing command. For example, if you have a subprogram in an application that prints a series of long reports, you may want to allow the user to interrupt the printing; or a user may need to stop printing because of a paper jam or some other reason.

Deciding what to do when Esc is pressed may be more complicated than deciding when to redefine the key. It depends on your application, but redefining the Esc key is usually complicated and requires more than a single command. Therefore, you must design and write a program to define the action to take when Esc is pressed. In the above example involving printing reports, you may want to allow the user to start printing the most recent report from the start, or to leave the printing subprogram all together.

Once you have isolated the group of commands for which you want the Esc key redefined, place the ON ESCAPE DO <redefinition program name> before the group of commands. After the commands, place ON ESCAPE with no parameter to reinstate the normal Esc key function.

Examples

The following example allows the user to press the Esc key during a subprogram that prints several reports. ON ESCAPE triggers a routine that decides what to do next based on user input. The first listing below, Reports.PRG, is a subprogram that is assumed to have been called by a main menu program:

```
* Reports.PRG
*
* This program prints several reports for the Employee database
* file.
SET CONSOLE OFF  && So reports don't show on screen
USE Employee
CLEAR
@ 10, 0 SAY "Press the Esc key at any time to interrupt reports."

* If the user presses the Esc key, execute WhatNext.PRG.
ON ESCAPE DO WhatNext

REPORT FORM Payroll TO PRINTER
REPORT FORM Taxes TO PRINTER
REPORT FORM Names TO PRINTER

ON ESCAPE  && Restore Esc key to its normal function
CLOSE DATABASES
SET CONSOLE ON
```

The WhatNext.PRG program listed below redefines the Esc key function. It allows the user to continue printing or return to the main menu program.

```
* WhatNext.PRG
*
* This program decides what to do if the Esc key is pressed
* during the Reports.PRG program execution.

response = SPACE(1)
CLEAR
@ 10, 0 SAY "Do you want to continue printing? (Y/N)" ;
        GET response PICTURE "Y"
READ
IF response = "N"

   * If the user does not want to continue,
   * close the database file,
   CLOSE DATABASES

   * restore the Esc key to its normal function,
   ON ESCAPE
```

```
   * turn the screen back on.
   SET CONSOLE ON

   * and return back to the main menu program.
   RETURN TO MASTER

ELSE

   * If the user wants to continue, give them a chance to get
   * ready before restarting last report.
   response = SPACE(1)
   @ 11, 0 SAY "Press any key when you are ready to restart " + ;
               "the last report at the beginning." GET response
   READ
   RETRY  && Restart last report
ENDIF
```

Warnings

If SET ESCAPE is OFF, the Esc key is completely disabled; the ON ESCAPE redefinition of the Esc key is ignored until you SET ESCAPE ON.

By redefining the Esc key with ON ESCAPE, it is possible to put a program into an infinite loop. Always make sure your programs have a way out, especially if you use ON ESCAPE or SET ESCAPE OFF.

The validity of the command used as the ON ESCAPE command line option is not checked when ON ESCAPE is executed; instead, the command is interpreted at the time ON ESCAPE is triggered by pressing the Esc key.

Tips

ON ESCAPE takes precedence over ON KEY; if there is an ON ESCAPE and an ON KEY in effect, pressing the Esc key activates the ON ESCAPE rather than the ON KEY.

Remember to disable the Esc key trap when it is no longer needed by using ON ESCAPE with no parameter.

ON ESCAPE SUSPEND speeds up debugging by suppressing the prompt that asks if you want to suspend.

ON KEY

Syntax `ON KEY [<command>]`

Overview

The ON KEY command controls what action is taken when a user presses any key during the execution of certain dBASE III PLUS commands. It affects all commands except the full-screen commands (e.g., APPEND, MODIFY STRUCTURE, CREATE REPORT), and commands that accept input from the keyboard (e.g., WAIT, READ, and ACCEPT).

After ON KEY <command> is executed, dBASE III PLUS stores the keypress in the typeahead buffer. (See SET TYPEAHEAD.) If you press one or more keys while another command is executing, dBASE III PLUS executes the command that you specify as the ON KEY command line argument. Unlike with ON ESCAPE, ON KEY does not interrupt the execution of the current command when you press a key; ON KEY is triggered only after the other command is finished executing. The key trap remains in effect until you disable it by issuing ON KEY with no arguments.

Procedure

Although it can be used at the dot prompt, ON KEY is almost always used in a program. You must first decide at what point in the program you want to begin trapping keyboard entry, and what you want to do when a key is pressed. Remember that if the user presses a key while another command is executing, ON KEY will be triggered only after the other command has completed execution.

When you isolate the portion of your program where you want to trap keyboard entry, you must design and code a program that decides what to do with the keypress. Usually, this program uses INKEY( ) to get the keypress out of the typeahead buffer, or to identify what key was pressed. Otherwise, the keypress will be used as input to subsequent commands which expect keyboard entry (e.g., ACCEPT, READ, and WAIT). The program then either decides what to do based on the key pressed or prompts the user to find out what to do.

Insert ON KEY DO <key trap program> before the group of commands that you have isolated. After the commands, place ON KEY with no parameter to disable the key trap.

Examples

The following program, Clock.PRG, displays the time in the upper right corner of the screen until the user presses a key:

```
* Clock.PRG
*

SET TYPEAHEAD TO 1  && Only allow a single keypress
SET SCOREBOARD OFF  && Using line zero
SET TALK OFF
stop = .F.  && This flag variable is changed to true by Stop.PRG

* Activate key trap before continuous loop begins.  Stop.PRG
* changes the stop flag variable used as the DO WHILE loop
* condition to .T.
ON KEY DO Stop

* Displays the new time on the screen every second.
DO WHILE .NOT. stop
   cur_time = TIME()
   IF cur_time <> TIME()
      @ 0, 72 SAY TIME()
   ENDIF
ENDDO

ON KEY  && Disable key trap
SET TALK ON
SET SCOREBOARD ON
SET TYPEAHEAD TO 20
```

Stop.PRG, listed below, is triggered by ON KEY DO Stop whenever the user presses a key. This program clears the keypress from the typeahead buffer (see INKEY( )) and sets the stop flag variable to .T..

```
* Stop.PRG
*
* This program stops the clock display.

i = INKEY()  && Clear ON KEY key from typeahead buffer
stop = .T.   && Set stop flag to true to terminate display loop
CLEAR        && Erase the screen
RETURN
```

Warnings

ON KEY cannot be used to trap the Ctrl-S or Left Arrow keys. These keys are reserved by dBASE III PLUS at all times to stop and start screen scrolling.

The validity of the command used as the ON KEY command line option is not checked when ON KEY is executed; instead, the command is interpreted at the time ON KEY is triggered by a keypress.

Tips

If your ON KEY key trap program assumes that only a single key is in the typeahead buffer, you may want to SET TYPEAHEAD TO 1 in the calling program before executing ON KEY; otherwise, a user can press many keys, the first of which triggers ON KEY and the rest of which remain in the typeahead buffer. (See CLEAR TYPEAHEAD.)

ON ESCAPE takes precedence over ON KEY; if there is an ON ESCAPE and an ON KEY in effect, pressing the Esc key activates the ON ESCAPE rather than the ON KEY. To trap the Esc key with ON KEY you must have SET ESCAPE OFF and must not have an ON ESCAPE in effect.

Operator. *See* **Expression**

OS( )

Syntax `OS()`

Overview

The OS( ) function has no arguments.

Procedure

OS( ), short for operating system, returns a character string and can be used anywhere in the language where a character expression is appropriate.

Examples

OS( ) identifies the name and version number of the operating system under which dBASE III PLUS is running. For example,

```
? OS()
DOS 3.10
```

Warnings

Because of its simple syntax, there are no error messages associated with OS( ).

Tips This function was added to the language when dBASE was intended to run on operating systems other than DOS. At the time of this writing, dBASE III PLUS is available only under the MS/PC-DOS operating system.

OTHERWISE. *See* DO CASE

PACK

Syntax `PACK`

Overview The PACK command is used to remove permanently the records marked for deletion from the active database file. Any index files that are open with the database file when PACK is executed are automatically reindexed (see REINDEX) after the deleted records are removed from the database file. The database and index files remain open after PACK is finished.

Procedure To remove the records marked for deletion from a database file with PACK, you must first open the file. (See USE.) If you are using dBASE III PLUS in a network environment, exclusive use (see SET EXCLUSIVE, USE) of the active database file is required to do a PACK.

Before you PACK a file, you may want to review the records marked for deletion to ensure that you are not removing records that you want to keep. LIST FOR DELETED( ) lists all the records marked for deletion. (See RECALL if you want to reinstate records marked for deletion.)

Issue PACK when you are sure that you want to remove permanently the deleted records.

Examples Suppose that you want to discontinue the Black patent leather shoe because of lack of sales. The following commands DELETE this record from the Inventry file and permanently remove it using PACK:

```
. USE Inventry INDEX Part_No
. SEEK "BL861"  && The shoe has BL861 as the part number
. DISPLAY Part_No, Descrip
Record#  Part_No Descrip
      5  BL861   Black high heel patent leather pump.

. DELETE
      1 record deleted
. DISPLAY Part_No, Descrip  && Note the asterisk in the display
Record#  Part_No Descrip
      5 *BL861   Black high heel patent leather pump.

. PACK
      5 records copied
Rebuilding index - C:Part_No.ndx
  100% indexed            5 Records indexed
. CLOSE DATABASES
```

Warnings

If you use PACK in the network version of dBASE III PLUS, exclusive use of the active database file is required. If you attempt to PACK a database file that was opened for shared use, the error message *Exclusive open of file is required* is displayed. Either SET EXCLUSIVE ON and reopen file, or reopen the file with USE <filename> EXCLUSIVE and issue PACK again.

Once you PACK a file, there is no way to recover the lost data. This command does not prompt you before removing the records that are marked for deletion, regardless of the status of SET SAFETY. Thus, if you accidentally PACK a file, the only way to get back your original file is to use your backup. If you don't make backups regularly, the data is permanently lost.

Make backups of your important database files using the dBASE III PLUS COPY TO or COPY FILE commands, or use the operating system COPY or BACKUP utility to make backup copies of your files.

Tips

You can ignore the records that are marked for deletion in the active database file without permanently removing them from the file with PACK. (See SET DELETED for more information.)

When you PACK a database file, the number of records that remain in the file is displayed on the screen. If there are open index files, the indexing information is also displayed. You can suppress these displays with SET TALK OFF.

See DELETE for information on marking records for deletion; see RECALL for information on reinstating records marked for deletion.

PACK does not recover diskspace from memo field data stored in .DBT files. Use COPY TO to "pack" those memo files.

PARAMETERS

Syntax `PARAMETERS <memory variable list>`

Overview

PARAMETERS is the receiving command for DO <filename> WITH <parameter list>. (See DO.) The DO...WITH command that executes the program or procedure passes a list of parameters to the routine, and the routine makes its own private copy (see PRIVATE) of the parameter values using the memory variable list that is part of the PARAMETERS command.

The routine can make any changes at all to the parameters. When the execution of the routine is complete, the private copy of the memory variable is either lost or is passed back to the calling program (i.e., the program containing the DO...WITH command). If the corresponding parameter in the original DO...WITH parameter list is a memory variable, the value of the PARAMETERS memory variable is transferred to the original memory variable. If the corresponding parameter is a more complicated expression or a field name, the PARAMETERS memory variable is lost. In either case, the private copy of the memory variables created by the PARAMETERS command is released before control is returned to the calling program.

Procedure

The PARAMETERS command must be used in a program or procedure that is executed by the DO...WITH command. (See DO.) The memory variables named in the list must be separated by commas and must be equal in number to the parameters in the DO...WITH parameter list.

In a program, the PARAMETERS statement must be the first executable command; the only exception is comment command lines. (See * (Asterisk).) In a procedure, it must be the first executable command after the PROCEDURE command. Executable commands that precede the PARAMETERS command are ignored; no error message is displayed.

Examples

The following example illustrates how to pass a parameter to a program and receive a new value back:

```
* Calc.PRG
SET TALK OFF

* Formula contains the procedures for calculating area and volume.
SET PROCEDURE TO Formula

* Initialize all variables to zero.
STORE 0 TO area, volume, length, width, height

* Prompt user for dimensions.
CLEAR
@  9, 0 SAY "Enter the dimensions of a rectangular solid " + ;
            "in inches."
@ 11, 0 SAY "Length " GET length
@ 12, 0 SAY "Width  " GET width
@ 13, 0 SAY "Height " GET height
READ

* Compute the area using the length and width.
* The area is passed as a parameter so that the computed
* value will be returned.
DO Area WITH area, length, width

* Compute the volume using the area and height.
* The volume is passed as a parameter so that the computed
* value will be returned.
DO Volume WITH volume, area, height

* The computed values, area and volume, are displayed.
@ 15, 0 SAY "The area is " + LTRIM(STR(area)) + " square inches."
@ 16, 0 SAY "The volume is " + LTRIM(STR(volume)) + ;
            " cubic inches."
```

The procedure file, Formula.PRG, is listed below:

```
* Formula.PRG

******************************************************************
*                                                                *
* This procedure file contains procedures that compute the area *
* and volume of a rectangular solid, and pass these values back *
* to the calling routine.                                        *
*                                                                *
******************************************************************

PROCEDURE Area  && Computes area of a rectangle
PARAMETERS area, length, width
area = length * width
RETURN

PROCEDURE Volume  && Computes volume of rectangular solid
PARAMETERS volume, area, height
volume = area * height
RETURN
```

If you execute the Calc program by typing `DO Calc` at the dot prompt, your screen should look like the one in Figure 67. Type 200 for the length, 30 for the width, and 12 for the height (each value followed by Enter). Your screen should look like the one in Figure 68.

Warnings Passing fields and expressions other than memory variables as parameters with the DO...WITH command is permitted, but the value of the corresponding PARAMETERS memory variable is returned to the calling program for memory variable parameters only.

If the number of memory variables in the PARAMETERS list does not match the number of parameters in the corresponding DO...WITH command, the error message *Wrong number of parameters* is displayed. There must be a one-to-one correspondence between these two lists. It is not possible to have "optional" parameters.

```
Enter the dimensions of a rectangular solid in inches.

Length _          0
Width             0
Height            0
```

Figure 67

```
Enter the dimensions of a rectangular solid in inches.

Length        200
Width          30
Height         12

The area is 6000 square inches.
The volume is 72000 cubic inches.
```

Figure 68

If you execute a program that is expecting parameters (i.e., one that has a PARAMETERS command) and neglect to specify the WITH option as part of the DO command, the PARAMETERS command will not be recognized by the dBASE III PLUS command interpreter, and the error message *** *Unrecognized command verb* will be displayed.

If you execute a program that does not have a PARAMETERS command using the DO...WITH command, the error message *No PARAMETER statement found* is displayed.

Tips

You can use the same memory variable names in the DO...WITH parameter list and the PARAMETERS list without fear of conflict. Changes made to PARAMETERS variables are also made to the DO...WITH variables.

Using PARAMETERS adds to the number of memory variables in use even if you use the same variable names. Remember that you can have a maximum of 256 memory variables in use at one time.

DISPLAY MEMORY shows the PARAMETERS variables with references to the expressions in the DO...WITH list. The @ symbol is used to indicate that a variable is linked to an expression as a parameter.

PCOL( )

Syntax `PCOL()`

Overview

The PCOL( ) function, short for print column, has no arguments. This function determines and returns the column number of the current printer position.

Procedure

PCOL( ) returns a number and can be used anywhere in the language where a numeric expression is appropriate.

Examples

PCOL( ) is used when sending the result of @...SAY commands to the printer. It tells @...SAY to begin printing in the column where the last printed output ended. This function is useful when you want to avoid conversion functions and @...SAY commands that are too long (the maximum command line length in dBASE III PLUS is 254 characters including blank spaces). The following routine prints a form letter for all customers whose accounts are overdue. The program makes extensive use of the PCOL( ) function to break up the @...SAY commands:

```
* Letter.PRG
*
SET TALK OFF
SET DEVICE TO PRINTER
USE Customer
LOCATE FOR Deadline < DATE()
DO WHILE FOUND()
   @  6, 0      SAY TRIM(First_Name) + " " + Last_Name
   @  7, 0      SAY TRIM(Address1)
   @  8, 0      SAY TRIM(City) + ", " + State + "  " + Zip
   @  9,70      SAY DATE()
   @ 10, 0      SAY "Dear " + TRIM(First_Name) + " "
   @ 10, PCOL() SAY TRIM(Last_Name) + ":"
   @ 12, 0      SAY "Our records show that your account is "
   @ 12, PCOL() SAY "overdue.  "
   @ 12, PCOL() SAY "Your balance is $"
   @ 12, PCOL() SAY LTRIM(STR(Amt_Owed, 10, 2)) + "."
   @ 13, 0      SAY "This amount was due and payable on "
   @ 13, PCOL() SAY Deadline
   @ 13, PCOL() SAY ".  Please send payment immediately."
   @ 14, 0      SAY "If you have already submitted your payment,"
   @ 14, PCOL() SAY " disregard this notice."
   CONTINUE
ENDDO
USE
EJECT
SET DEVICE TO SCREEN
SET TALK ON
```

Warnings

Because of its simple syntax, there are no error messages associated with PCOL( ).

Tips PCOL( ) works only when addressing the printer. Use COL( ) for addressing the screen.

When used in conjunction with the @...SAY command, the $ symbol can be used in place of PCOL( ). This is a carryover from dBASE II that maintains consistency with that language.

PICTURE

Syntax PICTURE <template>

Overview The PICTURE < template > allows you to specify limited display rules for the @...GET and @...SAY commands and the TRANSFORM( ) function. (With TRANSFORM( ), only the template is specified – not the PICTURE keyword). PICTURE also allows you to define limited data validation criteria for @...GET.

The < template > is a character expression. The resulting string consists of certain symbols that have a special meaning. These symbols are referred to as PICTURE template and function symbols, and are listed below:

TEMPLATE	RULES
!	Forces letters (input and display) to uppercase. Has no effect on other characters.
$	Displays the leading zeros in a number as dollar signs. For data types other than numeric, treated as a non-template symbol.
*	Displays the leading zeros in a number as asterisks. For data types other than numeric, treated as a non-template symbol.
.	Displays a decimal point. For data types other than numeric, treated as a non-template symbol.
,	Displays a comma if non-zero numbers exist to the left of the comma. For data types other than numeric, treated as a non-template symbol.
#	Allows input of numbers, signs, and blanks only. Has no effect on data display.
9	Allows input of numbers (and signs for numeric data type) only. Has no effect on data display.
A	Allows input of letters only. Has no effect on data display.

TEMPLATE	RULES
L	Allows input of logical values (Y, N, T, and F) only. Also works with character data types, but displays any character other than Y, N, T or F as a blank.
N	Allows input of letters and numbers only. Has no effect on data display.
X	Allows input of any character. Has no effect on data display.
Y	Allows input of a Y or an N only. Works with character data types also, but displays any character other than Y, N, T or F as a blank. T is displayed as Y and F is displayed as N.

FUNCTION	RULES
!	Forces letters (input and display) to uppercase. Has no effect on other characters.
(	Displays negative numbers surrounded by parentheses. Has no effect if used with a data type other than numeric or if used with @...GET.
A	Allows input of letters only. Has no effect on data display.
B	Left-justifies the display of numeric type data.
C	Displays positive numbers followed by the letters CR (for credit). Has no effect if used with a data type other than numeric or if used with @...GET.
D	Displays dates in default date format, MM/DD/YY. Also, works with character and numeric data types if they are formatted properly. Characters should be of the form "MM/DD/[CC]YY", and numbers of the form MMDDCCYY (where MM is month, DD is day, CC is century and YY is year). The order of the date components depends on SET DATE and the use of the century depends on SET CENTURY. (See those commands for details.)
E	Displays dates in European date format, DD/MM/YY. Works with character and numeric data types also as described above for the D function.
R	Causes non-template symbols in PICTURE template to be treated differently for character type data. Without the R function, non-template symbols are displayed instead of the corresponding character in the string and are stored in the resulting string. Using R inserts the non-template symbol in the character string display and does not store them in the result.
S<n>	Displays a character string using the specified width, <n>, where n is an integer. If there are more than n characters in the string, the data is scrolled horizontally for input only.

FUNCTION	RULES
X	Displays negative numbers followed by the letters DB (for debit). Has no effect if used with a data type other than numeric or if used with @...GET.
Z	Displays zeros as blanks.

PICTURE functions and template symbols are used differently because functions apply to the entire expression (i.e., the @...SAY or TRANSFORM( ) expression or the @...GET variable) result, whereas template symbols apply only to a single character in the expression result.

PICTURE functions and template symbols have different syntax as well as different uses. A PICTURE template is formed by stringing together several template symbols, one for each character in the expression result. Function symbols, if used as part of a PICTURE template (see Tip below), must always be preceded by the @ character. If both a template and a function are used, the function must appear first in the PICTURE template, followed by a space before the template.

When a PICTURE template is used with @...SAY or TRANSFORM( ), the rules of the function and template symbols are applied to the expression result. With @...SAY, the display of the result is affected by the PICTURE template. With TRANSFORM( ), the actual result is affected.

When a PICTURE template is used with @...GET, the rules of the function and template symbols are applied to the variable, and it is displayed accordingly. When the cursor is positioned in the data entry area for the variable, the function and template symbols are used again to restrict data entry.

Procedure

Use a PICTURE <template> with @...SAY and TRANSFORM( ) to specify how the display is to look. Use it with @...GET to specify data entry validation criteria and display rules.

Examples

The following examples illustrate the use of various PICTURE templates with character type data. The first LIST command shows the data as it appears in the database file. The second one uses TRANSFORM( ) with the ! PICTURE function to capitalize the entire Last_Name field. The third LIST uses the template "!XXXXXXXXXXX" to capitalize the first letter and display the rest of the Last_Name as it appears in the database file. The last uses a PICTURE template along with the @R function to capitalize the

Last_Name and insert a blank space between the letters. (Note that the ! symbol is the only one that affects character data display.)

```
. USE Mail
. LIST Next 5 Last_Name
Record#  Last_Name
      1  SMITH
      2  Corbbit
      3  Roman
      4  Gurly
      5  King

. GO TOP
. LIST Next 5 TRANSFORM(Last_Name, "@!")
Record#  TRANSFORM(Last_Name, "@!")
      1  SMITH
      2  CORBBIT
      3  ROMAN
      4  GURLY
      5  KING

. GO TOP
. LIST Next 5 TRANSFORM(Last_Name, "!XXXXXXXXXXX")
Record#  TRANSFORM(Last_Name, "!XXXXXXXXXXX")
      1  SMITH
      2  Corbbit
      3  Roman
      4  Gurly
      5  King

. GO TOP
. LIST Next 5 TRANSFORM(Last_Name, "@R ! ! ! ! ! ! ! ! ! ! ! !")
Record#  TRANSFORM(Last_Name, "@R ! ! ! ! ! ! ! ! ! ! ! !")
      1  S M I T H
      2  C O R B B I T
      3  R O M A N
      4  G U R L Y
      5  K I N G

. CLOSE DATABASES
```

For data validation of character variables, use @...GET with a PICTURE template. The following routine uses several different PICTURE templates, each of which is commented by a preceding @...SAY command to explain its effect:

```
* At_Char.PRG
*
SET TALK OFF
* Several character variables are initialized.
STORE SPACE(10) TO char_one, char_two, char_three, char_four, ;
                   char_five, char_six
STORE SPACE(80) TO long_char
CLEAR

@ 4, 0 SAY "First character must be a letter, and the rest " + ;
           "must be numbers..."
@ 5,10 GET char_one PICTURE "A999999999"

@ 6, 0 SAY "All characters must be numbers..."
@ 7,10 GET char_two PICTURE "9999999999"

@ 8, 0 SAY "All characters are forced to uppercase, and " + ;
           "must be letters..."
@ 9,10 GET char_three PICTURE "@!A"

@ 10, 0 SAY "First four characters must be numbers..."
@ 11,10 GET char_four PICTURE "9999-XXXXX"

@ 12, 0 SAY "First five characters must be numbers, and " + ;
            "the rest must be letters..."
@ 13,10 GET char_five PICTURE "@R 99999-AAAAA"

@ 14, 0 SAY "First character must be a letter, and all " + ;
            "letters are converted to uppercase..."
@ 15,10 GET char_six PICTURE "@! AXXXXXXXXX"

@ 16, 0 SAY "This character is longer than the rest, " + ;
            "but it scrolls in ten columns..."
@ 17,10 GET long_char PICTURE "@S10"

READ
SET TALK ON
```

To execute, type `DO At_Char` at the dot prompt, and your screen should look like the one in Figure 69.

```
First character must be a letter, and the rest must be numbers...

All characters must be numbers...

All characters are forced to uppercase, and must be letters...

First four characters must be numbers...

First five characters must be numbers, and the rest must be letters...

First character must be a letter, and all letters are converted to uppercase...

This character is longer than the rest, but it scrolls in ten columns...
```

Figure 69

If you try to enter invalid data into any of the data entry areas, the bell rings and the cursor remains in the same position until you enter the correct data.

The following examples illustrate the use of various PICTURE templates with numeric type data. In all of the examples, the first LIST command shows the data as it appears in the database file. The second one uses TRANSFORM( ) with a PICTURE function or template to change the display of the data:

```
. USE Inventry
. LIST OFF Quantity - Reorder
 Quantity - Reorder
                -3
                 1
                 0
                -5
                 0
                 1

. LIST OFF TRANSFORM(Quantity - Reorder, "@(")
 TRANSFORM(Quantity - Reorder, "@(")
 (          3.00)
            1.00
            0.00
 (          5.00)
            0.00
            1.00
```

```
. LIST OFF Price
      Price
      23.95
      65.99
      47.99
      75.99
      63.87
      23.98

. LIST OFF TRANSFORM(Price, "@B")
 TRANSFORM(Price, "@B")
 23.95
 65.99
 47.99
 75.99
 63.87
 23.98

. USE Employee
. LIST OFF Salary
      Salary
   43252.29
   38712.23
   43712.00
   25003.23
   27832.12
  123000.00
  250000.00
   21987.33
   57612.12
   53137.77

. LIST OFF TRANSFORM(Salary, "999,999,999.99")
 TRANSFORM(Salary, "999,999,999.99")
      43,252.29
      38,712.23
      43,712.00
      25,003.23
      27,832.12
     123,000.00
     250,000.00
      21,987.33
      57,612.12
      53,137.77
```

```
. LIST OFF TRANSFORM(Salary, "$$$,$$$,$$$.99")
TRANSFORM(Salary, "$$$,$$$,$$$.99")
$$$$$43,252.29
$$$$$38,712.23
$$$$$43,712.00
$$$$$25,003.23
$$$$$27,832.12
$$$$123,000.00
$$$$250,000.00
$$$$$21,987.33
$$$$$57,612.12
$$$$$53,137.77

. CLOSE DATABASES
```

Warnings

If the error message *Variable not found* is displayed as a result of a PICTURE template, you probably neglected to enclose the template in delimiters. Be sure to enclose the template in single quotes, double quotes, or square brackets.

If both a PICTURE and a RANGE template are used with @...GET, the PICTURE template must come first; otherwise, the error message *Unrecognized phrase/keyword in command* is displayed.

Tips

Composite functions can be made by combining one or more function symbols. For example, a function that displays positive numbers followed by CR and negative numbers followed by DB would look like "@CX". A function that allows letters only and forces them to uppercase would look like "@!A".

If you want to save some space in your database files, do not store unnecessary characters (e.g., parentheses, dashes) in character fields such as phone number and social security number. Instead, store only the pertinent data and use the @R PICTURE function to insert the formatting characters whenever you display or edit that field. For example, a phone number can be stored in a ten-character field and formatted for display or editing with the PICTURE template "@R (999)999-9999". A social security number can be stored in a nine-character field and formatted with the PICTURE template "@R 999-99-9999". The @R function inserts the special characters in the display but does not store them as part of the variable.

Instead of using the function symbol as part of a PICTURE template, you can use the FUNCTION keyword followed by one or more of the function symbols. If you use FUNCTION, it must precede any PICTURE that you use. The function symbols must be enclosed in delimiters and must not be preceded by the @ character. If both a PICTURE and a FUNCTION template are used, the FUNCTION template must come first; otherwise, the error message *Unrecognized phrase/keyword in command* is displayed. For example, instead of using PICTURE "@! AAAAA", use FUNCTION "!" PICTURE "AAAAA".

PRIVATE

Syntax

```
PRIVATE <memory variable list>
PRIVATE ALL [LIKE|EXCEPT <skeleton>]
```

Overview

The PRIVATE command declares memory variables that are private to the program in which the command is issued. Private memory variables can be accessed only by the program that declares them and programs that it calls (directly or indirectly). Any memory variable with the same name already in existence is temporarily hidden from access. The private variables are automatically released from memory as soon as the program that declared them returns to its calling program. Any variables hidden by that program become accessible at that time.

There are two forms of PRIVATE. The first, PRIVATE <memory variable list>, lets you list by name the private memory variables that you want to declare. The list is separated by commas.

The second, PRIVATE ALL [LIKE | EXCEPT <skeleton>], lets you describe the variable names that you want to declare as private. PRIVATE ALL indicates that all of the variables used by a program are private. PRIVATE ALL LIKE <skeleton> indicates that all the variable names of a particular form are private. PRIVATE ALL EXCEPT <skeleton> indicates that all the variable names except those of a particular form are private. (See Skeleton for more information of how to compose a skeleton.)

Procedure

Because memory variables initialized at the dot prompt are always public (see PUBLIC), you cannot use PRIVATE effectively at the dot prompt. Furthermore, by default, all memory variables created in a program are automatically private to that program; therefore, you do not need to use PRIVATE when creating a new memory variable.

PRIVATE is used in programs in order to use a memory variable name that already exists, disregarding the existing memory variable completely. Essentially, you create a new, private copy of the memory variable that remains in effect until the program returns to its calling program.

When you decide what variables you want to make private, put PRIVATE near the beginning of the program before using any of the variables. The variables will be automatically released from memory at the end of the program.

Examples

The following example illustrates how you can use PRIVATE to ensure that a subroutine does not interfere with any existing variables. All variables used in the routine are declared private. Consequently, this subroutine cannot access or change any variable names used in other parts of the application, so you do not have to ensure that the variable names in the subroutine are unique. In the example, the main, calling program is not listed; assume that the program listed below is part of a larger application:

```
* RptMenu.PRG
*

PRIVATE ALL  && All variables used by this subroutine are local

* All reports use the following view.
USE Orders
SELECT 2
USE Inventry INDEX Part_No
SELECT 1
SET RELATION TO Part_No INTO Inventry

* All reports require total number of orders, total price, and
* average price.  After these are computed, Orders database file
* is positioned at first record.
COUNT TO ord_num
SUM Quantity * Inventry->Price TO tot_price
AVERAGE Quantity * Inventry->Price TO avg_price
GO TOP

DO WHILE .T.

   choice = 0
   CLEAR
```

```
    * Display report submenu
    @  6, 29 SAY "0 - Exit to main menu"
    @  8, 29 SAY "1 - Print Orders"
    @ 10, 29 SAY "2 - Print Invoices"
    @ 12, 29 SAY "3 - Print Inventory"
    @  4, 20 TO 14, 54 DOUBLE
    @ 14, 37 GET choice PICTURE "9" RANGE 0, 3
    READ

    * Execute programs based on menu choice
    DO CASE

       CASE choice = 0
          CLOSE DATABASES
          * Automatically releases all variables created.
          RETURN

       CASE choice = 1
          DO Ord_Rpt

       CASE choice = 2
          DO Invoices

       CASE choice = 3
          DO Inv_Rpt

    ENDCASE
ENDDO
```

Warnings

Remember that PRIVATE hides all existing memory variables that it references, including public memory variables. (See PUBLIC.) If you use PRIVATE ALL in a program, that program will be denied access to all existing memory variables.

Although PRIVATE can be used to have several different memory variables with the same name, each variable uses a memory slot. The maximum number of memory variables available at one time is 256.

Tips

DISPLAY MEMORY indicates with the word (*hidden*) that a memory variable is hidden by a private variable.

The PUBLIC or PRIVATE status of memory variables is not saved to the memory file. (See SAVE.) Instead, the status of the restored variables is decided when the memory file is restored. (See RESTORE.) Restoring memory variables from a memory file is the same as initializing the variables for the first time. By default, variables are initialized as public at the dot prompt. Therefore, issuing RESTORE from the dot prompt restores all of the variables as public variables. Similarly, RESTORE restores all variables in a program as private to that program. If you want variables in a memory file to be public when they are restored in a program, use PUBLIC to declare those variables, then use RESTORE FROM...ADDITIVE. Using the ADDITIVE keyword forces RESTORE to look at the current memory variables and to retain their PUBLIC or PRIVATE status.

PROCEDURE

Syntax `PROCEDURE <procedure name>`

Overview

The PROCEDURE command is used to name the procedures in a procedure file and to identify where each procedure begins in the file.

The procedure name follows the same naming conventions as file names (i.e., the procedure name can be from one to eight characters in length, and must begin with a letter; the remaining characters can be any combination of letters, numbers, and underscores).

Procedure

A procedure file is a text file that can contain a maximum of thirty-two complete dBASE III PLUS programs or procedures that you create using the built-in text editor (see MODIFY COMMAND), or a word processor of your choice. Like a program file, a procedure file has a .PRG extension by default.

When you create the procedure file, use PROCEDURE at the beginning of each new procedure in the file. The name that you give the procedure with this command is the one that you will use when you execute the procedure. (See DO.)

Once the procedure file is created, you must first open the file (see SET PROCEDURE) to execute the procedures in the file. Once the file is open, the individual procedures in the file can be executed just like program files. (See DO). When you are finished with the procedure file, you must close it. (See CLOSE PROCEDURE.)

Examples

The following example illustrates how to open a procedure file, execute the procedures stored in the file, and close the file:

```
* Compute.PRG
*
SET TALK OFF
SET PROCEDURE TO Stats  && Open the procedure file
USE Mail
* The field name on which you want to gather statistics
* must be passed as a character string.
field_name = "Age"
* The variables used in the procedure are initialized.
STORE 0 TO mean, sum_total, variance, std_dev
* Statistics are computed.
DO SumTotal WITH field_name
DO Mean WITH field_name
DO Variance WITH field_name, mean
DO Std_Dev WITH variance
* Statistics are displayed.
? "Sum: " + LTRIM(STR(sum_total, 10, 2))
? "Mean: " + LTRIM(STR(mean, 10, 2))
? "Variance: " + LTRIM(STR(variance, 10, 2))
? "Standard deviation: " + LTRIM(STR(std_dev, 10, 2))
CLOSE DATABASES
CLOSE PROCEDURE
SET TALK ON
```

The Stats procedure file is listed below. Note the use of PROCEDURE to identify each of the procedures in the file.

```
* Stats.PRG is a procedure file that computes statistical
* values based on a field name that is passed to the individual
* procedures.

PROCEDURE SumTotal
* This procedure computes the sum of the numbers stored in the
* field name that is passed as a parameter, field_name.
PARAMETERS field_name
SUM &field_name TO sum_total
RETURN
```

```
PROCEDURE Mean
* This procedure computes the mean of the numbers stored in the
* field name that is passed as a parameter, field_name.
PARAMETERS field_name
AVERAGE &field_name TO mean
RETURN

PROCEDURE Variance
* This procedure computes the variance of the numbers stored in
* the field name that is passed as a parameter, field_name.
PARAMETERS field_name, mean
square_sum = 0
GO TOP
DO WHILE .NOT. EOF()
   square_sum = &field_name ^ 2 + square_sum
   SKIP
ENDDO
variance = square_sum / RECCOUNT() - mean ^ 2
RETURN

PROCEDURE Std_Dev
* This procedure computes the standard deviation of the numbers
* stored in the field name passed as a parameter, field_name.
PARAMETERS variance
std_dev = SQRT(variance)
RETURN
```

If you execute the program, you will get the following statistics based on the age of the people in the mailing list:

```
. DO Compute
Sum: 583.00
Mean: 32.39
Variance: 40.68
Standard deviation: 6.38
```

Note that with this program you can compute statistics for any numeric field in any database file by changing the database file and the memory variable field_name.

Warnings There is no error message if you open a procedure file with more than thirty-two procedures; instead, any procedure past the thirty-second is ignored. Attempting to execute such a procedure results in the error message *File does not exist*, unless there is a .PRG file with the same name. In that case, the program is executed instead of the procedure.

Similarly, bad procedure names are not detected when you open the file, but you will not be able to execute a procedure with an incorrect name. The error message *File does not exist* is displayed if you attempt to do so.

Unlike a program file, a procedure can call itself without causing an error; however, there is a limit to the number of DO commands that you can execute without issuing a RETURN. If you call the same procedure more than twenty times, the error message *DOs nested too deep* is displayed. This message can also occur if you have procedures that execute other procedures in the same file. If the level of nesting (i.e., DO commands without a corresponding RETURN) is too deep, this error message will occur.

Although executing a procedure from within the same procedure file is not trapped as an error when you do it, this form of recursion is a bad programming practice in dBASE III PLUS and should be avoided. You won't be able to use this same practice with program files because of the error message *File is already open.*

Tips

Using a procedure file can save you time, since thirty-two programs may be kept in the same file. Instead of opening a file each time you execute a program with DO, open a procedure file only once with SET PROCEDURE. Once the procedure file is open, executing a procedure with DO does not require another open file and, therefore, decreases execution time. Of course, using procedures also decreases the number of files open. (The maximum is fifteen.)

If you have several program files that you want to turn into procedures, use the ^KR (read file) feature in MODIFY COMMAND to read the .PRG file into the procedure file. After you enter the program file name with its extension, the contents of the program file is added to the end of the procedure file. Insert a line before the first line of the program file using Ctrl-N, and type in a PROCEDURE command to identify the new procedure; you can use the same name as the original .PRG file. When you have an open procedure file, a procedure with the same name as a .PRG file takes precedence over the file (i.e., DO executes the procedure instead of the program file).

If you have one program file that calls several procedures, the procedures can be located in that program file rather than in a separate procedure file. The procedures must be located after the program's code; the program simply SETs PROCEDURE TO itself. The example above would put all procedures from Stats.PRG into Compute.PRG after the Compute's existing code. Change the command `SET PROCEDURE TO Stats` to `SET PROCEDURE TO Compute`.

Protect

Overview

The Protect facility is used with dBASE III PLUS in a network environment to provide password protection for your database files. When you use Protect, the information that you define is saved to a file named Dbsystem.DB. This file forces users to go through a log-in sequence rather than directly entering dBASE III PLUS. Protect is an external utility packaged with dBASE III PLUS. It is not a command.

Protect assigns a user name, password, group name, and access level for each dBASE III PLUS user on the network. Once the elements are defined, the user must provide a user name, password, and group name when prompted to log-in.

Assign each database file to a particular group. This tells Protect that you want to use that particular group name to encrypt the database file in order to prevent unauthorized access to the file; it also provides for security in and out of dBASE III PLUS. When a user logs in, the user's group name is used to determine which database files can be accessed. Outside of dBASE III PLUS, users cannot use other means (e.g., the DOS Debug Utility) to decipher the data in encrypted files.

You can assign file and field privileges for up to eight access levels, thereby further securing the file against unauthorized access by users in the same group. The available file privileges are Delete, Extend, Read, and Update. The field privileges are None, Full, and Read-Only. The user's access level (also defined in Protect) is compared to the file and field privileges for that level to determine exactly what operations the user is allowed to perform on a particular file.

Procedure

Once you have installed dBASE III PLUS for use on your network, you can use the Protect facility whenever you want to. The file, Protect.EXE, should be located in the same directory as the dBA files used to execute dBASE III PLUS. To use Protect, type `Protect` at the DOS prompt, then press Enter. You should have everything well-planned before attempting to secure your database files.

After you use Protect and save your work, no other user can access dBASE III PLUS without a log-in sequence. This requires that you know all users and their roles in the database management system. That is, you must know what group or groups of people each user works with and what database files each group needs to access. Furthermore, if the individuals in the group need varying levels of access to the files assigned to their group or to the fields in those files, you must have all of this information thought out and recorded in advance. The volume of data that you must deal with to use Protect effectively can be staggering. You must keep track of it manually since there is no reporting capability in Protect to give you a printout of your work.

Before you use Protect, divide the users into logical groups according to the tasks that they have in common. For example, you may have a group of people who use the database management system for processing orders and another group that does the payroll. Once you have established the groups, decide what files the group needs to access. You can put the same user in more than one group, but a file can belong only to a single group because the group name is used as the encryption key. Make up a group name for each group, and let the users decide on their own user name and password.

To assign an access level for a user, you must know the relative importance of that user's job in the group. If all of the users have the same job, they should all have the same access level and should probably all have full file and field privileges at that access level. If one of them is the supervisor or in some other position of authority, that user should be assigned a lower access level than the other users so that you can grant different privileges. If there is a user whose access you want to restrict more than the others in the group for any reason, assign a higher access level to that user. For example, in the Payroll group you may want to restrict who has the authority to change the Salary field and to add new employees to the file; in the Orders group, you may want to restrict who can change customer numbers, part numbers, and supplier numbers.

The following is an example of how you might represent this information:

		ACCESS
GROUP NAME:	Payroll	
USERS/PASSWORDS:	Tom/Tomcat	1
	Mark/Ricecake	8
	Chris/Columbus	8
FILES:	Employee	
	TaxTable	

		ACCESS
GROUP NAME:	Orders	
USERS/PASSWORDS:	Chris/Columbus	8
	Debby/Doodahday	1
	Len/Skinhead	8
	Orders	
	Inventry	
	Customer	
FILES:	Supplier	

You must next determine for each database file the privileges associated with each access level number. For example, access level 1 may have all privileges to all files, while access level eight cannot add records to certain files or even see the data in a particular field.

For the Orders group, the assumption is that any user at any level can process the Orders file in any way. Only access level 1 can change the key fields (i.e., Part_No in Inventry, Cust_No in Customer, and Supplier in Supplier); access level 8 can only read these fields. Finally, only access level 1 can add and delete records to the Inventry file. This means that you must define file privileges for the Inventry file, and field privilege levels for Inventry, Customer, and Supplier. (Orders does not require any access level definitions since its use is not restricted.) The following form can be used to record file access level privileges:

File name: Inventry	FILE PRIVILEGES							
ACCESS LEVELS	1	2	3	4	5	6	7	8
FILE PRIVILEGES								
READ								Yes
UPDATE								Yes
EXTEND	Yes							
DELETE	Yes							

The following forms can be used to record field access level privileges:

File name: Inventry	FIELD PRIVILEGES							
ACCESS LEVELS	1	2	3	4	5	6	7	8
FIELD NAME								
Part_No	Full							R/O

File name: Customer	FIELD PRIVILEGES							
ACCESS LEVELS	1	2	3	4	5	6	7	8
FIELD NAME								
Cust_No	Full							R/O

File name: Supplier	FIELD PRIVILEGES							
ACCESS LEVELS	1	2	3	4	5	6	7	8
FIELD NAME								
Supplier	Full							R/O

Once you have recorded all of this information, you need only execute the Protect.EXE utility and use the menus it provides to enter the information. The menu navigation keys are listed in Appendix B. The example below shows you how to use the forms above to implement the Orders group by adding its users and defining its file and field privileges.

Examples Execute the Protect utility by typing `Protect` at the DOS prompt then pressing Enter. Your screen should look like the one in Figure 70. If you have not already established a password, create one now, type it as prompted, then press Enter. The first time you use a password you are prompted again to make sure that you and Protect agree on your password. Write down your password and store it in a safe place. You must enter your password each time you use Protect. Your password prevents other users from inadvertently changing the security system you have established.

After you verify your password, the Protect menu is displayed and your screen should look like the one in Figure 71. The first menu on the Protect menu bar is called Users. This menu defines groups in terms of the users that belong to them.

For the Orders group, the user information is as follows:

		ACCESS
GROUP NAME:	Orders	
USERS/PASSWORDS:	Chris/Columbus	8
	Debby/Doodahday	1
	Len/Skinhead	8

Figure 70

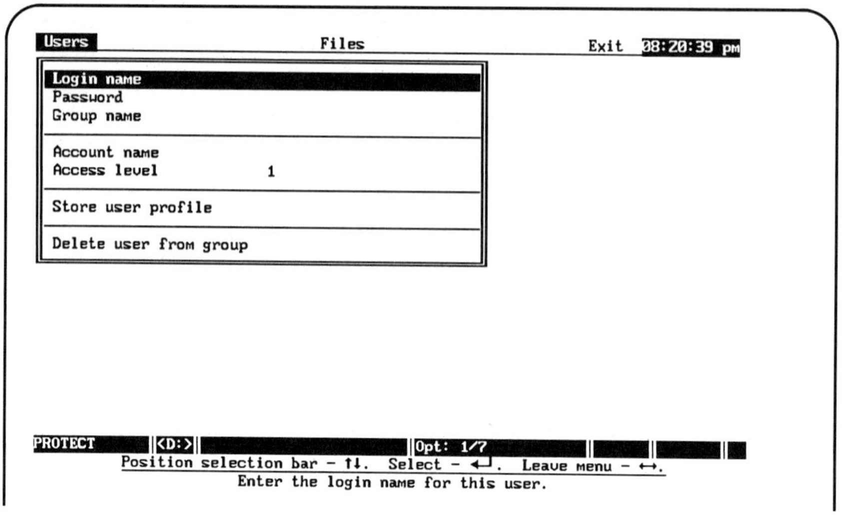

```
Users                       Files                           Exit  08:20:39 pm
 Login name
 Password
 Group name

 Account name
 Access level           1

 Store user profile

 Delete user from group

PROTECT    ||<D:>||                    ||Opt: 1/7   ||   ||   ||
     Position selection bar - ↑↓.  Select - ↵.  Leave menu - ↔.
               Enter the login name for this user.
```

Figure 71

The *Login name* menu option is used to define the user names. Press Enter when this option is highlighted, and type CHRIS followed by Enter. Highlight the *Password* option to type in the password for this user, press Enter, and type Columbus followed by Enter. Highlight the *Group name* option, press Enter, and type ORDERS followed by Enter to put Chris in the order processing group. Highlight the *Access level* option, press Enter, and type 8 followed by Enter to assign Chris an access level of eight. To save this user security profile, highlight *Store user profile* and press Enter. Repeat this procedure to add the other two users listed above to the order processing group. Make sure that you store the user profile each time.

You are now ready to define file and field privileges. Open the Files menu by pressing the Right Arrow. Your screen should look like the one in Figure 72.

With the *Select new file* option highlighted, press Enter to obtain a submenu of database files. Find the Inventry file in the submenu, highlight it, and press Enter. Highlight the *Group name* option and press Enter. Type ORDERS, then press Enter to add the Inventry file to the order processing group. Using the following chart, assign file privileges for this file:

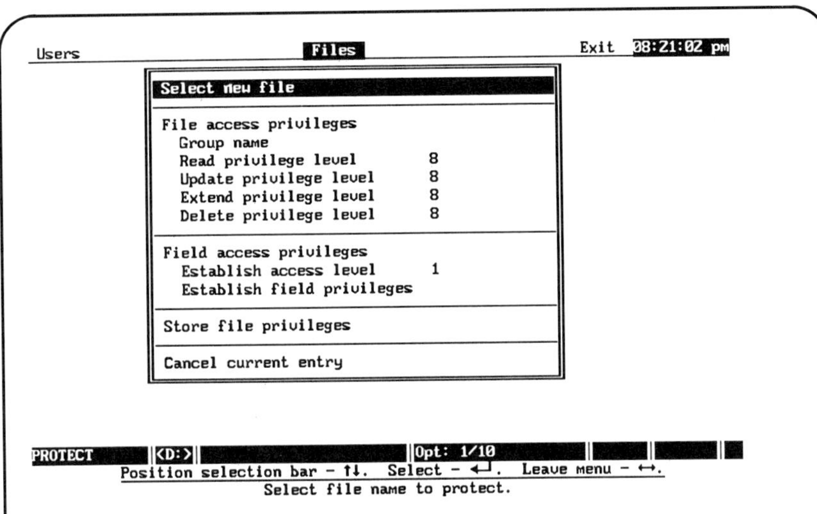

Figure 72

File name: Inventry	FILE PRIVILEGES							
ACCESS LEVELS	1	2	3	4	5	6	7	8
FILE PRIVILEGES								
READ								Yes
UPDATE								Yes
EXTEND	Yes							
DELETE	Yes							

To assign file privileges, highlight the appropriate file *privilege level* menu option (i.e. *Delete, Extend, Read,* or *Update*), press Enter, and type the number associated with the column marked YES in the chart. Use the following chart to specify field privileges for the Inventry file:

File name: Inventry	FIELD PRIVILEGES							
ACCESS LEVELS	1	2	3	4	5	6	7	8
FIELD NAME								
Part_No	Full							R/O

To specify field privileges, highlight *Establish access level*, press Enter, type 8, then press Enter. Highlight *Establish field privileges* and press Enter, and a field list submenu appears to the right of the main menu. Highlight the Part_No field and press Enter until R/O appears to the right of the field name as in Figure 73.This changes the field privilege to read only for users at access level 8. To close this submenu, press the Left or Right Arrow. The default for all field privileges at every level is FULL, so you don't have to repeat this procedure for level 1. Save the file and field privileges for this file by highlighting *Store file privileges* and pressing Enter.

For the Customer and Supplier files, you need only define the field privilege for access level 8. There are no special file privileges for these files. Highlight *Select new file* and press Enter, and this time select the Customer file from the submenu. Type ORDERS for the *Group name* and, as you did with the Part_No field of the Inventry file, define the Cust_No field to be read only for access level eight. The steps are as follows:

1. Highlight *Establish access level* and press Enter.
2. Type 8 and press Enter.
3. Highlight *Establish field privileges* and press Enter.
4. Highlight Cust_No field in the submenu.
5. Press Enter until R/O appears beside field name.

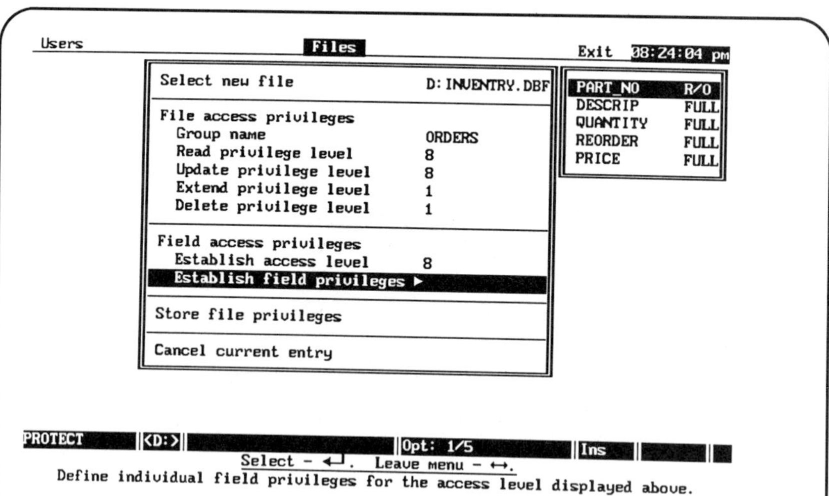

Figure 73

6. Press Left Arrow to close submenu
7. Highlight *Store file privileges* and press Enter.

Repeat this process using the Supplier file and its key field, Supplier. You do not need to define any file or field privilege levels for the Orders file. Simply select the Orders file as the *Select new file* option and type ORDERS for its *Group name* to ensure that other group members cannot access the file.

To exit Protect and save all of the security information, press the Right Arrow to open the Exit menu. Highlight the *Save* option and press Enter to ensure that everything is saved to disk, then select the *Exit* option to leave Protect. When you do this, encrypted forms of the database files that you selected in the Files menu are written to the disk, and a file called Dbsystem.DB is created to keep track of the groups, users, and passwords. For your safety, the original, unencrypted forms of the files are left intact on the disk. The encrypted files are assigned the same name as the original database file but with a .CRP extension.

To use the encrypted files, remove the original database files and rename the encrypted files with .DBF extensions by using the following DOS commands. (You may want to make backup copies of the original .DBF files before issuing these commands.)

```
C> COPY *.CRP TO *.DBF
C> ERASE *.CRP
```

Now that you have used Protect, the log-in screen shown in Figure 74 is displayed whenever a user on the network accesses dBASE III PLUS. Each user must enter the requested information.

Warnings

The Dbsystem.DB file created by Protect is vital to your security system. Make a backup of this file each time you use Protect to make additions or deletions in your security scheme. Backing up this file is important: if this

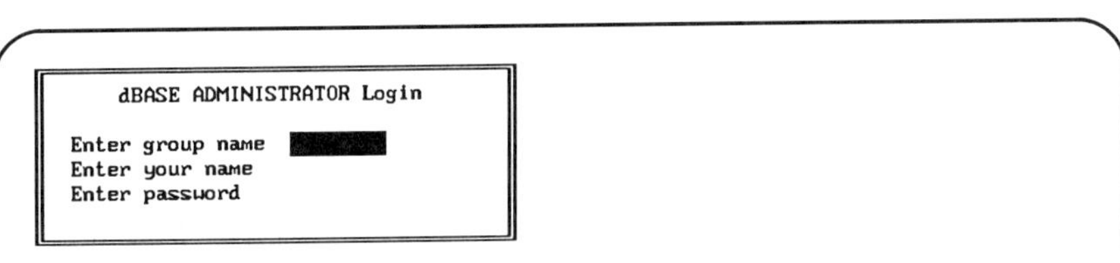

Figure 74

file gets erased or damaged, no user will be able to access the encrypted database files.

Tips Ignore the *Account name* option in the Users menu. It is of no consequence to you or to dBASE III PLUS.

See ACCESS( ), LOGOUT, and SET ENCRYPTION for more information on protected files.

PROW( )

Syntax `PROW()`

Overview The PROW( ) function, short for print row, has no arguments. This function determines and returns the row number of the current printer position.

Procedure PROW( ) returns a number and can be used anywhere in the language where a numeric expression is appropriate.

Examples PROW( ) is used when sending the result of @...SAY commands to the printer. It tells @...SAY to begin printing on the same line as the last printed output. This function is useful when you want to avoid conversion functions and @...SAY commands that are too long (the maximum command line length in dBASE III PLUS is 254 characters, including blank spaces). The following routine prints the Last_Name of the first customer in the Customer database file next to the current date and the amount that the customer owes—all without conversion functions:

```
* Amt_Owed.PRG
*
SET TALK OFF
SET DEVICE TO PRINTER
USE Customer
@ 10, 0 SAY TRIM(Last_Name)
@ PROW(), PCOL()+1 SAY DATE()
@ PROW(), PCOL()+1 SAY Amt_Owed
CLOSE DATABASES
EJECT
```

```
SET DEVICE TO SCREEN
SET TALK ON
```

Consider the equivalent @...SAY command:

```
@ 10, 0 SAY TRIM(Last_Name) + " " + DTOC(DATE()) + " " +;
        STR(Amt_Owed, 10, 2)
```

Warnings Because of its simple syntax, there are no error messages associated with PROW( ).

Tips PROW( ) works only when addressing the printer; use ROW( ) for addressing the screen.

When used in conjunction with @...SAY, the $ symbol can be used in place of PROW( ). This is a carryover from dBASE II in order to maintain consistency with that language.

PUBLIC

Syntax `PUBLIC <memory variable list>`

Overview The PUBLIC command declares a list of memory variables that can be accessed and changed by any program at any level. Such memory variables are called public, or global, variables.

By default, a memory variable created (see STORE) in a program is private to that program (see PRIVATE). This means that the memory variable is available only to the program in which it is first initialized and to programs that are called (directly or indirectly) by this initializing program. (See DO.) When the initializing program returns control to its calling program (see RETURN), all memory variables that it created are removed from memory. (See RELEASE.)

When PUBLIC is issued, each memory variable listed is initialized to a Logical false (.F.) and tagged as a PUBLIC variable unless the variable already exists in memory as public. Any variable listed that exists and has been previously declared as PUBLIC is left with its current value. The variable can then be reinitialized, accessed, and changed by any program at any level. Public memory variables are not automatically removed from memory like private variables; you must explicitly remove them from memory. (See CLEAR MEMORY or RELEASE.)

Procedure

Memory variables initialized at the dot prompt are always PUBLIC; however, in a program, you must explicitly declare the memory variables that you want to be PUBLIC; otherwise, memory variables that you initialize in programs are private. (See PRIVATE.) Thus, it does not make any sense to use the PUBLIC command at the dot prompt.

Furthermore, by default, all memory variables that are initialized in the main program (e.g., the main menu program) are available to all other programs in the application. Even though the variables are private, they are private to the main program, which means that all lower level programs can use and change them; therefore, you do not need to use PUBLIC to allow lower-level programs to use certain memory variables.

If a lower level program, or a subprogram, in an application initializes a memory variable whose value is needed by the calling program, you may want to use PUBLIC at the beginning of the subprogram to make the variable global before initializing it. Otherwise, the variable will be private to the subprogram and will be released before control is returned to the calling program. As a result, the calling program won't be able to access the variable.

Using PUBLIC to pass a variable from a subprogram to the calling program is not recommended because the programs are difficult to understand if you must read and change them later. It is better to initialize the variable to some arbitrary value in the calling program and pass it as a parameter to the subprogram. (See DO and PARAMETERS.) This solution is more straightforward and makes it easier to read the programs and determine what variables are shared by what programs.

Finally, after the application is complete, you may want to use certain memory variables that are created by an application. Since private variables are automatically released, you might consider naming these particular variables with a PUBLIC command; however, there is a better alternative. Instead of declaring these variables to be public, save them to a memory file (see SAVE) just before the final command in the application. Then, when you want to use the variables, restore them from the file into memory. (See RESTORE.)

PUBLIC is seldom used; there is always a better alternative. PUBLIC variables are difficult to work with because you must explicitly remove them from memory when you are finished with them (see RELEASE) and you must be careful that the variables that you declare with PUBLIC do not already exist as private variables.

If you want to use PUBLIC to explicitly declare which variables are to be shared throughout an application, the best way to do so is to use a single PUBLIC command near the beginning of the main program that lists all of the global variables. After the PUBLIC command, use STORE or the assignment statement (see STORE) to initialize each variable to some meaningful value. Then, somewhere near the end of the main program, use the RELEASE command listing all of the public variables, or CLEAR MEMORY to release the variables from memory.

Examples

Rather than illustrating PUBLIC in an application, the following example shows how public memory variables can be changed and hidden by subroutines. The three programs are listed below:

```
* Main.PRG
*
SET TALK OFF
PUBLIC number1, number2
DISPLAY MEMORY  && 1st display

STORE 1 TO number1, number2
DISPLAY MEMORY  && 2nd display

DO Sub1  && Sub1 uses one public variable and hides the other
DISPLAY MEMORY  && 4th display

DO Sub2  && Sub2 uses both public variables
DISPLAY MEMORY  && 5th display

CLEAR MEMORY && Remove all variables from memory
SET TALK ON


* Sub1.PRG
*
* By declaring a PRIVATE number2, the PUBLIC number2 is
* temporarily hidden from access.  A new value is assigned
* to the private number2 that is used in the calculation.
PRIVATE number2
number2 = 5
number1 = number1 + number2
DISPLAY MEMORY  && 3rd display
RETURN
```

```
* Sub2.prg
*
number1 = number1 + number2
RETURN
```

DISPLAY MEMORY is used at various intervals to show what is going on with the memory variables. If you execute main program by typing `DO Main` at the dot prompt, you will see a series of memory displays. These displays are broken up and discussed in the figures below.

The screen in Figure 75 is the result of the first DISPLAY MEMORY command, and it shows how PUBLIC automatically initializes the memory variables to logical values and tags them as public.

The screen in Figure 76 is the result of the second DISPLAY MEMORY command and shows the variables after they are reinitialized to 1 with STORE.

The screen in Figure 77 is the most interesting. It is the result of the DISPLAY MEMORY command issued from the Sub1.PRG subprogram. It shows the original public variable, number2, as hidden because a private copy has been created for use by this subprogram. You can see that the private copy of the variable is used in the calculation by the value of number1.

```
NUMBER1      pub   L  .F.
NUMBER2      pub   L  .F.
    2 variables defined,         4 bytes used
  254 variables available,    5996 bytes available
```

Figure 75

```
NUMBER1      pub   N          1  (          1.00000000)
NUMBER2      pub   N          1  (          1.00000000)
    2 variables defined,        18 bytes used
  254 variables available,    5982 bytes available
```

Figure 76

```
NUMBER1      pub   N          6  (          6.00000000)
NUMBER2      pub   (hidden)  N         1  (          1.00000000)
NUMBER2      priv  N          5  (          5.00000000)          C:Sub1.prg
    3 variables defined,        27 bytes used
  253 variables available,    5973 bytes available
```

Figure 77

After Sub1 returns control to Main, the screen in Figure 78 is displayed. Note that the private copy of number2 with a value of 5 is gone, and the original number2 is unchanged and no longer hidden. Furthermore, notice that number1 has its new value of 6.

Finally, after Sub2 does a calculation involving number1 and number2, the screen in Figure 79 results from the last DISPLAY MEMORY command in Main. It shows both public variables; number1 has a new value based on the calculation in the subprogram.

Warnings If you include an existing private memory variable in the PUBLIC memory variable list, a *Syntax error* is displayed. You can initialize a PUBLIC memory variable and later hide its value by creating a PRIVATE variable with the same name, but you cannot do the reverse.

In a program, RELEASE ALL and RELEASE ALL LIKE does not affect public variables. To remove a public variable in a program, use RELEASE with the explicit name of the memory variable. You can also use CLEAR MEMORY, but this command releases all variables, both public and private.

Tips The PUBLIC or PRIVATE status of memory variables is not saved to the memory file. (See SAVE.) The status of the restored variables is decided when the memory file is restored. (See RESTORE.)

Restoring memory variables from a memory file is the same as initializing the variables for the first time. At the dot prompt, variables are initialized as public by default; therefore, issuing RESTORE from the dot prompt restores all of the variables as public variables. Similarly, in a program, RESTORE restores all variables as private variables.

```
NUMBER1      pub   N          6  (          6.00000000)
NUMBER2      pub   N          1  (          1.00000000)
    2 variables defined,        18 bytes used
  254 variables available,    5982 bytes available
```

Figure 78

```
NUMBER1      pub   N          7  (          7.00000000)
NUMBER2      pub   N          1  (          1.00000000)
    2 variables defined,        18 bytes used
  254 variables available,    5982 bytes available
```

Figure 79

If you want variables in a memory file to be public when they are restored in a program, use PUBLIC to declare those variables, and use RESTORE FROM...ADDITIVE. Using the ADDITIVE keyword forces RESTORE to look at the current memory variables and to retain their PUBLIC or PRIVATE status.

Unlike with PRIVATE, you cannot use an ALL LIKE <skeleton> with PUBLIC. If dBASE III PLUS allowed something like PUBLIC ALL LIKE a*, because of the way PUBLIC is designed, it would have to initialize all memory variable names that could possibly begin with the letter a. This is not possible.

A public memory variable can be hidden from access by using PRIVATE to declare a private variable with the same name.

QUIT

Syntax `QUIT`

Overview The QUIT command is used to exit dBASE III PLUS. This command closes all files, frees all of the memory it uses, and returns you to the operating system level.

Procedure If you are using the interactive mode (i.e., the dot prompt) in dBASE III PLUS, enter QUIT at the dot prompt when you are finished with your work.

Use QUIT as the exit command in your main program if you do not want the user to have access to the interactive mode of dBASE III PLUS (i.e., the dot prompt).

Examples In the following example, QUIT is used as the exit command in the main menu program. When this program is executed and the user selects Exit from the menu, QUIT is executed, and the user is left at the operating system level:

```
* Menu.PRG
*
SET TALK OFF
SET STATUS ON
```

```
SET MESSAGE TO "Enter a menu choice."
CLEAR
DO WHILE .T.  && Display the menu until the user selects Exit
   choice = 0

   * Display menu and prompt for user's choice.
   @  6,29 SAY "0 - Exit"
   @  8,29 SAY "1 - Add Records"
   @ 10,29 SAY "2 - Edit Records"
   @ 12,29 SAY "3 - Print Reports"
   @  4,20 TO 14, 54 DOUBLE
   CLEAR TYPEAHEAD
   @ 14,37 GET choice PICTURE "9" RANGE 0, 3
   READ

   * Use DO CASE to execute a different program for each choice.
   DO CASE

      * If the user chooses 0, QUIT dBASE III PLUS.
      * QUIT automatically closes all open files.
      CASE choice = 0
         QUIT

      * If the user chooses 1, do program to add records.
      CASE choice = 1
         DO Add_Recs

      * If the user chooses 2, do program to edit records.
      CASE choice = 2
         DO EditRecs

      * If the user chooses 3, do program to print reports.
      CASE choice = 3
         DO Reports

   ENDCASE  && End the DO CASE control structure
ENDDO
```

Warnings

QUIT dBASE III PLUS before turning off or rebooting your computer; otherwise, you can lose some valuable data or corrupt one of your files beyond use.

Tips

See RETURN for another method of exiting a program that leaves the user at the dot prompt instead of terminating dBASE III PLUS.

RANGE

Syntax RANGE [<expression>], [<expression>]

Overview

The RANGE keyword is used with @...GET to specify an upper and lower limit for a numeric or a date variable. The first expression represents the lower limit, and the second the upper limit. The type of each expression must be the same, and they both must match the data type of the @...GET variable with which they are used.

As the syntax indicates either one or both of these limits can be omitted, but the comma must be included. Leaving out the lower limit indicates that there is no lower boundary for the @...GET variable; omitting the upper limit indicates that there is no upper boundary for the @...GET variable. Omitting both the lower and upper limits is equivalent to specifying no RANGE at all.

If it has a RANGE clause, when an @...GET is executed you will be able to enter only a number or date that falls between the specified upper and lower limit, inclusive.

Procedure

Use a RANGE clause to place an upper and lower boundary for numbers and dates with @...GET. When @...GET is executed, only values within the specified RANGE are accepted. If a value outside of the RANGE is entered, the bell rings and a message is displayed on the screen. The message indicates the valid range and instructs you to press the space bar to continue data entry.

Examples

The following example illustrates the use of the RANGE clause with both date and numeric variables:

```
* Limits.PRG
*
SET TALK OFF
CLEAR
* Initialize some numeric and date variables.
STORE 0 TO num_1, num_2, num_3
STORE CTOD("  /  /  ") TO date_1, date_2, date_3

@  4, 0 SAY "Enter a number between 15 and 20..."
@  5,10 GET num_1 RANGE 15, 20
```

```
@  6, 0 SAY "Enter a number that is greater than 100..."
* Since the range is inclusive, the lower limit must be 101.
* No upper limit is specified.
@  7,10 GET num_2 RANGE 101,

@  8, 0 SAY "Enter a number that is less than or equal to 100..."
* No lower limit is specified.
@  9,10 GET num_3 RANGE ,100

@ 10, 0 SAY "Enter a date in the future..."
* The smallest date that you can enter is today's date plus one
* day, which is tomorrow; therefore, the date you enter must
* be in the future.  No upper limit is specified.
@ 11,10 GET date_1 RANGE DATE() + 1,

@ 12, 0 SAY "Enter a date in the past..."
* The latest date that you can enter is today's date minus one
* day, which is yesterday; therefore the date you enter must
* be in the past.  No lower limit is specified.
@ 13,10 GET date_2 RANGE ,DATE() - 1

@ 14, 0 SAY "Enter a date in the month of July, 1987..."
@ 15,10 GET date_3 RANGE CTOD('07/01/87'), CTOD('07/31/87')

READ
```

If you execute this program, your screen should look like the one in Figure 80.

If you try to enter a value that is not in the allowable range, the bell rings and a message is displayed on the screen indicating the correct RANGE. You must press the space bar and enter a valid value.

Warnings You can leave the value in any @...GET variable unchanged by pressing Enter when the cursor is positioned in the data entry area for that variable.

```
Enter a number between 15 and 20...
              0
Enter a number that is greater than 100...
              0
Enter a number that is less than or equal to 100...
              0
Enter a date in the future...
           /  /
Enter a date in the past...
           /  /
Enter a date in the month of July, 1987...
           /  /
```

Figure 80

This is true even if a RANGE is specified and the @...GET variable is already outside the range of valid values. (In other words, the RANGE criteria is applied to the variable only if you change its value.)

If either or both of the RANGE expressions does not match the data type of the @...GET variable, the error message *Data type mismatch* is displayed.

If the lower limit of a RANGE clause is greater in value than the upper limit, a *Syntax error* is displayed.

If a RANGE clause is used with an @...GET variable whose data type is not numeric or date, a *Syntax error* is displayed.

If both a RANGE and a PICTURE clause are used with @...GET, the PICTURE clause must come first; otherwise, the error message *Unrecognized phrase/keyword in command* is displayed.

Tips

To limit a numeric variable to positive numbers, use RANGE Ø, . Omitting the upper limit allows you to enter any number that is greater than or equal to zero (i.e., all positive numbers).

READ

Syntax `READ [SAVE]`

Overview

If used in a program with an open format file (see SET FORMAT TO) in the current work area, the READ command executes the @ commands in the format file (see @...CLEAR, @...GET, @...SAY, @...TO) and activates the @...GET variables for editing. READ is one of the full-screen editing commands (see APPEND, CHANGE, EDIT and INSERT) and is able to make use of the full-screen cursor movement and editing keys. These keys are listed in a table in Appendix A.

If used in a program when there is no open format file in the current work area, READ activates the @...GET variables already displayed on the screen.

After the @...GET variables have been edited and saved, the @...GET commands are released from READ access. (See CLEAR GETS.) Using the SAVE keyword as part of READ retains the @...GET commands so that you can repeat READ to edit the variables again.

In a format file, you can use READ (without the SAVE keyword) to get the effect of a multi-page form. Put READ in the format file where you want a new page to begin. Then, whenever you use the format file by opening it and activating it with one of the full-screen commands, the @ commands up to the next READ in the format file are displayed and activated for editing. When this set of @...GET variables has been edited and saved, the screen is cleared and the @ commands up to the next READ are activated for editing. This process continues until all of the @ commands in the format file have been executed.

Procedure

You can create a multiple-page format file with a maximum of thirty-two pages, by inserting READ in the format file wherever you want a new page to begin. Do not use READ as the last command in the format file, and do not use READ SAVE in a format file.

Use READ in a program to edit a group of memory variables or a single record at a time in the active database file. If you want to edit information in a database file, you must have the file in use (see USE) and the record pointer positioned to the record (see GO, LOCATE or SEEK) whose fields you want to edit. Next, issue the @ commands to paint the screen and present the fields and memory variables for editing. This can be done by issuing the @ commands in the program or by opening a format file (see SET FORMAT TO) that already has the appropriate @ commands. Issue READ when you are ready to edit.

Examples

The following examples illustrate how to use READ to edit records in the mailing list. The user enters the last name so that the program can find the correct record. The fields are then displayed on the screen and edited using READ:

```
* MailEdit.PRG
*
SET TALK OFF
USE Mail INDEX Last

* Set up the screen so that the user can enter a last name.
* The labels for the other fields are displayed here because
* they are the same for each record and need only be shown once.

CLEAR
@ 3, 5 SAY "Last Name"
```

```
@ 4, 5 SAY "First Name"
@ 5, 5 SAY "Street"
@ 6, 5 SAY "Apartment"
@ 7, 5 SAY "City"
@ 8, 5 SAY "State"
@ 9, 5 SAY "Zip Code"

m_error = .F.  && Initialize error flag

DO WHILE .T.

   * A different prompt is displayed depending on the error flag.
   IF m_error
      @ 1,5 SAY "The name you entered was not found.  Try again."
      m_error = .F.  && Reset error flag
   ELSE
      @ 1,5 SAY "Enter the last name of the person to find.      "
   ENDIF

   m_last = SPACE(20)     && Make m_last blank
   @ 3, 17 GET m_last     && Enter a name into a memvar
   @ 4, 17 CLEAR TO 9,79  && Clear previous record from screen

   READ  && Enables user to edit the memvar, m_last

   IF "" = TRIM(m_last)
      EXIT   && Exit from the loop if no name is entered
   ENDIF

   SEEK m_last  && Locate the last name entered

   IF .NOT. FOUND()   && Test to make sure that name is on file

      * If the name is not found, set the error flag to true
      * and start the loop over.
      m_error = .T.
      LOOP

   ELSE  && Display contents of record on screen for editing

      @ 1,  5  && Erase prompt
      @ 3, 17 GET Last_Name
      @ 4, 17 GET First_Name
      @ 5, 17 GET Address1
      @ 6, 17 GET Address2
      @ 7, 17 GET City
```

```
        @ 8, 17 GET State
        @ 9, 17 GET Zip

        READ  && Allow user to edit the fields
    ENDIF
ENDDO
CLEAR
CLOSE DATABASES
SET TALK ON
```

Warnings

If you use READ SAVE, be aware that you must clear the gets from read access (see CLEAR GETS) after every 128 @...GET commands, at least; otherwise, the error message *Insufficient memory* is displayed.

If you are using dBASE III PLUS in a network environment, you must obtain a manual file or record lock (see FLOCK( ), RLOCK( )), or open the database file for exclusive use (see SET EXCLUSIVE, USE) before using @...GET on a field followed by a READ. The error message *Record is not locked* is displayed if you attempt to READ an @...GET under these circumstances.

Tips

The @...GET command used in conjunction with READ (or one of the other full-screen editing commands) is the only way to edit the contents of a memory variable in dBASE III PLUS. Other commands such as ACCEPT and INPUT create new memory variables, and any variable that happens to exist with the same name is released from memory.

READ is the only full-screen editing command that can activate @...GET commands without the use of a format file.

READKEY( )

Syntax `READKEY()`

Overview

The READKEY( ) function has no arguments. The function determines which key the user pressed to exit a full-screen editing command (i.e., APPEND, CHANGE, EDIT, INSERT and READ) and returns a number representing that key. The number indicates not only what key was pressed, but also whether or not data was changed in the current record. Table 12 shows the READKEY( ) return values.

TABLE 12

READKEY( ) Return Values

KEY	(NO CHANGE)	(CHANGE)
◁, ^S, ^H	0	256
BackSpace	0	256
▷, ^D, ^L	1	257
Home, ^A	2	258
End, ^F	3	259
⇧, ^E, ^K	4	260
⇩, ^X, ^J	5	261
PgUp, ^R	6	262
PgDn, ^C	7	263
Esc, ^Q	12	n/a
^End, ^W	n/a	270
(type past end)	15	271
Enter, ^M	15	271
Enter, ^M *	16	n/a
^Home, ^]	33	289
^PgUp, ^-	34	290
^PgDn, ^^	35	291
F1	36	292

Note that for ^End, the (no change) column is not applicable. The same is true for the (change) column for the Esc and Enter keys. This is because Esc never saves data, and ^End always does.

* This entry in the READKEY( ) table is specifically for when the Enter (or ^M) key is typed as the first letter during the interactive APPEND. The first entry is for all other cases of Enter. The (change) column is not applicable because the Enter key, in this case, is designed to terminate the APPEND without saving the blank record.

Procedure READKEY( ) returns a number and can be used anywhere in the language where a numeric expression is appropriate.

Examples READKEY( ) can be used to test how a full-screen editing command was exited and make decisions based on that information. For example, the following routine is almost identical to the one used in the RECCOUNT( ) example, but instead of asking the user whether he wants to add more records each time, it lets him enter data until the Esc key is pressed. When this key is pressed, the last record is deleted to avoid having blank records saved in the database file.

```
* Cust_Add.PRG
*
CLEAR
SET TALK OFF
USE Customer
SET FORMAT TO Cust_Add
DO WHILE RECCOUNT() < 100
   APPEND BLANK
   READ
   IF READKEY() = 12 && Esc has a READKEY() value of 12
      DELETE
      EXIT          && EXIT leaves the DO WHILE loop
   ENDIF
ENDDO
CLOSE DATABASES
SET TALK ON
```

For a listing of the format file used in this example, Cust_Add.FMT, see the example for RECCOUNT( ). Remove the @...SAY command that asks about adding more records.

Warnings Because of its simple syntax there are no error messages associated with READKEY( ).

Tips READKEY( ) can be used effectively only in command files.

RECALL

Syntax `RECALL [<scope>] [WHILE <condition>] [FOR <condition>]`

Overview

The RECALL command reinstates records in the active database file that are marked for deletion. (See DELETE.) If used with no parameters, it reinstates only the current record; however, a scope, a FOR clause, and a WHILE clause can be used to mark records within a specific range that meet certain conditions. Each of these command line options is discussed separately. (See Scope, FOR, and WHILE.)

If SET TALK is ON when records are reinstated, a message is displayed on the screen showing the number of records recalled. SET TALK OFF to suppress the message.

A record marked for deletion is indicated by an asterisk when the record is displayed using LIST or DISPLAY. In full-screen editing, the word *Del* on the scoreboard or the status bar indicates that a record is marked for deletion. The Ctrl-U key is used in full-screen editing as a toggle to mark records for deletion and to reinstate them.

Procedure

Use RECALL when you have records in your database file that you no longer want to have marked for deletion. If there are only a few records with nothing in common, position the record pointer to each record using GOTO, LOCATE, or some other positioning command, and enter RECALL with no parameters. Use RECALL with a FOR, or WHILE clause to reinstate a group of records that meet a particular condition.

Examples

Suppose that you mark a record for deletion when you no longer have the current address for an individual in your mailing list. If you later obtain the new address, you can reinstate the record and update it. Assuming that the record in question is already marked for deletion (see DELETE), the following commands illustrate the RECALL command:

```
. USE Mail
. LOCATE FOR First_Name = "Gloria"  && Find the record you want
Record =       3
. DISPLAY First_Name, Last_Name  && Notice the asterisk
Record#  First_Name   Last_Name
      3 *Gloria       Roman

. RECALL  && Reinstate the current record only
      1 record recalled
. DISPLAY First_Name, Last_Name  && The asterisk does not appear
Record#  First_Name   Last_Name
      3  Gloria       Roman
```

You can make the changes to the record using a command such as EDIT or REPLACE.

Warnings

The PACK command permanently removes records that are marked for deletion from the active database file. Before you PACK the database file, you can reinstate records that are marked for deletion using RECALL; however, once you have packed a database file, the deleted records cannot be recovered.

If you are using dBASE III PLUS in a network environment, RECALL, if used with a scope, FOR, or WHILE clause, attempts an automatic file lock unless the database file is already locked (see FLOCK( )) or is opened for exclusive use (see SET EXCLUSIVE, USE). If for any reason the command cannot lock the database file, the error message *File is in use by another* is displayed. RECALL with no scope, FOR, or WHILE clause attempts an automatic record lock (see RLOCK( )) instead. In this case, the error message *Record is in use by another* is displayed.

Tips

In dBASE III PLUS, records marked for deletion are processed by other commands just like any other record. In order to make a particular command ignore deleted records, use the clause FOR .NOT. DELETED( ) as part of the command syntax. To make all commands ignore deleted records, SET DELETED ON or SET FILTER TO .NOT. DELETED( ).

If SET DELETED is ON, or if you have a SET FILTER TO expression that includes the condition .NOT. DELETED( ) to ignore deleted records, RECALL ignores deleted records just like any other command. Thus, if you RECALL ALL under these conditions, no records are recalled.

The only way to RECALL records when deleted records are being ignored is to access the record directly (see GO) and use RECALL with no parameters.

RECCOUNT( )

Syntax `RECCOUNT()`

Overview

The RECCOUNT( ) function, short for record count, has no arguments. The function returns the total number of records in the active database file. The record count is the number that you see to the right of the words *Number of data records* when you do a LIST STRUCTURE.

If used with no open database file, RECCOUNT( ) returns a zero.

Procedure

In order to use RECCOUNT( ) effectively, there must be a database file in use in the current work area. (See USE.) Otherwise, the function automatically returns a value of zero.

RECCOUNT( ) returns a number and can be used anywhere in the language where a numeric expression is appropriate.

Examples

RECCOUNT( ) can be used to prompt a user for a record number to GOTO. By making use of RECCOUNT( ), the following routine continues to ask for a record number until the user enters a valid one:

```
* Rec_Check.PRG
*
SET TALK OFF
SET BELL OFF
CLEAR
USE Customer
number = 0
DO WHILE number <= 0 .OR. number > RECCOUNT()
   @ 10, 5 SAY "Enter the record number to edit " GET number
   READ
ENDDO
GO number
EDIT
```

```
CLOSE DATABASES
SET BELL ON
SET TALK ON
```

RECCOUNT( ) is also used to control the number of records in a file at one time. You may need this kind of control if you do not have a hard disk on which to store your data. If you determine, for example, that your floppy drive has room to hold only one hundred records, you would want to check the number of records in the file each time you want to add more records. The following record-add routine checks for this condition:

```
* Cust_Add.PRG
*
SET TALK OFF
USE Customer
SET FORMAT TO Cust_Add
more = .T.
DO WHILE RECCOUNT() < 100 .AND. more
   APPEND BLANK
   READ
ENDDO
CLOSE ALL
SET TALK ON
```

This example uses a format file called Cust_Add.FMT which is listed below for your convenience:

```
* Cust_Add.FMT
*
@  0,  0 SAY RECNO()
@  1,  0 SAY "CUST_NO    " GET Cust_No
@  2,  0 SAY "FIRST_NAME" GET First_Name
@  3,  0 SAY "LAST_NAME " GET Last_Name
@  4,  0 SAY "ADDRESS1   " GET Address1
@  5,  0 SAY "ADDRESS2   " GET Address2
@  6,  0 SAY "CITY       " GET City
@  7,  0 SAY "STATE      " GET State PICTURE "@A!"
@  8,  0 SAY "ZIP        " GET Zip PICTURE "99999"
@  9,  0 SAY "PHONE      " GET Phone PICTURE "(999)999-9999"
@ 10,  0 SAY "AMT_OWED   " GET Amt_Owed
@ 11,  0 SAY "DEADLINE   " GET Deadline
* Remove the next line for use with READKEY() example.
@ 14,  0 SAY "Add more records? (Y/N)" GET more PICTURE "Y"
```

Warnings

Because of its simple syntax, there are no error messages associated with RECCOUNT( ).

Tips

Although dBASE III PLUS has commands such as SET DELETED ON and SET FILTER TO <condition> that hide certain records from view, RECCOUNT( ) always returns the total number of records in the file. Use COUNT if you want to know the number of records you are actually using of this total.

RECNO( )

Syntax `RECNO()`

Overview

The RECNO( ) function, short for record number, has no arguments. The function returns the record number of the current record in the active database file.

If used with no open database file, RECNO( ) returns a zero.

Procedure

To use RECNO( ) effectively, there must be a database file in use in the current work area. (See USE.) Otherwise, the function automatically returns a value of zero.

RECNO( ) returns a number and can be used anywhere in the language where a numeric expression is appropriate.

Examples

RECNO( ) can be used to mark your current position in a database file so that you can perform another operation and return to that location. For example, if you want to get some statistical information on a subset of a database file, you need a way to return the record pointer to the first record in the sample for each command. The following routine calculates the average and sum of all numeric fields in the active database file, beginning with the current record and ending after ten records. The database file is repositioned after each command.

```
* Position.PRG
*
SET TALK OFF
current = RECNO()
AVERAGE NEXT 10 TO avg_amt
GO current
SUM NEXT 10 TO sum_amt
```

```
GO current
? avg_amt, sum_amt
SET TALK ON
```

Warnings Because of its simple syntax, there are no error messages associated with RECNO( ).

Tips If a FIND or SEEK command results in a .NOT. FOUND( ) condition, the record pointer in the active database file is positioned to the end of file. You can save the value of RECNO( ) before doing a FIND or SEEK if you want to return the record pointer to that location in the event that the record you are looking for is not found. This technique is identical to the above example.

RECORD. *See* Scope

RECSIZE( )

Syntax `RECSIZE()`

Overview The RECSIZE( ) function, short for record size, has no arguments. The function returns the record size of the active database file. The record size is the number that you see to the right of the word *Total* when you do a LIST STRUCTURE. This number is the sum of all the field lengths plus one byte that is reserved for the deletion mark.

If used with no open database file, RECSIZE( ) returns a zero.

Procedure In order to use RECSIZE( ) effectively, there must be a database file in use in the current work area. (See USE.) Otherwise, the function automatically returns a value of zero.

The RECSIZE( ) function returns a number and can be used anywhere in the language where a numeric expression is appropriate.

Examples RECSIZE( ) can be used to approximate the size of a database file. The following formula produces a number that is close to the actual size in bytes of the active database file:

```
RECSIZE() * RECCOUNT() + 4129
```

The number 4129 is added to the amount of space used by the data because this is the maximum size of the header record that is used to store the structure of the database file.

Warnings Because of its simple syntax, there are no error messages associated with RECSIZE( ).

Tips This function is useful in backup procedures. (See DISKSPACE( ) for an example.)

REINDEX

Syntax `REINDEX`

Overview The REINDEX command recreates one or more existing index files. The command uses the index key expression that is stored in the index file so that you do not have to specify it as you did when you originally created the index file. (See INDEX.)

Procedure If one or more of the index files for a particular database file is out of date, you can recreate it with REINDEX. Open the database file and all of the invalid index files (see USE and SET INDEX) in the current work area, and issue REINDEX to recreate all of the open index files. If SET TALK is ON, a message is displayed for each index as it is being recreated.

Index files can be invalidated if you add or change information in the database file without opening the index file. Getting the error message *Record is not in index* when you try to access a record or a not found condition (see FIND, SEEK, and FOUND( )) when you are sure the key exists are symptoms of an index file that is out of date. REINDEX can solve these problems.

If you are using dBASE III PLUS in a network environment, exclusive use (see SET EXCLUSIVE, USE) of the active database file is required to REINDEX.

Examples Assuming that all of the index files belonging to the Customer file are out of date, the following commands can be used to recreate them:

```
. USE Customer INDEX Cust_No, C_Fname, C_Lname, C_Zip
. REINDEX  && All four open index files are recreated
Rebuilding index - C:Cust_No.ndx
  100% indexed          10 Records indexed
Rebuilding index - C:C_Fname.ndx
  100% indexed          10 Records indexed
Rebuilding index - C:C_Lname.ndx
  100% indexed          10 Records indexed
Rebuilding index - C:C_Zip.ndx
  100% indexed          10 Records indexed
. CLOSE DATABASES
```

Warnings

The error message *Index file does not match database* cannot be corrected with REINDEX. This message indicates that the index key expression stored in the index file uses one or more field names that cannot be found in the active database file structure. This can mean one of several things:

- The index file may actually belong to another database file. Check the file name to ensure that you have used the correct one.
- The database file structure may have been altered (see MODIFY STRUCTURE) and one of the key fields changed. In this case, you must recreate the index file from scratch using the new field name(s). (See INDEX.)

If you use REINDEX in the network version of dBASE III PLUS, exclusive use of the active database file is required. The error message *Exclusive open of file is required* is displayed if you attempt to REINDEX a database file that was opened for shared use. Either SET EXCLUSIVE ON and reopen file, or reopen the file with USE <filename> EXCLUSIVE, and issue REINDEX again.

Tips

The need to REINDEX can be minimized if you keep your index files up to date with the database file. Be sure that all index files are open whenever you make additions to a database file. If you make changes to existing records in a database file, be sure that you have opened the index files whose key field values are subject to change.

If you are using dBASE III PLUS in a network environment and have installed Protect (see Protect) to protect your database files from unauthorized access, you may want to REINDEX your index files. When you Protect a database file, the file gets encrypted for further protection, but Protect does not know about index files. If you want your index files to be encrypted, simply REINDEX them once after you Protect the associated database file. New index files that you create (see INDEX) are automatically encrypted if the database file is encrypted.

RELEASE

Syntax

```
RELEASE <memory variable list>
RELEASE ALL [LIKE¦EXCEPT <skeleton>]
```

Overview

The RELEASE command releases from memory variables that you no longer need. The command has two forms.

The first form, RELEASE <memory variable list>, lets you list by name the memory variables that you want to release from memory. The list is separated by commas. In a program, the only way to release a public memory variable (see PUBLIC) from memory with RELEASE is to use this form of the command and name the public variable in the list.

The second form, RELEASE ALL [LIKE ¦ EXCEPT <skeleton>], lets you describe which variable names you want to release from memory. This form of the command behaves differently in a program than at the dot prompt. In a program, it affects only private memory variables. (See PRIVATE.) At the dot prompt, it affects only public memory variables because there are no private memory variables at the dot prompt.

RELEASE ALL means that you want all memory variables released; RELEASE ALL LIKE <skeleton> means that you want all the variable names of a particular group to be released; RELEASE ALL EXCEPT <skeleton> means that you want all the variable names except those of a particular group to be released from memory. (See Skeleton for information on how to compose a skeleton.)

Procedure

Memory variables created in a program are, by default, private and are automatically released from memory at the end of the program (i.e., when the program returns to its calling program or the dot prompt); thus, there is almost never a need to use RELEASE in a programming application that uses only private variables. If you create a private memory variable in a program that you want to release midway through the program, you can use either form of RELEASE for this purpose.

If you use public memory variables in your programming application, you must explicitly remove them from memory unless you want them to remain until you leave dBASE III PLUS. (See QUIT.) Use RELEASE with a memory variable list to name explicitly the public variables that you want released from memory.

If you are working with memory variables at the dot prompt, you can use either form of RELEASE to indicate that you no longer want to use the memory variables.

Examples

The following commands demonstrate the use of RELEASE at the dot prompt, where it is most often used:

```
. firstname = "Debby"
Debby
. last_name = "Moody"
Moody
. birthday = CTOD("12/20/59")
12/20/59
. STORE 10 TO number1, number2, number3
10
. DISPLAY MEMORY
FIRSTNAME    pub   C  "Debby"
LAST_NAME    pub   C  "Moody"
BIRTHDAY     pub   D  12/20/59
NUMBER1      pub   N          10  (        10.00000000)
NUMBER2      pub   N          10  (        10.00000000)
NUMBER3      pub   N          10  (        10.00000000)
    6 variables defined,       50 bytes used
  250 variables available,   5950 bytes available

. RELEASE ALL LIKE ?????name  && Releases firstname and last_name
. DISPLAY MEMORY
BIRTHDAY     pub   D  12/20/59
NUMBER1      pub   N          10  (        10.00000000)
NUMBER2      pub   N          10  (        10.00000000)
NUMBER3      pub   N          10  (        10.00000000)
```

```
    4 variables defined,        36 bytes used
  252 variables available,    5964 bytes available

. RELEASE ALL LIKE num*  && Releases all of the number variables
. DISPLAY MEMORY
BIRTHDAY     pub   D  12/20/59
    1 variables defined,         9 bytes used
  255 variables available,    5991 bytes available

. RELEASE ALL  && Remaining memory variables are released
. DISPLAY MEMORY
    0 variables defined,         0 bytes used
  256 variables available,    6000 bytes available
```

Warnings If you include a non-existent variable name in the RELEASE memory variable list, no error message is displayed; instead, the variable name is ignored. If there is a memory variable in existence that you know you released, check the spelling of the variable names in the RELEASE command; RELEASE does not warn you if a variable name is misspelled.

Tips RELEASE ALL [LIKE | EXCEPT <skeleton>] does not affect public memory variables in a program. Use CLEAR MEMORY if you want to release all memory variables, both public and private, in a program.

See PUBLIC and PRIVATE for more information on public and private memory variables. See ACCEPT, INPUT, STORE, and WAIT for information on how to create memory variables.

RELEASE MODULE

Syntax `RELEASE MODULE <binary module name>`

Overview The RELEASE MODULE command releases binary modules from memory. The binary module is given its name when you load the binary file into memory. (See LOAD.) The module name is the root portion of the file name (i.e., up to an eight-character file name with no drive specification, directory name, or extension).

Procedure

Use LOAD to load a binary file into memory as a module. Execute the binary module with CALL. (See CALL.) RELEASE MODULE when you no longer want to use the module, or if you want to make room to load other modules.

Examples

The following commands illustrate how to LOAD, CALL, and RELEASE a binary MODULE. (See LOAD for a listing of the assembly language program, Redirect, and a more complete example.)

```
. LOAD Redirect
. filename = "Atsay.TXT"
Atsay.TXT
. CALL Redirect WITH filename
. RELEASE MODULE Redirect
```

Warnings

If you attempt to RELEASE a MODULE that you did not LOAD, the error message *File was not LOADed* is displayed. Use DISPLAY STATUS to see a list of the loaded module names.

Tips

No other command except QUIT releases binary modules from memory. Use RELEASE MODULE to unload binary modules when you are finished with them in order to free the memory they use for other purposes.

RENAME

Syntax `RENAME <filename> TO <new filename>`

Overview

The RENAME command changes the name of a file and moves a file from one directory to another (see Tips below). This command is very similar to the DOS RENAME command.

Procedure

The first file name in the RENAME command syntax is the one that you want to change. You must specify the file extension since none is assumed by the command. If the file is in a directory other than the current one, you must also specify that directory because RENAME does not use the dBASE III PLUS path setting (see SET PATH) to find the file.

The file name following the TO keyword is the new name that you want to give to the file. You must specify the extension if you want the new file to have one. After RENAME has completed its execution, the new file will be in the current directory unless you explicitly name a different one as part of the file name.

Examples

The following commands illustrate how to change the name of a database file that has a corresponding memo file. In this example, the mailing list file name is changed from Mail to MailList.

```
. CLOSE DATABASES  && Just in case the file is in use
. RENAME Mail.DBF TO MailList.DBF  && Rename database file
. RENAME Mail.DBT TO MailList.DBT  && Rename memo file
. USE MailList  && Open file using new name
```

Warnings

If you want to RENAME a database file, remember to RENAME any existing memo file. The memo file has the same name as the database file, but with a .DBT extension. If you neglect to rename the memo file and then attempt to use the newly-named database file, the error message *.DBT file cannot be opened* is displayed.

Because of their similarity, you may confuse the dBASE III PLUS RENAME command with its DOS equivalent. If this occurs and you neglect to specify the TO keyword between the two file names, a *Syntax error* message is displayed.

If you attempt to RENAME TO a file name that already exists, the error message *File already exists* is displayed. This same error message occurs if the TO file name has a drive specification other than the current drive or contains wildcard charcters. Although you can use RENAME to change the directory name of a file, you cannot use it to move the file to a different drive or to move more than one file at a time.

If you attempt to RENAME a file name that cannot be found, the error message *File does not exist* is displayed.

The message *File is already open* means that you are attempting to RENAME a file that is open. Use the appropriate command to close the file (see CLOSE) that you want to rename, and try the command again.

Tips

In one sense, the dBASE III PLUS RENAME command is more powerful than the DOS RENAME command since it can be used to move a file from one directory to another. In DOS, you cannot specify a directory name with the second file name without getting an error message because the second file is assumed to be in the same directory as the first file. In dBASE III PLUS, you are required to specify the directory name of the second file. If not, the resulting file is automatically moved to the current directory.

The following command shows how dBASE III PLUS users can give a file a new name and, at the same time, move it to a new directory.

```
. RENAME \Reports\Party.FRM TO \Dbase\NewParty.FRM
```

The DOS equivalent, RENAME \Reports\Party.FRM \Dbase\NewParty .FRM, produces an error message.

REPLACE

Syntax

```
REPLACE <fieldname> WITH <expression>
[, <fieldname> WITH <expression>...]
[<scope>] [WHILE <condition>] [FOR <condition>]
```

Overview

The REPLACE command replaces one or more fields in the active database file with new values. The replacement values are specified as expressions.

When the command is executed, the WITH expression is evaluated for each field name specified, and the current contents of the field is replaced with the value of the expression. The expression and the field must be the same data type. The default scope of REPLACE is the current record; however, a scope, a FOR clause, and a WHILE clause can be used to include all of the records within a specific range that meet certain conditions. Each of these command line options is discussed separately. (See Scope, FOR, and WHILE.)

If SET TALK is ON when records are replaced, a message is displayed on the screen showing the number of records replaced. Use SET TALK OFF to suppress the message.

Procedure

In programming, REPLACE is often used to control user input into a database file.

Several memory variables are initialized that are used to hold the user input. (See STORE.) The variables are given the same length and data type as the fields to which they correspond in the active database file.

The @...GET and READ commands are used to allow the user to input data into the memory variables; these variables are verified for accuracy before REPLACE enters them into the database file. Verification of the memory variable values depends on your application.

This procedure can be used to add new records to a database file and to make changes to existing records. To add a new record, APPEND BLANK before issuing REPLACE. To change an existing record, locate the record and initialize the memory variables to the current field values before doing the @...GET and READ commands. Issue REPLACE as soon as the variables have been verified.

Examples

The following example illustrates how to use REPLACE to add records to the Orders database file after the data has been verified. When the user enters the customer and part numbers, SEEK is used to verify that the customer number is on file in the Customer file and that the part number is on file in the Inventry file. Information is then displayed from the Inventry file, and the user enters the quantity to order.

```
* Orders.PRG
*

SET TALK OFF

* Set up the database file environment.
SELECT 3
USE Customer INDEX Cust_No
SELECT 2
USE Inventry INDEX Part_No
```

```
SELECT 1
USE Orders

* Clear screen and display this part of the screen only once.
CLEAR
@  1, 3 TO  17,69 DOUBLE
@  2,30 SAY "O R D E R S"
@  3,29 TO  3,41
@  5,10 SAY "Customer Number"
@  6,10 SAY "Part Number"
@  8,10 SAY "Amount to Order"
@  9, 4 TO  9,68
@ 11, 6 SAY "Description:"
@ 15,42 SAY "Unit Price"
@ 16,42 SAY "Total Cost"

* Infinite loop has an EXIT inside for when the user does
* not enter a customer number.
DO WHILE .T.

   * Reset color to default.
   SET COLOR TO

   * Erase data from previous record from the screen.
   @  8,28 CLEAR TO  8,68
   @ 12, 6 CLEAR TO 12,68
   @ 15,57 CLEAR TO 15,68
   @ 16,54 CLEAR TO 16,68
   @ 19, 0 CLEAR TO 19,79

   * Initialize memory variables for the next order.
   m_cust_no  = SPACE(4)
   m_part_no  = SPACE(5)
   m_quantity = 0

   * Get the customer and part numbers.
   @  5,28 GET m_cust_no  PICTURE "@! A999"
   @  6,28 GET m_part_no  PICTURE "@! AX999"
   READ

   * Erase error message, if any, from previous order.
   @ 13, 6 CLEAR TO 13,68

   * If no customer number is entered, EXIT the loop.
   IF "" = TRIM(m_cust_no)
      EXIT
   ENDIF
```

```
* Change the standard display to black on white to call
* attention to the SAY fields.
SET COLOR TO N/W

* Check to see if the customer number is on file.
SELECT Customer
SEEK m_cust_no

* If it is not, display an error message and go back to
* the beginning of the DO WHILE loop.
IF .NOT. FOUND()
   @ 13, 6 SAY "Customer number is not on file.  Try again."
   LOOP
ENDIF

* Check to see if part number is on file.
SELECT Inventry
SEEK m_part_no

* If it is not, display an error message and go back to
* the beginning of the DO WHILE loop.
IF .NOT. FOUND()
   @ 13, 6 SAY "Part number is not on file.  Try again."
   LOOP
ENDIF

* If you get this far, it means that both the customer number
* and part number are on file.  Display the Inventry fields
* on the bottom half of the screen.
@ 12, 6 SAY Descrip FUNCTION "S62"
@ 15,57 SAY Price PICTURE "99999999.99"

* Now, get the quantity using the quantity-on-hand field in
* the Inventry file as the upper limit of the RANGE.
@  8,28 GET m_quantity PICTURE "9999999999" RANGE 1, Quantity
READ

* Display the total price for this order and wait for the
* user to see it and press any key.
@ 16,54 SAY Price * m_quantity PICTURE "99999999999.99"
goahead = SPACE(1)
* Deny typeahead so that user is sure to see order.
CLEAR TYPEAHEAD
@ 19,15 SAY "Press any key to enter the next order.";
        GET goahead
READ
```

```
    * Update the Orders file with the information that
    * was entered.  First, a blank record is added to the
    * end of the database file with APPEND BLANK.  REPLACE
    * is then used to replace the blank field names in the
    * new blank record with the memory variables.

    SELECT Orders
    APPEND BLANK
    REPLACE Cust_No WITH m_cust_no, Part_No WITH m_part_no,;
            Quantity WITH m_quantity
ENDDO
CLOSE DATABASES
SET TALK ON
```

Warnings

Never use REPLACE with a scope, FOR, or WHILE clause to replace the contents of a field used as part of the key expression of the controlling index file. (See SET INDEX, SET ORDER.) This syntax will not work because each replacement repositions the record according to the value of its new key; when the command attempts to move the record pointer to do the next replacement, the record that it encounters is not likely to be the one you expect. For example, suppose that you want to give all of your employees a ten percent raise and that you want the result displayed in order of ascending salary. You might try the following command sequence:

```
. USE Employee INDEX Salary  && Salary.NDX is indexed on Salary
. LIST Salary
Record#       Salary
      8     21987.33
      4     25003.23
      5     27832.12
      2     38712.23
      1     43252.29
      3     43712.00
     10     53137.77
      9     57612.12
      6    123000.00
      7    250000.00

. REPLACE ALL Salary WITH Salary * 1.1  && Perform 10% raise
      8 records replaced
. LIST Salary  && Note that only 8 records were replaced
```

```
Record#      Salary
      8    24186.06
      4    27503.55
      5    30615.33
      2    42583.45
      3    43712.00
      1    47577.52
      9    57612.12
     10    58451.55
      6   135300.00
      7   275000.00

. CLOSE DATABASES
```

In this example, record numbers 3 and 9 were not updated. The reason for this is clear if you analyze the numbers. The record before record 3 in the index file before the REPLACE was record 1. When the Salary field in record 1 was updated from 43252.29 to 47577.52, record 1 took its new place in the index after record 3 and before record 10. Thus, the next record in the REPLACE scope was record 10 (record 3 was skipped). Similarly, when record 10 was updated, its new key value moved it past record 9, and record 9 was also skipped by REPLACE. The correct way to accomplish this update is to perform REPLACE without the index file and to recreate the index afterward. (See REINDEX.)

Since REPLACE requires using an expression, a number of errors are possible when the expression is evaluated. The most common error messages are *Variable not found* and *Data type mismatch.*

Data type mismatch indicates that the WITH expression and the field do not have the same data type; this could be caused by attempting to replace a Date field with a character string. Use the proper data conversion function (see DTOC( ), CTOD( ), VAL( ), and STR( )) to convert the expression to the same data type as the field, and try REPLACE again.

Variable not found indicates that you have used a variable name that does not exist either as a field or a memory variable. Check the expression to make sure that you did not misspell one of the variable names. If you are replacing a Character field with a constant value, be sure that you put the constant value in quotes. For example,

```
. USE Mail
. APPEND BLANK
. REPLACE First_Name WITH Debby  && It thinks Debby is a memvar
Variable not found.
                              ?
REPLACE First_Name WITH Debby
. REPLACE First_Name WITH "Debby"  && Quoting "Debby" fixes this
      1 record replaced
```

Variable not found is also displayed if the field name that you are replacing does not exist. Be sure that you did not misspell the field name, and that it is included in the SET FIELDS list (see SET FIELDS) if you are using one.

If you are using dBASE III PLUS in a network environment, REPLACE, if used with a scope, FOR, or WHILE clause, attempts an automatic file lock unless the database file is already locked (see FLOCK( )) or is opened for exclusive use (see SET EXCLUSIVE, USE). If for any reason the command cannot lock the database file, the error message *File is in use by another* is displayed. If used without a scope, FOR, or WHILE clause, you must obtain a manual file or record lock (see FLOCK( ), RLOCK( )), or open the database file for exclusive use (see SET EXCLUSIVE, USE) before a REPLACE. If you attempt to do a REPLACE under these circumstances, the error message *Record is not locked* is displayed.

Tips

Whenever possible, use a single REPLACE command to replace several fields rather than using several consecutive REPLACE commands to replace one field at a time. Continue the REPLACE command to make it as long as possible (up to a maximum of 254 characters) before beginning a new REPLACE command. For example,

```
REPLACE First_Name WITH "Debby", Last_Name WITH "Moody",;
        Age WITH 27, Birthday WITH CTOD("12/20/59")
```

is functionally equivalent to, but much faster than

```
REPLACE First_Name WITH "Debby"
REPLACE Last_Name WITH "Moody"
REPLACE Age WITH 27
REPLACE Birthday WITH CTOD("12/20/59")
```

However, using individual REPLACE commands can be useful when you are debugging because if an error occurs it will be obvious which REPLACE is at fault. Use individual REPLACE commands until your program is debugged, then combine them into a single command for maximum performance once everything is running smoothly.

REPLICATE( )

Syntax `REPLICATE(<expC>, <expN>)`

Overview The REPLICATE( ) function requires two arguments:

- A character expression which represents the character string that is to be replicated
- A numeric expression which represents the number of times that the character string is to be replicated

The function concatenates the character string onto itself the specified number of times and returns the result.

Procedure REPLICATE( ) returns a character string and can be used anywhere in the language where a character expression is appropriate.

Examples REPLICATE( ) can generate a bar graph based on data in a database file. The following example generates a bar graph of the ages of all the people in your mailing list:

```
* AgeGraph.PRG
*
SET TALK OFF
USE Mail
DO WHILE .NOT. EOF()
   ? First_Name + " ¦ " + REPLICATE("*", Age)
   SKIP
ENDDO
CLOSE DATABASES
SET TALK ON
```

To execute this program and see the results,

```
. DO AgeGraph
MICHELLE       ¦ ***************************
Rebecca        ¦ ***************************
Gloria         ¦ **********************************
David          ¦ ***********************
Julia          ¦ *****************************
Perry          ¦ ************************
Cathy          ¦ **********************************
Doug           ¦ *****************************************
Wade           ¦ ****************************************
Sandy          ¦ ******************************
VELMA          ¦ **************************************************
Mala           ¦ ********************************
Lawrence       ¦ ********************************
Nancy          ¦ *********************************
Jeff           ¦ **********************************
Linda          ¦ **************************************
Jerry          ¦ *************************************
Chris          ¦ ************************************
```

Warnings If either function argument evaluates to the wrong data type, the error message *Invalid function argument* is displayed.

If the function results in the error message *Variable not found,* you probably used a literal character string as the first function argument and it is being interpreted as a variable name. The character string, in this case, must be enclosed in single quotes, double quotes, or square brackets.

If the numeric expression evaluates to a number other than an integer, the numbers after the decimal place are truncated before REPLICATE( ) is executed.

REPORT FORM

Syntax

```
REPORT FORM <filename>¦? [<scope>] [WHILE <condition>]
[FOR <condition>] [TO PRINTER] [TO FILE <filename>]
[PLAIN] [HEADING <expC>] [NOEJECT] [SUMMARY]
```

Overview

The REPORT FORM command displays on the screen or printer the report defined in a report file. Report files are created and changed using CREATE REPORT (see CREATE REPORT) and are assumed to have a .FRM extension.

The ?, or catalog query clause, can be used instead of a file name if there is an active catalog. (See SET CATALOG.) This activates a menu of all cataloged report files that belong to the active database file and allows you to select the report that you want to use.

A scope, a FOR clause, and a WHILE clause can be used to display records within a specific range that meet certain conditions. Each of these command line options is discussed separately. (See Scope, FOR, and WHILE.) The default scope for the REPORT FORM command is ALL records in the active database file.

The TO PRINTER option prints the report on the printer. If this option is not specified, the report is displayed only on the screen.

The report can be directed to a text (.TXT) file using the TO FILE option. Sending the output of REPORT FORM to a text file is not exclusive of printing the file. You can use the TO PRINTER and TO FILE options together in order to print the report and send the output to a text file at the same time.

The PLAIN option determines whether or not the date and page number are printed at the top of each page of the report just before the page title, and whether or not the page title appears on all pages. By default, a page number and the current date are displayed on the first two lines of each report page and the page title is printed at the top of each page. To display the page title on only the first page and to suppress the other headings entirely (including the HEADING option), use the PLAIN option as part of the REPORT FORM command.

The HEADING option is used to specify an additional report page title. Specify the heading using a character expression; when you run the report the value of the expression is displayed at the top of each new page on the same line as the page number. Using the PLAIN option suppresses the heading display.

The NOEJECT option determines if there is an initial page eject before the report is printed. By default, all reports begin with a page eject. If you specify NOEJECT with the REPORT FORM command, the report will begin printing at the current print location. This is useful if you want to print several short reports on the same page or if you know your printer is already set to its top-of-form mark.

The SUMMARY option lets you specify whether or not the report detail lines are displayed. By default, the detail lines are displayed along with subtotal and total lines unless you specified *Summary report only* during report creation. (See CREATE REPORT.) You can suppress the detail lines and display only the subtotal and total lines of the report by using SUMMARY with the REPORT FORM command.

Procedure

Use REPORT FORM to print a report that you have already defined using CREATE REPORT. The database file for which the report was designed must be open (see USE), and any memory variables that are used in the report design must be initialized (see STORE) before you issue the REPORT FORM command. If the report was designed to use fields from more than one database file, be sure that all of the necessary files are open and that the relations between the files are established (see CREATE REPORT Example) before running the report with REPORT FORM.

Examples

In the following example, the report designed earlier using CREATE REPORT is displayed using several of the REPORT FROM command line options. (See CREATE REPORT for the example in which the Orders report form was designed.) The environment is established and the report printed with the following commands:

```
. CLOSE DATABASES  && Close all open files
. SELECT 2
. USE Inventry INDEX Part_No
. SELECT 1
. USE Orders INDEX O_PartNo
. SET RELATION TO Part_No INTO Inventry  && Link files on Part_No
. REPORT FORM Orders TO PRINTER
```

The report should look like the one you see in Figure 81.

To print the report with an additional heading, issue the following command:

```
. REPORT FORM Orders TO PRINTER HEADING "July, 1987"
```

The report should look like the one you see in Figure 82.

To display a summary of the report without detail lines, issue the following command:

```
. REPORT FORM Orders TO PRINTER SUMMARY
```

The report should look like the one you see in Figure 83.

Warnings

The PLAIN and HEADING options of the REPORT FORM command are mutually exclusive, but using them both does not cause an error message; instead, the HEADING option is ignored.

If the report file cannot be found, the error message *File does not exist* is displayed.

If you are using dBASE III PLUS in a network environment, REPORT FORM attempts an automatic file lock unless the database file is already locked (see FLOCK( )) or is opened for exclusive use (see SET EXCLUSIVE, USE). If for any reason, the command cannot lock the database file, the error message *File is in use by another* is displayed.

Tips

If you issue REPORT FORM...TO PRINTER and the printer is not turned on or is off-line, one of two things may happen.

```
Page No.     1
07/27/87
                                         Monthly Orders

Part   Product                          Quantity  Quantity     Price      Total
Number Description                       Ordered   On Hand   Per Unit     Price


** Part Number B-254
 B-254  Blue leather pump.                    2         5      65.99     131.98
** Subtotal **
                                                                         131.98

** Part Number G-165
 G-165  Green leather slip                    2         7      23.98      47.96
        on.
** Subtotal **
                                                                          47.96

** Part Number R-123
 R-123  Red high top tennis                   1         2      23.95      23.95
        shoe.
 R-123  Red high top tennis                   1         2      23.95      23.95
        shoe.
** Subtotal **
                                                                          47.90
*** Total ***
                                                                         227.84
```

Figure 81

```
Page No.     1                          July, 1987
07/27/87
                                         Monthly Orders

Part   Product                          Quantity  Quantity     Price      Total
Number Description                       Ordered   On Hand   Per Unit     Price


** Part Number B-254
 B-254  Blue leather pump.                    2         5      65.99     131.98
** Subtotal **
                                                                         131.98

** Part Number G-165
 G-165  Green leather slip                    2         7      23.98      47.96
        on.
** Subtotal **
                                                                          47.96

** Part Number R-123
 R-123  Red high top tennis                   1         2      23.95      23.95
        shoe.
 R-123  Red high top tennis                   1         2      23.95      23.95
        shoe.
** Subtotal **
                                                                          47.90
*** Total ***
                                                                         227.84
```

Figure 82

```
Page No.     1
07/27/87
                               Monthly Orders

Part   Product                  Quantity  Quantity     Price      Total
Number Description               Ordered   On Hand   Per Unit     Price

** Part Number B-254
** Subtotal **
                                                                  131.98
** Part Number G-165
** Subtotal **
                                                                   47.96
** Part Number R-123
** Subtotal **
                                                                   47.90
*** Total ***
                                                                  227.84
```

Figure 83

If the prompt *Printer not ready. Retry? (Y/N)* is displayed, you should correct the problem and then respond by typing `Y`. If you get this prompt and type `N`, the report goes to the screen.

However, instead of this prompt, there may be a long pause with no warning message after which the report goes to the screen. If you turn the printer on before the screen display begins, the report will print.

The SUMMARY, NOEJECT, and PLAIN options override the equivalent settings that are saved as part of the report file. (See CREATE REPORT Procedure for more information on these settings.)

REST. *See* Scope

RESTORE

Syntax `RESTORE FROM <memory filename> [ADDITIVE]`

Overview The RESTORE command is used to restore into active memory the contents of a memory (.MEM) file. (See SAVE.)

If the command is issued without the ADDITIVE keyword, all current memory variables, both public and private, are released from memory, and the variables stored in the memory file are placed in memory. If the command is issued from the dot prompt, all variables are created as public (see PUBLIC); if issued from a program, all variables are created as private (see PRIVATE).

Using the ADDITIVE keyword keeps the current variables in memory and adds the variables that are stored in the memory file. If there is a variable in memory with the same name as one in the memory file, the current value of the variable is replaced with its value in the memory file. Existing variables, even if their value is changed by RESTORE, retain their public or private status.

Procedure

Use RESTORE to retrieve variables from a memory file that you have previously created using SAVE. These two commands are used together to pass the value of one or more memory variables from one application to another or to save the value of variables that change in the application for use by the same application in subsequent sessions.

SAVE is used at the end of the main program (e.g., the exit option of the main menu) in an application to save specified variables to a memory file. RESTORE is used at the beginning of the main program in an application to reinstate the variables saved in the memory file.

Examples

The following example is a check printing program. It assumes that you have check forms to use in your printer and that the printer is set up to handle the forms. (See CHR( ).) The program uses a memory file to keep track of the next available check number and the current balance. The check printing program, Ck_Print.PRG, is not listed because it is not pertinent to the illustration of RESTORE.

```
* Checks.PRG
*
SET ESCAPE OFF
SET TALK OFF
CLEAR

* The balance and check number are retrieved from the Chk_Book
* memory file, if it exists.
IF FILE("Chk_Book.MEM")
   RESTORE FROM Chk_Book
```

```
* If the memory file does not exist, it means that this is the
* first time the program has been run.  The user must enter the
* current balance and check number.  The variable names begin
* with s_ to identify them later in the SAVE command.
ELSE
   s_check_no = 0
   s_balance = 0
   @ 3,29 SAY "Enter the first check number" GET s_check_no ;
          PICTURE "9999"
   @ 5,34 SAY "Enter the balance" GET s_balance ;
          PICTURE "9999999.99"
   READ
ENDIF

* Checks.DBF is the name of the file used to record your checks.
USE Checks

* This part of the screen remains constant, so it is displayed
* here rather than in the DO WHILE loop.
CLEAR
@  3,35 SAY "Check Number"
@  4,35 SAY "Date             " + DTOC(DATE())
@  5,35 SAY "Balance"
@  7, 0 SAY "Pay To"
@  8, 0 SAY "The Order Of"
@  8,56 SAY "$"
@ 10, 0 SAY "For"

* There is an EXIT in this otherwise infinite loop.
DO WHILE .T.

   * Initialize variables.
   m_pay_to = SPACE(40)
   m_amount = 0
   m_for = SPACE(20)

   * Display current check number and balance.
   @  3,54 SAY s_check_no PICTURE "9999"
   @  5,48 SAY s_balance PICTURE "9999999.99"

   * Allow user to enter other pertinent check information.
   @  8,13 GET m_pay_to
   @  8,57 GET m_amount PICTURE "9999999.99"
   @ 10,13 GET m_for
   READ

   * If no pay to value is entered, exit the loop.
   IF "" = TRIM(m_pay_to)
```

```
    EXIT
  ENDIF

  * Add check information to database file.
  APPEND BLANK
  REPLACE Check_No WITH s_check_no, Pay_To WITH m_pay_to, ;
          Amount WITH m_amount, For WITH m_for

  * Print the check.
  DO Ck_Print

  * Update check number and balance variables for next check.
  s_check_no = s_check_no + 1
  s_balance = s_balance - m_amount

ENDDO

* Any variable whose name begins with s_ is saved to the
* Chk_Book memory file.  These variables are the new check
* number and balance that will be used the next time this
* program is run.
SAVE ALL LIKE s_* TO Chk_Book

CLOSE DATABASES
SET TALK ON
SET ESCAPE ON
```

Warnings

Any variables in memory at the time you issue RESTORE are released from memory before the memory file is restored. If you want to maintain the existing variables, be sure that you use the ADDITIVE keyword with RESTORE. ADDITIVE also retains the public and private status of existing variable names.

If the file that you RESTORE FROM cannot be found, the error message *File does not exist* is displayed.

If the memory file does not match the format that the RESTORE command expects, the error message *Memory Variable file is invalid* is displayed. This message will occur if you attempt to create a memory file using anything other than SAVE.

Tips

When you are writing a program that uses a memory file, test for the existence of the memory file before RESTORE is issued. Remember that the file may get deleted by accident, in which case the user must enter the appropriate values in order for the program to continue.

RESUME

Syntax `RESUME`

Overview RESUME continues the execution of a suspended program. (See SUSPEND.) Program execution begins with the command following the one where the program was suspended. Usually, this is the command following a SUSPEND command, but if SET ESCAPE is ON you can interrupt a program at any point by pressing the Esc key and typing S when prompted, *Cancel, Ignore, or Suspend? (C, I, or S).*

Procedure When debugging a new program, you often need to suspend its execution (see SUSPEND) to check the contents of memory (see LIST MEMORY), the history buffer (see SET DOHISTORY, LIST HISTORY), or the status of certain flags (see LIST STATUS). After you are finished and want to continue with the execution of the suspended program, enter RESUME from the dot prompt.

Examples See SUSPEND for an example using RESUME.

Warnings If you attempt to use MODIFY COMMAND to change a suspended program, the error message *File is already open* is displayed. Cancel the suspended program (see CANCEL) before attempting to make changes to it.

RETRY

Syntax `RETRY`

Overview RETRY is functionally identical to RETURN, except that when control is returned to the calling program, execution of the program continues beginning with the last command that was executed instead of the one following it.

Procedure

RETRY is almost always used in an error recovery program that is triggered by one of the ON commands. (See ON ERROR, ON ESCAPE, and ON KEY.) Of these commands, ON ERROR is most often used with RETRY. The ON ERROR DO < recovery program > command is embedded in a program at particular points (see ON ERROR) to trap certain errors. In the recovery program, commands are issued to correct the situation based on the error that occurred (see ERROR( )), and RETRY is used to reexecute the command that triggered the error recovery program.

Examples

The following example illustrates RETRY. The first listing below, Open.PRG, is a partial program that is called from a main menu.

```
* Open.PRG
*
    .
    .
    .

* The recovery program for database and index open errors is
* called Recover.PRG.  The ON ERROR trap is activated to execute
* this recovery program in case the USE...INDEX command results
* in an error.

ON ERROR DO Recover
USE Inventry INDEX Part_No
ON ERROR  && Disable error trap

    .
    .
    .
```

The next listing is of the error recovery program, Recover.PRG. This program tests for certain known errors likely to occur as the result of USE...INDEX that is isolated in the Open.PRG program. Depending on the error, a different recovery path is taken.

```
* Recover.PRG
*
* This is a recovery program for trapping potential database
* and index file opening errors.

DO CASE
```

```
* ALIAS name already in use, or File is already open.
CASE ERROR() = 24 .OR. ERROR() = 3

   * Both of these errors can be corrected by closing
   * all database files and reexecuting the USE...INDEX.
   CLOSE DATABASES
   RETRY  && Reexecutes the USE command

* File does not exist.
CASE ERROR() = 1

   * If the file does not exist, it is assumed that
   * the path is not set to the directory where the file
   * is stored.  This gives the user the opportunity to
   * enter the correct directory name.
   setpath = SPACE(40)
   CLEAR
   @ 10, 0 SAY "Either the Inventory file or its index"
   @ 11, 0 SAY "file cannot be found.  Enter the name"
   @ 12, 0 SAY "of the directory where the file is stored."
   @ 14, 0 GET setpath
   READ
   SET PATH TO &setpath
   RETRY  && Reexecutes the USE command

* Index file does not match database.
CASE ERROR() = 19

   * The index must be recreated from scratch to recover
   * from this error.  RETRY is used to reopen the database
   * and the newly created index file just to make sure that
   * the complete index file is written to disk.
   INDEX ON Part_No TO Part_No
   RETRY  && Reexecutes the USE command

* Not a dBASE database file.
CASE ERROR() = 15

   * This is a serious error that requires restoring the
   * database file from a backup.
   go_ahead = SPACE(1)
   CLEAR
   @ 10, 0 SAY "The Inventory file is corrupted."
   @ 11, 0 SAY "Insert the backup diskette in drive A."
   @ 12, 0 SAY "Press any key to restore from backup." ;
           GET go_ahead
```

```
        READ
        COPY FILE A:Inventry.DBF TO Inventry.DBF
        USE Inventry

        * The index is recreated from scratch just in case it
        * is also corrupted.
        INDEX ON Part_No TO Part_No
        RETRY  && Reexecutes the USE command

   OTHERWISE

        * This takes care of any unexpected error.
        CLEAR
        @ 10, 0 SAY "Unanticipated error encountered."
        @ 11, 0 SAY "No recovery available."

        * All files are closed.
        CLOSE DATABASES

        * The ON ERROR trap is disabled here since there will
        * not be a return to the calling program.
        ON ERROR

        * The application cannot continue due to an
        * unrecoverable error.
        RETURN TO MASTER

ENDCASE
```

Warnings Never use RETRY as the normal way of returning from a subprogram since this will result in the infinite execution of the subprogram (i.e., the DO <subprogram> command is executed over and over again). Use RETURN as the normal way of returning from a subprogram, and reserve using RETRY for error recovery situations.

Tips See ON ESCAPE for another programming example that uses RETRY.

RETURN

Syntax `RETURN [TO MASTER]`

Overview

The RETURN command ends a program by returning control to its calling program or to the dot prompt if it is the main program. When control is returned to a program, execution of the program continues beginning with the command following the last command that was executed. Usually, the last command executed is DO <program filename>, but this is not necessarily the case since ON commands (see ON ERROR, ON ESCAPE, and ON KEY) can be used to interrupt a program at any point.

RETURN also closes the current program and releases all private memory variables (see PRIVATE) belonging to it. All parameters passed as memory variables are replaced with their new values if the program was called with parameters. (See DO and PARAMETERS.)

The TO MASTER option causes the program to return control to the highest level program in the application (i.e., the program that was initiated at the dot prompt).

In a program, encountering RETURN is equivalent to encountering the end of file of the program. In a procedure (see PROCEDURE, SET PROCEDURE), it is equivalent to the procedure encountering another PROCEDURE command or its own end of file. Thus, RETURN is not always necessary.

Procedure

There are two kinds of programs in dBASE III PLUS. The first program executes its commands from beginning to end and returns control to its calling program after the last command executes. Although you can have a RETURN command as the last command in such programs, it is not necessary since the RETURN command is implied. A program encountering its own end of file is equivalent to encountering a RETURN command.

The second type of program returns to its calling program when some other condition is met. A good example of this kind of program is a menu. A menu program is usually an infinite DO WHILE loop. One of the menu options allows the user to get out of the menu program. When the user selects this option, the program does a RETURN. The following program skeleton illustrates this use of RETURN.

```
DO WHILE .T.
   .
   . <menu display and user selection>
   .
   DO CASE
      .
      . <other menu selections>
      .
      CASE choice = 0
         CLOSE DATABASES
         RETURN
   ENDCASE
ENDDO
```

Examples The following program is a submenu program that returns to the main menu program when the user selects the exit option. (See DO CASE for an example showing the main menu program.)

```
* RptMenu.PRG
*

PRIVATE ALL  && All variables used by this subroutine are local

* All reports use the following view.

USE Orders
SELECT 2
USE Inventry INDEX Part_No
SELECT 1
SET RELATION TO Part_No INTO Inventry

* All reports require total number of orders, total price, and
* average price.  After these are computed, the Orders database
* file is positioned at first record.
COUNT TO ord_num
SUM Quantity * Inventry->Price TO tot_price
AVERAGE Quantity * Inventry->Price TO avg_price
GO TOP

DO WHILE .T.

   choice = 0
   CLEAR
```

```
* Display report submenu.
@  6, 29 SAY "0 - Exit to main menu"
@  8, 29 SAY "1 - Print Orders"
@ 10, 29 SAY "2 - Print Invoices"
@ 12, 29 SAY "3 - Print Inventory"
@  4, 20 TO 14, 54 DOUBLE
@ 14, 37 GET choice PICTURE "9" RANGE 0, 3
READ

* Execute programs based on menu choice.
DO CASE

   CASE choice = 0
      CLOSE DATABASES
      * Automatically releases all variables created and
      * returns control to the main menu program.
      RETURN

   CASE choice = 1
      DO Ord_Rpt

   CASE choice = 2
      DO Invoices

   CASE choice = 3
      DO Inv_Rpt

   ENDCASE
ENDDO
```

Tips

See ON ESCAPE for a good example of using RETURN TO MASTER. RETURN TO MASTER is often used with the ON commands (see ON ESCAPE, ON KEY) in exception to the rule that programs should return up to the top through each program that is called. More often, you will use RETURN with no parameter to return back through the same sequence in which the program was called.

Although not always necessary, the explicit use of RETURN in applications programs makes the code easier to read.

RIGHT( )

Syntax `RIGHT(<expC>, <expN>)`

Overview The RIGHT( ) function, short for right substring, requires two arguments:

- A character expression representing the original string from which the substring is to be extracted
- A numeric expression representing the number of characters to be extracted from the original string

The function returns the substring of the specified character string starting in the rightmost position and extending left the specified number of characters.

Procedure RIGHT( ) returns a character string, and can be used anywhere in the language where a character expression is appropriate.

Examples Usually, a substring extraction is done from left to right, but RIGHT( ) starts at the end of the original string and extends left. You might use RIGHT( ) to add programmatically a string onto the end of a character field. If so, first be sure that there is enough blank space at the end of the field to accommodate the new information. The following routine uses the RIGHT( ) in combination with LEN( ) and SPACE( ) to determine if there is enough available space based on user input:

```
* SpaceChk.PRG
*
SET TALK OFF
USE Employee INDEX Emp_Code
ACCEPT "Enter the employee code to find: " TO m_emp_code
SEEK m_emp_code
IF FOUND()
   ACCEPT "Enter comments for this employee: " TO m_comment
   * Test to see if there is enough SPACE to accommodate the
   * additional comments.
   IF RIGHT(Comment, LEN(m_comment)) = SPACE(LEN(m_comment))
      REPLACE Comment WITH TRIM(Comment) + "  " + m_comment
   ELSE
      ? "There isn't enough space for your comments"
      WAIT
```

```
   ENDIF
ELSE
   ? "Employee code not found."
   WAIT
ENDIF
CLOSE DATABASES
SET TALK ON
```

Warnings If the function argument evaluates to a data type other than character, the error message *Invalid function argument* is displayed.

If the numeric expression evaluates to a number other than an integer, the numbers after the decimal place are truncated before RIGHT( ) is executed.

RLOCK( )

Syntax `RLOCK()|LOCK()`

Overview The RLOCK( ) function, short for record lock, does not have any arguments. It can be used effectively only if you are using dBASE III PLUS in a network environment.

The function attempts to lock the current record in the active database file. If the file is related to other files (see SET RELATION), it also attempts to lock the records in these files that are related to the current record. If no other user on the network has a record lock for those records, the current record in the active database file and all of its related records are locked and the function returns a logical True (.T.). A separate record lock can be obtained for each work area that has an open file.

If any of the needed records are already locked by another user, the function returns a logical False (.F.) and no records are locked.

Procedure RLOCK( ) is used in network programming to prevent a user from making changes to a database file record while others may also be changing data in the same record. It is necessary to use record locking only if the file was opened with shared access (i.e., SET EXCLUSIVE was OFF when the file was opened and USE was issued without the EXCLUSIVE keyword) and the file is not already locked. (See FLOCK( ).)

You must use record locking in dBASE III PLUS to use the @...GET (see @...GET) to edit the contents of one or more fields in the current record. You cannot use @...GET to edit the contents of a record in a shared, unlocked database file without getting an error message.

To use RLOCK( ) in a program, first open all of the database and index files that you want to use and establish the relationships between them. (See SELECT, SET RELATION, USE.) Then, use RLOCK( ) in a DO WHILE loop that has some sort of time-out capability. After the DO WHILE loop, check again to make sure that the loop did not time-out. If you obtain the record lock before running out of time, perform the commands you want (e.g., series of @...GETs followed by READ), then unlock the record (see CLOSE, UNLOCK) when you are finished with it. If you run out of time without obtaining the record lock, display an error message for the user.

Examples

The following example illustrates the correct use of RLOCK( ). Before issuing a series of @...GET commands to edit a particular record in the mailing list file, the record is locked.

```
* MailEdit.PRG
*
SET TALK OFF
SET EXCLUSIVE OFF  && For shared access to database files
USE Mail INDEX Last

* Set up the screen so that the user can enter a last name.
* The labels for the other fields are displayed here because
* they are the same for each record and need only be shown once.

CLEAR
@ 3, 5 SAY "Last Name"
@ 4, 5 SAY "First Name"
@ 5, 5 SAY "Street"
@ 6, 5 SAY "Apartment"
@ 7, 5 SAY "City"
@ 8, 5 SAY "State"
@ 9, 5 SAY "Zip Code"

m_error = 0   && Initialize error number

DO WHILE .T.

   * A different prompt depending on the error number.
   DO CASE
```

```
    CASE m_error = 0  && No error
       @ 1,5 SAY "Enter the last name of the person to find."

    CASE m_error = 1
       @ 1,5 SAY "The name you entered was not found.       "

    CASE m_error = 2
       @ 1,5 SAY "The record cannot be locked.              "

    CASE m_error = 3
       @ 1,5 SAY "The record was changed by another user.   "

 ENDCASE

 m_error = 0           && Reset error number
 m_last = SPACE(20)    && Make m_last blank
 @ 4,17 CLEAR TO 9,79  && Clear previous record from screen

 @ 3,17 GET m_last     && Enter a name into a memory variable
 READ

 IF "" = TRIM(m_last)
    EXIT   && Exit from the loop if no name is entered
 ENDIF

 SEEK m_last  && Locate the last name entered

 IF .NOT. FOUND()   && Test to make sure that name is on file

    * If the name is not found, set the error flag to true
    * and start the loop over.
    m_error = 1  && Error number 1 means not found
    LOOP

 ELSE  && Obtain record lock and edit contents of record

    time_out = 0

    * Try to lock the record 100 times.
    DO WHILE .NOT. RLOCK() .AND. time_out < 100
       time_out = time_out + 1  && Increment time_out variable
    ENDDO

    * If time_out equals 100, it means that the DO WHILE loop
    * timed out without obtaining a file lock.  Set the error
    * flag to true and start loop over.
```

```
      IF time_out = 100  && File lock was not successful
         m_error = 2  && Error number 2 means not locked
         LOOP

      * Otherwise, the record lock was successful.
      ELSE

         * Before allowing the edit, check to make sure that no
         * change was made to the Key field between the SEEK
         * command completion and the RLOCK().

         IF Last_Name = m_last  && Key field still the same
            @ 1, 5  && Erase prompt
            @ 3,17 GET Last_Name
            @ 4,17 GET First_Name
            @ 5,17 GET Address1
            @ 6,17 GET Address2
            @ 7,17 GET City
            @ 8,17 GET State
            @ 9,17 GET Zip

            READ  && Allow user to edit the fields
            UNLOCK  && Unlock record after edit

         ELSE  && Someone changed key field before lock
            m_error = 3  && Error number 3 means changed.
            UNLOCK       && Unlock changed record
            LOOP
         ENDIF  && Record changed check

      ENDIF  && Record lock time out check

   ENDIF  && Record found check
ENDDO
CLEAR
CLOSE DATABASES
SET EXCLUSIVE ON  && Return exclusive flag to its default value
SET TALK ON
```

If you execute this program, a screen appears that allows you to enter a name. If the appropriate record cannot be locked after one hundred tries, or the name you enter is not in the database file, or the name you originally sought gets changed between the time the record was found and the record lock was obtained, an error message is displayed instead of the normal prompt. When the name that you enter is found and the record is successfully locked, the prompt is erased and the record is displayed for you to edit.

Warnings

RLOCK( ) does not produce an error message if the record lock is unsuccessful because this is not considered an error. The function tells you with its return value whether or not it succeeded; you can continue to try the record lock until it is successful.

When using RLOCK( ), always allow for a time out; otherwise, your program will get stuck in an infinite loop if another user forgets to release a lock or close an exclusively used database file.

The error message *Record is not locked* is displayed if you attempt to use REPLACE to change the current record (i.e. no scope, no FOR, and no WHILE clause) without first obtaining a record lock. Use REPLACE NEXT 1 if you want the command to do an automatic file lock, or use RLOCK( ) to lock the record before issuing REPLACE. This same error message occurs if you use the @...GET command with a field name followed by a READ without first obtaining a record lock. You must use FLOCK( ) or RLOCK( ) to obtain a file or record lock before you can use @...GET/READ to edit the contents of a record in a shared database file. (See SET EXCLUSIVE, USE.)

Unless there is already a record or file lock in place (or unless the file(s) involved have been opened exclusively), the DELETE and RECALL commands automatically attempt a record lock if you do not specify a scope, a FOR clause, or a WHILE clause. Although this suggests that RLOCK( ) is not necessary under these circumstances, RLOCK( ), in fact, allows you to control how an unsuccessful record lock is handled. Automatic record locking results in the error message *Record is in use by another* if it is unsuccessful; this forces you to use an ON ERROR trap (see ON ERROR, ERROR( )) to handle the error message and to avoid program failure.

The message *Record is in use by another* can occur under a number of different circumstances and is handled differently depending on when it happens. For example, if the message is the result of an automatic record lock, the ON ERROR routine (if one is in effect) is triggered. If you attempt to SKIP over, GO directly to, or SEEK (also FIND) the key of a locked record, dBASE III PLUS considers this an error and triggers the ON ERROR routine. However, if you do a LIST or DISPLAY ALL on a file that has a locked record, it is not considered an error (i.e., ON ERROR is not triggered), and the message is simply displayed as part of the listing.

If you try to LIST or DISPLAY a locked record using a RECORD number scope (see Scope), no error occurs; instead, a blank record is displayed with the record number of the locked record.

Tips

If you are using dBASE III PLUS in a single-user environment, RLOCK( ) always returns a value of .T. This allows programs written for the network version to be used by the single-user version without producing an error. In the program example given above, SEEK locates a particular record based on a key field value entered by a user. This is a common practice that allows a user to bring up quickly a desired record for editing; sometimes LOCATE is used for this purpose also.

In network programming, you don't know what happens to a record in a database file between the time that you access it and the time that you obtain a record lock. For example, suppose that SEEK is successful, and another user locks the record before your program gets to the DO WHILE .NOT. RLOCK( ) .AND. time_out < 100 command. The other user can change the Last_Name field and UNLOCK the record before the loop executes one hundred times. When the record is displayed on the screen with the series of @...GET commands, it will have a different Last_Name than the one you originally sought. For this reason, it is a good idea to check the search condition again after you have the record locked.

EDIT allows you to do interactive record locking and unlocking, rather than having to obtain a file or record lock in advance. (See EDIT for more information.)

See FLOCK( ) for information on locking an entire file. RLOCK( ) and FLOCK( ) are unique among the dBASE III PLUS functions because they not only return a value but also perform an operation.

A user-controlled timeout provides a more flexible interface. If a record is locked, display a message stating that the program is waiting for a locked record and that the user can press a key at any time to stop waiting. Then, enter a loop that tests for INKEY( ) while trying to lock the record instead of counting to a fixed number. (See INKEY( ) for more information.)

ROUND( )

Syntax `ROUND(<expN1>, <expN2>)`

Overview

The ROUND( ) function requires two numeric expressions as its arguments:

- A numeric expression representing the number to be rounded
- A second numeric expression representing the number of decimal places to be used in rounding

The second number can be zero, positive, or negative. If it is zero, the first number is rounded to the nearest whole number; if it is positive, the first number is rounded to the right of the decimal place, and if it is negative, the first number is rounded to the left of the decimal place. The function rounds the first number accordingly and returns the result.

Procedure

ROUND( ) returns a number and can be used anywhere in the language where a numeric expression is appropriate.

Examples

In dBASE III PLUS, the result of certain mathematical operations can result in more decimal places than you want. For example, multiplying two numbers results in an answer that has a number of decimal places equal to the sum of the number of decimal places in the original two numbers. When dealing with dollars and cents, you probably want to round such results to two decimal places. The following example computes the sales tax of a number and rounds the result:

```
* RoundOff.PRG
*
SET TALK OFF
CLEAR
dollar_amt = 0.00
@ 10, 0 SAY "Enter the dollar amount: " GET dollar_amt
READ
* The California sales tax is 6.5
tax = ROUND(.065 * dollar_amt, 2)
sale_price = dollar_amt + tax
```

```
SET FIXED ON
? "Amount   ", dollar_amt
? "Tax      ", tax
? "----------------------"
? "Total    ", sale_price
SET FIXED OFF
SET TALK ON
```

Warnings If either function argument evaluates to a data type other than numeric, the error message *Invalid function argument* is displayed.

Tips Although ROUND( ) rounds numbers to a particular number of decimal places, the result may show more decimal places than you want. Since the result is rounded, the extra places all have a value of zero, but the places are still displayed. To fix the display to a particular number of decimal places, use the SET DECIMALS TO and SET FIXED commands. The following example shows how a display looks before and after the number of decimals is fixed:

```
SET TALK OFF
number = 1.66666666666
? "This list has too many decimal places showing"
? "---------------------------------------------"
DO WHILE number < 2
   ? ROUND(number, 5)
   number = number + .1
ENDDO
number = 1.66666666666
SET DECIMALS TO 5
SET FIXED ON
?
?
? "This list is correct"
? "--------------------"
DO WHILE number < 2
   ? ROUND(number, 5)
   number = number + .1
ENDDO
SET FIXED OFF
SET DECIMALS TO 2
SET TALK ON
```

```
This list has too many decimal places showing
---------------------------------------------
          1.66667000000
          1.76667000000
          1.86667000000
          1.96667000000

This list is correct
--------------------
          1.66667
          1.76667
          1.86667
          1.96667
```

ROW( )

Syntax `ROW()`

Overview The ROW( ) function has no arguments. This function determines and returns the row number of the current screen position of the cursor.

Procedure ROW( ) returns a number and can be used anywhere in the language where a numeric expression is appropriate.

Examples ROW( ) is most frequently used for relative screen addressing (i.e., the display of data at screen coordinates relative to where the last screen output ended). The @...SAY command is only capable of displaying the value of a single expression. For this reason, it may appear necessary to use complicated conversion functions to display different data types on the same line; however, you can avoid this complication by using ROW( ). The following routine displays the Last_Name of the first customer in the Customer database file next to the current date and the amount that the customer owes—all without conversion functions:

```
* Amt_Owed.PRG
*
SET TALK OFF
```

```
USE Customer
CLEAR
@ 10, 0 SAY TRIM(Last_Name)
@ ROW(), COL()+1 SAY DATE()
@ ROW(), COL()+1 SAY Amt_Owed
CLOSE DATABASES
SET TALK ON
```

Consider the following equivalent @...SAY command:

```
@ 10, 0 SAY TRIM(Last_Name) + " " + DTOC(DATE()) + " " +;
        STR(Amt_Owed, 10, 2)
```

Warnings ROW( ) works only when addressing the screen. When directing output to the printer with SET DEVICE TO PRINTER, use PROW( ).

Tips When used with @...SAY and @...GET, the $ symbol can replace ROW( ). This carryover from dBASE II maintains consistency with that language.

RTRIM( ). *See* TRIM( )

SAVE

Syntax

```
SAVE TO <memory filename>
[ALL LIKE¦EXCEPT  <skeleton>]
```

Overview The SAVE command saves the contents of existing memory variables to a memory file. By default, the file is given a .MEM extension.

Unless you specify an ALL LIKE or ALL EXCEPT skeleton, all existing memory variables are saved to the named memory file. SAVE...ALL LIKE <skeleton> indicates that you want to save all the variable names of a particular form to the memory file. SAVE...ALL EXCEPT <skeleton> indicates that you want to save all the variable names except those of a particular form to the memory file. (See Skeleton for information on how to compose a skeleton.)

Procedure

To use SAVE effectively, decide in advance which memory variables you want to save and give these variables similar names so that you will be able to describe them using a skeleton. The easiest way to do this is to use the same letter(s) to begin the names of the variables that you want to save and to name all other variables differently. Then, when you are ready to save the variables to a file, use SAVE...ALL LIKE <skeleton> to describe the variables. For example, if you use s_ to begin the names of the variables that you want to save, you SAVE TO <memory file> ALL LIKE s_*.

The alternative to this method is to do the opposite: give all the variables that you do not want to save similar names, name the variables that you want to save differently, then use SAVE...ALL EXCEPT <skeleton>. For example, you could name all variables that you do not want to save with m_, and use SAVE...ALL EXCEPT m_* to create the memory file.

Use SAVE with no skeleton phrase to save all of the existing memory variables to the memory file.

SAVE and RESTORE (see RESTORE) are used together to pass the value of one or more memory variables from one application to another, or to save the value of the variables for use by the same application.

SAVE is used in an application at the end of the main program (e.g., the main menu) in an application to save specified variables to a memory file. RESTORE is used in an application at the beginning of the main program to reinstate the variables saved in the memory file.

Examples

See RESTORE for a complete illustration of the use of SAVE.

Warnings

If the safety flag is set off (see SET SAFETY), SAVE overwrites an existing memory file without warning.

Unlike most other commands that allow a skeleton to describe a group of memory variables (see PRIVATE and RELEASE), SAVE does not allow you to use the ALL keyword without LIKE or EXCEPT. The default for SAVE is all memory variables; if you use ALL without LIKE or EXCEPT, the error message *Unrecognized phrase/command in command* is displayed.

Tips

Another difference between SAVE and other commands that allow a skeleton to describe a group of memory variables (see PRIVATE and RELEASE) is that SAVE does not have an alternate syntax that allows you to specify a list of variables. Therefore, if you do not want to save all variables to a memory file, you must give similar names either to the variables that you want to save or to the ones that you do not want to save.

Scope

Syntax A scope is represented in command syntax as <scope>. Whenever it appears, you can use any of the following:

```
ALL
NEXT <expN>
RECORD <expN>
REST
```

Overview Specifying a scope as part of a command tells the command how many records to process and which record to start with. The meaning of each scope is stated below:

SCOPE	MEANING
ALL	Start with the first record in the file, and process all records.
NEXT <expN>	Start with the current record and process the specified number of records.
RECORD <expN>	Go to the record with the specified number and process only that record.
REST	Start with the current record and process the rest of the records.

Procedure All dBASE III PLUS commands that allow a scope as part of their syntax have a default scope that is assumed. For example, the COPY and LIST commands have a default scope of ALL records, and the DISPLAY command has a default scope of the current record (i.e., NEXT 1).

The use of a FOR clause without a scope changes the default scope of any command to ALL records, and the use of a WHILE clause without a scope changes the default scope of any command to the REST of the records.

To change the default scope of a command, specify a scope as part of its syntax. The command will begin with the appropriate record and only process those within the specified scope.

Examples The following example uses the LIST and DISPLAY commands to demonstrate all of the different scopes:

```
. USE Mail
. LIST NEXT 5 First_Name, Last_Name FOR Age < 30
Record#  First_Name   Last_Name
      1  MICHELLE     SMITH
      2  Rebecca      Corbbit
      4  David        Gurly
      5  Julia        King

. LIST REST First_Name, Last_Name
Record#  First_Name   Last_Name
      5  Julia        King
      6  Perry        Lester
      7  Cathy        Moore
      8  Doug         Smith
      9  Wade         Adams
     10  Sandy        Richardson
     11  VELMA        MOODY
     12  Mala         Schaefer
     13  Lawrence     Arthur
     14  Nancy        Long
     15  Jeff         Potter
     16  Linda        Roberts
     17  Jerry        Samuels
     18  Chris        Whiteside

. DISPLAY RECORD 3 First_Name, Last_Name, Age
Record#  First_Name   Last_Name                Age
      3  Gloria       Roman                     33

. DISPLAY ALL First_Name, Last_Name, Age
Record#  First_Name   Last_Name                Age
      1  MICHELLE     SMITH                     26
      2  Rebecca      Corbbit                   26
      3  Gloria       Roman                     33
      4  David        Gurly                     22
      5  Julia        King                      28
      6  Perry        Lester                    23
      7  Cathy        Moore                     33
      8  Doug         Smith                     40
```

```
     9  Wade        Adams           39
    10  Sandy       Richardson      29
    11  VELMA       MOODY           49
    12  Mala        Schaefer        31
    13  Lawrence    Arthur          31
    14  Nancy       Long            32
    15  Jeff        Potter          33
    16  Linda       Roberts         37
    17  Jerry       Samuels         36
    18  Chris       Whiteside       35

. CLOSE DATABASES
```

Warnings If the expression used with NEXT or RECORD evaluates to a data type other than numeric, the error message *Not a numeric expression* is displayed.

Tips You can use a scope and a WHILE clause to retrieve a specific number of records that meet a particular condition, but the database file must be in the correct order. For example, suppose that you want to see the names of two people in your mailing list who are thirty-three years old. You might try the following commands:

```
. USE Mail
. LOCATE FOR Age = 33
Record =       3
. LIST NEXT 2 FOR Age = 33 First_Name, Last_Name, Age
Record#  First_Name   Last_Name            Age
      3  Gloria       Roman                 33
```

Since the person following record number three is not thirty-three years old, LIST NEXT 2 with a FOR condition does not solve the problem. You might try using LIST NEXT 2 with a WHILE clause, but you would have the same problem because the file is not in order by age.

The problem is solved by engaging an index file called Ages whose key field is Age. With the index file engaged, all of the records with age thirty-three are in consecutive order, and the WHILE clause solves the problem:

```
. SET INDEX TO Ages
. SEEK 33
. LIST NEXT 2 WHILE Age = 33 First_Name, Last_Name, Age
Record#  First_Name   Last_Name           Age
      3  Gloria       Roman                33
      7  Cathy        Moore                33

. CLOSE DATABASES
```

SEEK

Syntax `SEEK <expression>`

Overview

The SEEK command locates the first record in the active database file that has a particular index key value. The key value is specified as an expression.

Procedure

Use SEEK with an indexed database file to locate a record with a particular key value using the controlling index file. (See SET INDEX or SET ORDER.) SEEK can be used with any index file, as long as the SEEK expression and the index key expression are of the same data type.

When SEEK is executed, the expression is evaluated, and the record pointer is positioned to the first record whose key value matches the value of the SEEK expression. After SEEK is issued, FOUND( ) should be used to determine whether or not the record was located. A DO WHILE loop or another command with a WHILE clause can be used to process all occurrences of the same key.

Examples

The following routine allows the user to add new orders to the Orders file. When the user enters the customer and part numbers, SEEK verifies that the customer number is on file in the Customer file and that the part number is on file in the Inventry file. Information is then displayed from the Inventry file and the user enters the quantity to order.

```
* Orders.PRG
*

SET TALK OFF

* Set up the database file environment.
SELECT 3
USE Customer INDEX Cust_No
SELECT 2
USE Inventry INDEX Part_No
SELECT 1
USE Orders

* Clear screen and display the part of the screen that remains
* constant only once.
CLEAR
@  1, 3 TO  17,69 DOUBLE
@  2,30 SAY "O R D E R S"
@  3,29 TO  3,41
@  5,10 SAY "Customer Number"
@  6,10 SAY "Part Number"
@  8,10 SAY "Amount to Order"
@  9, 4 TO  9,68
@ 11, 6 SAY "Description:"
@ 15,42 SAY "Unit Price"
@ 16,42 SAY "Total Cost"

* Endless loop has an EXIT inside for when the user does
* not enter a customer number.
DO WHILE .T.

   * Reset color to default.
   SET COLOR TO

   * Erase data from previous record from the screen.
   @  8,28 CLEAR TO  8,68
   @ 12, 6 CLEAR TO 12,68
   @ 15,57 CLEAR TO 15,68
   @ 16,54 CLEAR TO 16,68
   @ 19, 0

   * Initialize memory variables for the next order.
   m_cust_no  = SPACE(4)
   m_part_no  = SPACE(5)
   m_quantity = 0
```

```
* Get the customer and part numbers.
@  5,28 GET m_cust_no  PICTURE "@! A999"
@  6,28 GET m_part_no  PICTURE "@! AX999"
READ

* Erase error message, if any from previous order.
@ 13, 6 CLEAR TO 13,68

* If no customer number is entered, EXIT the loop.
IF "" = TRIM(m_cust_no)
   EXIT
ENDIF

* Change the standard display to black on white to call
* attention to the SAY fields.
SET COLOR TO N/W

* Check to see if the customer number is on file.
SELECT Customer
SEEK m_cust_no

* If it is not, display an error message and go back to
* the beginning of the DO WHILE loop.
IF .NOT. FOUND()
   @ 13, 6 SAY "Customer number is not on file.  Try again."
   LOOP
ENDIF

* Check to see if part number is on file.
SELECT Inventry
SEEK m_part_no

* If it is not, display an error message and go back to
* the beginning of the DO WHILE loop.
IF .NOT. FOUND()
   @ 13, 6 SAY "Part number is not on file.  Try again."
   LOOP
ENDIF

* If you get this far, it means that both the customer number
* and part number are on file.  Display the Inventry fields
* on the bottom half of the screen.
@ 12, 6 SAY Descrip FUNCTION "S62"
@ 15,57 SAY Price PICTURE "99999999.99"
```

```
    * Now, get the quantity using the quantity-on-hand field in
    * the Inventry file as the upper limit of the RANGE.
    @  8,28 GET m_quantity PICTURE "9999999999" RANGE 1, Quantity
    READ

    * Display the total price for this order and wait for the
    * user to see it and press any key.
    @ 16,54 SAY Price * m_quantity PICTURE "99999999999.99"
    goahead = SPACE(1)
    * Deny typeahead so that user is sure to see order.
    CLEAR TYPEAHEAD
    @ 19,15 SAY "Press any key to enter the next order.";
            GET goahead
    READ

    * Update the Orders file with the information that
    * was entered.
    SELECT Orders
    APPEND BLANK
    REPLACE Cust_No WITH m_cust_no, Part_No WITH m_part_no,;
            Quantity WITH m_quantity
ENDDO
CLOSE DATABASES
SET TALK ON
```

Warnings

If you use SEEK with a database file that does not have an open index file, the error message *Database is not indexed* is displayed.

The warning message *No find* is displayed if SEEK is unsuccessful. Since this is a warning message rather than an error message, you can suppress it with SET TALK OFF.

Since SEEK requires that you use an expression, a number of errors are possible when the expression is evaluated. The most common error messages are *Variable not found* and *Data type mismatch.*

Data type mismatch indicates one of two things – either the SEEK expression and the index key expression do not have the same data type, or the SEEK expression uses two variables with differing data types. For example, this error will result if you attempt to add a number to a character string. Correct this error by using the proper data conversion function. (See DTOC( ), CTOD( ), VAL( ), and STR( )).

Variable not found means that you have used a variable name that does not exist. Check the SEEK expression to ensure that you did not misspell one of the variable names. If you are trying to use SEEK with a constant character value, be sure to put the constant value in quotes.

Tips

If you use a complicated key expression when you initially create the index file (see INDEX), use the same expression form when you SEEK the index. For example, suppose that you use the following commands to create an index file called Amt_Ord.NDX:

```
USE Orders
INDEX ON STR(Quantity, 10) + Part_No TO Amt_Ord
```

Later on, you may use the following to prompt a user to look for a particular record using this index file:

```
USE Orders INDEX Amt_Ord
m_quantity = 0
m_part_no = SPACE(5)
@ 10, 0 SAY "Enter the amount ordered" GET m_quantity;
        PICTURE "9999999999"
@ 11, 0 SAY "Enter the part number" GET m_part_no;
        PICTURE "@! AX999"
READ
```

To correctly SEEK using these variables, you would use:

```
  SEEK STR(m_quantity, 10) + m_part_no
```

If there are multiple occurrences of the same key in your database file, SEEK can only locate the first one. In order to process all occurrences of a particular key, use a DO WHILE loop with the SKIP command. For example,

```
SEEK key
DO WHILE key = KeyField
   <commands>
   SKIP
ENDDO
```

You can also use a WHILE clause with any command that allows it to process all of the keys. For example,

```
SEEK key
LIST WHILE key = KeyField
```

If you are using a memory variable to store the key value, it is faster to use SEEK than FIND since FIND requires macro substitution and SEEK does not.

SELECT

Syntax `SELECT <work area number>|<alias name>`

Overview The SELECT command switches between the ten database file work areas available in dBASE III PLUS. The work areas are numbered from 1 to 10 but also can be identified by the alias name of the database file that is open in the work area. (See USE.)

Each work area is assigned a default alias name that can be used to identify the work area instead of using the work area number. These alias names are the letters A through J; A is assigned to work area number 1, B is assigned to number 2, and so on. (See Alias for more information on alias names and their uses.)

Procedure When you enter dBASE III PLUS, the current work area is number 1. Unless you use SELECT to access another work area, all database files that you open (see USE) are put into use in work area 1, thus closing each previously open file.

If you want to work simultaneously with two or more database files, SELECT a new work area number before opening each file. Once the database files are open in different work areas, use SELECT with the database alias name to access whichever database you want.

Examples The following example shows how to use SELECT to establish a database file environment and to access the individual files once they are open:

```
* Invoice.PRG
*
SET TALK OFF
SET DEVICE TO PRINTER  && Send @...SAY result to printer

* Establish environment for printing invoices.
SELECT 3
USE Inventry INDEX Part_No
SELECT 2
USE Customer INDEX Cust_No
SELECT 1
USE Orders INDEX O_CustNo
SET RELATION TO Part_No INTO Inventry
```

```
* The memory variable, previous, is used to determine if the
* current customer number is the same as it is in the previous
* record of the Orders file.  This way, Orders for the same
* customer go on a single invoice.
previous = SPACE(4)

DO WHILE .NOT. EOF()

   * Since there may be more than one order for a particular
   * customer number, this IF...ENDIF block prints the customer
   * number, name, and address only once per invoice.
   IF Cust_No <> previous

      * Find the Customer record for this order.  The SELECT
      * command is used with the database alias name instead
      * of the work area number.

      SELECT Customer
      SEEK Orders->Cust_No
      SELECT Orders

      * The @...SAY command is used to print a single character
      * field from the Orders file and to print fields from the
      * Customer file that are concatenated with other fields
      * and character string contents.  Functions are also
      * applied to some fields, demonstrating the ability of
      * the @...SAY command to work with complicated character
      * expressions.

      @ 2,50  SAY Cust_No
      @ 3, 5  SAY TRIM(Customer->First_Name) + " " + ;
                  Customer->Last_Name
      @ 4, 5  SAY Customer->Address1
      @ 5, 5  SAY Customer->Address2
      @ 6, 5  SAY TRIM(Customer->City) + ", " + ;
                  Customer->State + "  " + Customer->Zip
   ENDIF

   * This next DO WHILE loop prints the line items on the
   * invoice.  A line counter, this_line, and total price
   * accumulator are initialized.
   this_line = 10
   tot_price = 0

   * The previous customer number becomes the current customer
   * number before the line items are printed.
```

```
  previous = Cust_No

  * The printing of line items continues until the customer
  * number changes.
  DO WHILE Cust_No = previous

     * The @...SAY command is used with a variable row number
     * to print fields from Orders and Inventry.

     @ this_line, 0 SAY Part_No
     @ this_line, 8 SAY SUBSTR(Inventry->Descrip, 1, 45)
     @ this_line,54 SAY Quantity

     * The @...SAY command is used to calculate a numeric
     * expression and print its result.
     @ this_line,57 SAY Quantity * Inventry->Price

     * The total price accumulator for this customer is
     * updated.
     tot_price = tot_price + Quantity * Inventry->Price

    * Time to print the next line item of the invoice.
     SKIP
     this_line = this_line + 1
  ENDDO

  * The @...SAY command is used to print the total price
  * which is stored in the memory variable, tot_price.
  @ this_line,65 SAY tot_price

ENDDO
EJECT
CLOSE DATABASES
SET DEVICE TO SCREEN
SET TALK ON
```

Warnings If you try to SELECT a work area number that is outside of the allowable range from 1 to 10, the error message *Cannot select requested database* is displayed.

Similarly, if you use the work area alias names instead of the numbers, the error message *ALIAS not found* is displayed. This message indicates that you tried to SELECT a work area alias name other than A through J, or that you misspelled the alias name of a database file.

Since the letters A through J are reserved as default alias names for the ten work areas, you cannot create database files with these names. The error message *ALIAS name already in use* is displayed if you use CREATE with one of these reserved alias names. Using RENAME or some other method to create a database file with one of the reserved alias names as its name will result in this same error message if you attempt to open the file. (See USE.)

Tips

Although it is not necessary to use the work areas in consecutive order, it is probably a good idea. In an applications program, use the work area number only when initially setting up the database file environment. After that, to SELECT a database file, use its alias name.

See SET RELATION for information on relating database files once they are in use in different work areas.

SET

Syntax `SET`

Overview

The SET command, often referred to as full-screen SET, uses a menu-driven system to change certain dBASE III PLUS environmental settings. The majority of commands that begin with the verb SET (see, for example, SET BELL and SET FUNCTION) can be changed using this command.

Procedure

SET is normally used at the dot prompt to customize the dBASE III PLUS environment. No preparation is necessary for using the command; simply type SET to activate the menu system. When you are finished changing the settings, press Esc. The menu navigation and selection keys are detailed in Appendix B.

Note that the value of any SET menu option differs depending on the status of its corresponding SET command. The following instructions assume that all SET commands are at their default settings.

Options The Options menu changes most of the ON ¦ OFF SET commands as well as SET DEVICE. If you are in a network environment, the additional SET options, *Encryption* and *Exclusive* (see SET ENCRYPTION, SET EXCLUSIVE), are listed in this menu. If you are using a catalog (see SET CATALOG), the *Catalog* menu option will be available as an ON ¦ OFF setting. Excluded from this menu are commands such as SET DEBUG and SET ECHO, which are normally used in debugging.

All of the options in this menu are toggles. To change an option, highlight it and press Enter. (See SET followed by the menu option name for more information on the effect of changing any of these options.)

Screen The Screen menu specifies the screen color and attributes; the menu differs for color and monochrome monitors. The *Display Type* menu option shows what monitor type you are using based on whether set COLOR is ON or OFF. You cannot change the *Display Type* menu option unless you have two monitors attached to your computer or have an extended graphics color display (EGA). If you have an EGA, this menu option allows you to switch to a 43-line display.

Some of the options in this menu are toggles; the rest are just like toggles, but with more than two possible values. To change an option, highlight it and press Enter. For options that have more than two possible values, press Enter several times until the value that you want appears in the menu.

As soon as you begin changing options in this menu, a box appears to the right to show the effect of your changes on the display. (See SET COLOR for more information on the effect of changing any of these options.)

Keys The Keys menu changes the function key settings. To change the value of a function key, highlight its key label in the menu and press Enter. Type in the new value and press Enter to indicate that you are finished. Remember to include a semicolon as the last character if you want the carriage return to be automatic when the function key is pressed. (See SET FUNCTION for more information.)

Disk The Disk menu specifies the dBASE III PLUS default drive (see SET DEFAULT) and the search path (see SET PATH). To change the default drive, highlight the option and press Enter until the correct drive is displayed in the menu. To change the search path, highlight the option and press Enter. Type in the path setting, and press Enter to indicate that you are finished. Although SET PATH lets you have a path up to sixty characters long, this menu option only allows you to enter twenty characters. If you type the maximum number of characters, you do not have to press Enter when you are finished.

Files The Files menu specifies the SET commands that open files. (See SET ALTERNATE, SET FORMAT, and SET INDEX.) Note that you cannot specify a catalog file even though SET CATALOG ON ¦ OFF is available in the Options menu.

To open an alternate file, highlight the *Alternate* menu option and press Enter. Type in the name of the file and press Enter when you are done.

Use of the *Format* and *Index* menu options depends on whether or not there is an open database file in the current work area. (See SELECT, USE.) If there is not, you must start by highlighting the *Index* option and pressing Enter. Because there is no open database file, you are presented with a menu of database rather than index files, and you must select one before you can open index files. After selecting a database file, a menu of index files appears from which you can select a maximum of seven. When you have selected all of the index files that you want, press Right or Left Arrow to close the menu. Then, highlight the *Format* option, press Enter, and select a format file from the menu.

If there is already an active database file, you can select the index files and format file as described above, but no database file menu will be displayed when you select the *Index* option since there is already one in use. You do not have to open the index files before opening the format file.

Margin The Margin menu specifies the margin (see SET MARGIN) and memo field display width (see SET MEMOWIDTH) settings. To change either of these options, highlight it and press Enter. Type in a new number between zero and 80. If the number that you type is a single digit, press Enter when you are finished.

Decimals The Decimals menu specifies the number of decimals you want to use in numeric displays. (See SET DECIMALS.) To change the number of decimals, press Enter and type in number between zero and 15. If the number that you type is a single digit, press Enter when you are finished.

Examples

In this example, SET is used to SET BELL OFF and to change the default drive to A. To begin, enter SET from the dot prompt. Your screen should look like the one in Figure 84. Highlight the *Bell* option in the Options menu using the Down Arrow key and press Enter to change its value from ON to OFF.

Next, instead of using the Right or Left Arrow to cursor to the menu, open the Disk menu by typing D. (This is a shortcut that you can use with any menu-driven command in dBASE III PLUS to open a menu.) Your screen should look like the one in Figure 85. To change the *Default disk drive* from C to A, press Enter until A appears in the menu. The number of times you press Enter corresponds to the number of drives you have (e.g., if you have two drives, press Enter once).

Press Esc to leave full-screen SET, and put these new environmental settings into effect.

Warnings

If you do not already have an open database file in the Files menu, selecting a Format file before opening a database and index files with the *Index* option results in the closing of that format file. (This is caused by the way in which the SET FORMAT and USE commands work.) Remember to use the *Index* option first.

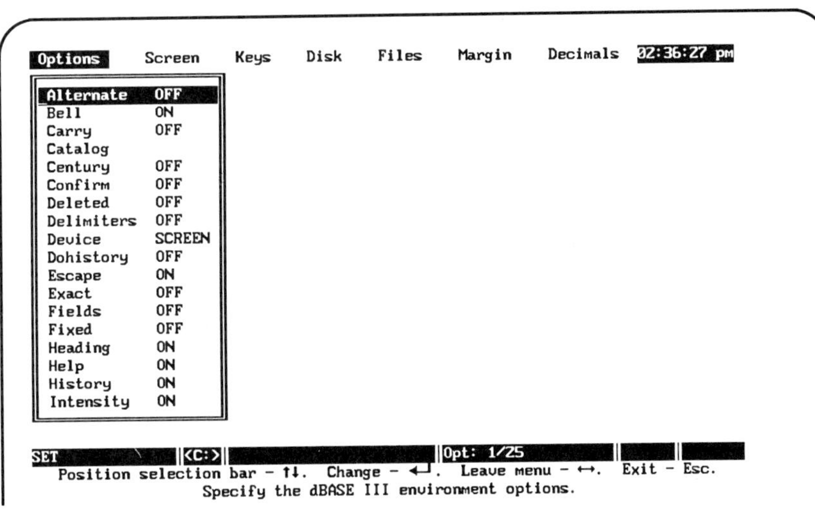

Figure 84

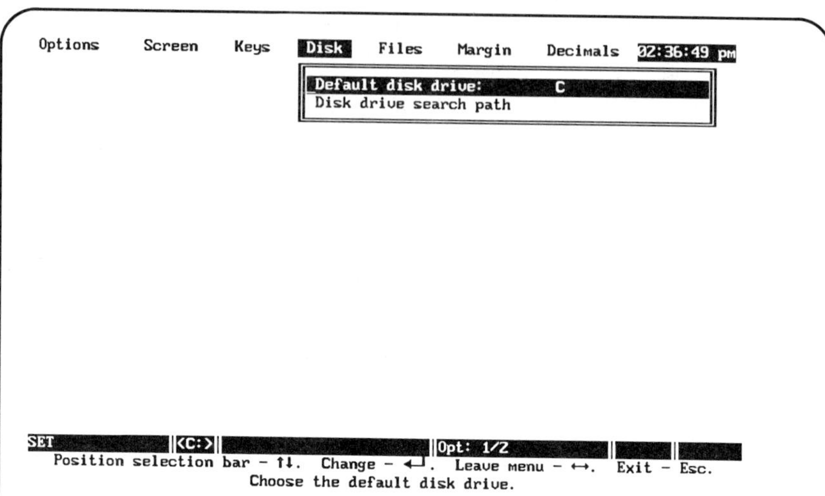

Figure 85

Although SET PATH lets you have a path up to sixty characters long, the *Disk drive search part option* in the Disk menu only allows you to enter twenty characters.

If you enter a number greater than 80 for the *Left report margin* and *Memo field display width* options in the Margin menu, the value of the menu option automatically reverts to 80. This is not consistent with the range of values allowed for SET MARGIN and SET MEMOWIDTH. Also, the *Memo field display width* option allows you to enter a number that is less than 8, which is also not consistent with the corresponding command. If you enter a value from zero to 6, you get a memo width display of six characters, and a value of 7 results in a memo width display of seven characters, neither of which can be accomplished using the SET MEMOWIDTH command. For both options in the Margin menu, entering a negative number results in the error message *Illegal value.*

If you enter a number greater than 15 for the *Decimal places* option in the Decimals menu, the value automatically reverts to 15. If you enter a negative value, the error message *Illegal value* is displayed below the status bar, and you must correct the error.

Tips

SET is a good way to become familiar with the environmental set options available to you in dBASE III PLUS, but it is impractical to use this command

each time you customize the environment. A better solution is to use the dBASE configuration file (see Config.DB) to change the default settings if you disagree with the default status of certain SET options.

SET ALTERNATE

Syntax

```
SET ALTERNATE TO [<filename>]
SET ALTERNATE ON¦OFF
```

Overview The SET ALTERNATE TO <filename> command creates and opens the named text file, which is referred to as the alternate file. The file is given a .TXT extension unless one is supplied as part of the file name. The alternate file is an alternative destination for the screen output in dBASE III PLUS (except for the screen output of the @...SAY command).

Once the alternate file is created and opened with SET ALTERNATE TO <filename>, SET ALTERNATE ON ¦ OFF controls what is written to the file. By default, SET ALTERNATE is OFF and nothing is written to the alternate file. To begin writing the screen output to the alternate file, SET ALTERNATE ON. To discontinue writing to the file, SET ALTERNATE OFF.

To close the alternate file when you are finished writing to it, use either SET ALTERNATE TO with no file name or CLOSE ALTERNATE; these are equivalent commands. Closing the alternate file automatically does a SET ALTERNATE OFF.

Procedure Use the SET ALTERNATE commands to control writing to the alternate file. SET ALTERNATE TO the file name to which you want to write the text. SET ALTERNATE ON before issuing the commands whose output you want to write to the alternate file. If you want to skip over certain commands and not record their output in the file, SET ALTERNATE OFF before issuing these commands and SET ALTERNATE ON again when you want to continue writing to the alternate file. Use CLOSE ALTERNATE to close the file when you are finished with it.

Examples Suppose that you have your payroll checks printed by your bank each week and that they require a text file containing the name and weekly salary for each employee, followed by a total salary amount. The following routine opens an alternate file in order to build the payroll file for the bank. The name and weekly salary of each employee is recorded in the file while the total is accumulated. The total is then recorded and the alternate file is closed:

```
* Payroll.PRG
*
SET TALK OFF
* Payroll text file is opened...
SET ALTERNATE TO Payroll
* and made ready for recording.
SET ALTERNATE ON
tot_salary = 0.00
USE Employee
DO WHILE .NOT. EOF()
   * Weekly salary is Salary divided by 52 weeks.
   weekly = ROUND(Salary / 52, 2)
   tot_salary = tot_salary + weekly
   ? Last_Name, First_Name, weekly
   SKIP
ENDDO
? tot_salary
CLOSE ALTERNATE
CLOSE DATABASES
SET TALK ON
```

Warnings

Although SET ALTERNATE TO <filename> creates a text file, this command does not respect the status of SET SAFETY and will always overwrite the named file without warning. If this presents a problem, use FILE( ) to test for the existence of the file before issuing the SET ALTERNATE TO command. You cannot add text to an existing alternate file.

Tips

Remember that the screen output is not suppressed when you are writing to the alternate file. Use SET CONSOLE OFF if you want to suppress the screen output when you are writing to the alternate file.

Certain commands (e.g., LABEL FORM and REPORT FORM) have a built-in TO FILE command line option that is equivalent to using SET ALTERNATE. Use the command line option when it is available, since it is more convenient and faster than SET ALTERNATE.

In dBASE III PLUS, the result of @...SAY (see @...SAY) cannot be captured in the alternate file. (See LOAD for an assembly language program that you can use to redirect the result of the @ command from the printer to a file.)

SET BELL

Syntax `SET BELL ON¦OFF`

Overview The SET BELL command controls whether or not the bell rings during data entry with any of the full-screen commands (i.e., APPEND, BROWSE, CHANGE, EDIT, INSERT, READ, and all CREATE commands). By default, SET BELL is ON, and the bell rings if you fill a data entry field or if you make an error such as attempting either to enter an incorrect date or to enter letters into a numeric field. SET BELL OFF disables the bell in these circumstances.

Procedure Use SET BELL OFF to disable the bell during data entry, and use SET BELL ON to enable it again.

Examples The following routine deactivates the bell before adding records to the mailing list and activates it after the records are added:

```
* Bell.PRG
*
SET BELL OFF
USE Mail
APPEND
CLOSE DATABASES
SET BELL ON
```

Warnings When you enter an incorrect date, dBASE III PLUS usually warns you with a message and makes you press the space bar to continue; no further input is accepted until you press the space bar. The same is true for RANGE errors. If SET BELL is ON, the warning message is accompanied by a ring of the bell to draw your attention to the error.

When you SET BELL OFF, the bell will not ring if you make a data entry error. If you enter data without looking at the screen, you could be typing without realizing that you made an error.

Tips If the bell annoys you, change the default value of SET BELL using the BELL = OFF entry in your dBASE III PLUS configuration file. (See Config.DB).

You can manually ring the bell using ?? CHR(7).

SET CARRY

Syntax `SET CARRY ON¦OFF`

Overview The SET CARRY command controls whether or not the data from the previous record is carried forward when records are added to a database file using the APPEND, BROWSE or INSERT commands. By default, SET CARRY is OFF, and no data is carried forward (i.e., you are presented with a blank record). If you SET CARRY ON, all of the data from the previous record is carried forward when records are added with one of these commands.

Procedure Use SET CARRY ON to add records to a database file in which several of the fields seldom change from one record to the next. Issue SET CARRY ON before the APPEND, BROWSE, or INSERT command, and SET CARRY OFF after you are finished adding records.

Examples If you want to add some people who live in the same city to your mailing list, SET CARRY ON before adding these records. Instead of being presented with a blank record each time, you are presented with the contents of the previous record, and you need only edit those fields that need to be changed.

```
* Carry.PRG
*
SET CARRY ON
USE Mail
APPEND
CLOSE DATABASES
SET CARRY OFF
```

Tips When using a format file with APPEND or INSERT, or a FIELDS list with BROWSE, you can exclude certain fields. Remember, though, that SET CARRY ON carries all of the fields forward, regardless of whether the field appears on the screen during the append operation.

SET CATALOG

Syntax

```
SET CATALOG TO [<filename>¦?]
SET CATALOG ON¦OFF
```

Overview

The SET CATALOG TO <filename> command creates and opens the named catalog file if it does not already exist, and opens the named catalog if it does exist. You are prompted with *Create new file catalog? (Y/N)* and must type Y before a new catalog is created. Catalog files are database files that are assumed to have a .CAT extension unless you supply a different one as part of the file name. The catalog file can be selected from a menu of all catalogs by using the ?, or catalog query clause. The catalog is always opened in work area 10.

The SET CATALOG ON ¦ OFF controls whether or not information is recorded in the open catalog. By default, SET CATALOG is OFF, but opening a catalog with SET CATALOG TO switches it ON. When a catalog is open and SET CATALOG is ON, files (e.g., database files, reports, labels, indices) are automatically recorded in the catalog as they are used. SET CATALOG OFF discontinues this automatic recording of files in the catalog. Once a catalog is open, you can use the ? clause with designated commands to select cataloged files from a menu, regardless of whether SET CATALOG is ON or OFF.

To close the catalog, use SET CATALOG TO with no parameters. Closing the catalog automatically does a SET CATALOG OFF.

Procedure

Catalogs are a useful way of organizing related files. Use SET CATALOG TO when you want to use a catalog.

Use SET CATALOG TO <filename> to open an existing catalog and begin using it, or to create a new catalog and begin using it. SET CATALOG ON when you want to record files in the catalog, and SET CATALOG OFF when you do not.

When you no longer want to use the catalog, use SET CATALOG TO with no parameters or CLOSE CATALOG.

Examples

The following example shows you how to activate a catalog and select a database file from it. The Business catalog keeps track of all the business files. When you open and query the catalog with the following commands, your screen should look like the one in Figure 86.

```
. SET CATALOG TO Business
. USE ?
```

Warnings

Catalog file names themselves are maintained in a master catalog assigned the name Catalog.CAT. If this file is not present and you attempt to SET CATALOG TO ?, a new master catalog is created and the error message *Master catalog is empty* is displayed.

SET VIEW TO opens database, index, and format files that are saved as a view. This command is somewhat incompatible with using a catalog because the catalog does not recognize that the individual files in the view file have been opened. If you get the error message *File not cataloged since SET CATALOG was OFF when the active database was USEd,* it usually does not mean what it says. Chances are that SET CATALOG was ON when the database file was opened, but that the database file was opened using SET VIEW TO instead of USE. Keep this in mind, and avoid using views and catalogs together if at all possible.

Tips

Remember that a catalog is simply a database file. If you are experienced with the structure of the catalog and how it organizes data, you can alter

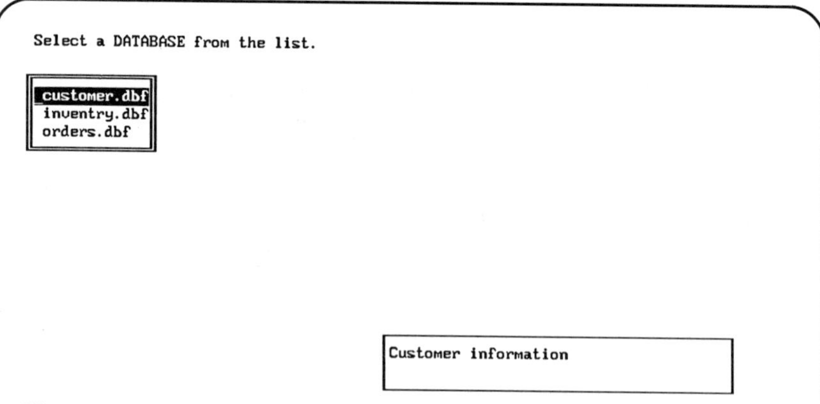

Figure 86

its contents whenever you want. Just USE it by supplying the .CAT extension or SELECT 10 after opening it with SET CATALOG TO and make the necessary changes to the file. (See Catalogs for more information on how catalogs are organized and maintained.)

SET CENTURY

Syntax `SET CENTURY ON¦OFF`

Overview The SET CENTURY command controls whether or not the century is displayed as part of the default date format. By default, SET CENTURY is OFF, all dates default to the twentieth century, and the century is not displayed. If you SET CENTURY ON, you have to supply the century when entering dates, and the century is displayed as part of the date.

Procedure Use SET CENTURY ON to use dates that are not in the twentieth century or to display the century as part of the default date display. SET CENTURY OFF to return to using a two-digit year.

Examples Use the following routine to display the birthdays in your mailing list with the century as part of the date format:

```
* Century.PRG
*
SET CENTURY ON
USE Mail
LIST OFF First_Name, Birthday
CLOSE DATABASES
SET CENTURY OFF
```

To execute this program and see its results,

```
. DO Century
 First_Name   Birthday
 MICHELLE     09/28/1960
 Rebecca      09/11/1960
 Gloria       06/08/1953
 David        06/08/1964
 Julia        11/01/1958
 Perry        04/25/1963
 Cathy        07/16/1953
 Doug         01/20/1946
 Wade         06/12/1947
 Sandy        12/04/1957
 VELMA        05/18/1922
 Mala         09/22/1955
 Lawrence     07/02/1955
 Nancy        10/30/1954
 Jeff         12/18/1953
 Linda        05/11/1949
 Jerry        02/25/1950
 Chris        06/26/1951
```

Tips

CTOD( ) always accepts a century but never requires one, regardless of the status of the SET CENTURY flag. This means that you can create non-twentieth century dates with SET CENTURY OFF. However, if you have a non-twentieth century date stored in a field or variable, and you edit it with any of the full-screen editing commands, the date will automatically revert back to the twentieth century if SET CENTURY is OFF.

Be consistent in dealing with SET CENTURY. If you often use non-twentieth century dates, use the CENTURY = ON entry in your dBASE III PLUS configuration file. (See Config.DB.) If you never use non-twentieth century dates but want to see the century when dates are displayed, SET CENTURY ON before doing the display, and SET CENTURY OFF after the display is complete.

SET COLOR

Syntax

```
SET COLOR TO [<standard foreground>
             [/ <standard background>]]
             [,<enhanced foreground>
             [/ <enhanced background>]]
             [,<border>] [,<background>]
SET COLOR ON¦OFF
```

Overview

The SET COLOR TO command specifies the colors that are used for the standard and enhanced displays and for the border. The command is designed so that it can be used effectively with a variety of types of monitors. Use this command to specify a foreground and background color for the standard and enhanced displays, a border color, and a single background color (if your monitor is not capable of having a different background color for each character position on the screen). Any of the four color options can be omitted, leaving that option unchanged from its previous setting.

dBASE III PLUS distinguishes whether the primary display monitor is driven by a color or a monochrome card. If the monitor is driven by a color card, the following set of codes can be used for the SET COLOR TO options:

CODE	EFFECT
N ¦ <space>	Black
W	White
R	Red
G	Green
B	Blue
BG	Cyan
BR	Magenta
GR	Brown
X	Blank

If the monitor is driven by a monochrome card, fewer options are available:

CODE	EFFECT
N ¦ <space>	Black
W	White
U	Underline
I	Inverse (black on white)
X	Blank

In both cases, the foreground can be made to blink and can be displayed in a higher intensity than normal by following any of the SET COLOR TO options with an asterisk (*) and/or a plus sign (+). The asterisk is for blinking, and the plus sign is for high intensity. For example, GR+ is bright brown, or yellow.

SET COLOR TO with no parameters returns the colors to their default settings (i.e., standard display is white on black; enhanced display is black on white with a black border).

dBASE III PLUS determines whether or not the primary display is driven by a monochrome or a color card, and uses this information to determine what color codes should be used with SET COLOR TO. If the primary display is driven by a color card, the SET COLOR ON ¦ OFF flag has a default setting of ON. If the primary display is driven by a monochrome card, this flag has a default setting of OFF.

The SET COLOR ON ¦ OFF flag can be used effectively only if you have two display monitors attached to your computer, one of which is a color display and the other monochrome. The purpose of having two display monitors is to allow switching back and forth between a primary and secondary display device. If you use SET COLOR ON ¦ OFF without having a second monitor, the flag is not changed from its default value and there is no error message.

Procedure

Use SET COLOR TO to change the various display colors. Use SET COLOR ON ¦ OFF to switch between a color and a monochrome display device, if you have both.

Examples

The next few examples illustrate how to use SET COLOR TO with a color display (a display driven by a color card).

This command changes the standard display to yellow (i.e., bright brown) letters on a blue background, the enhanced display to red letters on a black background, and the border to blinking green:

```
. SET COLOR TO GR+/B, R/N, G*
```

If the blinking green border is distracting, but you like the other attributes, the following command changes the border color to magenta without changing the standard and enhanced displays:

```
. SET COLOR TO ,,BR  && Using comma leaves attribute unchanged
```

To change the color settings back to their defaults,

```
. SET COLOR TO
```

The rest of the examples illustrate how to use the SET COLOR TO command with a monochrome display (a display driven by a monochrome card).

This command changes the standard display to black letters on a white background (inverse), the enhanced display to white letters on a black background, and the border to white:

```
. SET COLOR TO I, W/N, W
```

If the white border is distracting, but you like the other attributes, the following command changes the border to black without changing the standard and enhanced displays:

```
. SET COLOR TO ,,N  && Using comma leaves attribute unchanged
```

To change the screen attributes back to their default settings,

```
SET COLOR TO
```

Warnings Some computers, such as Compaq machines, sometimes use a monochrome monitor that is driven by a color card. If you are unaware of this arrangement, it can cause problems: you will think that you are using a monochrome screen (since that is what you see), but dBASE III PLUS thinks you are using a color screen because it sees the color card. If you have this kind of set-up and use the codes designed for use with a monochrome monitor, you may no longer be able to see anything on your screen. Solve this problem by using the SET COLOR TO codes that are designed for use with a color monitor. You will not, of course, see the colors on your screen, but you will be able to get a wide range of intensities on the monochrome display.

To check what kind of monitor dBASE III PLUS thinks you are using, use the full-screen SET command and look at the Screen menu. You can also use this menu interactively to change the color settings and see the effects on your screen. ISCOLOR( ) reports the kind of monitor dBASE III PLUS believes you have.

Tips

If you have an extended graphics color display (EGA), you will not be able to set the border color in dBASE III PLUS; however, this type of color display is capable of a forty-three line display. You can use the Screen menu of the full-screen SET command to switch between the twenty-five and forty-three line displays by pressing Enter on the first menu option. There is no SET COLOR command equivalent for achieving this effect.

Use the full-screen SET command to interactively change the color settings and see what screen colors appeal to you. Make note of the colors that you want to use, and construct the appropriate SET COLOR TO command. To change the default colors, use the entry COLOR = <attributes> in your dBASE III PLUS configuration file. (See Config.DB.)

SET CONFIRM

Syntax `SET CONFIRM ON¦OFF`

Overview

The SET CONFIRM command controls whether or not you must press the Enter key to exit a data entry area when it reaches capacity. SET CONFIRM affects all full-screen command data entry, not just the full-screen editing commands. By default, SET CONFIRM is OFF; when you fill a field, the cursor automatically advances to the next field. If you SET CONFIRM ON, you must press Enter to advance the cursor to the next field; if you do not press Enter, the data that you type will continue to overwrite the last position in the field.

Procedure

When you are entering data into a database file, some fields will always be filled to capacity (e.g., phone number and zip code) while others will seldom be completely filled (e.g., name and address). To make data entry faster, dBASE III PLUS advances automatically to the next field when you fill a field to capacity. Thus, sometimes you type data and press Enter to get to the next field, and other times you type data that are automatically placed in the next field. If this feature seems inconsistent or causes a problem when you are entering data, SET CONFIRM ON.

Examples

The following example enables the CONFIRM feature before allowing you to add records to a database file, and disables it again when you are done:

```
* Confirm.PRG
*
SET CONFIRM ON
USE Mail
APPEND
CLOSE DATABASES
SET CONFIRM OFF
```

Warnings

If SET BELL and SET CONFIRM are both ON, the bell rings for each character that you type into a field after it is filled; SET CONFIRM ON also causes each additional character that you type to overwrite the last character in the field until you press Enter. This results from the user's inability to control the typeahead feature in full-screen commands with the SET TYPEAHEAD TO command.

Tips

SET CONFIRM affects all of the full-screen commands (including the CREATE commands) as well as the database file editing commands.

SET CONSOLE

Syntax `SET CONSOLE ON¦OFF`

Overview

The SET CONSOLE command controls whether or not output is displayed on the screen. By default, SET CONSOLE is ON, and all output is displayed on the screen. Even if you print the output using the SET PRINTER ON command or a TO PRINTER command line option, the output is displayed both on the screen and printer. Use SET CONSOLE OFF to suppress the screen display of any command except @...SAY.

Procedure

Use SET CONSOLE OFF to suppress screen output. This command is effective only when used in a program.

SET CONSOLE is always ON at the dot prompt. Issuing SET CONSOLE OFF at the dot prompt does not cause an error message, but it does not turn the console off. This is a safety feature—as you would not be able to see what you were typing if you could SET CONSOLE OFF at the dot prompt.

Examples

Use the following routine if you want to print the names in your mailing list without seeing the output on the screen:

```
* Console.PRG
*
SET CONSOLE OFF
USE Mail
LIST Name TO PRINTER
CLOSE DATABASES
SET CONSOLE ON
```

Tips

SET CONSOLE does not affect @...SAY. The destination of this command is controlled by SET DEVICE. If you have SET DEVICE TO PRINTER, the result of the @...SAY is seen only on the printer, not on the screen. Similarly, if you have SET DEVICE TO SCREEN, the result of @...SAY is seen only on the screen, not on the printer.

SET DATE

Syntax `SET DATE AMERICAN¦ANSI¦BRITISH¦FRENCH¦GERMAN¦ITALIAN`

Overview

The SET DATE command controls the date format in dBASE III PLUS.

By default, SET DATE is AMERICAN, though a variety of different date formats are available. The format for each of the date settings follows. In the format, MM is month, DD is day, YY is year, and CC is century (which is optional, depending on the status of SET CENTURY):

SETTING	FORMAT
AMERICAN	MM/DD/CCYY
ANSI	CCYY.MM.DD
BRITISH	DD/MM/CCYY
FRENCH	DD/MM/CCYY
GERMAN	DD.MM.CCYY
ITALIAN	DD-MM-CCYY

Procedure

Use SET DATE whenever you want to change the default date format.

Examples

In the following example, SET DATE is used to customize the date format in a form letter that is printed for each member of your mailing list. The field called Country is used to change the date format before each letter is printed.

```
* Date_Set.PRG
*
SET TALK OFF
USE Mail
DO WHILE .NOT. EOF()

   * Field names cannot be used in macro substitution,
   * so Country is stored in a memory variable.

   m_country = Country

   * The date format is customized to the country.
   * This program will not work with countries other
   * than those allowed by dBASE III PLUS.

   SET DATE &m_country
   DO Letter  && Subroutine to output one letter
   SKIP
ENDDO
CLOSE DATABASES
SET DATE AMERICAN
SET TALK ON
```

Warnings

When you INDEX on a character field and a date field together, you must convert one to the other to make up the index expression. Usually, the date is converted to a character string using CTOD( ). Although this conversion may seem appropriate, it does not work correctly. (See CTOD( ) for an explanation and a good solution.)

Since SET DATE ANSI converts a date into a format suitable for ordering when concatenated with character strings, a natural use for this command might seem to be indexing dates with character fields. This will work correctly; however, if you choose this method, SET DATE ANSI must be in effect not only when the index file is created, but also whenever the index file is updated. As a result, the date will have to be entered as ANSI when you add records, and this may not seem natural to a user. It is better to use the method described under the entry for DTOC( ) since this method works for all dates, regardless of the status of SET DATE.

Tips

dBASE III PLUS is translated into many languages. The primary reason for the existence of the SET DATE command is to make these translations easier. In European countries where it is available, dBASE III PLUS is shipped with the appropriate date format as the default.

SET DEBUG

Syntax `SET DEBUG ON¦OFF`

Overview

The SET DEBUG command controls whether the results of SET STEP and SET ECHO are displayed on the screen or printed. By default, SET DEBUG is OFF, and the results of these commands are shown on the screen. SET DEBUG ON sends their results to the printer instead of the screen.

Procedure

Use SET DEBUG ON when you are debugging a program with SET ECHO ON and/or SET STEP ON and do not want their results to clutter your screen display.

Examples

The following commands illustrate how to get a program to ECHO its commands to the printer as they are executed:

```
. SET ECHO ON
. SET DEBUG ON
. DO New_Prog
. SET DEBUG OFF
. SET ECHO OFF
```

Warnings

When stepping through a program with SET STEP ON, SET DEBUG ON causes the step prompt to display only on the printer. Although you cannot see the prompt on your screen, you must respond to it in order for the program to continue to execute.

The SET DEBUG command does not control the output of SET TALK.

Tips

If you need to debug only a portion of a program, temporarily embed SET ECHO and SET DEBUG in the program to get a better idea of what is happening. Use SET ECHO and DEBUG ON before the problem area of the program, and turn them off afterwards.

SET DECIMALS

Syntax `SET DECIMALS TO [<expN>]`

Overview

The SET DECIMALS TO <expN> command serves two purposes:

1. It determines the minimum number of decimal places to be displayed as a result of numeric operations
2. It specifies the number of decimal places to be displayed when SET FIXED is ON

The numeric expression must evaluate to a value between zero and fifteen, inclusive. By default, the number of decimals is set at two; however, SET FIXED is OFF, and the rules for determining the number of decimal places that result from a calculation have little to do with the value of SET DECIMALS TO. The rules are as follows:

- In multiplication, the number of decimal places in the result is equal to the sum of the number of decimal places in the both multiplicands (e.g., 1.23 * 2.000 = 2.46000).
- In division, addition, and subtraction results, it is equal to the maximum number of decimal places in the two numbers involved (e.g., 1.23 + 1.23450 = 2.46450).
- In exponentiation, it is equal to the number of decimal places in the root number (e.g., 2.00 ^ 2.00000 = 4.00).
- In numeric functions, it is the maximum of the number of decimal places in the function argument and the SET DECIMALS TO value.

If you SET FIXED ON, all numbers are rounded to the SET DECIMALS TO value before they are displayed.

SET DECIMALS TO with no parameter is equivalent to SET DECIMALS TO 0.

Procedure

Use SET DECIMALS in conjunction with SET FIXED ON to fix the number of decimal places to a particular value.

Examples

As stated above, the result of certain mathematical operations can result in more decimal places than you want. When dealing with dollars and cents, you probably want to round such results to two decimal places. The following example computes the sales tax of a number and rounds the result:

```
* Tax.PRG
*
SET TALK OFF
CLEAR
dollar_amt = 0.00
@ 10, 0 SAY "Enter the dollar amount: " GET dollar_amt
READ
* The California sales tax is 6.5%.
tax = ROUND(.065 * dollar_amt, 2)
sale_price = dollar_amt + tax
SET FIXED ON
? "Amount   ", dollar_amt
? "Tax      ", tax
? "----------------------"
? "Total    ", sale_price
SET FIXED OFF
SET TALK ON
```

If you execute this program and type 1234 in response to the prompt, you will see the following displayed on your screen:

```
Amount          1234.00
Tax               80.21
----------------------
Total           1314.21
.
```

Warnings Unlike most other SET commands, using SET DECIMALS TO without a parameter changes the number of decimals to zero, rather than its default value of 2.

The numeric expression used with SET DECIMALS must evaluate to a value between zero and 15, inclusive. Otherwise, the command results in a *Syntax error*.

Tips Use SET DECIMALS along with SET FIXED ON to format a list of numbers when you want to display them in a column. This command ensures that the numbers will have the same number of decimal places and line up at the decimal point.

SET DEFAULT

Syntax `SET DEFAULT TO <drive letter>`

Overview The SET DEFAULT command changes the disk drive that dBASE III PLUS uses as its default. This command does not change the operating system logged-in drive.

Procedure When you bring up the dBASE III PLUS program, its default drive is the same as the operating system logged-in drive. If you are frequently accessing data from another disk drive, you may want to SET DEFAULT to that drive letter; this allows you to access files from that drive without needing to enter the drive letter as part of the file name.

Examples Assuming that your mailing list is on Drive A and the default is Drive C, the following commands use two different methods to access the file on the Drive A:

```
. USE A:Mail        && Specify A: as part of the file name
. SET DEFAULT TO A && Change the default drive to A...
. USE Mail         && and use the file.
```

Warnings SET DEFAULT does not change the operating system logged drive, but only the drive that dBASE III PLUS uses as its default. If you use RUN to execute an external program, be aware of this because the operating system default drive and the dBASE III PLUS default may differ. If the external program is not on the operating system logged-in drive, be sure that you specify the correct drive letter as part of its file name.

Tips If you keep your data and programs on a drive other than the one on which you keep the dBASE III PLUS program, use the DEFAULT = <drive letter> entry in your dBASE III PLUS configuration file. (See Config.DB.)

SET DELETED

Syntax `SET DELETED ON¦OFF`

Overview The SET DELETED command controls whether deleted records (i.e., those marked for deletion) are processed or ignored. By default, SET DELETED is OFF and deleted records are processed just like any other record. SET DELETED ON causes dBASE III PLUS to ignore deleted records.

Procedure Use SET DELETED ON to ignore deleted records without having to permanently remove them from your database file. Use SET DELETED OFF to include those records again.

Examples

You can use SET DELETED ON whenever you want to ignore the deleted records in a database file without permanently removing those records. For example, suppose that one of the people in your mailing list is moving across the country and plans to spend two or three months touring before settling down. You cannot send mail to that individual until you get the new address, but you don't want to remove her from your mailing list. In such a case, you might use this command sequence:

```
. USE Mail
. LOCATE FOR Last_Name = "Roman"
Record =       3
. DELETE
      1 record deleted
. DISPLAY NEXT 1 First_Name, Last_Name
Record#  First_Name   Last_Name
      3 *Gloria       Roman

. SET DELETED ON
. LIST First_Name, Last_Name
Record#  First_Name   Last_Name
      1  MICHELLE     SMITH
      2  Rebecca      Corbbit
      4  David        Gurly
      5  Julia        King
      6  Perry        Lester
      7  Cathy        Moore
      8  Doug         Smith
      9  Wade         Adams
     10  Sandy        Richardson
     11  VELMA        MOODY
     12  Mala         Schaefer
     13  Lawrence     Arthur
     14  Nancy        Long
     15  Jeff         Potter
     16  Linda        Roberts
     17  Jerry        Samuels
     18  Chris        Whiteside

. CLOSE DATABASES
```

Notice that Gloria doesn't show up on the list. SET DELETED ON each time you want to process your mailing list without using her record.

Warnings Even if you SET DELETED ON, records marked for deletion can still be addressed and accessed directly using either GO or the RECORD keyword for commands that have a scope. RECALL is no exception.

Tips SET DELETED ON is equivalent to SET FILTER TO .NOT. DELETED( ). However, SET FILTER has an advantage over SET DELETED since a different filter can be set for each work area, while SET DELETED affects all open database files.

Records are marked for deletion using either DELETE or Ctrl-U in full-screen editing. Deleted records are reinstated using either RECALL or Ctrl-U in full-screen editing. Deleted records are permanently removed using PACK.

SET DELIMITERS

Syntax

```
SET DELIMITERS TO <expC>¦DEFAULT
SET DELIMITERS ON¦OFF
```

Overview The SET DELIMITERS ON ¦ OFF command controls whether or not the data entry area in full-screen editing commands (see APPEND, CHANGE, EDIT, INSERT, and READ) is delimited on either side. By default, SET DELIMITERS is OFF and the data entry area is not delimited. To have this area delimited by a colon on either side, SET DELIMITERS ON.

SET DELIMITERS TO <expC> is used to change the delimiter characters. The character expression should evaluate to a string that is either one or two characters in length. If the string is a single character, that character is used as the beginning and ending delimiter. If the string is two characters, the first one is used as the beginning delimiter and the second one the ending delimiter. If the string is more than two characters long, all characters beyond the second one are ignored.

SET DELIMITERS TO DEFAULT changes the delimiter character back to its default value. This command is equivalent to SET DELIMITERS TO ":".

Procedure

Use SET DELIMITERS to control how and when the data entry area in full-screen editing commands is delimited. SET DELIMITERS ON before issuing the full-screen command. Use SET DELIMITERS TO <expC> if you prefer to use delimiters that are different from the default. SET DELIMITERS TO DEFAULT to return to using the default delimiters. When you no longer want to use the delimiters, SET DELIMITERS OFF.

Examples

The following routine shows you several data entry screens with different delimiters:

```
* Expermnt.PRG
*
SET TALK OFF
SET MENU OFF
USE Mail
* The delimiters are enabled.
SET DELIMITERS ON
* The left and right brackets are defined as delimiters.
SET DELIMITERS TO "[]"
EDIT NEXT 1 FIELDS First_Name, Last_Name
* The asterisk is defined as both delimiters.
SET DELIMITERS TO "*"
EDIT NEXT 1 FIELDS First_Name, Last_Name
* The delimiters are changed back to the default colon.
SET DELIMITERS TO DEFAULT
EDIT NEXT 1 FIELDS First_Name, Last_Name
CLOSE DATABASES
* Delimiters are disabled.
SET DELIMITERS OFF
SET MENU ON
SET TALK ON
```

If you execute this program by typing

```
DO Expermnt
```

and press the PgDn key on each screen, you will see three screens with different delimiters.

Tips

If you prefer having the data entry area delimited, use the DELIMITERS = ON entry in your dBASE III PLUS configuration file. If you also prefer a delimiter other than the colon (e.g., square brackets), use the entry DELIMITERS = [ ] in Config.DB. (See Config.DB for more information .)

You can have multiple delimiters on a single screen using different SET DELIMITER TO commands interspersed with @...GET commands. This combination of commands, however, cannot be used in a format file because SET commands are not allowed there.

SET DEVICE

Syntax `SET DEVICE TO SCREEN¦PRINTER`

Overview The SET DEVICE command controls which device displays the result of @...SAY. By default, SET DEVICE is TO SCREEN, and the result of @...SAY is displayed on the screen. If you SET DEVICE TO PRINTER, the command result is displayed on the printer instead.

Procedure Use SET DEVICE TO PRINTER when you want to use @...SAY to print a form where the data must be positioned precisely on the page (e.g., a preprinted form such as a paycheck). After @...SAY, SET DEVICE TO SCREEN to resume sending output to the screen.

Examples The following routine prints the names, addresses, and phone numbers from your mailing list on rolodex cards:

```
SET TALK OFF
SET DEVICE TO PRINTER
USE Mail
* Set the Epson FX-86e printer to 7 lines per page.
@ 0, 0 SAY CHR(27) + CHR(67) + CHR(7)
DO WHILE .NOT. EOF()
   @ 0,25 SAY Phone
   @ 1, 5 SAY TRIM(First_Name) + " " + Last_Name
   @ 2, 5 SAY Address1
   @ 3, 5 SAY Address2
   @ 4, 5 SAY TRIM(City) + ", " + State + "  " + Zip
   SKIP
ENDDO
* Reset the printer to 66 lines per page.
@ 0, 0 SAY CHR(27) + CHR(67) + CHR(66)
CLOSE DATABASES
SET DEVICE TO SCREEN
SET TALK ON
```

Warnings Before using SET DEVICE TO PRINTER or any other printing command, be sure that your printer is properly connected to your computer and that it is turned on and on-line. dBASE III PLUS tries to be forgiving about printing errors either by providing an error message or by simply not printing when you tell it to, but there are some printing errors which can cause the program to hang. If this happens to you, check the printer to make sure that it is turned on and on line before making the decision to reboot your machine and thereby possibly losing some data. Sometimes turning on the printer and/or bringing it on line will make dBASE III PLUS operational again.

Tips @...GET is ignored if SET DEVICE TO PRINTER is in effect. If you want this information printed, the only way to do it is to change the GET to a SAY.

SET DOHISTORY

Syntax `SET DOHISTORY ON¦OFF`

Overview The SET DOHISTORY command controls whether or not commands executed from within a program are recorded in the HISTORY buffer. By default, SET DOHISTORY is OFF, and only commands issued from the dot prompt and from ASSIST are recorded in the HISTORY buffer. SET DOHISTORY ON causes commands that are executed from programs to be recorded in HISTORY also.

Procedure Use SET DOHISTORY ON to record the commands that are executed from a program in HISTORY. When the program exits to the dot prompt, you can trace the flow of control by examining the contents of the HISTORY buffer. SET DOHISTORY OFF when this feature is not needed.

Examples SET DOHISTORY ON is generally used to debug a program when an error in logic cannot be figured out. You can imbed this command in your program at a problem point and later SUSPEND the program. Then, you can examine the HISTORY buffer using LIST HISTORY to find out the order of execution of the commands in the problem area of the program.

Warnings SET HISTORY OFF overrides SET DOHISTORY ON. If you SET HISTORY OFF, SET DOHISTORY has no effect.

SET DOHISTORY ON slows down the execution of your program. Use this feature only when it is necessary for debugging.

Tips The default size of the HISTORY buffer is twenty lines. Although this might be a practical size for use in the interactive mode, it may be insufficient for a complicated program. In addition to using SET DOHISTORY ON, you may want to SET HISTORY TO a larger number to take full advantage of this feature.

SET ECHO

Syntax `SET ECHO ON¦OFF`

Overview The SET ECHO command controls whether or not commands are echoed to the screen as they are executed. By default, SET ECHO is OFF, and the commands are not shown on the screen. SET ECHO ON displays them on the screen just before they are executed.

Procedure Use SET ECHO ON when you want to debug a program by following the order in which the commands are executed.

Examples The following commands illustrate how to get a program to ECHO its commands to the screen as they are executed:

```
. SET ECHO ON
. DO New_Prog
. SET ECHO OFF
```

Tips If you want to print the results of SET ECHO ON, use SET DEBUG ON to prevent the screen from becoming cluttered.

SET ENCRYPTION

Syntax `SET ENCRYPTION ON|OFF`

Overview

You have the option of installing a security utility (see Protect) if you are using dBASE III PLUS in a network environment. If you have installed Protect, each database file that you include using the Files menu is automatically encrypted. As a result, only users assigned to a group with access to a particular file may read it. Furthermore, network users who are not using dBASE III PLUS cannot use other means such as the DOS Debug utility to read the data in the file.

Database files that have not been protected using the Protect utility remain in their regular, unencrypted form and any user can access them. If you are using dBASE III PLUS in a network environment and have not installed Protect, no database files are encrypted and SET ENCRYPTION has no effect.

If a database file is encrypted and a user of dBASE III PLUS has access to that file, the user can copy its contents to another file in an unencrypted form using the SET ENCRYPTION command.

By default, SET ENCRYPTION is ON, and copying an encrypted database file (see COPY, COPY STRUCTURE, JOIN, SORT and TOTAL) creates a new database file with the same encryption key as the original file. Consequently, the new file is assigned the same group name and access levels as the original file.

If you SET ENCRYPTION OFF before copying an encrypted database file, the new file will not be encrypted and can be used by anyone.

Procedure

SET ENCRYPTION can be used effectively only in a network environment where Protect has been installed. By default, SET ENCRYPTION is ON and any file that you create using an existing database file (i.e., COPY, COPY STRUCTURE, JOIN, SORT, and TOTAL) is encrypted in the same way as the original file.

If you want to create a copy of the database file that is not encrypted, SET ENCRYPTION OFF before issuing the command to create the new file. When the new file is created, SET ENCRYPTION ON again. If you want, you can then leave dBASE III PLUS (see QUIT) and use Protect to specify different privileges for the new file.

Examples

The following example shows the correct way to export a database file that is encrypted:

```
. USE Orders                  && Orders.DBF is encrypted
. SET ENCRYPTION OFF          && Turn off encryption flag to export
. EXPORT TO Orders TYPE PFS
     4 records copied         && Turn encryption flag on again
. SET ENCRYPTION ON
```

Warnings

The error message *Database is encrypted* is displayed if you attempt to open an encrypted database file without passing through the dBASE III PLUS log-in procedure. Usually, you are forced to enter by logging-in once the Protect facility has been installed (see Protect); however, it is possible to circumvent the log-in procedure. Protect creates a file named Dbsystem.DB that controls the logging-in of users. If this file cannot be found when you enter dBASE III PLUS, you will not see the normal log-in screen. The Dbsystem.DB file should be in the same directory as the Dba.COM file that you use to enter dBASE III PLUS in a network environment.

Database is encrypted also occurs if you attempt to COPY to a non-database file (e.g., DELIMITED or other TYPE), or EXPORT or COPY STRUCTURE EXTENDED on an encrypted file. You must SET ENCRYPTION OFF to use these commands on an encrypted file.

If a user attempts an unauthorized operation on an encrypted file, the error message *Unauthorized access level* is displayed. Examples of unauthorized operation are to USE a database file that belongs to another group or to EDIT the file when your access level is defined as read only.

You cannot make an encrypted database file simply by using SET ENCRYPTION ON before you COPY an unencrypted file. SET ENCRYPTION ON simply tells dBASE III PLUS to create the new file with the same encryption key as the original file; therefore, if the original file does not have an encryption key, neither will the new one. Using Protect is the only way to encrypt a database file.

In dBASE III PLUS, only database files and index files (see REINDEX) are encrypted. This means that you cannot protect the information that you store in memo fields, for example, from other network users who may want to tamper with it.

Tips See Protect for more information on database file encryption.

If you want to change the default setting of the SET ENCRYPTION flag to OFF, you can do so with the dBASE III PLUS configuration file (see Config.DB) by using the entry ENCRYPTION = OFF.

The single-user version of dBASE III PLUS cannot use encrypted database files. To use a database file that is encrypted in the single-user version, SET ENCRYPTION OFF and COPY the file. For example,

```
. USE Mail                  && Mail.DBF is encrypted
. SET ENCRYPTION OFF        && Turn off encryption flag to copy
. COPY TO S_U_Mail
    18 records copied
. SET ENCRYPTION ON         && Turn encryption flag on again
```

SET ESCAPE

Syntax `SET ESCAPE ON¦OFF`

Overview The SET ESCAPE command controls whether or not the Esc key can terminate program execution. By default, SET ESCAPE is ON, and pressing the Esc key during program execution results in a dialogue that allows you to Cancel, Ignore, or Suspend the program. SET ESCAPE OFF prevents the termination of a program using the Esc key.

Procedure When developing a program, it is useful to have SET ESCAPE ON so that you can stop the program at any point for debugging purposes; however, in a finished program, you do not want a user to be able to stop a program in the middle of an important process simply by pressing the Esc key. For this reason, SET ESCAPE OFF is often used in completed programs.

Examples

SET ESCAPE OFF is generally used in completed programs to prevent the user from interrupting a program during an important process. A well-behaved program will provide a normal exit for the user and eliminate the need for using the Esc key. The following menu program disables the Esc key, gives the user an exit option on the menu, and traps the Esc key with INKEY( ) as an alternative exit option:

```
* Menu.PRG
*
SET ESCAPE OFF
SET TALK OFF
SET SCOREBOARD OFF  && To use row zero
prompt1 = "Add"
prompt2 = "Edit"
prompt3 = "Quit"

DO WHILE .T. && Display menu continuously
   CLEAR
   * The menu display always starts on prompt one.  GET is used
   * to enhance the display of the current prompt.
   current = 'one'
   @  0, 0 GET prompt1
   @  0,10 SAY prompt2
   @  0,20 SAY prompt3
   @ 21, 0 SAY "Use arrow keys to navigate and Enter to select."

   * Infinite loop that constantly updates the menu display as
   * the user navigates until a selection is made.
   DO WHILE .T.
      key = 0
      * Waits for a key to be pressed using INKEY() function.
      DO WHILE key = 0
         key = INKEY()
      ENDDO

      DO CASE
      * If prompt1 is highlighted and the Right Arrow is pressed,
      * or if prompt3 is highlighted and the Left Arrow is
      * pressed, highlight prompt2.
      CASE (current = 'one' .AND. key = 4) .OR.;
           (current = 'three' .AND. key = 19)
         @ 0, 0 SAY prompt1
         @ 0,10 GET prompt2
         @ 0,20 SAY prompt3
         current = 'two'
```

```
* If prompt2 is highlighted and the Right Arrow is pressed,
* or if prompt1 is highlighted and the Left Arrow is
* pressed, or if the End key is pressed, highlight prompt3.
CASE (current = 'two' .AND. key = 4) .OR.;
     (current = 'one' .AND. key = 19) .OR.;
     (key = 6)
   @ 0, 0 SAY prompt1
   @ 0,10 SAY prompt2
   @ 0,20 GET prompt3
   current = 'three'

* If prompt3 is highlighted and the Right Arrow is pressed
* or if prompt2 is highlighted and the Left Arrow is
* pressed, or if Home is pressed, highlight prompt1.
CASE (current = 'three' .AND. key = 4) .OR.;
     (current = 'two' .AND. key = 19) .OR.;
     (key = 1)
   @ 0, 0 GET prompt1
   @ 0,10 SAY prompt2
   @ 0,20 SAY prompt3
   current = 'one'

* If Esc is pressed, QUIT dBASE III PLUS.
CASE key = 27
   QUIT

* If Enter is pressed...
CASE key = 13

   * ...this nested DO CASE performs menu selection.
   DO CASE
   * If menu prompt one was selected, DO Add_Recs routine.
   CASE current = 'one'
      DO Add_Recs
      EXIT  && Exit to main menu display loop

   * If menu prompt two was selected, DO Edit_Recs routine.
   CASE current = 'two'
      DO Edit_Recs
      EXIT  && Exit to main menu display loop

   * If prompt three was selected, QUIT dBASE III PLUS.
   CASE current = 'three'
      QUIT
   ENDCASE

ENDCASE
```

```
    ENDDO  && End menu navigation loop

ENDDO  && End main menu display
SET ESCAPE ON
SET TALK ON
SET SCOREBOARD ON
```

Warnings

SET ESCAPE OFF temporarily disables ON ESCAPE if one is in effect.

Tips

SET ESCAPE OFF simply disables the Esc key for the purpose of terminating a program; use ON ESCAPE with SET ESCAPE ON to control what happens when the Esc key is pressed.

SET EXACT

Syntax `SET EXACT ON¦OFF`

Overview

The SET EXACT command controls how character strings are compared. Character string comparisons are done either directly using the relational operators (i.e., >, > =, <, < =, =, #, and < >) or indirectly when you do a FIND or SEEK on a character key field.

By default, SET EXACT is OFF, and strings are compared character-for-character from left to right. If at any position, two characters are not the same, then one string is greater or less than the other based on that position, and no further comparison is done. Otherwise, the comparison continues until the string on the right side of the relational operator is exhausted. If all of the characters compare equally, then the strings are equal. With this method of comparison, two strings compare equally if they are equal up to the point where the string on the right ends. Note that if the string on the right has more characters than the one on the left, and the two have compared equally up to the end of the string on the left, the string on the left is less than the string on the right.

If you SET EXACT ON, comparisons are done according to matching characters and length. In order for two strings to compare equally, they must have exactly the same characters and exactly the same length. If two strings are equal up to the end of one of the strings, the shorter string is always less than the longer one, and the longer string is always greater than the shorter one.

Procedure

Use SET EXACT ON when you want character strings to be compared using their length as well as their content.

Examples

If you have an index file which has a unique key value for each record in your database file, a particular record can be positively identified by its key value. In an application, you may want to require that records be located only on the basis of the entire key so that the program can be sure that the user has the right record; however, the FIND and SEEK commands that are used to locate records in an index can locate records based on one or more characters in the key value.

The Emp_Code field in the Employee database file is an example of an index key field that is unique (i.e., no two employees should have the same employee code). The following routine is designed to print special bonus checks based on employee numbers that are input by the user. SET EXACT ON is used so that SEEK will not locate a record unless the user enters the entire four-character key. Otherwise, the user could enter a partial key and print a bonus check for the wrong employee.

```
* Special.PRG
*
SET EXACT ON
SET TALK OFF
USE Employee INDEX Emp_Code
DO WHILE .T.
   CLEAR
   m_code = SPACE(4)
   @ 10,10 SAY "Enter employee code: " GET m_code PICTURE "A999"
   READ
   IF "" = TRIM(m_code)
      EXIT  && Exit loop if no employee code entered
   ENDIF
   m_code = UPPER(m_code)  && Convert m_code to uppercase
   SEEK m_code
   IF FOUND()
      * Print 5% Salary bonus check.
      DO Bonus WITH Salary * .05
   ELSE
```

```
        @ 12, 0 SAY "Employee not found.  Make sure that you"
        @ 13, 0 SAY "enter all four characters of the code."
        WAIT
    ENDIF
ENDDO
CLOSE DATABASES
SET TALK ON
SET EXACT OFF
```

Warnings Because of the way comparisons are done when SET EXACT is OFF, all character strings will compare equally to a null string if you put the null string on the right side of the relational operator. When comparing any string to a null string, either SET EXACT ON before the comparison or make sure that you put the null string on the left side of the operator so that the comparison will be accurate.

Tips If you find that you are using SET EXACT ON for all of your character string comparisons, change its default value using the EXACT = ON entry, in your dBASE III PLUS configuration file. (See Config.DB.)

SET EXCLUSIVE

Syntax `SET EXCLUSIVE ON¦OFF`

Overview The SET EXCLUSIVE command controls whether database files are opened (see USE) for the exclusive use of the current user or for shared use by all users. This SET command can be used effectively only if you are using dBASE III PLUS in a network environment.

By default, SET EXCLUSIVE is ON, and all database files are opened for the exclusive use of the current user. This means that no other user on the network can open any database file if that file is being used by someone else. SET EXCLUSIVE OFF causes all subsequent database files to be opened for the shared use of all the dBASE III PLUS users on the network.

Procedure SET EXCLUSIVE can be used effectively only in a network environment. By default, SET EXCLUSIVE is ON and all database files that you are able to open (see USE) cannot be opened by any other user on the network until you close them. If SET EXCLUSIVE is ON, there is no need for any other file or record locking since no sharing of data can take place.

If you want to use the network version of dBASE III PLUS to its maximum capacity, SET EXCLUSIVE OFF. This way, all database files are opened in shared mode, and many users on the network can gain access to the same database file at once. To make changes to a database file, you may want to obtain a file or record lock (see FLOCK( ), RLOCK( )) first, depending on the command that you use to make the changes. Some commands provide automatic locking (see Tips section) if you do not obtain the lock beforehand.

Other commands require exclusive use of the database file to operate correctly. (See INSERT, MODIFY STRUCTURE, PACK, REINDEX, and ZAP.) To use one of these commands, either specify the EXCLUSIVE keyword when you open the database file (see USE), or SET EXCLUSIVE ON before opening the file. If you use SET EXCLUSIVE ON, make sure that you turn it back off after you are finished unless you want subsequent database files also opened in exclusive mode.

Examples See FLOCK( ) and RLOCK( ) for examples that use SET EXCLUSIVE.

Warnings Certain operations in dBASE III PLUS (see INSERT, MODIFY STRUCTURE, PACK, REINDEX, and ZAP) require that the database file be used exclusively. With these commands, the error message *Exclusive open of file is required* is displayed if the database file was opened for shared use. Either SET EXCLUSIVE ON and reopen the file, or reopen the file with USE <filename> EXCLUSIVE, and issue the command again.

Tips By default, SET EXCLUSIVE is ON, but this setting does not allow you to take full advantage of the capabilities of dBASE III PLUS in a network environment. It is ON in order to provide you with a certain amount of safety in case you are unfamiliar with file sharing and to make the network and single-user versions compatible. If you want to allow the sharing of data by several users, you can change the default setting of the SET EXCLUSIVE flag to OFF with the dBASE III PLUS configuration file (see Config.DB) by using the EXCLUSIVE = OFF entry.

The USE command has an EXCLUSIVE keyword that can be used to override the SET EXCLUSIVE flag. (See USE for more information.)

The commands that provide automatic locking (either file or record, depending on the circumstances) if SET EXCLUSIVE is OFF are listed below. See the individual command entries for more information: APPEND, APPEND FROM, AVERAGE, BROWSE, COPY, COPY STRUCTURE, COUNT, DELETE, INDEX, JOIN, RECALL, REPLACE, REPORT FORM, SORT, SUM, TOTAL, and UPDATE.

SET EXCLUSIVE is always ON in the single-user version of dBASE III PLUS. As with other commands that are intended for use in a network environment, if you issue SET EXCLUSIVE in the single-user version, the command is completely ignored. This allows programs written for the network version to be used by the single-user version without producing an error.

SET FIELDS

Syntax

```
SET FIELDS TO [<field list>¦ALL]
SET FIELDS ON¦OFF
```

Overview

The SET FIELDS TO command limits the fields that are accessible and specifies the default field list for commands that have a FIELDS clause. SET FIELDS ON ¦ OFF determines whether this field list is used or ignored.

By default, SET FIELDS is OFF. When you open a database file, all fields are accessible; the default field list for commands that have a FIELDS clause is all fields in the file. Fields from database files in unselected work areas can only be accessed using the <alias name> –> <fieldname> form of the field name.

Using SET FIELDS TO <field list> limits access to the fields specified in the field list. The ALL option is a shortcut for listing all of the field names in the active database file. This command automatically does a SET FIELDS ON so that the newly defined field list goes into effect immediately. Consecutive SET FIELDS TO commands add to the existing field list instead of overwriting it.

When you have established a field list with one or more SET FIELDS TO commands and SET FIELDS is ON, the default field list for commands that have a FIELDS phrase in their syntax is no longer all fields in the active database file. Instead, the SET FIELDS TO field list is used along with the

SET RELATION TO command to determine the default field list for these commands. The default field list is composed of all fields in the active database and all fields in related files that are in the SET FIELDS TO field list.

SET FIELDS TO with no parameters removes all fields in the active database file from the existing field list but leaves the SET FIELDS flag ON so that none of the fields in the active database file is accessible. Use CLEAR FIELDS to remove all fields from the field list (not just those in the active database file).

Any command that opens or closes a database file (e.g., CLOSE DATABASES and USE) automatically does a SET FIELDS OFF.

Procedure

Use SET FIELDS TO <field list> to limit access to a subset of the available fields. Use SET FIELDS ON to respect this field list and SET FIELDS OFF to ignore it.

Examples

SET FIELDS TO can be used to treat the fields in two related database files as if the fields were in the same file. This is illustrated in the following example which relates Orders and Inventry by the Part_No field, selects fields from each, and does a LIST that shows fields from both files:

```
. SELECT 2
. USE Inventry INDEX Part_No
. SELECT 1
. USE Orders
. SET RELATION TO Part_No INTO Inventry
. SET FIELDS TO Part_No, Quantity  && Select fields from Orders
. SET FIELDS TO Inventry->Price    && Select fields from Inventry
. LIST  && Files are related - LIST all fields in SET FIELDS list
Record#  PART_NO   QUANTITY      PRICE
      1  R-123            1      23.95
      2  B-254            2      65.99
      3  G-165            2      23.98
      4  R-123            1      23.95

. CLOSE DATABASES
```

Warnings

If any of the fields in the SET FIELDS TO field list cannot be found, the error message *Field not found* is displayed. If you get this error message, check the spelling of the fields in the list and also make sure that you used the

<alias name> – > <fieldname> form to specify a field from a database file in another work area.

SET FIELDS TO with no parameters removes all fields in the active database file from the existing field list but does not SET FIELDS OFF; therefore, if you attempt to issue a command that uses a FIELDS list, an error message is displayed. The error message varies depending on the command. For example, with EDIT, the error message is *No fields to process*, with COPY it is *No fields were found to copy*, and with AVERAGE and SUM it is *Variable not found*. LIST and DISPLAY do not display error messages in this case, but list only the record number with no data.

Remember to SET FIELDS OFF if you want to return to using all fields in the active database file.

Tips

The commands APPEND, INDEX ON, LOCATE, SET FIELDS, SET FILTER, and SET RELATION have access to all fields, regardless of the SET FIELDS TO list or the status of SET FIELDS ON ¦ OFF.

Since each SET FIELDS TO adds to the existing field list, removing one or more fields from the field list is difficult. You must remove all fields in the database file from the field list by doing a SET FIELDS TO with no parameters and then do another SET FIELDS TO <field list> that does not include the unwanted field or fields.

SET FILTER

Syntax `SET FILTER TO [<condition>] ¦ [FILE <filename>¦?]`

Overview

The SET FILTER command controls whether the records in the active database file are processed in their entirety or according to some logical condition. Each open database file can have its own SET FILTER condition.

By default, there are no filter conditions on a database file. After you open a database file, you can use SET FILTER to impose a logical condition which must be met by each record in order for it to be processed. Using the first form of the command, SET FILTER TO <condition>, the condition is specified directly as part of the command syntax (e.g., SET FILTER TO Name="Smith"). Using the SET FILTER TO FILE form of the command, the filter condition is taken from a query (.QRY) file. The query file can be

specified by using its file name or, if a catalog is in use (see SET CATALOG), can be selected from a menu of catalogued query files by using the ?, or catalog query clause. Query files are created with the CREATE QUERY command.

SET FILTER TO with no parameters disables the filter condition so that all records are processed again.

Procedure

Use SET FILTER TO <condition> to process only those records in the active database file that meet a particular condition. Use SET FILTER TO FILE ? to select from a menu of cataloged query files.

Use SET FILTER TO with no parameters to process all records.

Examples

You can use SET FILTER to process a subset of a database file. For example, suppose that you are having a party and want to send invitations only to those individuals in your mailing list who live close by. The following routine sets up a filter to print labels only for people who live in Pasadena, Los Angeles, or Hollywood:

```
* Party.PRG
*
SET TALK OFF
USE Mail
SET FILTER TO UPPER(City) = "LOS ANGELES";
         .OR. UPPER(City) = "HOLLYWOOD";
         .OR. UPPER(City) = "PASADENA"
LABEL FORM Mail TO PRINTER
CLOSE DATABASE  && Closing database file gets rid of filter
SET TALK ON
```

The resulting printout seen in Figure 87 shows labels only for local friends.

Warnings

Even if you have a filter in effect, records that do not meet the condition can still be addressed and accessed directly using either GO or the RECORD keyword for commands that have a scope.

Tips

After you SET FILTER TO some condition, do a GO TOP if the next command that you want to execute has a scope that begins with the current record. Otherwise, the current record will be processed, even if it does not meet the filter condition. For example,

```
. USE Mail
. SET FILTER TO Last_Name = "MOODY"
. DISPLAY Last_Name  && SMITH shows up even though it shouldn't
Record#  Last_Name
      1  SMITH

. GO TOP
. DISPLAY Last_Name  && GO TOP fixes the problem
Record#  Last_Name
     11  MOODY

. CLOSE DATABASES
```

```
Gloria Roman
1922 Kant Street
Los Angeles, CA 90029


Perry Lester
38 Merrily Circle
Pasadena, CA 94033


Mala Schaefer
1822 Hollywood Blvd.
Los Angeles, CA 90038


Nancy Long
242 Beach Road
Los Angeles, CA 90069


Jeff Potter
858 Laughing Lane
Los Angeles, CA 90029


Jerry Samuels
4184 Maryland Road
Los Angeles, CA 90042


Chris Whiteside
1432 Gentleman Avenue
Hollywood, CA 90043
```

Figure 87

SET FIXED

Syntax `SET FIXED ON¦OFF`

Overview The SET FIXED command controls whether the number of decimal places used in numeric displays is fixed or variable. By default, SET FIXED is OFF, and the number of decimals places depends on the calculation used when a number is derived.

The rules for determining the number of decimal places that result from a calculation are as follows:

- In multiplication, the number of decimal places in the result is equal to the sum of the number of decimal places in the both multiplicands (e.g., 1.23 * 2.000 = 2.46000).
- In division, addition, and subtraction results, it is equal to the maximum number of decimal places in the two numbers involved (e.g., 1.23 + 1.23450 = 2.46450).
- In exponentiation, it is equal to the number of decimal places in the root number (e.g., 2.00 ^ 2.00000 = 4.00).
- In numeric functions, it is the maximum of the number of decimal places in the function argument and the SET DECIMALS TO value.

With SET FIXED ON, all numbers are rounded to the SET DECIMALS TO value before they are displayed.

Procedure Use SET FIXED ON to display a list of numbers using the same number of decimal places.

Examples As stated above, the result of certain mathematical operations can result in more decimal places than you want. When dealing with dollars and cents, you probably will want to round such results to two decimal places. The following example computes the sales tax of a number and rounds the result:

```
* Tax.PRG
*
```

```
SET TALK OFF
CLEAR
dollar_amt = 0.00
@ 10, 0 SAY "Enter the dollar amount: " GET dollar_amt
READ
* The California sales tax is 6.5%.
tax = ROUND(.065 * dollar_amt, 2)
sale_price = dollar_amt + tax
? "Amount    ", dollar_amt
? "Tax       ", tax
? "----------------------"
? "Total     ", sale_price
SET TALK ON
```

If you execute this program and type 1234 in response to the prompt, you will see the following displayed on your screen:

```
Amount          1234.00
Tax               80.21000
----------------------
Total           1314.21000
```

If the Tax program is executed with SET FIXED ON, the display looks a lot more presentable:

```
Amount          1234.00
Tax               80.21
----------------------
Total           1314.21
```

You could alter the above program, Tax.PRG, by putting `SET FIXED ON` before the first ? command and `SET FIXED OFF` after the last one.

Warnings

SET FIXED ON fixes the number of decimal places for all numeric output including functions like RECNO( ) that normally return an integer. Remember this when using SET FIXED.

SET FORMAT

Syntax `SET FORMAT TO [<filename>|?]`

Overview The SET FORMAT TO <filename> command opens a format file in the current work area for use with subsequent full-screen editing commands. The format file (.FMT) can be specified by using its file name or, if a catalog is in use (see SET CATALOG), can be selected from a menu of cataloged format files by using the ?, or catalog query clause. Format files are created using MODIFY COMMAND or CREATE SCREEN.

SET FORMAT TO with no parameters closes the format file in the active work area and is equivalent to CLOSE FORMAT. Closing and/or opening a database file also closes any format file that is open in the current work area.

Procedure Use SET FORMAT TO <filename> to open a format file in the current work area. When you later issue a full-screen editing command (i.e., APPEND, CHANGE, EDIT, INSERT, or READ), the @...SAY...GET commands in the open format file are executed, resulting in a customized screen display. Use SET FORMAT TO ? to select from a menu of cataloged format files.

Use SET FORMAT TO with no parameters to close the format file in the current work area.

Examples You can use SET FORMAT TO <filename> to activate a customized data entry screen before adding or editing records in any of your database files. The following routine activates a format file for use in adding records to the Employee database file:

```
* Emp_Add.PRG
*
SET TALK OFF
SET STATUS ON
SET MESSAGE TO "Enter new employee information."
USE Employee
SET FORMAT TO Emp_Add
APPEND
CLOSE DATABASES && Also closes format file
SET MESSAGE TO
SET STATUS OFF
SET TALK ON
```

The Emp_Add.FMT format file is listed below for your convenience:

```
@  2, 7 SAY "Employee Number"
@  2,24 GET Emp_Code PICTURE "@! A999"
@  2,42 SAY "Hire Date"
@  2,59 GET Hire_Date
@  3,42 SAY "Social Security"
@  3,59 GET Ssn PICTURE "999-99-9999"
@  4,42 SAY "Starting Salary"
@  4,59 GET Salary
@  6, 4 SAY "Name"
@  6,13 GET Last_Name PICTURE "AAAAAAAAAAAAAAAAAAAA"
@  6,35 GET First_Name PICTURE "AAAAAAAAAAAA"
@  7,16 SAY "(last)               (first)"
@  9, 4 SAY "Address"
@  9,13 GET Address1
@ 10,16 SAY "(street)"
@ 11,13 GET Address2
@ 12,16 SAY "(apartment #)"
@ 13,13 GET City
@ 13,46 GET State PICTURE "@! AA"
@ 13,55 GET Zip PICTURE "99999"
@ 14,16 SAY "(city)                     (state)    (zip)"
@ 16, 4 SAY "Phone"
@ 16,13 GET Phone PICTURE "(999)999-9999"
@ 18, 4 SAY "Comments"
@ 18,13 GET Comment PICTURE "@S64"
@  0, 0 TO 20,79 DOUBLE
```

If you execute the Emp_Add.PRG program, your screen should look like the one in Figure 88.

Warnings

It is possible to have an open format file without an open database file because format files can be used to edit memory variables. However, to use a format file with a database file, you must open the database file first since opening the database file automatically closes any previously open format file.

Tips

Because it executes faster and does not open an additional file, you might want to use a procedure instead of a format file in a program. The procedure is created by putting the commands from the format file in your procedure file, giving it a name with the PROCEDURE command, and DOing <procedure> where you would have SET FORMAT TO <filename>.

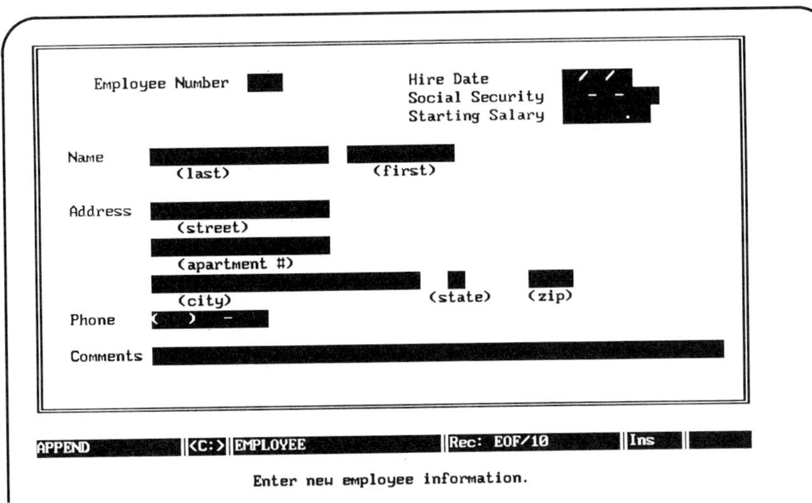

Figure 88

SET FUNCTION

Syntax `SET FUNCTION <key number>|<key label> TO [<expC>]`

Overview The SET FUNCTION command specifies the output of a function key when it is pressed. With this command, a function key is identified either by a number or a label. If the <key number> is used, it is specified by a numeric expression; if the <key label> is used, it is specified by a character expression.

SET FUNCTION evaluates the TO character expression and stores the resulting character string in the specified function key. Subsequently, that string is output each time the function key is pressed. Semicolons are translated into carriage returns when the string is output.

There are ten function keys on an IBM PC. dBASE III PLUS allows you to program nine of them and reserves F1 for help. The function keys are labeled F2 through F10 and are numbered 2 through 10. (Although some keyboards have more than ten function keys, only keys 2 through 10 can be set using dBASE III PLUS.)

If you use SET FUNCTION without the optional parameter, the specified function key is changed back to its default value. The default values for the programmable function keys are as follows:

FUNCTION KEY	DEFAULT VALUE
F2	assist;
F3	list;
F4	dir;
F5	display structure;
F6	display status;
F7	display memory;
F8	display;
F9	append;
F10	edit;

Procedure

Use SET FUNCTION to change the default value of a function key.

Examples

The following routine allows you to program all of the available function keys. The functions FKLABEL( ) and FKMAX( ) are used to make the program more flexible.

```
* FKeys.PRG
*
SET TALK OFF
num_key = 1
DO WHILE num_key <= FKMAX()
   ACCEPT "Enter the command to perform when ";
          + FKLABEL(num_key) + " is pressed: " TO command
   SET FUNCTION FKLABEL(num_key) TO command + ";"
   num_key = num_key + 1
ENDDO
SET TALK ON
```

Warnings

If you attempt to SET FUNCTION using a key number or label that is not available, the error message *Unknown function key* is displayed.

Tips

You can program a single function key to perform several different commands by separating the individual commands with semicolons. For example,

```
SET FUNCTION 2 TO "x = 12; y = 13; name = [John]; DO Test WITH
x, y, name;"
```

initializes the memory variables x, y, and name, and executes a program called Test using these variables as parameters.

You can also program the function keys for data entry. If, for example, you are adding records to your mailing list, and the City field is almost always Los Angeles, Glendale, or San Francisco, you could issue the following commands before adding records to your file:

```
. SET FUNCTION 2 TO "Los Angeles;"
. SET FUNCTION 3 TO "Glendale;"
. SET FUNCTION 4 TO "San Francisco;"
```

Now, when you APPEND and are ready to enter the City field, simply press F2 for Los Angeles, F3 for Glendale, or F4 for San Francisco. The semicolon causes the carriage return to the next field to be automatic.

If you want to disable the function keys so that they do not interfere with your data entry, set them all to a null string using the following routine:

```
* Null_Key.PRG
*
SET TALK OFF
num_key = 2
null = ""
DO WHILE num_key <= 10
   SET FUNCTION num_key TO null
   num_key = num_key + 1
ENDDO
SET TALK ON
```

SET HEADINGS

Syntax `SET HEADINGS ON|OFF`

Overview The SET HEADINGS command controls whether or not headings are displayed with the AVERAGE, DISPLAY, LIST, and SUM commands. By default, SET HEADINGS is ON and headings are displayed with these commands. SET HEADINGS OFF prevents the display of the headings.

Procedure

Use SET HEADINGS OFF when you want to provide your own headings or when you do not want any headings at all; use SET HEADINGS ON when you want to see headings.

Examples

Usually, the headings that are displayed with these commands are convenient when you are using the commands interactively and working with fields only. When used in this way, the heading that is displayed is the name of the field and the display looks fine. However, when you use an expression list with these commands, the heading is the entire expression, and it can look sloppy. Notice the difference in the following example:

```
. USE Mail
. LIST TRIM(First_Name) + " " + TRIM(Last_Name)
Record#  TRIM(First_Name) + " " + TRIM(Last_Name)
      1  MICHELLE SMITH
      2  Rebecca Corbbit
      3  Gloria Roman
      4  David Gurly
      5  Julia King
      6  Perry Lester
      7  Cathy Moore
      8  Doug Smith
      9  Wade Adams
     10  Sandy Richardson
     11  VELMA MOODY
     12  Mala Schaefer
     13  Lawrence Arthur
     14  Nancy Long
     15  Jeff Potter
     16  Linda Roberts
     17  Jerry Samuels
     18  Chris Whiteside
```

```
. SET HEADINGS OFF
. LIST TRIM(First_Name) + " " + TRIM(Last_Name)
     1  MICHELLE SMITH
     2  Rebecca Corbbit
     3  Gloria Roman
     4  David Gurly
     5  Julia King
     6  Perry Lester
     7  Cathy Moore
     8  Doug Smith
     9  Wade Adams
    10  Sandy Richardson
    11  VELMA MOODY
    12  Mala Schaefer
    13  Lawrence Arthur
    14  Nancy Long
    15  Jeff Potter
    16  Linda Roberts
    17  Jerry Samuels
    18  Chris Whiteside

. CLOSE DATABASES
. SET HEADINGS ON
```

Warnings

If SET TALK is OFF, the AVERAGE and SUM commands have no screen output or headings. To see the result of these commands, be sure that SET TALK is ON, then SET HEADINGS ON or OFF to control the heading, and issue the AVERAGE or SUM command.

SET HELP

Syntax `SET HELP ON¦OFF`

Overview

The SET HELP command controls whether or not you are prompted when you make a mistake entering a command at the dot prompt. By default, SET HELP is ON and you are prompted with *Do you want some help? (Y/N)* if you make an error. If you respond by typing Y, dBASE III PLUS presents you with a help screen. SET HELP OFF disables the help prompt.

Procedure

Use SET HELP OFF to disable the help prompt. SET HELP can be issued at the dot prompt or in a program, but the effect of this command can be seen only when entering commands interactively.

Examples

The following example illustrates the difference with SET HELP ON and SET HELP OFF:

```
. USE Maal
File does not exist.
          ?
USE Maal
Do you want some help? (Y/N) No
```

The name of the Mail database file was misspelled, resulting in an error and the help dialogue. The same error is repeated with SET HELP OFF:

```
. SET HELP OFF
. USE Maal
File does not exist.
          ?
USE Maal
```

The error message is displayed without the help dialogue.

Warnings

The dBASE III PLUS help file, Help.DBS, must be available, or a Y reply results in the error message *HELP text not found.*

Tips

If the help prompt annoys you, change the default value of SET HELP using the HELP = OFF entry in your dBASE III PLUS configuration file. (See Config.DB.)

You can get help for any command or function by using the HELP command, regardless of the state of SET HELP.

SET HISTORY

Syntax

```
SET HISTORY TO <expN>
SET HISTORY ON¦OFF
```

Overview

The SET HISTORY TO <expN> command specifies the maximum number of commands that can be saved in the history buffer. The value of the numeric expression can range from zero to 16000, inclusive. The default size of the history buffer is twenty.

SET HISTORY ON ¦ OFF controls whether or not commands are saved in the history buffer. By default, SET HISTORY is ON, and commands issued at the dot prompt are stored in the history buffer. If SET DOHISTORY is ON, commands issued from programs and procedures are also saved in the history buffer. Commands in the history buffer can be retrieved, edited, and executed from the dot prompt. To discontinue saving commands in the history buffer, SET HISTORY OFF.

Procedure

The history feature in dBASE III PLUS is useful when you are entering commands interactively from the dot prompt. If you make an error such as misspelling a field or memory variable name, omitting a delimiter, or forgetting a comma, you can use the Up Arrow key to bring the erroneous command back to the dot prompt. You can then use any of the full-screen editing and cursor movement keys to correct the command, and press Enter to execute it.

Use SET HISTORY OFF if you do not want to use the history feature.

Use SET HISTORY TO <expN> to make the history buffer larger or smaller than the default value. This is particularly useful when you use SET DOHISTORY ON to record program commands in the history buffer since twenty commands may be insufficient.

Examples

If you are using SET DOHISTORY ON to debug a newly written program, you may want to increase temporarily the size of the history buffer so that you can examine more commands. The following command increases the size of the history buffer to one hundred before executing the new program:

```
. SET HISTORY TO 100
. SET DOHISTORY ON
. DO New_Prog
```

Warnings If you attempt to SET HISTORY TO a value outside of the allowable range, the error message *Invalid value* is displayed.

If you SET HISTORY TO a value that is smaller than the current history buffer size, you will lose the commands that are already stored in the buffer.

Tips Although the allowable range is from zero to 16000, a large history buffer uses additional memory. If your machine has only 256K of memory, you cannot maintain a history buffer of the maximum allowable size; in fact, the maximum for you may be considerably smaller. Remember this if you are using a large history buffer and encounter the *Insufficient memory* error message.

SET INDEX

Syntax `SET INDEX TO [<index filename list>¦?]`

Overview The SET INDEX TO <index filename list> command opens a maximum of seven index files for use with the active database file. Subsequently issued commands that update the data in the database file also update all of the open index files if a key field value is updated. The index file list can be specified by using a list of index (.NDX) file names separated by commas; if a catalog is in use (see SET CATALOG), it can be selected from a menu of catalogued index files by using the ?, or catalog query clause. (See INDEX for information on creating index files.)

The first index in the index file list (or the first one that you select if you use the catalog query clause) is the controlling index file. The controlling index file controls the order in which the database file is processed, and is used with the FIND and SEEK commands. The other index files in the list are assigned an order number according to their position in the list. The

SET ORDER command uses that order number to change the controlling index file.

SET INDEX TO with no parameters closes all of the index files in the active work area and is equivalent to CLOSE INDEX. Closing and/or opening a database file also closes all index files that are open in the current work area.

Procedure

Use SET INDEX TO <index filename list> when your database file is already open and you want to open one or more of its associated index files. Use SET INDEX TO ? to select from a menu of cataloged index files.

Use SET INDEX TO with no parameters to close the index files in the current work area.

Examples

Usually, when you want to use index files you open them with the database file using the INDEX parameter of the USE command; however, there are occasions when you want to either open the index files after the database file is in use or close them leaving the database file in use. In these cases, SET INDEX is used.

Open index files slow down the execution of commands that process the database file sequentially (e.g., AVERAGE, LIST, LOCATE), and you may want to disengage index files for operations where they are not needed. The following routine uses the Employee database file to calculate the average salary and to display a list of employees with salaries below this average. The list is in order by Salary, but in order to speed up the execution of the AVERAGE command the index file is not engaged until after the average is computed:

```
* Avg_Sal.PRG
*
SET TALK OFF
USE Employee
AVERAGE Salary TO m_salary
SET INDEX TO Salary  && Index file is engaged for the LIST OFF
LIST OFF Last_Name, Salary FOR Salary < m_salary
CLOSE DATABASES
SET TALK ON
```

Executing this program by typing `DO Avg_Sal` results in the following output:

```
Last_Name          Salary
Schaefer          21987.33
King              25003.23
Moore             27832.12
Corbbit           38712.23
SMITH             43252.29
Roman             43712.00
Roberts           53137.77
Long              57612.12
```

Warnings

Because records are rearranged in the index file as soon as a key field is changed, attempting to do a REPLACE on a key field when an index file is engaged may not work as you expect it to if the scope of the command is more than one record. REPLACE follows the order of the controlling index file, and the potential exists for large blocks of records to be ignored by this command. To do a global REPLACE on an index key field, disengage the index file with SET INDEX TO, do the REPLACE, open the index file, and REINDEX.

The index key expression is stored in the header record of each index file when it is created. Each time an index file is open, dBASE III PLUS attempts to evaluate that expression; if it is unable to do this, the error message *Index file does not match database* is displayed. This error occurs if you attempt to open an index file that was created for a different database file or if you MODIFY STRUCTURE on a database file and change any of the fields used in the index key expression.

Tips

You can use index files created for a particular database file whenever you want to control the order in which that file is processed or whenever you want to locate records quickly based on the index key using FIND or SEEK. You must, however, use the index files when adding records to or changing key field information in the associated database. If you do not use the index files, they will not be updated and will have to be REINDEXed the next time you want to use them. Save time by opening the index files when you intend to make changes to the database file rather than REINDEXing the files later on.

SET INTENSITY

Syntax `SET INTENSITY ON¦OFF`

Overview The SET INTENSITY command controls whether or not you see both a standard and an enhanced display. By default, SET INTENSITY is ON, and dBASE III PLUS uses both displays. The standard display (e.g., output of LIST, ?, and @...SAY) appears as white letters on a black background and the enhanced display (e.g., status bar and output of @...GET) appears as black letters on a white background (inverse video). SET INTENSITY OFF disables the enhanced display, and all screen output uses the standard display attributes.

Procedure Use SET INTENSITY OFF to disable the enhanced display if you do not want to see this distinction.

Examples The following routine lets you BROWSE through your mailing list with SET INTENSITY OFF:

```
. USE Mail
. SET INTENSITY OFF
. BROWSE
```

Notice the effect of SET INTENSITY on the status bar and the BROWSE (Ctrl-Home) menu bar in Figure 89.

Warnings Certain full-screen commands automatically SET INTENSITY ON because they need both display attributes to convey information to you. These include ASSIST and all of the CREATE commands. The full-screen editing commands (i.e., APPEND, EDIT, and BROWSE), however, respect the status of SET INTENSITY.

Tips SET COLOR changes the attributes of the enhanced and standard displays. If you do not like inverse video but want both a standard and an enhanced display, change the enhanced display with SET COLOR rather than disabling it with SET INTENSITY OFF.

```
Bottom           Top           Lock           Record No.         Freeze  11:13:31 am
NAME--------------------------------------  FIRST_NAME-- LAST_NAME----------
MICHELLE SMITH                               MICHELLE     SMITH
Rebecca Corbbit                              Rebecca      Corbbit
Gloria Roman                                 Gloria       Roman
David Gurly                                  David        Gurly
Julia King                                   Julia        King
Perry Lester                                 Perry        Lester
Cathy Moore                                  Cathy        Moore
Doug Smith                                   Doug         Smith
Wade Adams                                   Wade         Adams
Sandy Richardson                             Sandy        Richardson
VELMA MOODY                                  VELMA        MOODY
Mala Schaefer                                Mala         Schaefer
Laurence Arthur                              Laurence     Arthur
Nancy Long                                   Nancy        Long
Jeff Potter                                  Jeff         Potter
Linda Roberts                                Linda        Roberts
Jerry Samuels                                Jerry        Samuels


BROWSE        ||<C:>||MAIL                  ||Rec: 1/18          ||      ||
        Position selection bar with ↔.  Select with ↵.
                     Go to end of the file.
```

Figure 89

SET MARGIN

Syntax `SET MARGIN TO <expN>`

Overview The SET MARGIN command specifies the left margin used for printed output. This margin is respected by all commands capable of printed output, including @...SAY. The default left margin is zero; the numeric expression should evaluate to between zero and 32767, inclusive.

Reports and labels have their own left margin which is specified when they are created. The value of SET MARGIN TO is added to this internal left margin when reports and labels are printed.

Procedure Use SET MARGIN to change the left margin for printed output to a value other than the default.

Examples The following example changes the left margin to 10 before printing letters stored in a memo field in the mailing list. The field named Send is a logical field that is .T. if there is a letter to print and .F. if there is none.

```
* Letter.PRG
*
SET TALK OFF
SET MEMOWIDTH TO 65
SET MARGIN TO 10
SET PRINTER ON
USE Mail
DO WHILE .NOT. EOF()
   IF Send  && Logical field
      ?
      ?
      ?
      ?
      ? SPACE(56), DATE()
      ?
      ?
      ? Letter  && Memo field
      EJECT
   ENDIF
   SKIP
ENDDO
CLOSE DATABASES
SET PRINTER OFF
SET MARGIN TO 0
SET MEMOWIDTH TO 50
SET TALK ON
```

Warnings

SET MARGIN TO does not give an error message if the margin setting is too small or too large, but sets the margin to zero. The upper limit on the margin setting is large enough so that you will probably never encounter it.

If you SET MARGIN TO a value larger than the number of columns available on your printer, dBASE III PLUS still displays this number of blank spaces before printing each line. If your printer is set up to wrap around, and the value of SET MARGIN is very large, several blank lines are displayed before each line is printed.

Unlike other SET...TO commands, SET MARGIN does not allow you to omit the TO expression; if you do so, a *Syntax error* is displayed.

Tips

If you consistently use a margin setting other than the default, you can change its default value in your dBASE III PLUS configuration file. (See Config.DB.) For example, if you prefer a margin of 10, use the MARGIN = 10 entry.

SET MEMOWIDTH

Syntax `SET MEMOWIDTH TO [<expN>]`

Overview The SET MEMOWIDTH TO <expN> command specifies the display width of memo fields. The display of a memo field never breaks in the middle of a word. As a result, some of the lines of display may be less than this specified width, but no line will be longer.

The default display width for memo fields is 50, and the minimum width is 8. The maximum is larger than the width of any screen or printer and, therefore, you will probably never encounter it.

Memo fields can only be displayed using the ?, DISPLAY, LIST, and REPORT FORM commands. With REPORT FORM, SET MEMOWIDTH sets the default width when the report is created, but this default can be changed whenever the report is modified. Thus, a REPORT FORM can display memo fields using a variety of widths, all of which may differ from the value of SET MEMOWIDTH.

SET MEMOWIDTH TO with no parameter resets the memo field display width to its default value of 50.

Procedure Use SET MEMOWIDTH to display one or more memo fields with a width other than the default.

Examples In the following example, a memo field called Letter is printed for certain people in the mailing list. In order for the letters to fit properly on 8½-by-11 paper, SET MEMOWIDTH TO 65 is used before the letters are printed. Unfortunately, in dBASE III PLUS there is no way to determine whether or not a memo field is empty, so a logical field called Send is employed. This field is manually changed to .T. if there is a letter for a particular individual and to .F. if there is none.

```
* Letter.PRG
*
SET TALK OFF
SET MEMOWIDTH TO 65
SET MARGIN TO 10
SET PRINTER ON
USE Mail
```

```
DO WHILE .NOT. EOF()
   IF Send  && Logical field
      ?
      ?
      ?
      ?
      ? SPACE(56), DATE()
      ?
      ?
      ? Letter  && Memo field
      EJECT
   ENDIF
   SKIP
ENDDO
CLOSE DATABASES
SET PRINTER OFF
SET MARGIN TO 0
SET MEMOWIDTH TO 50
SET TALK ON
```

Warnings The numeric expression used with SET MEMOWIDTH TO must evaluate to at least 8, but its upper limit is large enough so that you will probably never encounter it. If the SET MEMOWIDTH TO value is outside of the allowable range, the error message *Illegal value* is displayed.

Tips If you consistently display memo fields with a width other than the default, you can change its default value in your dBASE III PLUS configuration file. (See Config.DB.) For example, if you prefer a memo field display width of 65, use the MEMOWIDTH = 65 entry.

SET MENUS

Syntax `SET MENUS ON¦OFF`

Overview The SET MENUS command controls whether or not you see a cursor navigation menu when using any of the full-screen commands. By default, SET MENUS is ON, and you see a cursor navigation menu when you use these commands. SET MENUS OFF turns the cursor navigation menu display off.

Procedure

Use SET MENUS OFF once you are familiar with the full-screen editing and cursor navigation keys and no longer wish to be reminded of them.

Examples

The following routine lets you BROWSE through your mailing list without the display of a cursor navigation menu:

```
. USE Mail
. SET MENUS OFF
. BROWSE
```

Notice that once you are browsing, you can toggle the menu on and back off again using the F1 key.

Warnings

Once you are in the full-screen mode you can toggle the menu on and off using the F1 key regardless of the status of SET MENUS. With a few exceptions, pressing this key to turn the menu on and off actually changes the status of the SET MENUS flag. The exceptions are CREATE LABEL and CREATE REPORT, both of which return the SET MENUS flag to its status prior to their execution.

CREATE REPORT ignores SET MENUS and always displays a cursor navigation menu when executed.

Neither CREATE VIEW nor QUERY have cursor navigation menus.

Tips

After you become familiar with the cursor navigation and editing keys, you will not need the menu to constantly remind you of them. You can change the default value of SET MENUS using the MENUS = OFF entry, in your dBASE III PLUS configuration file. (See Config.DB.)

SET MESSAGE

Syntax `SET MESSAGE TO [<expC>]`

Overview

The SET MESSAGE TO <expC> command specifies the message displayed on the bottom line of your screen when SET STATUS is ON. The character expression should evaluate to a string between zero and 79 characters in length, inclusive.

The message is displayed at the dot prompt as well as in APPEND, CHANGE, EDIT, INSERT, and READ. SET MESSAGE does not affect commands such as ASSIST and BROWSE; these commands always have a status bar and predefined messages.

SET MESSAGE TO with no parameter changes the message back to its default value (i.e., *Enter a dBASE III PLUS command* at the dot prompt and nothing in the other modes.)

Procedure

Use SET MESSAGE in combination with SET STATUS ON to change the default message at the dot prompt or to define a message for APPEND, CHANGE, EDIT, INSERT, and READ.

Examples

The following routine defines a message for adding records to your mailing list. The message gives instructions on exiting the routine.

```
* Add_Mail.PRG
*
SET TALK OFF
SET MENUS OFF
SET MESSAGE TO "Add new records to the mailing list.  " +;
               "Press Enter on a blank record to stop."
SET STATUS ON
USE Mail
APPEND
CLOSE DATABASES
SET STATUS OFF
SET MESSAGE TO
SET MENUS OFF
SET TALK ON
```

Warnings

If the character expression evaluates to a string longer than 79 characters, SET MESSAGE TO does not give an error message but truncates the string to 79 characters.

SET MESSAGE TO is evaluated only once. Consequently, if you use a memory variable as part of the SET MESSAGE TO character expression and later change the value of that variable, the message is not updated to reflect this change. At the time of evaluation, the value of the memory variable is saved as a constant and the fact that a memory variable was used is lost. In other words, these commands

```
. var_msg = "This is my message."
This is my message.
. SET MESSAGE TO var_msg
```

are equivalent to this command:

```
. SET MESSAGE TO "This is my message."
```

Tips

If you do not want to see a message when SET STATUS is ON at the dot prompt, you might try SET MESSAGE TO "", but this will not work. SET MESSAGE TO "" is equivalent to SET MESSAGE TO with no parameter. You can SET MESSAGE TO SPACE(79) to change the default message to a blank string.

SET ODOMETER

Syntax `SET ODOMETER TO <expN>`

Overview

The SET ODOMETER command specifies the value at which the record counter (the odometer) is incremented when SET TALK is ON for commands such as APPEND FROM, COPY TO, and REPLACE. The default increment value is 1, and the value of the numeric expression has no practical limitations. If the value is a negative number, its absolute value is used.

SET ODOMETER TO 0 prevents incrementing of the record counter until all records are processed.

Procedure

SET ODOMETER is probably the least frequently used command in dBASE III PLUS. Originally undocumented, it has little, if any, practical application. If you want, you can use SET ODOMETER to change the default value at which the record counter is incremented. Use SET TALK OFF if you do not want to see the record counter at all.

Examples Use the following command to change the odometer increment to 10:

```
. SET ODOMETER TO 10
```

To see the result, USE a database file with more than ten records and COPY it before and after you change the odometer setting.

Warnings SET ODOMETER is very accommodating and does not have any associated error messages. Its upper limit is more than four million; since you cannot have this many records in a single database file the maximum is more than sufficient; however, if you somehow exceed this upper limit, SET ODOMETER reverts back to its default value of 1.

Tips If you use the record counter in your programs to give the user feedback (e.g., SET TALK ON before a PACK or COPY TO), increasing the odometer increment can save a great deal of screen output time if your database file is very large. A benchmark test on a database file with slightly more than 21,000 records showed the amount of time to copy the file was less than half when the SET ODOMETER value was changed from its default value to 100. The actual time a user saves depends on several factors including the number of records and the structure of the file. (See TIME( ) for an example of a benchmark program.)

SET ORDER

Syntax `SET ORDER TO [<expN>]`

Overview The SET ORDER TO <expN> command specifies which index file is the master index. The master index file controls the order in which the database file is processed; its index key is the one used with the FIND and SEEK commands. The value of the numeric expression must be between zero and the number of index files open in the active work area, inclusive. The number of an index file is determined by its position in the index file name list when the file is opened using SET INDEX TO <index filename list> or USE...INDEX <index filename list>. The first file name in the list is number 1, the second is number 2, and so on. By default, the first file name in the list is the master index.

SET ORDER TO 0 is equivalent to SET ORDER TO with no parameters. Each of these forms of the SET ORDER command causes all index files to be completely ignored. If you SET ORDER TO 0, the database file is processed in its natural record number order and no updates are made to any of the index files, although they remain open. You cannot do index-related commands such as SEEK and REINDEX when you have the order set to zero.

Procedure

Use SET ORDER when working with a database file that has several associated index files. It is more efficient to open all index files at once and to switch between them using SET ORDER.

Examples

The following example illustrates how SET ORDER works. In this example, the files C_Lname, C_Fname, and Cust_No are indexed on Last_Name, First_Name, and Cust_No, respectively.

```
. USE Customer INDEX Cust_No, C_Fname, C_Lname
. SET ORDER TO 2  && Activates C_Fname index file
Master index: C:C_Fname.ndx
. LIST First_Name && List is in order by First_Name
Record#  First_Name
      5  Cathy
      3  Gloria
      4  Julia
      9  Linda
      1  MICHELLE
     10  Mala
      8  Nancy
      2  Rebecca
      6  Sandy
      7  VELMA

. SET ORDER TO 3  && Activates C_Lname index file
Master index: C:C_Lname.ndx
```

```
. LIST Last_Name  && List is in order by Last_Name
Record#  Last_Name
      2  Corbbit
      4  King
      8  Long
      7  MOODY
      5  Moore
      6  Richardson
      9  Roberts
      3  Roman
      1  SMITH
     10  Schaefer

. SET ORDER TO 1  && Activates Cust_No index file
Master index: C:Cust_No.ndx
. LIST Cust_No  && List is in order by Cust_No
Record#  Cust_No
      4  A109
      2  A123
      1  A254
     10  A452
      3  A753
      8  A935
      9  F107
      5  F126
      6  F876
      7  M198

. SET ORDER TO 0  && Ignores all index files
. LIST Cust_No, Last_Name, First_Name  && Record number order
Record#  Cust_No Last_Name            First_Name
      1  A254    SMITH                MICHELLE
      2  A123    Corbbit              Rebecca
      3  A753    Roman                Gloria
      4  A109    King                 Julia
      5  F126    Moore                Cathy
      6  F876    Richardson           Sandy
      7  M198    MOODY                VELMA
      8  A935    Long                 Nancy
      9  F107    Roberts              Linda
     10  A452    Schaefer             Mala

. CLOSE DATABASES
```

Warnings If you use an index number for which there is no corresponding index file, the error message *Invalid index number* is displayed.

Remember that SET ORDER TO 0 is similar to closing the index files because the files are ignored altogether. Index files are not updated when the order is set to zero.

SET PATH

Syntax `SET PATH TO [<path list>]`

Overview The SET PATH TO <path list> command defines a list of directory paths that are searched when a file cannot be found in the default directory. The paths in the list are separated by commas or semicolons. The length of the search path cannot exceed sixty characters.

By default, there is no path list defined, and when you attempt to access a file only the current directory is searched. If the file is not found there, an error message similar to *File not found* is displayed. If you define a path list with SET PATH TO, all of the paths in the list are searched in the order of their appearance in the list, and the file is accessed from the first path in which it exists. An error message is displayed only if the file cannot be found in any of these paths.

SET PATH TO with no parameters removes the path list so that only the current directory is searched.

Procedure Use SET PATH TO <path list> when working with files that may be stored in one of several directories. This command prevents you from having to specify the path as part of the file name each time you want to access a file. Use SET PATH TO with no parameters to return the search path to the current directory only.

Examples SET PATH in dBASE III PLUS is similar to SET PATH in DOS except that the syntax is slightly different. dBASE III PLUS does not use the DOS path setting, but you can easily make the dBASE path and the DOS path the same with the following routine:

```
* Set_Path.PRG
*
SET TALK OFF
path_name = GETENV("PATH")  && Get the DOS path setting
SET PATH TO &path_name      && Set dBASE path to DOS path
SET TALK ON
```

Warnings

When you issue SET PATH, dBASE III PLUS does not check the validity of the path names. If you get an error message such as *File does not exist* when trying to access a file that you know exists in a specified path, use DISPLAY STATUS to check the spelling of the path names on the path list.

If the length of the path setting is more than the maximum of sixty characters, the error message *Maximum path length exceeded* is displayed .

SET PRINTER

Syntax `SET PRINTER ON¦OFF`

Overview

The SET PRINTER command controls whether or not screen output (excepting that of the @...SAY...GET command) is also printed. By default, SET PRINTER is OFF and the screen output is not printed. SET PRINTER ON turns the printer on and subsequent screen output is echoed to the printer.

Procedure

Use SET PRINTER ON to echo screen output to the printer.

Examples

The most common use of SET PRINTER ON is to send the result of the ? command to the printer. It can also be used to send the result of many other commands (e.g., LIST and REPORT FORM) to the printer; most of these commands, however, have a TO PRINTER option that makes SET PRINTER ON unnecessary. The following example prints the names of the people in your mailing list:

```
USE Mail
SET TALK OFF
SET PRINTER ON
DO WHILE .NOT. EOF()
   ? TRIM(First_Name), Last_Name
   SKIP
ENDDO
```

```
CLOSE DATABASES
SET PRINTER OFF
SET TALK ON
EJECT
```

Notice that you do not need SET PRINTER ON to do an EJECT.

Warnings Before using SET PRINTER ON or any other printing command, be sure that your printer is properly connected to your computer and that it is turned on and on-line. dBASE III PLUS tries to be forgiving about printing errors either by providing an error message or by simply not printing when you tell it to, but there are some printing errors which can cause the program to hang. If this happens to you, check the printer to make sure that it is turned on and on-line before making the decision to reboot your machine and possibly lose some of your data. Sometimes turning on the printer and/or bringing it on line will make dBASE III PLUS operational again.

Tips SET CONSOLE OFF to prevent output from appearing on your screen while it is printed with SET PRINTER ON.

To print @...SAY results, use SET DEVICE TO PRINTER.

SET PRINTER TO

Syntax

```
SET PRINTER TO [<device name>]
SET PRINTER TO [\\<computer name>\
<printer name> = <device name>]
SET PRINTER TO [\\SPOOLER]
```

Overview If you have more than one printer attached to your computer, the SET PRINTER TO command specifies which one dBASE III PLUS uses for all of its printed output. (See SET DEVICE, SET PRINTER.)

If you are using dBASE III PLUS in a network environment, one of the second two forms of SET PRINTER TO can also be used. These two forms of the command are used to spool printer output to a network printer instead of printing on a local print device.

```
SET PRINTER TO \\<computer name>\<printer name> = <device name>
```

is for use with an IBM network printer. The computer name and printer name are assigned by the network shell rather than by dBASE III PLUS. In this case, the device name can be LPT1, LPT2, or LPT3. The second form,

```
SET PRINTER TO \\SPOOLER
```

is used with a Novell network printer. This form of the command is equivalent to issuing SPOOL from the network shell. Both of these commands spool all subsequent printed output so that it can be printed on the network printer at a later time. The form of SET PRINTER TO used with the IBM network is more complicated than the one used with Novell because in DOS 3.1 you can use any local printer as the network printer as long as it has been declared public. (See your operating system documentation for details.)

SET PRINTER TO with no parameters returns the print device to its default. If you are using dBASE III PLUS on a network, this command also sends all spooled output to be printed on the network printer. If you are using the Novell network, SET PRINTER TO is equivalent to issuing END-SPOOL from the network shell.

Procedure

When you have two or more printers attached to your computer, use SET PRINTER TO to select the printer you want to use. dBASE III PLUS assumes that the primary print device is connected to the DOS list device, which is normally PRN or LPT1. To redirect the output to another printer, SET PRINTER TO the device name to which it is connected. The valid device names are LPT1, LPT2, LPT3, COM1, and COM2.

If you are using dBASE III PLUS in a network environment and want to print on the network printer, use one of the last two forms of the command (depending on the network you are using) to spool the printed output, and use SET PRINTER TO with no parameters to print the spooled output on the network printer.

Examples

If you have both a dot matrix and a laser printer connected to your computer, you can print draft copies of your mailing list letters on the dot matrix printer and the final copy on the laser printer. Assuming that the dot matrix is connected to LPT1 and the laser printer is connected to LPT2, the following routine lets you choose:

```
* PrSelect.PRG
*
```

```
SET TALK OFF
CLEAR
answer = SPACE(1)
DO WHILE .NOT. UPPER(answer) $ ("YN")
   @ 10, 0 SAY "Print letter quality? (Y/N)" GET answer
   READ
ENDDO
* Only need to change printer if answer is Yes since the
* other printer is the default.
IF UPPER(answer) = "Y"
   SET PRINTER TO LPT2  && Switch to laser printer
ENDIF
DO Letters  && Print letters on correct printer
SET PRINTER TO  && Return printer to default device
SET TALK ON
```

If you are using dBASE III PLUS on the IBM network and want to redirect a set of mailing labels to a network printer that is always set up for label printing, you could use the following commands. The following example assumes that the computer name is Labels and the printer name is Laser:

```
. USE Mail
. SET PRINTER TO \\Labels\Laser = LPT1  && Redirect output
. LABEL FORM Party TO PRINTER           && Spool output
. SET PRINTER TO                        && Print spooled output
```

On the Novell network, the equivalent commands would be as follows:

```
. USE Mail
. SET PRINTER TO \\SPOOLER    && Redirect output
. LABEL FORM Party TO PRINTER && Spool output
. SET PRINTER TO              && Print spooled output
```

Before allowing the labels to print, the network administrator must ensure that the printer is set up with the correct form.

Warnings

If you SET PRINTER TO a device name that is not connected to your computer, the error message *Invalid printer port* is displayed.

If you SET PRINTER TO a device name which either does not have a printer connected to it or has a printer connected that is not turned on, the error message *Printer is either not connected or turned off* is displayed.

Tips

When using a serial printer, be sure that you use the DOS MODE command to set the proper baud rate and to reroute this printer to LPT1 if you want it to be your default printer. The following DOS commands set the baud rate to 9600 and reassign the serial printer attached to COM1 to the list device:

```
C> MODE COM1: 9600, n, 8, 1, p
C> MODE LPT1: = COM1:
```

Since a portion of MODE stays resident in memory once it is executed, you should execute this command before entering dBASE III PLUS rather than running it from dBASE III PLUS (see !). In fact, if you use any programs that remain resident in memory, you must execute them before executing dBASE III PLUS.

SET PROCEDURE

Syntax `SET PROCEDURE TO [<filename>]`

Overview

The SET PROCEDURE TO <filename> command opens the named procedure file. The file is assumed to have a .PRG extension unless another one is supplied as part of the file name.

A procedure file is a special dBASE III PLUS program file that may contain up to thirty-two separate routines which are called procedures. In this file, each individual procedure begins with the command PROCEDURE <procedure name>. When a procedure file is open with SET PROCEDURE, the procedures in the file can be executed using DO <procedure name>.

SET PROCEDURE TO with no parameters closes the procedure file and is equivalent to CLOSE PROCEDURE.

Procedure

Use SET PROCEDURE TO <filename> to open a procedure file. Once the file is open, use DO <procedure name> to execute the procedures stored in the file. When you no longer want access to the procedures in the procedure file, close the file using either CLOSE PROCEDURE or SET PROCEDURE TO with no parameter.

Examples

The following example illustrates how to open a procedure file, to execute the procedures stored in the file, and to close the file:

```
* Compute.PRG
*
SET TALK OFF
SET PROCEDURE TO Stats  && Open the procedure file
USE Mail
* The field name on which you want to gather statistics
* must be passed as a character string.
field_name = "Age"
* The variables used in the procedure are initialized.
STORE 0 TO mean, sum_total, variance, std_dev
* Statistics are computed.
DO SumTotal WITH field_name
DO Mean WITH field_name
DO Variance WITH field_name, mean
DO Std_Dev WITH variance
* Statistics are displayed.
? "Sum: " + LTRIM(STR(sum_total, 10, 2))
? "Mean: " + LTRIM(STR(mean, 10, 2))
? "Variance: " + LTRIM(STR(variance, 10, 2))
? "Standard deviation: " + LTRIM(STR(std_dev, 10, 2))
CLOSE DATABASES
CLOSE PROCEDURE
SET TALK ON
```

The Stats procedure file is listed below:

```
* Stats.PRG is a procedure file that computes statistical
* values based on a field name that is passed to the individual
* procedures.

PROCEDURE SumTotal
* This procedure computes the sum of the numbers stored in the
* field name that is passed as a parameter, field_name.
PARAMETERS field_name
SUM &field_name TO sum_total
RETURN
```

```
PROCEDURE Mean
* This procedure computes the mean of the numbers stored in the
* field name that is passed as a parameter, field_name.
PARAMETERS field_name
AVERAGE &field_name TO mean
RETURN

PROCEDURE Variance
* This procedure computes the variance of the numbers stored in
* the field name that is passed as a parameter, field_name.
PARAMETERS field_name, mean
square_sum = 0
GO TOP
DO WHILE .NOT. EOF()
   square_sum = &field_name ^ 2 + square_sum
   SKIP
ENDDO
variance = square_sum / RECCOUNT() - mean ^ 2
RETURN

PROCEDURE Std_Dev
* This procedure computes the standard deviation of the numbers
* stored in the field name passed as a parameter, field_name.
PARAMETERS variance
std_dev = SQRT(variance)
RETURN
```

If you execute the program, you will get the following statistics based on the ages of the people in the mailing list:

```
. DO Compute
Sum: 583.00
Mean: 32.39
Variance: 40.68
Standard deviation: 6.38
.
```

Note that you can compute statistics for any numeric field in any database file by changing the database file and the memory variable field_name.

Warnings If you SET PROCEDURE TO a file name that cannot be found, the error message *File does not exist* is displayed.

Tips

To avoid conflict when using a combination of procedures and programs, make sure that program files and procedures do not have the same names. The procedure name always takes precedence when a procedure file is open; a naming conflict may cause unusual problems for a user who is unaware of this order of precedence.

Using a procedure file is faster than using many separate program files since the procedure file only has to be opened one time.

If you have one program file that calls several procedures, the procedures can be located in that program file rather than in a separate procedure file. The procedures must be located after the program's code and the program simply SETs the PROCEDURE TO itself. For instance, the example above would put all procedures from Stats.PRG into Compute.PRG after the Compute's existing code. Then, change `SET PROCEDURE TO Stats` to `SET PROCEDURE TO Compute`.

SET RELATION

Syntax `SET RELATION TO [<expression> INTO <alias name>]`

Overview

The SET RELATION command relates the records in one database file to the records in another one, based on matching index keys or record numbers. To relate two database files, both files must be in use in different work areas. (See USE and SELECT.)

When you issue SET RELATION TO <expression> INTO <alias name>, a link is established between the active database file and the database file with the named alias. If the database file that you are relating into has an open index file, the files are related based on an index key; otherwise, they are related based on record number. You can establish a relation chain that links several files together by having several open database files and issuing several SET RELATION commands from different work areas.

Once a relation is established between two files, each time the record pointer in the active database file is moved, the record pointer in the related file also moves.

To be related based on an index key means that each time the record pointer in the active database file is moved, the SET RELATION TO expression is evaluated and a SEEK is done in the related file in order to update its record pointer.

To be related based on record number means that you must use a numeric expression as the SET RELATION TO expression. Each time the record pointer in the active database file is moved, the numeric expression is evaluated to obtain a number, and the record pointer in the related file is advanced to that record number.

Procedure

When using SET RELATION the database files that you want to relate must be open in different work areas, and the database file that you want to relate from must be in the active, or selected, work area. If you want to relate the files on an index key, the index file with that key must also be in use as the controlling index with the unselected database file. If there is no index file open with the unselected database file, SET RELATION requires a numeric expression, and the files are related by record number. Use this command whenever you want to treat two database files as one.

Use SET RELATION TO with no parameters to break the relation between the files. Closing either of the database files involved in the relation also breaks the relation.

Examples

The following example relates the Orders and Customer database files and then lists fields from both files. This is an example of a relation based on an index key, which in this case is Cust_No.

```
. SELECT 2
. USE Customer INDEX Cust_No  && Indexed on Cust_No field
. SELECT 1
. USE Orders
. SET RELATION TO Cust_No INTO Customer  && Relate by Cust_No
. LIST Part_No, Quantity, Cust_No, Customer->First_Name
Record#  Part_No   Quantity Cust_No Customer->First_Name
      1  R-123            1 A254    MICHELLE
      2  B-254            2 F126    Cathy
      3  G-165            2 A452    Mala
      4  R-123            1 A452    Mala

. CLOSE DATABASES  && Closes databases and breaks relation
```

Note that in this example the Customer file is indexed on its Cust_No field to an index file that is also called Cust_No, and the SET RELATION TO expression refers to the field Cust_No from the Orders file. By coincidence, the key fields have the same name, but this is not necessary. For example, if the customer number field in the Orders database was called Cust_Num, SET RELATION TO Cust_Num INTO Customer would be used. The name of the key expression is not important, but the key expression used with the SET RELATION command and the key expression of the controlling index file in the related database file must match in data type and length.

The next example illustrates how to relate two files based on the record number. In this example, students in a class are given one of three possible multiple choice tests. The tests are numbered, and each student enters his or her name, test number, and test answers into a database file record. The test results are consolidated into a single database file called Tests.

The correct answers to each test are stored in a second database file called Answers. The answers for test number one are in record number one, those for test two are in record two, and those for test three are in record three.

Using SET RELATION TO, the Test_Num field in the Tests database file is linked to the record number in the Answers database file; hence, if the Tests record for a student shows he took test number two, the test results are compared to record number two in the Answers database file. Similarly, if the Tests record for another student shows she took test number three, her test results are compared to record number three in the Answers database file. In this way, each student's test responses are compared to the correct response for the particular test that the student took.

```
* Grade.PRG
*
SET TALK OFF

* The Answers database file contains a different set of
* answers for each test.  The answers to test number 1 are
* in record 1, the answers to test 2 in record 2, and so on.
SELECT 2
USE Answers

* The Tests database file contains each student's responses
* to the test questions.  The number of the test that each
* student took is stored in a field called Test_Num.
```

```
SELECT 1
USE Tests

* The Tests database file is related to the test Answers using
* the Test_Num field.  Since the Answers file is not indexed,
* the relation is based on the record number in this file.
SET RELATION TO Test_Num INTO Answers

* Each student's test results are processed and each one
* graded.
DO WHILE .NOT. EOF()
   question = "1"
   correct = 0

   * For each student, all 10 answers are compared to the correct
   * answers in the Answers database file.
   DO WHILE VAL(question) <= 10
      IF Answer&question = Answers->Answer&question
         * The number of correct answers is accumulated.
         correct = correct + 1
      ENDIF
      * Go on to the next question.
      question = LTRIM(STR(VAL(question) + 1, 2))
   ENDDO
   * Since there are 10 questions, the score is the number
   * correct multiplied by 10.
   REPLACE Score WITH correct * 10
   SKIP
ENDDO
CLOSE DATABASES
SET TALK ON
```

The database file structures for the Tests and Answers database files are listed below and will enhance your understanding of the program:

```
. USE Tests
. LIST STRUCTURE
```

```
Structure for database: C:Test.dbf
Number of data records:       6
Date of last update   : 05/08/87
```

```
Field  Field Name  Type       Width    Dec
    1  STUDENT     Character     50
    2  TEST_NUM    Numeric        1
    3  SCORE       Numeric        3
    4  ANSWER1     Character      1
    5  ANSWER2     Character      1
    6  ANSWER3     Character      1
    7  ANSWER4     Character      1
    8  ANSWER5     Character      1
    9  ANSWER6     Character      1
   10  ANSWER7     Character      1
   11  ANSWER8     Character      1
   12  ANSWER9     Character      1
   13  ANSWER10    Character      1
** Total **                      65
```

```
. USE Answers
. LIST STRUCTURE
```

```
Structure for database: C:Answers.dbf
Number of data records:       3
Date of last update   : 05/08/87
```

```
Field  Field Name  Type       Width    Dec
    1  ANSWER1     Character      1
    2  ANSWER2     Character      1
    3  ANSWER3     Character      1
    4  ANSWER4     Character      1
    5  ANSWER5     Character      1
    6  ANSWER6     Character      1
    7  ANSWER7     Character      1
    8  ANSWER8     Character      1
    9  ANSWER9     Character      1
   10  ANSWER10    Character      1
** Total **                      11
```

Warnings

In dBASE III PLUS, you cannot directly relate the same file to more than one other file, but there is a way to accomplish this indirectly. (See the Tips section.) Each SET RELATION command overrides any existing relation from the active database file.

If you issue SET RELATION without first opening the file to be related into in another work area, the error message *ALIAS not found* is displayed.

When relating two files based on an index key, the SET RELATION TO expression must evaluate to the same data type as the controlling index for the related database file, or the *Data type mismatch* error message is displayed.

If the related database file has no open index file, SET RELATION assumes that you want to relate the files based on record number; in this case the SET RELATION TO expression must be a numeric expression or the *Database is not indexed* error message is displayed.

Tips

To relate two database files based on matching record numbers, use RECNO( ) as the SET RELATION TO expression. You might use this command if you want more than the 128 fields that dBASE III PLUS allows in a database file. By creating a second file with 128 fields, you can relate the two on RECNO( ) and effectively have 256 fields in a file.

You can relate several files together by doing a SET RELATION from the first file into the second, selecting the second file, and doing a SET RELATION from it into the third, and so on. This is illustrated in the following example in which commands link the Inventry file, the Orders file, and the Customer file together and list fields from all three:

```
. SELECT 3
. USE Customer INDEX Cust_No  && Cust_No is indexed on Cust_No
. SELECT 2
. USE Orders INDEX O_PartNo   && O_PartNo is indexed on Part_No
. SET RELATION TO Cust_No INTO Customer  && Relate by Cust_No
. SELECT 1
. USE Inventry
. SET RELATION TO Part_No INTO Orders  && Relate by Part_No
. SET FIELDS TO Part_No, Orders->Cust_No, Orders->Quantity
. SET FIELDS TO Customer->First_Name
. LIST
Record#  PART_NO CUST_NO   QUANTITY FIRST_NAME
      1  R-123   A254             1 MICHELLE
      2  B-254   F126             2 Cathy
      3  BL890
      4  B-735
      5  BL861
      6  G-165   A452             2 Mala
```

Because there are no orders for some parts, the customer number, quantity, and name do not appear. Also note that though there are actually two orders for part number R-123, only the first one shows up in the list.

SET RELATION cannot access multiple occurrences with the same key values in the related file, so this particular example is not very useful. When you are using SET RELATION, remember this and always set the relation from the database file containing multiple occurrences of the same key value into the database file with unique key values. This will enable you to access all of the records.

If you do not require related data every time the record pointer is moved, use SEEK when you need to instead of setting a relation.

To relate a file to more than one other file, each related file can use the first file's alias to form its own SET RELATION expression. This way, whenever the first file's record pointer is moved, all related files will be positioned according to that file's key expression.

```
* Open four files.  The three index files should all be
* indexed on the same key.
SELECT 4
USE File_4 INDEX Ndx_4
SELECT 3
```

```
USE File_3 INDEX Ndx_3
SELECT 2
USE File_2 INDEX Ndx_2
SELECT 1
USE File_1

* Set all relations based on key in file 1.
SET RELATION TO Keyfield INTO File_2
SELECT 2
SET RELATION TO File_1->Keyfield INTO File_3
SELECT 3
SET RELATION TO File_1->Keyfield INTO File_4
SELECT 1
* Files 2, 3, and 4 are now each related to the key in file 1.
```

SET SAFETY

Syntax `SET SAFETY ON¦OFF`

Overview The SET SAFETY command controls whether or not you are prompted before dBASE III PLUS overwrites an existing file. By default, SET SAFETY is ON; before an existing file is overwritten, you are prompted with *<filename> already exists, overwrite it? (Y/N)* If SET SAFETY is ON, you are prompted with *Zap <filename> ? (Y/N)* when you attempt to ZAP a database file. SET SAFETY OFF disables these prompts so that the operations are done without warning.

Procedure Use SET SAFETY OFF if you do not want to be warned each time an existing file is about to be overwritten.

Examples Often, you will want to overwrite a file that you know exists, and having SET SAFETY ON will interfere with the flow of your program. For example, the following routine makes a backup copy of your mailing list on the drive A, and will overwrite the existing backup file without warning:

```
SET TALK OFF
SET SAFETY OFF
USE Mail
COPY TO A:Mail.BAK
```

```
CLOSE DATABASES
SET SAFETY ON
SET TALK ON
```

Warnings SET ALTERNATE TO ignores the SET SAFETY flag and always overwrites an existing file without warning. (See SET ALTERNATE.) If you do not want to overwrite an existing file, use FILE( ) to test for the existence of the file before using SET ALTERNATE TO.

Tips If you are not worried about overwriting existing files, change the default value of SET SAFETY by using the SAFETY = OFF entry in your dBASE III PLUS configuration file. (See Config.DB.)

SET SCOREBOARD

Syntax `SET SCOREBOARD ON¦OFF`

Overview The SET SCOREBOARD command controls whether or not the scoreboard, or line zero, is reserved by dBASE III PLUS for displaying status information and messages. By default, SET SCOREBOARD is ON; if SET STATUS is OFF, dBASE III PLUS reserves line zero for displaying certain information. This information includes the status of the Ins, Caps Lock, and Num Lock keys, the Del marker for records that are marked for deletion in the full-screen editing commands, and RANGE error messages. SET SCOREBOARD OFF if you want to use line zero for your own display purposes.

Procedure Use SET SCOREBOARD OFF along with SET STATUS OFF to control the entire screen in dBASE III PLUS.

Examples The following commands illustrate how to use line zero for data display. The example assumes that SET STATUS is at its default setting of OFF:

```
SET TALK OFF
SET SCOREBOARD OFF
USE Mail
@ 0,45 SAY DATE()
@ 1, 0 SAY "First Name" GET First_Name
@ 2, 0 SAY "Last Name " GET Last_Name
```

```
@ 3, 0 SAY "Address 1 " GET Address1
@ 4, 0 SAY "Address 2 " GET Address2
@ 5, 0 SAY "City      " GET City
@ 6, 0 SAY "State     " GET State
@ 7, 0 SAY "Zip Code  " GET Zip PICTURE "99999"
@ 8, 0 SAY "Phone     " GET Phone PICTURE "(999)999-9999"
READ
SET SCOREBOARD ON
SET TALK ON
CLOSE DATABASES
```

Warnings

If you display information on line zero when SET SCOREBOARD is ON, it will eventually be overwritten or erased. Be sure that you SET SCOREBOARD OFF before attempting to display data on line zero.

If SET SCOREBOARD and SET STATUS are OFF, you will not be able to see the status of the Ins, Caps Lock, or Num Lock keys.

Tips

If SET STATUS is ON, the status of SET SCOREBOARD is ignored, and the information that would normally be displayed on line zero is shown either on the status bar or on the message line. Line zero is always available if SET STATUS is ON.

SET STATUS

Syntax `SET STATUS ON|OFF`

Overview

The SET STATUS command controls whether or not the status bar is displayed at the dot prompt and for all of the full-screen editing commands except BROWSE (i.e., APPEND, CHANGE, EDIT, INSERT, and READ). By default, SET STATUS is OFF, but dBASE III PLUS is shipped with a configuration file (see Config.DB) that contains a STATUS = ON entry to turn it on. Use SET STATUS OFF to turn the status bar off in these modes.

Procedure

Use SET STATUS ON if you want the status bar on your screen. SET STATUS OFF if you prefer not to use the status bar.

Examples The following commands illustrate the appearance of the EDIT screen using the status bar:

```
. USE Mail
. SET FORMAT TO MailEdit
. SET STATUS ON
. EDIT
```

The screen you see should look like the one in Figure 90.

To turn the status bar off again and close the mailing list file,

```
. SET STATUS OFF
. CLOSE DATABASES
```

Warnings Using the status bar can slow down the execution of some dBASE III PLUS commands considerably. Remember this if you are trying to improve the performance of your programs.

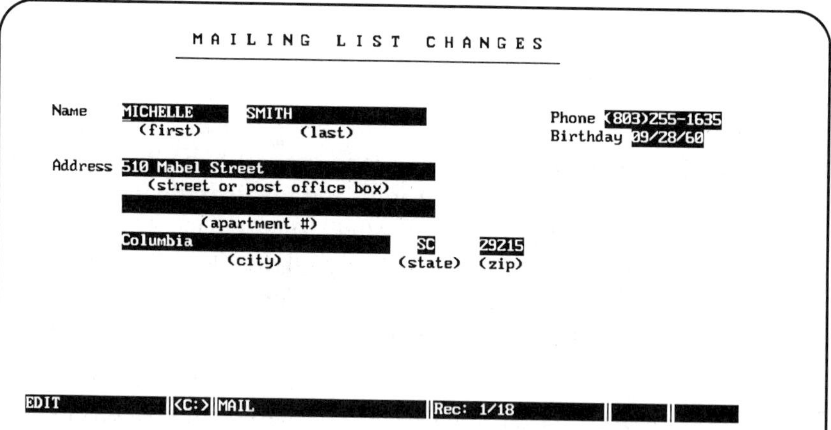

Figure 90

The status bar is always on in ASSIST, BROWSE, and CREATE regardless of SET STATUS because all of these commands have a menu bar (it is optional in BROWSE, CREATE, and MODIFY STRUCTURE). There is no way to suppress the status bar when using these commands.

Tips

If SET STATUS is ON, the status of SET SCOREBOARD is ignored, and the information that would normally be displayed on line zero is shown either on the status bar or on the message line. Line zero is always available for your use if SET STATUS is ON.

The configuration file (see Config.DB) that is shipped with dBASE III PLUS contains the STATUS = ON entry to turn the status bar, but the default for SET STATUS is OFF. If you prefer not to use the status bar, modify the Config.DB file with any word processor and remove this entry.

SET MESSAGE allows you to define a message that is displayed below the status bar.

SET STEP

Syntax `SET STEP ON¦OFF`

Overview

The SET STEP command controls whether or not you are allowed to step through a program by answering a prompt each time a command is executed. By default, SET STEP is OFF, and programs run without interruption. If you SET STEP ON and run a program, you will be prompted with *Press SPACE to step, S to suspend, or Esc to cancel...* after each command in the program is executed. You must respond to this prompt by pressing the space bar to execute the next command, typing S to suspend the program, or pressing Esc to cancel it.

Procedure

Use SET STEP ON when you want to debug a program by stepping through it one command at a time.

Examples

The following commands illustrate how to step through a program one command at a time:

```
. SET ECHO ON
. SET STEP ON
. DO New_Prog
. SET STEP OFF
. SET ECHO OFF
```

Warnings

When stepping through a program with SET STEP ON, SET DEBUG ON causes the step prompt to display only on the printer. This means that you cannot see the prompt, but you are expected to respond to it; otherwise, the program will not continue to execute.

Tips

Use SET STEP ON in conjunction with SET ECHO ON to see which command was executed. If you want to print the results of these commands, SET DEBUG ON; this command prevents the screen from becoming cluttered.

SET TALK

Syntax `SET TALK ON|OFF`

Overview

The SET TALK command controls whether or not dBASE III PLUS talks back to you when you issue commands. By default, SET TALK is ON and the majority of commands give you a screen response. For example, the STORE command shows you the value that it stores in the memory variable; COPY shows you how many records it is copying. SET TALK OFF suppresses this automatic screen output.

Procedure

Use SET TALK OFF whenever you do not want the screen display to be interrupted.

Examples

SET TALK is probably the most frequently used SET command. In almost every program example in this book, SET TALK OFF is the first line in the program and prevents command responses from displaying while the program is executing. At the end of the program, SET TALK ON appears, which allows the user to get visual feedback during command entry when the program exits to the interactive mode.

Tips

In a program with SET TALK OFF, you should offer your own visual feedback when conducting lengthy operations. For example, if you are REINDEXing a large database file in the middle of a program, a user who does not get any visual feedback may think that the program is stuck and, as a result, might do something drastic. Before executing the command, either display a message with ?, or @...SAY, or SET TALK ON. If you SET TALK ON for a particular command, be sure that you SET TALK OFF after the command has executed.

SET TITLE

Syntax `SET TITLE ON¦OFF`

Overview

The SET TITLE command controls whether or not you are prompted for a Title when a file name is added to the open catalog. (See SET CATALOG.) By default, SET TITLE is ON and you are prompted to enter a Title each time a file name is added to the catalog. SET TITLE OFF suppresses this prompt and causes the Title field in the catalog to be left blank.

Procedure

Use SET TITLE OFF whenever you do not want the catalog Title prompt to interfere with your screen display.

Examples

The way a catalog is set up in dBASE III PLUS can be tedious because file names are added automatically to the catalog whenever they are created or used, and dBASE III PLUS uses many files. Each time a file name is added to the catalog, you are prompted for a Title. This can be annoying when you are setting up a catalog for the first time. SET TITLE OFF if you would rather go back at a later time and fill in the Title field by editing the catalog file.

Tips

If SET TITLE is OFF, the Title field in the catalog is left blank when subsequent file names are added to the catalog; you can fill them in later because you can USE and EDIT the catalog just like any other database file.

SET TYPEAHEAD

Syntax `SET TYPEAHEAD TO <expN>`

Overview The SET TYPEAHEAD TO <expN> command specifies the size of the typeahead buffer. The value of the numeric expression must be between zero and 32000, inclusive. The default typeahead buffer size is twenty characters. No additional characters are accepted from the keyboard when the buffer is full.

Procedure If you type faster than dBASE III PLUS can respond, SET TYPEAHEAD TO a larger value. You cannot make dBASE III PLUS respond any faster, but you will be able to type ahead of it without interruption.

Examples The following example shows how to change the typeahead buffer to one hundred characters:

```
. SET TYPEAHEAD TO 100
```

Warnings If you attempt to SET TYPEAHEAD TO a value outside of the allowable range, the error message *Invalid value* is displayed.

Tips If you prefer a typeahead buffer that is larger or smaller than the default twenty characters, change the default size using the TYPEAHEAD = <number> entry in the dBASE III PLUS configuration file. (See Config.DB.)

SET UNIQUE

Syntax `SET UNIQUE ON¦OFF`

Overview The SET UNIQUE command controls whether all records or only those with unique index keys are kept in a particular index file. By default, SET

UNIQUE is OFF, and all index files that you create using INDEX are flagged to keep track of all records that are added to the database file.

With SET UNIQUE ON, any subsequent index file that you create is flagged so that only those records with key values not already in the index file will be maintained in the index file.

Procedure Use SET UNIQUE ON to create unique index files. Once a unique index file is created, it will automatically be maintained as a unique index file, regardless of the status of SET UNIQUE.

Examples SET UNIQUE ON creates an index file that will be maintained as a unique index. The following example shows how to create a unique index file:

```
. USE EMPLOYEE
. SET UNIQUE ON
. INDEX ON Emp_Code TO Emp_Code
  100% indexed          10 Records indexed
. SET UNIQUE OFF
. CLOSE DATABASES
```

Records are ignored by the Emp_Code index file if you either add a record with an existing key value or edit a record so that its key value matches that of another record in the Employee database file. However, dBASE III PLUS does not automatically warn you that records are being ignored or dropped from an index file. The following routine allows you to add records to the Employee database file and, using ON ERROR along with ERROR( ), the program warns you if you enter an existing employee code and prevents you from adding that record to the file:

```
SET TALK OFF
SET BELL OFF
SET MENUS OFF
USE Employee INDEX Emp_Code  && Emp_Code is a UNIQUE index file
DO WHILE .T.
   CLEAR
   APPEND BLANK
   okay = .T.  && Is it okay to add this record?
   rec = RECNO()  && Save number of added blank records
   @ 1, 0 SAY "Enter new employee code" GET Emp_Code
   READ
```

```
    * If no employee code is entered, delete the blank record
    * and exit the loop.
    IF "" = TRIM(Emp_Code)
       DELETE
       EXIT
    ENDIF
    * The error trap is set.  GO rec will result in error no. 20,
    * Record is not in index, if the key was already in the index.
    ON ERROR DO Unique
    GO rec
    ON ERROR  && Disable error trap
    * If this record is not already in the index, put in the
    * remaining fields.  Otherwise, display an error message.
    IF okay
       EDIT NEXT 1 FIELDS First_Name, Last_Name, Address1, ;
                          Address2, City, State, Zip, Phone, ;
                          Ssn, Hire_Date
    ELSE
       @ 4, 0 SAY "This employee is already on file."
       WAIT
    ENDIF
ENDDO
PACK   && Permanently erase records deleted by this routine
CLOSE DATABASES
SET MENUS ON
SET BELL ON
SET TALK ON
```

The program Unique.PRG is listed below to complete this example:

```
* Unique.PRG
* Error number 20 is "Record is not in index."
* The record is deleted and a flag is passed to the calling
* routine indicating that it is not okay to add this record.
IF ERROR() = 20
   DELETE RECORD rec
   okay = .F.
ENDIF
RETURN
```

Warnings

The only command whose action is determined by the SET UNIQUE flag is INDEX, and even this command ignores the flag if the UNIQUE parameter is used as part of the command syntax. If you have created a unique index file, you cannot make it into a non-unique index file by using SET UNIQUE OFF followed by REINDEX. You must, in this case, recreate the index file using the INDEX command with SET UNIQUE OFF. REINDEX ignores the SET UNIQUE status, and looks to the index file itself to evaluate its uniqueness.

Tips

In the original release of dBASE III, SET UNIQUE was designed to be a global flag, and it was impossible to maintain both a unique and a non-unique index for one database file. In dBASE III PLUS, SET UNIQUE was changed to make uniqueness an attribute of the index file, and the UNIQUE keyword was added to the INDEX command syntax. When you create a unique index file, the header of the file indicates this property so that the index can be maintained properly without regard to the current status of SET UNIQUE.

You can override the SET UNIQUE OFF flag by using the UNIQUE parameter of the INDEX command when you create an index file.

SET VIEW

Syntax `SET VIEW TO <filename>¦?`

Overview

The SET VIEW TO command opens the named view file to establish the environment, or view, that is stored in the file. The file is assumed to have a .VUE extension unless you specify another one as part of the file name. View files are created using either the CREATE VIEW or CREATE VIEW FROM ENVIRONMENT.

The ?, or catalog query clause, can be used instead of a file name if there is an active catalog. (See SET CATALOG.) This presents you with a menu of cataloged view files from which you can select the one you want to use.

The view that is established is, at minimum, a single database file. It may also include several database files, their alias names and index files, relations between the database files, a field list, a filter condition, and a format file. The commands USE...INDEX, SELECT, SET RELATION, SET FIELDS, SET FORMAT, and SET FILTER are used by SET VIEW to establish the view.

Procedure

Use SET VIEW to establish a view that you have stored in a view file. A view file is a convenient way of storing a frequently used environment. By creating the view file once, you can establish the environment with a single SET VIEW command rather than a series of commands.

Examples

If you find the full-screen CREATE VIEW command less complicated than entering the command equivalents to establish a view, you can create a view file using CREATE VIEW FROM ENVIRONMENT. First, enter all of the appropriate commands to set up the environment that you want; once the environment is established, use CREATE VIEW FROM ENVIRONMENT. The following commands establish and create a view file called Invoices:

```
. SELECT 3
. USE Customer INDEX Cust_No
. SELECT 2
. USE Inventry INDEX Part_No
. SELECT 1
. USE Orders
. SET RELATION TO Part_No INTO Inventry
. SET FIELDS TO Cust_No, Part_No, Quantity
. SET FIELDS TO Inventry->Descrip, Inventry->Price
. SET FIELDS TO Customer->First_Name, Customer->Last_Name
. SET FIELDS TO Customer->Address1, Customer->Address2
. SET FIELDS TO Customer->City, Customer->State, Customer->Zip
. CREATE VIEW Invoices FROM ENVIRONMENT
```

This set of commands sets up the environment for printing invoices. All of the database and index files required are opened, the relation between the Orders and Inventry file is established, and the necessary fields are set. A view file is then created to store this environment.

Instead of entering all of these commands each time you print invoices, enter SET VIEW TO Invoices and execute the program to print them. Such a program might look like this:

```
* Invoices.PRG
*
SET TALK OFF
SET VIEW TO Invoices
SET DEVICE TO PRINTER
DO WHILE .NOT. EOF()
   * Get the correct customer information for this order.
   SELECT Customer
```

```
    SEEK Orders->Cust_No
    SELECT Orders
    * Invoices.FMT is a format file that does the @...SAY
    * commands to display a formatted invoice.
    DO Invoices.FMT
    SKIP
ENDDO
SET DEVICE TO SCREEN
CLOSE DATABASES  && This clears the field list, relations, etc.
SET TALK ON
```

Warnings

This command is best utilized interactively to avoid setting up the environment repeatedly. However, its use in a program makes the program difficult to read because you cannot see what files are in use or what their relationships are.

Unlike most other files in dBASE III PLUS, the view file stays open only long enough to establish the view, and then it is closed. For this reason, SET VIEW TO with no parameters has no meaning and causes a *Syntax error.*

If the named view file cannot be found, the error message *File does not exist* is displayed.

Tips

SET VIEW TO <filename> does a CLOSE DATABASES before establishing the view. If you want to save the current environment before setting up a new one, use CREATE VIEW FROM ENVIRONMENT to save it in a view file. This enables you to reestablish the old environment after you are finished working with the other view. For example,

```
. CREATE VIEW Current FROM ENVIRONMENT  && Save environment
. SET VIEW TO New_View  && Establish new environment
   .
   . <work with new environment>
   .
. SET VIEW TO Current  && Establish original environment
```

Skeleton

Overview

The term <skeleton> often occurs in dBASE language syntax. A skeleton describes a group of object names such as files or memory variables by using special symbols to ignore certain characters in the name and other symbols to match characters in the name.

The special symbols are the asterisk (*) and the question mark (?). The ? indicates that the character in its position of the name is to be ignored, and the * indicates that all remaining characters are to be ignored. For a file name, you can specify a separate skeleton for the eight-character root portion of the file name and for the extension; therefore, an * used in the root portion of the file name skeleton only ignores characters up to the period. Any other symbols such as letters or numbers are taken literally to be in the name.

Procedure

You construct a skeleton just as you would a name except that you can mask characters in the name so that they are ignored using the ? and * (often called "wildcard characters"). When the command containing the skeleton as one of its command line parameters is executed, each object (i.e., either file or memory variable, depending on the command) is compared to the skeleton to determine if it matches. Depending on whether the command uses the phrase LIKE or EXCEPT with the skeleton, the object is either processed or ignored.

Examples

See DIR for an example using several file skeletons.

Warnings

The * symbol, when used as part of a skeleton, ignores all remaining characters in the name; therefore, it is meaningless to include literal characters after an asterisk in a skeleton. This means you cannot mask an unspecified number of characters in the middle of a name. For example, you might think that the following command could be used to release all of the memory variables that begin with the letter m and end with the letter t:

```
RELEASE ALL LIKE m*t
```

However, since everything after the * is ignored, this command is equivalent to

```
RELEASE ALL LIKE m*
```

Tips

In file name skeletons, the file name and the extension can be specified as separate skeletons. For example,

```
DIR A*.??X
```

The file name skeleton ends at the period where the extension skeleton begins.

SKIP

Syntax `SKIP [<expN>]`

Overview The SKIP command is used to move the record pointer in the active database file relative to its current position in the file. With no parameters, the command moves the record pointer forward a single record.

The number of records that you want to skip over is specified with the SKIP command as a numeric expression. If the numeric expression evaluates to a positive number, the record pointer moves forward that number of records. If it is a negative number, the record pointer moves backward that number of records.

If the database file has a controlling index (see SET INDEX, SET ORDER), the record pointer is moved according to the logical indexed order of the file rather than the natural record number order.

Procedure SKIP with no parameters is most often used in programs to process the records in a database file one at a time. To accomplish this, SKIP is used in a loop. (See DO WHILE.)

Examples There are many dBASE III PLUS commands that process an entire database file sequentially, but often you want more control than any single command can give you. In these cases, use SKIP in a DO WHILE loop to perform several commands for each record in a database file. The following example updates the area code for a particular range of zip codes and displays each record that is changed:

```
* New_Zip.PRG
*
SET TALK OFF
USE Customer
DO WHILE .NOT. EOF()
   IF "90029" <= Zip .AND. Zip <= "90037"
      REPLACE Phone WITH STUFF(Phone, 2, 3, "818")
      ? Last_Name, Zip, Phone
   ENDIF
   SKIP
```

```
ENDDO
CLOSE DATABASES
SET TALK ON
```

To execute this program and see its results,

```
. DO New_Zip
Roman                   90029 (818)485-5955
```

See BOF( ) for an example that processes a database file from bottom to top using SKIP −1 instead of SKIP.

Warnings

If you issue SKIP with a negative parameter when the active database file is already positioned at the beginning of file (see BOF( )), the error message *Beginning of file encountered* is displayed. Similarly, if you issue SKIP with a positive parameter when the active database file is already positioned at the end of file (see EOF( )), the error message *End of file encountered* is displayed. When using SKIP, be sure to check the EOF( ) or BOF( ) flag to avoid these error messages.

Tips

Although you can use SKIP to skip any number of records in order to access a record that you know is in a particular place, GO (see GO) is generally used when you know precisely where a record is in a database file. Using GO can be much faster than SKIP if you know the record number.

SORT

Syntax

```
SORT ON <key fieldname>
[/[A¦D][C] ¦ ASCENDING ¦ DESCENDING]
[, <key fieldname> [/[A¦D][C] ¦ ASCENDING ¦
DESCENDING]...] TO <filename> [<scope>]
[WHILE <condition>] [FOR <condition>]
```

Overview

The SORT command copies the contents of the active database to another database file in sorted order. You specify the sort order by supplying up to ten fields that you want to SORT ON. Specifying more than one sort key field results in a cascading sort with the first field as the major sort key and the last field as the most minor. Each key field that you list is sorted in ascending ASCII order (see Appendix C) unless you specify an option after the field name. For each field, specify ASCENDING or DESCENDING, or use one or more of the / (slash) options. A stands for ascending, D for descending, and C for case-independent. In a case-independent, or dictionary, sort, no case distinction is made in the ordering process.

When the command is executed, the TO database file is created with a structure that is identical to the active database file, and the records in the active database file are sorted according to the list of fields that you specify with the ON keyword. When the SORT process is complete, the sorted records are written to the new file, and the active file remains in its unsorted order.

A scope, a FOR clause, and a WHILE clause can be specified to limit the records that are sorted. Each of these command line options is discussed separately. (See Scope, FOR, and WHILE.) Unless one of these clauses is specified, all records in the active database file are sorted.

SORT displays the number of records sorted and the number of records written to the new file if SET TALK is ON. SET TALK OFF suppresses this screen output.

Procedure

In order to SORT a database file, the file must be open in the current work area. (See USE.) You can issue the SORT command once the file is open.

Decide which fields you want to SORT ON and list them as part of the command. You cannot use logical or memo fields as SORT key fields: key fields must be character, date, or numeric. The order in which you list the key fields is significant, the first field being the major sort key, and the last the most minor. If you want the sort order for any key field to be other than ascending order, specify the appropriate slash option. /D gives a descending ASCII sort, /C gives an ascending dictionary sort, and /DC gives a descending dictionary sort. There is never a need to specify /A or ASCENDING, since it is the default, and the DESCENDING keyword is equivalent to /D.

Use a scope, WHILE, and/or FOR clause to limit the records processed by SORT. Finally, specify the TO < filename > and execute the SORT command.

Once SORT has executed, the original file remains in use. To view the contents of the sorted database file, USE the file and CLOSE DATABASES to close all of the files when you are finished.

Examples

In the following example, the SORT command sorts the Orders database file in several different ways. The first example sorts using the Cust_No as the major sort key and the Part_No as the secondary key. The customer number is sorted in ascending order and the part number in descending order.

```
. USE Orders
. SORT ON Cust_No, Part_No/D TO CustSort
   00% Sorted   100% Sorted            4 Records sorted
. USE CustSort
. LIST  && Note that customer A452's orders are descending
Record#  CUST_NO PART_NO    QUANTITY
      1  A254    R-123             1
      2  A452    R-123             1
      3  A452    G-165             2
      4  F126    B-254             2
```

In the next example, the Orders file is sorted using the part number as the major sort key and the customer number as the secondary key. Notice how this SORT groups like-part numbers together, whereas the previous one grouped like-customer numbers:

```
. USE Orders
. SORT ON Part_No, Cust_No TO PartSort
   00% Sorted   100% Sorted            4 Records Sorted
. USE PartSort
. LIST FIELDS Part_No, Cust_No
Record#  Part_No Cust_No
      1  B-254   F126
      2  G-165   A452
      3  R-123   A254
      4  R-123   A452
```

In the last two examples, the Mail database file is used to illustrate the difference between an ASCII and a dictionary sort order:

```
. USE Mail
. SORT ON Last_Name TO Ascii
  100% Sorted           18 Records sorted ... Copying text file.
. USE Ascii
. LIST Last_Name  && Note SMITH comes before Samuels
Record#  Last_Name
      1  Adams
      2  Arthur
      3  Corbbit
      4  Gurly
      5  King
      6  Lester
      7  Long
      8  MOODY
      9  Moore
     10  Potter
     11  Richardson
     12  Roberts
     13  Roman
     14  SMITH
     15  Samuels
     16  Schaefer
     17  Smith
     18  Whiteside

. USE Mail
. SORT ON Last_Name/C TO Dict
  100% Sorted           18 Records sorted ... Copying text file.
. USE Dict
. LIST Last_Name  && Note SMITH is now just before Smith
Record#  Last_Name
      1  Adams
      2  Arthur
      3  Corbbit
      4  Gurly
      5  King
      6  Lester
      7  Long
      8  MOODY
      9  Moore
     10  Potter
     11  Richardson
     12  Roberts
```

```
      13  Roman
      14  Samuels
      15  Schaefer
      16  SMITH
      17  Smith
      18  Whiteside

. CLOSE DATABASES
```

Warnings

The syntax for the SORT ON slash options is [/[A ¦ D][C]], which means that you are allowed to use /A, /AC, /D, and /DC only; however, SORT does not trap as an error any combination of these three letters following a slash. Therefore, you can specify an impossible combination such as /AD even though it is impossible to do an ascending and a descending sort at the same time. Instead, the last slash option (in this case D) is used to do the sort. Using any letter besides A, C, and D after the slash results in a *Syntax error*.

Remember that unless you specify /C, the key field is sorted in ASCII order in which all lowercase letters come after all uppercase letters. (See Appendix C and the INDEX command for more information on ASCII order.)

The SORT ON key fields cannot be logical or memo. If you use a field type other than character, date, or numeric, either *Operation with Logical field invalid* or *Operation with Memo field invalid* is displayed, depending on the type of field that you try to use.

If you exceed the ten fields limitation, the error message *Too many sort key fields* is displayed.

If you are using dBASE III PLUS in a network environment, SORT attempts an automatic file lock unless the database file is already locked (see FLOCK( )) or is opened for exclusive use (see SET EXCLUSIVE, USE). If for any reason the command cannot lock the database file, the error message *File is in use by another* is displayed.

Tips

Unlike most other commands, SORT does not allow a FIELDS list as part of its syntax. See MODIFY STRUCTURE for information on how to eliminate fields from the new file structure.

The SORT command is slow and rarely used in dBASE III PLUS. An index file (see INDEX) is a more efficient manner of ordering a database file since it can make the database file appear in order and easily maintain that order. An index file is preferable to a physically sorted file, in which maintaining the order of the file is almost impossible.

If you are using dBASE III PLUS in a network environment and the database file that you SORT is encrypted (see Protect), the new file is also encrypted unless you SET ENCRYPTION OFF (see SET ENCRYPTION).

SPACE( )

Syntax `SPACE(<expN>)`

Overview The SPACE( ) function accepts a numeric expression as its argument. The function evaluates the expression and returns a character string consisting of the specified number of blank spaces.

Procedure SPACE( ) returns a character string and can be used anywhere in the language where a character expression is appropriate.

Examples SPACE( ) can be used to format displays when you must right-justify character data. This capability is illustrated in the following program which displays five return address labels with the telephone number right justified on the first line of the label. The example prints labels that are forty columns wide and four lines long after prompting you for the necessary information.

```
* RetLabel.PRG
*
SET TALK OFF
SET BELL OFF
STORE SPACE(25) TO name, address, city
state = SPACE(2)
zip = SPACE(5)
phone = SPACE(13)
CLEAR
@ 10, 5 SAY "PLEASE ENTER THE FOLLOWING INFORMATION"
@ 12, 0 SAY "Name:           " GET name
@ 13, 0 SAY "Street address:" GET address
@ 14, 0 SAY "City:           " GET city
@ 15, 0 SAY "State:          " GET state PICTURE "!!"
```

```
@ 16, 0 SAY "Zip Code:          " GET zip PICTURE "99999"
@ 17, 0 SAY "Phone Number:  " GET phone PICTURE "(999)999-9999"
READ
CLEAR
SET PRINTER ON
num_labels = 1
DO WHILE num_labels <= 5
   * The phone number always takes up 13 spaces, so that
   * the left part of the first line must use exactly 27 spaces.
   * The SPACE() function below displays a number of blank
   * spaces based on the length of the name you enter.
   ? TRIM(name) + SPACE(27 - LEN(TRIM(name))) + phone
   ? address
   ? TRIM(city) + ", " + state + "   " + zip
   ?
   num_labels = num_labels + 1
ENDDO
SET PRINTER OFF
CLOSE DATABASES
SET TALK ON
SET BELL ON
```

Warnings

If the function argument evaluates to a data type other than numeric, the error message *Invalid function argument* is displayed.

Tips

SPACE( ) can be used to initialize a memory variable to blanks. This is necessary if you want to use @...GET to enter data into a memory variable, because this command can edit but not create memory variables. The previous example illustrates this technique.

SQRT( )

Syntax `SQRT(<expN>)`

Overview

The SQRT( ) function, short for square root, accepts any numeric expression as its argument. The function evaluates the expression and then returns the square root of that resulting number.

Procedure

The SQRT( ) function returns a number and can be used anywhere in the language where a numeric expression is appropriate.

Examples

The SQRT( ) function can be used whenever you want to obtain the square root of a number. The following routine lists all of the perfect squares between 1 and 100:

```
* Squares.PRG
*
SET TALK OFF
number = 1
? "          x          SQRT(x)"
? "    -----------------------"
DO WHILE number <= 100
   IF SQRT(number) = INT(SQRT(number))
      ? number, SQRT(number)
   ENDIF
   number = number + 1
ENDDO
SET TALK ON
```

To execute this program and see its results,

```
. DO Squares
         x          SQRT(x)
     -----------------------
         1           1.00
         4           2.00
         9           3.00
        16           4.00
        25           5.00
        36           6.00
        49           7.00
        64           8.00
        81           9.00
       100          10.00
```

Warnings

If the function argument evaluates to a data type other than numeric, the error message *Invalid function argument* is displayed.

If the function argument evaluates to a negative number, the error message ****Execution error on SQRT( ) : Negative* is displayed.

Tips

The SQRT( ) function can be applied to itself any number of times to obtain other even roots. For example, SQRT(SQRT(x)) returns the fourth root of the number x, and SQRT(SQRT(SQRT(x))) returns the eighth root of x. To obtain odd roots and even roots that are not a power of two, use the exponentiation operator (^ or **) with a fractional exponent. For example, the third root of the number x is equivalent to x**1/3.

STORE

Syntax

```
STORE <expression> TO <memory variable list>
<memory variable name> = <expression>
```

Overview

The STORE command assigns values to initialize, or give a new value to, one or more memory variables.

To assign a value to a memory variable, you must use an expression to represent the value. The data type of the expression becomes the data type of the memory variable to which you assign it.

You can assign the value to as many memory variables as you want, provided that you do not exceed the maximum command line length of 254 characters or the maximum of 256 memory variables. After the TO keyword, use one or more memory variable names separated by commas.

Memory variables follow the same naming convention as fields (i.e., the name can have a maximum of ten characters). It must begin with a letter, and can contain any combination of letters, digits, and underscores for the remaining nine characters.

The assignment statement, formed by using <memory variable> = <expression>, is a faster way of initializing a memory variable, but it only works for a single memory variable at a time.

Procedure

Use STORE in a program to initialize more than one memory variable using the same value. Otherwise, use the assignment statement to initialize each variable separately.

If SET TALK is ON, the value of the variable is displayed on the screen after it is initialized. SET TALK OFF to suppress this output.

Examples

The following example shows how to use the STORE command and the assignment statement to create memory variables with different data types.

```
. name = "Debby Moody"  && initialize a Character variable
Debby Moody
. STORE 35 TO number1, number2, number3  && create three Numerics
35
. birthday = 12/20/59  && attempt to make a Date variable fails
    0.01
. birthday = CTOD("12/20/59")  && must use CTOD() to make it work
12/20/59
. STORE SUBSTR(name, 1, 5) TO first  && name used to create two
Debby
. STORE SUBSTR(name, 6) TO last      && new Character variables
 Moody
. age = (DATE() - birthday) / 365.00  && Numeric age computed
          27.65
. DISPLAY MEMORY
NAME        pub  C  "Debby Moody"
NUMBER1     pub  N          35  (        35.00000000)
NUMBER2     pub  N          35  (        35.00000000)
NUMBER3     pub  N          35  (        35.00000000)
BIRTHDAY    pub  D  12/20/59
FIRST       pub  C  "Debby"
LAST        pub  C  " Moody"
AGE         pub  N          27.65  (        27.64657534)
    8 variables defined,       73 bytes used
  248 variables available,   5927 bytes available

. CLEAR MEMORY
```

Almost every programming example in this book uses the assignment statement or STORE. (See SEEK for a good example.)

Warnings

STORE does not check to see if the memory variable that you are initializing already exists in memory; as a result, it overwrites existing memory variables without warning. If this concerns you, use TYPE( ) to determine if a memory variable exists. (See TYPE( ) for more information.)

Enclose the string in quotes when initializing a character memory variable with a constant character string; otherwise, the error message *Variable not found* is displayed.

If you make a mistake in naming a memory variable, STORE results in a *Syntax error.*

When naming memory variables, do not give them names that are reserved by dBASE III PLUS for commands and keywords. If you make this mistake, the assignment statement might result in various error messages (depending on the reserved word that you use). Avoid this potential difficulty by prefacing all memory variable names with a prefix such as m_.

dBASE III PLUS allows only 256 variables in memory at a time. If STORE exceeds this limitation, the error message *Out of memory variable slots* is displayed.

The total size of the variables cannot exceed 6,000 bytes. (See Config.DB for information on how to increase the total size limitation, MVARSIZ.) *Out of memory variable memory* indicates that this limitation has been exceeded. Character variables use their length (see LEN( )) plus two bytes; date and numeric variables use nine bytes each, and logicals use two bytes each.

Tips

See ACCEPT, AVERAGE, COUNT, INPUT, PUBLIC, SUM, and WAIT for information on other commands that create memory variables.

See SAVE and RESTORE for information on saving memory variables to a value and retrieving them at a later time.

See RELEASE for information on releasing variables from memory.

To initialize a date memory variable with a constant date value, you must use CTOD( ). (See CTOD( ) for more information.)

When a database file is in use, field names that have the same name as memory variable names take precedence. You can use the prefix, M->, with the memory variable name to override this precedence and access a memory variable with the same name as a field. For example,

```
. USE Mail
. first_name = "Debby"  && Assign first_name memory variable
Debby
. ? first_name  && First_name is also a field in Mail.DBF
MICHELLE
. ? M->first_name  && Using M-> prefix gives memvar value
Debby
. CLOSE DATABASES
```

STR( )

Syntax `STR(<expN> [, <length> [, <decimals>]])`

Overview

The STR( ) function, short for string, is the numeric-to-character conversion function. It requires one argument but accepts up to three. The three arguments are as follows:

- <expN> is a numeric expression representing the number to be converted.
- <length> is an optional numeric expression representing the length of the resulting string. The default value is 10.
- <decimals> is an optional numeric expression representing the number of decimal places to use. If this argument is not specified, no decimal places are returned.

This function converts the number to a character string of specified length containing the digits of the number. Unless the third argument is used, the function only converts the portion of the number before the decimal place. If the third argument is used, the function also converts the decimal point and the specified number of digits following the decimal point. The original number is rounded if necessary.

Procedure

STR( ) returns a character string and can be used anywhere in the language where a character expression is appropriate.

Examples

STR( ) converts numbers to characters, and you can used it with a single command to display text and numbers on the same line. For example, the following routine prints a memo for each employee in the Employee file informing them of a ten percent pay raise:

```
* Raise.PRG
*
SET TALK OFF
SET DEVICE TO PRINTER
USE Employee
DO WHILE .NOT. EOF()
   REPLACE Salary WITH Salary * 1.1
   @  4,20 SAY "M E M O R A N D U M"
   @  6, 0 SAY "To:       " + TRIM(First_Name) + " " + Last_Name
   @  8, 0 SAY "From:     Personnel Department"
   @ 10, 0 SAY "Subject: 10% Pay Raise"
   @ 12, 0 SAY "This is to inform you that you are receiving a " +;
               "10% pay"
   @ 13, 0 SAY "raise.  Your new salary is " +;
               LTRIM(STR(Salary, 10,2)) + "."
   SKIP
ENDDO
CLOSE DATABASES
EJECT
SET DEVICE TO SCREEN
SET TALK OFF
```

To execute this program, type `DO Raise`. A sample of the printed output is shown in Figure 91.

Warnings

If any of the function arguments evaluates to a data type other than what is expected, the error message *Invalid function argument* is displayed.

```
                    M E M O R A N D U M
To:       MICHELLE SMITH
From:     Personnel Department
Subject: 10% Pay Raise
This is to inform you that you are receiving a 10% pay
raise.  Your new salary is 47577.52.
```

Figure 91

If either of the numeric expressions evaluates to a number other than an integer, the numbers after the decimal place are truncated before the STR( ) is executed.

STR( ) returns a null string if the length argument evaluates to zero.

The length argument must evaluate to a number between zero and 19, and the decimals between zero and 16, inclusive. Furthermore, the number of decimals must always be less than the specified length; otherwise, the error message ***Execution error on STR( ) : Out of range* is displayed.

If the length argument is −1, the function behaves as if the argument were omitted.

If the number has more digits than the specified length, STR( ) attempts to truncate the decimal places to fit in the specified width. For larger numbers, the function attempts to use scientific notation. If neither of these solutions works, the function results in a character string of asterisks, which is the indicator of a numeric overflow condition.

STUFF( )

Syntax `STUFF(<string>, <begin>, <remove>, <insert>)`

Overview The STUFF( ) function is used to insert, or stuff, characters into an existing character string. In addition to specifying the original character string and the character string to be inserted, the function must specify where the insertion is to begin and how many characters, if any, are to be removed from the original string when the insertion takes place. The STUFF( ) function requires four arguments:

- <string> is a character expression representing the original character string.
- <begin> is a numeric expression representing the position in the original string where insertion is to begin.
- <remove> is a numeric expression representing the number of characters to be removed from the original string.
- <insert> is a character expression representing the new string to be inserted into the original string.

Beginning at the specified position, the function removes the designated number of characters from the original string, inserts the new string starting in that same position, and returns the resulting string.

Procedure

STUFF( ) returns a character string and can be used anywhere in the language where a character expression is appropriate.

Examples

STUFF( ) replaces a substring of characters in a field or memory variable. For example, suppose "outstanding" has been consistently misspelled as "oustanding" in the Comment field of your Employee file. You can correct this problem using the following routine:

```
* Misspell.PRG
SET TALK OFF
USE Employee
wrong = "oustanding"
correct = "outstanding"
length = LEN(wrong)
DO WHILE .NOT. EOF()
   DO WHILE wrong $ Comment
      start = AT(wrong, Comment)
      REPLACE Comment WITH ;
      STUFF(SUBSTR(Comment, 1, 253), start, length, correct)
   ENDDO
   SKIP
ENDDO
CLOSE DATABASES
SET TALK ON
```

To demonstrate the result of this program on the Employee database file, the number of occurrences of "oustanding" is counted before and after the program is executed.

```
. USE Employee
. COUNT FOR "oustanding" $ Comment
     2 records
. DO Misspell
. USE Employee
. COUNT FOR "oustanding" $ Comment
No records
. CLOSE DATABASES
```

Warnings If any of the function arguments evaluate to a data type other than what is expected, the error message *Invalid function argument* is displayed.

If the function results in the error message *Variable not found*, you probably used a literal character string as either the first or the last function argument, and it is being interpreted as a variable name. The character string, in this case, must be enclosed in single quotes, double quotes, or square brackets.

If either of the numeric expressions evaluates to a number other than an integer, the numbers after the decimal place are truncated before STUFF( ) is executed.

If the numeric expression representing the starting position evaluates to a number less than 1, the function behaves as if the number were 1.

If the numeric expression representing the number of characters to remove evaluates to a number that is less than zero, the function behaves as if the number were zero.

Tips STUFF( ) removes characters from a string if you specify a null string as the last argument to the function.

To insert the new string without overwriting any characters in the original string, use zero as the third function argument.

To overlay the new string by overwriting characters in the original string, use LEN(<new string>) as the third function argument.

SUBSTR( )

Syntax `SUBSTR(<expC>, <begin> [, <length>])`

Overview The SUBSTR( ) function, short for substring, extracts a subset of the characters from a given string. The function takes either two or three arguments:

- <expC> is a character expression representing the original character string.
- <start> is a numeric expression representing the starting position of the substring in the original string.

- <length> is a numeric expression representing the number of characters to be extracted from the original string (i.e., the length of the resulting substring). This argument is optional; if it is not used the substring extraction continues to the end of the original string.

This function returns a substring that begins in the starting position of the original string. The length of the substring is either specified by the third function argument or is determined by the length of the original string.

Procedure

SUBSTR( ) returns a character string and can be used anywhere in the language where a character expression is appropriate.

Examples

SUBSTR( ) works with portions of an existing string. Suppose that you designed your mailing list with a single field to hold the entire name, and you have now decided to split up the name into two fields (one for the first name and the other for the last name). First, use MODIFY STRUCTURE to add two fields called First_Name and Last_Name to the mailing list file. Assuming that the original names were entered with one space between the first and last name (omitting titles and middle initials), you could split up the Name field with the following routine:

```
* NameSplt.PRG
*
SET TALK OFF
USE Mail
* The SUBSTR() function is used to split up the Name field
* into first and last name.
REPLACE ALL First_Name WITH SUBSTR(Name, 1, AT(" ", Name))
REPLACE ALL Last_Name WITH SUBSTR(Name, AT(" ", Name) + 1)
CLOSE DATABASES
SET TALK ON
```

To clearly demonstrate the effect of this program on the Mail database file, the Name field is listed, and the First_Name and Last_Name field are blanked out before the program is executed.

```
. USE Mail
. LIST OFF Name
 Name
 MICHELLE SMITH
 Rebecca Corbbit
 Gloria Roman
 David Gurly
 Julia King
 Perry Lester
 Cathy Moore
 Doug Smith
 Wade Adams
 Sandy Richardson
 VELMA MOODY
 Mala Schaefer
 Lawrence Arthur
 Nancy Long
 Jeff Potter
 Linda Roberts
 Jerry Samuels
 Chris Whiteside

. REPLACE ALL First_Name WITH SPACE(12), Last_Name WITH SPACE(20)
    18 records replaced
. CLOSE DATABASES
```

When the program is executed, the first and last names in the Name field are successfully split up into two fields.

```
. DO NameSplt
. USE Mail
. LIST OFF First_Name, Last_Name
 First_Name   Last_Name
 MICHELLE     SMITH
 Rebecca      Corbbit
 Gloria       Roman
 David        Gurly
 Julia        King
 Perry        Lester
 Cathy        Moore
 Doug         Smith
```

```
Wade          Adams
Sandy         Richardson
VELMA         MOODY
Mala          Schaefer
Lawrence      Arthur
Nancy         Long
Jeff          Potter
Linda         Roberts
Jerry         Samuels
Chris         Whiteside

. CLOSE DATABASES
```

Warnings

If a function argument evaluates to a data type other than what is expected, the error message *Invalid function argument* is displayed.

If either of the numeric expressions evaluates to a number other than an integer, the numbers after the decimal place are truncated before the SUBSTR( ) is executed.

The error message ****Execution error on SUBSTR( ) : Start point out of range* occurs if the starting position argument is either negative or larger than the length of the original string.

SUBSTR( ) returns a null string if either of the numeric arguments is zero. It also returns a null string if the third argument is less than or equal to −2.

If the third argument is −1, the function behaves as if the argument were omitted.

Tips

LEFT( ) and RIGHT( ) are special case substring functions that can be used as shortcuts.

SUM

Syntax

```
SUM [<scope>] [WHILE <condition>] [FOR <condition>]
[<expN list>] [TO <memory variable list>]
```

Overview

The SUM command computes the total, or sum, of one or more numbers by processing a specified set of records in the active database file. If this command is issued when there is no file in use in the current work area, you are prompted to enter the name of a database file. The sum is computed by taking a running total of each numeric field.

The result of the command is displayed on the screen with headings if both SET HEADING and SET TALK are ON. SET HEADING OFF suppresses the field name headings, and SET TALK OFF completely suppresses the screen output of the SUM command.

In its simplest form (i.e., no command line arguments are specified), SUM calculates the sum of all numeric fields for each record in the active database file.

A scope, a FOR clause, and a WHILE clause can be specified to limit the records which are processed. Each of these command line options is discussed separately. (See Scope, FOR, and WHILE.) The default scope of the SUM command is all records.

The expression list limits the fields and specifies more complicated numbers to be totaled. If used, the list must consist of one or more numeric expressions separated by commas.

The result of SUM can be saved in one or more memory variables using the TO clause. Items in the list must be separated by commas.

Procedure

Use SUM to compute the total of one or more fields in the active database file. The result is displayed if SET TALK is ON and can be saved in one or more memory variables for later use.

Examples

The following example relates the Orders and Inventry files on Part_No, then computes the total price of all orders using an expression involving a field from each file:

```
. SET TALK OFF
. USE Orders
. SELECT 2
. USE Inventry INDEX Part_No
. SELECT 1
. SET RELATION TO Part_No INTO Inventry
. SUM Quantity * Inventry->Price TO totprice
. ? totprice
      227.84
. CLOSE DATABASES
. SET TALK ON
```

Warnings If the number of memory variables listed in the TO clause does not match the number of numbers to be totaled (i.e., the number of expressions in the list or the number of numeric fields in the database file), *Syntax error* is displayed.

If an expression in the expression list evaluates to a data type other than numeric, the error message *Not a numeric expression* is displayed.

If you misspell a field name or include a memory variable that has not been initialized in the expression list, the error message *Variable not found* is displayed.

If you are using dBASE III PLUS in a network environment, SUM attempts an automatic file lock unless the database file is already locked (see FLOCK( )) or is opened for exclusive use (see SET EXCLUSIVE, USE). If for any reason, the command cannot lock the database file, the error message *File is in use by another* is displayed.

Tips dBASE III PLUS also has an AVERAGE command to compute the arithmetic mean of one or more numbers. AVERAGE and SUM are the only statistical functions available in the command language at the time of this writing. (See SET PROCEDURE for an example that calculates a few other statistical values.)

SUSPEND

Syntax `SUSPEND`

Overview The SUSPEND command is used to stop temporarily the execution of a program file for debugging purposes. If SET ESCAPE is ON, a program can also be suspended by pressing the Esc key and typing S when prompted to *Cancel, Ignore, or Suspend? (C, I, or S)*. This same prompt is presented if any command in a program is in error. The program will be suspended as if you had pressed Esc.

When a program is suspended, the message *Do suspended* is displayed. This message cannot be suppressed with SET TALK OFF.

Procedure When debugging a program, you may occasionally want to SUSPEND it to the dot prompt to check the values of certain variables and perhaps also to check the contents of the history buffer. (See SET DOHISTORY.)

Insert SUSPEND in a program following the commands that you suspect are causing the problem. When SUSPEND is executed, you are presented with the dot prompt with all files and variables intact as they were established by the program. At the dot prompt, use commands such as LIST MEMORY, LIST HISTORY, and LIST STATUS to determine if the program is proceeding correctly.

If SET ESCAPE is ON, you can interrupt the program at any point by pressing the Esc key and typing S when prompted to *Cancel, Ignore, or Suspend? (C, I, or S)*. This puts you at the dot prompt in suspend mode just as if you had issued SUSPEND.

If an error is encountered for any command in the program file, the *Cancel, Ignore, or Suspend? (C, I, or S)* prompt is displayed as part of the error message dialogue. Typing S puts you at the dot prompt in suspend mode just as if you had issued SUSPEND.

If you find that you want to make a program change while at the dot prompt in suspend mode, issue CANCEL to terminate the suspend mode and close all program files. (Database, index, format, and procedure files remain open until you close them with the appropriate CLOSE command.) Otherwise, issue RESUME (see RESUME) to continue program execution.

Remove all SUSPEND commands from the program file when you finish debugging the program.

Examples

In the following example, a program is suspended due to an error in one of the commands that results from an uninitialized memory variable. The program displays and counts the zip codes in the mailing list that begin with the digit 9 and displays the total count of these zip codes.

```
* ZipCode.PRG
*
SET TALK OFF
USE Mail INDEX Zip
SEEK "9"
DO WHILE Zip = "9"
   zipcount = zipcount + 1
   ? Zip
   SKIP
ENDDO
?
?
? "Total: " + LTRIM(STR(zipcount))
```

```
CLOSE DATABASES
SET TALK ON
```

If you execute this program, an error is encountered on the command zipcount = zipcount + 1 because the memory variable, zipcount, is never initialized. Your screen should look like this:

```
. DO ZipCode
Variable not found.
                           ?
  zipcount = zipcount + 1
Called from - C:ZipCode.prg
Cancel, Ignore, or Suspend? (C, I, or S)
```

If you respond by typing S, you can correct the error and continue with the program:

```
Variable not found.
                           ?
  zipcount = zipcount + 1
Called from - C:ZipCode.prg
Cancel, Ignore, or Suspend? (C, I, or S) Suspend
Do suspended
. DISPLAY MEMORY  && No memory variables show up
    0 variables defined,        0 bytes used
  256 variables available,   6000 bytes available

. zipcount = 1  && initialize to 1 - one record already processed
. RESUME        && and resume the program.
90029
90029
90038
90042
90043
90069
94033
94315
98230

Total: 9
```

This is only a temporary solution. To correct the program, you must insert the command zipcount = 0 before the DO WHILE command. You can use MODIFY COMMAND to make this change. The new version of the program should look like the one below:

```
* ZipCode.PRG
*
SET TALK OFF
USE Mail INDEX Zip
SEEK "9"
zipcount = 0
DO WHILE Zip = "9"
   zipcount = zipcount + 1
   ? Zip
   SKIP
ENDDO
??
? "Total: " + LTRIM(STR(zipcount))
CLOSE DATABASES
SET TALK ON
```

Warnings If you attempt to use MODIFY COMMAND to change a suspended program, the error message *File is already open* is displayed. Cancel the suspended program (see CANCEL) before attempting to make changes to it. Use CLOSE PROCEDURE if you are using a procedure file.

Tips See SET DEBUG, SET DOHISTORY, SET ECHO, and SET STEP for information about other debugging commands available in dBASE III PLUS.

TEXT

Syntax

```
TEXT
   <text>
ENDTEXT
```

Overview The TEXT command is part of a program construct in dBASE III PLUS referred to as TEXT...ENDTEXT. This construct allows you to display with ease large blocks of text on the screen without quoting the text or using any other display commands.

Procedure

The TEXT...ENDTEXT construct is designed for use in programs only. You cannot use it at the dot prompt.

In a program, use TEXT to begin displaying text. On the following lines, type the text where you want it to appear on the screen. Do not put the text in quotes unless you want the quote marks to appear on the screen. Put a carriage return at the end of each line of text to keep it from wrapping around. Lines that you allow to wrap will also wrap on the screen. Place ENDTEXT on the line following the last line of text.

When you execute the program and TEXT is encountered, all lines following this command are displayed on the screen until ENDTEXT is encountered. Blank lines and leading spaces are displayed, and lines of text that are too wide for the screen wrap around. If there are more lines of text than will fit on a single screen, the text scrolls up the screen. If SET PRINTER is ON, the text is also printed.

Examples

The following example uses the TEXT...ENDTEXT construct to display a menu:

```
* TextMenu.PRG
*
SET TALK OFF
DO WHILE .T.
   CLEAR

   * Menu is displayed using TEXT...ENDTEXT construct
   TEXT

          0 - Exit
          1 - Add Records
          2 - Edit Records
          3 - Print Reports

   ENDTEXT

   choice = 0
```

```
* The user is prompted for a value between zero and three
@ 11, 0 SAY "Enter your selection";
     GET choice PICTURE "9" RANGE 0, 3
READ

* The users response is evaluated in order to determine
* what to do next.
DO CASE

   CASE choice = 0
      SET TALK ON
      RETURN

   CASE choice = 1
      DO Add_Recs

   CASE choice = 2
      DO EditRecs

   CASE choice = 3
      DO PrtRprts

  ENDCASE
ENDDO
```

Warnings If you issue TEXT at the dot prompt, the error message *Valid only in programs* is displayed.

Tips To print the text in a TEXT...ENDTEXT construct without displaying it on the screen, SET PRINTER ON and SET CONSOLE OFF before TEXT. After ENDTEXT, SET PRINTER OFF and SET CONSOLE ON.

TIME( )

Syntax `TIME()`

Overview The TIME( ) function has no arguments. The function returns the system time as a character string of the form "hh:mm:ss", where hh is hours, mm is minutes, and ss is seconds.

Procedure

TIME( ) returns a character string and can be used anywhere in the language where a character expression is appropriate.

Examples

TIME( ) can be used to do benchmark tests. Benchmark tests are useful when there are several ways of accomplishing the same task and you want to know which way is faster. For example, the following routine uses LIST and a DO WHILE .NOT. EOF( ) loop to display the contents of the Customer file. TIME( ) is calculated before and after each routine and the elapsed times are computed and displayed at the end of the routine.

```
* Benchmrk.PRG
*
SET TALK OFF
USE Customer
beg_list = TIME()
LIST First_Name, Last_Name
end_list = TIME()
GO TOP
beg_do = TIME()
DO WHILE .NOT. EOF()
   ? First_Name, Last_Name
   SKIP
ENDDO
end_do = TIME()
* The elapsed time is calculated by converting the starting
* and ending times to seconds, and subtracting.
ltime = VAL(SUBSTR(end_list, 1)) * 3600 +;
        VAL(SUBSTR(end_list, 4)) * 60 +;
        VAL(SUBSTR(end_list, 7)) -;
        VAL(SUBSTR(beg_list, 1)) * 3600 +;
        VAL(SUBSTR(beg_list, 4)) * 60 +;
        VAL(SUBSTR(beg_list, 7))
dtime = VAL(SUBSTR(end_do, 1)) * 3600 +;
        VAL(SUBSTR(end_do, 4)) * 60 +;
        VAL(SUBSTR(end_do, 7)) -;
        VAL(SUBSTR(beg_do, 1)) * 3600 +;
        VAL(SUBSTR(beg_do, 4)) * 60 +;
        VAL(SUBSTR(beg_do, 7))
? "The LIST took " + LTRIM(STR(ltime)) + " seconds."
? "The DO WHILE took " + LTRIM(STR(dtime)) + " seconds."
CLOSE DATABASES
SET TALK ON
```

You can decide which method is faster by comparing the screen output of the elapsed times.

Warnings

Because of its simple syntax, there are no error messages associated with TIME( ).

Tips

Note that although there is a separate data type for dates, there is not a time data type; therefore, there are no built-in capabilities for doing time arithmetic. Consequently, some fairly complicated routines are necessary to extract the components of the time and to convert the components to numbers.

To compute the elapsed time between two times, convert both times to seconds and subtract them using the following formula:

```
elapse = VAL(SUBSTR(end, 1)) * 3600 +;
         VAL(SUBSTR(end, 4)) * 60 +;
         VAL(SUBSTR(end, 7)) -;
         VAL(SUBSTR(start, 1)) * 3600 +;
         VAL(SUBSTR(start, 4)) * 60 +;
         VAL(SUBSTR(start, 7))
```

TOTAL

Syntax

```
TOTAL ON <key fieldname> TO <filename>
[FIELDS <field list>] [<scope>] [WHILE <condition>]
[FOR <condition>]
```

Overview

The TOTAL command adds together the numeric fields in the active database file based on the value of a specified key field and stores the result in a new database file.

When the command is executed, the TO database file is created with a structure that is identical to the active database file (excluding all memo fields), and a record is added to the file for the first set of totals. The contents of all fields not being totaled is written to this record, and then the totaling process begins. For each record processed, a running total is kept for each numeric field until the value of the ON key field name changes. At this point, the totals are written to the TO database file. This process is repeated for each new key field value encountered until the end of the active database file is encountered.

A scope, a FOR clause, and a WHILE clause can be specified to limit the records which are processed. Each of these command line options is discussed separately. (See Scope, FOR, and WHILE.) Unless one of these clauses is specified, all records in the active database file are totaled.

If no FIELDS phrase is specified, the resulting file contains totals for all numeric fields in the active database file. Specifying a FIELDS list limits the numeric fields that are totaled but does not affect the structure of the resulting database file. All fields in the active database file are included in the structure of the resulting database file. (See FIELDS for more information.)

TOTAL displays the number of records totaled and the number of records written to the new file if SET TALK is ON. SET TALK OFF suppresses this screen output.

Procedure

In order to TOTAL a database file, the file must be open in the current work area (see USE) and should be in order according to the key field (see INDEX, SORT) that you intend to TOTAL ON. Otherwise, the resulting totaled database file will contain more than a single record for some of the keys in the file. The key field cannot be a logical or a memo field. It must be character, date, or numeric.

Once the file is open and in order, issue TOTAL. The ON <key fieldname> and TO <filename> phrases must be specified, but all others are optional. If you want to total all numeric fields in the entire file, do not specify any of the optional phrases. Use a FIELDS list to limit the numeric fields that are totaled and use a scope, WHILE, and/or FOR clause to limit the records that are processed by TOTAL.

Once TOTAL has executed, the original file remains in use. To view the contents of the new database file, USE the file and CLOSE DATABASES to close all of the files when you are done.

Examples

In the following example, TOTAL builds a database file that contains a single record for each part number that has been ordered:

```
. USE Orders INDEX O_PartNo
. TOTAL ON Part_No TO OrdTotal
      4 Record(s) totalled
      3 Records generated
. USE OrdTotal
. LIST
Record#  CUST_NO PART_NO   QUANTITY
      1  F126    B-254            2
      2  A452    G-165            2
      3  A254    R-123            2
```

In the example given above where the Orders file was totaled, the Cust_No field is a part of the resulting database file but is not pertinent because the information about the customer's order is lost. TOTAL has no way of limiting the fields that are written to the file, but it has a FIELDS list as part of its syntax and, therefore, respects a SET FIELDS list if one is in effect. (See SET FIELDS.) The above example could be improved by using the following commands:

```
. USE Orders INDEX O_PartNo
. SET FIELDS TO Part_No, Quantity
. TOTAL ON Part_No TO OrdTotal
      4 Record(s) totalled
      3 Records generated
. USE OrdTotal
. LIST
Record#  PART_NO   QUANTITY
      1  B-254            2
      2  G-165            2
      3  R-123            2
. CLOSE DATABASES
```

Warnings If a resulting total is larger than its field size, the result is a numeric overflow (i.e. asterisks in the field) in the new database file; the error message *Numeric overflow (data was lost)* is displayed. MODIFY STRUCTURE to enlarge numeric fields to their maximum potential size before using TOTAL.

If you include a non-numeric field in the FIELDS list of the TOTAL command, the error message *Data type mismatch* is displayed. This same error message occurs if the key field name that you TOTAL ON is a logical or a memo field. You can only TOTAL ON a character, date, or numeric field.

The error message *File is already open* indicates that the TO database file is open in another work area. Close the file (see USE) and try TOTAL again.

If you are using dBASE III PLUS in a network environment, TOTAL attempts an automatic file lock unless the database file is already locked (see FLOCK( )) or is opened for exclusive use (see SET EXCLUSIVE, USE). If for any reason the command cannot lock the database file, the error message *File is in use by another* is displayed.

Tips

See SUM for information about obtaining totals for numeric fields without saving the result in a database file. TOTAL does not allow you to obtain totals based on an expression that is more complicated than a single field name. For example, suppose that the Orders file contained several records for each customer, and that some customers order the same item several different times. You may want to see a total based on the Part_No field within the Cust_No field (i.e., the key would be Cust_No + Part_No). The following program accomplishes this using SUM instead of TOTAL:

```
OrdTotal.PRG
SET TALK OFF

USE Orders INDEX CustPart    && Index key is Cust_No + Part_No
COPY STRUCTURE TO OrdTotal   && Set up the structure for totals

* Open the OrdTotal file in another work area to record the
* totals as they are computed.
SELECT 2
USE OrdTotal

SELECT Orders

DO WHILE .NOT. EOF()

   * Before the SUM is computed, the customer and part number
   * fields are placed in the total file.  This is because once
   * the SUM command is complete, the record pointer will be
   * positioned on the next key value.
   SELECT OrdTotal
   APPEND BLANK
   REPLACE Cust_No WITH Orders->Cust_No, ;
           Part_No WITH Orders->Part_No
```

```
    * Go back to the Orders file and compute the total for the
    * first group of keys.  Save the result in a memvar so that
    * it can be used to update the total file.
    SELECT Orders
    key = Cust_No + Part_No
    SUM WHILE Cust_No + Part_No = key TO m_quantity

    * Select the total file to put in the total quantity.
    SELECT OrdTotal
    REPLACE Quantity WITH m_quantity

    * Go back to the Orders file to continue the process.
    SELECT Orders

ENDDO

* List the contents of the total file.
SELECT OrdTotal
LIST

SET TALK ON
CLOSE DATABASES
```

This program is not illustrative with the Orders database file that we are using because there are no two records with the same customer and part number; however, you can add more data to the file in order to demonstrate the program. You can see the result by adding another record for customer F126 ordering three more of part number B-254 and one for customer A452 ordering one more of part number G-165.

```
. DO OrdTotal
Record#  CUST_NO PART_NO   QUANTITY
      1  A254    R-123            1
      2  A452    G-165            3
      3  A452    R-123            1
      4  F126    B-254            5
```

If you are using dBASE III PLUS in a network environment and the database file that you TOTAL is encrypted (see Protect), the new file is also encrypted unless you SET ENCRYPTION OFF (see SET ENCRYPTION).

TRANSFORM( )

Syntax `TRANSFORM(<expression>, <expC>)`

Overview

The TRANSFORM( ) function converts dates, numbers, character strings, and logical values to formatted character strings. It requires two arguments:

- A date, numeric, character, or logical expression. The result of this expression is converted to the character string that is formatted.
- A character expression which represents an @...SAY PICTURE clause. (See PICTURE for a complete explanation of PICTURE clauses.)

TRANSFORM( ) returns a character string equivalent to what @...SAY would display using the same PICTURE clause.

Procedure

TRANSFORM( ) returns a character string and can be used anywhere in the language where a character expression is appropriate.

Examples

This function is useful when you want to format the output of the LIST or ? commands. The following routine lists the Last_Name and the Salary of all the employees in the Employee file. The output is formatted using TRANSFORM( ).

```
* Salaries.PRG
*
SET HEADINGS OFF
SET TALK OFF
USE Employee
LIST TRANSFORM(Last_Name,"@!"), TRANSFORM(Salary,"$,$$$,$$$.99")
CLOSE DATABASES
SET TALK ON
SET HEADINGS ON
```

Notice that the example uses a PICTURE function for Last_Name and a template for Salary. To execute this program and see its results,

```
. DO Salaries
     1  SMITH                   $$$43,252.29
     2  CORBBIT                 $$$38,712.23
     3  ROMAN                   $$$43,712.00
     4  KING                    $$$25,003.23
     5  MOORE                   $$$27,832.12
     6  RICHARDSON              $$123,000.00
     7  MOODY                   $$250,000.00
     8  SCHAEFER                $$$21,987.33
     9  LONG                    $$$57,612.12
    10  ROBERTS                 $$$53,137.77
```

Warnings

If any of the function arguments evaluate to a data type other than what is expected, the error message *Invalid function argument* is displayed.

Like @...SAY, TRANSFORM( ) cannot be used with a memo field. If you attempt to use a memo field with this function, the error message *Operation with a Memo field invalid* is displayed.

If a literal character string is used for the PICTURE portion of TRANSFORM( ), it must be quoted using single quotes, double quotes, or square brackets. If the function results in *Syntax error* or *Variable not found*, the error message is most likely caused by the omission of quotes or brackets.

Tips

You can use TRANSFORM( ) to customize the output of a REPORT FORM (created with CREATE REPORT). However, if it is used to format a number, you will be unable to total that number since TRANSFORM( ) converts it to a character string.

TRIM( )

Syntax `TRIM|RTRIM(<expC>)`

Overview

The TRIM( ) function accepts a character expression as its argument. The function evaluates the expression to obtain the resulting character string and then returns that character string without any trailing blank spaces.

RTRIM( ), short for right trim, is an alternative function name for TRIM( ).

Procedure

TRIM( ) returns a character string and can be used anywhere in the language where a character expression is appropriate.

Examples

TRIM( ) can be used to format the display of a list of character fields that are to appear on the same line. Since the contents of a character field seldom occupies the entire field length, using this function prevents the display of the extra blank spaces. For example, to list the First_Name and Last_Name fields from your mailing list database, you might try the following commands:

```
. USE Mail
. LIST OFF First_Name, Last_Name
 First_Name   Last_Name
 MICHELLE     SMITH
 Rebecca      Corbbit
 Gloria       Roman
 David        Gurly
 Julia        King
 Perry        Lester
 Cathy        Moore
 Doug         Smith
 Wade         Adams
 Sandy        Richardson
 VELMA        MOODY
 Mala         Schaefer
 Lawrence     Arthur
 Nancy        Long
 Jeff         Potter
 Linda        Roberts
 Jerry        Samuels
 Chris        Whiteside
```

Using TRIM( ) makes a much cleaner display:

```
. LIST OFF TRIM(First_Name) + " " + Last_Name
TRIM(First_Name) + " " + Last_Name
MICHELLE SMITH
Rebecca Corbbit
Gloria Roman
David Gurly
Julia King
Perry Lester
Cathy Moore
Doug Smith
Wade Adams
Sandy Richardson
VELMA MOODY
Mala Schaefer
Lawrence Arthur
Nancy Long
Jeff Potter
Linda Roberts
Jerry Samuels
Chris Whiteside
```

Warnings If the function argument evaluates to a data type other than character, the error message *Invalid function argument* is displayed.

Tips TRIM( ) can be applied to LTRIM( ) to trim all leading and trailing blank spaces from a character string (i.e., TRIM(LTRIM(<expc>))).

To determine if a string is empty, compare its TRIM( ) with a null character, produced by placing two matching quote marks together. The null must appear on the left side of the relational operator.

```
IF "" = TRIM(string)
   <commands>
ENDIF
```

TYPE

Syntax `TYPE <filename> [TO PRINTER]`

Overview The TYPE command displays the contents of an ASCII text file on the screen or the printer. By default, the file listing is displayed on the screen; use the TO PRINTER option to print it. The file that you TYPE cannot be open when you issue this command.

Procedure TYPE is most often used with the TO PRINTER option to obtain a printed copy of dBASE III PLUS programs and format files. You must specify the extension as part of the file name because TYPE does not assume one.

You can also TYPE label and report text files that were created using the TO FILE command line option. (See LABEL FORM, REPORT FORM.) Typing these files with the TO PRINTER option prints the report or the labels just as REPORT FORM TO PRINTER or LABEL FORM TO PRINTER would have.

Examples The following example prints the MailEdit format file. The printout looks like the one you see in Figure 92.

```
.TYPE MailEdit.FMT TO PRINTER
```

```
@  2, 19 SAY "M A I L I N G   L I S T   C H A N G E S"
@  6,  3 SAY "Name"
@  6, 11 GET  First_Name
@  6, 25 GET  Last_Name
@  6, 59 SAY "Phone"
@  6, 65 GET  Phone PICTURE "(999)999-9999"
@  7, 13 SAY "(first)           (last)                        Birthday"
@  7, 68 GET  Birthday
@  9,  3 SAY "Address"
@  9, 11 GET  Address1
@ 10, 14 SAY "(street or post office box)"
@ 11, 11 GET  Address2
@ 12, 20 SAY "(apartment #)"
@ 13, 11 GET  City
@ 13, 44 GET  State PICTURE "@A !!"
@ 13, 51 GET  Zip PICTURE "99999"
@ 14, 23 SAY "(city)                 (state)  (zip)"
@  3, 17 TO  3, 59
```

Figure 92

Warnings The file that you TYPE cannot be open when you issue this command. If you get the error message *File is already open*, close the file and try again. (See CANCEL and CLOSE for information on how to close program, alternate, format, and procedure files.)

When using the TO PRINTER option, make sure the printer is turned on and on-line to avoid printer errors.

Attempting to TYPE a binary file such as dBASE.EXE results in a meaningless display of characters.

Tips You can use TYPE to show the contents of any text file, including alternate files. (See SET ALTERNATE.) TYPE, however, is not useful for listing non-text files such as database files, memo files, and index files.

TYPE( )

Syntax `TYPE(<expC>)`

Overview The TYPE( ) function accepts any character expression as its argument. The function evaluates the expression and then returns the type of the expression represented by that character string.

The result of TYPE( ) is always a single uppercase letter. Its value is "C" for a character expression, "N" for a numeric expression, "D" for a date expression, "L" for a logical expression, "M" for a memo field, and "U" if the expression is undefined.

Procedure TYPE( ) returns a character value, and can be used anywhere in the language where a character expression is appropriate.

Examples TYPE( ) is used to ensure that dBASE III PLUS can evaluate an expression before using that expression as part of another command or function. For example, suppose that you want to prompt the user for a filter condition. In order to make sure that the condition entered is a logical expression, you could use the following routine:

```
* UDfilter.PRG
* This program lets the User Define a filter condition.
* Assumes an open database file.
```

```
ACCEPT "Enter a filter condition for the " + DBF() + " file: ";
       TO condition
IF TYPE(condition) = "L"
   SET FILTER TO &condition
ELSE
   ? "The formula entered is not a logical expression."
ENDIF
RETURN
```

This routine assumes that a database file is in USE in the active work area. To activate the routine either from a program or from the dot prompt, use the following command:

```
DO UDfilter
```

Warnings

If the function argument evaluates to a data type other than character, the error message *Invalid function argument* is displayed.

If the function unexpectedly results in a U, you probably used a literal character string as the function argument. The function argument must be a character expression (i.e., a literal character string enclosed in single quotes, double quotes, or square brackets.)

Tips

Use TYPE( ) to determine whether a memory variable is initialized or not. If it is not initialized, TYPE( ) returns a "U"; otherwise, TYPE( ) returns a valid data type. Remember to enclose the memory variable name in quotes when using it with TYPE( ) (e.g., TYPE("m_name")).

UNLOCK

Syntax `UNLOCK [ALL]`

Overview

The UNLOCK command releases file and record locks. (See FLOCK( ), RLOCK( ).) UNLOCK without a parameter releases the lock in the current work area (i.e., either the file or record lock, since there can only be one in effect at a time). Locks for related database files are also released. (See SET RELATION.)

There can be unrelated locks in different work areas. UNLOCK ALL releases all locks in all work areas with a single command.

Procedure UNLOCK is used in network programs that use file and/or record locking. When you no longer need the lock to do your work, use this command to release it so that other users can proceed with any desired changes.

Examples See RLOCK( ) and FLOCK( ) for two examples that use UNLOCK.

Warnings Remember to release locks on a particular database file; in a network environment, most database files are shared by many users, one of whom may be waiting to obtain a file lock.

Tips Other commands that close database files (see CLOSE, CLEAR ALL, USE, and QUIT) also release file and record locks.

UPDATE

Syntax

```
UPDATE ON <key fieldname> FROM <alias name> [RANDOM]
REPLACE <fieldname> WITH <expression>
[, <fieldname> WITH <expression>...]
```

Overview The UPDATE command replaces fields in the active database file with data from another database file based on the value of a specified key field.

When UPDATE is executed, each record in the active database file is processed with one exception: if there is more than one record with the same index key field value in the file, only the first record with a given key is processed, and the rest are ignored. The update process for a record is to REPLACE the specified field names with values for each record in the FROM file with a matching key field value. Multiple occurrences of the same key field value in the FROM file are processed as part of UPDATE.

UPDATE displays the number of records updated if SET TALK is ON. SET TALK OFF suppresses this screen output.

Procedure To UPDATE successfully, the database file to be updated must be open in the current work area (see USE) and must be in order according to the key field (see INDEX, SORT) that you intend to UPDATE ON. The key field must be character, date, or numeric, and must have the same field name as the one in the file you intend to UPDATE FROM.

Once the file that you are going to update is open and in order, open the file that you are going to UPDATE FROM in another work area. This file may or may not be in order according to the key field. (See SET INDEX, SET ORDER.) A different form of UPDATE is used depending on whether or not the FROM file is in order.

When both files are open, activate the one you want to update (see SELECT), and issue UPDATE. The ON key field name is the name of the field by which the active database file is ordered and also the name of the field that is common to both database files. Specify the FROM file using its alias name. (See Alias.)

If the FROM file is not in order, the active database file must have as its controlling index (see SET INDEX, SET ORDER) a file whose key is the ON key field name; in this circumstance, you must use the RANDOM keyword with UPDATE.

In other situations, the active database file must still be in order according to the key field, but can either be indexed or sorted (see INDEX, SORT) and you must not use RANDOM. Execution of UPDATE is faster if you do not have to use the RANDOM keyword.

Use the REPLACE keyword with a list of fields whose values you want to update. You must specify at least one REPLACE field in order for UPDATE to be syntactically correct. This keyword operates like REPLACE (see REPLACE), except that UPDATE has its own method for deciding which records should be updated and under what circumstances. The WITH expression must be the same data type as the field it is replacing, and it is usually a field in the FROM file. Be sure to use the <alias> - > <fieldname> form for fields in the FROM file that you specify in the WITH expression.

Once UPDATE has executed, the updated file and the FROM file both remain in use. When you are finished with these files, use CLOSE DATABASES to close them.

Examples

In the following example, UPDATE is used to reduce the Quantity on hand field in the Inventry database file by the Quantity ordered which comes from the Orders database file. In this example, the RANDOM keyword is used because the Orders file is not in order. Although the UPDATE command wraps around in the screen below, do not press Enter until you type the entire command.

```
. USE Inventry INDEX Part_No
. LIST Part_No, Quantity
Record#  Part_No    Quantity
      2  B-254             5
      4  B-735            15
      5  BL861             3
      3  BL890            10
      6  G-165             7
      1  R-123             2
. SELECT 2

. USE Orders
. LIST Part_No, Quantity
Record#  Part_No    Quantity
      1  R-123             1
      2  B-254             2
      3  G-165             2
      4  R-123             1

. SELECT Inventry
. UPDATE FROM Orders ON Part_No RANDOM REPLACE Quantity WITH
Quantity - Orders->Quantity
      4 records updated
. LIST Part_No, Quantity  && Quantities have been reduced
Record#  Part_No    Quantity
      2  B-254             3
      4  B-735            15
      5  BL861             3
      3  BL890            10
      6  G-165             5
      1  R-123             0

. CLOSE DATABASES
```

The same example below uses the Orders file with an index so that UPDATE can be used without the RANDOM keyword:

```
. USE Inventry INDEX Part_No
. SELECT 2
. USE Orders INDEX O_PartNo
. SELECT Inventry
. UPDATE FROM Orders ON Part_No REPLACE Quantity WITH Quantity -
Orders->Quantity
      4 records updated
. CLOSE DATABASES
```

Warnings

UPDATE results in the error message *Database is not indexed* if you use the RANDOM keyword when the active database file does not have an open index file. Remember that RANDOM is used when the FROM file is in random order, and its use requires that the active database file be indexed rather than sorted. (See INDEX, SET INDEX, SET ORDER.)

If the active database file is not in order, no error message is displayed, but only the first record in the file is updated.

If you are using dBASE III PLUS in a network environment, UPDATE attempts an automatic file lock unless the database file is already locked (see FLOCK( )) or is opened for exclusive use (see SET EXCLUSIVE, USE). If for any reason the command cannot lock the database file, the error message *File is in use by another* is displayed.

Tips

UPDATE has several limitations:

1. It cannot update based on an expression that is more complicated than a single field name.
2. The file to be updated must be ordered on the update key.
3. The file to be updated and the FROM file must have the same key field name.
4. Only the first occurrence of a key value that is repeated in the active file gets updated.

The following, more general purpose update program addresses the limitations of UPDATE. There are two versions of the program listed below. In

each program, the user must make the appropriate substitutions where angle brackets occur. The first version of the program assumes that the FROM file is not indexed.

```
* Update1.PRGSET TALK OFF
SET TALK OFF

* Set up database file environment.
SELECT 2
USE <from database file>   && Substitute name of FROM file
SELECT 1
USE <update database file>  && Substitute name of UPDATE file

DO WHILE .NOT. EOF()
   * Below, <update key expression> and <from key expression>
   * are the key expressions from the respective database files.
   * These can be simple field names, or more complicated
   * expressions.  Substitute the appropriate values.

   m_key = <update key expression>

   * This loop is to update all occurrences of each key,
   * not just the first one.

   DO WHILE <update key expression> = m_key
      SELECT <from database file>
      LOCATE FOR <from key expression> = m_key

      * This loop is to update the current record using each
      * occurrence of the same key value in the from file.
      DO WHILE FOUND()
         SELECT <update database file>

         * Substitute the fields and expressions for the REPLACE
         REPLACE <field> WITH <exp> [, <field> WITH <exp>...]
         SELECT <from database file>
         CONTINUE
      ENDDO

      SELECT <update database file>
      SKIP

   ENDDO
ENDDO
```

```
SET TALK ON
CLOSE DATABASES
```

The next version of the update program assumes that the FROM file is indexed on the key expression. This version is much faster than the previous one since it uses SEEK instead of the sequential LOCATE.

```
* Update2.PRG

SET TALK OFF

* Set up database file environment.  All file names must be
* substituted.  The <index file> must be indexed on the
* <from key expression>.
SELECT 2
USE <from database file> INDEX <index file>
SELECT 1
USE <update database file>

DO WHILE .NOT. EOF()

   * Below, <update key expression> and <from key expression>
   * are the key expressions from the respective database files.
   * These can be simple field names, or more complicated
   * expressions.  Substitute the appropriate values.

   m_key = <update key expression>

   * This loop is to update all occurrences of each key,
   * not just the first one.

   DO WHILE <update key expression> = m_key
      SELECT <from database file>
      SEEK m_key

      * This loop is to update the current record using each
      * occurrence of the same key value in the from file.
      DO WHILE <from key expression> = m_key
         SELECT <update database file>
```

```
            * Substitute the fields and expressions for the REPLACE
            REPLACE <field> WITH <exp> [, <field> WITH <exp>...]
            SELECT <from database file>
            SKIP
         ENDDO

         SELECT <update database file>
         SKIP

      ENDDO

   ENDDO

   SET TALK ON
   CLOSE DATABASES
```

UPPER( )

Syntax UPPER(<expC>)

Overview The UPPER( ) function accepts a character expression as its argument. The function evaluates the expression to obtain the resulting character string and then returns that character string in all uppercase letters.

Procedure UPPER( ) returns a character string and can be used anywhere in the language where a character expression is appropriate.

Examples UPPER( ) can be used in combination with LOWER( ) and SUBSTR( ) to format the display of character data when the data is entered into the database file in a free form fashion. For example, to display all of the Last_Name fields from your mailing list with the first letter capitalized and the remaining ones in lowercase, use the following commands:

```
. USE Mail
. LIST UPPER(SUBSTR(Last_Name, 1, 1)) + LOWER(SUBSTR(Last_Name, 2))
Record#  UPPER(SUBSTR(Last_Name, 1, 1)) + LOWER(SUBSTR(Last_Name, 2))
      1  Smith
      2  Corbbit
      3  Roman
      4  Gurly
      5  King
      6  Lester
      7  Moore
      8  Smith
      9  Adams
     10  Richardson
     11  Moody
     12  Schaefer
     13  Arthur
     14  Long
     15  Potter
     16  Roberts
     17  Samuels
     18  Whiteside

. CLOSE DATABASES
```

Warnings If the function argument evaluates to a data type other than character, the error message *Invalid function argument* is displayed.

USE

Syntax

```
USE [<database filename>|?
[INDEX <index filename list>] [ALIAS <alias name>]
[EXCLUSIVE]]
```

Overview The USE command opens a database file in the current work area. (See SELECT.) Used with no command line parameters, USE closes the active database file and all of its ancillary files. (See SET INDEX, SET FORMAT.)

When opening the database file, you can also open a maximum of seven of its associated index files by using the INDEX keyword followed by a list of seven index file names separated by commas. Using the INDEX keyword with USE is equivalent to opening the index files after the database file is opened. (See SET INDEX.)

Use the ALIAS keyword to assign an alias name to the database. If you do not assign an alias name, the database file name or the work area alias name (see SELECT) can be used as the default alias name. The alias name is used to SELECT the work area containing the database file without knowing its work area number and to identify its fields when the file is not active (i.e., in USE in an unselected work area). (See Alias for more information on alias names and their uses.)

The EXCLUSIVE keyword is used only in a network environment. It opens the database file in exclusive mode, which prevents other users from accessing the file until the file is closed. When a user has a database file open in exclusive mode, file or record locks (see FLOCK( ), RLOCK( )) are unnecessary since use of the file is not shared by anyone. Exclusive use of a database file is required for certain operations. (See INSERT, MODIFY STRUCTURE, PACK, REINDEX, and ZAP.) Use of the EXCLUSIVE keyword with USE is necessary only if the SET EXCLUSIVE flag is OFF; by default, it is ON (see SET EXCLUSIVE) and all files are opened automatically in exclusive mode. In a single-user environment, this keyword is ignored.

If there is an open catalog (see SET CATALOG), the ?, or catalog query clause, can be used instead of a database file name to activate a menu of cataloged database files. Using this menu allows you to select the database file you want to open. After selecting the database file, you are presented with a second menu of all index files associated with that file in the catalog. You can select up to seven index files. Press the Left or Right Arrow key to close the menu after you have selected all of the index files you want to open. If you use the catalog query clause with the USE command, all other USE command line arguments are ignored.

Procedure

USE is the only command other than SET VIEW that can open database and index files. Used in conjunction with SELECT and SET RELATION, USE can open several related database and index files that are processed like a single file. (See SET VIEW.)

Issue USE to open a database file in the current work area so that you can examine and make changes to the data in the file. If you plan to make changes to index key fields or if you are going to add records to the file, use the INDEX keyword with USE to open all associated index files so that they will be updated automatically.

Specify an ALIAS if you want to refer to the database file using a name other than its file name or work area number. If you use cryptic file names derived from your own unique file name/numbering system, ALIAS names are useful to give the file a more meaningful reference name. The alias name can be up to ten characters in length; the first character must be a letter, and the remaining ones can be any combination of letters, numbers, and underscores.

If you are using dBASE III PLUS in a network environment and SET EXCLUSIVE is OFF, use the EXCLUSIVE keyword to open the database file in exclusive mode to perform an operation that requires exclusive use of the file. (See INSERT, MODIFY STRUCTURE, PACK, REINDEX and ZAP.)

When you are finished with the database file, close it using a USE with no parameters or close all open files with CLOSE DATABASES or CLOSE ALL. (See CLOSE.)

Examples

In the following example, USE is used with SELECT, SET FIELDS, and SET RELATION to work with the Orders and Customer database files as a single unit. The program lists the phone numbers of all customers who have placed an order.

```
* Clients.PRG
*
SET TALK OFF

* Open Orders with index O_PartNo in current work area.
USE Orders INDEX O_PartNo

* Customer is opened in work area 2 and given an alias name of
* Clients by which it will be referred throughout this program.
SELECT 2
USE Customer ALIAS Clients INDEX Cust_No

* Orders is made the active database file to establish relation
* with Customer, ALIAS Clients.
```

```
SELECT Orders
SET RELATION TO Cust_No INTO Clients
SET FIELDS TO Part_No, Quantity, Clients->Cust_No, Clients->Phone

* Fields from both files are listed.
LIST
CLOSE DATABASES
SET TALK ON
```

To execute this program and see its results,

```
. DO Clients
Record#  PART_NO   QUANTITY CUST_NO PHONE
      2  B-254            2 F126    (803)235-3205
      3  G-165            2 A452    (213)465-5723
      1  R-123            1 A254    (803)255-1635
      4  R-123            1 A452    (213)465-5723
```

Warnings

If you USE a database file that has the same ALIAS name as a file already in use in another work area, the error message *ALIAS name already in use* is displayed. This same error message occurs if you attempt to open a database file that uses for its name a letter A through J. These are the reserved alias names of the ten work areas (see SELECT) and cannot be used as database file names.

If the memo file corresponding to the database file that you are trying to USE cannot be found, the error message *.DBT file cannot be opened* is displayed. Perhaps you used RENAME to change the name of the database file and forgot to change the memo file name, or you used COPY FILE to move the database file to a new directory without also copying the memo file. Remember that any database file with one or more memo fields in its file structure has an associated memo file, and the file has the same name as the database file but with a .DBT extension. Be sure to remember the memo file when operating on a closed database file (see COPY FILE, ERASE, RENAME); dBASE III PLUS does not automatically check for it.

If you misspell the database file name or the file cannot be found in the current directory or any other directory in the path (see SET PATH), the error message *File does not exist* is displayed. If the file is in another directory, be sure to include it in the path. If the file has been inadvertently erased from the disk, use your most recent backup to recover the file. (See COPY FILE.)

If you try to use a file that is already in use in an unselected work area, the error message *File is already open* is displayed. Select the work area using the alias name (see SELECT) to access the file.

If a database file is corrupted, the error message, *Not a dBASE database* is displayed. The only recovery from this error is to use your most recent backup to recover the file. (See COPY FILE.)

If you use the INDEX keyword to open one or more index files with the database file, the error message *Index file does not match database* is displayed. This message indicates that one of the index files has a key expression that cannot be evaluated. If you are opening more than one index file, the ? part of the error message appears above the command just after the name of the offending index file name. In the following example, Salary.NDX belongs to another database file:

```
. USE Customer INDEX Cust_No, Salary, C_Lname
Index file does not match database.
                                           ?
USE Customer INDEX Cust_No, Salary, C_Lname
```

This error can occur if you have changed the name or data type of an index key field in the database file structure. (See MODIFY STRUCTURE.) Recreate the index file (see INDEX) and try the USE command again.

If you attempt to open more than seven index files with USE...INDEX, the error message *Too many indices* is displayed.

The error messages below can occur only if you are using dBASE III PLUS in a network environment:

Database is encrypted means that you have attempted to open the database file without using the correct log-in procedure. This should never happen if the dBASE ADMINISTRATOR system has been set up properly.

File is in use by another means that another user has the file open in exclusive mode. Try to access the file again later.

Unauthorized access level means that you do not have the appropriate access level to open the file. If you need to access this file, speak with the individual who administers your network.

Tips

Although USE with no parameters closes the active database file, CLOSE ALL and CLOSE DATABASES have the same function. CLOSE commands are more readable in a program, but these commands close all database files in addition to the active one. If you want to close only the active database file, USE with no parameters is the only way to do so.

If you want to open a format file for use with a database file (see SET FORMAT), you must open the database file first. It is possible to use a format file without using a database file (e.g., the format file could use only memory variables). In this case, USE closes all files (including the format file) that happen to be open in the current work area. The correct procedure is

```
USE <database filename>
SET FORMAT TO <format filename>
```

USE closes the current file before opening a new one. You can save changes to the disk by periodically reissuing the same USE command that opened the current file. Remember, however, that this also moves the record pointer the same as issuing a GO TOP. (See GO.)

VAL( )

Syntax `VAL(<expC>)`

Overview

The VAL( ) function accepts a character expression as its argument. The function evaluates the expression to obtain the resulting character string and converts the string to a numeric data type.

Procedure

VAL( ) returns a number and can be used anywhere in the language where a numeric expression is appropriate.

Examples

VAL( ) is helpful when manipulating a pseudo-array since you use the same variable for both the loop counter and the array index. The array index must be a character data type to work with the macro substitution symbol, and the loop counter must be a numeric data type so that it can be incremented. In the following example, a two-dimensional pseudo-array called "day" is initialized and displayed:

```
* Array.PRG
*
SET TALK OFF
USE Mail
* Pseudo array is initialized.  Second column will store the
* name of the day and first column will store the number of
* people born on that day.
STORE 0 TO day11, day21, day31, day41, day51, day61, day71
STORE "" TO day12, day22, day32, day42, day52, day62, day72
DO WHILE .NOT. EOF()
   num = STR(DOW(Birthday), 1)
   day&num.1 = day&num.1 + 1
   day&num.2 = CDOW(Birthday)
   SKIP
ENDDO
CLEAR
num = "1"
* The VAL() function converts the array index to a number
* so that it can be used as the loop counter and for the
* row coordinate of the @...SAY command.
DO WHILE VAL(num) <= 7
   @ VAL(num), 0 SAY STR(day&num.1, 1) + " born on ";
                 + day&num.2
   * The VAL() function is used to increment the loop counter
   * and the STR() function is used to convert the result back
   * to a character string.
   num = STR(VAL(num) + 1, 1)
ENDDO
CLOSE DATABASES
SET TALK ON
```

To execute this program, type `DO Array` and you will see the following:

```
2 born on Sunday
2 born on Monday
2 born on Tuesday
3 born on Wednesday
4 born on Thursday
1 born on Friday
4 born on Saturday
```

Warnings If the function argument evaluates to a data type other than character, the error message *Invalid function argument* is displayed.

The VAL( ) function only operates on numeric characters and a single decimal point. If there are other characters in the original string (e.g., commas, letters, or a second decimal point) the conversion process stops and VAL( ) returns what it has converted thus far; hence, VAL( ) returns zero if the original string begins with a non-numeric character other than a decimal point.

Tips

VAL( ) returns the number of decimal places specified by SET DECIMALS, which is, by default, two. If the original character string has more decimal places than specified by SET DECIMALS, the result of VAL( ) is rounded to that number of decimal places. To see all of the numbers following the decimal, SET DECIMALS TO a larger number as in the following example:

```
. character = "123.4477777"
123.4477777
. ? VAL(character)
       123.45
. SET DECIMALS TO 7
. ? VAL(character)
       123.4477777
```

When designing a database file, assign the appropriate data type to numbers. Only numbers used in mathematical calculations are numeric and all others are character. If you frequently manipulate a field with VAL( ), use MODIFY STRUCTURE to change the data type of that field from character to numeric.

VERSION( )

Syntax `VERSION([<expN>])`

Overview

The VERSION( ) function is normally used with no argument. The function returns the name and version number of the product.

Procedure

VERSION( ) returns a character string and can be used anywhere in the language where a character expression is appropriate.

Examples

Use VERSION( ) to avoid making your program version specific. This is particularly desirable if many people use your application and you want to take advantage of some of the latest product features. Because you can't be sure what version of dBASE III each person will be using, you can conditionally use new features with VERSION( ). For example, since the original version of dBASE III did not have the IIF( ) function, the following sequence tests for the version number and uses either IIF( ) or the IF... ELSE...ENDIF equivalent:

```
* Ver_Test.PRG
*
IF VERSION() = "dBASE III PLUS"
   ? IIF(Married, "Married", "Single")
ELSE
   IF Married
      ? "Married"
   ELSE
      ? "Single"
   ENDIF
ENDIF
```

Warnings

Because of its simple syntax, there are no error messages associated with VERSION( ).

Tips

An undocumented VERSION( ) feature is its ability to use any numeric expression as the argument to see the internal version number. The actual value of the argument does not matter. The internal version number includes the release date of the version that you are using. This information can be useful since Ashton-Tate often releases unannounced versions of dBASE.

WAIT

Syntax `WAIT [<prompt>] [TO <memory variable>]`

Overview

The WAIT command waits for the user to enter a single character from the keyboard. When the command is executed, the user must press a key to

continue. If the TO option is specified, the character that is typed is saved in the named character memory variable.

If used, the <prompt> is supplied in the form of a character expression. The expression is evaluated and the resulting character string is displayed on the screen to prompt the user for specific input. If no <prompt> is specified, the default prompt, *Press any key to continue...*, is displayed.

Procedure

Use WAIT with no parameters in a program when you want the user to see what is on the screen before continuing. Preceding WAIT by CLEAR TYPEAHEAD ensures that the user does not type ahead of WAIT.

Use WAIT TO <memory variable> in a program if your application requires a single character response that you need to analyze. Initialize the memory variable to any value that is not an acceptable response, and put WAIT in a DO WHILE loop that tests the user's response for validity. For example,

```
* Initialize waitvar to an unacceptable value so that it
* will pass through the DO WHILE loop.
waitvar = SPACE(1)

* Continue prompting until the user enters a Y or an N.
DO WHILE .NOT. waitvar $ "YyNn"
   WAIT "Do you want to continue? (Y/N) " TO waitvar
ENDDO

* Act based on the user's response
IF waitvar $ "Yy"
   DO NextProg
ELSE
   RETURN
ENDIF
```

Examples

A common use of WAIT is after an error message display to ensure that the user reads and acknowledges the error. The following example illustrates this use of WAIT to indicate when the program does not find a key that the user enters:

```
* Special.PRG
*
SET EXACT ON
```

```
SET TALK OFF
USE Employee INDEX Emp_Code
DO WHILE .T.
   CLEAR
   m_code = SPACE(4)
   @ 10,10 SAY "Enter employee code: " GET m_code PICTURE "A999"
   READ
   IF "" = TRIM(m_code)
      EXIT  && Exit loop if no employee code entered
   ENDIF
   m_code = UPPER(m_code)  && Convert m_code to uppercase
   SEEK m_code
   IF FOUND()
      * Print 5% salary bonus check.
      DO Bonus WITH Salary * .05
   ELSE
      @ 12, 0 SAY "Employee not found.  Make sure that you"
      @ 13, 0 SAY "enter all four characters of the code."

      * CLEAR TYPEAHEAD makes sure that the contents of the
      * typeahead buffer is not used to respond to the WAIT
      * command.  Otherwise, the user might not see the error
      * message.
      CLEAR TYPEAHEAD
      WAIT
   ENDIF
ENDDO
CLOSE DATABASE
SET TALK ON
SET EXACT OFF
```

Warnings

If used, the <prompt> must be a character expression. If you use a literal character string as the prompt and do not enclose the string in single quotes, double quotes, or square brackets, the error message *Variable not found* is displayed. If the expression used for the prompt evaluates to a data type other than character, the error message *Not a Character expression* is displayed.

Tips

Instead of using WAIT to prompt the user for a single character, you can initialize a memory variable to a single blank character (see STORE, SPACE()) and use @...GET followed by a READ to prompt the user for input. This allows you better control of what the user is allowed to enter (see PICTURE, RANGE) as well as the data type of the memory variable. @...GET and READ is faster than WAIT.

To use WAIT without displaying a prompt, use a null string as the prompt (e.g., WAIT "" TO waitvar).

Note that WAIT creates the named memory variable so that it does not have to be initialized before the command is executed; if it does exist, it is overwritten without any warning.

ACCEPT is very similar to WAIT, but it allows more than a single character to be entered. (See ACCEPT for more details.)

Pressing Enter in response to the WAIT command without typing anything else creates a memory variable containing a null string.

INKEY( ) in a DO WHILE loop behaves similarly to WAIT but adds the ability to detect the non-printable keypress such as Enter, Esc, and PgDn.

WHILE

Syntax `WHILE <condition>`

Overview

When you use a WHILE clause as part of a command, you specify a logical condition that is evaluated for each record that the command processes. As long as the condition evaluates to true (.T.), the command continues to process records. As soon as it evaluates to false (.F.), the command stops.

Procedure

Many dBASE III PLUS commands allow a WHILE clause as part of their syntax. If it is not specified, the command processes the records in the active database file unconditionally.

Use a WHILE clause to impose a condition that must evaluate to true (.T.) in order for the command to continue (or begin) execution.

Usually, a WHILE clause is used with an indexed database file, and the condition involves the index key field. The first record that meets the WHILE condition is found using SEEK or FIND. The records are processed using a command with a WHILE clause.

Examples

The following example uses LIST with a WHILE clause to list all people in the mailing list who are between the ages of twenty-nine and thirty-three:

```
. USE Mail INDEX Ages
. SEEK 29
. LIST Last_Name WHILE Age >= 29 .AND. Age <= 33
Record#  Last_Name
     10  Richardson
     12  Schaefer
     13  Arthur
     14  Long
      3  Roman
      7  Moore
     15  Potter

. CLOSE DATABASES
```

Warnings

The WHILE clause does not return an error message if the condition evaluates to a data type other than logical. Be aware of this if you are using a WHILE clause and it does not seem to work correctly.

Tips

A WHILE clause can be further limited using a FOR clause. The following example is similar to the one above, but it only shows the people between twenty-nine and thirty-three who have a zip code that begins with "900":

```
. USE Mail INDEX Ages
. SEEK 29
. LIST Last_Name WHILE Age >= 29 .AND. Age <= 33 FOR Zip = "900"
Record#  Last_Name
     12  Schaefer
     14  Long
      3  Roman
     15  Potter

. CLOSE DATABASES
```

As this example illustrates, WHILE has precedence over FOR when WHILE and FOR are used together.

YEAR( )

Syntax YEAR(<expD>)

Overview The YEAR( ) function accepts any date expression as its argument. The function evaluates the expression and returns the year portion as a number.

Procedure The YEAR( ) function returns a number and can be used anywhere in the language where a numeric expression is appropriate.

Examples Using YEAR( ) in combination with some of the other date manipulation functions, you can generate a wide variety of date displays. The following routine displays the current date in several different formats:

```
* Dates.PRG
*
SET TALK OFF
today = DATE()
? today
? LEFT(CMONTH(today), 3) + " " + LTRIM(STR(DAY(today))) + ", " +;
  LTRIM(STR(YEAR(today)))
? CMONTH(today) + " " + LTRIM(STR(DAY(today))) + ", " +;
  LTRIM(STR(YEAR(today)))
? CDOW(today) + ", " + LTRIM(STR(DAY(today))) + " " +;
  CMONTH(today)
? LTRIM(STR(DAY(today))) + " " + LEFT(CMONTH(today), 3) + " " +;
  LTRIM(STR(YEAR(today)))
SET TALK ON
```

Executing this routine results in the following output, assuming today's date is June 19, 1987.

```
. DO Dates
06/19/87
Jun 19, 1987
June 19, 1987
Friday, 19 June
19 Jun 1987
```

Warnings If the function argument evaluates to a data type other than date, the error message *Invalid function argument* is displayed.

Tips Note that the YEAR( ) function always returns a four-digit year, regardless of the status of the SET CENTURY flag. To get a two-digit year, use SUBSTR(STR(YEAR(< date >), 4), 3, 2).

ZAP

Syntax `ZAP`

Overview The ZAP command removes all of the records from the active database file; all open index files are kept up to date. If SET SAFETY is ON, the prompt *ZAP <filename> ? (Y/N)* is displayed before the command proceeds. Typing `N` cancels the ZAP command without removing any records.

Procedure After designing and coding the programs in a new application, you usually test the application before allowing someone else to use it. Testing an application almost always involves putting test records into the database files to see that the programs work correctly with various kinds of data.

ZAP is rarely used in applications programming. The most common use of this command is to remove test data from database files before turning a new application over to a user.

Before entering ZAP, open the database file where records will be deleted and all of its index files. (See USE.) If you are using dBASE III PLUS in a network environment, exclusive use (see SET EXCLUSIVE, USE) of the active database file is required. If you are prompted with *ZAP <filename> ? (Y/N)*, type `Y` to continue the process. It is important that the index files be in use at the time that you ZAP the database file so that they are kept up to date.

Examples The following example illustrates how to use ZAP at the dot prompt to empty the contents of the Orders database file along with its part number

and customer number index file. Before ZAP is issued, a backup copy of the file is put on drive A. This example assumes that SET SAFETY is ON and that you type Y when prompted.

```
. USE Orders
. COPY TO A:Orders  && Back up file to A drive
     4 records copied
. SET INDEX TO O_PartNo, O_CustNo
. ZAP
Zap C:Orders.dbf? (Y/N) Yes
```

Warnings If SET SAFETY is OFF, ZAP deletes all of the records in the database file without warning. Use this command with extreme caution.

If you use ZAP in the network version of dBASE III PLUS, exclusive use of the active database file is required. If you attempt to ZAP a database file that was opened for shared use, the error message *Exclusive open of file is required* is displayed. Either SET EXCLUSIVE ON and reopen file, or reopen the file with USE <filename> EXCLUSIVE, and issue ZAP again.

Tips In certain applications, you might occasionally want to empty a particular database file. In such cases, you can use ZAP in a program to remove all of the records in a file at the end of each week or month. Once you use ZAP, however, you will not be able to retrieve the data from a previous period. It is a good idea, therefore, to archive the contents of such database files before using ZAP. For example,

```
* Archive.PRG
*
* Orders.ARC is a database file used to archive data before it
* is permanently deleted from the main Orders file.
USE Orders.ARC
APPEND FROM Orders
USE Orders
ZAP
CLOSE DATABASES
```

This sequence allows you to recover data from any period. Remember to make backup copies of all of your files, including archive database files.

Appendices

Appendix A: Cursor Navigation and Editing Keys

KEY	CTRL-KEY EQUIVA-LENT	FUNCTION
Home	^A	Moves the cursor to the first character of the previous word in the current field or line. At the beginning of a field or line, the cursor moves to the last position in the previous field or line.
^→	^B	Moves the cursor to the end of the current field or line. In BROWSE, pans the screen by moving the leftmost field on the screen out of view and bringing another field into view on the right side of the screen.
PgDn	^C	Moves forward one page or record.
→	^D, ^J	Moves the cursor one position to the right. At the end of a field or line, the cursor moves to the beginning of the next field or line.
↑	^E, ^K	Moves the cursor up one field or line.
End	^F	Moves the cursor to the first character of the next word in the current field or line. At the end of a field or line, the cursor moves to the first position in the next field or line.
Del	^G	Deletes the character at the current cursor position and moves all characters to the right of the deleted character one space to the left. The cursor does not move.
Tab	^I	In text editing (i.e., MODIFY COMMAND, CREATE SCREEN blackboard, and memo field editing), moves the cursor several blank spaces to the right.
Enter	^M	Moves the cursor to the beginning of the next line.
	^N	In text editing (i.e., MODIFY COMMAND, CREATE SCREEN blackboard, and memo field editing), moves the text on the current line starting at the current cursor location to the next line. If the cursor is at the beginning of a line, a blank line is inserted since all text is moved to the next line. In CREATE QUERY, inserts a new line before the current line in the Set Filter menu. In CREATE REPORT, inserts a new column before the current one in the Columns menu. In CREATE LABEL, inserts a blank line before the current line in the Contents menu.
	^O	In the network version, locks the current record in CHANGE and EDIT.
	^P	In the interactive mode, toggles printer on and off.
Esc	^Q	Abandons full-screen mode without saving the changes that you have made to disk. In the full-screen database file editing commands, only the changes to the current record are not saved; all others are saved.

APPENDIX A: CURSOR NAVIGATION AND EDITING KEYS

KEY	CTRL-KEY EQUIVA-LENT	FUNCTION
PgUp	^R	Moves backward one page or record.
◁	^S, ^H	Moves the cursor one position to the left. At the beginning of a field or line, the cursor moves to the end of the previous field or line.
	^T	Deletes to the end of the current word starting at the current cursor location. The cursor does not move.
	^U	In BROWSE and EDIT, toggles the delete marker for the current record. In CREATE QUERY, deletes the current line in the Set Filter menu from the Condition box. In CREATE REPORT, deletes the current column in the Columns menu from the report definition. In CREATE LABEL, deletes the current line in the Contents menu from the label definition. In CREATE and MODIFY STRUCTURE, deletes the current field from the database file structure. In CREATE SCREEN, deletes the current field from the blackboard.
Ins	^V	Toggles between insert and overwrite mode.
^End	^W	Leaves full-screen mode and saves all changes that you have made to disk.
▽	^X, ^K	Moves the cursor down one field or line.
	^Y	In the full-screen editing commands APPEND, BROWSE, CHANGE, EDIT, INSERT, and READ, deletes to the end of the current line starting at the current cursor location and does not move the cursor. In text editing (i.e., MODIFY COMMAND, CREATE SCREEN blackboard, and memo field editing), moves the cursor to the beginning of the current line and deletes the entire line.
^◁	^Z	Moves the cursor to the beginning of the current field or line. In BROWSE, pans the screen by moving the rightmost field on the screen out of view and bringing another field into view on the left side of the screen.
BackSpace		Deletes the character to the left of the current cursor position and moves the cursor one position to the left.
F1	^\	Toggles the cursor navigation menu on and off.
^PgDn	^Home	In APPEND, EDIT, INSERT, and READ, allows editing of a memo field when the cursor is positioned on the *memo* icon.
^PgUp	^End	Leaves memo field editing and saves the changes to disk, and returns to full-screen editing command.

Appendix B: Menu Navigation Keys

KEY	CTRL-KEY EQUIVA-LENT	FUNCTION
Home	^A	Moves the highlight to the first option on the menu bar.
PgDn	^C	Moves the highlight to the last option in the menu or submenu. For file and field list menus, scrolls the list down one page at a time.
⇨	^D	Moves the highlight to the next option on the menu bar if you are in a main menu. In a submenu, closes the submenu and returns control to the main menu.
⇧	^E	Moves the menu highlight to the previous available option in the current menu or submenu. On the first option, the highlight moves to the last option.
End	^F	Moves the highlight to the last option on the menu bar.
Enter	^M	Selects the highlighted option in the menu. If the option is a YES/NO toggle or other selection of values, selects the next value.
Esc	^Q	Abandons full-screen mode without saving the changes that you have made to disk. In commands where the menu is optional, also deactivates the menu bar.
PgUp	^R	Moves the highlight to the first option in the menu or submenu. For file and field list menus, scrolls the list up one page at a time.
⇦	^S	Moves the highlight to the previous option on the menu bar if you are in a main menu. In a submenu, closes the submenu and returns control to the main menu.
⇩	^X	Moves the menu highlight to the next available option in the current menu or submenu. On the last option, the highlight moves to the first option.
F10	^Home	In commands where it is optional (e.g., BROWSE, MODIFY STRUCTURE), activates menu bar.

Appendix C: ASCII Code Tables

Characters zero through 31 are control codes. Characters number 32 through 126 are printable. 127 is the delete.

CODE	CHAR	CODE	CHAR	CODE	CHAR	CODE	CHAR
0	ctrl @	32	space	64	@	96	`
1	ctrl A	33	!	65	A	97	a
2	ctrl B	34	"	66	B	98	b
3	ctrl C	35	#	67	C	99	c
4	ctrl D	36	$	68	D	100	d
5	ctrl E	37	%	69	E	101	e
6	ctrl F	38	&	70	F	102	f
7	ctrl G	39	'	71	G	103	g
8	ctrl H	40	(	72	H	104	h
9	ctrl I	41	)	73	I	105	i
10	ctrl J	42	*	74	J	106	j
11	ctrl K	43	+	75	K	107	k
12	ctrl L	44	,	76	L	108	l
13	ctrl M	45	–	77	M	109	m
14	ctrl N	46	.	78	N	110	n
15	ctrl O	47	/	79	O	111	o
16	ctrl P	48	0	80	P	112	p
17	ctrl Q	49	1	81	Q	113	q
18	ctrl R	50	2	82	R	114	r
19	ctrl S	51	3	83	S	115	s
20	ctrl T	52	4	84	T	116	t
21	ctrl U	53	5	85	U	117	u
22	ctrl V	54	6	86	V	118	v
23	ctrl W	55	7	87	W	119	w
24	ctrl X	56	8	88	X	120	x
25	ctrl Y	57	9	89	Y	121	y
26	ctrl Z	58	:	90	Z	122	z
27	escape	59	;	91	[	123	{
28	ctrl \	60	<	92	\	124	|
29	ctrl]	61	=	93	]	125	}
30	ctrl ^	62	>	94	^	126	~
31	ctrl _	63	?	95	_	127	delete

Appendix C: Extended ASCII Graphics Character Set

CODE	CHAR	CODE	CHAR	CODE	CHAR	CODE	CHAR
128	Ç	160	á	192	└	224	α
129	ü	161	í	193	┴	225	β
130	é	162	ó	194	┬	226	Γ
131	â	163	ú	195	├	227	π
132	ä	164	ñ	196	─	228	Σ
133	à	165	Ñ	197	┼	229	σ
134	å	166	ª	198	╞	230	µ
135	ç	167	º	199	╟	231	τ
136	ê	168	¿	200	╚	232	Φ
137	ë	169	⌐	201	╔	233	Θ
138	è	170	¬	202	╩	234	Ω
139	ï	171	½	203	╦	235	δ
140	î	172	¼	204	╠	236	∞
141	ì	173	¡	205	═	237	ø
142	Ä	174	«	206	╬	238	ε
143	Å	175	»	207	╧	239	∩
144	É	176	░	208	╨	240	≡
145	æ	177	▒	209	╤	241	±
146	Æ	178	▓	210	╥	242	≥
147	ô	179	│	211	╙	243	≤
148	ö	180	┤	212	╘	244	⌠
149	ò	181	╡	213	╒	245	⌡
150	û	182	╢	214	╓	246	÷
151	ù	183	╖	215	╫	247	≈
152	ÿ	184	╕	216	╪	248	•
153	ö	185	╣	217	┘	249	•
154	ü	186	║	218	┌	250	·
155	¢	187	╗	219	█	251	√
156	£	188	╝	220	▄	252	η
157	¥	189	╜	221	▌	253	²
158	₧	190	╛	222	▐	254	■
159	ƒ	191	┐	223	▀	255	

Appendix D: dBASE III PLUS Command and Function Syntax

! ¦ RUN <command> ¦ <program> ¦ <batch file>

* ¦ NOTE <text>

? [<expression list>]

?? [<expression list>]

@ <coordinates> CLEAR [TO <coordinates>]

@ <coordinates> GET <variable> [PICTURE <template>]
[RANGE [<exp>], [<exp>]]

@ <coordinates> [SAY <expression> [PICTURE <template>]]

@ <coordinates> TO <coordinates> [DOUBLE]

ABS(<expN>)

ACCEPT [<prompt>] TO <memory variable>

ACCESS( )

APPEND [BLANK]

APPEND FROM <filename> ¦ ? [WHILE <condition>] [FOR <condition>]
[[TYPE] WKS ¦ SYLK ¦ DIF ¦ SDF ¦ DELIMITED
[WITH BLANK ¦ <delimiter>]]

ASC(<expC>)

ASSIST

AT(<expC1>, <expC2>)

AVERAGE [<scope>] [WHILE <condition>] [FOR <condition>]
[<expN list>] [TO <memory variable list>]

BOF( )

BROWSE [FIELDS <field list>] [LOCK <expN>] [FREEZE <fieldname>]
[WIDTH <expN>] [NOAPPEND] [NOFOLLOW] [NOMENU]

CALL <binary module name> [WITH <memory variable> ¦ <expC>]

CANCEL

CDOW(<expD>)

CHANGE [<scope>] [FIELDS <field list>]
[WHILE <condition>] [FOR <condition>]

CHR(<expN>)

APPENDIX D: DBASE III PLUS COMMAND AND FUNCTION SYNTAX

CLEAR

CLEAR ALL

CLEAR FIELDS

CLEAR GETS

CLEAR MEMORY

CLEAR TYPEAHEAD

CLOSE ALL ¦ ALTERNATE ¦ DATABASES ¦ FORMAT ¦ INDEXES ¦ PROCEDURE

CMONTH(<expD>)

COL( )

CONTINUE

COPY TO <filename> [FIELDS <field list>] [<scope>]
    [WHILE <condition>] [FOR <condition>]
    [[TYPE] WKS ¦ SYLK ¦ DIF ¦ SDF ¦ DELIMITED [WITH BLANK ¦ <delimiter>]]

COPY FILE <filename> TO <new filename>

COPY STRUCTURE [FIELDS <field list>] TO <filename>

COPY STRUCTURE EXTENDED TO <filename>

COUNT [<scope>] [WHILE <condition>] [FOR <condition>]
    [TO <memory variable>]

CREATE <filename>

CREATE <filename> FROM <extended filename>

CREATE ¦ MODIFY LABEL <filename> ¦ ?

CREATE ¦ MODIFY QUERY <filename> ¦ ?

CREATE ¦ MODIFY REPORT <filename> ¦ ?

CREATE ¦ MODIFY SCREEN <filename> ¦ ?

CREATE ¦ MODIFY VIEW <filename> ¦ ?

CREATE VIEW <filename> FROM ENVIRONMENT

CTOD(<expC>)

DATE( )

DAY(<expD>)

DBF( )

DELETE [<scope>] [WHILE <condition>] [FOR <condition>]

DELETE FILE <filename> ¦ ?

DELETED( )

DIR ¦ DIRECTORY [[ON] <drive>] [[LIKE] <skeleton>]

DISKSPACE( )

DISPLAY [[FIELDS] <expression list>] [<scope>]
  [WHILE <condition>] [FOR <condition>] [OFF] [TO PRINTER]

DISPLAY FILES [[ON] <drive>] [[LIKE] <skeleton>] [TO PRINTER]

DISPLAY HISTORY [LAST <expN>] [TO PRINTER]

DISPLAY MEMORY [TO PRINTER]

DISPLAY STATUS [TO PRINTER]

DISPLAY STRUCTURE [TO PRINTER]

DISPLAY USERS [TO PRINTER]

DO <command filename> ¦ <procedure name> [WITH <parameter list>]

DO CASE
  CASE <condition 1>
  <commands>
  [CASE <condition 2>
  <commands>
  .
  .
  .
  CASE <condition n>
  <commands>]
  [OTHERWISE
  <commands>]
ENDCASE

DO WHILE <condition>
  <commands>
  [LOOP]
  [EXIT]
ENDDO

DOW(<expD>)

DTOC(<expD>)

EDIT [FIELDS <field list>] [<scope>]
    [WHILE <condition>] [FOR <condition>]

EJECT

EOF()

ERASE <filename> ¦ ?

ERROR()

EXP(<expN>)

EXPORT TO <filename> [TYPE] PFS [FIELDS <field list>]
    [<scope>] [WHILE <condition>] [FOR <condition>]

FIELD(<expN>)

FILE(<expC>)

FIND <string>

FKLABEL(<expN>)

FKMAX()

FLOCK()

FOUND()

GETENV(<expC>)

GO ¦ GOTO [RECORD] <expN>
GO ¦ GOTO BOTTOM ¦ TOP

HELP [<screen name>]

IF <condition>
  <commands>
[ELSE
  <commands>]
ENDIF

IIF(<condition>, <exp1>, <exp2>)

IMPORT FROM <filename> [TYPE] PFS

INDEX ON <key expression> TO <filename> [UNIQUE]

INKEY()

INPUT [<prompt>] TO <memory variable>

INSERT [BEFORE] [BLANK]

INT(<expN>)

ISALPHA(<expC>)

ISCOLOR( )

ISLOWER(<expC>)

ISUPPER(<expC>)

JOIN WITH <alias> TO <filename> FOR <condition>
    [FIELDS <field list>]

LABEL FORM <filename> ¦ ? [SAMPLE] [<scope>] [WHILE <condition>]
    [FOR <condition>] [TO PRINTER] [TO FILE <filename>]

LEFT(<expC>, <expN>)

LEN(<expC>)

LIST [[FIELDS] <expression list>] [<scope>] [WHILE <condition>]
    [FOR <condition>] [OFF] [TO PRINTER]

LIST FILES [[ON] <drive>] [[LIKE] <skeleton>] [TO PRINTER]

LIST HISTORY [LAST <expN>] [TO PRINTER]

LIST MEMORY [TO PRINTER]

LIST STATUS [TO PRINTER]

LIST STRUCTURE [TO PRINTER]

LIST USERS [TO PRINTER]

LOAD <binary module filename>

LOCATE [<scope>] [WHILE <condition>] [FOR <condition>]

LOG(<expN>)

LOGOUT

LOWER(<expC>)

LTRIM(<expC>)

LUPDATE( )

MAX(<expN1>, <expN2>)

MESSAGE( )

MIN(<expN1>, <expN2>)

MOD(<expN1>, <expN2>)

MODIFY COMMAND <filename>

MODIFY FILE <filename>

MODIFY STRUCTURE

MONTH(<expD>)

NDX(<expN>)

ON ERROR [<command>]

ON ESCAPE [<command>]

ON KEY [<command>]

OS( )

PACK

PARAMETERS <memory variable list>

PCOL( )

PRIVATE <memory variable list>

PRIVATE ALL [LIKE ¦ EXCEPT <skeleton>]

PROCEDURE <procedure name>

PROW( )

PUBLIC <memory variable list>

QUIT

READ [SAVE]

READKEY( )

RECALL [<scope>] [WHILE <condition>] [FOR <condition>]

RECCOUNT( )

RECNO( )

RECSIZE( )

REINDEX

RELEASE <memory variable list>

RELEASE ALL [LIKE ¦ EXCEPT <skeleton>]

RELEASE MODULE <binary module name>

RENAME <filename> TO <new filename>

REPLACE <fieldname> WITH <expression>
[, <fieldname> WITH <expression>...]
[<scope>] [WHILE <condition>] [FOR <condition>]

REPLICATE(<expC>, <expN>)

REPORT FORM <filename> ¦ ? [<scope>] [WHILE <condition>]
[FOR <condition>] [TO PRINTER] [TO FILE <filename>]
[PLAIN] [HEADING <expC>] [NOEJECT] [SUMMARY]

RESTORE FROM <memory filename> [ADDITIVE]

RESUME

RETRY

RETURN [TO MASTER]

RIGHT(<expC>, <expN>)

RLOCK() ¦ LOCK()

ROUND(<expN1>, <expN2>)

ROW()

SAVE TO <memory filename> [ALL LIKE ¦ EXCEPT <skeleton>]

SEEK <expression>

SELECT <work area number> ¦ <alias name>

SET

SET ALTERNATE TO [<filename>]
SET ALTERNATE ON ¦ OFF

SET BELL ON ¦ OFF

SET CARRY ON ¦ OFF

SET CATALOG TO [<filename> ¦ ?]
SET CATALOG ON ¦ OFF

SET CENTURY ON ¦ OFF

SET COLOR TO [<standard foreground> [/ <standard background>]]
[, <enhanced foreground> [/ <enhanced background>]]
[, <border>] [, <background>]

SET COLOR ON ¦ OFF

SET CONFIRM ON ¦ OFF

SET CONSOLE ON ¦ OFF

SET DATE AMERICAN ¦ ANSI ¦ BRITISH ¦ FRENCH ¦ GERMAN ¦ ITALIAN

SET DEBUG ON ¦ OFF

SET DECIMALS TO [<expN>]

SET DEFAULT TO <drive letter>

SET DELETED ON ¦ OFF

SET DELIMITERS TO <expC> ¦ DEFAULT
SET DELIMITERS ON ¦ OFF

SET DEVICE TO SCREEN ¦ PRINTER

SET DOHISTORY ON ¦ OFF

SET ECHO ON ¦ OFF

SET ENCRYPTION ON ¦ OFF

SET ESCAPE ON ¦ OFF

SET EXACT ON ¦ OFF

SET EXCLUSIVE ON ¦ OFF

SET FIELDS TO [<field list> ¦ ALL]
SET FIELDS ON ¦ OFF

SET FILTER TO [<condition>] ¦ [FILE <filename> ¦ ?]

SET FIXED ON ¦ OFF

SET FORMAT TO [<filename> ¦ ?]

SET FUNCTION <key number> ¦ <key label> TO [<expC>]

SET HEADINGS ON ¦ OFF

SET HELP ON ¦ OFF

SET HISTORY TO <expN>
SET HISTORY ON ¦ OFF

SET INDEX TO [<index filename list> ¦ ?]

SET INTENSITY ON ¦ OFF

SET MARGIN TO <expN>

SET MEMOWIDTH TO [<expN>]

SET MENUS ON ¦ OFF

SET MESSAGE TO [<expC>]

SET ODOMETER TO <expN>

```
SET ORDER TO [<expN>]
SET PATH TO [<path list>]
SET PRINTER ON ¦ OFF
SET PRINTER TO [<device name>]
SET PRINTER TO [\\<computer name>\<printer name> = <device name>]
SET PRINTER TO [\\SPOOLER]
SET PROCEDURE TO [<filename>]
SET RELATION TO [<expression> INTO <alias name>]
SET SAFETY ON ¦ OFF
SET SCOREBOARD ON ¦ OFF
SET STATUS ON ¦ OFF
SET STEP ON ¦ OFF
SET TALK ON ¦ OFF
SET TITLE ON ¦ OFF
SET TYPEAHEAD TO <expN>
SET UNIQUE ON ¦ OFF
SET VIEW TO <filename> ¦ ?
SKIP [<expN>]
SORT ON <key fieldname> [/[A ¦ D][C] ¦ ASCENDING ¦ DESCENDING]
        [, <key fieldname> [/[A ¦ D][C] ¦ ASCENDING ¦ DESCENDING]...]
        TO <filename>
        [<scope>] [WHILE <condition>] [FOR <condition>]
SPACE(<expN>)
SQRT(<expN>)
STORE <expression> TO <memory variable list>
STR(<expN> [, <length> [, <decimals>]])
STUFF(<string>, <begin>, <remove>, <insert>)
SUBSTR(<expC>, <begin> [, <length>])
SUM [<scope>] [WHILE <condition>] [FOR <condition>]
    [<expN list>] [TO <memory variable list>]
SUSPEND
```

TEXT
<text>
ENDTEXT

TIME( )

TOTAL ON <key fieldname> TO <filename> [FIELDS <field list>]
[<scope>] [WHILE <condition>] [FOR <condition>]

TRANSFORM(<expression>, <expC>)

TRIM ¦ RTRIM(<expC>)

TYPE <filename> [TO PRINTER]

TYPE(<expC>)

UNLOCK [ALL]

UPDATE ON <key fieldname> FROM <alias name> [RANDOM]
REPLACE <fieldname> WITH <expression>
[, <fieldname> WITH <expression> ...]

UPPER(<expC>)

USE [<database filename> ¦ ? [INDEX <index filename list>]
[ALIAS <alias name>] [EXCLUSIVE]]

VAL(<expC>)

VERSION([<expN>])

WAIT [<prompt>] [TO <memory variable>]

YEAR(<expD>)

ZAP

Appendix E: Sample Database Files

This appendix lists the structure and content of the database files used for the examples in this book.

Answers.dbf
Checks.dbf
Customer.dbf
Employee.dbf
Inventry.dbf
Mail.dbf
Managers.dbf
Medical.dbf
Orders.dbf
Supplier.dbf
Tests.dbf

Answers.dbf

```
Structure for database: A:Answers.dbf
Number of data records:       3
Date of last update   : 08/18/87
Field  Field Name  Type        Width    Dec
    1  ANSWER1     Character       1
    2  ANSWER2     Character       1
    3  ANSWER3     Character       1
    4  ANSWER4     Character       1
    5  ANSWER5     Character       1
    6  ANSWER6     Character       1
    7  ANSWER7     Character       1
    8  ANSWER8     Character       1
    9  ANSWER9     Character       1
   10  ANSWER10    Character       1
** Total **                       11
```

Record#	ANSWER1	ANSWER2	ANSWER3	ANSWER4	ANSWER5	ANSWER6	ANSWER7	ANSWER8	ANSWER9	ANSWER10
1	A	C	E	D	A	B	A	A	D	D
2	B	E	D	A	A	B	A	C	D	E
3	E	A	B	D	E	C	A	B	E	A

Checks.dbf

```
Structure for database: A:Checks.dbf
Number of data records:       0
Date of last update   : 08/18/87
Field  Field Name  Type        Width    Dec
    1  CHECK_NO    Numeric         4
    2  PAY_TO      Character      40
    3  AMOUNT      Numeric        10      2
    4  WORDAMOUNT  Character      50
    5  FOR         Character      20
** Total **                      125
```

Customer.dbf

```
Structure for database: A:Customer.dbf
Number of data records:       10
Date of last update   : 08/18/87
Field  Field Name  Type        Width    Dec
    1  CUST_NO     Character       4
    2  FIRST_NAME  Character      12
    3  LAST_NAME   Character      20
    4  ADDRESS1    Character      35
    5  ADDRESS2    Character      35
    6  CITY        Character      30
    7  STATE       Character       2
    8  ZIP         Character       5
    9  PHONE       Character      13
   10  AMT_OWED    Numeric        10      2
   11  DEADLINE    Date            8
** Total **                      175
```

Record#	CUST_NO	FIRST_NAME	LAST_NAME	ADDRESS1	ADDRESS2	CITY	STATE	ZIP	PHONE	AMT_OWED	DEADLINE
1	A254	MICHELLE	SMITH	510 Mabel Street		Columbia	SC	29215	(803)255-1635	1000.00	04/04/87
2	A123	Rebecca	Corbbit	22 Winner Circle		Aiken	SC	29802	(803)645-5521	-25.00	/ /
3	A753	Gloria	Roman	1922 Kant Street		Los Angeles	CA	90029	(213)485-5955	30.00	04/01/87
4	A109	Julia	King	447 Spring Road		North Augusta	SC	29814	(803)279-2106	1500.00	05/01/87
5	F126	Cathy	Moore	88 Chris Street		Greenville	SC	29699	(803)235-3205	1500.43	05/15/87
6	F876	Sandy	Richardson	51 Constance Road		Aiken	SC	29801	(803)648-3421	27.50	04/01/87
7	M198	VELMA	MOODY	23 Clemson Drive		Aiken	SC	29801	(803)648-0684	-10.00	/ /
8	A935	Nancy	Long	242 Beach Road		Los Angeles	CA	90069	(213)444-7732	75.98	03/31/87
9	F107	Linda	Roberts	138 Briarpatch Road		Greenville	SC	29651	(803)271-2345	0.00	/ /
10	A452	Mala	Schaefer	1822 Hollywood Blvd.		Los Angeles	CA	90038	(213)465-5723	193.79	/ /

Employee.dbf

```
Structure for database: A:Employee.dbf
Number of data records:       10
Date of last update    : 08/20/87
Field  Field Name  Type        Width    Dec
    1  EMP_CODE    Character       4
    2  FIRST_NAME  Character      12
    3  LAST_NAME   Character      20
    4  SALARY      Numeric        10      2
    5  ADDRESS1    Character      20
    6  ADDRESS2    Character      20
    7  CITY        Character      30
    8  STATE       Character       2
    9  ZIP         Character       5
   10  PHONE       Character      13
   11  HIRE_DATE   Date            8
   12  SSN         Character      11
   13  COMMENT     Character     254
** Total **                      410
```

```
Record# EMP_CODE FIRST_NAME LAST_NAME  SALARY    ADDRESS1     ADDRESS2 CITY            STATE ZIP   PHONE         HIRE_DATE SSN COMMENT
     1  A254     MICHELLE   SMITH      43252.29 510 Mabel Street       Columbia        8C    29215 (803)255-1635 03/12/86      Michelle
    is an oustanding employee.  She always puts forth the extra effort needed to get the job done. Her special bonus for a job well done
    is a trip to Hawaii.  Have Julia arrange it.
     2  A123     Rebecca    Corbbit    38712.23 22 Winner Circle       Aiken           SC    29802 (803)645-5521 11/13/86      Becky
    has been late everyday for the past month.  Remind Linda about having a discussion with her.  This is unlike Becky because her
    performance is usually oustanding.
     3  A753     Gloria     Roman      43712.00 1922 Kant Street       Los Angeles     CA    90029 (213)485-5955 02/07/86      Gloria
    is very responsible.  She works very long hours to get the project done.  There is an interesting project coming up that she will be
    interested in but she must take a vacation first.
     4  A109     Julia      King       25003.23 447 Spring Road        North Augusta   SC    29814 (803)279-2106 01/07/87      Julia
    is very efficient and has learned the ropes in a very short time.  She will be an asset to the company.
     5  F126     Cathy      Moore      27832.12 88 Chris Street        Greenville      SC    29699 (803)235-3205 01/07/86      Cathy
    is ready for a management position.
     6  F876     Sandy      Richardson 123000.00 51 Constance Road     Aiken           SC    29801 (803)648-342101/07/85
     7  M198     VELMA      MOODY      250000.00 23 Clemson Drive      Aiken           SC    29801 (803)648-068401/05/85
     8  A452     Mala       Schaefer   21987.33 1822 Hollywood Blvd.   Los Angeles     CA    90038 (213)465-5723  02/01/87
     9  A935     Nancy      Long       57612.12 242 Beach Road         Los Angeles     CA    90069 (213)444-773206/15/86
    10  F107     Linda      Roberts    53137.77 138 Briarpatch Road    Greenville      SC    29651 (803)271-2345  07/18/86
```

Inventry.dbf

```
Structure for database: A:Inventry.dbf
Number of data records:       6
Date of last update   : 08/14/87
Field  Field Name  Type       Width    Dec
    1  PART_NO     Character      5
    2  DESCRIP     Character    254
    3  QUANTITY    Numeric       10
    4  REORDER     Numeric       10
    5  PRICE       Numeric       10      2
** Total **                     290
```

Record#	PART_NO	DESCRIP	QUANTITY	REORDER	PRICE
1	R-123	Red high top tennis shoe.	2	5	23.95
2	B-254	Blue leather pump.	5	4	65.99
3	BL890	Black penny loafer.	10	10	47.99
4	B-735	Blue suede fringe boot.	15	20	75.99
5	BL861	Black high heel patent leather pump.	3	3	63.87
6	G-165	Green leather slip on.	7	6	23.98

Mail.dbf

```
Structure for database: A:Mail.dbf
Number of data records:       18
Date of last update   : 08/20/87
Field  Field Name  Type       Width    Dec
    1  NAME        Character     40
    2  FIRST_NAME  Character     12
    3  LAST_NAME   Character     20
    4  ADDRESS1    Character     35
    5  ADDRESS2    Character     35
    6  CITY        Character     30
    7  STATE       Character      2
    8  ZIP         Character      5
    9  PHONE       Character     13
   10  BIRTHDAY    Date           8
   11  AGE         Numeric        3
   12  LETTER      Memo          10
   13  SEND        Logical        1
** Total **                     215
```

Record#	NAME	FIRST_NAME	LAST_NAME	ADDRESS1	ADDRESS2	CITY	STATE	ZIP	PHONE	BIRTHDAY	AGE	LETTER	SEND
1	MICHELLE SMITH	MICHELLE	SMITH	510 Mabel Street		Columbia	SC	29215	(803)255-1635	09/28/60	26	Memo	.F.
2	Rebecca Corbbit	Rebecca	Corbbit	22 Winner Circle		Aiken	SC	29802	(803)645-5521	09/11/60	26	Memo	.F.
3	Gloria Roman	Gloria	Roman	1922 Kant Street		Los Angeles	CA	90029	(213)485-5955	06/08/53	33	Memo	.F.
4	David Gurly	David	Gurly	P.O. Box 3640		Stanford	CA	94315	(415)424-9970	06/08/64	22	Memo	.F.
5	Julia King	Julia	King	447 Spring Road		North Augusta	SC	29814	(803)279-2106	11/01/58	28	Memo	.F.
6	Perry Lester	Perry	Lester	38 Merrily Circle		Pasadena	CA	94033	(818)449-7777	04/25/63	23	Memo	.F.
7	Cathy Moore	Cathy	Moore	88 Chris Street		Greenville	SC	29699	(803)235-3205	07/16/53	33	Memo	.F.
8	Doug Smith	Doug	Smith	7902 Queen Road		Orangeburg	SC	29115	(803)535-8675	01/20/46	40	Memo	.F.
9	Wade Adams	Wade	Adams	343 Sarah Drive		Aiken	SC	29802	(803)648-8888	06/12/47	39	Memo	.F.
10	Sandy Richardson	Sandy	Richardson	51 Constance Road		Aiken	SC	29801	(803)648-3421	12/04/57	29	Memo	.F.
11	VELMA MOODY	VELMA	MOODY	23 Clemson Drive		Aiken	SC	29801	(803)648-0684	05/18/37	49	Memo	.F.
12	Mala Schaefer	Mala	Schaefer	1822 Hollywood Blvd.		Los Angeles	CA	90038	(213)465-5723	09/22/55	31	Memo	.F.
13	Lawrence Arthur	Lawrence	Arthur	703 Main Street	#1	Seattle	WA	98230		07/02/55	31	Memo	.F.
14	Nancy Long	Nancy	Long	242 Beach Road		Los Angeles	CA	90069	(213)444-7732	10/30/54	32	Memo	.
15	Jeff Potter	Jeff	Potter	858 Laughing Lane		Los Angeles	CA	90029	(803)463-6443	12/18/53	33	Memo	.F.
16	Linda Roberts	Linda	Roberts	138 Briarpatch Road		Greenville	SC	29651	(803)271-2345	05/11/49	37	Memo	.F.
17	Jerry Samuels	Jerry	Samuels	4184 Maryland Road		Los Angeles	CA	90042	(213)635-1235	02/25/50	36	Memo	.F.
18	Chris Whiteside	Chris	Whiteside	1432 Gentleman Avenue		Hollywood	CA	90043	(213)622-5597	06/26/51	35	Memo	.F.

Managers.dbf

```
Structure for database: A:Managers.dbf
Number of data records:       3
Date of last update   : 08/18/87
Field  Field Name  Type        Width    Dec
    1  MG_CODE     Character       1
    2  FIRST_NAME  Character      12
    3  LAST_NAME   Character      20
    4  SALARY      Numeric        10      2
    5  ADDRESS1    Character      20
    6  ADDRESS2    Character      20
    7  CITY        Character      30
    8  STATE       Character       2
    9  ZIP         Character       5
   10  PHONE       Character      13
   11  HIRE_DATE   Date            8
   12  SSN         Character      11
   13  COMMENT     Character     254
** Total **                      407
```

Record#	MG_CODE	FIRST_NAME	LAST_NAME	SALARY	ADDRESS1	ADDRESS2	CITY	STATE	ZIP	PHONE	HIRE_DATE	SSN	COMMENT
1	A	Marilyn	Simpkins	40000.00	75 Big Wheel Road		Los Angeles	CA	90027	(213)664-8769	01/01/85	120-73-7712	
2	F	Michael	Johansen	75000.00	879 Alvarado		Los Angeles	CA	90037	(213)887-8721	02/25/85	786-55-6557	
3	M	Thomas	Redding	300000.00	138 North Terrace		Marina Del Rey	CA	90239	(213)721-2836	03/27/85	987-86-8898	

Medical.dbf

```
Structure for database: A:Medical.dbf
Number of data records:       1
Date of last update   : 08/18/87
Field  Field Name  Type        Width    Dec
    1  PAT_CODE    Character       4
    2  SYMPTOMS    Character     254
    3  TREATMENT   Character     254
** Total **                      513
```

```
Record#  PAT_CODE  SYMPTOMS              TREATMENT
      1  A123      Sniffles, headache,   Take two aspirin and
                   scratchy throat,      call me in the morning.
                   aching muscles
```

Orders.dbf

```
Structure for database: A:Orders.dbf
Number of data records:       4
Date of last update   : 08/11/87
Field  Field Name  Type        Width    Dec
    1  CUST_NO     Character       4
    2  PART_NO     Character       5
    3  QUANTITY    Numeric        10
** Total **                       20

Record#  CUST_NO PART_NO   QUANTITY
      1  A254    R-123            1
      2  F126    B-254            2
      3  A452    G-165            2
      4  A452    R-123            1
```

Supplier.dbf

```
Structure for database: A:Supplier.dbf
Number of data records:       6
Date of last update    : 08/18/87
Field  Field Name  Type        Width    Dec
    1  SUPPLIER    Character       4
    2  PART_NO     Character       5
    3  FIRST_NAME  Character      12
    4  LAST_NAME   Character      20
    5  ADDRESS1    Character      35
    6  ADDRESS2    Character      35
    7  CITY        Character      30
    8  STATE       Character       2
    9  ZIP         Character       5
   10  PHONE       Character      13
** Total **                      162
```

Record#	SUPPLIER	PART_NO	FIRST_NAME	LAST_NAME	ADDRESS1	ADDRESS2	CITY	STATE	ZIP	PHONE
1	A198	R-123								
2	A951	B-254								
3	C861	BL890								
4	J875	B-735								
5	K891	BL861								
6	S861	G-165								

Tests.dbf

```
Structure for database: A:Tests.dbf
Number of data records:        6
Date of last update   : 08/18/87
Field  Field Name  Type        Width     Dec
    1  STUDENT     Character      50
    2  TEST_NUM    Numeric         1
    3  SCORE       Numeric         3
    4  ANSWER1     Character       1
    5  ANSWER2     Character       1
    6  ANSWER3     Character       1
    7  ANSWER4     Character       1
    8  ANSWER5     Character       1
    9  ANSWER6     Character       1
   10  ANSWER7     Character       1
   11  ANSWER8     Character       1
   12  ANSWER9     Character       1
   13  ANSWER10    Character       1
** Total **                       65
```

Record#	STUDENT	TEST_NUM	SCORE	ANSWER1	ANSWER2	ANSWER3	ANSWER4	ANSWER5	ANSWER6	ANSWER7	ANSWER8	ANSWER9	ANSWER10
1	Michelle Brodie	1	90	A	C	E	B	A	B	A	A	D	D
2	Becky Corbin	1	80	A	E	E	D	B	B	A	A	D	D
3	Perry Lessing	2	70	B	E	D	B	A	A	B	C	D	E
4	Jeff Pott	2	90	A	E	D	A	A	B	A	C	D	E
5	Janette Gembitz	3	90	E	B	B	D	E	C	A	B	E	A
6	Mala Schein	3	100	E	A	B	D	E	C	A	B	E	A

Applications Index

General Index